HISTORY OF WOMEN IN THE UNITED STATES

HISTORY OF WOMEN IN THE UNITED STATES

Historical Articles on Women's Lives and Activities

Edited by Nancy F. Cott

Series ISBN 3-598-41454-4

1. Theory and Method in Women's History
   ISBN 3-598-41455-2 Part 1
   ISBN 3-598-41477-3 Part 2

2. Household Constitution and Family Relationships
   ISBN 3-598-41456-0

3. Domestic Relations and Law
   ISBN 3-598-41457-9

4. Domestic Ideology and Domestic Work
   ISBN 3-598-41458-7 Part 1
   ISBN 3-598-41475-7 Part 2

5. The Intersection of Work and Family Life
   ISBN 3-598-41459-5 Part 1
   ISBN 3-598-41476-5 Part 2

6. Working on the Land
   ISBN 3-598-41460-9

7. Industrial Wage Work
   ISBN 3-598-41461-7 Part 1
   ISBN 3-598-41693-8 Part 2

8. Professional and White-Collar Employments
   ISBN 3-598-41462-5 Part 1
   ISBN 3-598-41694-6 Part 2

9. Prostitution
   ISBN 3-598-41463-3

10. Sexuality and Sexual Behavior
    ISBN 3-598-41464-1

11. Women's Bodies: Health and Childbirth
    ISBN 3-598-41465-X

12. Education
    ISBN 3-598-41466-8

13. Religion
    ISBN 3-598-41467-6

14. Intercultural and Interracial Relations
    ISBN 3-598-41468-4

15. Women and War
    ISBN 3-598-41469-2

16. Women Together: Organizational Life
    ISBN 3-598-41470-6

17. Social and Moral Reform
    ISBN 3-598-41471-4 Part 1
    ISBN 3-598-41695-4 Part 2

18. Women and Politics
    ISBN 3-598-41472-2 Part 1
    ISBN 3-598-41697-0 Part 2

19. Woman Suffrage
    ISBN 3-598-41473-0 Part 1
    ISBN 3-598-41696-2 Part 2

20. Feminist Struggles for Sex Equality
    ISBN 3-598-41474-9

HISTORY OF WOMEN IN THE UNITED STATES

Historical Articles on Women's Lives and Activities

13. Religion

Edited with an Introduction by

Nancy F. Cott
Yale University

K · G · Saur
Munich · New Providence · London · Paris · 1993

Publisher's Note

The articles and chapters which comprise this collection originally appeared in a wide variety oof publications and are reproduced here in facsimile from the highest quality offprints anad photocopies available. The reader will notice some occasional marginal shading and text-cunrl common to photocopying from tightly bound volumes. Every attempt has been made to eitheer correct or minimize this effect.

Copyright information for articles reproduced in this collection appears at the end of this volume.

Library of Congress Cataloging-in-Publication Data

History of women in the United States : historical articles on
women's lives and activities / edited with
an introduction by Nancy F. Cott.
p. cm.
Includes bibliographical references and indexes.
Contents: 1. Theory and method in women's history -- 2. Household constitution and family relationships -- 3. Domestic relations and law -- 4. Domestic ideology and domestic work -- 5. The intersection of work and family life -- 6. Working on the land -- 7. Industrial wage work -- 8. Professional and white-collar employments -- 9. Prostitution -- 10. Sexuality and sexual behavior -- 11. Women's bodies -- 12. Education -- 13. Religion -- 14. Intercultural and interracial relations -- 15. Women and war -- 16. Women together -- 17. Social and moral reform -- 18. Women and politics -- 19. Woman suffrage -- 20. Feminist struggles for sex equality.
ISBN 3-598-41454-4 (set)
1. Women--United States--History. 2. Women--United States--Social conditions. I. Cott, Nancy F.
HQ1410.H57 1992
305.4'0973--dc20 92-16765
CIP

Die Deutsche Bibliothek - CIP - Einheitsaufnahme

History of Women in the United States: historical articles
on women's lives and activities / ed. with an introd. by Nancy F. Cott.
- Munich ; New Providence ; London ; Paris : Saur.
ISBN 3-598-41454-4
NE: Cott, Nancy F. (Hrsg.)
Vol. 13. religion - (1993)
ISBN 3-598-41467-6

Printed on acid-free paper/Gedruckt auf säurefreiem Papier

K.G. Saur Verlag GmbH & Co. KG, Munich 1993
A Reed Reference Publishing Company

Printed in the United States of America
Printed/Bound by Edwards Brothers Incorporated, Ann Arbor

ISBN 3-598-41467-6 (vol. 13)
ISBN 3-598-41454-4 (series)

Contents

CONTENTS

CONTENTS

Series Preface

In the space of one generation, women's history has become the fastest-growing area of scholarship in U.S. history. Since the resurgence of feminism in the late 1960s and 1970s, insistent questions about the historical meanings of "woman's place" have sowed and reaped a garden of scholarship. Where scholarly works used to be bare of mention of women, academic enterprise has now produced a vigorous growth of books and articles, bringing to light diverse women of every region, race, class and age. This research is marked by a renovating intent that refuses to accept as "human" history a history of men. Interest is lively and debate is stimulating and sought after: attendance at the Berkshire Conference on the History of Women rivals the size of the annual convention of the American Historical Association.

While books in women's history are daily increasing in numbers and strength, as in any fast-developing field the scholarly literature in the form of articles is most expansive and up-to-the-minute. All the history journals now publish articles on women's work, domestic settings, family relations, household matters, female politics and organizations and so forth, and new journals have sprung into being to concentrate on such topics. Women's historians publish in numerous regional and thematic history journals as well as in feminist outlets and in journals of other social science disciplines. This series brings together a collection of outstanding articles from the field, almost all written in the past twenty years and more than half published during the 1980s. It brings together, in volumes organized by topic, essays otherwise widely dispersed. These volumes reprint only articles that originally appeared in journals, not chapters of books; review articles are not included. Articles have been chosen for overall quality and for range. Each one was chosen for one or more of the following reasons: because it is the standard authority on its subject matter; represents an important statement on a topic by a recognized scholar; presages an important book to come; provides a first look at new evidence or new methods; or opens an untapped area or new controversy. Older articles have been reprinted if their data or interpretation have not been surpassed or if they marked an important stage in the historiography, even if since superseded.

The historical coverage of the series extends from the Revolutionary era to the 1960s. The articles themselves are dated from the 1940s through 1988. Volumes are organized by topic rather than time period. Within each volume, the articles are ordered chronologically (with respect to substance), so that the whole can be read as an historical overview. The only exception to this ordering principle is Volume One, on Theory and Method, in which the contents are arranged in order of publication. Within each volume there is an attempt to include articles on as diverse kinds of women as possible. None of the volume topics is regionally or racially defined; rather, all volumes are topically designed so as to afford views of women's work, family lives, and public activities which cut across races and regions. Any volume in the series stands on its own, supplying as full a treatment of a designated subject matter as the scholarly literature will provide. Several groupings of volumes also make sense; that is, volumes two through five all center around domestic and family matters; volumes five through nine consider other varieties of women's work; volumes nine through eleven concern uses and abuses of women's bodies; volumes twelve through fourteen look at major aspects of socialization; and volumes fifteen through twenty include organizational and political efforts of many sorts.

As a whole, the series displays in all its range the vitality of the field of women's history. Aside from imbuing U.S. history with new vision, scholarship in this area has informed, and should continue to inform, current public debate on issues from parental leave to the nuclear freeze. By bringing historical articles together under topical headings, these volumes both represent accurately the shape of historical controversy (or consensus) on given issues and make historians' findings most conveniently available for current reference.

Introduction

In Christian America, men have been the acknowledged religious leaders—theologians and pastors—but women have outnumbered men in church congregations since about 1700, and perhaps for even longer. Women's historians' stress on this fact that through the whole history of the United States, congregations of Christian churches were predominantly female, and models of piety were therefore "feminized," has caused a reorientation in religious history. No longer is it possible to regard the church without its gender dimension, to discuss and analyze male ministers' sermons or views without recognizing that the majority of the faithful who attended to them were women.

Certainly the decline in male converts and the swelling of female-dominated congregations between the seventeenth and the nineteenth centuries had a great deal to do with Protestant ministers' reevaluation of female character, and with their increasing look to the domestic hearth to create piety and rear Christians. Protestant Christianity from the time of the Reformation had stressed the equality, and similar access, of all individual souls (whether of males or females) before God. Yet early Protestant doctrine also emphasized the sin of Eve—first in transgression—and the legacy of corruptible nature deeded to her daughters. During the eighteenth century in America, as men were diverted from religion to secular concerns and women appeared the more faithful, pastoral views gradually embraced a more positive religious role for womanhood. Ministers turned their eyes from Eve to more reliable models of Biblical womanhood, such as the worthy woman of Proverbs 31, who was a useful and pious member of the community, a devoted wife, mother and housekeeper. Their sermons and discussions dwelt on the theme of reciprocal giving between women and Christianity. Only Christianity and the civilization it brought, they reasoned, elevated women to "proper" respect and rank; women in turn had the religious temperament which disposed them to piety and Christian nurture. By the early nineteenth century Protestant ministers were claiming that women were "fitted by nature" for piety and benevolence, and that family religion communicated from parents to children was the natural, divinely approved and most effective means of sustaining the stream of believers.[1] Throughout the century this set of assumptions persisted, pervasive in American culture, embraced by women themselves and used as the springboard to a host of voluntary activities.

Because women have been congregants, the faithful, doers of pious deeds rather than elaborators of theology or religious orthodoxy, the work on religion in women's history has not concentrated on doctrinal questions so much as on social actions and meanings. During the series of religious revivals known as the Second Great Awakening, spanning from 1798 through the 1830s and traveling from New England to the mid-Atlantic states to the South, female converts took leading roles. Not only were female models of confession and profession often highlighted in revivalist ministers' exhortations, but also, in practice, wives and mothers influenced their husbands and sons to convert, bringing a larger proportion of men into the churches than during non-revival times.[2] In the wake of the Second Awakening, women's prayer groups, charitable institutions, missionary and education associations, Sabbath School organizations, moral reform and maternal societies all multiplied phenomenally. These voluntary activities of women, like the less prolific but equally emphatic activities of evangelical Christian men, saw religious education not only as the route to true faith and salvation but also as a means to assure social order in the present world. Whether women prayed together, or raised money to support missionaries, or distributed Bibles and tracts among the poor and unchurched, or set up Sabbath Schools for children to begin the business of Christian training early, they intended to foster religious education, conversion and reformation of individual character with the dual aim of present and eternal salvation.

More than for men, however, for women such religious voluntarism also provided an approved arena of satisfying usefulness outside the home. The "awakened" Christian community defined itself by its adversary and evangelical relation to the outside world—the unconverted, the Roman Catholic—as well as by its functions for its members. It required members to be "up and doing," actively fostering the extension of like-minded belief. Piety implied group evangelical activity. Where men freely pursued a range of activities related to political, occupational and civic concerns, women's church-related work was the kind which most readily received approbation and support. In such activities women could press forward their conception of the good society, join a community of their peers, express themselves, gain the rewards of self-esteem and approval for pursuing a good cause within a like-minded group.

Much of the work in women's history and religion has explored the dual potential of women's evangelical Christian belonging. Women's occupation in prayer and charity societies, in moral reform and maternal associations, in Sabbath Schools, Bible societies and missionary support groups, has had the potential to encourage women's independence and self-definition within a supportive community, or to acclimate women to a limited, subordinate, clerically-defined role. As the nineteenth century wore on, the variations on this dual theme became additionally complex, as some women struggled to be preachers, others became missionaries themselves rather than only supporting men who would do so, many joined mass Christian-based social reform movements such as the Women's Christian Temperance Union, and utopians, Mormons, Catholics and Jews multiplied the models of religious experience in America. Bringing together signal articles on women's participation in religious life as congregants, models of conversion, missionaries, and voluntary religious workers, this volume makes clear how far women as a gender group have served the purposes of organized religion and also explores the functions of organized religion for women as individuals.

Notes

[1] Nancy F. Cott, *The Bonds of Womanhood: 'Woman's Sphere' in New England, 1780-1835* (New Haven, CT, Yale Univ. Press, 1977), 126-148.

[2] *See* Mary Ryan, "A Woman's Awakening: Evangelical Religion and the Families of Utica, N.Y. 1800-1840," *American Quarterly* 30 (Winter 1978), 602-623.

Religion

THE FEMINIZATION OF AMERICAN CONGREGATIONALISM, 1730–1835

RICHARD D. SHIELS
Ohio State University, Newark

"THERE ARE FAR MORE GODLY WOMEN IN THE WORLD THAN THERE ARE godly Men," Cotton Mather observed in 1691. To illustrate his point, he referred to the sex ratio of church members in Boston: "In a church of between three and four hundred Communicants, there are but a few more than One Hundred Men." Nearly a century and a half later, Frances Trollope recorded a similar observation: "I never saw, or read, of any country where religion had so strong a hold upon the women, or a lighter hold upon the men."[1]

Historians have noted the same phenomenon. Two decades ago, Edmund Morgan called for "another approach" to the study of Puritanism, one which would seriously examine the disproportionate number of women in seventeenth-century churches. More recently Cedric Cowing, Mary Maples Dunn, and Gerald Moran have documented the high percentage of women among eighteenth-century church members, and Nancy Cott and Barbara Welter have found a preponderance of women in nineteenth-century churches. Welter terms the refashioning of church teachings in response to this growing female audience the "feminization of American religion."[2]

[1] Mather, *Ornaments of the Daughters of Zion, or, the Character and Happiness of a Virtuous Woman* (Boston: Samuel Phillips, 1691), 56–57; Trollope, *Domestic Manners of the Americans* (1832; New York: Viking, 1949), 75.

[2] Morgan, "New England Puritanism: Another Approach," *William and Mary Quarterly*, 3d series, 18 (April 1961), 236–42; Cowing, "Sex and Preaching in the Great Awakening," *American Quarterly*, 20 (Fall 1968), 624–44; Dunn, "Saints and Sisters," *American Quarterly*, 30 (Winter 1978), 583–601; Moran, "The Puritan Saint," (Diss. Rutgers Univ., 1974); Cott, *The Bonds of Womanhood: "Woman's Sphere" in New England, 1780–1835* (New Haven: Yale Univ. Press, 1977), 126–60; Welter, "The Feminization of American Religion: 1800–1860," in Mary Hartman and Lois Banner, eds., *Clio's Consciousness Raised* (New York: Harper Torchbooks, 1973), 137–55.

Figure 1.
PERCENTAGE OF WOMEN ENTERING 97
NEW ENGLAND CHURCHES, 1730–1835

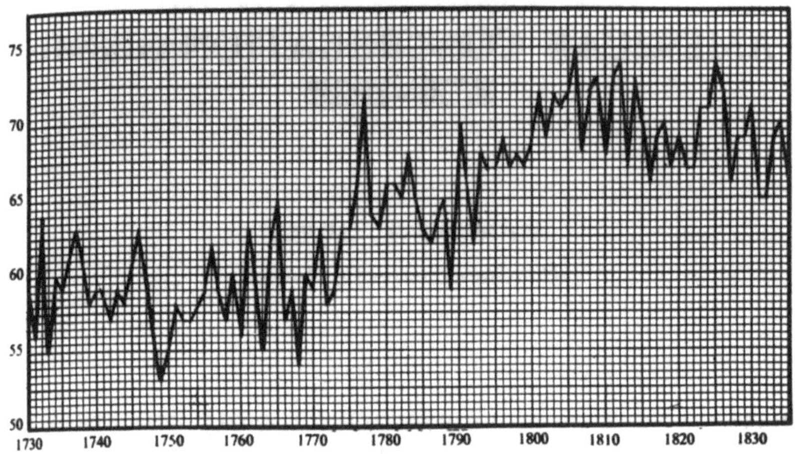

Note: Figure 1 is based upon 52,296 men and women who joined 97 churches over 105 years. Persons who joined by transfer from another church have been omitted.

As Mather's lament suggests, the audience was largely female long before the message was feminized. What has not been known, however, is that the feminine component of the audience increased during the American Revolution and then rose more dramatically after 1800. The constituency of New England's Congregational churches, which had long been predominantly female, was further feminized in the two generations following the Declaration of Independence.

* * *

As Figure 1 illustrates, the percentage of women among persons joining 97 Congregational churches in Massachusetts and Connecticut increased dramatically from 1730 to 1835.[3] The sex ratio of new members fluctuated

[3] Records from 46 Connecticut churches were consulted. From Fairfield County: Huntington, New Canaan, Redding, Stamford, Trumbull, and Wilton. From Hartford County: New Britain, Avon, Granby, and Wethersfield. From Litchfield County: North Canaan, Cornwall Second, Kent, New Milford, and Plymouth. From Middlesex County: East Haddam Second, Haddam, Hadlyme Second, and Clinton. From New Haven County: Cheshire, Oxford, East Haven, Guilford, Meriden, New Haven, Fair Haven, White Haven, North Haven, and Woodbridge. From New London County: Colchester, Colchester Second, Franklin, Goshen (Lebanon), Old Lyme, New London, Norwich, Preston, Stonington, and East Stonington. From Tolland County: Bolton, Columbia, Somers, and Vernon. From Windham County: Windham, Scotland, and Woodstock. Fifty-one church records were consulted from Massachusetts. From Barnstable County: West Barnstable and Falmouth. From Berkshire County: Great Barrington, Lee, Lenox, and Stockbridge. From Bristol County: Attleborough Second, Berkeley, and Easton. From Essex County: South Andover,

within distinct ranges in each of three periods: 1730–1776, 1777–1799, and 1800–1835. Moreover, the ratio of women to men increased from one period to the next. The female component never rose above 65 percent in any year prior to 1776 and fell below 60 percent 27 times in those 45 years. In 1777, the percentage of women rose to 72 percent, and it exceeded 65 percent 13 times in the final quarter of the century, falling below 60 percent only once. In 35 years beginning in 1800, the proportion of women never fell below 65 percent, and it reached or exceeded 70 percent on 13 occasions. In sum, 59 percent of all new members from 1730 to 1769 were women, compared to 64 percent of the new members from 1770 to 1799 and 69 percent of the new members from 1800 to 1835.

Never before in New England's history had the proportion of female converts been so great for so long. Figure 2, which includes data collected

Figure 2.
PERCENTAGE OF WOMEN ENTERING NEW ENGLAND CHURCHES, CALCULATED BY FIVE-YEAR INTERVALS

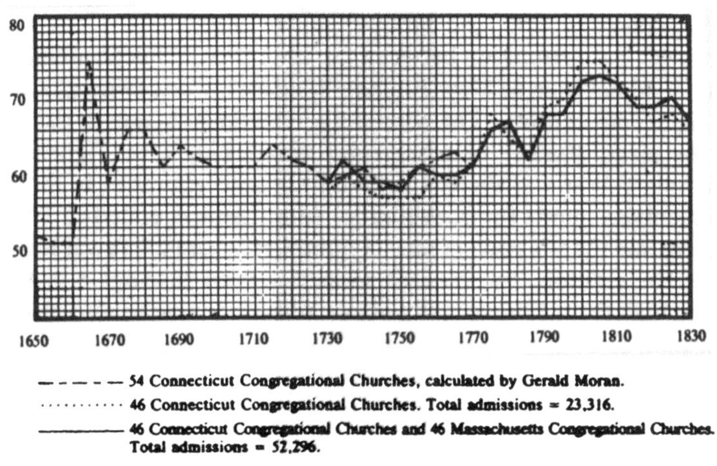

Boxford Second, Danvers, North Haverhill, West Haverhill, Lynn, Marblehead, Methuen, Middleton, Rowley, and South Salem. From Franklin County: Sunderland. From Hampden County: Springfield and Wilbraham. From Hampshire County: Belchertown and Ware. From Middlesex County: Cambridge, Framingham, Hopkinton, Lincoln, Newton, Newton Second, Reading, Stoneham, Tewksbury, Wilmington. In Norfolk County: Braintree, Foxborough, Medway Second, Millis, Randolph, and Weymouth. In Plymouth County: Hanover and Plymouth. In Suffolk County: Brattle Square, Old South, and West Boston. In Worchester County: Brookfield Third, Milford, Millbury, Sutton, and West Brookfield. Gaps occur in most of these records, and some of these churches had not yet formed in 1730. Hence, the sample for any given year is fewer than 97 churches. For 1730, the sample is 31 churches. It is never fewer than 40 churches after 1733, nor fewer than 50 after 1740, nor fewer than 60 after 1746, nor fewer than 75 from 1764 to 1832.

from 54 Connecticut churches and calculated by five-year intervals by Gerald Moran, suggests that the level remained remarkably constant from 1685 to 1775.[4] The percentage of women among new members prior to 1725 was slightly higher than it would be from 1725 to 1754, but the range of fluctuation was both narrow and consistent. Women constituted as much as 63 percent of the new members in only two five-year intervals (1695–1699 and 1715–1719) and as little as 57 percent in only one (1745–1749). Only once since 1650 had the percentage of women totalled over 65 percent (1665–1669). Hence the changing sex ratio after 1770 followed a prolonged period of stability. Moreover, the change after 1770 was not merely a momentary correction as had occurred in the 1660s. The percentage of women declined again after 1810 in Connecticut and after 1825 in Massachusetts, but it did not decline either as suddenly or as severely as it had in 1670.

The proportions of this change among church members rule out a correlation to changes in the population at large. Connecticut's population was 49.5 percent female in 1774, 50.5 percent in 1790, and 50.6 percent in 1830. In Massachusetts, women constituted 50.8 percent of the population in 1764, 51 percent in 1790, and 51.2 percent in 1830.[5]

Moreover, the correlation between the sex ratio of church members and the rate of admissions to New England churches was reversed at the end of the eighteenth century. The percentage of women began to rise in 1777, when the mean number of admissions was falling (see Figure 3). The Revolutionary War was disrupting New England churches in that period and probably accounts for both trends. After the war ended in 1783, both admissions and the sex ratio of new members returned to prewar levels temporarily. Nonetheless, the ratio of women to men rose again in 1790 and remained high from 1793 to 1835, while admissions were also rising. The feminization of church membership, which began in the Revolution, continued through the Second Great Awakening.

During the Second Awakening, an increasing proportion of women among church members coincided with an increase in the proportion of church members within the population at large. Consequently, the per-

[4] Moran, "The Puritan Saint," 327. Dunn has also studied the sex ratio of church members; using 28 churches in Massachusetts and Connecticut, she has calculated the percentage of females among new members by ten year intervals from 1632 to 1759. Dunn's figures are higher than either Moran's or mine. She finds the percentage of women fluctuated from 60 to 66 from 1680 to 1749, and then jumped to 70 for the period 1750–1759. Dunn, "Saints and Sisters," 591. See also Moran, "Sisters in Christ. Women and the Church in Seventeenth Century New England," in Janet Wilson James, ed., *Women in American Religion* (Philadelphia: Univ. of Pennsylvania Press, 1980), 47–67.

[5] U. S. Department of Commerce and Labor, Bureau of the Census, *A Century of Population Growth* (Washington: GPO, 1909), 166–69, 158–62, 192–94; *Abstract of the Returns of the Fifth Census* (New York: Arno, 1976), 5–7, 48.

Figure 3.
MEAN ANNUAL ADMISSIONS TO 97 NEW ENGLAND CHURCHES, BY FIVE-YEAR INTERVALS

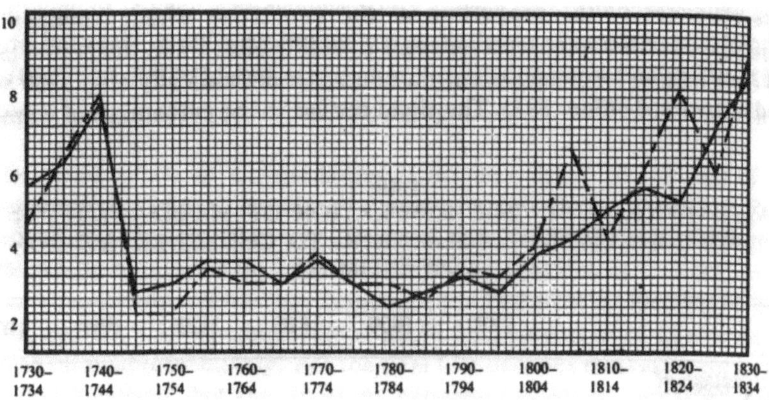

centage of New England women who joined the church rose dramatically. Unfortunately, there are no precise calculations of the percentage of New Englanders who joined churches, or even of the total number of New England church members. The most common estimate is that one out of fifteen Americans belonged to a church in 1800, and one out of eight in 1835. New Englanders may have been more religious than Southerners, but church membership requirements were more restrictive in New England than elsewhere. Hence, it is unclear whether these estimates should be raised for New England; it seems unlikely that they should be lowered. It is safe to assume, however, that the proportion of church members doubled in the first third of the century in New England as well as elsewhere.[6]

[6] Winthrop Hudson, *Religion in America: An Historical Account of the Development of American Religious Life* (New York: Scribner's, 1973), 128–30; Paul E. Johnson, *A Shopkeeper's Millennium: Society and Revivals in Rochester, New York, 1815–1837* (New York: Hill and Wang, 1978), 4–6; Frank H. Littell, *From State Church to Pluralism: A Protestant Interpretation of Religion in American History* (New York: Doubleday, 1962), 36–39. Robert Baird and Daniel Dorchester provide estimates of the total number of members in various denominations, but their figures are for the entire nation. Both estimate that there were 75,000 Congregationalists in 1800; Dorchester estimates 140,000 in 1830, and Baird estimates 197,196 in 1850. Baird, *The Christian Retrospect and Register: A Summary of The Scientific, Moral, and Religious Progress of the First Half of the 19th Century* (New York: M. W. Dodd, 1851), 220. Dorchester, *Christianity in the United States from the First Settlement* (New York: Phillips and Hunt, 1888), 373, 733, 749.

Using even imprecise estimates of the church-going component of the population, it is possible to demonstrate the increase in the proportion of New England women joining churches. Tables 1A and 1B employ different estimates of the proportion of the population which belonged to churches, but the same trend appears in both tables. First, the percentage of New England women joining churches rose dramatically after 1800 and did not decline before 1835. The slight decline in the percentage of women

Table 1.

A. PERCENTAGE OF THE POPULATION OF MASSACHUSETTS AND CONNECTICUT BELONGING TO CHURCHES, BY SEX; LOW ESTIMATE

	1790	1800	1810	1820	1830	1835
Percentage of total population in churches	7	7	8	10	12	15
Percentage of male population in churches	6	6	6	7	8	10
Percentage of female population in churches	8	8	10	13	16	20

B. PERCENTAGE OF THE POPULATION OF MASSACHUSETTS AND CONNECTICUT BELONGING TO CHURCHES, BY SEX; HIGH ESTIMATE

	1790	1800	1810	1820	1830	1835
Percentage of total population in churches	10	10	12	15	18	20
Percentage of male population in churches	8	8	9	10	12	14
Percentage of female population in churches	12	12	15	19	24	26

Note: Tables 1A and 1B are based upon census data and the sex ratios evident in Figure 2. Both tables assume that 10% of all church members either died or left town in each decade; the results are changed by only a fraction of a percentage when this mortality-migration estimate is doubled.

among new members, evident on Figure 2, was offset by an increase in the proportion of church members in the population. The probability that any woman would join the church was still rising in 1835. Second, by 1835, the percentage of women who belonged to a church was double the percentage of the male population belonging to churches. Church membership had become a woman's activity.

* * *

The feminization of Congregational churches began at the end of a century which had seen important changes in New England religion. Revivals of religion erupted in the 1730s and then swept the colonies in the Great Awakening of 1741–1742. The awakening subsided as suddenly as it had arisen, but not before New England churches were divided into New Lights and Old Lights, camps which might best be described as evangelical and rational respectively. For the next five decades revivals were both rare and localized, but the divisions between Christians remained well into the new century. The revivals of the Second Great Awakening began in the 1790s. One wave of revivals followed upon the crest of another, culminating in the revivals of 1831, which were more widespread and more intense than any others. How did two awakenings and deep divisions between Christians affect the sex ratio of church membership?[7]

The Great Awakening may have reduced the ratio of women to men converts from earlier levels. Contemporaries said that it did, and Cedric Cowing has identified six churches in which the decline in the proportion of female converts in these two years was dramatic. Cowing also found that the decline was less substantial in Boston, where some churches did not experience revivals in 1741–1742, and that the percentage of women among new members increased in these years in six churches in Essex County, where the awakening was weaker still. The total effect of the awakening upon seventeen churches which Cowing studied was a decrease in the percentage of females among new members from 64 percent for the years 1720–1740 to 57 percent in 1741–1742 (see Table 2).[8]

Although the present study relies upon different church records than those used by either Cowing or Moran, the statistics produced in all three projects are remarkably consistent. A decline in the percentage of women from 64 percent to 57 percent fits within the range of fluctuation illustrated above. Indeed, Figure 1 reveals a decline to 57 percent in 1742, and Figure

[7] John M. Bumsted and J. E. VandeWetering, *What Must I Do To Be Saved? The Great Awakening in Colonial America* (Hinsdale, Ill.: Dryden Press, 1976); Charles Roy Keller, *The Second Great Awakening in Connecticut* (New Haven: Yale Univ. Press, 1942).

[8] Cowing, "Sex and Preaching," 632–34. Table 2 summarizes data which Cowing presented.

Table 2.
PERCENTAGE OF WOMEN ENTERING NEW ENGLAND CHURCHES BEFORE, DURING, AND AFTER THE GREAT AWAKENING

	1720–40	1741–42	1743–48
Six New Light churches	66 (877)	50 (469)	53 (177)
Five Boston churches	65 (1,521)	64 (288)	58 (170)
Six Essex County churches	60 (1,649)	63 (193)	58 (115)
Seventeen churches combined	64	57	56

Note: The total number of both sexes included in each cell appears in parentheses.

2 indicates that the ratio of women to men fell to 57 percent for the period 1745–1749 among Moran's Connecticut churches. A more general decline of 3 to 4 percent appears in Moran's figures for the period 1725–1755; perhaps it is to be explained as the effect of the Awakening and of revivals which preceded it.

In our sample, however, the ratio of women to men among revival converts from 1730 to 1769 was no lower than among those persons who joined churches which were not in the midst of revival. Figure 4 separates revival converts from other converts, and illustrates the percentage of women among both groups by five-year intervals. Prior to 1770, the ratio of women to men was often highest among revival converts. In these years, 59 percent of all new members were women, and 60 percent of those converted in revivals.[9]

Once again the pattern changes after 1770. The ratio of women to men was lower among revival converts than among non-revival candidates from that date on. For five years beginning in 1785, the ratio was one man converted in a revival for every woman. For 25 years after 1770, women constituted 60 percent of the revival converts and 66 percent of the converts who joined outside of revivals.

[9] To identify revivals, the number of admissions in one church in one year was divided by the mean number of admissions to that church in all years; the result is a grand mean score for each church-year. A score less than or equal to 1.0 identified an average or worse-than-average year for the church in question. But what score best identified revivals? Figure 4 separates church-years with scores less than or equal to 1.0 from church-years with admissions greater than 20 and grand mean scores equal to or greater than 3.0. A running mean was also calculated, but the running mean identified nearly all of the same church-years; Figure 3 is based upon the grand mean scores.

Figure 4.
PERCENTAGE OF WOMEN ENTERING 97 NEW ENGLAND CHURCHES
IN REVIVALS AND IN AVERAGE YEARS, CALCULATED
BY FIVE-YEAR INTERVALS

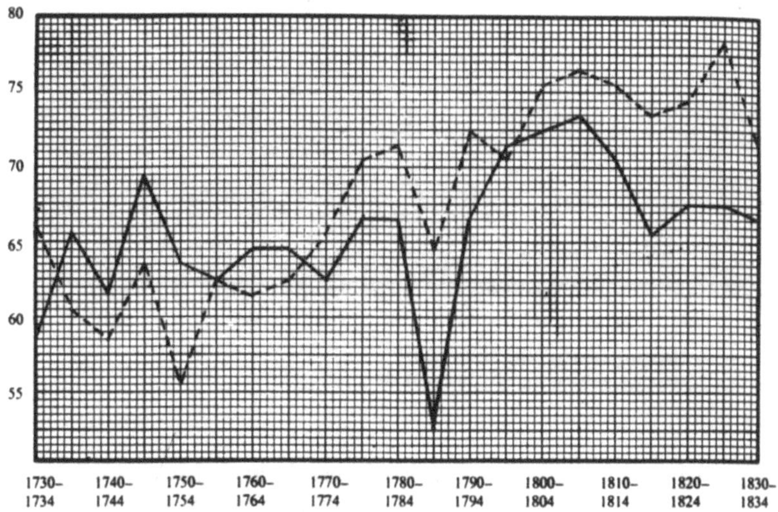

—— Percentage of persons converted during revivals who were women. Total number of both sexes converted in revivals = 17,294.

- - - - Percentage of persons converted in average years who were women. Total number of both sexes converted in average years = 14,207.

However, revivals were rare in this period, and New Light clergymen decried "declension." The decline in admissions was most marked from 1777 to 1798, and was proportionately greater among men than women (see Figure 5). Large numbers of women joined churches in western New England in a wave of revivals from 1798 to 1800. Clergymen declared a "Second Great Awakening," and lent male leadership to what was initially a woman's movement. Male laymen did not join churches in large numbers until the second and third waves of revivals in 1807–1809 and 1815–1816. From 1795 to 1815 women constituted 69 percent of all revival converts and 72 percent of the persons joining churches outside of revivals. Only after 1815 did revivals function to diminish the predominance of women joining churches. Even then, 64 percent of all revival converts from 1815 to 1835, and 72 percent of all other converts, were women. The final decades of the Second Awakening checked the feminizing process but did not reverse it.

What was the effect of the New Light–Old Light division? One way to measure that effect is to focus upon the education of New England cler-

Figure 5.
MEAN ANNUAL ADMISSIONS OF MEN AND WOMEN TO 97 NEW ENGLAND CHURCHES, BY FIVE-YEAR INTERVALS

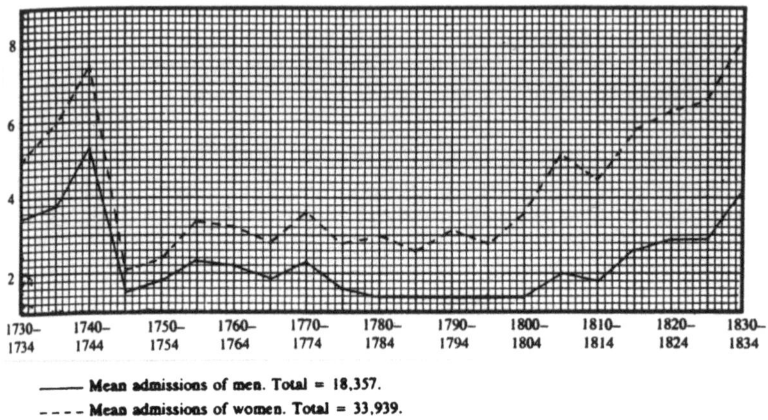

gymen. Education shaped the style of preaching and pastoral leadership. New Lights and moderate Old Lights developed a religious style which was conducive to revivalism; other Old Lights moved toward a rational style which was not. The evangelicals retained much of the Calvinistic tradition and even returned to the Puritan custom of requiring a conversion experience for admission to the church. The liberal rationalists challenged traditional doctrine while maintaining comprehensive church membership standards. By 1800, Yale College was a leading evangelical institution, and Harvard was so liberal that it would soon become Unitarian. The contrast between the two schools became most evident in the nineteenth century, but Yale nearly always had been more conservative than Harvard.[10]

Yale-trained clergymen converted a higher proportion of men than did their Harvard colleagues. The correlation, shown in Table 3, was consistent over time and within different geographical areas. The message

[10] Conrad Wright, *The Beginnings of Unitarianism in America* (Boston: Beacon, 1955); Edmund S. Morgan, *The Gentle Puritan: A Life of Ezra Stiles, 1727–1795* (New Haven: Yale Univ. Press, 1962); Joseph Haroutunian, *Piety versus Moralism: The Passing of the New England Theology* (Hamden, Conn.: Archon Books, 1964). Historians of theology have distinguished numerous schools within the two great camps, and have drawn more precise distinctions than I do here. Even the New Light–Old Light division is difficult to use in a quantitative study, because it is impossible to know how to label every clergyman. The college education of clergymen is at best an imprecise measure of their message or style, but Table 3 indicates that it is a meaningful variable.

Table 3.
PERCENTAGE OF WOMEN ENTERING CHURCHES WITH CLERGYMEN TRAINED AT HARVARD AND YALE, BY REGION

	1730–69	1770–99	1800–35
Massachusetts and Connecticut			
Harvard clergy	60	66	73
	(9,275)	(4,077)	(4,011)
Yale clergy	57	63	69
	(5,047)	(5,448)	(8,951)
Eastern Massachusetts			
Harvard clergy	60	65	72
	(7,137)	(3,340)	(3,677)
Yale clergy	72	63	69
	(153)	(671)	(962)
Western Massachusetts			
Harvard clergy	60	65	76
	(492)	(298)	(83)
Yale clergy	57	60	63
	(383)	(552)	(1,130)
Connecticut			
Harvard clergy	61	73	79
	(1,646)	(439)	(251)
Yale clergy	57	64	70
	(4,511)	(4,225)	(6,859)

Note: The number of both sexes included in each cell appears in parentheses. Eastern Massachusetts includes Barnstable, Bristol, Essex, Middlesex, Norfolk, Plymouth, Suffolk, and Worcester counties. Western Massachusetts includes Berkshire, Franklin, Hampden, and Hampshire counties. Eastern Massachusetts and Connecticut have not been divided into smaller regions, as on Figure 6, because there were few Yale clergymen in northeastern Massachusetts and few Harvard clergymen in southern Connecticut after 1770.

clergy learned in college and preached from their pulpits explains the difference. Yale graduates preached doctrines which incited revivals in both awakenings. The message of Harvard graduates became more rationalistic over time, and Harvard clergymen led few revivals after 1745. For the entire century, however, in revivals and in times of declension, the evangelical, Calvinistic Yale theology appealed to more men. In the Second Awakening, some Yale graduates established Williams College and taught an evangelical, Calvinistic message there. Williams graduates led revivals at a rate comparable to Yale graduates in succeeding years, and drew a similar proportion of men.[11]

New England Congregationalism was feminized in the midst of the Second Great Awakening, a movement in which evangelical preachers led revivals. Both revivals and evangelical preaching diminished the increasing proportion of women among new members; the more "liberal" or "rational" preaching did not. However, the more rational preachers were a dwindling minority in Congregational pulpits after 1800; their preaching was not the cause of the changing sex ratio which was so widespread.[12]

* * *

Social as well as religious change marked the eighteenth and early nineteenth centuries. Communalism gave way to individualism, deference to egalitarianism, Puritanism to Jacksonian democracy. The sex ratio of church members was transformed, not merely by innovations in theology or worship, but also by deep changes in the day-to-day lives of New Englanders.

Migration touched many lives very deeply. Children reared to cherish family ties and communal responsibilities left for the frontier in early adulthood. Each generation migrated greater distances. Early in the eighteenth century, New Englanders moved to the outskirts of their parents' towns. In the decades preceding the Great Awakening, many of them settled Windham County, Connecticut; in the decades following,

[11] In another article which is still in progress, I have identified revivals in the records of these 97 churches over 105 years, and have correlated revivals in these churches with the education of the clergymen. Prior to 1798, clergymen trained at Harvard and Yale led revivals at very similar rates. Neither led revivals very frequently from 1745 to 1798. In the Second Awakening, clergymen trained at Yale and Williams led many more revivals than those trained at Harvard. Women constituted 67% of the persons converted by Williams graduates from 1800 to 1835. On Williams, see Calvin Durfee, *A History of Williams College* (Boston: A. Williams, 1860).

[12] The diminishing proportion of Harvard graduates within the sample can be demonstrated with a table.

	1770	1790	1810	1830
Number of churches with Harvard clergy	33	31	23	18
Number of churches with Yale clergy	37	39	40	17
Number of churches with other clergy	8	20	28	52

they established Litchfield County, Connecticut. After the Revolution, migrants streamed into western Massachusetts, Vermont, and New Hampshire.[13] Berkshire, Hampden, Hampshire, and Franklin counties in western Massachusetts grew at tremendous rates between the census of 1764 and that of 1800, but at much slower rates thereafter. In the nineteenth century, New England's children moved to western New York, and Ohio, and beyond.[14]

The character of the migration affected the sex ratio of churches of the New England frontier. A disproportionate number of the earliest migrants in any area were male. Women constituted only 48 percent of the 1,530 people living in Berkshire County in 1764 and only 49.4 percent of the 29,940 who lived there in 1790. By contrast, 52.2 percent of the 22,139 inhabitants of Essex county were women in 1764 and 52.9 percent of 57,005 in 1790. Berkshire and Essex counties represent the extremes within New England, but the contrast they represent was typical. The sex ratio of the New England population varied from the frontier to the older settlements.[15]

Similarly, the sex ratio of church members varied from one region to another, as Figure 6 demonstrates. The percentage of new female church members was lowest in northern Connecticut during the period of its settlement and in western Massachusetts prior to 1800. In each period, however, the difference in the proportion of women joining churches in eastern and western Massachusetts is too great to be a reflection of the population at large. Perhaps the migration experience led men to desire participation in churches. Having forsaken their homes, migrants sought to build new communities. Churches represented the first and perhaps the primary communal institution. Men who wished to participate in the community joined the church.

Moreover, migration affected the sex ratio of church members in all areas, starting in the closing decade of the century. Families were torn apart, and women in particular felt concern for their departing kinsfolk. Prior to the Revolution, most Massachusetts and Connecticut migrants moved to other areas of their own colonies. As new towns were settled,

[13] The early movement to the outskirts of the oldest towns is described in several community studies; see Kenneth Lockridge, *A New England Town: The First Hundred Years, Dedham, Massachusetts, 1636–1736* (New York: Norton, 1970) for a good example. On the settlement of northern Connecticut, see Richard Bushman, *From Puritan to Yankee: Character and the Social Order in Connecticut, 1690–1765* (Cambridge: Harvard Univ. Press, 1967). On the migration after the Revolution, Lois K. Matthews, *Expansion of New England* (Boston: Houghton Mifflin, 1909).

[14] *Century of Population Growth*, 158–69, 192–94. *Abstract of the Returns of the Fifth Census*, 5–7.

[15] *Century of Population Growth*, 158–69, 192–94.

Figure 6.
PERCENTAGE OF WOMEN ENTERING 97
NEW ENGLAND CHURCHES, BY REGION

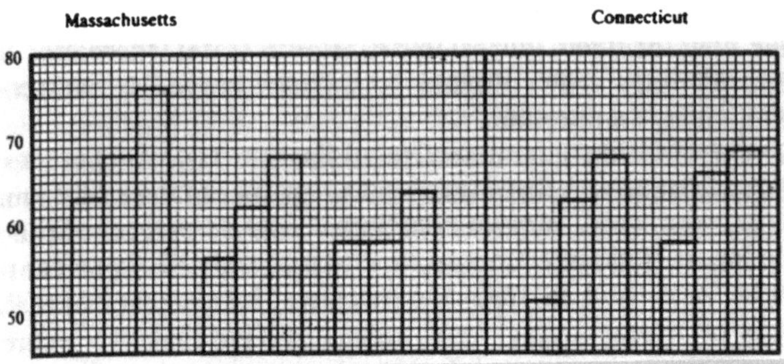

Eastern Massachusetts N = 12,564 | Middle Massachusetts N = 10,221 | Western Massachusetts N = 6,195 | Northern Connecticut N = 8,355 | Southern Connecticut N = 14,961

First bar — 1730–1769 Second Bar — 1770–1799 Third bar — 1800–1835

Eastern Massachusetts includes Essex, Suffolk, Bristol, Plymouth, and Barstable Counties.
Middle Massachusetts includes Middlesex, Worcester, and Norfolk Counties.
Western Massachusetts includes Berkshire, Franklin, Hampden, and Hampshire Counties.
Northern Connecticut includes Litchfield, Hartford, Tolland, and Windham Counties.
Southern Connecticut includes Fairfield, New Haven, Middlesex, and New London Counties.
N = total number of converts of both sexes.

the governments of these two colonies were expected to require that churches and schools be established and that each home have a Bible.[16] By the end of the century, however, neither government was faithfully executing these responsibilities, and most migrants were moving beyond the state borders anyway. Voluntary societies emerged to assume the task of supporting religion and morality on the frontier. The Connecticut Missionary Society, formed in 1798, sent missionaries to establish churches and schools in Vermont, New York, and Ohio. Soon a plethora of similar societies emerged, sending Bibles and tracts as well as clergymen to the West. These voluntary societies attracted New England women who were concerned about their children and kinsfolk who had left home. Most groups met in churches and were led by clergymen. Hence, joining a missionary society often led to joining a church.[17] The sharpest increase in the percentage of females among new church members, displayed on Figures 1 to 3, coincides chronologically with the formation of evangelical voluntary societies all over New England.

[16] Benjamin Trumbull, *A Complete History of Connecticut, Civil and Ecclesiastical*. . . , 2 vols. (New London, Conn.: H. D. Utley, 1898), 1:238, 240–42.

[17] Keller, *Second Awakening*, 71–140. Cott, *Bonds of Womanhood*, 132–42; Welter, "Feminization," 139.

At the same time that migration was disrupting family life, changes were occurring in the social role of the churches and the roles assigned by society to men and women. In the older settlements, churches were no longer central community institutions. The city of Boston had 64 churches by 1836; New Haven had 11 by 1829.[18] No one church could claim even a majority of the leadership in these cities, or could hope to speak for the community. Inevitably, dissenters challenged the traditional status of the established churches and many criticized clergy who spoke on political matters. In short, religion was a source of disunity at least in the older, urban areas. Moreover, other social, professional, and political organizations and ties were competing with churches for male members. Men might define themselves in professional or political rather than religious terms, and men might find personal support in other circles.[19] Indeed, men might feel uncomfortable in churches, where the clergy condemned the materialism of a new market economy and the divisiveness of a new partisan politics.

Displaced from the center of New England communities, churches assumed a more private role. Clergymen gave their attention to the salvation of individuals, to strengthening family life, improving morality and refining popular culture, and to supporting missionary activity. These were concerns of women as well. Women were excluded from politics and commerce and many of the new organizations which competed for men. Restricted to membership in churches and evangelical societies, women defined themselves in religious terms and found personal support in religious company. Like clergymen, women were expected to care deeply about the family in a period in which families were being dispersed, and about purity and morality in a period in which men were encouraged to participate in the amoral world of government and business. Women and clergymen were restricted to similar, overlapping spheres of activity.[20]

Both the role of the church and the role of women changed first in the older settlements and changed most emphatically in the cities. Figure 7 portrays the proportion of women joining churches in urban and rural areas in Connecticut and Massachusetts. Simply put, Figure 7 shows that the bigger the town the higher the percentage of women among its church members. The pattern for all towns of less than 4,000 people was very similar in Massachusetts and Connecticut. However, the proportion of women was higher in churches in the largest Massachusetts cities than in

[18] Justin Winsor, *The Memorial History of Boston, including Suffolk County, Massachusetts, 1630–1880*, 4 vols. (Boston: J. R. Osgood, 1882) 3:415–25; Rollin Osterweis, *Three Centuries of New Haven, 1638–1938* (New Haven: Yale Univ. Press, 1953), 215.

[19] Richard Brown, "The Emergence of Voluntary Associations in Massachusetts, 1760–1830," *Journal of Voluntary Action Research*, 2 (Winter 1973), 64–73.

[20] Welter, "Feminization," 138–40. See also Ann Douglas, *The Feminization of American Culture* (New York: Knopf, 1977).

Figure 7.
PERCENTAGE OF WOMEN ENTERING 97 NEW ENGLAND CHURCHES, BY TOWN SIZE

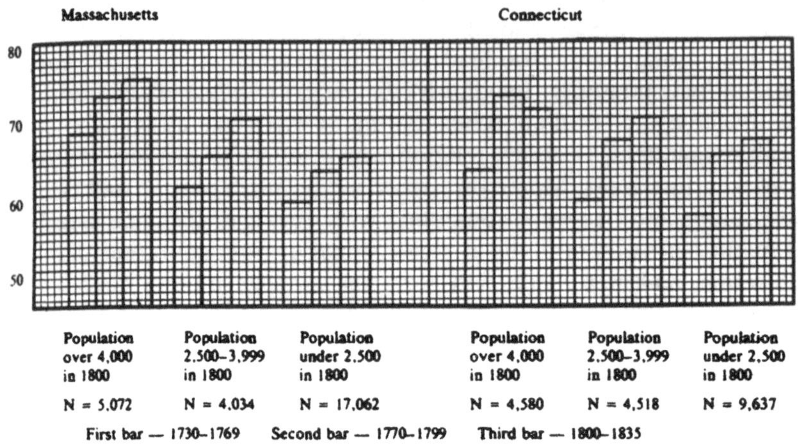

Note: Figure 7 includes 77% of the persons in the sample. The other 23% could not be included because of difficulties in determining an appropriate town size figure for some communities before they were incorporated. N = total number of converts of both sexes.

the largest Connecticut cities. The disparity is partially explained by the very principle which Figure 7 displays. These Massachusetts cities ranged in population from 5,211 to 24,937 in 1800; only Marblehead included fewer than 7,000. The Connecticut cities, on the other hand, ranged from 4,380 to 5,400. The largest cities had the greatest number of churches and competing organizations; these cities were the most commercial as well.

Still, why did the percentage of women decline slightly in Connecticut cities after 1800, while continuing to rise everywhere else? Connecticut's urban churches were led by Yale-trained clergymen. After 1810, many of them were led by men who had studied with Yale president Timothy Dwight. This group was particularly evangelical, led a remarkable number of revivals, and converted an unusually high proportion of men. Connecticut's cities were smaller than many Massachusetts cities; her churches were exposed to Calvinistic preaching more consistently; and, after 1810, Connecticut's urban churches were frequently engulfed with revivals which spread less often to the large urban areas in Massachusetts.[21]

[21] Historians have traditionally credited Dwight's students with leadership in revivals. See Stephen Berk, *Calvinism versus Democracy: Timothy Dwight and the Origins of American Evangelical Orthodoxy* (Hamden, Conn.: Archon Books, 1974). I find that Dwight's students did not instigate the Second Awakening, but led revivals at a remarkable rate after 1810; Shiels, "The Second Great Awakening in Connecticut: Critique of the Traditional Interpretation," in *Church History*, 49 (Winter 1980), 401–16. In my sample, Dwight's students held pulpits in four of the seven Connecticut cities with populations over 4,000, but in none of the Massachusetts cities.

Cotton Mather lamented the predominance of women in Boston churches. The feminization of New England Congregationalism was most extreme in the cities of eastern Massachusetts. Women constituted 73 percent of all new members in these cities in the period from 1770 to 1799 and 78 percent of all new members from 1800 to 1835.[22] A variety of factors conspired to produce these figures. The population of Suffolk County was 51.6 percent female in 1764, 52.7 percent female in 1790, and 52 percent female in 1830. The clergy were predominantly liberal. Many Boston churches became Unitarian by 1830. No Unitarian churches were included in this study, but three of the eight eastern Massachusetts urban churches were led by clergymen trained at Harvard; none were led by Yale graduates. A plethora of competing churches and community organizations provided alternatives for men, while voluntary evangelical societies drew women into churches.

The feminization of New England Congregationalism is both a chapter in the history of New England religion and in the history of the role of women. The preponderance of women in the pews inevitably colored the message from the pulpit; at the same time, religious rhetoric shaped new ideas of a "woman's sphere." The fall of Calvinism coincided with a new emphasis on the redemptive power of godly mothers. In many churches, the members refused to believe that infants who died before baptism were damned or that Christian child-rearing practices were in vain unless the child was elected by a Father-God. They turned from these Calvinistic teachings to the ideas of Horace Bushnell, who advised women in the ways of *Christian Nurture* and even wrote that God might regenerate a fetus in its mother's womb. Similarly, nineteenth-century Christians put away traditional hymnody in which Christ called sinners to repent, and sang new songs in which a gentle, feminine Jesus invited wanderers to come home. In short, they glorified motherhood and sanctified the home. By doing so, they changed the nature of New England religion, and they defined a lifestyle for religious women.[23]

[22] The figures cited are new members of the First Church in Marblehead, the South Church in Salem, and three churches in Boston: Brattle Square Church, Old South Church, and West Church.

[23] Welter, "Feminization," 139. Bushnell, *Views on Christian Nurture* (Hartford, Conn.: Edwin Hunt, 1847). Sandra Sizer, *Gospel Hymns and Social Religion. The Rhetoric of Nineteenth Century Revivalism* (Philadelphia: Temple Univ. Press, 1978).

* Research for this article was conducted while participating in an NEH Summer Seminar for College Teachers at Brandeis University, 1979. I am grateful to David Hackett Fischer, the seminar director, for his encouragement and advice. Three Brandeis programmers (Matthew Schuchman, Ben Westervelt, Evan Willette) and two Ohio State University students (Concha Hendershot and Steve George) also assisted. Louise Verhoek Shiels helped gather records and collate data.

YOUNG WOMEN IN THE SECOND GREAT AWAKENING IN NEW ENGLAND

Nancy F. Cott

In the first several decades of the nineteenth century, New England churches experienced a "Great Awakening." Converts appeared in Congregational, Presbyterian, Methodist, and Baptist churches in town after town beginning in the late 1790s, a time when revival seemed desperately necessary to churchmen and some lay persons. Calvinist piety and religious intensity had been undermined throughout the eighteenth century by worldly engagement, rationalism, and deism. The War for Independence had diverted attention away from religious salvation toward political survival. After the turmoil of the Revolutionary period, the membership and vitality of New England churches were at a low ebb.[1] New England pastors were further worried by the example and influence of "godless" revolutionary France,[2] and some began a campaign of countersubversion marked by vigorous preaching and encouragement of any sign of religious revival.[3] Their successes, reported in evangelical magazines, inspired other congregations to seek their own religious awakenings. After a first wave of revivals in New England towns between 1798 and 1801, revival peaks recurred every two to five years until the 1830s.[4]

A conspicuous feature of the second Great Awakening (the first having been during the 1740s in New England) was the predominance of female converts. There were at least three female converts to every two male converts between 1798 and 1826, according to the Reverend Ebenezer Porter's estimate in 1832.[5] An examination of women's attraction to evangelical preaching and religious commitment at this time should illuminate women's attitudes and self-perceptions, while providing some reasons for revival successes. Women's diaries and correspondence, and ministers' published accounts of the revivals, furnish the historical sources. Modernization theory and developmental psychology supply perspectives that allow the analysis of religious choices in the context of a more inclusive model of human behavior.

Although the second Great Awakening occurred episodically and under the aegis of ministers of several denominations, the revivals appear to have been remarkably uniform. New England ministers consistently preached, and "hopeful converts" accepted, what they acknowledged as "soul-humbling doctrines" or "hard sayings": the doctrines of "the divine sovereignty—the holiness, extent and inflexibility of the moral law—human depravity—our entire dependence on God—the special agency of the Holy Spirit in conviction and conversion—and mere grace through Jesus Christ as the Mediator."[6] This was Calvinist doctrine. New England Calvinism in the eighteenth century, however, in its struggle against skepticism, deism and rational Christianity, had begun to admit elements of the Arminian heresy—the doctrine that an individual's actions could affect his or her salvation. Revival preaching in the second Great Awakening stressed this idea by focusing on the necessity of active repentance. As the Reverend Increase Graves of Bridport, Vermont, explained, individuals were obliged "to do all they are able, just as much as if they could save themselves by their own works." The Reverend Ebenezer Porter aptly labeled this prevalent strain of preaching "doctrino-practical."[7]

According to ministers' reports, conversions during the second Great Awakening were restrained and serious, with "scarcely a single instance . . . of over-heated zeal, or flight of passion."[8] The main vehicles of the revivals were prayer or singing meetings and other group conferences, held in churches, schools, or homes, and usually segregated by age and sex. In prayer meetings, individuals expressed their religious anxieties or convictions extemporaneously, often inducing listeners to blurt out similar feelings. The Reverend Ammi Robbins described the impact that an individual profession of faith had in Norfolk, Connecticut in 1798:

> Numbers who had as yet remained unmoved, when . . . they beheld many of their intimate companions—a husband—a wife—a brother—a sister—a parent—a child—a near friend—a late jovial companion, with sweet serenity, solemnly giving up themselves to the Lord . . . they were pierced through, as it were, with a dart. They often went home full of distress, and could never find rest or ease until they had submitted to a sovereign God.[9]

Other features prompted repeated comment in revival after revival. The converted were neither self-assertive nor self-righteous—they expressed humility, and continued in self-doubt. Conversion usually came not as a lightning bolt, but through a gradual struggle.[10] And although ministers delighted in unexpected conversions of lifelong infidels, they had to report that the best subjects for conversion were young persons who had been reared in families of some piety.[11]

The most striking and consistent characteristic of the second Great Awakening was the youthfulness of its participants. Again and again ministers noted that religious concern and conversion occurred first and most frequently among youths. "Youth" was an inexact term, generally applied to those between twelve and twenty-five, but sometimes restricted to those between twelve and eighteen, or between twelve and twenty.[12] Most of the youths affected by the revivals were female. In revivals in Plymouth, Torrington, Bristol, and Norfolk, Connecticut, and in Lenox, Massachusetts, in 1798-1799, almost two-thirds of the converts were female. In Canton, Connecticut in 1805-1806, and in Farmington, Connecticut in 1826, the reporting ministers said the conversions occurred "chiefly" among females. And Reverend Ebenezer Porter, as mentioned, estimated that three-fifths of the converts in the New England revivals between 1798 and 1826 were female.[13]

Young women, then, made up the largest single age and sex grouping in these revivals. "Young" women usually meant unmarried women, since the average age at marriage was about twenty-two to twenty-three.[14] In the absence of detailed community studies and investigations of church registers, it is impossible to determine the exact social base of the Awakenings, or to figure the proportional relation that female converts bore to the population at large. Contemporary documents give the impression, however, that a broad middle range of the population was affected. Young female converts ranged from mill workers to students at selective female academies.[15] Were there circumstances peculiar to the lives and prospects of young unmarried women at this time that might make them especially susceptible to religious "awakening"?

In the decades following the American War for Independence, the removal of New England's economy from its agricultural and household base was perceptible in the rising density of population, the multiplication of nonfarming occupations, the expansion of commerce, and the beginnings of industrialization. Rationalization and specialization occurred. Commercial and market orientation appeared in the farm population in the forms of specialized agriculture, wage-earning (both in farm labor and in "given-out" industry), and greater reliance on cash purchase of household goods. Even before large-scale industrialization took place, a household economy in which families produced all the goods they needed was displaced by a market economy.[16]

These developments affected young unmarried women's work more noticeably than they affected married women's work. Married women's work in the preindustrial household economy included organization and management of the household, care of children, and domestic manufacture. Young unmarried women also contributed to the preindustrial economy in several ways: they performed general household work in their own families, or were hired out to do the same for pay in other families; they helped out in a family shop; at home they did varieties of handiwork, such as knitting and lace-making, and sold or exchanged their products; by the mid-eighteenth century they taught summer sessions of school. Their chief employment, however, was spinning, weaving, and needlework in their homes and also in the employ of other families.[17] As compared to matrons' work, young unmarried women's household work lay more exclusively in textile manufacture. Economic development in New England decreased the importance of this domestic manufacture. The textile industry was the first machine industry in New England. Spinning machinery was introduced in 1789; and when the power loom was installed in Waltham, Massachusetts in 1814, all the processes of turning raw fiber into finished cloth were first united under one factory roof.[18] The industrialization of spinning and weaving, virtually completed by 1830 in New England, was the single greatest factor affecting young women's work.

It is important to recognize that economic development—especially the decline in household manufacture—disrupted the daughter's usual place in the household before it disrupted the mother's. While the wife/mother's life continued to be defined (and consumed) in household management and rearing of children, the daughter's household contribution sank from vital to marginal significance. The *predictability* of the daughter's relation to and function in the family faltered. The decline of household manufactures compelled many young women to seek paid employment outside the family, to reproduce in cash their former domestic usefulness. Early textile mill operatives, almost all of them between fifteen and thirty years old, were women who followed their traditional occupations to their new location, the factory. The textile industry from its start employed vastly more women than men.[19] Other paid employments open to young women were industrial piece work, sewing for individuals, and school-teaching in summer sessions of public schools or in the growing number of academies. None of these employments was permanent or exclusive. Young women combined or alternated among them; for instance, some factory workers taught school part of the year.[20] Female academies attracted students who had new leisure time or a need for education.

In the search for training and income, many young women of this period experienced relative mobility and variety of experience. The scope of action opened to them enlarged but so did the uncertainty and insecurity. In contrast to the "settled" lives of married women, unmarried women's circumstances were—in the language of the day—"unsettled." For a wide middle range of the young female population, a predictable role in the household economy had ended. Their experience now very likely included repeated change—of work, of place, of associates. Their economic alternatives frequently required them to leave home and board with unfamiliar people in strange towns—perhaps in a succession of towns. The pursuit of work, or support, or education, strained their ties to family and native home. Educational experiences and certain employments also tended to emphasize rootless, age-peer relationships. Young women boarding together looked to each other for sympathy and emotional support, and in some cases this worked to devalue family ties. Teen-aged Rebeccah Root, for example, felt depressed after she left Hartford, Connecticut, where she had shared school and revival experiences with her friends Harriet Whiting and Weltha Brown. Back at home, she wrote to Weltha, "here is Mama but I cannot say anything to her although the best of Mothers, My sisters feel differently from me therefore cannot participate in my feelings I often think if I could see you or Harriet a few moments I should feel much more contented."[21]

Young women who did not enjoy secure places and predictable occupations in their families may also have had difficulty envisioning their future roles. Although the normative role for adult women was that of wife and mother, several factors may have complicated young women's expectation of this role for themselves. One was the surplus of women over men of marriageable age in the populous eastern towns of New England.[22] Perhaps even more important, a cultural focus on romantic love bloomed in the late eighteenth century, contemporaneously with a heightened perception of marriage as a commercial transaction. These developments accompanied a greater freedom of marital choice from parental management, and an increased separation of the conjugal pair from the larger kinship network.[23] In some young women's discourse, a fine distinction appeared between giving one's *hand* in marriage and giving one's *heart*. Mary Orne Tucker of Haverhill, Massachusetts, for instance, twenty-six years old and four years married, recognized that marriage could be a "galling chain": "*souls* must be *kindred* to make the bands silken; all other I call unions of *hands*, not *hearts*,—I rejoice that the knot which binds me was not tied with any mercenary feelings, and that my *heart* is under the same sweet subjection as my *hand*." Some young women expressed a preference for "single blessedness" above a less than ideal marriage. Some spinsters attributed their lifelong singleness to their high romantic ideals, which no man could actually approximate.[24]

Customarily, a woman could not choose her mate, but could only respond to an offer of marriage. As the importance of parents in arranging marriages declined, the power of young men in choosing wives increased and the leverage of marriageable young women decreased further.[25] Yet marrying was the most important step a woman would take: her marriage would probably determine her residence, her economic status, her acquaintances.[26] Women were aware, as well, that a wife's role prescribed subjection and obedience to her husband. A "Hint to a New-Married Sister" composed by a Connecticut woman in 1819 included the warning, "Now you have left your parents wing,/ Nor longer ask their care./ It is but seldom husbands bring/ A lighter yoke to wear."[27]

During the years of the second Great Awakening, then, it was likely that young women's experience contained one or more disorienting elements. It could include disruption of traditional domestic usefulness, uncertainty about means of financial support, separation from family, substitution of peer-group for family ties, unforeseen geographical relocation, ambiguous prospects for and attitudes toward marriage, and hence an insecure future. To be unable to anticipate marriage with equanimity was an occupational as well as emotional hazard, because wife/motherhood was the major occupation as well as status for adult women. It seems that the process of change that made social and economic functions more complex, rational, and specialized in New England brought young women uncertainty rather than opportunity; it brought them indeterminacy with little power to exercise personal choice. The commercialization and rationalization of the economy in this period made men's economic dominance, and women's economic dependence on men, more salient. Because there were severe social and economic constraints on women's means to earn money, the release of young women from their productive domestic roles did not transform them into economic individuals competing equally with men in the marketplace.[28] The gap between opportunities available to women and to men appears to have widened, as does the gap between personal decision making powers exercised by women and by men.[29] For young men, economic and social developments in this period created new opportunities and in the process added uncertainties; for young women, who were shut out from economic initiatives, such developments created insecurity without a compensating new range of choice.

In other words, women and men experienced the impact of modernization in different ways. I use the word modernization to mean the development of "the institutional concomitants of technologically induced economic growth."[30] In the economic sphere modernization implies rationalized production, mobilization of available resources, specialization, and increased scale and integration of the economy. In the social and political spheres it implies analogous developments toward rational, functional, and integrated structures: expanded political participation, centralization of authority, and and movement away from small, isolated, traditional communities with ascriptive or hereditary hierarchies toward one large (national) society with common and cosmopolitan values.[31]

In the United States, decisive modernization was under way within fifty years following the War for Independence. Moreover, American men seem to have exhibited by this time a modern personality type, one animated by secular, rational, and cosmopolitan values, demonstrating openness to new experience, abandoning reliance on hierarchical authority, and adopting initiative rather than passivity or resignation in the face of difficulties;[32] It is open to question, however, whether the same forces that were "making men modern" in the post-Revolutionary generation were also "making women modern." Women were largely shut out from speculative business ventures and popular politics, the two main avenues leading men to exhibit "modern" characteristics. The "calculating, dynamic approach to economic life and social mobility" which Richard D. Brown points to as a central manifestation of the modern personality in America did not apply to women, because of their economic and social subordination to men. Women could not take part in republican politics where the rule of deference to officeholders was replaced with ideas of popular will and public service.[33] Women were socialized to remain deferential to their traditional authority figures—men (especially husbands). They were taught to be passive and resigned, and were expected to exhibit self-renunciation rather than self-assertion.[34]

Yet societal modernization certainly affected women's roles and expectations. It may have had a crucial impact on young women in the process of establishing their adult identities, at just the age that so many responded to revival appeals. Erik Erikson' analysis of the psychosocial stage of adolescence is very useful here. Erikson says the "task" of adolescence is identity formation, "the selective repudiation and mutual assimilation of childhood identifications and their absorption in a new configuration." The child's observation of ordered social roles in and outside the family gives her a set of expectations regarding her future roles; but, Erikson observes, cultural and historical change can prove "traumatic to identity formation: it can break up the inner consistency of a child's hierarchy of expectations."[35] The lack of predictability in young women's economic resources and marriage prospects in the first decades of the nineteenth century may thus have made identity formation problematic for them.

In Erikson's view, the ego's specific tasks in adolescence are to defend against newly intense bodily impulses, to match important "conflict-free" achievements with work opportunities, and to put childhood identifications together in a way that is unique and yet accords with accepted social roles. Adolescents are eager "to be inspired by 'ways of life,' " Erikson maintains, and so are attracted by the "ideological potential of a society." Erikson also suggests a distinction between types of adolescent experience that seems pertinent to the differential impact of modernization on male and female youth:

> In any given period in history . . . that part of youth will have the most affirmatively exciting time of it which finds itself in the wave of a technological, economic, or ideological trend seemingly promising all that youthful vitality could ask for.
>
> Adolescence, therefore, is least "stormy" in that segment of youth which is gifted and well trained in the pursuit of expanding technological trends, and thus able to identify with new roles of competency and invention and to accept a more implicit ideological outlook. Where this is not given, the adolescent mind becomes a more explicitly ideological one, by which we mean one searching for some inspiring unification of tradition or anticipated techniques, ideas, and ideals.[36]

Early nineteenth-century adolescent males were, in general, better trained "to identify with new roles of competency and invention" in a time of rapid modernization, and to accept the modern ideology implicit in these roles, than were females, who looked for a "more explicitly ideological" framework such as that offered by religious conversion. This does not exclude the possibility that young male converts in the second Great Awakening were also attempting to resolve anxieties about their adult roles. Although their childhood identifications and the causes of their indeterminancy would have differed from young women's, religious conversion may have served analogous purposes for them.[37]

More detailed examination is in order to explain how conversion could provide young women with ideological ballast useful to stabilize their lives and identities. First of all, the "doctrino-practical" approach of the second Great Awakening allowed individuals to take an initiative in their own salvation. In bright contrast to the uncertainties that young women encountered in most pursuits and prospects, ministers proposed repentance and resignation of all to God as conscious choices that would affect their temporal and eternal salvation. Yet, the religious choice was actually a surrender—to God's will. One minister likened the sinner's obstinate heart in relation to God to a garrison surrounded by an army. "Many a garrison has been unable to *stand out*, and *resist*; but who ever heard of one that had not *power* to *surrender*!!"[38] The submission required of those who were to be saved was consistent with female socialization, but this submission was also an act of initiation and assertion of strength by female converts. Conversion set up a direct relation to God's authority that allowed female converts to denigrate or bypass men's authority—to defy men—for God. The appeal of this proposed religious choice may have been especially strong for young women because, as Erikson has emphasized, adolescent identifications urgently "force the young individual into choices and decisions which will . . . lead to commitments for 'life.' "[39]

Just as the doctrine of the revivals intersected at vital points with young women's needs, the means used to propagate revivals suited young women's predilections. Prayer meetings gave young women opportunity for public expressions of anxiety, and offered them sympathy and support perfectly attuned to the peer relationships they relied on at work or at school away from home. These small group meetings also put effective pressure on participants to become converts. Characterized by restraint, such practices did not frighten away "respectable" girls as the more exuberant Methodist practices frightened young Nancy Thomson in 1806:

> I attended a campmeeting at Sharon. I went praying that God would awaken and convert my companions but was very fearful that the exercises would be so alarming to my tender feelings that I should appear indecent and I thought If I could obtain religion in a still way without much ado I would be glad to do it but would rather remain without this blessing than to lose my strength or cry out as some did.[40]

The experience of Lucinda Read, as revealed in her diary, was probably typical. Oldest child of ten in a farming family of Greensboro, Vermont, she taught the summer session of a local school when she was seventeen, then departed from home the following January, in 1816, to spend a year with relatives in Farmington, Connecticut. After a few weeks in Farmington, she was sent by her uncle to an academy in Canton, Connecticut, where she boarded with a family. In Canton she began to attend "young female conferences" and to berate herself for not believing, seeking, and attaining grace. Four years earlier she had rejected a hope of conversion as specious. After hardly a week in the revival movement at Canton, however, she expressed religious convictions and felt she had experienced conversion. Thereafter she called Canton the place of her "second nativity."[41]

Conversion brought the young person a "new birth" into an extensive family of "sisters" and "brethren"—a family that promised to be more secure than her original family. As ministers noted, young converts tended to have had some religious upbringing, so their conversions suggested the persistence of childhood identifications that received support from sources outside the family. Achievement of secure identity in adolescence, according to Erikson, requires some form of recognition from society or from subsocieties. The young individual should "be responded to and be given function and status as a person whose growth and transformation make sense to those who begin to make sense to [her]." The community of professing Christians supplied precisely this response to the young believer. Converts were well aware of revivals occuring in towns other than their own, and this served to reaffirm their sense of membership in a growing camp. The support of other female converts particularly encouraged in young women the peer-group loyalties that Erikson has called an important part of testing and reinforcing identity formation.[42]

Conversion during a revival also proved a satisfying ideological commitment, supplying a person with an inspiring "way of life."[43] Providing both an immediate and a long-term purpose, conversion could resolve young women's uncertainties about the future. To summarize the meaning of her conversion in 1808 at age nineteen, Nancy Thomson of Connecticut wrote, "I made religion the principal business of my life." Likewise Lucinda Read vowed, upon her conversion, to devote all of her thought and action to God and righteousness.[44] Conversion did not mean complacency. The Reverend William Sprague advised ministers to impress young converts "with the consideration that *if they have really been renewed, they are just entering on a course of labor and conflict*."[45] One could never rest in certainty of salvation. But the convert's otherworldly concern could provide a source of fortitude in this world.[46]

As opposed to the vagaries encountered in social and economic pursuits, the Christian's struggle was comprehensible, its consequences were well-defined, and a supportive community echoed the individual's experience. Evangelical religion made each proselyte a proselytizer as well. The propagators of nineteenth-century orthodox religion acted on the notion that the best defense is a good offense. Lucinda Read, who was boarding with her students' families while she taught school, after her conversion, wrote in her diary: "Oh that my duty were plain while residing in an irreligious Family. Must I usurp the conversation and introduce religion in the midst of levity? Or must I try to engage the attention of the family individually and say something upon the all-important concerns of the soul: the never-dying immortal soul which they are selling for paltry pelf?"[47]

The revival demanded individual commitment in its central question, "What shall you do to be saved?" The community of converts offered supportive recognition to the person who repented and sought grace. The church required "fidelity" and an ideological stance against "infidelity." Conversion promised not only a lifetime's work in religious struggle, but also a loyal peer-group with whom to share it. For young women whose growth to adulthood in a period of modernization was marked by disruption and uncertainty, these elements together comprised a persuasive argument for forming a religious identity.[48] While evangelical Christianity confined women to private religious roles, sex-specific propriety, and subordinate public status, it also brought them vital strength and purpose that found confirmation among their peers. The reasons supporting young women's conversions during the second Great Awakening suggest why Christian identity was fundamental to the definition of "womanhood" through the nineteenth century.

NOTES

[1]Cf. William Warren Sweet, *Revivalism in America* (New York: Charles Scribner, 1944), p. 117: "[In post-Revolutionary America] religious and moral conditions of the country as a whole reached the lowest ebb tide in the entire history of the American people"; and Sydney E. Ahlstrom, *A Religious History of the American People* (New Haven: Yale University Press, 1972), p. 365: "The revolutionary era was a period of decline for American Christianity as a whole. The churches reached a lower ebb of vitality during the two decades after the end of hostilities than at any other time in the country's religious history." Lawrence Cremin, *American Education: The Colonial Experience* (New York: Harper Torchbooks, 1970), p. 493, concurs that Sweet's estimate that twenty to twenty-five percent of the New England population were church members in 1760 seems fair or a little high.

[2]The Rev. Nathan Perkins of West Hartford, Connecticut, for example, in 1798 attributed the errors and heresies of recent years to the corruption of morals during the American Revolution, to revolutionary events in Europe, and to the number of atheistic and infidel publications released "by the votaries of MODERN PHILOSOPHY, and the NEW THEORIES of liberty and equality." Quoted in William Wallis Woodward, *Surprising Accounts of the Revival of Religion, in the United States of America. . .* (Philadelphia: the author, 1802), p. 117.

[3]The best known of the New Divinity men were Samuel Hopkins of Newport, R.I., Stephen West of Stockbridge and Nathaniel Emmons of Franklin, Mass., and Ebenezer Porter, Asahel Hooker, Azel Backus and Abel Flint of Connecticut. Charles R. Keller, *The Second Great Awakening in Connecticut* (New Haven: Yale University Press, 1942), pp. 26, 33.

Richard D. Birdsall, in "The Second Great Awakening and the New England Social Order," *Church History* 39 (1970): 358, sees the first stage of the revivals as "the expression of intense religious feelings coming from solitary individuals and building into numerous close though temporary communities," and the second stage as "a kind of consolidation and crystalization of this spirit, in which the clergy rather than the people played the more active role."

[4]Charles Keller notes revival peaks in 1798-1801, 1805-1806, 1807-1808, 1812, 1815-1816, 1818, 1820-1821, and 1825-1826: *Second Great Awakening*, pp. 37, 42.

[5]Ebenezer Porter, *Letters on Revivals of Religion* (Andover, Mass.: Revival Association, 1832), p. 5. Women constituted the majority of New England church members from about the middle of the seventeenth century onwards. See Edmund S. Morgan, "New England Puritanism: Another Approach," *William and Mary Quarterly* 3rd ser., 18 (1961): 236-42; Darrett Rutman, "God's

Bridge Falling Down—'Another Approach' to New England Puritanism Assayed," *William and Mary Quarterly* 3d ser., 19 (1962): 408-21; and Mary Maples Dunn, "Colonial Women and Religion: Quaker and Puritan Compared," paper delivered at the Second Berkshire Conference on the History of Women, Cambridge, Mass., October 26, 1974. Nevertheless, the great influx of female converts during the second Great Awakening requires explanation. Donald Mathews, "The Second Great Awakening as an Organizing Process," *American Quarterly* 21 (1969): p. 42, and Whitney R. Cross, *The Burned Over District* (New York: Harper Torchbooks, 1965), esp. pp. 84-89, have noted the potential significance of the disproportionate numbers of female converts during these revivals. In the first Great Awakening of the 1730s-1740s, according to Cedric Cowing, "Sex and Preaching in the Great Awakening," *American Quarterly* 20 (1968): 624-44, male converts brought the sex ratio to parity in New Light churches.

[6]The Rev. Alexander Gillet, regarding the revival in Torrington, Connecticut, 1798-1799, quoted in Bennet Tyler, *New England Revivals, as they existed at the close of the eighteenth and the beginning of the nineteenth centuries. Compiled principally from narratives first published in the Connecticut Evangelical Magazine* (Boston: Sabbath School Association, 1846), pp. 90-91. See also Keller, *Second Great Awakening*, pp. 29-30, 204, 366-67; William B. Sprague, *Lectures on Revivals of Religion . . . with an Appendix, consisting of letters from . . . [many ministers]*, 2d ed. (New York: Daniel Appleton, 1833), p. 238, 271; and Ebenezer Porter, *Letters*, p. 15.

Ahlstrom, *Religious History*, p. 417, notes that before Western, Methodist, and "New School" practices took hold, the second Great Awakening in New England broadcast simple and uniform doctrine: God's absolute sovereignty, man's total depravity, Christ's atoning love.

[7]Graves was quoted in an account of the Bridport revival of 1813-1814 in Tyler, *N. E. Revivals*, pp. 366-67. Porter, *Letters*, pp. 13, 15, explained that the doctrino-practical approach stressed "the entire alienation of the sinner's heart from God:—his voluntary, inexcusable, and yet certain rejection of the gospel, till his heart is subdued by divine influence; his complete obligation, as a moral agent, to repent, and do all that God requires of him, and to do it immediately; his need of an infinite Saviour to make atonement for him, for an infinite Sanctifier to renovate him, and take away his only obstacle to obedience, the guilty opposition of his heart; and his dependence on free grace through faith to justify and save him."

Cf. William McLoughlin's summary of the idea of "compliance with the terms of salvation," introduced by the New Divinity pastor Nathaniel Taylor: "The process of conversion thus became a shared act, a complementary relationship. Man striving and yearning; God benevolent and eager to save; the sinner stretching out his hands to receive the gift of grace held out by a loving God. This belief in man's free will or his partial power to effect his own salvation had in earlier Calvinist days been condemned as the heresy of Arminiansim. For this reason most nineteenth-century ministers preferred to call themselves Evangelicals," (*The American Evangelicals 1800-1900* [New York: Harper Torchbooks, 1968], p. 10).

[8]Thomas Baldwin, *A Brief Account of the Late Revivals of Religion in a Number of Towns in the New-England States* (Boston, Manning and Loring, 1799), p. 6. See also Woodward, *Surprising Accounts* pp. 8, 11, 25; Joshua Bradley, *Account of Religious Revivals in Many Parts of the United States from 1815 to 1818* (Albany, New York: G. J. Loomis and Co., 1819), pp. 30, 40, 51-53; Tyler, *N. E. Revivals*, pp. 57-58. In fact, this claim appears in almost every revival account of the period, intending, no doubt, to disarm critics who associated revivals with "enthusiasm." Did the minister-reporters "protest too much"? The absence of accusations of enthusiasm, and honest admission of a few instances of over-zealous behavior, suggest that the ministers were reporting the circumstances fairly.

[9]Quoted in Tyler, *N. E. Revivals*, pp. 186-87; also in *New England Tracts, No. 1; Narratives of Reformations, in Canton and Norfolk, Connecticut, in four letters* (Providence, Barnum Fields, n.d.), p. 16.

For a description of prayer meetings by an opponent of them, see Menzies Rayner, *A Dissertation upon Extraordinary Awakenings* (New Haven: Herald Office, 1816), pp. 43-51.

[10]Tyler, *N. E. Revivals*, pp. 76, 148, 159, 189; Porter, *Letters*, p. 35. Part of this emphasis was probably due to ministers' desire to ward off criticism of enthusiasm.

[11]Tyler, *N. E. Revivals*, pp. 197, 209, 318, 342, 357; Sprague, *Lectures*, p. 114; Porter, *Letters*, p. 5. Many ministers joined Ammi Robbins in recognizing and exploiting the influence a person's conversion could have on other members of her or his family; e.g., Woodward, *Surprising Accounts*, pp. 7, 238-42; Tyler, *N. E. Revivals*, pp. 186-87; *New England Tracts*, p. 16.

[12]See Tyler, *N. E. Revivals*, pp. 24-27, 55, 84, 93, 120, 155, 196, 284-86, 322, 339, 356; Sprague, *Lectures*, pp. 272, 295; Porter, *Letters*, p. 6; Woodward, *Surprising Accounts*, pp. 7, 12, 18, 22; Baldwin, *Brief Account*, pp. 4, 5, 7; Bradley, *Account*, pp. 13-22, 26-29, 34-35, 36-38, 38-41, 41-42, 49-50, 51, 53-59, 65-77, 85-95, 130-32.

The largest pool of possible converts obviously consisted of youths. There were also reasons of self-interest and church-interest that would have led ministers to emphasize the youth of their new professors. Conversion of young persons promised most for the future stability of church and society, and contradicted the notion that orthodox doctrines were old-fashioned and irrelevant to post-Revolutionary America. Neverthless it is unlikely that ministers exaggerated the role of youths, because such claims were also subject to the accusation that young people were volatile and susceptible to enthusiasms, and their professions of faith often specious.

Joseph Kett has written about "youth" (male) in New England in "Growing Up in Rural New England, 1800-1840," in *Anonymous Americans: Explorations in Nineteenth-Century Social History*, ed., Tamara K. Hareven (Englewood Cliffs, N.J.: Prentice-Hall, 1971), pp. 1-16, and "Adolescence and Youth in Nineteenth-Century America," in *The Family in History*, eds., Theodore K. Rabb and Robert I. Rotberg (New York: Harper Torchbooks, 1973), pp. 95-110.

[13]Tyler, *N. E. Revivals*, pp. 95, 84-85, 187, 155, 322-32; Sprague, *Lectures*, p. 295; Porter, *Letters*, p. 5.

[14]On age of marriage in this period, see Robert V. Wells, "Quaker Marriage Patterns in a Colonial Perspective," *William and Mary Quarterly* 3d ser., 29 (1972): 418-21; and Bernard Farber, *Guardians of Virtue; Salem Families in 1800* (New York: Basic Books, 1972), pp. 41-43.

[15]E.g., Catherine Sedgwick reported to her brother in a letter of September 15, 1833, from Lenox, Massachusetts, "We have had the religious agitators among us lately—They have produced some effect on the factory girls & such light & combustible materials—." Sedgwick, a Unitarian, objected to evangelical religion. CS to Robert Sedgwick, Sedgwick Collection, Massachusetts Historical Society.

See also Almond H. Davis, *The Female Preacher, or Memoir of Salome Lincoln* (Providence, R.I.: J. S. Mowry, 1843), the memoir of a Massachusetts factory worker who became a Freewill Baptist preacher.

Numerous conversions at such academies as Miss Pierce's in Litchfield, Connecticut, indicated that middle-class and elite group responded to revival appeals. A student at Miss Pierce's in 1814-15 wrote to a friend about the success of revival meetings in Litchfield, "We trust that more than half the school have been made the subjects of renewing grace." Abigail Bradley to Eliza Nash, September 14, 1815, Bradley—Hyde Collection, Schlesinger Library.

[16]See Percy Wells Bidwell, "The Agricultural Revolution in New England," *American Historical Review* 26 (1920): 683-702, David Montgomery, "The Working Classes of the Pre-Industrial American City," in *New Perspectives in American History*, eds., Stanley Katz and Stanley Kutler, 2d ed. (Boston: Little-Brown, 1972), I, pp. 222-37; Douglass C. North, *The Economic Growth of the United States, 1790-1860* (New York: W. W. Norton, 1966), pp. 156-77; and Nancy F. Cott, "In the Bonds of Womanhood: Perspectives on Female Experience and Consciousness in New England, 1780-1830," (Ph.D. dissertation, Brandeis University, 1974), chapter 1.

[17]See Cott, "In the Bonds," pp. 11-19.

[18]The first manufactories, established during the 1760s in major American cities, were merely places of business to collect yarn spun and cloth woven by women in their homes by traditional hand methods. Then, by the 1780s, some employers put spinning wheels and looms on their own

premises, and hired women to work them there. In general, at this stage a small number of women were employed on the premises, and a much larger number worked at home. After the introduction of spinning machinery, and the subsequent spread of spinning mills, these circumstances were reversed. Spinning became a machine industry more than two decades before weaving did. The first factories produced yarn only, not cloth. With the introduction of the power loom, weaving also became a factory rather than a domestic occupation. See Edith Abbott, *Women in Industry* (New York: D. Appleton, 1918), pp. 36-39, 41-47; and Rolla M. Tryon, *Household Manufactures in the United States 1640-1860* ([1917] New York: Augustus M. Kelly, 1966), pp. 274-77.

[19]Abbott, *Women in Industry*, pp. 89-90, 121.

[20]Ibid., p. 119; Lucy Larcom, *A New England Girlhood* ([1889] New York: Corinth Books, 1961), p. 223. For examples of women who spent their youth pursuing various means of economic support see *The Life and Letters of Mrs. Emily C. Judson*, ed., A. C. Kendrick (Boston: Gould and Lincoln, 1861), pp. 15-26, and Davis, *The Female Preacher*.

[21]Rebeccah Root to Weltha Brown, August 7, 1815, Weltha Brown Correspondence, Schlesinger Library.

According to operatives like Lucy Larcom, Harriet Hanson Robinson, and the contributors to the Lowell magazines, work in the Lowell-area mills also emphasized age-peer relationships among operatives.

[22]There was a surplus of women above age sixteen in the eastern counties of Massachusetts from the latter part of the eighteenth century. See the 1764-1765 census in *Early Census-Making in Massachusetts*, ed., J. H. Benton, Jr. (Boston: Boston University Press, 1905). David Montgomery reports that the sex ratio in Massachusetts in 1810 was 103 (women) to 100(men) for the age group 16-45; for the age group over 26 it was 107 to 100. The sex ratio in Boston was 127 to 100. "Working Classes," pp. 235-36.

[23]Data assembled by Daniel Scott Smith indicate a shift toward individual autonomy and away from parental control in marriage choice beginning markedly during the Revolutionary period. "Parental Power and Marriage Patterns—An Analysis of Historical Trends in Hingham, Massachusetts," *Journal of Marriage and the Family* 35 (1973): 419-28. See Herman R. Lantz, *et al.*, "Pre-Industrial Patterns in the Colonial Family in America: A Content Analysis of Colonial Magazines," *American Sociological Review* 33 (1968): 413-26, on the existence of romantic love ideals by the late eighteenth century. See also Ian Watt, "The New Woman: Samuel Richardson's *Pamela*," in *The Family: Its Structure and Functions*, ed., Rose Laub Coser(New York: St. Martin's Press, 1964), pp. 269-72, on the implications of freeing the conjugal pair from the larger family network.

[24]Manuscript diary of Mary Orne Tucker, April 17, 1802, Essex Institute Library, Salem, Massachusetts. Eliza Chaplin of Salem asserted in 1820 that she would never give her hand without her heart, having as she did a romantic ideal of the perfect mate. "Rather than be subject to the 'eternal strife,' which . . . prevails . . . where minds are 'fettered to different moulds,' " she said, she would "ever remain in 'single blessedness' and deem it felicity thus to live." Eliza Chaplin to Laura Lovell, July 26, 1820, Chaplin-Lovell correspondence, Essex Institute Library.

Cf. Mrs. A. J. Graves (pseud.), *Girlhood and Womanhood* (Boston: T. H. Carter, 1844), p. 210; and Catherine Sedgwick's musing, at 45, that her rejections of marriage offers may have been because "romantic imaginative persons formed a *beau ideal* to which nothing in life approximated near enough to satisfy them." Manuscript diary of Catherine Sedgwick, May 24, 1834; Massachusetts Historical Society.

[25]A nineteen-year-old of Maine wrote with sarcasm in 1802 on this point, "We ladies, you know, posesss that 'sweet pliability of temper' that disposes us to enjoy any situation, and we must have no choice in these things till we find what is to be our destiny, then we must consider it the best in the world." Eliza Southgate to Moses Porter, May 1802, reprinted in *Root of Bitterness: Documents of the Social History of American Women*, ed., Nancy F. Cott (New York: E. P. Dutton, 1972), p. 109. "There are more blanks than prizes in the matrimonial lottery," Mary Orne Tucker admitted in her diary, April 28, 1802.

[26]Cf. the opinion of an eligible bachelor—a student at Litchfield Law School in 1820—who felt that the advantage in marital choice should be on the woman's side, "because the contract is so much more important in its consequences to females than to males—for besides leaving everything else to unite themselves to one man they subject themselves to his authority—they depend more upon their husband than he does upon the wife for society & for the happiness & enjoyment of their lives—he is their all—their only relative—their only hope—but as for him—business leads him out of doors, far from the company of his wife . . . & then it is upon his employment that he depends almost entirely for the happiness of his life." Journal of George Younglove Cutler, 1820, quoted in *Chronicales of a Pioneer School*, ed., Emily Vanderpoel (Cambridge, Mass.: Harvard University Press, 1903), p. 196. With increased migration of population out of New England after 1800, the likelihood multiplied that marriage would remove a young woman from her native place, family, and friends, and make her husband's influence on her life all the more salient.

[27]Manuscript journal of Lucy Beckley, 1819, Connecticut Historical Soceity.

[28]Women's wages were generally about one-fourth to one-half as high as men's for comparable work. See Abbott, *Women in Industry*, pp. 76n, 157, 192, 262-316, 249.

[29]See Gerda Lerner, "The Lady and the Mill-Girl: Changes in the Status of Women in the Age of Jackson," *Mid-Continent American Studies Journal* 10 (1969): 5-15, for a discussion of the relative status-deprivation felt by some middle-class women circa 1820-1840.

[30]The phrase is that of Peter L. Berger, Brigitte Berger, and Hansfried Kellner, *The Homeless Mind: Modernization and Consciousness* (New York: Random House, 1973), p. 10. I would also adopt their caution that there are "reciprocal relations of causality" between "the technological transformation of the economy, and the gamut of modern institutions," and that "the great transformation could not have taken place without antecedent processes that were neither technological nor economic (as, for example, religious and ethical interpretations of the world)." Modernization is a loaded word, since it has usually been used to indicate the superiority of the industrialized West over the Third World, while implying that all social values and structures accompanying modern industrial capitalism are positive goods. I intend to use the word modernization without these connotations, if possible.

[31]My summary of the model of modernization relies on Richard D. Brown, "Modernization and the Modern Personality in Early America, 1600-1865: A Sketch of a Synthesis," *Journal of Interdisciplinary History* 2 (1972): 201-202. See also E. A. Wrigley, "Modernization and the Industrial Revolution in England," *Journal of Interdisciplinary History* 3 (1972); North, *Economic Growth*, esp. pp. 156-77; William N. Chambers, *Political Parties in a New Nation* (New York: Oxford University Press, 1963), pp. 14-15, 95-96; and, on the implications of modernization for women's roles, Cott, "In the Bonds," Chapters 1 and 2.

[32]Other "modern" characteristics are readiness to form opinions about distant or abstract problems; belief that one can conquer one's environment rather than being dominated by it; orientation toward the present and future rather than the past; and adoption of time-discipline, scheduling, and planning ahead as ways to organize life. Alex Inkeles, "Making Men Modern: On the Causes and Consequences of Individual Change in Six Developing Countries," *American Journal of Sociology* 75 (1969): 210, and "The Modernization of Man," in *Modernization: the Dynamics of Growth*, ed., Myron Weiner (Voice of American Forum Lectures, 1967), pp. 153-57. For the application of the concept of modern personality to American history, see Brown, "Modernization and Modern Personality," pp. 201-222.

[33]On these aspects of "modern" behavior, see Brown, "Modernization and Modern Personality," pp. 216-19. See David David H. Fischer, *The Revolution of American Conservatism* (New York: Harper Torchbooks, 1965) on the general theme of the decline of political deference between 1790 and 1815.

[34]Cf. Hannah More's advice, which echoed through subsequent American tracts: "Girls should be led to distrust their own judgment; they should learn not to murmur at expostulation; they should be accustomed to expect and to endure opposition. It is a lesson with which the world

will not fail to furnish them; and they will not practice it the worse for having learnt it the sooner. It is of the last importance to their happiness, that they should early acquire a submissive temper and a forbearing spirit" (*Strictures on the Modern System of Female Education*, 9th ed. [London: A. Strahan, 1801], I, pp. 183-84.

[35]Erik H. Erikson, *Identity: Youth and Crisis* (New York: W. W. Norton, 1968), p. 159. Erikson's theoretical model of the life cycle is valuable for this analysis despite the fact that it is implicitly more male than androgynous. Erikson intends his analysis to apply to the *human* personality, and does use some case studies of females to illustrate his general points about adolescence and identity.

[36]Ibid., pp. 128-30, 156.

[37]On young men in the second Great Awakening, cf. Lois Banner, "Religion and Reform in the Early Republic: The Role of Youth," *American Quarterly* 23 (1971): 677-95.

[38]Quoted in Porter, *Letters*, p. 16.

[39]Erikson, *Identity*, p. 155.

[40]"A Short Sketch of the life of Nancy Thomson," written c. 1813, manuscript included in the diaries of Nancy Thompson [*sic*] Hunt, Connecticut Historical Society. On the contribution of Methodist measures to Congregational and Presbyterian revival practice in the Northeast before Finney, see Richard Carwardine, "The Second Great Awakening in the Urban Centers: An Examination of Methodism and the 'New Measures,'" *Journal of American History* 59 (1972): 327-41.

[41]Manuscript diary of Lucinda Read, 1815-1816, Massachusetts Historical Society, esp. entries for January 19; February 1, 23, 25, 27; March 23, 1816.

[42]Erikson, *Identity*, pp. 156, 132-33. For an example of converts' correspondence noting revivals in other towns, see Rebeccah Root to Weltha Brown, April 1829, Weltha Brown Correspondence.

[43]Erikson maintains that "fidelity" or "the search for something and somebody to be true to," is "in the center of youth's most passionate and most erratic striving" (*Identity*, pp. 233,235).

[44]Thomson, "Short Sketch," and Lucinda Read diary, March 30, 1816. Cf. Birdsall, "Second Great Awakening," p. 357: "From this new and brief community a new sense of individual and social possibility could develop; for the individual was no longer existing in the broad and somewhat abstract social pattern of the formal law with its universal prescription of what was criminal and what was not, but rather within a community of belief in which he was encouraged to make a decision that would be a positive organizing principle for his own life. For this instant he experienced a radical freedom—in which he could make a personal decision and this in a new community of mutual concern."

[45]Sprague, *Lectures*, p. 151.

[46]Professing faith implied earthly self-denial, but for sufficient cause; as one female convert confided to another, "I long to become 'crucified to the world, that the world may become crucified to me.' The greatest joy of a christian is, that while he is in the world he is out of it" (Rebeccah Root to Weltha Brown, September 27, 1816, Weltha Brown Correspondence).

[47]Lucinda Read diary, September 20, 1816.

[48]An example of the consoling power of a religious identity may be seen in the case of Rachel Stearns, of Greenfield, Massachusetts. Descended from solidly respectable New England families, she nevertheless endured financial stringency from her youth as a result of her father's early death. In the mid-1830s, when she was in her early twenties, she pursued a variety of types of work—sewing, teaching—and seemed to suffer a sense of isolation and class displacement as one of the genteel poor. In 1835 she deserted her family's traditional Congregationalism and became a Methodist convert, though this set her off even more from her relatives. In her diary she recorded the encouragement she gained from the Methodist doctrine of God's perfect love, and the sole happiness she found in feeling that she was living for God and in Christ: "Yes, through the grace and mercy of God, it is possible that *I*, the 'self-willed' 'obstinate' 'head-strong' and at the same time 'inefficient' 'shiftless' and 'ill-tempered' *Rachel*, that girl whose very name conveys the idea of the essence of ugliness, and who added to all her other faults, pride and self-conceit, who conscious that this long catalogue of

evil things applied to her by her friends did not apply in its full extent, thence concluded that none of them knew, and that she was in reality very good superior to most people, Yes, *this girl, this Rachel*, may live to fear God without committing sin" (Rachel Willard Stearns diary, September 14, 1836, volume 6, Stearns Collection, Schlesinger Library; see also entries for May 3, July 19, November 15, 19, 1835).

Domesticity and Religion in the Antebellum Period: The Career of Phoebe Palmer

By

ANNE C. LOVELAND*

It is well known that women enlisted enthusiastically in the ranks of the antebellum evangelical crusade. At prayer meetings and revivals, through missionary, education, and other "female benevolent societies," they engaged in the work of converting sinners to Christ.[1] Moreover, as Barbara Welter has observed, such efforts were generally sanctioned by the "cult of true womanhood." Advocates of the cult, both male and female, noted approvingly that religious activity did not take woman from her proper sphere, nor did it make her less domestic or submissive.[2] Nevertheless, the experience of one woman, Phoebe Palmer, belied the confident statements of the cult. Instead of harmony, she discovered a conflict between domestic and religious duties, and in the course of resolving the conflict she enlarged the boundaries of woman's proper sphere. Though her prominence as an evangelist prevents her from being categorized as a "typical" woman, it seems likely that other women of the antebellum period, whose lives were also shaped by evangelical religion, underwent similar experiences and conflict.

Phoebe Palmer was a leader in the perfectionist or holiness

* The author is Associate Professor of History at Louisiana State University. She wishes to acknowledge the assistance of the National Endowment for the Humanities in the form of a Younger Humanist Fellowship.

[1] See, for example, Whitney R. Cross, *The Burned-Over District: The Social and Intellectual History of Enthusiastic Religion in Western New York, 1800-1850* (New York, 1950), 84-89, 177, 237; Timothy L. Smith, *Revivalism and Social Reform: American Protestantism on the Eve of the Civil War* (New York, 1957), 82-83, 124, 143-44; Ronald W. Hogeland, "'The Female Appendage': Feminine Life-Styles in America, 1820-1860," *Civil War History* 17 (June 1971): 109-10; Barbara Welter, "The Feminization of American Religion: 1800-1860," in William L. O'Neill, ed., *Insights and Parallels: Problems and Issues in American Social History* (Minneapolis, Minn., 1973), 307, 309, 313, and n; Keith Melder, "The Beginnings of the Women's Rights Movement in the United States, 1800-1840," (Ph.D. dissertation, Yale University, 1964), 47-48, 61, 70-76.

[2] Barbara Welter, "The Cult of True Womanhood: 1820-1860," *American Quarterly* 18 (Summer 1966): 153.

movement which dominated American Methodism in the 1840s and 1850s. She also participated in missionary, Sunday School, tract, and other benevolent activities, including an orphanage, a prison ministry at the Tombs in New York City, and the Five Points Mission. A prolific writer, she was editor of *The Guide to Holiness* and author of several books. Her most popular work, *The Way of Holiness*, had sold 24,000 copies by 1851 and was published in thirty-six editions before the Civil War. But she exercised even more influence through the Tuesday Meetings for the Promotion of Holiness, which were held in her New York City home, and through the revival meetings which she attended, sometimes with her husband, sometimes alone, through the Northeast and in Canada and Great Britain as well. Given what she admitted was her "passion for soul-saving"[3] and the energy with which she exercised it, it is not surprising that Bishop John P. Newman should describe her as "the Priscilla who taught many an Appolos 'the way of God more perfectly.'" Few women exerted as much influence as she did on evangelical religion in the antebellum period.[4]

As a young girl, Phoebe was not troubled by a conflict between domesticity and religion. Her parents were both pious Methodists, the father, Henry Worrall, having been converted by John Wesley; and family worship was a regular and important part of the household activities. Most of the ten Worrall children became members of the church at an early age.[5] Indeed, religion was so much a part of the life of the Worrall family that Phoebe found it difficult to pinpoint the exact time of her conversion.[6] She seems to have been the product of the kind of "familial grace" that Horace Bushnell described.[7] Yet Phoebe was dissatisfied with her religious condition. She chided herself for having a wandering

[3] Phoebe Palmer to Brother Harper, undated, in Rev. Richard Wheatley, *The Life and Letters of Mrs. Phoebe Palmer* (New York, 1876), 137.

[4] John Leland Peters calls Phoebe Palmer one of the "outstanding" exponents of Christian perfection. *Christian Perfection and American Methodism* (New York, 1956), 110. For biographical information on Phoebe see Smith, *Revivalism and Social Reform*, 105, 116-17, 122-24, 141, 144, 158, 169-71, 212; Matthew Simpson, ed., *Cyclopaedia of Methodism. Embracing Sketches of Its Rise, Progress, and Present Condition, with Biographical Notices and Numerous Illustrations* (Philadelphia, 1880), 691-92; Edward T. James, ed., *Notable American Women, 1607-1950: A Biographical Dictionary*, 3 vols. (Cambridge: Harvard University Press, Belknap Press, 1971), 3: 12-14; Rev. J. A. Roche, "Mrs. Phoebe Palmer," *The Ladies Repository* 26 (February 1866): 65-70.

[5] Wheatley, *Life and Letters*, 13-17.

[6] Roche, "Mrs. Phoebe Palmer," 65.

[7] Wheatley, *Life and Letters*, 18-19. On Horace Bushnell's notion of "familial grace" see William G. McLoughlin, *The American Evangelicals, 1800-1900* (New York, 1968), 17.

heart and for being distracted from the duty of secret prayer. She longed for "the full assurance of faith."[8]

At age twenty Phoebe became betrothed to a young physician, Dr. Walter C. Palmer. Recording her satisfaction that the forthcoming marriage was approved not only by her parents but by God, Phoebe noted in her diary that Palmer's moral and intellectual "endowments" were of the highest order. But, she continued, "The best of all is, that he is a servant of the Lord." Writing a few months after the wedding, Phoebe reiterated her conviction that "our union is of the Lord." She noted that the "family altar" had been established and that she and her husband were "aiming mutually to acknowledge the Lord in all our ways." Thus marriage seemed to reinforce the equation between domesticity and piety that Phoebe had taken for granted as a young girl. Religion was to be as pervasive an element in the Palmer household as it had been in the Worrall family. Still, her own vague feelings of religious inadequacy persisted. "I am so often fearful and unbelieving," she confessed. "I shrink from crosses, and often bring condemnation upon my soul. I approve of the things that are excellent, but am wanting in courage, faith, and fervour. . . . my timid nature too often shrinks when duty is presented."[9]

Not until her infant son died in 1831 did Phoebe think she understood the reason for her religious failings. It was the second time in less than three years that she had undergone the "crushing trial" of losing a child, and she viewed the experience as a further, necessary test of her religious faith. "God takes our treasure to heaven, that our hearts may be there also," she wrote. "The Lord has declared himself a jealous God, He will have no other Gods before him." She saw now that in devoting herself to her children, she had neglected religion. "After my loved ones were snatched away, I saw that I had concentrated my time and attentions far too exclusively, to the neglect of the religious activities demanded. Though painfully learned, yet I trust the lesson has been fully apprehended. From henceforth, Jesus must and shall have the uppermost seat in my heart."[10]

[8] Journal, January 1, 1826, in Wheatley, *Life and Letters*, 21.

[9] Journal, August 12, 1827, and November 24, 1827, *ibid.*, 23-24.

[10] Journal, September 28, 1831, *ibid.*, 26. For Phoebe, the "lesson" derived from the death of her son was not a momentary rationalization devised to cope with overwhelming grief. It continued to shape her thinking, and when a third child died in 1835 she interpreted that tragedy in a similar way, as an additional lesson on the necessity of a proper balance between domesticity and religion. God had taken the first two children to point out her neglect of religious activity; now the death of her third child led her to resolve to spend the time she would have devoted to her "darling" in working for Jesus. She was consoled by the conviction that God would make her daughter's "translation to heaven, the occasion of many

Phoebe resolved to devote herself to the duty of converting others to Christ. But she was hampered by continued feelings of religious inadequacy. She remained timid and unsure of her religious condition. Even when she obtained a quickening of piety during a revival in the Allen Street Church, she was unable to suppress a twinge of jealousy over the religious labors of her husband. "My beloved was greatly blest," she reported. (Characteristically, it was he who had led the way to the altar when both went forward to secure a deeper work of grace.) "He seems to be filled with the Spirit, and labors so excessively, that I sometimes fear he will kill himself," she wrote. She knew such worries were wrong: "I chide myself for the feeling I have, in regard to this matter, and keep my fears to myself, as I would not dare to hinder him from adding stars to the crown of his rejoicing." Her own awakening was only temporary. She was "getting on feebly in the divine life;—not so much lacking in good purposes, as in carrying out my ever earnest resolve." She wished she could be "more openly active."[11]

In July 1837 Phoebe experienced the deeper work of grace she had long been seeking. She underwent what Wesley had referred to as a "second blessing," resulting in "entire sanctification."[12] Phoebe declared that sanctification occurred only when she was able to enter into a covenant with God which was *"absolute,* and *unconditional."* "I was to be united in eternal oneness with the Lord my Redeemer, requiring unquestioning allegiance on my part . . . ." She declared herself willing to give up everything—even "life" or "friends"—for the Lord. "I am wholly Thine. There is not a tie that binds me to earth. Every tie has been severed."[13]

Thus in her experience of July 26—which she afterwards always referred to as "the day of days"—Phoebe achieved that otherworldliness, that deadness to the world and its ties, that the death of her children had suggested. Her path to holiness had entailed a gradual weaning of affection, first for her children and then finally for her husband, the person in whom she once declared she found "all my earthly happiness." Sanctification came only when she was able to obey the Christian injunction to reserve her highest love for God. She recalled that "the last object that was

being translated out of the kingdom of darkness, into the kingdom of His dear Son." Journal, July 29, 1836, *ibid.*, 31-32.

[11] Journal, April 28, 1832, *ibid.*, 25.

[12] It was this experience of sanctification that was the focus of the holiness movement in American Methodism. See Smith, *Revivalism and Social Reform*, chapter 8.

[13] Journal, July 27, 1837, in Wheatley, *Life and Letters*, 36-41.

presented as a barrier to the entire santification of all my powers was my precious companion." This was because, as she explained, her love for him "was far too exclusive."

> Before, there were always dregs in the cup of my enjoyment, if he was not a partaker. . . . If I went even to the house of God, and experienced the visits of His grace, they were hardly prized to the same degree, unless he also was a sharer. But now, how different. Though my *genuine* affection has increased, I can see him go with a contented heart about his Father's business in his own sphere, and I can go with a light heart to that assigned to me. He is perhaps more useful, knowing that I am satisfied with his absence, and I *know* that I am far more useful now.[14]

Phoebe's religious experience was similar in certain respects to that of other young women of the time. Nancy Cott has noted the paradoxical character of the experiences of young women converted during the Second Great Awakening. For them, conversion involved both an act of submission and "an act of initiative and assertion of strength."[15] Similarly, sanctification meant for Phoebe an "unconditional" but at the same time voluntary surrender of herself to God. Cott also suggests that "conversion set up a direct relation to God's authority which allowed female converts to denigrate or bypass men's authority—to defy men, for God."[16] While sanctification did not lead Phoebe to denigrate or defy her husband, it did give her a sense of independence and strength that she had not had before. The woman who had once let her husband lead the way to the altar would soon be leading others to "the way of holiness."[17] Her dependence was now on God; it was to Him that she looked for support, for guidance, for protection.[18] More-

[14] Journal, September 11, 1837, *ibid.*, 47. In describing her experience for her sister the next morning, Phoebe said, "It was suggested to my mind that the Lord would take away my dear husband, and I thought, 'How can I let him go? O, let me die, but let him stay!'" Hesitating at first, weeping, she finally said, "Yes, Lord, take life or friends away." Having made that declaration, "it seemed to her that the last tie was broken, and she was all the Lord's. She thought, 'What is this but holiness?' And she kept saying, *'O, I am set apart; I am sanctified to God!'"* Quoted by Mrs. Sarah Lankford Palmer, February 9, 1886, in Rev. George Hughes, *Fragrant Memories of the Tuesday Meeting and Its Fifty Years' Work for Jesus* (New York, 1886), 112. See also Roche, "Mrs. Phoebe Palmer," 66.

[15] Nancy F. Cott, "Conversion of Young Women in the Second Great Awakening," paper presented at the Second Berkshire Conference on the History of Women, Radcliffe College, October 26, 1974, p. 15.

[16] *Ibid.*

[17] Phoebe's book, *Promise of the Father*, which was addressed specifically to the clergy, provides an even better instance of the way in which conversion could lead one woman to challenge the authority of men. See below, pp. 466-470.

[18] Journal, July 27, 1837, in Wheatley, *Life and Letters*, 39. Cf. Phoebe's "very vivid and significant dream" which she related in a letter to Bishop and Mrs.

over, Phoebe's second work of grace provided her with a sense that her own experience was meaningful, whether or not her husband shared in it. She no longer denigrated her own experience, or was jealous of his, because sanctification had provided her with a new identity, a new commitment to serve God. Indeed, it was the same kind of commitment which she had once envied in her husband. Having acquired the proper detachment from the world, having entered into a direct relationship with God, Phoebe was able to be "more openly active," "more useful" in the cause of religion.

For Phoebe the experience of sanctification involved a kind of liberation from earthly affections and domestic obligations. But it is important to recognize that her liberation (if indeed that is the proper word) did not develop out of a discontent with family ties, but rather out of an awareness that she was only too willing to make family ties everything, even to the exclusion of religion. After the sanctification experience Phoebe continued to see her religious work as involving a partial renunciation of her "much loved husband" and children.[19] When a revival meeting or some other activity required her to be away from home, she viewed the separation from her family as a sacrifice she had agreed to make in the cause of holiness. But she never felt easy about the separation, and she never was impelled to abandon home and family entirely. For she continued to believe that "Home, and home duties" were "the place of mother and wife, and from these high responsibilities, none can relieve them." Christianity itself dictated such obligations. "A religion that would lead to coolness of affection, or want of attachment to family endearments, or domestic ties, in any of its various relations, is not of God," Phoebe declared; "and Bible Christianity is incompatible with such a course." Torn between

---

Leonidas Hamline, dated New York, November 29, 1855. In the dream she was attacked by a fierce lion. She seized hold of its mouth and, "with a strength which I knew could only have been supernatural, kept his mouth closed. . . . The fury of the lion seemed so tremendous. . . . Every particle of my *physical* and *mental* strength seemed called into exercise, while no prospect of human aid was at hand. O, thought I, if my husband was only here, to help me in this awful conflict. But again, I thought, if he was here, how could he help me, for his very efforts to belabor the animal would only infuriate, and make his strength greater, and then his strength might wholly exceed the power of my grasp. Added to this, I seemed left in one sense without *Divine* aid, but I reasoned thus, 'How could I possibly, by my own feeble grasp, keep the mouth of this lion closed. Supernatural aid, or rather *Divine* aid, must surely be given, though I have no sensible perception of it, or otherwise how could I possibly endure?" *Ibid.*, 93-94.

[19] The Palmers had six children, three of whom died in childhood. Journal, September 28, 1872, *ibid.*, 144. See also Phoebe to "Much Loved Husband," Groton Hollow, July 1, 1850, and to Walter Palmer, New Haven, January 19, 1854, *ibid.*, 143, 145.

"family endearments" and the cause of religion, impelled to advance the work of holiness but never absenting herself from her family longer "than what duty seems to demand," she spent much of her life seeking the proper balance between domestic and spiritual obligations.[20]

Following the sanctification experience, Phoebe undertook a variety of religious activities. She had already begun to teach a Young Ladies Bible Class in the Allen Street Church Sabbath School. Membership increased to some fifty students and the class became so crowded with visitors that a larger meeting place had to be found.[21] In religious meetings she found herself able for the first time to testify to the workings of grace within her soul. On July 2, 1838, she described in her journal the way that "grace triumphed gloriously over nature" at the experience meeting. "In the early part of the meeting, I felt an unusual shrinking, when the duty of speaking was presented. I felt desirous to avail myself of the opportunity, if assured of its being duty; but the enemy, by repeated suggestions, endeavored to darken my mind." But then "I felt conscious assistance from on high, while speaking of the riches of grace manifested toward me in the experience of the past week."[22] Gradually Phoebe overcame her shyness and took up greater responsibilities. Occasionally, when her husband was required to be absent, she led his class meeting; at other times she visited with different classes in the Church. In December 1839 the Rev. J. L. Gilder put her in charge of a class of her own.[23]

The evangelistic career to which she had dedicated herself involved Phoebe in an ever-widening range of activities. A journal entry for June 1848 described a "day filled and almost crowded." There was a home mission meeting in the morning, followed by dinner with a presiding elder and his family visiting from New Jersey. In the afternoon Phoebe attended another meeting, after which she had several friends to tea and entertained company till late in the evening. Besides attending several meetings each week, Phoebe also answered many requests to visit individuals for "religious conversation." And she listed as "among the most monopolizing demands upon my time, the many letters which I am required to write."[24] Perhaps her best-known religious activity was the Tuesday Meeting for the Promotion of Holiness. The Meeting had been held in the Palmer house since 1835, and after

[20] Journal, 1844, *ibid.*, 159; Journal, June 15, 1857, *ibid.*, 156-57; and see also 597.

[21] *Ibid.*, 34-35.

[22] Journal, July 2, 1838, *ibid.*, 176.

[23] *Ibid.*, 177-78.

[24] Journal, June 6, 1848, *ibid.*, 156.

her sanctification experience Phoebe became its leader.[25] Until 1839 it was a ladies' meeting, after which the prayer group was opened to men as well. Soon ministers and laymen were attending in great numbers, and the weekly gathering became a center for the promotion of Methodist holiness doctrines in the 1840s and 1850s.[26]

While taking up a variety of religious and benevolent activities, Phoebe continued to fulfill her duties as wife, mother, and housekeeper. Social engagements absorbed much of her time. As the wife of a prominent Methodist layman, Phoebe received numerous callers. The hospitality of the Palmers, according to Timothy Smith, was "a byword among Methodist ministers."[27] But whatever the social occasion, Phoebe always attempted to "give such a turn to conversation" as she conceived would "best tell on the pages of eternity." Thus in a journal entry for September 2, 1839, she described a day "very much taken up in seeing company" and noted thankfully that "I do not have many trifling visitors. My friends seem to have learned what to expect from me, and if afraid of serious conversation, do not make long visits—unless they become interested in the subject, which, in all companies, I feel it a duty to bring forward as most prominent."[28]

Phoebe's determination to utilize social occasions for spiritual ends is even more clearly seen in the Tuesday Meeting for Holiness. The Meeting, according to Richard Wheatley, was regarded as "a social religious company" rather than a formal religious convocation. Significantly, it was held in a home rather than a church; debate, controversy, and sermonizing were proscribed; and there were no set devotional exercises. Instead, freedom and spontaneity were the rule. "Any one has perfect liberty to rise and request prayers, or relate the dealing of God with his soul, drop a word of exhortation, exposition, or consolation, or pour out his heart in prayer or praise," Wheatley reported. Such "testimony," interspersed with singing and prayer, was the substance of the Meeting.

[25] For a description of the way Phoebe conducted the Meeting and of her "powers in speaking," see Roche, "Mrs. Phoebe Palmer," 67-69.

[26] On the origin of the Tuesday Meeting see Wheatley, *Life and Letters*, 238; Smith, *Revivalism and Social Reform*, 105; Hughes, *Fragrant Memories*, 10-11, 29. Hughes puts a somewhat later date on Phoebe's becoming leader of the Meeting than that cited by Wheatley and Smith. He says that when Phoebe's sister, Mrs. Sarah Lankford, moved away from New York City in 1840, it became necessary for Phoebe to take over the responsibility of conducting the Meeting. According to Hughes, "She had, while her sister was with her, shrunk from this, but the time had now come for her to stand before the people of the Lord in the holy place, and boldly declare the wonders of redeeming grace."

[27] Smith, *Revivalism and Social Reform*, 123.

[28] Journal, May 17, [?], in Wheatley, *Life and Letters*, 166; Journal, September 2, 1839, *ibid.*, 165.

Indeed, the Meeting is perhaps best described as a communal version of the "religious conversations" Phoebe conducted as part of her holiness crusade. Wheatley further underscored the social, conversational character of the Meeting in elaborating on its purposes and design:

> The children of this world have their social gatherings, where, in intelligent, social converse, heart meets heart in unrestrained fellowship. We can conceive how undesirable any set forms would be under such circumstances, and this social gathering is designed to be, in the religious world, answerable to this want of our social nature as children of the kingdom.[29]

Though Phoebe was convinced that domestic and spiritual activities were compatible—and could even be made to complement one another—she also recognized the difficulty of making them so. The antebellum cult of the home might portray the home as the antithesis of "the world"—"a refuge from the care and strife of the world of business and politics," a place where true piety could flourish.[30] But Phoebe knew that the reality could be very different from the idealization. Her own experience as housewife and mother showed her that on occasion "domestic concerns" and "care" could be "extremely pressing" and distracting. She had found that only by stealing a few hours "from the season usually devoted to sleep" could she secure an "uninterrupted time" for secret prayer and meditation.[31] So she sympathized with a young woman, Mrs. Mary James, whose new baby precluded her engaging in "those outward active services to which you have been accustomed. . . ." Too many women, Phoebe noted, who were active in the cause of the Lord "when free from the otherwise vexatious cares of a little family," lost their religious zeal and "entire devotedness" when thrust into "the unceasing trial of patience and untold care . . . [involved] in rearing a family." This was especially true of those possessed of "minds of a higher grade," she observed. Perhaps thinking of her own experience, she noted that they were "exposed to severe mental conflict on this point." She urged her friend to see the birth of her child as initiating a test of faith, placing her "in circumstances where thousands of Christian mothers are placed, and where, alas, too many are prone to let go their hold on the all-sufficiency of grace."[32]

[29] *Ibid.*, 250-54.

[30] McLoughlin, *American Evangelicals*, 19.

[31] Journal, August 16, 1839, in Wheatley, *Life and Letters*, 76; Journal, 1838, *ibid.*, 153.

[32] Phoebe to Mrs. Mary D. James, New York, March 29, 1846, *ibid.*, 592-94; also published as "'He Led Them Forth By the Right Way,' Letter to a Pious Literary Lady on Domestic, Literary and Religious Habits," dated New York, April 9, 1846, and signed "P.P.," in *Guide to Holiness* 9 (1846): 135-37.

Phoebe's advice was to place domestic and religious duties in the proper balance. "Home, on the whole, or speaking in general terms, is the sphere of woman's action," she declared; "and yet she must not be unmindful of the example of Him who 'lived not to please Himself.' "[33] She was critical of women who weighted the balance too far in either direction. Thus on the one hand she disapproved of a woman who had visited with the Shakers and "become so far deluded, during her residence with them, that she renounced all earthly obligations to her husband and family . . . ."[34] On the other hand she was equally critical of women who engaged in what she considered to be unnecessary household drudgery. Phoebe told of a pious lady, in comfortable circumstances, who was blessed with "literary taste, and a heart inclining her to be variously engaged in doing good, and talents capacitating her nobly for the work. But in view of laying up treasures on earth, she permits herself to bear unaided the cares of her family, while perhaps some poor woman in her neighborhood may be pining in penury, for want of employment." Such a woman was "consuming her energies in doing the work which God has fitted the other to do for her." Phoebe did not doubt that when the pious lady was called to her accounting, God would find that "there has been a misappropriation of talents."[35]

Apparently Phoebe expounded her views on domesticity and religion at the Tuesday Meeting, which attracted large numbers of women. The way in which holiness doctrines might be applied to "the requirements of the *female* heart, and the exactions of domestic and household duty" is suggested by a woman who set down the thoughts that had come to her while attending the Meeting. She wrote that

> my heart yearned over those, who, in the petty annoyances to which most females are subjected, lose their sense of religious enjoyment . . . . what but the proper appreciation of the command, "*Whatsoever* ye do, do all for the glory of God," . . . can redeem from the feeling of littleness, the thousand petty demands which are constantly made upon us? Should we so often hear complaints of want of time to attend to religion, if we fully understood that *all duty was religious* . . . . The domestic avocations, to some minds so peculiarly repugnant, can not only be sustained, but are actually ennobled by the consideration that this is work placed before us by our heavenly Employer . . . .

[33] Quoted in Wheatley, *Life and Letters*, 597. See also Roche, "Mrs. Phoebe Palmer," 67.

[34] Journal, 1847, in Wheatley, *Life and Letters*, 603.

[35] Quoted, *ibid.*, 597-98.

The woman confessed that she had not always viewed domestic duties in such a light. When "altered circumstances" had forced her to withdraw from "public" activities and confine herself to "home duties," she had resented not being able to work in "a wider sphere of usefulness." She said she had "felt a sort of contempt for the household avocation . . . and shrunk from taking pleasure in the discharge of these duties, *because they were not religious.*" Only gradually had she come to the kind of awareness that Phoebe had urged on Mrs. James. Thus it would seem that holiness doctrines could serve to reconcile some women to the confined sphere of household duties, at the same time that, as in Phoebe's case, they could impel others to move outside the domestic sphere.[36]

The rule which Phoebe herself tried to follow and which she urged on other women was that religious duties took priority over domestic ones. She said she endeavored always "to make all things subservient to the duties of religion, showing manifestly before my family that I seek *first* the kingdom of God and its righteousness . . . ."[37] Though she sometimes offered her own life as an example of the proper balance between domesticity and religion, she more often pointed to the lives of other women. One such woman was her sister, Sarah Lankford, who had organized the Tuesday Meeting for Holiness. Phoebe credited her with effecting a profound change in the religious and moral climate of the country district in which she labored. There was a lesson in her achievement: "Had sister pleaded important domestic engagements, as she truly might have done, and have thought the spiritual and moral culture of the inhabitants less pressing than household cares, she would not have gone with tract in hand over hill and dale, two, three or four miles distant, informing the parents that religious services were about to commence in the neighborhood, and inviting the children to Sunday School . . . ."[38]

But it was Susannah Wesley, wife of the founder of Methodism, for whom Phoebe reserved the greatest praise. In Phoebe's eyes Susannah was not only a model wife and mother but a woman of immeasurable piety and devotion to God. Endowed with "a mind of the highest order," Mrs. Wesley possessed "the most marked independence of character, and original turn of thought, which capacitated her to act for herself . . . ." Yet, Phoebe noted admiringly, she never challenged her husband's "lordly prerogative." Had she done so, Phoebe observed, she would have violated not

[36] "Reflections in Meeting," signed "E. M. B.," dated September 19, 1848, in *Guide to Holiness* 14 (1848): 89, 90.

[37] Journal, June 15, 1857, in Wheatley, *Life and Letters*, 157. See also *ibid.*, 164.

[38] Phoebe to Mrs. James, Coney Island, New York, August 14, 1846, *ibid.*, 107.

only domestic duties but scriptural ones as well. "Had she contended the point, from a knowledge that her intellectual capacities fitted her for equal authority, how disastrous would the consequence have been to her own peace, and the well-being of her family." Indeed, Phoebe feared that "republican principles" had had an unfavorable effect on American wives, "inducing a forgetfulness of some express Scriptural injunctions on this point." Besides exhibiting the submissiveness proper to a wife, Susannah Wesley was an exemplar in other respects. She had nineteen children ("think of the amount of physical suffering and care") and "no woman was ever more diligent in business, or attentive to family affairs . . . ." Yet, Phoebe noted, she managed to allot two hours a day for meditation and private prayer. The secret of her achievement was her capacity "for *method* and good management, both in her studies and business," by which she conserved time and energy and "kept her mind from perplexity."[39] Maintaining the proper balance between domestic and religious duties was not only a way of serving God, Phoebe seemed to be saying; it also preserved one from the "mental conflict" which seemed to afflict so many intelligent women in the nineteenth century.

As Phoebe continued her religious work she moved gradually into activities which were considered to be outside woman's proper sphere. Her appointment as class leader, for example, was an innovation among the Methodists of New York City, though in Great Britain women had served in that capacity since Wesley's time. What Phoebe achieved in terms of an enlarged sphere of religious work—largely by happenstance rather than design—she began to argue was the right and duty of all Christian women. Thus she criticized the general practice of limiting class leaders to men as a "glaring departure" from "primitive usages" as well as a "deviation" from the General Rules of the Methodist Church. Moreover, she noted that the practice also entailed a great waste of the "talent" of hundreds of "pious females" within the Church—a waste of talent (though on a far larger scale) similar to that exemplified in the life of the pious lady who did her own housework. Phoebe was no less sure that "for these unimproved talents, God will hold the church accountable." The Church, she declared, "needs that a reforming spirit be raised up in the midst of her, possessed of the enlightened zeal, firmness, and independence of *character* which marked her founder, under God."[40]

Ultimately Phoebe came to contend, in *Promise of the Father,* published in 1859, that women who had been brought to "an

[39] Phoebe to Mrs. James, New York, March 29, 1846, *ibid.*, 594-95. See also Journal, June 15, 1857, *ibid.*, 157.

[40] Journal, 1847, *ibid.*, 612-13.

experimental knowledge of the grace of Christ" should be allowed to pray and preach in mixed, public assemblies.[41] In defining the word "preach," she dissociated herself from the "technical" meaning which the modern age attached to it. "The word *preach,* taken in connection with its attendant paraphernalia, oratorical display, onerous titles, and pulpits of pedestal eminence, means . . . much more than we infer was signified by the word *preach,* when used in connection with the ministrations of Christ and his apostles," she noted. In its "scriptural," as opposed to its "technical sense," to preach meant simply "to herald, to announce, to proclaim, to publish . . . or be the messenger of good news." That women had the right to do so was clear from the fact that on the day of Pentecost God had visited his grace on women as well as men. Women had been endowed with the "gift of prophecy"; and Phoebe observed that "though prophesying sometimes means predicting, or foretelling future events, it means preaching in the common acceptation of the word . . . ." She believed that "all Christ's disciples, whether male or female, should covet to be endued [*sic*] with the gift of prophecy; then will they proclaim, or, in other words, *preach* Christ crucified, as far as in them lies, under all possible circumstances."[42] At the very least Phoebe was urging the kind of activity she herself had undertaken in conducting informal worship at the Tuesday Meeting for Holiness and, later, in various revival meetings. Her use of the word "preach" was perhaps purposely vague and though she denied advocating "women's preaching in the technical sense," she was certainly calling for an enlarged religious role for women.[43]

Phoebe attributed the modern-day prohibition against women's praying and preaching in public to two things: an incorrect reading of Scripture by the churches,[44] and, more generally, the distorted and un-Christian view which most men had of the opposite sex. Too many men believed "that woman . . . was formed mainly

[41] [Mrs. P. Palmer], *Promise of the Father; or, A Neglected Speciality of the Last Days. Addressed to the Clergy and Laity of all Christian Communities* (Boston, 1859), 33.

[42] *Ibid.*, 22-23, 34, 36, 43, 328-30.

[43] *Ibid.*, 36. Wheatley quotes Phoebe on this subject as follows: "It is our aim, in addressing the people previous to the prayer-meeting services, to simplify the way of faith, to seekers of pardon . . . . Preach we do not; that is, not in a *technical sense.* We would do it, if called; but we have never felt it our duty to sermonize in any way by dividing and subdividing with metaphysical hair-splittings in theology. We have nothing to do more than Mary, when, by the command of the Head of the Church, she proclaimed a risen Jesus to her brethren; or than Peter and John, who talked to the people about a crucified, exalted Saviour . . . . We occupy the desk, platform, or pulpit, as best suited to the people, in order that all may hear and see." *Life and Letters,* 614.

[44] [Palmer], *Promise of the Father,* 4-8.

to minister to the sensuous nature of man . . . ."[45] They revered woman as a domestic creature, but scorned her spiritual gifts. "Women whose wisdom is acknowledged, and whose position is venerated, when thrown in the society of men of refinement, either of the ministry or laity in polite circles, are, when brought into the church circle, treated by the same men with a coldness which shows that her opinions are lightly esteemed, and her position but little regarded."[46] Phoebe could not but believe that "the children of the world" were wiser than "the children of light" in their attitudes toward women. No worldling would forbid woman to grace the social circle with "her refined sensibilities and social qualities." Indeed, women not only graced the social circle "in converse and song"; a few—like Jenny Lind or Fanny Kemble—appeared on the stage and received the "gaze and admiration of tens of thousands." How singular then, "that when the talents of a lovely female are turned into a sanctified channel, and, instead of ministering by her attractive eloquence to the intellectual pleasures and amusement of the children of this world, she seeks only to allure her audience away from the fleeting things of time and the pleasures of sense, to the Saviour of sinners and joys beyond the grave, she should be looked upon coldly by some professed followers of the Saviour, as though her call were questionable!"[47]

While advocating the right of women to pray and preach in mixed assemblies, Phoebe explicitly dissociated her viewpoint from the cause of "Women's Rights." "We believe woman has her legitimate sphere of action, which differs in most cases materially from that of man; and in this legitimate sphere she is both happy and useful," she declared. Though a few exceptional women might, by the providence of God, "be brought out of the ordinary sphere of action, and occupy in either church or state positions of high responsibility," the proper sphere for most women was the home, where they assumed the "high and holy trust" of providing moral and intellectual training for children. Thus Phoebe was not proposing "a change in the social or domestic relation."[48] Indeed, she contended that woman's spiritual gifts were enhanced by domesticity. To illustrate her point, she compared the spiritual condition of the ordinary Christian woman with that of the typical businessman. The latter she described as "a man of ordinary intellectual ability" who had "never taken much time to cultivate his intellect." His attention was almost completely engrossed by the "ever-varying whirl" of the business world. He

[45] *Ibid.*, 345.
[46] *Ibid.*, 361.
[47] *Ibid.*, 315-19.
[48] *Ibid.*, 1-3, 12-13.

might be a professed Christian, but "too seldom, during the six days of the week, does he find time for little more than a few moments to read the Holy Word in the morning and evening of the day." Phoebe estimated that he probably spent "far more of his precious time . . . in reading the news of the day, and with interests connected with his citizenship in this world, than with interests connected with his citizenship in heaven." She asked, "Can we imagine a man, whose daily routine of life is about thus, in a state of spirituality that would particularly fit him for close and effective communion with God in leading the devotions of others, either in prayer or in speaking?" Yet such a man was often a leader in religious meetings.[49]

In sharp contrast to the businessman, with his sporadic piety, Phoebe drew a portrait of the "consistently pious, earnest, Christian woman, whose every-day life is an ever-speaking testimony of an indwelling Saviour . . . ." There were many such women, who,

> though earthly solicitudes may press upon them, such is the absorption of their zeal that they make even their every-day cares a means of grace, and subservient to their increased ability for usefulness! Knowing that they serve the Lord Christ in serving their household, and in training their children for immortality and eternal life, being answerable to all the various social duties of life, their oft pressures of worldly care are made subservient to greater spirituality of mind, by pressing them more closely to the heart of Christ, as their almighty Friend, and the compassionate bearer of all their burdens. The Bible is their companion, and daily do they live by every word that proceedeth out of the mouth of God. Though their spiritualized affections may not have disposed them, nor their time have been sufficient, to familiarize themselves particularly with many worse than useless newspaper recordings, yet with the recordings which educate the mind, and fit it for a spiritual appreciation of the responsibilities of man's short citizenship here on earth, and an eternal citizenship in heaven, they have cultivated an earnest acquaintance.[50]

In Phoebe's comparison, women acting in their "legitimate sphere" were much more likely than men to exhibit true piety. The man of business, she implied, worked daily in an arena whose principles and purposes were at variance with the cause of Christ, whereas the mother and housewife in serving her family served the Lord. While the businessman's concerns distracted him from religion, woman's suffering and cares only caused her to press "more closely to the heart of Christ . . . ." Such a woman was

[49] *Ibid.*, 162.
[50] *Ibid.*, 4, 163.

obviously more fitted than the businessman to testify to "the power of an ever-present Jesus . . . ."[51] Thus in advocating the right of women to preach and pray in mixed assemblies, Phoebe was led to challenge the ability—and therefore the right—of men to lead such assemblies.

At first glance Phoebe's argument in *Promise of the Father* appears somewhat contradictory. On the one hand, in contending that domesticity enhances woman's piety, she seems to defer to traditional attitudes about woman's nature and proper sphere. Yet she uses the contention as a basis for challenging the generally accepted notion that women should refrain from leading religious assemblies. The seeming paradox is better understood if *Promise of the Father,* like Phoebe's effort to establish a proper balance between domestic and religious duties, is viewed as an attempt to create an ideology which, while recognizing woman's domestic obligations (even elevating them to a spiritual level by suggesting that home duties could be translated into spiritual ones), would not restrict her to the domestic sphere—which would offer her an enlarged sphere of action quite beyond that accepted by spokesmen for the "cult of true womanhood" and evangelical religion.

Thus Phoebe's career and thought would seem to substantiate Keith Melder's thesis that evangelical religion contributed in a significant, if subtle, way in altering attitudes toward woman's sphere and in expanding her status in the antebellum period.[52] Unlike some other women, Phoebe did not move from religious and benevolent work into the women's rights movement. She never shed a sense of uneasiness at neglecting domestic duties, and she always was aware of the possibility of conflict between domestic and religious duties, even though she protested—perhaps too much—that no real conflict existed. Perhaps this is why she never took up the cause of women's rights; it was too radical, calling for a redefinition of woman's sphere beyond what Phoebe herself was able to accept. It is also true that Phoebe's evangelical orientation caused her to be more concerned with woman's spiritual than with her earthly state.[53] *Promise of the Father* can be read as a declaration of woman's spiritual independence and rights, a demand that woman be allowed to work out her own salvation, unhampered by restrictions which would confine her "spiritual gifts." In making such a demand Phoebe declared that nothing less than the moral and religious destiny of the world was at stake. Woman must be allowed to exercise her spiritual gifts as a means of ushering in "the last act in the great drama of man's redemption

[51] *Ibid.,* 4.
[52] Melder, "The Beginnings of the Women's Rights Movement," 43, 61, 76, 92-93.
[53] Cf. Smith, *Revivalism and Social Reform,* 212.

. . . ."[54] The Church would experience "a resurrection of power . . . when . . . women shall come forth, in a very great army, engaging in all holy activities; when, in the true scriptural sense, and answerable to the design of the God of the Bible, woman shall have become the 'help meet' to man's spiritual nature!" Arguing in this vein, Phoebe was simply following the logic of an essentially evangelical approach. But she concluded her declaration with a statement that any women's rights advocate would have accepted: "The idea that woman, with all her noble gifts and qualities, was formed mainly to minister to the sensuous nature of man, is wholly unworthy a place in the heart of a Christian."[55]

[54] [Palmer], *Promise of the Father*, 328, and see also 64, 258.
[55] *Ibid.*, 345.

A WOMEN'S AWAKENING: EVANGELICAL RELIGION AND THE FAMILIES OF UTICA, NEW YORK, 1800–1840

MARY P. RYAN
State University of New York at Binghamton

WRITING MORE THAN A QUARTER CENTURY AGO, WHITNEY CROSS OBSERVED that women "should dominate a history of enthusiastic movements, for their influence was paramount."[1] Although Cross retreated from the question of the relationship between sex and revivalism, his history of religion and reform in western New York state was riddled with evocative references to women. The women of the "Burned-Over District" still stand in the sidelines of antebellum history ready to play a variety of roles. First of all, there is woman as convert, piously, at times hysterically, approaching the anxious seat. Then there is her more audacious sister, perhaps her alter ego, who grasped for social power under cover of religious enthusiasm as she led men in private prayer or even preached. Finally, hidden in the history of American revivalism, is woman the power behind the pulpit, the minister's financial and moral support, the convert's evangelizing wife or mother.

A trail of anecdotes leads out of this literature into the eastern section of the Burned-Over District, to the county of Oneida and its bustling regional marketplace, the town of Utica. The grand master of antebellum re-

[1] Whitney R. Cross, *The Burned-Over District: The Social and Intellectual History of Enthusiastic Religion in Western New York, 1800 to 1850* (Ithaca: Cornell Univ. Press, 1950), 84.

vivalism, Charles Finney, experienced childhood, courtship, and conversion in Oneida County. More to the point, Finney's career as an evangelist began with a tour of Oneida funded by the Female Missionary Society of the Western District. The direct antecedent of this organization had been established in 1806 at a tiny trading post in the frontier township of Whitestown, the village of Utica. For nearly 20 years the women of Utica carefully prepared the soil, planted and nourished the seeds for Finney's renowned evangelical harvest of 1825 and 1826. Utica, then, is an appropriate place to begin writing the women's history of the Burned-Over District.[2]

Utica and its environs, like other bounded localities, also provides the specific population and a concrete and manageable body of records through which to identify the precise roles women played in the Second Great Awakening. The names of converts were inscribed in the registries of four local churches: the First Presbyterian Church of Utica; its parent church, the First Presbyterian Society of Whitestown, located in the adjacent town of Whitesboro; its offshoot, the Second Presbyterian Church; and one of its denominational rivals, the Whitesboro Baptist Church. Each of these lists of church members was arranged according to the date when a parishioner formally professed his or her faith. Admissions to all churches clustered in a similar chronological pattern with each peak of new entries matching the dates of revivals designated by contemporary observers. Altogether, these lists yield a revival population consisting of over 1,400 men and women who proclaimed their salvation during the years 1814, 1819, 1826, 1830 to 1832, and 1838. The distribution of Christian names within this population indicates that women were in the majority during each revival and at every church. The proportion of female converts ranged from a low of approximately 52 percent in the Whitesboro Baptist Church in 1814 to a high of around 72 percent during the revival that occurred in the same church in 1838. All these proportions were above the sex ratio of the population at large: women constituted slightly less than 50 percent of the combined population of Utica and Whitestown at the beginning of the revival cycle and accounted for only 51.3 percent by 1838. Within the membership of each church, however, women outnumbered men by a larger margin, accounting for 62 to 65 percent of the total admissions. The ratio of females to males occasionally fell below this percentage during seasons of revival. In other words, most revivals, and particularly those of the 1820s and 1830s, saw a relative

[2] Charles Finney, *Memoirs of Reverend Charles G. Finney* (New York, 1876), chaps. 1 and 2; "Records of the Female Charitable Society of Whitestown," MS, The Whitestown Collection, Oneida Historical Society, Utica, N. Y. (hereafter OHS).

increase in the proportion of male church members and hence, an actual diminution of the female majority (see Tables 1 and 4).[3]

In addition to sex ratios, these simple church lists contain other demographic evidence: kin relationships as signaled by common surnames. The church records of Utica and Whitesboro are meshed with these suggestions of kin ties (see Tables 1 and 2).[4] Depending on which church or revival year is considered, from 17 to 54 percent of the converts professed their faith in the company of relatives. The same records suggest significant differences between men and women: on the one hand the majority of men, as opposed to only one third of the women, assumed full church membership during the same revival period as did persons of the opposite sex and same surname; on the other hand, approximately half the female converts, compared to 41 percent of the males, made their appearance in the church lists unaccompanied by relatives of either sex.

These data evoke at least two hypotheses about the position of women in Utica's evangelical history. First of all, the proportion of solitary female converts suggests that by joining a church independently of relatives many women exercised a degree of religious autonomy during seasons of revival. A second hypothesis can be shakily constructed around the propensity of men to profess their faith in the company of female kin. This statistic could be read as an indication that the male converts were led into the churches by pious wives, mothers, and sisters. This intriguing hypothetical relationship is given further credence by the analysis of the larger kin networks that laced the church membership. Approximately 30 percent of the revival converts were preceded into full church membership by persons who shared their surname. The first family member to enter the church was twice as likely to be female than male. It would follow that women, in addition to constituting the majority of revival converts, were also instrumental in a host of other conversions among their kin of both sexes.

[3] The records of the First Presbyterian, Utica, and the First Presbyterian, Whitesboro were transcribed from the original by the New York Genealogical and Biographical Society in 1920, edited by Royden Woodward Vosburgh; these typescripts along with the original records from the Second Presbyterian Church and the Whitesboro Baptist Church are found at the Oneida Historical Society and the Utica Public Library. Church records are unavailable for the local Methodist Congregation, which reportedly played a small role in Utica's revivals. The records of Trinity Episcopal Church revealed no significant increase in membership during revival years. Sex ratios were calculated from published summaries of the Federal Census, 1800–1840.

[4] Of the total number of converts 49.9 percent of the females entered the church alone, 17.6 percent in the company of relatives of the same sex, and 32.5 percent with relatives of the opposite sex; the comparable figures for males are 41.2 percent, 5.5 percent and 53.3 percent.

Table 1. PERCENTAGE OF CONVERTS BY SEX AND BY SURNAME

Year of Revival	Utica First Presbyterian			Whitesboro Presbyterian			Utica Second Presbyterian			Whitesboro Baptist		
	N*	% Female	% with same surname	N	% Female	% with same surname	N	% Female	% with same surname	N	% Female	% with same surname
1814	65	69.2	41.5	45	69.6	36.9	—	—	—	44	52.3	52.2
1819	90	67.9	27.7	65	56.9	54.5	—	—	—	70	70.0	44.2
1826	123	59.3	35.1	134	67.1	26.9	53	71.6	30.0	87	63.2	40.2
1830	121	58.6	29.7	110	55.4	44.8	236	59.3	31.0	—	—	—
1838	57	56.1	42.1	—	—	—	76	69.7	17.0	82	71.9	46.0

* Total Number of Converts

Table 2. FAMILY PRECEDENTS OF CONVERSION 1800 TO 1838

	Utica First Presbyterian N = 456 %	Whitesboro Presbyterian N = 354 %	Whitesboro Baptist N = 201 %
Converts related to church members	29.7	29.3	30.0
Cases in which males are the first professors	20.7	15.3	29.5
Cases in which females are the first professors	48.3	61.2	43.1
Cases in which couples are the first professors	37.0	23.5	36.2

To test these hypotheses requires reference to the records that specify the kin relations that may underlie common surnames. Unfortunately, the volatile communities of antebellum New York are unlikely places in which to find reliable sets of vital statistics. The First Presbyterian Church of Utica compiled the only extensive series of marriage and baptismal records for the revival period. These parish records provide information about the 476 men and women who flocked into the church during the revival seasons. Upon initial examination, these records seem unpromising; more than 60 percent of the men and women admitted to the First Presbyterian church during the revivals left no trace in the birth and marriage records. There is no indication that they underwent baptism, married, or had their children christened in the same church in which they first professed their faith. Thus their age, marital status, and kin associations remain unknown. This poorly documented majority can be described only through a series of negative inferences.

In most cases these elusive church members left the First Presbyterian Church shortly after their revival experiences: fully 30 percent of the converts requested official letters of dismissal within five years of their conversions. Countless others must have left the church more hastily and without this formality. Although women registered their intention of leaving the church less frequently than men, more than a quarter of them had also removed from the place of their conversion within five years (see

Table 3. INDICES OF MOBILITY, AGE AND STATUS FOR UTICA FIRST PRESBYTERIAN CONVERTS

Year of Revival	N	% in Church Records	% Dismissed within 5 Years	% in Directory	% (of Males) Boarders
1814	65	48	8	14 (1817)	—
1819	90	38	31	9 (1817)	—
1826	123	34	35	17 (1828)	—
1830	121	25	38	22 (1832)	28
1838	57	44	25	24 (1838)	44

Table 3).[5] Thus it is safe to draw one conclusion about this historically silent majority: they were, at least in the short run, a peripatetic lot with shallow roots in church and community.

There is reason to suppose that the bulk of revival converts was not only mobile but also young and of relatively low social status. Evidence of youth is convincing in the case of male converts. The low enumeration of converts in city directories compiled soon after the revivals cannot be attributed entirely to mobility. It is also plausible that large numbers of converts failed to meet the qualification for inclusion in the directory, namely, being a head of household. Conversely, when the compilers of the directories changed their policy and began to include young men 17 years of age and over regardless of family status, the number of identifiable converts tended to increase. For example, 44 percent of the male converts of 1838 appeared in that year's directory and were identified as boarders. Almost 65 percent of the male converts whose names appeared in the directory at all exhibited the status of boarder, one which often connoted not only youth but also deracination from the conjugal family.[6] There is little reason to believe that female converts differed markedly from males in age or family status. The absence of almost 60 percent of the female converts from the records either of marriage or of the parents of newly baptized infants suggests that few of them were adult married women.[7]

The inference that large numbers of Utica's converts were young and single was repeatedly affirmed by contemporary observers. Ministers

[5] The church records list formal professions of faith made several months after the peak of the revival and exclude professions made in a second church. As such they may underestimate the mobility of converts.

[6] Of the 13 known boarders who converted in 1830, 7 resided with persons of a different surname whereas 8 of the 11 boarders were in this position in 1838.

[7] See Tables 3 and 5.

Table 4. INDICES OF HOUSEHOLD AND FAMILY CHANGE

Year of Census	Mean Household Size	Sex Ratio*	Child/ Woman Ratio**	% Boarders (in Directory Listings)
1800 (Whitestown Township)	6.19	108.2	2,091	—
1810 (Whitestown Township)	6.22	107.8	2,018	—
1820 (Utica)	6.24	105.6	1,387	—
1830 (Utica)	6.48	103.1	1,008	28 (1835)
1840 (Utica)	6.82	96.9	885	30 (1845)

* Men per 100 women.
** Children aged 0–9 per 1,000 women aged 15–49.

sympathetic to the revivals admitted that only a choice minority of their converts ranked among the community's respectable heads of households. The opponents of revivalism unleashed apocalyptic rhetoric as they described the age and social status of Finney's recruits. The conservative ministers of Oneida County penned a pastoral letter in 1827 which indicted the leaders of the recent revival for "disregard of the distinctions of age and station," and charged the converts with acts of rebellion against patriarchal authority. A typical crime, the ministers alleged, was to address a church elder as follows: "You old, grey headed sinner, you deserved to have been in hell long ago."[8]

The religious history of Oneida county contains hints of evangelical disregard for the distinctions of sex as well as age. From the town of Paris, located a few miles south of Utica, came a defense of female preaching in the incendiary tones of Deborah Peirce. The author demanded that sinful males "remove the yoke from my sisters' necks," and challenged timid women to "rise up ye careless daughters," and give public testimony for Christ.[9] Another inspired and daring woman toured the environs of Utica

[8] "Pastoral Letter of the Ministers of the Oneida Association to the Churches under their Care on the Subject of Revivals of Religion" (Utica, 1827), 13–14.
[9] Deborah Peirce, "A Scriptural Vindication of Female Preaching, Prophesying, or Exhortation" (n.d., n.p.), OHS.

preaching against the practice of infant baptism. Martha Howell's evangelism elicited a jeremiad and the accolade Jezebel from James Carnahan, Utica's first Presbyterian minister. Yet a Baptist defender of Martha Howell pointed out that on at least one occasion a woman had spoken before a promiscuous audience in the Reverend Carnahan's own meetinghouse.[10]

These examples of bold female piety were concentrated in rural areas during the first decade of the nineteenth century and were typical of the relatively youthful Baptist and Methodist sects. As such they may be more a symptom of frontier leniency than an example of beneficent evangelical policy toward women. The revivals themselves occasioned only a minor expansion of woman's public role, her right to pray aloud and speak out during religious services. There is evidence that women exercised even this limited new freedom with constraint. In a report favorable to revivals, a committee of the Oneida Presbytery observed; "We have also had various small circles for prayer, as well as stated and public prayer-meetings, and in the former females, in some cases, though more seldom than we could wish, have taken part."[11] In short there is little direct evidence that the young women who swelled Utica's church rolls during the Second Great Awakening were in open and militant defiance of male authority.

These young women, and men, who passed so quickly and quietly through the evangelical history of Utica left little direct evidence of the motivations surrounding conversion. The personal meaning of conversion can only be illuminated by speculative references to the social world encountered during a sojourn in Utica between 1814 and 1838. The strongest reaction inspired by this time and place was probably a heady sense of change, bustle, and impermanence. The military post known as Fort Schuyler during the Revolution had become a village of some 3,000 inhabitants by 1817. Stimulated by the completion of the Erie Canal in 1825, the town of Utica had grown to a city of four times that population before 1840. Stores, workshops, banks, insurance companies, shipping offices, and law firms proliferated as quickly as the population and apace with the evangelical harvest. In sum, Utica was the archetypal commercial town, the bustling marketplace for a maturing agricultural economy.

[10] James Carnahan, "Christianity Defended Against the Cavils of Infidels and the Weakness of Enthusiasts" (Utica, 1808), 29; Elias Lee, "A Letter to the Rev. James Carnahan, Pastor of the Presbyterian Churches in Utica and Whitesborough Being a Defense of Martha Howell and the Baptists Against the Misrepresentations and Aspersions of that Gentleman" (Utica, 1808), 22.

[11] "A Narrative of the Revival of Religion in the County of Oneida, Paticularly in the Bounds of the Presbytery of Oneida" (Utica, 1826), 26.

The sheer volatility and newness of this way of life and making a living might well have augured uncertain futures for Utica's young of either sex.

Young Uticans, however, were spared the direct experience of industrialization and the accompanying challenge to traditional sex roles that beset their neighbors in Whitestown. The influx of young women into the cotton mills of this nearby village had made the men of Whitestown a minority group by the 1820s. Utica's men, by contrast, were nearly equal to women numerically until the advent of the city's first textile factories in 1845. Their preindustrial city offered young Uticans an expanding range of occupations and opportunities, which male converts seemed to have exploited to the fullest. Men entered the revival rolls from the ranks of merchants, shopkeepers, artisans, professionals, white collar workers, and clerks. The lowly class of common laborers, however, contributed only two converts to the entire revival roster. The city directory also recorded a twofold increase in female occupations during the revival era. Yet females still accounted for a mere 3.3 percent of the directory's entries in 1835. The limited ranks of female occupations, chiefly milliners, dressmakers, washerwomen, and teachers, sent only two women, both seamstresses, into the revivals of the First Presbyterian Church. Thus, whatever economic uncertainty might have propelled women to the anxious seat remained hidden in the homes and home economics of the busy city.[12]

Although the majority of the women of Utica remained in the households of shopkeepers and artisans, the advances of a market economy encroached upon their roles. First, the domestic manufactures that once occupied so much of woman's time were almost nonexistent in Utica. The entire town produced only 2,500 yards of homespun in 1835, or slightly more than a yard per household. The products of home gardens and dairies were also miniscule within the city limits, at a time when newspapers advertised everything from flour to candles to crockery, all for sale in cash. Utica's market economy was also absorbing the female roles of shopkeeper's assistant and artisan's helper. The cash revenues that accrued to the petty bourgeoisie could pay the wages of a growing number of clerks and hired laborers, all of whom were male. Finally an increasing number of the town's women were removed from the source of their families' livelihood. As early as 1817 approximately 14 percent of the entries in the village directory listed separate addresses for home and workplace.

[12] Calculations based on: *Census for 1820* (Washington, 1821); *Census of the State of New York for 1835* (Albany, 1836); Manuscript Schedules of the Federal Census for 1840; *Utica City Directory*, 1817, 1837–38. Too few of Utica's converts were traceable in the city directories to provide a precise description of their class backgrounds. For an excellent portrait of male converts, see Paul Johnson, "A Shop Keepers' Millennium: Society and Revivals in Rochester, N. Y., 1815–1837," Diss. UCLA, 1975.

Twenty years later this measure of the disintegration of the home economy combined with an extraordinarily high rate of boarding. According to the city directory of 1837–38 a full 28 percent of the entries identified boarders, men and women who resided apart from their kin and remote from their place of work.[13]

The structure of the family as well as the work force changed during the revival era. Although mean household size remained at the same high level (more than six resident members), household composition was changing in important ways. The practice of boarding brought the brittle monetary relations of commercial capitalism into the household itself. Moreover, the proliferation of boarders and boarding houses coincided with a decline in Utica's birth rate. Extrapolating from the federal census of 1820, there were 1,390 children between the ages of zero and ten for every thousand women of childbearing age. This crude measure of fertility had declined to 885, or by 36 percent, at the time of the 1840 census (see Table 4). This drop in the child-woman ratio is due in part to an increase in the proportion of young adult women in the city's population. These unmarried females, rather than shunning motherhood, had simply not yet begun the reproductive period of their life cycles. Nonetheless, the overall role of Utica's women in reproduction, as well as production, declined during the revival period.

Referring to a similar social setting, Nancy Cott has demonstrated how such changes in the history of the family and the economy worked a particular hardship on America's daughters.[14] Cott has argued that the young women who experienced or anticipated changes in their social and economic roles early in the nineteenth century might assuage their anxieties and affirm a modern identity in the act of religious conversion. This interpretation may constitute the best possible explanation for the behavior of the youthful and anonymous majority of Utica's converts. Such inferences do not, however, fully differentiate women's experience from that of the many men who converted at the same time and place. Nor do they account for the dense network of kin ties that riddled church membership lists, often linking male to female in one evangelical process. The kinship of conversion is particularly significant because it invites a revision of the frequent understanding of antebellum revivalism as exemplary of youthful, independent, and individualistic Jacksonian America.

Only an examination of the select minority of converts who left evidence of kin ties in Utica can yield a more satisfying description of the

[13] Calculations based on *Census of the State of New York for 1835; Utica City Directory*, 1817, 1837–38.

[14] Nancy F. Cott, "Young Women in the Second Great Awakening in New England," *Feminist Studies*, 3 (Fall 1975), 14–29.

relation between women and revivalism. Thus the remainder of this analysis is based on the experience of the 160 men and women who left more substantial testimony in the records of Utica's First Presbyterian Church. They may or may not be representative of the bulk of converts who made a minor appearance in the annals of local churches. Nonetheless, the minority commands attention both in its own right and because its more durable church ties insured a greater capacity to affect the course of evangelism itself. Many even of these converts, however, made but a single appearance in the vital records—at the time of their marriage, their baptism, or their children's christening. Thus any conclusions based solely on these fragmentary records are heuristic—rare and suggestive tracks through an uncharted historical landscape.

In the case of Utica's first revival, that of 1814, these tracks lead in a specific direction: toward a religious awakening among Utica's parents. Although less than half of those men and women who professed their faith in the 1814 revival left any trace in the vital records, 65 percent of these (or almost a third of all converts) left evidence of being married and 23 percent of them baptized an infant child within a year of their conversion. In addition more than a dozen older children were promptly brought forward to be christened by their newly converted parents. All these relationships reappeared with the second revival in 1819. The subsequent revivals seem to follow naturally upon these first two, as progeny came to supplant parentage as the predominant family status of converts. Despite an increase in the proportion of mobile and independent converts during and after the revival of 1826, approximately 20 percent of the new communicants can be identified as the children of church members. Many of the parents in question had presented these very children for baptism in the full flush of their own conversion in 1814 or 1819. By 1838 more than 40 percent of the converts could be identified as the offspring of this firmly entrenched first generation. In some cases the lineage of conversion had passed unbroken through each stage of the revival cycle. Seventy converts, 15 percent of the total, had a relative who joined the church during a previous or subsequent revival (see Table 5).

Thus beneath the febrile evangelism of Utica's First Presbyterian Church there lay a solid infrastructure, the family cycle of the church's first generation. During the revivals of the 1810s Utica's first settlers took the opportunity to plant religious roots in the frontier soil. These revivals of 1814 and 1819 also coincided with the highest marriage and birth rates in the church's history. The revivals of the 1820s and 1830s can then be attributed to the echo effect of this high birth rate, as the children of the prolific first generation came of age, grew in grace, and professed their faith in the church of their parents. In short, the family pattern of the

Table 5. PARENT/CHILD CONVERSIONS, UTICA FIRST PRESBYTERIAN CHURCH

Year of Revival	N	Number of Converts in Vital Records	Infants baptized within year	Children of Church members
1814	65	31	15	0
1819	90	33	7	0
1826	123	41	1	25
1830	121	30	1	22
1838	57	25	0	24
Total	456	160	24	71

revivals is in part a reflection of the peculiar demographic history of the First Presbyterian Church.

The family cycle is a partial but hardly sufficient explanation of either revivalism or the conversion of Utica's second generation. Certainly the Presbyterian ministry did not rely on demography as a means of salvation. In fact, they were preoccupied with admonishing Oneida's parents of their obligation to guide their offspring into the church. The theologians of Oneida County steered a treacherous path through Calvinist dogma and simultaneously conducted pamphlet and sermon warfare against the local Baptists—all in defense of infant baptism and the Abrahamic covenant interpreted as a kind of birthright of salvation for their progeny. Every human agency, both pastoral and parental, was mobilized to bring the children of the frontier into full church membership. The Synod of Utica instructed pastors to preach every November on "the privileges and obligations of the Abrahamic covenant, presenting distinctly the duty of pious parents to dedicate their infant children to God in baptism." The annual sermon should also remind parents of their "responsibilities in connection with their [children's] religious training and the precious grounds of expectation and confidence that, if found faithful, saving blessings would follow." This rather Antinomian interpretation of the lineage of salvation was reinforced by the revival of 1826, which brought so many of the children of the first generation to the ranks of the elect. The report of the clergymen of Oneida on the Finney revival closed with this lesson: "One great end of the baptism of households is that parents and ministers and church may be impressed with the obligation of bringing [their children] up in the nurture and admonition of the Lord." Oneida County was littered with pamphlets, sermons, and ecclesiastical resolutions testifying to this same religious imperative, devising practical ways to guide a second generation toward salvation and full allegiance to the church of their parents.[15]

This same literature, addressed to "heads of households" or "parents," did not acknowledge the conscientious guardians of this religious inheritance, the mothers. A review of the records of Utica's First Presbyterian Church exposes the female agency of the Second Great Awakening with striking clarity. At the time of the first revival women constituted 70 percent of the church population. The mothers, in other words, first planted the families' religious roots on the frontier. Women certainly claimed a maternal role in the first revival, for 12 percent of all the converts of 1814 appear to have been pregnant when they professed their faith. Mothers, unaccompanied by their mates, also accounted for approximately 70 percent of the baptisms that followed in the wake of revivals in 1814 and 1819.[16] Nancy Lynde exemplified this maternal fervor. Within two years of her conversion in 1814, she had given six children to the Lord in baptism. The church records referred to the children's father, who was not a member of the congregation, by the perfunctory title of Mr. Lynde. This family failed to appear in the village's first directory, compiled in 1817.

Yet in some later revival, perhaps somewhere to the west, the children of Nancy Lynde may have swelled the membership of another evangelical church. At any rate many of Nancy Lynde's peers who remained in Utica enrolled their children in the church during the sequence of revivals that began in 1826. Of those children of church members who dominated the revival of 1838, for example, more than 60 percent professed the faith of their mothers, but not their fathers.[17] These later revivals brought some of Utica's mothers a pious sense of achievement, when after years of prayer and instruction their children pledged their souls to Christ. Harriet Dana must have felt this satisfaction when her son John joined the ranks of the saved in 1826, and again with the belated conversion in 1838 of her son James Dwight Dana, who would soon acquire a national reputation as a Yale professor of natural science. Mrs. Dana's own conversion had occurred in July of 1814, at the zenith of Utica's first revival. She was most likely pregnant at the time; her son James was baptized the following September, his brother John two years thereafter. The religious biog-

[15] P. H. Fowler, *Historical Sketch of Presbyterianism Within the Bounds of the Synod of Central New York* (Utica, 1844), 110; *Narrative of the Revival*, 54

[16] The Baptismal Records of the First Presbyterian Church reveal that 8 converts of 1814 baptized infant children within nine months of their profession of faith. Of the 28 children of recent converts baptized in 1814 and 1819, 15 had mothers among converts, 11 had 2 parents converting, and only 2 children had merely a father in full church membership.

[17] During this revival 24 children of church members converted: 16 of them were preceded into the church by a mother alone, 5 by two parents, and 3 by a father alone.

raphies of an additional eight children are outside the purview of Utica's church records and beyond the time span of the revival cycle.

Another episode in the private revival of Harriet Dana is worthy of note, however. In 1826 James Dana, Senior, joined the church in which his wife had been ensconced for a dozen years. This conjugal dimension of the kinship of conversion was not unusual. In the revival occasioned by Finney's appearance in Utica, for example, seven husbands followed their wives into full church membership after many years of recalcitrance. This trend continued in the revivals that followed, much to the delight of the local ministry, ever eager to snare a head of household. One church history written 40 years after the event recalled with special pride the conversion in 1838 of Mr. John H. Ostrom, lawyer, bank officer, and prominent Utica politician. The author failed to mention that Ostrom's wife, then the young Mary Walker (notable church member and community leader in her own right) had converted in a revival that occurred almost a quarter-century earlier.[18]

Another example illustrates the matrilineage that runs through the history of revivalism in the Utica Presbyterian Church. This story of domestic evangelism began with the conversion of Sophia Bagg, who professed her faith on July 7, 1814, in the company of seven women and two men. Her daughter Emma was baptized the following September; the baptismal covenant was recited for her son Michael 14 months later; and two more sons were christened before 1820. When Finney arrived in Utica, Emma Bagg was at least 11 years old and promptly entered the church. A Mary Ann Bagg who was examined for admission to the church at about the same time may have been another of Sophia's daughters whose baptism was not recorded in the church records. At any rate the family of Sophia Bagg figured prominently in the revival of 1826, for in that year Moses Bagg, the wealthy and respected son of one of Utica's very first entrepreneurs, joined his wife and children in church membership. Moses Bagg was one of those "gentlemen of property and standing" who helped to organize Utica's anti-abolitionist riot in 1835.[19] Amid the uproar of the 1830s the Bagg family continued quietly to play out the family cycle of revivals. Moses Junior ranked among the converts of 1831, and his brother Egbert enrolled in the church in 1838. The Bagg family may be atypical only in social stability, public prominence, and the consequent wealth of historical documentation. Perhaps countless anonymous women left a similar legacy of conversions across the frontier or in poorly documented evangelical denominations, the Baptist and the Methodist.

[18] Fowler, 222.

[19] See Leonard L. Richards, *Gentlemen of Property and Standing: Anti-Abolitionist Mobs in Jacksonian America* (New York: Oxford Univ. Press, 1970).

Nor do the church records reveal the more extended kinship ties that underpinned the revival. Utica supplies one anecdote illustrating this wider network of revivalism and at the same time suggests the modes of evangelism peculiar to women. The central female character in this religious homily generally appears in the church's history under the name of Mrs. C or Aunt Clark. During the revival of 1825 and 1826 Mrs. C was visited by a nephew, a student at nearby Hamilton College. The nephew in question came from conservative Calvinist stock and looked with disdain upon the vulgar evangelist Charles Finney, a friend and temporary neighbor of his aunt. Thus Aunt Clark resorted to a pious deception to entice her young kinsman to a revival meeting at the Utica Presbyterian Church. She persuaded him to attend a morning service on the pretense that Finney would not be preaching until later in the day. Once in the church and in the presence of the despised preacher, the young man realized that he was caught in a trap of woman's making. He recalled it this way: "When we came to the pew door [Aunt Clark] motioned me to go in and followed with several ladies and shut me in." When he attempted a second escape his pious and wily aunt whispered in his ear, "You'll break my heart if you go!" Woman's role in the conversion that ensued would have remained forever unrecorded were it not that the convert in question was none other than Theodore Dwight Weld.[20] The famed abolitionist's aunt was Sophia Clark, whose many accomplishments included the enrollment of at least three children among the revival converts.

Such anecdotes would have to be compounded hundreds of times in order to demonstrate a causal rather than a coincidental relationship between women's revival fervor and the subsequent conversion of their kin. Obtaining such proof would entail an exhaustive and probably futile search through women's diaries and letters for confessions of bringing extreme evangelical pressure to bear upon members of their families. This exercise is not entirely necessary in Utica, where woman's role in the revival was not confined to her private efforts. Rather, it was conducted publicly and collectively within two women's organizations, the Female Missionary Society and the Maternal Association. Both these organizations left membership lists, the first for the year 1814, the second dating from 1840 but including the names of deceased members. Despite the sporadic and incomplete nature of these records almost one third of the revival converts can be traced to one of these documents, either directly or through their mothers (see Table 6). For example, Harriet Dana, Mary

[20] Charles Beecher, ed., *Autobiography, Correspondence, Etc., of Lyman Beecher, D.D.* (New York, 1865), 2: 310–12.

Table 6. LINKS BETWEEN REVIVALS AND WOMEN'S ORGANIZATIONS

Year of Revival	N*	Number of Female Converts	Converts in Female Missionary Society	Converts in Maternal Association	Mothers of Converts in Female Missionary Society	Mothers of Converts in Maternal Association
1814	65	45	23	3	0	0
1819	90	57	13	4	0	0
1826	123	73	1	4	18	16
1830	121	71	4	3	7	21
1838	57	32	0	1	6	18
Total	456	278	41	15	31	55

* Utica First Presbyterian Church only.

Walker Ostrom, Sophia Bagg, and Sophia Clark all subscribed to one or both of these organizations.

During the earliest revivals the strongest connection was between female converts and the Missionary Society. More than one third of the women who professed their faith in the revival of 1814 can be found among the members of the Female Missionary Society. In the 1820s and 1830s the links between women and revivalism were more often forged by mothers of converts enrolled in the Maternal Association. By 1838 over 30 percent of the converts had mothers in the Maternal Association alone. Neither missionary societies nor maternal associations were unique to Utica or to the Presbyterian Church. The city's Baptists, for example, established analogues to both these women's groups. Within these associations—the female contribution to the "new measures" of the Second Great Awakening—the historian can see women weaving the social and familial ties that ran through the revival.

Female missionary activity actually predated the formal organization of both the church and the village of Utica. In 1806 women associated with the First Religious Society of Whitestown met at the nucleus of stores and houses that would become the city of Utica and formed themselves into the Female Charitable Society. These women, who had assembled at the home of Sophia Clark, pledged a small annual contribution toward the support of missionary tours of the New York frontier. By 1824 this women's organization had evolved into the Female Missionary Society of the Western District, which spawned over 70 auxiliaries and contributed more than $1,200 annually for the support of eleven missionaries. The

Table 7. SOCIAL CHARACTERISTICS OF MEMBERS OF WOMEN'S ORGANIZATIONS

Class Composition	Female Missionary Society (N = 55) %	Maternal Association (N = 65) %	Total Directory Listings 1817 %	Total Directory Listings 1828 %
Merchants and Merchant Manufacturers	31	25	19	10
Professionals and White Collar	33	18	14	12
Artisans	16	35	40	42
Shopkeepers and Farmers	11	14	8	13
Laborers	—	—	15	14
Widows	7	5	4	6
Female Occupations	2	3	2	3

treasurer's report for 1824 revealed that $192 from the Society's coffers had gone to an untried young preacher named Charles Finney.[21]

The organizational and financial sophistication of this woman's organization invites comparison with the trading network built up by Utica's merchant capitalists. In fact the missionary society's officers almost mimic these entrepreneurs. The Female Charitable Society appeared under the heading of "Corporations" in the Utica Almanack for 1810,[22] in the company of a glass factory, a cotton factory, and a bank, as well as the village corporation. Throughout their history and in the style of businessmen the Female Missionary Society elected presidents, vice presidents, and trustees; met in formal meetings; and kept accounts.

The ties between female missionaries and male merchants were more substantial than such analogies. In fact 31 percent of the members of the missionary society were married to "merchants." The men who went by this title in the city directory were rarely shopkeepers but rather substantial retail and wholesale dealers involved in the regional market, men like James and Jerimiah Van Rensselaer, import merchants and scions of the

[21] "Minutes of the Whitestown Female Charitable Society," Oct. 21, 1806, MS., OHS; "Constitution of the Female Missionary Society of Oneida" (Utica, 1814); "First Annual Report of the Trustees of the Female Missionary Society of the Western District" (Utica, 1817); "Eighth Annual Report of the Trustees of the Female Missionary Society of the Western District," (Utica, 1824), 19, 20, 24.

[22] *Utica Almanack* (Utica, 1810), n.p.

New York aristocracy, or Samuel Stocking, shoe merchant and manufacturer who would amass one of Utica's largest fortunes. The wives of professional men had almost equal representation in the Missionary Society, and the wives of attorneys contributed almost one third of the membership (see Table 7).[23] Notable among these women were Ann Breese and Sophia Clark, who along with Susan and Adaline Van Rensselaer and Phoebe Stocking served as officers of the Society. By contrast, few wives of artisans, the largest occupational group in Utica, found berths among the officers or membership of the Female Missionary Society. Involvement in the missionary society seems characteristic of the sexual division of labor within Utica's more prominent merchant and professional families. By joining the Female Missionary Society women of the upper class publicly assumed the moral and religious responsibilities of their mercantile households. By efficiently and visibly fulfilling such social obligations these women enhanced the status of their busy mates.

At the same time these groups expanded woman's social role, and in a sphere that was organizationally independent of the male head of the household. Accordingly, another related social characteristic of the members of the Female Missionary Society is as significant as their husbands' class standing. Analysis of the city directories indicates that 66 percent of these women were married to men who maintained a business address detached from their place of residence. This percentage, which is too large to be attributed to a single class within the society's membership, compares with a figure of only 14 percent for the total population listed in the city directory (see Table 7). In other words, the members of the Female Missionary Society differed from the other women of Utica in that they had experienced the removal of basic economic activities from the household to the shops and offices of Genesee Street, hub of Utica's commercial life. It might follow that involvement in religious benevolence filled the consequent vacuum in woman's everyday life. To put it another way, participation in the Female Missionary Society might be one way of exercising the first breath of freedom from the duties and restrictions of a patriarchal home economy.

The alternative roles and activities that these women devised for themselves within the missionary society were more social than domestic. That is not to say that the society's officers eschewed heartrending appeals to women's domestic sensibilities. Their circular for 1819 begged the women of western New York to "imagine a pious mother, surrounded with a numerous family—none of them give evidence of possessing an interest in

[23] The term "shopkeepers" refers to such business designations as "grocery," "drug store," or "hardware store," and conveys fewer pretensions of economic stature than the self-proclaimed title of "merchant."

Christ."[24] Yet, although this image may have reflected the personal sentiments of many of the society's members, it led rhetorically to some remote frontier town where a paid agent might save unknown children from damnation. The Female Missionary Society presented itself primarily as the financial support of male missionaries who wrought the conversion of other women's children. This approach typified the early female benevolence that subordinated personal domestic relations to a wider ranging, more highly rationalized, more hierarchical, and more characteristically masculine mode of organization. In 1827 the Female Missionary society was absorbed into a masculine organization. In that year the society voted to accept an invitation to consolidate with their recently founded male counterpart, the Western Domestic Missionary Society. In the process many of these enterprising women forfeited evangelical leadership to their own husbands. Before this abdication, however, the members of the female missionary society saw their homes, their churches, and the surrounding countryside set ablaze with the evangelical fervor of 1825 and 1826.

The demise of the Female Missionary Society did not mark the retirement of Utica women from the battle for souls. Three years earlier eight members of the First Presbyterian Church, including the ubiquitous Sophia Clark, had formed one of the first Maternal Associations outside New England. Utica's Maternal Association shared the evangelical purpose of its sister organization and contributed financially to the education of missionaries. Yet most of the association's energy focussed in a novel direction. The constitution pledged each member to perform religious and parental duties—praying for each of her children daily, attending meetings every other Wednesday, renewing her child's baptismal covenant regularly, reading systematically through the literature of Christian childrearing, setting a pious example to her offspring at all times, and, finally, spending the anniversary of each child's birth in prayer and fasting. With the formation of the Maternal Association, the evangelical energies of Utica's women seemed to change course. The current that once gushed forth from Utica to inundate countless villages of the Western District was now diverted toward the homes of individual women, where it nurtured grace in the souls of their own children and kindled private family revivals.[25]

This transition from the Female Missionary Society to the Maternal Association hardly occurred in a single movement. Only six of the women

[24] "The Third Annual Report of the Trustees of the Female Missionary Society of the Western District" (Utica, 1819), 26.

[25] "Constitution of the 'Maternal Association of Utica' Adopted June 30, 1824," printed copy, New York State Library, Albany.

associated with the revivals held membership in both organizations. These women represented the pioneer generation; all were converted before 1820 and half of them came from lawyer families. Yet the professional classes were poorly represented in the membership of the Maternal Association. In fact they were outnumbered by the wives of common mechanics. Women of the artisan class accounted for 35 percent of the association's identifiable members and assumed the dominant position granted to merchants' wives within the Missionary Society (see Table 7). The class composition of the Maternal Association reflected the social structure of Utica in the canal era, when the city's economy was geared to small-scale artisan production for the local farm market.

The presence of these representatives of Utica's middling sort introduced some distinctive domestic concerns and relations into the Maternal Association. Consider, for example, the case of the Merrill family, four of whose members (Harriet, Lucina, Maria, and Julia) enrolled in the Maternal Association of the First Presbyterian Church. All these women were linked by marriage to a family of artisan printers and bookbinders. The clan's partriarch, Bildad Merrill, Sr., constructed an extended family economy out of such materials as a series of business partnerships among his sons, brothers, and nephews, and two strategic marital alliances with the family of his first business partner, Talcott Camp. The women who married into this family network inhabited an intricate and difficult domestic environment. In 1834, for example, Julia Merrill appeared before the session meeting of the First Presbyterian Church to charge her mother-in-law, Nancy Camp Merrill, with acts of personal abuse. The trial that ensued brought several of Julia's in-laws to her defense and exposed a frenetic and embittered household to historical scrutiny.

Julia Merrill's home, inhabited by four small children and replete with visiting neighbors, relatives, and customers, was further cluttered by two boarders, her father-in-law and his cranky wife. Nancy Merrill's animosity toward her daughter-in-law became unbearable when the elder Mrs. Merrill, to use Julia's phrase, "Took hold of me with violence." Such domestic contention could not but interfere with the pious mother's fulfillment of her maternal responsibilities. Julia Merrill herself testified that "My little children have often asked why Gramma talked so to me and why mama cried so."[26] The turmoil in this household may have been rare among Utica's families. Yet there is reason to believe that many members of the Maternal Association inhabited equally complex if more harmoni-

[26] "Records of the Session Meetings of the First Presbyterian Church," MS, The First Presbyterian Church, Utica, Vol. II, Nov. 10–Nov. 28, 1834. The Merrill family history was reconstructed from church records, the city directories, and Moses Bagg, Jr., *Pioneers of Utica* (Utica, 1877).

ous households. Only 45 percent of the members of the Maternal Association, as opposed to 66 percent of the Missionary Society's members, resided in homes that were separated from the husband's place of work (see Table 7). These women, like Julia Merrill, were likely to reside and work in households that retained many of the economic functions of the "little commonwealth." For many women of the Maternal Association, then, the demands of what they called "Christian Motherhood" came as an addition to the "arduous duties" that continued to characterize the households of Utica's middling sort.

A busy mistress of one of these households, recently awakened to her responsibility for her child's salvation, would seek out a special kind of organization. Accordingly, the founders of the Maternal Association eschewed the elaborate system of officers, trustees, and corporate charters that typified the Female Missionary Society. They resorted instead to the cooperative style exemplified by Article Six of the Association's charter. It stipulated that each mother should "suggest to her sister members such hints as her own experience may furnish, or circumstances seem to render necessary."[27] The Maternal Association may have formalized a longstanding network of neighborly advice and consultation, yet the articulation of common maternal responsibilities and the intention of fulfilling them in such a systematic fashion marked a crucial historical twist both in woman's roles and the methods of evangelism.

The casual organizational structure of the Maternal Association resembles the female prayer groups that Charles Finney discovered in Utica in 1825. The First Presbyterian Church had employed this "new measure" as early as 1822, and there were rumors of a quickening of grace within the woman's prayer group during the same year.[28] The idea for a maternal association probably emerged in one of these religious circles as women shared their anxiety about their children's souls.

It is easy to discern the material conditions that might breed this anxiety. The first decade in the Maternal Association's history coincided with the opening of the Erie Canal, the doubling of the city's population, and the accompanying proliferation of grog shops, boarding houses, and brothels. Neither the social elite represented by the Female Missionary Society nor relics of the New England social order such as the Presbyterian church trials could successfully oversee public morality. By turning their religious fervor as well as methods of childhood education on their own offspring, the women of the Maternal Association hoped to reinforce the Abrahamic Covenant against the assaults of a secular and individualistic culture. The revivals of 1826, 1831, and 1838 seemed to proclaim their enterprise a success. Known members of the Maternal Association saw at least 55 of their children enter the church during these years.

[27] "Constitution of the Maternal Association."
[28] Session Records, I, Apr. 1822; II, July 10, 1822.

Toward the end of the revival cycle, Maternal Associations evangelized as much in behalf of their own institutions as for the church itself. In 1833 the Presbyterian Maternal Association voted to establish a magazine that would circulate advice to mothers throughout central New York. The early issues of *The Mother's Magazine* depicted women guiding children and husbands toward salvation. Yet ministers and revival churches that once mediated the kin relations of conversion rarely appeared in these accounts. In fact, the typical reference to clergymen was a polite rebuke for their failure to foster Maternal Associations within their congregations. The Maternal Association seemed to be outgrowing the need for ministers and revivals. In 1835 the female editor of *The Mother's Magazine* put it this way: "The Church has had her seasons of refreshing and her returns of decay; but here in the circle of mothers, it is felt that the Holy Spirit condescends to *dwell*. It seems his blessed 'rest.'"[29] In other words mothers may have ultimately surplanted ministers as the agents of religious conversion and of its functional equivalent, the Christian socialization of children.

More to the point, the experience of a small group of mothers in upstate New York suggests an alternative interpretation of antebellum revivalism. Propelled by the fervor of their own conversions and strengthened by the female institutions that grew up around revivals, Utica women conducted a systematic evangelical campaign. As wives and mothers, and earlier as the trustees of an extensive missionary organization, women's contribution to revivalism did not stop with their own conversions. It exceeded their numbers in the revival population as it expanded to gather in converts of both sexes and spread throughout the revival cycle. The success of this woman's evangelism contradicts the interpretation of the Second Great Awakening as a rite of youthful independence. Quite the contrary, maternal evangelism in particular led scores of young men and women to an active, intensive, and deeply personal affirmation of the faith of their parents. The proliferation of such conversions among the sons and daughters of the middling sort moderated nineteenth-century individualism as it demonstrated the internalization of parental values. Simultaneously, the women who orchestrated the domestic revivals played a central part in creating a narrowly maternal role and image for their sex, with all its attendant contradictions. Thus, if the case of Utica, New York, at all represents the hundreds of communities enbroiled in antebellum revivalism, then women were more than the majority of the converts, more even than the private guardians of America's souls. The combination and consequence of all these roles left the imprint of a women's awakening on American society as well as on American religion.*

[29] *The Mother's Magazine*, Jan. 1833, 4–5; June 1833, 93–95.

* I would like to thank Paul Johnson, Louise Knauer, and Kathryn Kish Sklar for their helpful criticism of an earlier draft of this paper.

Maternity . . . of the Spirit: Nuns and Domesticity in Antebellum America*

Joseph G. Mannard

"In America the independence of woman is irrevocably lost in the bonds of matrimony." Thus wrote Alexis de Tocqueville in his famous description of the restricted position of married women in the American ideology of domesticity. "If an unmarried woman is less constrained there than elsewhere," he continued:

> a wife is subjected to stricter obligations. The former makes her father's house an abode of freedom and of pleasure; the latter lives in the home of her husband as if it were a cloister. . . . Thus in the United States the inexorable opinion of the public carefully circumscribes woman within the narrow circle of domestic interests and duties and forbids her to step beyond it.[1]

Tocqueville's comparison of the home to a cloister suggests a parallel between the lives of American wives and mothers and Roman Catholic nuns. Ironically, at the time he wrote, religious sisters were establishing numerous convents, schools, and charitable institutions in America,

*Presented at the Cushwa Center Conference on American Catholicism, October 4, 1985.

1. Alexis de Tocqueville, *Democracy in America*, 2 vols., ed. Phillips Bradley, trans. Henry Reeve (New York, 1945), II, 212. In 1840, the year Tocqueville's second volume appeared in the United States, there existed in the country a total of twenty-eight Catholic "female religious institutions," whose members directed and staffed nearly all of the forty-seven female academies and seventy-six charitable institutions of Catholic affiliation. By 1860, the number of convents had mushroomed to 160, the number of female academies to 202, and the number of charitable institutions to 183. Figures are taken from *The Metropolitan Catholic Almanac and Laity's Directory* (Baltimore, 1840, 1860). Hereafter referred to as the *Catholic Almanac*.

thereby proving apparent exceptions to his assertion that public opinion would not tolerate female divergence from domestic norms. Taking a cue from Tocqueville, this paper analyzes the relationship of women religious to the antebellum ideology of domesticity by examining the views of Protestant critics, Catholic defenders, and nuns themselves. Did the convent vocation primarily conform to or conflict with dominant cultural beliefs and assumptions about woman's nature and proper place? Did the work of women religious tend to challenge or reinforce the domestic doctrine of separate male and female spheres? What attitudes toward domesticity did nuns try to instill in the females under their care and instruction? Answers to such questions suggest much about the opportunities and limitations of the convent, and religion generally, as an avenue to women's fuller participation in nineteenth-century society.[2]

Carmelite nuns founded the first community of women religious in the United States in Port Tobacco, Maryland in 1790. It was not until the Jacksonian era, however, that the presence of convents generated great public outcry. Anti-convent sentiments emerged as part of the revived spirit of anti-Catholicism in the 1830s. Anti-Catholic nativism was reflected in hostility to the rising tide of immigrants from Ireland and Germany, in the popularity of publications like the Rev. Lyman Beecher's *A Plea for the West* (1835) and Samuel F. B. Morse's *Foreign Conspiracy against the Liberties of the United States* (1835)—both of which alleged the existence of Catholic plots to capture the American Republic for the Pope—and, most notoriously, in the burning of the Ursuline Convent in Charlestown, Massachusetts by a Protestant mob in August 1834.[3]

The growth of convents in American society profoundly alarmed many Protestants, not simply because nuns were Catholic and often foreign-born, but also because their vocation seemed in various ways to challenge the "cult of true womanhood" and the ideal of "Republican motherhood." By renouncing marriage and motherhood for themselves, by allegedly proselytizing Protestant children and attempting to enlist Protestant daughters into their ranks, nuns appeared to endanger the essential links

2. This paper uses the word "nun" in its popular sense to describe any woman religious, whether contemplative or active, who takes holy vows, whether solemn or simple.

3. An Ursuline Convent was founded in New Orleans in 1727, when that city was still a French possession. It became the fourth convent in the United States in 1803, following the American purchase of the Louisiana Territory from France. Sr. Mary Ewens, OP, *The Role of the Nun in the Nineteenth Century: Variations on an International Theme* (New York, 1978), 22, 33. Ray A. Billington, *The Protestant Crusade, 1800–1860: A Study in the Origins of Nativism* (New York, 1938), 119–129; though dated, Billington's book remains the best survey of anti-Catholic nativism before the Civil War.

Joseph Mannard

between family, church, and state enunciated in the ideology of domesticity.[4]

Originating in the Northeast among middle-class Protestants at the end of the eighteenth century, the ideology of domesticity crystallized in the 1830s and 1840s as advances in printing made possible its wide dissemination in ministers' sermons and women's magazines and advice literature. Domesticity emphasized the central role of the nuclear family in transmitting cultural values and maintaining social order, and especially stressed the significant contribution of woman as the chief agent in this process. Woman as wife and mother represented a beacon of stability, a preserver of tradition, in a society undergoing unprecedented industrial development, urban growth, and geographical expansion. While a man was to be preoccupied with the public sphere of business and politics, a woman's responsibilities lay fundamentally within the family circle where

4. On "true womanhood," see Barbara Welter, "The Cult of True Womanhood: 1820–1860," *American Quarterly* 18 (Summer 1966): 151–174. On "Republican motherhood," see Linda Kerber, *Women of the Republic: Intellect and Ideology in Revolutionary America* (Chapel Hill, NC, 1980), chapter 9. The ideology of domesticity reflected and shaped social, economic, and demographic transformations begun in the late eighteenth century that increasingly moved men's workplace outside the home and shifted women from being primarily producers in a family economy to being consumers in a market economy. The discussion of the origins and tenets of domesticity presented in this paper has been drawn principally from Nancy F. Cott, *The Bonds of Womanhood: "Woman's Sphere" in New England, 1780–1835* (New Haven, 1977); Mary P. Ryan, *The Empire of the Mother: American Writing about Domesticity, 1830–1860* (New York, 1982); and Kathryn Kish Sklar, *Catharine Beecher: A Study in American Domesticity* (New Haven, CT, 1973).

her main duties included instructing her children in religion, morality, and patriotism. Limiting in theory, domesticity could prove flexible in practice. The female sphere sometimes expanded outside the home in order that women might better protect those values peculiarly entrusted to them.

Some Protestants, then, saw nuns as veiled threats to American domesticity as they defined it. Convent opponents did not always agree among themselves as to the nature of this threat, because male and female convent critics tended to focus on those points most in conflict with their respective gender interests. Males made up the chief leadership and membership of the "convent reformers"—supporters of legislation for state inspection and regulation of nunneries. First voicing demands for convent reform in the early 1830s, these male writers, ministers, and editors expressed a common set of concerns but lacked the formal organization that characterized the antislavery and temperance crusades. It was not until the emergence of the anti-Catholic, anti-foreign American, or Know-Nothing, Party in the 1850s that convent reformers found the mechanism to put their demands into action. Anti-convent petition campaigns in Massachusetts and Maryland resulted in the legislatures of those states appointing "Nunnery Committees" to examine the issue. This temporary success for convent reform backfired, however, when these investigations failed to substantiate reformers' claims that women were being held in convents against their will.[5]

Females provided the principal spokespersons and the majority of what could be "convent competitors"—advocates of Protestant-financed female seminaries and teachers to compete with convent schools. In the mid-1840s and early 1850s, convent competitors successfully formed female education societies to effect their goals. Although convent competitors and reformers shared a mutual suspicion of the subversive nature of Catholic female academies, women most commonly directed their energies to providing an alternative to the convent menace, while men were likely to be more disturbed by the fear that nunneries were "priests' prisons for women."[6]

While expressing concern for the plight of females in convents, male reformers denounced the vocation of the nun as a form of social deviance

---

5. Ray A. Billington, *The Protestant Crusade, 1800–1860,* 414; John R. Mulkern, "Scandal Behind the Convent Walls: The Know-Nothing Nunnery Committee of 1855" *Historical Journal of Massachusetts* 11 (January 1983): 22–34; *Journal of the Proceedings of the House of Delegates of the State of Maryland* (Annapolis, 1856), 641–643; Sr. M. St. Patrick McConnville, *Political Nativism in the State of Maryland, 1830–1860* (Washington, DC, 1928), 108–111; Jean Baker, *Ambivalent Americans: The Know-Nothing Party in America* (Baltimore, 1977), 88–99.

6. Polly Welts Kaufman, *Women Teachers on the Frontier* (New Haven, CT, 1984). Andrew B. Cross, *Priests' Prisons for Women* (Baltimore, 1854).

directly at odds with a woman's sacred roles of wife and mother within the home. Reformers attacked the celibacy of women religious as flouting the laws of God and Nature. The publisher's introduction to the American edition of Scipio de Ricci's classic exposé *Female Convents: Secrets of Nunneries Disclosed* warned that celibacy was "unnatural . . . unjust and ruinous." He concluded that "nunneries and the conventual way of life, are altogether contradictory to the Divine appointments respecting the order of nature, and the constitution of mankind and human society."[7]

The maverick Catholic James Gordon Bennett also questioned the purpose of nunneries in a modern republic. Bennett, editor of the *New York Herald*, condemned celibacy publicly in his newspaper, charging that insanity resulted from its practice. "The natural position of a woman is to marry—have a family—and be surrounded by blooming children," he wrote. "To be shut up in a convent, and restricted from the happiness of a husband, is enough to drive any woman out of her senses." Bennett concluded that convents were antithetical to the American way of life and proposed their abolition throughout the land.[8]

In their arguments against celibacy, reformers also revealed their own sexual anxieties. The thought of females living without traditional male guidance stimulated the imaginations of reformers. Scurrilous works such as Maria Monk's best-selling *Awful Disclosures of the Hotel Dieu Nunnery of Montreal* (1836) decried celibacy as a deliberate sham that permitted debauched priests to violate helpless females. "The popish doctrine of celibacy—the unreserved obedience due to bishops and priests from all nuns and females in all the holy orders, opens the way for the corruptions that would be expected," concluded Rev. Robert J. Breckinridge and Rev. Andrew B. Cross in their journal, the *Baltimore Literary and Religious Magazine*. "Unmarried men have the charge of unmarried women, and hear them confess in these secret abodes. Need more be said?" asked Rev. Edward Beecher.[9]

Reformers also believed that the well-being of the community depended upon American women assuming responsibilities in their proper domain—the home. Anti-convent petitions to the Maryland legislature in 1856 charged that nunneries were detrimental to the "positive welfare of society" because they "cut off so many from their social duty and a sphere

7. Scipio de Ricci, *Female Convents: Secrets of Nunneries Disclosed* (New York, 1834), x–xi.

8. *New York Herald*, August 22–23, 1839.

9. Cross, *Priests Prisons for Women; Pope or President? Startling Disclosures of Romanism as Revealed by Its Own Writers* (New York, 1850; facsim. ed. New York, 1977), 88–122; *Baltimore Literary and Religious Magazine* 2 (September 1836): 359; Edward Beecher, *The Papal Conspiracy Exposed* (Boston, 1855), 418.

Mother Catherine McAuley

of usefulness." Another anti-convent writer admonished that "no woman can be justified for abandoning all the obligations which she owes to society." According to the American and Foreign Christian Union, any woman who entered a nunnery forsook her duties "to the family, and to society."[10]

Not only abjuring marriage and motherhood for themselves, women religious reportedly directed many of their female students into taking the veil, thus creating a self-perpetuating system in direct opposition to the domestic roles of true womanhood. Lewis H. J. Tonna neatly expressed this fear in his *Nuns and Nunneries*, a work originally published in England but widely circulated in the United States in the early 1850s. "At an early age when the heart is especially open to those impressions which may be called romantic or sentimental," warned Tonna, ". . . [a girl] is beset with continued commendations of the heavenly state of a nun. The duties of a wife, the cares of a mother, are denounced as dangerous, and interfering with the soul's health."[11]

Reformers' objections to the convent vocation reflected underlying concerns about maintaining the patriarchal authority of fathers and

10. *Frederick Examiner* (MD), February 13, 1856; Ricci, *Female Convents*, xiv; American and Foreign Christian Union, *Eighth Annual Report*, 29.

11. Lewis H. J. Tonna, *Nuns and Nunneries* (London, 1852), 17. Convent reform became a trans-Atlantic issue in the 1850s, with much sharing of information between Great Britain and the United States. See Walter S. Arnstein, *Protestant versus Catholic in Mid-Victorian England: Mr. Newdegate and the Nuns* (Columbia, MO, 1982).

husbands. Upholding a highly restrictive standard of domesticity, reformers focused on how nuns rejected the forms of domesticity—marriage, motherhood, and home. In contrast, the mainly female convent competitors stressed how Catholic sisters threatened to usurp the principal functions of domesticity—the care, education, and religious training of children—and, thereby, replace American mothers as the moral and cultural arbiters of the nation. In their view, nuns imperilled what historian Mary P. Ryan has labelled "the Empire of the Mother" in antebellum society. Much as native-American craftsmen looked upon Irish laborers as undercutting their social status and economic security, Protestant women who formed female education societies identified nuns as their chief rivals in a struggle to shape the cultural identity of the United States.[12]

Echoing Lyman Beecher's warnings of a Papal conspiracy to win the West for Catholicism, important female theorists of domesticity such as Sarah J. Hale and Catharine Beecher—Lyman's daughter—sounded the alarm about the dangerous growth of convent schools, especially on the frontier. Hale, editor of the Boston-based *American Ladies Magazine,* dedicated her publication to the cause of convent competition with a vow and a warning. "Female education and its results shall be the ruling theme of our Magazine," she wrote in 1834. "Female education must be provided for—otherwise convents will increase and Catholicism become permanently rooted in our country." Abigail G. Whittelsey expressed similar concerns in her journal, *The Mother's Magazine,* published in Utica, New York. The cover of the May, 1835 issue listed the number of Catholic schools and nunneries then existing in the United States. In the adjoining article Whittelsey warned her readers that Catholic sisters attempted to convert Protestant daughters who attended their schools. As one letter to the editor explained, "When these young ladies become mothers, they will educate their children for the special service of the Pope of Rome, and their Catholic sons will become our rulers, and our nation a nation of *Roman Catholics.*"[13]

---

12. Ryan, *The Empire of the Mother,* 18. Ryan contends that mothers in the home commanded a critical social position, providing "the vital integrative tissue for an emerging middle class." See also, Mary P. Ryan, *Cradle of the Middle Class: The Family in Oneida County, New York, 1780–1865* (Cambridge, 1980).

13. *The American Ladies' Magazine* 7 (December 1834): 564. Though concerned about the growing influence of convent schools, Hale bore no personal animosity towards the sisters who taught in them. She considered the Mother Superior of the Ursuline Convent in Charlestown to be a friend and publicly condemned the burning of that institution as an outrage upon all women; *The American Ladies' Magazine* 7 (September 1834): 419. *The Mother's Magazine* 3 (May 1835): 76–77. Fears similar to those expressed by Whittlesey are found in *General View of the Principles and Designs of the Mount Holyoke Female Seminary* (n.p., 1837), 8–10; and *Roman Catholic Female Schools: A Letter of an American Mother to an American Mother* No. 360 (New York, n.d.).

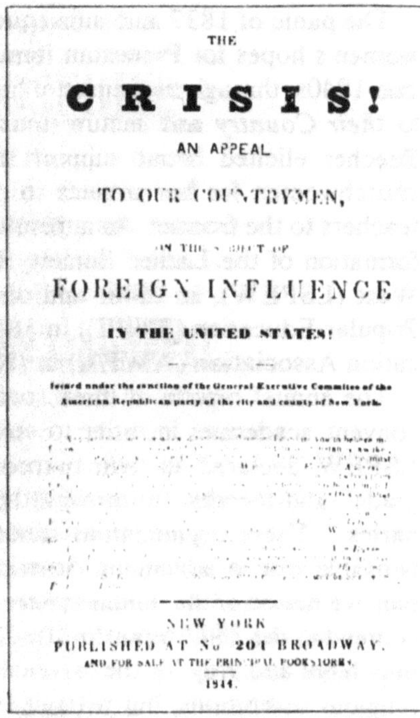

THE

CRISIS!

AN APPEAL

TO OUR COUNTRYMEN,

ON THE SUBJECT OF

FOREIGN INFLUENCE

IN THE UNITED STATES!

Issued under the sanction of the General Executive Committee of the American Republican party of the city and county of New York.

NEW YORK

PUBLISHED AT No 201 BROADWAY.

AND FOR SALE AT THE PRINCIPAL BOOKSTORES.

1844.

Above, "Maria Monk" and child, a "scandal" that threatened Catholics in 1836; at right, one of the flood of "Nativist" pamphlets that agitated against immigrants and Catholics in the 1840s; below, cartoon from 1844 in which Archbishop Hughes of New York is attacked by editor James Gordon Bennett, and defended by unruly Irishmen.

The panic of 1837 and subsequent economic depression delayed these women's hopes for Protestant female education for several years. In the mid-1840s, through the impact of her book *The Duty of American Women to their Country* and lecture tours to major Northern cities, Catharine Beecher elicited broad support from Protestant clergymen and local churchwomen for her projects to provide female education and women teachers to the frontier. As a result of her efforts, Beecher encouraged the formation of the Ladies' Society for the Promotion of Education at the West (LSPEW), in 1846; and directly founded the Board of National Popular Education (BNPE), in 1848; and the American Woman's Education Association (AWEA), in 1852.[14]

The annual reports of these societies regularly invoked the specter of convent academies in order to solicit funds for their work. Indeed, the LSPEW declared its twin purpose was "to furnish teachers of every grade" and thereby "to prevent the necessity of patronizing papal seminaries." These organizations fundamentally believed in women's indispensable role in advancing American institutions and argued for an expansive notion of the female sphere. "Politicians may plan and legislate," contended the 1847 report of the LSPEW, "and the ministers of religion may labor and pray for the extension and perpetuity of our free, civil, and religious institutions, but without the cooperation of *educated women* in the nursery and schoolroom, they will prove a failure." Catholic sisters, however, threatened to unravel this delicately spun web of family, church, and state, by undermining the value and influence of Republican motherhood, and creating a new generation of "Romish mothers." As the AWEA ruefully noted in 1854, "Nine-tenths of their schools are for females, showing that they mean to make the *mothers* who will make the nation." These educational associations justified teaching by women as an extension of the maternal duty to mold the character of the young, but they believed that nuns subverted the true purpose of that instruction—transmission of Protestant and republican values.[15]

For convent competitors like Beecher and Hale, the idea of female education was central to their theory of domesticity, which sought to elevate the position of American women by using the home as the base of female influence in society. Because their version of domesticity was inextricably linked to Protestantism and republicanism, convert competitors

14. Catharine Beecher, *Educational Reminiscences and Suggestions* (New York, 1874), 84, 105–115, 153–154.

15. Ladies Society for the Promotion of Education in the West, *First Annual Report* (Boston, 1847), 21, 31; American Woman's Educational Assocation, *Second Annual Report* (New York, 1854), 20. See also, Ladies Society, *Third Annual Report* (1849), 21–29; Board of National Popular Education, *Third Annual Report* (Cleveland, 1850), 37–40.

AWFUL DISCLOSURES,

BY

MARIA MONK,

OF THE

HOTEL DIEU NUNNERY OF MONTREAL,

REVISED, WITH AN

APPENDIX,

CONTAINING,

PART I. RECEPTION OF THE FIRST EDITIONS.
PART II. SEQUEL OF HER NARRATIVE.
PART III. REVIEW OF THE CASE.

ALSO, A SUPPLEMENT,

GIVING MORE PARTICULARS OF THE NUNNERY AND GROUNDS.

ILLUSTRATED BY A PLAN OF THE NUNNERY, &c.

NEW-YORK:
PUBLISHED BY MARIA MONK,
AND SOLD BY BOOKSELLERS GENERALLY.
1836.

This bestseller caused many Americans to be suspicious of nuns

perceived Catholic sisters as their rivals in a struggle to confirm the preeminence of American mothers in the moral and cultural life of the nation.

Just as American Catholics defended the compatibility of their religion and republicanism, they also argued for the nun's complementary relationship to American motherhood within the ideology of domesticity.

Compared to the flood of didactic literature emanating from Protestant pens, the amount of Catholic writings on domesticity before the Civil War was but a trickle. Catholic newspapers and periodicals reserved most of their space for theological, political, and economic matters. Nevertheless, in an area like Maryland, with its deep-rooted Catholic elite, and in cities with a nascent Catholic middle-class, the prescriptions of domesticity often appeared in articles in the Catholic press. European clergymen supplied most of this material, which was first translated and then reprinted for American consumption.[16]

An exemplary statement of the Catholic version of domesticity appeared in a series of essays written by Charles Sainte-Foi and collectively entitled "The Mission of Woman." *The Metropolitan,* a popular Catholic journal based in Baltimore, published translations of these articles from September 1853 to August 1854. Though little is known of Sante-Foi, the orthodoxy of his views is attested to by the fact that the magazine's clergyman editor refused to print anything "in the least at variance with the principles of Catholic faith and morals."[17]

Sainte-Foi defined a feminine ideal that in most essentials was virtually indistinguishable from that of mainstream Protestantism. He extolled marriage and motherhood as the proper roles for the vast majority of Catholic women. By their nature, females were expected to follow their hearts over their minds, relying more on intuition than logic. To mothers was entrusted the character formation of their children, especially their early religious training.[18]

Although the family was "the natural and primary sphere of her action," a woman could extend her domain of activities by joining with others of her sex in order to uphold her moral and spiritual responsibilities. Sainte-Foi recommended:

> If there are other women around her whom she can associate with herself, let her remember that two are stronger than one, and that in union there is strength. . . . Having on their side

16. Gerald P. Fogarty, S.J., "Public Patriotism and Private Politics: The Tradition of American Catholicism" U.S. Catholic Historian 4 (no. 1, 1984): 4–17; Jay P. Dolan, *The American Catholic Experience: A History from Colonial Times to the Present* (Garden City, NY, 1985): 108–109, 304–305. Mary Colleen McDannell, "The Home as Sacred Space in American Protestant and Catholic Popular Thought, 1840 to 1900" (Ph.D. diss., Temple University, 1984), 111–112, 181. Although focusing primarily on the second half of the nineteenth century, McDannell's work is the fullest examination and analysis of Catholic attitudes about domesticity. Especially valuable is her explicit comparison of Catholic and Protestant views.

17. The articles ran in the following issues: *The Metropolitan* 1 (September 1853): 388–390, (October 1853): 435–437, (November 1853): 536–538; (December 589–591); 2 (April 1854): 139–142, (August 1854): 395–398. *The Metropolitan* 1 (February 1853): 1. The magazine had as one of its primary aims to "form a valuable repertory of information for the Catholic family"; *The Metropolitan* 1 (February 1853): 2.

18. *The Metropolitan* 1 (September 1853): 388–390, (October 1853): 435–437.

the power which right and truth confer, they could, in setting about it properly, reform the tone and habits of the city; or at least oppose a salutary check to the evil tendencies that exist.[19]

Like their Protestant counterparts, middle- and upper-class Catholic females might form local benevolent societies to address the plight of orphans, widows, and other unfortunates. The Church considered such female activities outside the home as legitimate and good if carried out in a self-effacing manner and as part of women's aspostleship of "preaching Christ" in their everyday acts.[20]

For all their similarities, the glaring difference between Catholic and Protestant interpretations of domesticity was the former's contention that religious life is a higher calling than married life, that for women virginity is superior to maternity. According to Sainte-Foi, "The first and most perfect state that a woman can embrace, is virginity or the religious life." For Catholics, however, this belief in the primacy of virginity remained compatible with the maternal ideal of domesticity for two reasons. First, most women had no vocation for the convent.

The religious life, being a life of perfection, is the portion of but a small number of privileged souls for whom God reserves His most intimate communication, and most precious favors. The greater number of women are called to live in the world, and to serve God in the married state.

Every Catholic woman chose between these two options, "according to her inclinations and the manifestation of the divine will."[21]

Second, even virgins who entered the convent embraced maternity of a sort. "Maternity is for woman the aim of life," asserted Sainte-Foi.

If to follow a higher vocation, she renounces the joys which the maternity derived from the flesh and blood imparts, it is to consecrate herself to the functions of a more holy and sublime maternity, which is entirely of the spirit in its nature and in its end.[22]

This "maternity of the spirit" derived from the nun's status as a spiritual "bride of Christ" and from her works of teaching, nursing, orphan care, and moral reform.

---

19. *The Metropolitan* 1 (November 1853): 536–538. Sainte-Foi may have been unusual in advocating for Catholic lay women a social role beyond the home. McDannell contends that most Catholic didactic literature of the nineteenth century discouraged Catholic mothers from becoming involved in the type of reform activities occupying their Protestant counterparts, rather the tasks of "social housekeeping" were assigned to nuns.

20. *The Metropolitan* 1 (November 1853): 536–538.

21. *The Metropolitan* 1 (December 1853): 589; 2 (April 1854): 139.

22. *The Metropolitan* 1 (September 1853): 388–389.

Ruins of the Ursuline convent in Charlestown, MA, 1834

> She becomes the spouse of Jesus Christ in order to become, through mercy and charity, the mother of the little children whom she feeds with the milk of the doctrine of life, or of the sick and infirm whom she surrounds with her care, ... or else, ... she becomes the mother of those poor sinners who have wearied themselves in the ways of iniquity, and she brings them forth to Jesus Christ.[23]

Even contemplative orders of women religious, who dedicated themselves solely to lives of prayer within the cloister, practiced spiritual motherhood. Indeed, they engaged in "a still more exalted occupation" than active works of mercy in the world. Although contemplatives withdrew from the world, Sainte-Foi contended:

> They do not on this account forfeit the glorious privilege of maternity, for it is in their heart ever glowing with charity that are formed those germs of salvation and life, which the breath of the Spirit carries into languishing or withered souls, and which are afterwards fertilized by the action of divine grace.[24]

Mary the mother of Jesus embodied this Catholic notion of a "two-fold maternity, that of the spirit and that of the flesh." In her person, Mary

---

23. *Ibid.*
24. *Ibid.*

united the two states of virginity and maternity. Every other woman had to choose between these two states; but all, whether wife or nun, could share in the functions of maternity.[25]

In their personal and public documents, women religious expressed beliefs and assumptions conforming to the principles of the ideology of domesticity. Although the office of Mother Superior most clearly exemplified spiritual maternity within the convent, all members were committed to this concept in their lives and work. The four qualities identifying the antebellum true woman basically dovetailed with the virtues of the ideal nun as defined in the rules and constitutions of various religious sisterhoods. The convent institutionalized the true woman's attributes of piety, purity, and submissiveness in a nun's religious calling and her vows of chastity and obedience. For example, in recommending a prospective candidate to the Sisters of Charity, a New York priest noted her practical talents, including needlework. "This," he said, "together with her great piety, her modesty, . . . her agreeable manners, leads me [to] think that she will be a good and useful Sister of Charity." Catholic sisters took these virtues seriously as their standard of behavior. Typical was Sr. M. Clotilda Smith of the Visitation Order, who on her deathbed continually repeated the phrase "Obedience makes the religious, obedience and submission."[26]

Although not domestic in the formal sense, women religious often provided to clergymen and seminarians the kind of household services—cooking, washing, sewing—that fathers and sons expected from female family members. Above all, the nun in the cloister shared with the mother in the home a commitment to self-sacrifice for the sake of others. For both women, a spirit of self-denying benevolence formed the core of their being.

With more cleverness than honesty, Catharine Beecher argued a distinction between the self-sacrifice of Catholic sisters and Protestant mothers. "[I]t is often asserted," she remarked, "that the Catholics exhibit more self-denying zeal than Protestants, while these sisterhoods are specially pointed at as evidence." But, she contended, "[I]t has not been

25. *Ibid.*

26. Welter, "The Cult of True Womanhood: 1820–1860," 151–174. On convent rules and constitutions, see, for example, *An Abridgement of the Interior Spirit of the Religious of the Visitation of the Blessed Virgin Mary,* translated from the French (Washington, 1834); or *Regulations for the Society of Sisters of Charity in the United States,* printed as Appendix A in Ellin M. Kelly, comp. and ed., *Numerous Choirs: A Chronicle of Elizabeth Bayley Seton and Her Spiritual Daughters: Volume I: The Seton Years 1774–1821* (Evansville, IN, 1981). Rev. James Quinn to Mother Xavier Clark, November 26, 1843, Archives St. Joseph's Central House (Emmitsburg, MD), RG7-10, LV4, #123. "Life of Sr. M. Clotilda Smith," Baltimore Visitation Convent *Vow Book,* Vol. 1, 55, 65.

the benevolent self-denial of Christ, but a selfish and ascetic self-denial, aiming mainly to save self by inflictions and losses." Beecher's argument ignored the innumerable charitable works performed by active communities of women religious like the Sisters of Charity and Sisters of Mercy, of whose existence she was clearly aware. She also misrepresented the motives of contemplative orders, whose prayers were offered not only for the perfection of self but also, and necessarily, for the salvation of others.[27]

Women religious testified explicitly to their practice of maternity of the spirit by the language used in their school prospecti printed annually in the *Catholic Almanac*. Nuns assured parents and guardians of their complementary role to the mother in the nursery. A typical example appeared in the 1848 statement of the Sisters of Mercy of Charleston, South Carolina, promising that "the strictest attention is paid to the health, comfort, manners, and literary improvement of the pupils. The discipline or government, though firm and uniform, is mild and parental. The sick are attended with maternal tenderness." An 1841 announcement for the highly-respected Ursuline academy in New Orleans proclaimed:

> The object kept in view . . . is the adorning of their pupils' minds with knowledge and the forming of their hearts to virtue. The young ladies are accustomed to habits of order, cleanliness and polite manners. They are never suffered to go beyond the reach of a watchful but maternal superintendence, whose vigilance secures the preservation of morals and the willing observance of the rules.[28]

Catholic sisterhoods applied the same maternal sentiments to the care of orphans and widows and the tending of the sick, a fact to which lay persons bore witness. The Catholic press sometimes published letters of praise for nuns like the one from a visitor to St. Vincent's Asylum in Washington, D.C., who described the Sisters of Charity as "pious mothers of the orphan."[29]

Nuns also encouraged greater awareness of domesticity among others of their sex. After religious training, the chief educational objective of convent academies was to prepare girls to assume positions as refined wives in middle- and upper-class homes. True, nuns welcomed those girls who felt called to a convent vocation, but they recognized that the majority of their pupils would eventually take vows of matrimony not religion. Mother Elizabeth Seton, famous founder of the Daughters of Charity in the United States, explicitly articulated this view to her students at the St.

27. Catharine Beecher, *Address to the Protestant Clergy of the United States* (New York, 1846), 32; 28–29.
28. *Catholic Almanac*, 1848, 114; 1841, 158.
29. *Catholic Mirror* (Baltimore), August 27, 1853.

Catherine Beecher, the most important theorist of domesticity of her time

Joseph's Academy in Emmitsburg, Maryland. "Your little mother . . . does not come to teach you how to be good nuns or Sisters of Charity;" she said, "but rather I would wish to fit you for that world in which you are destined to live; to teach you how to be good mistresses and mothers of families."[30]

The curriculum in convent academies was mainly ornamental in intent, concentrating on basic subjects—reading, writing, arithmetic—and the arts—music, painting, and especially French, a must for any "accomplished" young lady. Convent academies closely paralleled the genteel education offered in secular female seminaries of the pre-Civil War years and often were more accessible financially and geographically. This fact explains why many Protestant families entrusted the training of their daughters to Catholic sisters despite the warnings of convent critics.[31]

30. Quoted in Charles I. White, *The Life of Mrs. Eliza Seton* (New York, 1853), 362.

31. Edmund J. Goebel, *A Study of Catholic Secondary Education During the Colonial Period up to the First Plenary Council of Baltimore, 1852* (Washington, DC, 1936), 220–230; Mother M. Benedict Murphy, RSHM, "Pioneer Roman Catholic Girls Academies: Their Growth, Character, and Contribution to American Education: A Study of Roman Catholic Education for Girls from Colonial Times to the First Plenary Council of 1852" (Ph.D. diss., Columbia University, 1958). For a detailed examination of curriculum change over time at one of the oldest and most prestigious convent academies, see Mada-Anne Gell, "A History of the Development of Curriculum: Georgetown Visitation Preparatory School 1865–1965" (Ph.D. diss., The Catholic University of America, 1983). Despite its title, this study also contains a good review of the antebellum years.

Convent academies, however, were often too expensive for a Catholic population comprised mostly of working-class immigrants. Yet nuns helped facilitate the acceptance of domesticity among these economically less-fortunate groups as well. Women religious particularly addressed the needs of members of their own sex at each stage of their lives: female foundlings and orphans, school girls, single working women, working-class wives and mothers, and dependent widows.

The tuition from convent academies usually helped fund benevolent schools for orphan girls and daughters of poor families in the parish. Mother Eleanora Walsh of the Order of the Visitation conducted such a free school for seventeen years in the basement of the cathedral in Wheeling, in western Virginia. By her selfless dedication, Walsh "produced such an impression upon the children under her charge, that no fewer than thirty of them became religious . . . while many others have become equally distinguished in domestic life as model wives and mothers of families."[32]

Arriving from Germany in 1848, the School Sisters of Notre Dame specialized in educating girls of that nationality. In 1854, Sr. M. Theresa Gerhardinger, Superior General of the congregation, wrote to Rome about the importance of female education in America. "If the sisters succeed in giving a good education," she predicted, ". . . there will always be enough of these young women becoming mothers, and thus a better generation will spring up."[33]

One of the two congregations of Afro-American women religious established in the antebellum era, the Oblate Sisters of Providence focused on educating the daughters of the free Black community in Baltimore. An advertisement for their school in the 1839 edition of the *Catholic Almanac* revealed that they trained their pupils to serve the ideal of domesticity in either one of two ways:

> . . . these girls will either become mothers of families, or household servants. In the first case, the solid virtues, the religious and moral principles which they acquired when in this school, will be carefully transferred as a legacy to their chldren. . . . As to such are to be employed as servants, they will be instructed in domestic concerns, and the care of young children.[34]

Members of the Sisters of Mercy opened "houses of protection" to relieve the condition of some of the thousands of ill-educated and unem-

32. "Life of Eleanor Walsh," Mount De Chantal Visitation Convent *Vow Book*, Vol. 1, 35–36.

33. Mother M. Theresa Gerhardinger to Cardinal Protector Clarelli, 1854, in S. M. Hester Valentine, SSND, ed., *The North American Foundations: Letters of Mother M. Theresa Gerhardinger* (Winona, MN, 1977), 116.

34. *Catholic Almanac*, 1839, 95.

ployed females arriving from Ireland, who might otherwise have fallen prey to lives of vice or crime in American cities. The object of these houses was to admit "distressed women of good character" for instruction in religion and domestic service. Each house acted as a kind of employment agency supplying the servant needs of elite Protestant and Catholic families. Convent annals recorded that "Ladies would call at the convent, or again drive up to the door in elegant carriages, to solicit a chambermaid, a nurse, or a cook." By such means nuns introduced immigrant women to middle- and upper-class homes where they became acquainted with the ideology of domesticity, sometimes imbibing its principles and passing them on to their own families.[35]

Women religious, such as the Sisters of Notre Dame de Namur in Boston, also instructed poor Irish mothers in techniques of home management and personal hygiene that encouraged aspiration to middle-class respectability. The nuns educated these women in habits of industry and discipline:

> teaching the untaught and overworked creatures how to make everything clean, tidy, and bright about them: helping them to have the children regular in their attendance at school, neatly dressed, with their clothes mended and all marks of degrading poverty removed . . . aiding every wife and mother to be herself, to husband and children, a model of sobriety, thrift, and gentleness.[36]

Nuns had an ambiguous relationship to the ideology of domesticity, but one that was ultimately compatible with a flexible interpretation of it. Superficially, the lives of women religious did transgress several of the outward forms and institutions of domesticity. Nuns renounced marriage, motherhood, and home. The convent served as an alternative to the nuclear household so central to the domestic ideal. Entry into a convent, ironically, provided a woman with unprecedented avenues for participation in the public realm. Catholic sisters were among the first women in nineteenth-century America to work outside the home on a permanent basis, and they became models for the quickly feminized professions of teaching and nursing. As convent superiors, hospital administrators, and academy directors, they held positions of power, influence, and responsibility denied to most women in antebellum society.[37]

---

35. "Annals of the Sisters of Mercy, Baltimore," 10–11. (Manuscript in possession of the Sisters of Mercy Provincialate, Baltimore, MD).

36. Quoted in Hasia R. Diner, *Erin's Daughters in America: Irish Immigrant Women in the Nineteenth Century* (Baltimore, 1983), 131.

37. Most recent scholarly research on women religious in the nineteenth century has emphasized their positive personal experiences and significant institutional contributions. See, for example, Sr. Mary Ewens, OP, *The Role of the Nun in the Nineteenth Century*; "Removing the Veil: The Liberated

Motherine Caroline Friess of the School Sisters of Notre Dame

Nevertheless, for women religious such pathbreaking activities and behavior did not reflect or foster changes in their values. There is little evidence to suggest that nuns criticized the male-exclusiveness of the Catholic clergy and hierarchy, or challenged their own subordination, or that of other women, to males generally. In this respect, their belief in spiritual motherhood closely resembled the so-called domestic feminism of women like Sarah Hale, Catharine Beecher, and, in the latter half of the nineteenth century, Frances Willard, president of the Women's Christian

American Nun," in Rosemary R. Ruether and Eleanor McLaughlin, eds., *Women of the Spirit: Female Leadership in the Jewish and Christian Traditions* (New York, 1979), 255-278; and "The Leadership of Nuns in Immigrant Catholicism," in Rosemary R. Ruether and Rosemary S. Keller, eds., *Women and Religion in America: Vol. I—The Nineteenth Century* (San Francisco, 1981), 101-149; Sr. Frances Jerome Woods, CDP, "Congregations of Religious Women in the Old South," in Randall M. Miller and Jon L. Wakelyn, eds., *Catholics in the Old South* (Macon, GA, 1983), 99-123; and Sr. Barbara Misner, SCSC, "A Comparative Social Study of the Members and Apostolates of the First Eight Permanent Communities of Women Religious within the Original Boundaries of the United States, 1790-1850" (Ph.D. diss., The Catholic University of America, 1980). Mary J. Oates, "The Professional Preparation of Parochial School Teachers, 1870-1940" *Historical Journal of Massachusetts* 12 (January 1984): 60-72; and "Organized Voluntarism: The Catholic Sisters in Massachusetts, 1870-1940" *American Quarterly* 30 (Winter 1978): 652-680 finds a relative decline in the social opportunities and professional training of women religious as they became more restricted to parochial school teaching following the Civil War. For a highly critical interpretation of the effects of religious life on women, see William Jarvis, "Mother Seton's Sisters of Charity" (Ph.D. diss., Columbia University, 1984).

Temperance Union—all of whom justified women widening their traditional sphere of behavior, but who also retained a belief in naturally ordained sex roles and the moral superiority of women. The failure of women religious to question the legitimacy of male domination meant that, as a women's institution, the convent remained at a "prefeminist" stage of consciousness.[38]

Nuns fundamentally accepted the gender distinctions and complementary sex-roles defined by the ideology of domesticity, and attempted to pass these ideals on to other women. Though Catholic sisterhoods pioneered new forms of participation for women beyond the immediate family circle, the effect was only to create new variations on traditional roles, to broaden the meaning of the female sphere without questioning the validity of that concept. Rather than being subversive of domesticity, nuns, by their practice of maternity of the spirit, fulfilled its functions and conformed to its assumptions about the female nature.

38. The term "prefeminist" is taken from Estelle Freedman, "Separatism as Strategy: Female Institution Building and American Feminism, 1870–1930," *Feminist Studies* 5 (Fall 1979): 527, f.7. Freedman suggests that "any female-dominated activity that places a positive value on women's social contributions, provides personal support, and is not controlled by antifeminist leadership has feminist political potential." Nineteenth-century convents meet the first two of these requirements but not the last. Freedman further contends, "When the group experience leads to insights about male domination," its members, ". . . often become politicized as feminists." This process failed to occur among religious sisterhoods in the nineteenth century, only becoming evident in the last half of the twentieth century following the Second Vatican Council.

EVANGELICAL WOMANHOOD IN THE NINETEENTH CENTURY: THE ROLE OF WOMEN IN SUNDAY SCHOOLS

ANNE M. BOYLAN

Recent work in women's history has traced the origin of modern roles for women and modern prescriptions for female behavior to the nineteenth century. Although disagreeing over the significance of these events, historians of women have pointed to the nineteenth century as a time when increasing numbers of middle-class women lost direct involvement in the productive process, were isolated in the home and removed from the work-world, and as a consequence developed a consciousness of themselves as a group with concerns and interests separate from those of men. These prescriptions, usually grouped together under the term "the cult of true womanhood," established for women a special "sphere" with activities and concerns circumscribed by their supposedly natural capabilities for nurturing, caring, and teaching.[1]

Some historians, focusing on the prescriptive literature written for nineteenth-century women, have attempted to determine exactly which roles the literature sanctioned. Initially, examinations of the literature suggested that "the cult of true womanhood" was narrowly restrictive, permitting only one "accepted ideal of femininity toward which all women would strive." More recently, however, Ronald Hogeland has demonstrated that there were several alternative prescriptions, several "distinctive lifestyles" available to middle-class women. Hogeland termed these prescriptions Ornamental womanhood (synonymous with the cult of the lady), Romanticized womanhood (or the cult of true womanhood), Evangelical womanhood, and Radical womanhood, and noted that they offered women a choice of acceptable behaviors ("lifestyles") within nineteenth-century culture. Thus, although the prescriptive literature delineated only ideal types, not real women, the study of it has enabled us to understand the range of roles considered acceptable in the nineteenth century.[2]

Exactly how these roles evolved and why women accepted them are issues which have also interested historians of women. In delineating a monolithic "cult of true womanhood," Barbara Welter argued that it was a creation of nineteenth-century men who, during the antebellum period, sought to make women hostages in the home in order to assuage men's guilt over their embrace of materialistic values. While refining Welter's model of available female roles, Hogeland still maintained that it was men, not women, who were "responsible for defining the dimensions of femininity and the roles which . . . [women] were able to play." In this view, women accepted, willingly or unwillingly, an essentially male vision of feminine roles. Two important exceptions to this approach were Nancy Cott's examination of New England women in the period 1780-1835 and Kathryn Sklar's biography of Catharine Beecher. Sklar demonstrated that Beecher, beginning in the 1820s, self-consciously developed an ideal of womanhood which stressed self-sacrifice but permitted women to adopt active social roles in areas such as teaching and moral leadership. Sklar showed that in pursuit of her goal, Beecher created many organizational opportunities for women. Similarly, Cott, dealing with the earlier period, delineated the attractions to women of an ideology which exercised their special capabilities, provided a positive self-image, and offered opportunities for public service.[3]

Related to these issues is the question of interpreting the rise of women's organizations in the early nineteenth century. Founded and staffed by women, the groups, most of which were devoted to benevolent purposes, emerged at the turn of the nineteenth century and proliferated rapidly in succeeding decades. Through these associations, women found outlets for their unused energies, developed a sense of group identity, and learned important organizational talents. Historians have demonstrated that it was in these groups that some women first gained a personal awareness of the disabilities suffered by their sex and moved into women's rights agitation. Some historians have interpreted these organizations as essentially responses, albeit creative ones, to a repressive male ideology. Women's increasingly public activities, in this view, represented a "subtle subversion" of the cult of true womanhood whereby women took a restrictive ideology and cleverly turned it to their own ends. If one examines these organizations more closely, however, it becomes clear that they emerged simultaneously with new ideals of womanhood, not in response to them. It then appears that associations were a logical extension of this emerging conception of womanhood, and that women themselves devised both the organizations and the ideology to express their view of female nature.[4]

My purpose in the following pages is to examine more fully the issues outlined above by looking at the women who founded and taught Sunday schools in the nineteenth century. This examination will illuminate how the ideal of Evangelical womanhood evolved during the first and second decades of the century and what role women themselves played in the evolution of this ideal. The examination will also show how the exponents of this ideal designed means of carrying it into practice and of transmitting it to succeeding generations. By showing what motivated women who founded Sunday schools and how they gave institutional shape to their concerns, I will argue that these women took an active part in molding the role of the evangelical woman. By examining the Sunday school teaching experience itself, I will point out what the experience meant to female teachers and why it appealed to them. Finally, by following the activities of Sunday school workers through the nineteenth century, I will demonstrate that the role of the evangelical women (as seen in Sunday school teachers' lives) was susceptible to a wide range of interpretations by the women who chose it. In general, Sunday school teachers remained at the conservative end of the interpretive spectrum; but perhaps they typified the nineteenth-century woman better than the handful of women who became feminists.

The founding of Sunday schools in the early nineteenth century grew out of the sequence of religious revivals termed the Second Great Awakening, which lasted from about 1790 to 1835. Almost all Sunday school founders and most early teachers were either recent converts or those hopeful of experiencing conversion. Like participants in the Awakening as a whole, these individuals were generally quite young, and a majority of them were women. For them, conversion, whether actual or imminent, was a defining life experience which they commonly regarded as a "re-birth." In their new lives, they were to have recognizably different patterns of activity, characterized by exemplary behavior as well as action to evangelize others. Their search for appropriate evangelizing agencies led Protestants to create a variety of benevolent institutions, among them Sunday schools, which simultaneously met the objective needs of a society without welfare agencies and the subjective needs of energetic converts without meaningful work.[5] As the writings of Sunday school organizers reveal, a two-pronged process led women from the conversion experience to benevolent work. First, they rejected prevailing ideas about women and created new ideals rooted in evangelical Protestantism; and second, they found institutional means of enacting and promulgating their new ideals.

At the turn of the nineteenth century, the image of woman most widely disseminated in popular magazines and novels was that of the lady. These publications presented woman as a creature who cultivated fashion, charm, and the "ornamental arts," so as to enhance the reputations of the men in her life, or to acquire men who valued these accomplishments. At one extreme, the lady was also one who shunned childbearing as indelicate (and figure-ruining), viewed childrearing as boring, and regarded churchgoing primarily as a means of displaying her latest fashionable outfit. In more moderate interpretations, the lady merely delegated as many routine tasks as possible to servants, in order to have time for herself.[6]

However popular, this image was seen by many as antithetical to American values, encouraging as it did an unrepublican concern with fashion and idle devotion to the self. Vigorously protesting this "aristocratic" image of women as frivolous and fashionmongering, many commentators urged American women to devote themselves instead to cultivating the image of the "Republican mother." Serious-minded and patriotic, the republican mother knew that her highest achievement lay in raising good citizens for the republic and in exemplifying those virtues–prudence, frugality, industriousness–which the country needed.[7]

The popular image of the lady was also incompatible with the tenets and social ideals of evangelical Protestantism. Echoing the republican rejection of this image, evangelical Protestant women at the turn of the century worked to create an alternative ideal of womanhood. A recurrent theme in their writings–that before conversion they had led frivolous, gay, and useless lives–points to their consciousness that conversion was inconsistent with the life of the lady. A related theme–the need to do something to signify one's conversion–reflects their concern with being useful, doing something meaningful with their lives. A third theme–the desire to save other women from the traps they had encountered–suggests their desire to develop concrete, alternative ways of life. As converted women, they must cast aside the cultural prescription of ornamental womanhood, develop a new female ideal, and take on new lives.[8]

Evangelical womanhood combined the traditional Protestant ideal of the "vertuous woman" with a new evangelical stress on action. It portrayed woman as nurturing, sensitive, pious; more aware than man of injustice, and more capable of providing comfort to those in need. Although stressing the essential differences between the sexes, this image suggested that the differences were divinely appointed for what Hannah More called the "better economy of the world," and did not imply inequalities between the sexes. Rather, men and women were complementary equals, with equally important roles to play in society. Evangelical women were to "be up and doing" and although their work differed from that of men–concerned as it was with care of children, the weak, and the oppressed–it was by no means less valuable.[9] Indeed, the exponents of this ideal came to see women's work as more important than that of men; men could be presidents, but only women could do society's most important work–rearing good children.[10]

In conjunction with this new image, women created an alternative social role: substituting a self-sacrificing dedication to others for the lady's concern with self, evangelical women designed activities for women of all ages and stations in life. A woman's central role, they knew, was that of wife and mother, and so they drew the outlines of a cult of selfless motherhood which eventually pervaded the nineteenth century. Devoting herself to husband and children, the evangelical mother sought to lead them all to salvation and useful lives. The only activity she allowed herself beyond the family circle was attendance at religious observances or membership in a maternal association (an association of mothers dedicated to improved methods of childrearing). Yet the greatest need was for meaningful work to engage young single women. With the age of first marriage rising, and with uneven sex ratios coming to prevail in the northeastern states (especially in cities), women stayed single longer; and more women did not marry at all. Reflecting on their own experiences, evangelical women argued that it was critical for the young to have some occupation which would protect them from the seductions of a leisured life. Later they might have motherhood to employ them; now they needed other work.[11]

Evangelical womanhood, then, was a role choice whereby individuals shaped their lives around their religious convictions, forming friendships, undertaking activities, even choosing jobs that would best further their image of themselves as converted persons. The existence of this role can be seen in the biographies, autobiographies, and diaries of countless Sunday school teachers. One example will reveal the general pattern.

Harriet Lathrop, Sunday school organizer and missionary, was born into a pious family in Connecticut in 1796. At the age of 13, she experienced conversion and joined her town's Presbyterian church as its youngest member. Like other evangelicals, she interpreted her conversion as a mandate to relinquish "amusements" and "gay" friends and to attempt "to be useful to all around me." "I desire," she wrote to her mother, "to spend my life in the service of my Maker." But how? She puzzled over what "a weak, ignorant female" could do, apart from pray, in order to evangelize others, and confessed she was "almost ready to wish myself a man" that she might become a missionary. By the time she was 18, Lathrop had begun to find an answer through activities which were not only "useful" but also in keeping with her self-definition as a converted Christian. Several hours a week were devoted to a Society for the Relief of Poor Women and Children: visiting poor women in their homes or at the almshouse, praying with them and distributing tracts, soliciting donations from well-do-to Christians, and teaching poor children in a free school. One evening a week she conducted a prayer meeting which quickly metamorphosed into a missionary society, raising funds "for the education of heathen youth." Sundays were spent teaching the Sunday school which she organized in 1816. Founded upon her return from a trip to New York where she had observed the work of the New York Female Union for the Promotion of Sabbath Schools, this school involved both Sunday teaching and weekly visits to her students at home. Much of her other free time was spent in letter writing to friends and relatives on religious subjects, or in seeking out neighbors for "Christian conversation." At the age of 23, she chose her future career by marrying a minister and accompanying him to Ceylon as a missionary. Even after the move, Lathrop continued to correspond with her Sunday school, with individuals to whom she had delivered tracts, as well as with family and close friends.[12]

Lathrop's life was typical of the pattern which other evangelical women created. They considered their conversions to be the defining experience in their lives and sought ways of leading others to the same experience. Conversion marked the beginning of a life devoted to Christian growth, involving intensive self-examination about matters of daily living. Intimate friendships could be cultivated only with pious individuals, and marriage with a nonpious person was out of the question. Teaching Sunday school facilitated this quest for right living not only because it reinforced religious commitment and provided an arena for influencing others in the same direction, but also because it presented a ready source of like-minded friends. Diaries, letters, and autobiographies reveal patterns of close, exclusive, and at times intense friendships between Sunday school students and teachers, friendships which frequently traversed time and distance.[13]

Individuals such as Lathrop did not develop their lives in isolation. Rather, they existed within an intricate network of personal relationships among fellow evangelicals. Although these relationships existed primarily among converted individuals within the same community, they were also extended beyond the local level by visits and letters among evangelical friends and by new evangelical magazines such as the *Religious Intelligencer*. Lathrop, for example, learned about Sunday schools while on a visit to New York where she sought out those attractions which offered "familiar Christian communion"; as another tourist might visit Castle Garden or New York's Battery, Lathrop attended the churches with the most inspiring preachers, and sat in on a meeting of the Sunday school society. Similarly, the founding of the first Sunday school in Utica, New York, can be traced to a visit to Utica by a young woman familiar with New York city's schools. Her host on that visit, a newly converted young woman, gathered four teenage friends with a similar commitment and founded a Sunday school.[14]

Once they had helped create the ideal and lifestyle of the evangelical woman, Sunday school workers devised ways of extending it to succeeding generations. Using a common contemporary understanding, Sunday school workers argued that "youth" (a term generally referring to age 14 and over) was "the most critical period of life" during which "the mind generally takes a decided turn, and the happiness and usefulness of the character is ensured or destroyed." Because the teenage years constituted such a crucial stage, female teachers sought ways of making their schools the central shaping force in a girl's life. Through the schools they hoped to disseminate the ideal of evangelical womanhood and secure early adherence to it among their pupils. In pursuit of this goal, they developed a rationale for Sunday school teaching; organized special classes to train adolescents to become teachers; and worked to make their own teachers significant role models in the lives of young women.[15]

Their rationale for Sunday school work stressed its long-term benefits to the young woman. It was a pious activity, they pointed out, so it maintained continuity with a youth's religious education. It was a demanding work, so it would counteract the "love of ease" which seemed to characterize youth, and the commitment it required helped to mitigate the natural tendency of the young to "indecision." Finally, it was work that existed in a growing number of locations, so that when young people moved to new areas they could, simply by offering their services to the local Sunday school, place themselves under good influences. Best of all, the experience of teaching Sunday school had been shown to promote conversion, the central experience of the evangelical life, and continuance in the work offered a sure "preservative against declension."[16]

Sunday school organizers also shaped the schools' program both to fit young people's needs and to ease the transition from childhood to youth by providing proper guidance during that "eventful and critical period." One type of guidance was personal. Envisioning the teacher as "an elder . . . sister" to her pupils, Sunday school organizers suggested that the formation of close personal and spiritual ties between teachers and their students could crucially affect the formation of the child's character. As one organizer wrote, a close relationship would give the teacher "a moral influence" over the student which would have "beneficial and enduring results," especially at adolescence when the student was choosing her future course in life. For female students, then, the female teacher was to provide a powerful model of evangelical womanhood, on which the students would want to shape their lives.[17] A second type of guidance was institutional and involved training students as future teachers. Individual teachers encouraged students who experienced conversion to bring the experience to fruition by becoming teachers. Former teacher Lydia Bacon expressed this expectation when she heard that a former student had been converted. "Tell her that I am happy to hear it," she wrote to a mutual acquaintance, "and that I trust she will be a firm, active Christian, taking up her cross in her youth. I presume she has a class in the Sabbath school." Teachers also set up formal "Bible classes" for teenagers aimed at, among other things, training these students to become teachers.[18]

Evidence from the experiences of the first generation of Sunday school teachers suggests that these strategies did in fact meet the needs of young Protestants. Material from teachers' diaries and letters, as well as from teachers' organizations, shows that teachers and students often became close friends and that the friendships served important reciprocal functions. Visiting students in their homes was a common practice which created "strong reciprocal affections" between student and teacher. Even when separated by distance, dedicated teachers frequently carried on correspondence with their former pupils. Indeed one teacher was able to claim on the fiftieth anniversary of her first Sunday school that of the nine students in her class, six were still her correspondents. (In her case, the closeness was reinforced because she taught many of the same students in daily school.) Caroline Richards, a student and later teacher in a Canadaigua, New York, Sunday school recorded numerous instances of female teachers and students meeting socially to make quilts or other gifts for women teachers who were leaving the school. When she herself was getting married, her class of eight girls "had their ambrotypes taken with me" and made plans to "dress in white and sit on the first seat in church." These close friendships, facilitated by the generally small size of Sunday school classes, enabled teachers to pass on to succeeding generations of students the model of evangelical womanhood to which they subscribed.[19]

Bible classes and weekly teachers' meetings were also significant means of disseminating and cultivating the ideal of evangelical womanhood. In the Bible class, usually kept to between six and ten students, a young woman could meet and develop friendships with other pious young women, including the teacher. Later, when they themselves became teachers, the young women would enter a world of activities which would reinforce their commitment to evangelicalism and provide alternatives to the diversions of the world. In the teachers' meetings, which were sex-segregated for the first few decades, young women could socialize with like-minded contemporaries, share prayers and narratives of religious experiences, and initiate new teachers into the community of workers through prayer and fellowship. By engaging in decision making about matters relating to the school, they received training in organization and leadership. Later on, when teachers' meetings integrated the sexes, they provided socially acceptable opportunities for meeting potential mates: in a world in which young women were constantly warned against strange men, they could be reasonably sure that men encountered at Sunday school shared their beliefs and lifestyle.[20]

These social and psychological benefits aside, Sunday school teaching attracted succeeding generations of women because it offered them an appealing vision of themselves as useful and significant individuals. To take one example, the speeches of successive presidents of the Baltimore Female Sabbath School Society indicate that women saw Sunday school work as one of the few areas where they could influence, however indirectly, the course of society. Our "exertions," argued one president, multiply "the virtues that establish the comfort of society." Sunday school teaching, suggested another, by "fitting the present generation to act their parts upon the great stage of human action," was a powerful means of shaping the future of society. If children represented that future, then those involved in their training would perhaps help to determine whether society languished under a "torrent of vice" or benefited from "those great moral influences upon which all prosperity and happiness" were founded. It fit the "diffidence and retirement so becoming" to women, another president proposed, that their power be exerted indirectly. "What though your names may not be emblazoned on the historical page?"

asked another; your influence is as great, perhaps greater, than that of those (men) whom history does remember. You are engaged, she concluded, in "mighty operations"; "you are attending to the moral and intellectual culture of youthful immortals."[21] These sentiments expressed the belief that evangelical activities enabled women to be as important and effective as men—perhaps even more so.

The achievement of the first women Sunday school founders and teachers during the 1810s and 1820s lay in establishing their work as useful and significant, and in drawing succeeding generations into it. In doing this, they were helping to establish evangelical womanhood as an alternative role choice for nineteenth-century women, and Sunday school teaching as a key part of that role.

The definition of evangelical womanhood was never static; indeed, some of its appeal lay in its flexibility and its varying interpretations. One could select one's own level and style of commitment to the ideal, whether it be devotion to family and home, teaching Sunday school once a week, engaging in numerous benevolent activities at once, or becoming a full-time missionary. For the individual, also, a particular choice need not be a final one: many women were content to do Sunday school teaching solely, but for others teaching led into an expanding round of benevolent activities. During the 1830s and 1840s, evangelical women, many of whom began their careers as Sunday school teachers, extended the boundaries of evangelical womanhood by engaging in increasingly activist and full-time forms of benevolence. Women who saw themselves as inheritors of the mantle of evangelical womanhood became foreign missionaries, moral reformers, abolitionists, or even advocates of women's rights, all the while arguing that their activities were merely different ways of exerting female influence in the world.[22]

For some women, teaching became a stepping-stone to other more public or more time-consuming activities. Women applying to become missionaries of the American Board of Commissioners for Foreign Missions, for example, invariably used their Sunday school teaching as evidence of their suitability for the job and their general good character; letters of recommendation from their ministers echoed this view. Other women found that teaching led them into involvement in related benevolent causes. Joanna Graham Bethune, organizer of the New York Female Union for the Promotion of Sabbath Schools in 1816, extended her activities into the formation of infant schools in the 1820s and gradually developed a full-time career in benevolence. In addition, there were a large number of anonymous women teachers who shaped writing careers for themselves by feeding the seemingly insatiable appetites of Sunday school publishers for books and magazine articles.[23]

Other Sunday school teachers, especially those who were trained as common school teachers or who were married to ministers, forged careers as missionaries to the American West. Combining a willingness to teach both day and Sunday schools, these women came to frontier communities as exemplars of evangelical womanhood. They conducted school during the week, larding their instruction with heavy doses of religious teaching, and also taught Sunday school. There are numerous examples of this type of career–from the ministers' wives who did dual duty in countless American communities to the missionaries who went South during Reconstruction to teach the freed slaves–and there is good evidence that their ability to teach Sunday school made these women doubly attractive to communities seeking teachers. National Sunday school publications even appealed to "pious females in single life" during the 1830s to move to "destitute" areas of the West precisely to fill this dual function.[24]

The career of Harriet Bishop provides a good example of a Sunday school missionary. A devoted evangelical Baptist and an admirer of women missionaries, Bishop was teaching school in New York when she heard about the National Board of Popular Education, an organization founded by Catharine Beecher to recruit female teachers for Western schools. Attending a course offered by the Board in 1847, Bishop answered an appeal for a teacher in Minnesota. Organizing the first day school and the first Sunday school in St. Paul, Bishop became a missionary both of evangelical religion and of the cultural values she associated with it, in the process creating a full-time career which reflected those of hundreds of evangelical women like her.[25]

Before 1850, however, most women Sunday school teachers continued to adhere to an interpretation of evangelical womanhood which stressed invisible influence. They did not seek, or gain, access to leadership positions within Sunday schools; instead they were content to see women exerting power and influence in silent, invisible ways. Situations of overt power, such as administrative jobs, were left to male Sunday school workers. Even when women made up a large majority of teachers in a school, as was frequently the case, the superintendent and other officers were always male.[26]

Female teachers did not begin to expand their definition of evangelical womanhood and hence take more active public roles until the 1850s. During that decade, teachers' associations began electing female officers (although the superintendent's position generally remained a male preserve); and some urban Sunday school organizations began hiring women for local missionary work. The late 1850s and 1860s saw the growth of local teachers' conventions and institutes, which women attended as delegates, and at which women occasionally conducted sessions. The percentage of women delegates to the New York State Sunday School Teachers' Convention, for example, rose from 16% in 1863 to 32% in 1878. In the same way women made up 30% of the delegates to Kentucky's 1875 convention; but they were 45% of the 1878 delegates. More married women were engaging in Sunday school teaching, also; at least 45% of the women delegates to the 1867 Illinois State Sunday School Convention were married.[27]

Even though their expanded activity came more than two decades after other evangelical women had begun to assert their right to lead and to speak on religious questions, female Sunday school workers in the 1850s and 1860s encountered resistance from male leaders who invoked traditional arguments against such public activity. Women, claimed one minister in a national magazine, have special qualities which suit them to teaching but not to supervising. To another, it appeared "evident that God never intended that women should be public speakers; or that, in his church, and in related organizations, women should occupy the position of public teachers and rulers." "It would be better," he concluded, "to have a man of *very* moderate ability as superintendent, than to have a very gifted woman." At the first national Sunday school teachers' summer school in Chautauqua, New York, in 1873, the organizers barred women from addressing a mixed assembly of teachers, requiring them instead to hold separate receptions for women only.[28]

Despite such opposition, women justified their movement into more authoritative positions in much the same way as their predecessors had justified organizing and teaching the schools. They had special talents to offer as women and special work to do as evangelicals, they argued, and could best perform that work by speaking and conducting sessions at conventions. Believing that they had a "peculiar power" to do good, to take the lead in "elevating society," they confidently dismissed opposition. Thus, three years after women were denied permission to speak to the Chautauqua assembly, the barrier came down as Frances Willard addressed the mixed gathering.[29]

In the 1860s and 1870s, female Sunday school workers found two new areas of activity: promoting new teaching methods and campaigning for temperance education. Women who came to Sunday school work with normal school training brought with them an enthusiasm for new teaching techniques and a belief that these techniques could improve Sunday school teaching. Among the techniques they were instrumental in adapting to Sunday schools were those based on the philosophy of Swiss educator Johann Pestalozzi. Because Pestalozzi's system was predicated upon an understanding of the child's "nature" and the achievement of "empathy" between teacher and pupil, women claimed a special competence for teaching the system. By using arguments similar to those which had justified the employment of women for primary public school teaching, they suggested that women were best qualified to teach children.[30]

The wholesale adoption of new methods by the 1870s and the introduction of new standards of professionalism into Sunday school work brought several women to national prominence. One was Sara J. Timanus, a teacher at the Minnesota State Normal School, who developed a second career lecturing to Sunday school teachers' institutes and writing for teachers' magazines. By the early 1870s, she was also preparing a set of weekly lessons for a national periodical. After her marriage in 1874 to another Sunday school worker (whom she had met while working on a book for teachers),[31] Timanus worked her second career into a full-time one.

Another Sunday school innovation particularly associated with women was the adoption of kindergartens. Beginning in the early 1870s women such as Matilda Kriege, principal of Boston's kindergarten training school, contributed numerous articles to teachers' magazines on the principles and practices of kindergartens and their adaptation to Sunday schools. Kriege and others like her also traveled to teachers' institutes and conventions, conducting "model classroom" sessions designed to familiarize teachers with kindergartens. Through these sessions, they taught techniques associated with Pestalozzi and with Friedrich Froebel, offered practical lessons in the use of such techniques, and emphasized that only women should teach kindergarten Sunday schools. They succeeded in convincing a growing number of Sunday schools to create kindergarten divisions and established kindergarten teaching as a special area of expertise reserved for women.[32]

Temperance workers developed a different set of leadership roles for women in Sunday schools. Although temperance work had traditionally attracted evangelical women, only in the late 1860s did they begin to use Sunday school magazines to suggest that teachers could win the battle against "the rum-power" by converting children to total abstinence. From these individual efforts came lectures on the importance of instructing Sunday school pupils on temperance, and finally, meetings of women temperance workers at the first national Sunday school teachers' summer school in Chautauqua, New York, in 1873, and again in 1874. These gatherings, in turn, led to the formation of the Woman's Christian Temperance Union, which quickly established committees on Juvenile Temperance Work and Sunday Schools. The idea of using Sunday schools as the means of reaching young people came naturally to WCTU organizers, many of whom—like Jennie Fowler Willing, Emily Huntington Miller, and Frances Willard—were Sunday school teachers. During the organization's first five years, they planned and executed two successful programs: organizing Sunday school students into Juvenile Temperance Unions, complete with banners and abstinence pledges; and lobbying for the adoption of temperance lessons within each denomination's schools. The lessons, written and developed by Sunday school and temperance advocates Sara Timanus (Crafts) and Emily Huntington Miller, achieved widespread adoption by 1879.[33]

These women, although more assertive and visible than earlier generations of Sunday school teachers, were nevertheless acting within the broad outlines of evangelical womanhood drawn in the early nineteenth century. They believed as did their predecessors that women possessed certain innate qualities which suited them for particular kinds of activity. Like them, too, they used the argument for female qualities to press for special social roles for women—as teachers, temperance leaders, kindergarten workers. No longer preoccupied with defining evangelical womanhood, they expanded it to include public speaking, conducting teachers' conventions, and writing Sunday school lessons.

The concept of evangelical womanhood, as I have elaborated it in the preceding pages, helps to delineate a particular ideal and style of female behavior in the nineteenth century. Although nineteenth-century evangelical women did not use the term themselves, they recognized that their lives and social ideals, as shaped by evangelical Protestantism, were different enough to set them apart from their contemporaries. Just as evangelicalism contained an inherent critique of the values and lifestyles of the leisured classes, so too did the concept of the evangelical woman encompass a critique of "the butterflies of the *fashionable* world."[34]

In evangelicalism, women found an alternative to uselessness. They also found ideals and values which not only reflected their own view of women's nature, but also encouraged their desire to create broader educational and social opportunities for women. Hence when evangelical women developed seminaries, benevolent societies, and church groups, they were creating alternative institutions through which the evangelical ideal of woman could be developed, taught, and promulgated. Sunday schools provide only one example of this process; the discussion presented here might also by extension be applied to developments within other institutions as well. For example, Sunday school workers' methods of transmitting the evangelical ideal, especially their use of conscious role models, were also practiced in seminaries and benevolent socities. None of these institutions existed alone; rather, their activities supported and reinforced each other, creating varied opportunities for women wishing to pursue the evangelical ideal.

This analysis also demonstrates the meaning of religious behavior for nineteenth-century women. Women had consistently made up a majority of church members in colonial America. What was new in the nineteenth century was their redefinition of the conversion experience to mandate social action. As in the past, religious behavior offered women a means of signifying their values and goals; but now it also offered them means of shaping active, even public lives. Precisely because nineteenth-century women had fewer acceptable avenues to usefulness and activity, religious behavior became a more important means of self-expression for them than it was for men.

In arguing, as I have here, that women themselves developed the ideal of evangelical womanhood and then elaborated on the ideal through varied interpretations, I do not mean to suggest that nineteenth-century women chose this role without constraints. They did not. The constraints upon them were not, however, the simple ones of male authority, which some historians have postulated. Rather, these women acted within a complex series of constraints formed by their social class, current public opinion, and the historical realities of women's subordinate status. Yet within these limits, evangelical women manifested a clear drive to take hold of their lives and shape goals and activities based on their own conception of womanhood.

NOTES

[1]See Janet Wilson James, "Changing Ideas about Women in the United States, 1776-1825" (Ph.D. dissertation, Radcliffe, 1954); Gerda Lerner, "The Lady and the Mill Girl: Changes in the Status of Women in the Age of Jackson," *Midcontinent American Studies Journal* 10 (1969): 5-14; Barbara Welter, "The Cult of True Womanhood, 1820-1860,"

American Quarterly 18 (1966): 151-74; Daniel Scott Smith, "Family Limitation, Sexual Control, and Domestic Feminism in Victorian America," *Feminist Studies* 1 (1973): 40-57. For a useful review of the literature on nineteenth-century sex roles, see Barbara Sicherman, "American History," *Signs* 1 (1975), especially pages 470-80.

[2]Welter, "Cult of True Womanhood," p. 151; Lerner, "Lady and the Mill Girl," p. 11; Ronald W. Hogeland, " 'The Female Appendage': Feminine Lifestyles in America, 1820-1860," *Civil War History* 17 (1971): 101-14.

[3]Welter, "Cult of True Womanhood," pp. 152-53; Glenda Riley, "Origins of the Argument for Improved Female Education," *History of Education Quarterly* 9 (1969): 456; Glenda Riley McIntosh, "The Origins of the Feminist Movement in America," *Forums in History* (St. Louis: Forum Press, 1973), p. 13; Hogeland, " 'The Female Appendage,' " p. 102; Nancy F. Cott, *The Bonds of Womanhood: "Women's Sphere" in New England, 1780-1835* (New Haven: Yale University Press, 1977). Kathryn Kish Sklar, *Catharine Beecher: A Study in American Domesticity* (New Haven: Yale University Press, 1973).

[4]Mary Bosworth Treudley, " 'The Benevolent Fair': A Study of Charitable Organizations among American Women in the First Third of the Nineteenth Century," *Social Service Review* 14 (1940): 509-22; Keith Melder, "The Beginnings of the Women's Rights Movement in the United States, 1800-1840" (Ph.D. dissertation, Yale University, 1963), chapter 2; Melder, "Ladies Bountiful: Organized Women's Benevolence in Early Nineteenth-Century America," *New York History* 48 (1967): 231-53; Glenda G. Riley, "The Subtle Subversion," *The Historian* 32 (1970): 210-27.

[5]Lois W. Banner, "The Protestant Crusade: Religious Missions, Benevolence, and Reform in the United States, 1790-1840" (Ph.D. dissertation, Columbia University, 1970), pp. 288-305; and "Religion and Reform in the Early Republic: The Role of Youth," *American Quarterly* 23 (1971): 677-95; Nancy F. Cott, "Young Women in the Second Great Awakening in New England," *Feminist Studies* 3 (1975): 15-29; Edwin Wilbur Rice, *The Sunday-School Movement, 1780-1917, and the American Sunday-School Union, 1817-1917* (Philadelphia: American Sunday-School Union, 1917). See also Carroll Smith-Rosenberg, *Religion and the Rise of the American City: The New York City Mission Movement, 1812-1870* (Ithaca: Cornell University Press, 1971), pp. 97-124.

[6]Robert Elno McGlone, "Suffer the Children: The Emergence of Modern Middle-Class Family Life in America, 1820-1870" (Ph.D. dissertation, UCLA, 1971), chapter 1; Julia C. Spruill, *Women's Life and Work in the Southern Colonies* (Chapel Hill: University of North Carolina Press, 1938; reprinted, 1972), pp. 208-31.

[7]For a good example of critiques of this image, see Thomas Branagan, *The Excellency of the Female Character Vindicated* (Philadelphia: J. Rakestraw, 1808), especially chapters 1 and 2. The concept of the "Republican mother" is set forth in Linda K. Kerber, "The Republican Mother: Women and the Enlightenment—An American Perspective," *American Quarterly* 28 (1976): 187-205.

[8]See especially Joanna Bethune, ed., *The Power of Faith: Exemplified in the Life and Writings of the Late Mrs. Isabella Graham of New York* (New York: American Tract Society, 1843).

[9]On the eighteenth century, see Lonna Myers Malmsheimer, "New England Funeral Sermons and Changing Attitudes Toward Women, 1692-1792" (Ph.D. dissertation, University of Minnesota, 1973), especially chapter 4; also Laurel Thatcher Ulrich, "Vertuous Women Found: New England Ministerial Literature, 1668-1735," *American Quarterly* 28 (1976): 20-40; and Mary Sumner Benson, *Women in Eighteenth-Century America: A Study of Opinion and Social Usage* (New York: Columbia University Press, 1935), chapters 3-4. Hannah More, a British evangelical, was very influential in the United States; see her *Strictures on the Modern System of Female Education* (London: T. Cadell & W. Davies, 1799).

[10]The best explication of this ideal, as articulated by Catharine Beecher a generation later, is in Sklar, *Catharine Beecher*, especially part IV.

[11]Anne L. Kuhn, *The Mother's Role in Childhood Education: New England Concepts, 1830-1860* (New Haven: Yale University Press, 1947) discusses some later manifestations of these ideas. For their origins, see especially Joanna Bethune, ed., *The Unpublished Letters and Correspondence of Mrs. Isabella Graham, From the Year 1767 to 1814* (New York: John S. Taylor, 1838), pp. 179-82, 222-24; Bethune, ed., *The Power of Faith*, pp. 82, 129-33; and *Diary of Sarah Connell Ayer* (Portland: n.p., 1910), pp. 226, 231, 358-59.

[12]Miron Winslow, *Memoir of Mrs. Harriet L. Winslow, Thirteen Years a Member of the American Mission in Ceylon* (New York: American Tract Society, 1840), pp. 18, 25, 29-30, 34, 37-40, 64-66.

[13]See Bethune, ed., *The Power of Faith*, pp. 167, 229-30, 235, 243, 368; J. Bethune to F. A. Packard, 4 August 1829, Gratz Collection, Historical Society of Pennsylvania, Philadelphia, Pennsylvania; B. K. Peirce, *One Talent Improved: or, The Life and Labors of Miss Susan B. Bowler, Successful Sunday-School Teacher* (New York: Carlton and Porter, 1845); *Biography of Mrs. Lydia B. Bacon* (Boston: Massachusetts Sabbath School Society, 1856).

[14]Winslow, *Memoir of Mrs. Harriet L. Winslow*, pp. 54-68; First Presbyterian Church, Utica, *Semi-Centennial of the Sunday School* (Utica, N.Y.: First Presbyterian Church, 1866), pp. 39-40.

[15]W. F. Lloyd, *Teacher's Manual: or, Hints to a Teacher on Being Appointed to the Charge of a Sunday School Class* (Philadelphia: American Sunday School Union, 1825), p. 82; Archibald Alexander, "Suggestions in Vindication of Sunday Schools" (Philadelphia: American Sunday School Union, 1829), p. 7; Elizabeth, New Jersey, First Presbyterian Church, Sunday School Teachers' Association Minutes, April 2, 1827, Presbyterian Historical Society, Philadelphia, Pennsylvania; *Religious Intelligencer* 3 (July, 1818): 105; Joseph F. Kett, "Adolescence and Youth in Nineteenth-Century America," *Journal of Interdisciplinary History* 2 (1971): 283-98.

[16]James Milnor, "Address to the Sunday School of St. George's Church, New York" (New York: New York Sunday School Union, 1817), p. 5; *Religious Intelligencer* 3 (December, 1818): 431; *Sabbath School Herald* 1(May, 1829): 76-77.

[17]Frederick A. Packard, *The Teacher Taught: An Humble Attempt to Make the Path of the Sunday School Teacher Straight and Plain* (Philadelphia: American Sunday School Union, 1839), pp. 87, 162.

[18]Boston, Twelfth Congregational Society, "Address Delivered Before . . . the Sunday School . . . At their Sixth Anniversary, March 29, 1833. By one of the Superintendents" (Boston: Twelfth Congregational Society, 1833), p. 13; Lydia Bacon to Elizabeth C., February 15, 1832, in *Biography of Mrs. Lydia B. Bacon*, pp. 115-16; "Second Annual Report of the New Hampshire Baptist Sabbath-School Union," *American Sunday-School Magazine* 7 (1830): 318-19; New York Female Union for the Promotion of Sabbath Schools, *Third Annual Report* (1819), p. 4.

[19]Peirce, *One Talent Improved*, pp. 112-15; letter of Susan Burchard Taintor, printed in First Presbyterian Church, Utica, *Semi-Centennial*, pp. 41-43; *Biography of Mrs. Lydia B. Bacon*; Caroline Cowles Richards, *Village Life in America, 1852-1872* (New York: Henry Holt and Co., 1912), p. 199.

[20]Philadelphia, Spruce Street Baptist Sabbath School Society, Minutes, 1855-57, American Baptist Historical Society, Rochester, New York; Baltimore Female Sabbath School Society, Minutes, 1816-1822, Lovely Lane Methodist Museum, Baltimore, Maryland. New York Sunday School Union Society, Methodist Branch Minutes, 1816-1820, New York Public Library, New York. For a description of a Sunday school courtship, see Richards, *Village Life in America*, entry of June, 1860, pp. 132-33.

[21]Baltimore Female (McKendrean) Sabbath School Society, Minutes: November 3,

1831; November 1, 1828; October 4, 1836; October 16, 1837; October 1, 1838.

22See Melder, "Beginnings of the Women's Rights Movement," chapters 3 and 4; Alice S. Rossi, "Social Roots of the Woman's Movement in America," in Rossi, ed., *The Feminist Papers* (New York: Bantam Books, 1974), pp. 241-81; McIntosh, "The Origins of the Feminist Movement."

23Louise T. Knauer, "Foot Soldiers in the Kingdom of God: Backgrounds and Motivations of Single Women Missionaries" (paper delivered at the Third Berkshire Conference on the History of Women, Bryn Mawr, Pennsylvania, June 9-11, 1976); George W. Bethune, ed., *Memoirs of Mrs. Joanna Bethune* (New York: American Tract Society, 1863). The incoming correspondence in the Frederick A. Packard file, Gratz Collection, Historical Society of Pennsylvania, Philadelphia, Pennsylvania, contains letters from some of the most prolific women writers for the American Sunday School Union.

24"An Appeal from the West," *American Sunday-School Magazine* 7 (October, 1830): 310-11; see also Ellen Harriet Thomsen, "The Interest of the Eastern Churches in Western Emigration, 1830-1839" (M.A. thesis, Columbia University, 1947), pp. 20-21; and Asa Bullard, *Fifty Years with the Sabbath Schools* (Boston: Lockwood, Brooks, and Co., 1876), p. 21.

25See her autobiographical work, *Floral Home* (New York: Sheldon, Blakeman and Co., 1857) and the biographical essay by Winifred D. Bolin in Barbara Stuhler and Gretchen Kreuter, eds., *Women of Minnesota: Selected Biographical Essays* (St. Paul: Minnesota Historical Society Press, 1977), pp. 7-19.

26See, for example, New York, Seventh Presbyterian Church Sunday School Teachers' Association, Minutes, 1827-1857, Presbyterian Historical Society.

27Philadelphia Sunday School Association, *Annual Report* (1859); New York State Sunday School Teachers' Association, *Proceedings* (Troy, 1863 and Albany, 1878), appendices; Kentucky State Sunday School Association, *Proceedings* (Lexington, 1875, 1878); Illinois State Sunday School Convention, *Proceedings of the Ninth Annual Convention* (Decatur, 1867), pp. 117-36.

28Rev. James Pierce Root, "Woman's Work in the Sabbath School," *National Sunday School Teacher* 6 (August 1871): 281-84; J. W. Willmarth, "Women and Men in Sunday Schools," *Baptist Teacher* 5 (October, 1874): 110-11; Jesse L. Hurlbut, *The Story of Chautauqua* (New York: G. P. Putnam's Sons, 1921), p. 77.

29National Woman's Christian Temperance Union, *Minutes of the First Convention* (Chicago, 1874), p. 6.

30Sara J. Timanus, "Pestalozzi in Sunday School Work," *Sunday School Journal* 3 (December, 1871): 266-67; Timanus, "Object Teaching in Sunday-schools," *Sunday-School World* 5 (1865): 98; J. H. Vincent, *Sunday School Institutes and Normal Classes* (New York: Nelson and Phillips, 1872); Timanus, "Questioning," *National Sunday School Teacher* 6 (1871): 245-49; Ned Harland Dearborn, *The Oswego Movement in American Education* (New York: Teachers' College, Columbia University, 1925).

31Sara J. Timanus, *The Infant Class: Hints on Primary Religious Instruction* (Chicago: Adams, Blackmer, and Lyon, 1870); *National Sunday School Teacher* 9 (July, 1874): 275.

32See the articles by Matilda H. Kriege in the *National Sunday School Teacher*: 6 (February, 1871): 41-43; 6 (September, 1871): 321-22; 7 (June, 1872): 208-10. See also Lizzie L. Woolman, "The Kindergarten System in the Sunday School," *Baptist Teacher* 1 (March, 1870): 19; Jennie Fowler Willing, "Keep the Little Children in Sunday School," *Sunday School Journal* 2 (June, 1870): 194-95.

33Jennie Fowler Willing, "Sunday-School Temperance Work," *National Sunday School Teacher* 4 (October, 1869): 293-94; Helen E. Tyler, *Where Prayer and Purpose Meet: The WCTU Story, 1874-1949* (Evanston: The Signal Press, 1949), pp. 11-28; National Woman's Christian Temperance Union, *Minutes of the Second Convention*

(Chicago, 1875), pp. 66-67; *Fourth Convention* (1877), pp. 202-203; *Fifth Convention* (1878), pp. 87-89; *Sixth Convention* (1879), pp. 81-89.

[34]Sarah Grimké, *Letters on the Equality of the Sexes and the Condition of Women* (Boston: Isaac Knapp, 1838), p. 86.

MEMORANDA AND DOCUMENTS

THE FEMINIZATION CONTROVERSY: SEXUAL STEREOTYPES AND THE PARADOXES OF PIETY IN NINETEENTH-CENTURY AMERICA

DAVID S. REYNOLDS

DAVID SCHUYLER's "Inventing a Feminine Past" (NEW ENGLAND QUARTERLY, September, 1978), an attack on Ann Douglas' *The Feminization of American Culture,* was a lively moment in the increasingly heated scholarly controversy about the nineteenth-century American woman. After noting the praise initially lavished on *Feminization,* Schuyler censured the book as a piece of "feminist" mythmaking, imprecise historicism, tendentious literary analysis, and pedestrian psychology.[1] However, in this corrective to Douglas, Schuyler did not offer an interpretation to replace hers. Nor did he judge Douglas' thesis against the often contradictory arguments made during the past two decades by other commentators on the American woman. More significantly, Schuyler said little about the long-debated topic which is one of Douglas' chief concerns—woman's role in the liberalization of American religion, as manifested in the sentimental-domestic novel and in the larger sphere of culture and popular piety.

A brief review of some prominent investigations of this topic reveals two contrasting critical camps: the "feminist" and the "feminine," in or between which most scholars can be placed. Despite Schuyler's judgment that Douglas has a "feminist" orientation, she can be more properly placed in the "feminine" camp, since she takes a rather negative view of some of the same women praised by others as heralds of American feminism.

According to the "feminist" interpretation, romantic liberalism

1 "Inventing a Feminine Past," NEW ENGLAND QUARTERLY, LI, 291-308 (Sept., 1978). Less acerbic and less thorough rebuttals to Douglas' thesis are found in the following reviews of *Feminization:* Gerda Lerner, "With Benefit of the Clergy," *New York Times Book Review,* June 26, 1977, p. 13 and Steven Schnur, "Pink and White Tyranny," *Commentary,* LXIV, 68-71 (Nov., 1977). Nina Baym, who questions the popular scholarly concept of a powerful cult of domesticity in nineteenth-century America, takes issue with Douglas in *Woman's Fiction: A Guide to Novels by and about Women in America, 1820-1870* (Ithaca, 1978).

was a liberating force, resulting in increased female participation in literature, reform, and intellectual and religious inquiry. In 1956 Helen Papashvily led in considering such novelists as Catherine Sedgwick, Lydia Maria Child, and Susan Warner as inchoate feminists who used fiction to advance reform and militant optimism. In Papashvily's view, "the quiet women revolted, . . . and waged their own devious, subtle, undeclared war against men—their manual of arms, their handbook of strategy was the sentimental domestic novel."[2] More recently, Susan Conrad has studied the careers of thirteen women writers between 1830 and 1860 with the aim of linking romantic self-confidence to female productivity in literary and aesthetic criticism, in translating foreign works, and in the writing of history.[3]

Those who endorse the "feminization" theory, in contrast, charge liberalism with emasculating American culture, stripping it of intellectual rigor, and replacing firm Calvinism with feeble sentimentality. This argument is rooted in an idea—one propounded by such commentators as Orestes Brownson, William James, George Santayana, and Van Wyck Brooks—that in the nineteenth century America became divided between "toughminded" business enterprise and "tenderminded" aesthetic culture. The feminization outlook has been most fully developed by Douglas, who uses a control group of thirty liberal clergymen and thirty women novelists between 1820 and 1875 to argue that theological, patriarchal Calvinism softened into an emotional, weakly feminine liberalism embodied in effeminate ministers and in timid fictional heroines.[4]

Some scholars appear to balance the two outlooks without advancing a clear thesis. Barbara Welter, for example, recalls Papashvily when she describes the popular novel as "a vehicle of protest"

2 *All the Happy Endings: A Study of the Domestic Novel in America* (New York, 1956), p. 24.

3 *Perish the Thought: Intellectual Women in Romantic America, 1830-1860* (New York, 1976).

4 *The Feminization of American Culture* (New York, 1977). George B. Forgie has applied the feminization idea to the antebellum political scene, arguing that orations and novels on topical social issues were often rhetorically designed to answer a prevailing "celebration of so-called feminine—specifically maternal—values" such as gentleness, quiescence, and conciliation (*Patricide in the House Divided: A Psychological Interpretation of Lincoln and His Age* [New York, 1979], p. 170).

promoting "temperance, women's rights, prolabor and antilabor, slavery and abolition."[5] Elsewhere Welter mirrors Conrad in her discussion of female intellectualism and, paradoxically, Douglas' claim that nineteenth-century American religion became "feminized, . . . more domesticated, more emotional, more soft and accommodating" (pp. 83-84). Two other mediating critics are Nancy F. Cott and Ernest Earnest. Cott holds that "the 'feminization' of Protestantism in the early nineteenth century was conspicuous," but that while the cult of pious domesticity restricted women, religion also helped to nurture feminism by fostering women's associations.[6] Earnest sees a split between the "American Eve" in fact and in fiction: whereas in real life women were likely to be intellectual and reformist, "the novel became feminized," presenting heroines who were little more than "a gallery of nincompoops, self-righteous prudes, and naive innocents."[7]

In face of these interpretations, reviewers have often betrayed puzzlement. Willie Rose, for instance, notes that four of Conrad's "intellectual" women appear on Douglas' list of those who brought about religious "feminization." After reviewing Douglas' work, Rose writes: "To come upon Susan Conrad's *Perish the Thought* after reading Douglas is to confront a different point of view: . . . *Intellectual* women? *Romantic* America?"[8] Indeed, Douglas' study has come to epitomize the problems connected with the analysis of female sensibility and popular piety. The present revaluation of religion and the popular novel in nineteenth-century America aims to show that Douglas did not, as David Schuyler argues, wholly "invent" a feminine past. Rather, she exaggerated one, just as other scholars have exaggerated a feminist past and still others have made disparate efforts to combine the two without defining their critical terminology. As a result of the widespread interest in women's history during the past two decades, no one

[5] *Dimity Convictions: The American Woman in the Nineteenth Century* (Athens, Ohio, 1976), p. 103. Future pagination for works quoted more than once in a single paragraph will be cited parenthetically in the text after an initial footnote.

[6] *The Bonds of Womanhood: Woman's Sphere in New England, 1780-1835* (New Haven, 1976), p. 132.

[7] *The American Eve in Fact and Fiction, 1775-1914* (Urbana, 1974), pp. 140, 10.

[8] "The Emergence of American Women," *New York Review of Books*, XXIV, 21 (July, 1977).

has recognized that a strong case can be made for a "masculine" past as well.

Because of its recent vogue and present questionable status, the feminization theory merits further consideration. To generalize that nineteenth-century American religion became feminized—i.e., more yielding, effeminate—is to overlook the fact that during this period a fervent muscular Christianity began to take shape. This is obvious in the circuit riders of the old Southwest, who in four decades (1800-1840) transformed Methodism from one of the smallest to the largest of American Protestant denominations. Frontier religion, which produced several novels before 1850, would be celebrated in Edward Eggleston's *The Circuit Rider: A Tale of the Heroic Age* (1878). This heroic kind of faith was not confined to the southern frontier: it was seen in the revivalism of Charles G. Finney, the evangelical orthodoxy of Lyman Beecher, and the reformism of the Benevolent Empire.

Moreover, it appeared in liberal circles, in Boston Unitarianism. To move, as Douglas has done, from an account of "the timid exploits of innumerable pale and pious heroines" through a description of liberal writers as either sentimental women or "delicate, even sickly homebound little boys," to the conclusion that American culture was emasculated by literary liberalism is to misinterpret the intention and achievement of Unitarian clergymen and authors.[9] The argument that a strong "masculine" Calvinism gave way to a shrinking "feminine" liberalism is almost a direct reversal of fact. We should recall that the Unitarian belief in human perfectibility helped spawn Emersonian self-reliance. Also, there had been strict Calvinists, including Jonathan Edwards and David Brainerd, who were known to be gentle and even timid in their private lives.

Many prominent liberals, in fact, saw Calvinism as a repressive system which not only thwarted human effort but created languor and listlessness. William Ellery Channing declared that the doctrines of predestination and human depravity were "destructive of the sense of moral responsibility, degrading man into a chattel slave of Power," rather than elevating him to "a freely obedient son of Love."[10] Calvinism, said Channing, nurtures "a slavish

[9] Douglas, *Feminization*, pp. 1, 117.

[10] Quoted in Elizabeth P. Peabody, *Reminiscences of Rev. William Ellery Channing* (Boston, 1880), p. 30.

spirit of fear." "All is passive," he went on, "both the sin and the deliverance of sin" (p. 245). Disturbed by Benjamin Constant's definition of religion as "a sigh of weakness," Channing called Christianity *"the spirit of martyrdom,"* "the Courage of pure Love, which is man's strength and special inheritance from God the Father" (pp. 190, 195).

William Ware also wrote that Calvinism "prostrates the independence of the mind, as it teaches men that they are naturally incapable of discerning religious truth, as it thus generates a timid and superstitious dependence."[11] Those who rejected Calvinism, in Ware's opinion, were typically strong and independent: Aaron Bancroft was notable for his "manliness, activity and free inquiry" (I, 174); John Allyn had a "striking originality" distant from any "timid and unmanly pliancy" (I, 215); there was "none more firm" than Henry Ware (I, 227); Joseph S. Buckminster possessed great "manliness of mind" (II, 225). Similarly, O. B. Frothingham wrote that the theological caution of liberals was complemented by masculine firmness: Theodore Parker, for example, was charged with "stern mental force," becoming a "Titan" who was religiously "muscular"; John Pierpont, too, "was essentially a fighter" with a "vein of heroism, . . . courage, determination, vigor."[12]

Henry Ware, Jr.'s *Formation of the Christian Character* (1829), which Frothingham called the *Imitatio* of Boston liberalism, translated this heroic conception of faith into an Arminian paean to man's capabilities. Ware castigated Calvinism's tendency "to supersede human exertion" and to provide "a reason for indolence and religious neglect."[13] Rather than complain of feebleness and passively await God's grace, Ware wrote, one must realize "that a man's labors are essential to his salvation" (p. 30). Religion for Ware was not a matter of retreat but of active soldiership. Thus, Ware converted meditation into the "surveying and burnishing of the soldier's arms" and religious practice into "the daily drill of a soldier" (pp. 80, 149).

In the nineteenth century, as normative Calvinism became liberalized, the Unitarian notion of Arminian heroism infiltrated

11 *American Unitarian Biography* (Boston, 1851), I, 77.

12 Frothingham, *Boston Unitarianism, 1820-1850* (New York, 1890), pp. 9, 185-186.

13 *Formation of the Christian Character* (Boston, 1867), p. 28.

mainstream religion. Prototypes for Calvinist muscularity could be found among various reformers and evangelical preachers before 1850. In the 1860's Horace Bushnell, drawing "an analogy between the Christian and the military discipline," demanded "rugged vigor and muscle" in religion, asserting "that our human nature is made to go a great deal more heroically than some of us think."[14] By 1881 the nation's most visible Liberal Protestant, Henry Ward Beecher, was denouncing "that crawling, that prostration, that takes the very manhood out of man."[15] Vocalizing the muscular religious outlook of the Gilded Age, Beecher told his congregation: "The object of religion is not to make dreamy speculators, but real, earnest, vigorous men. It is not to remove the burden from our path, but to enable us to bear it."[16] Between 1890 and 1920 this impulse found heightened expression in the virile ethic of such varied public figures as T. De Witt Talmage, Richard Harding Davis, Theodore Roosevelt, and Billy Sunday.

It would be easy to overstate this theme by positing "the masculinization of American culture." But we should recognize that liberals and modified Calvinists were intent on dissolving strict orthodoxy in many ways at once: the idea of Arminian self-help was aimed at the predestinarian, gloomy, tyrannical side of traditional Calvinism. The logical or excessively intellectual nature of orthodoxy was attacked from a different angle—that of emotionalism and sentimentality. Proponents of the feminization thesis magnify the latter quality while minimizing the former.

Discussion of nineteenth-century American religion, therefore, is distorted when based on a single sexual stereotype. In its endorsement of reform, perfectibility, and soldierly endeavor religion of the period tended to be "masculine" or "feminist." In its advocacy of benevolence and emotion it tended to be "feminine."

Popular fiction reflected this paradoxical combination of values. On one hand, such novelists as Lydia Maria Child, Elizabeth Oakes Smith, Sarah J. Hale, and Harriet Beecher Stowe advanced reform in novels whose pious protagonists often endured tribulation with almost superhuman strength. At the same time, these and other novelists endorsed a largely creedless religion of divine

[14] *Sermons on Living Subjects* (New York, 1872), pp. 416-417, 412.

[15] *Yale Lectures on Preaching* (New York, 1881), II, 280-281.

[16] *Proverbs from the Plymouth Pulpit* (New York, 1887), p. 125.

love and human emotion that was aligned against the logical side of received doctrine. In most novels these divergent tendencies met in a theologically benign but actively heroic center. In time such crises, with their accompanying "masculine" heroism, would almost totally displace theological discussion in American religious novels, as is evidenced by the extended scenes of martial conflict and Christian bravery in novels like Lew Wallace's *Ben-Hur* (1880) and Lloyd Douglas' *The Robe* (1942). But before the appearance of such muscular Christians as Wallace's Ben-Hur or Douglas' Marcellus, there were many fictional protagonists who were far more heroic than is implied in the studies by Ann Douglas and Ernest Earnest. Instead of purveying a weak piety, the religious novel almost from the start combined praise of God's attentive love with illustration of man's triumphant ability to survive setbacks and battle toward Christian victory.

In some novels published before the Civil War, the liberal concept of Calvinism as an enslaving system causing feebleness and defeatism was enacted in fictional contrasts between tyrannical religionists and their sturdily pious opponents. As early as 1790, Enos Hitchcock's *Memoirs of the Bloomsgrove Family* said that strict Calvinism made the weak "abject and servile" and the bold "totally negligent of religion," while liberal views helped make man "free from servile dread."[17] Three decades later, Catherine Sedgwick in *A New England Tale* (1822) characterized orthodoxy as a "demoralizing" system which makes people "languid, and selfish, and careless of their most obvious duties."[18] Having shown the fruits of a Calvinist upbringing to be indolence and immorality, Sedgwick in her later novels fashioned liberal protagonists of increasing strength and independence, including one who was "a fit heroine for the nineteenth century: practical, efficient, direct, and decided."[19] In Hannah Lee's *The Backslider* (1835), a novel commissioned by Henry Ware, Jr., anti-Calvinist self-confidence is embodied in a heroine who believes that "we have weapons given us and instructions how to use them, and it is because we are unfaithful to ourselves, if we do not gain the victory."[20] This Arminian heroism found secularized expression in the patriotic soldiers

[17] *Memoirs of the Bloomsgrove Family* (Boston, 1790), II, 201, 203.

[18] *A New England Tale* (New York, 1822), p. 24.

[19] *Clarence; or, A Tale of Our Own Times* (Philadelphia, 1830), I, 240.

[20] *The Backslider* (Boston, 1835), pp. 17-18.

and brawny backwoodsmen who figured in the novels of such authors as John Neal, Timothy Flint, William Gilmore Simms, and John Pendleton Kennedy. Kennedy's Horse-shoe Robinson, for example, is both a soldierly attacker of despotism and a frontier "minister" who believes that "'when God appoints a thing to be done, he gives it to them that's to do it all the wherewithals!'"[21]

More overtly anti-Calvinist variations of this theme were offered by Elizabeth Oakes Smith and H. W. Herbert. Puritan discipline, Smith stressed in her autobiography, had the tendency of "making the children not only submissive but passive."[22] In both her feminist essays and her reformist novels, Smith was wont to "point proudly to the God-like, of whatever creed or condition—the Heroes, Martyrs, Patriots and Poets of the earth."[23] Similarly, Herbert drew a fictional portrait of Calvinist children who "were mere passive, listless, senseless, almost soulless, agents of a will to which they bowed." Herbert contrasted these feeble products of orthodoxy to heroines who were "thinking, active, energetic, and impulsive creatures" with the ability to "support trials . . . better and with more fortitude than sterner and more hardy characters."[24]

Other novelists dramatized the passage from feebleness to strength on the part of protagonists who gain confidence in man's perfectibility and God's fairness. Eliza Lee wrote *Delusion* (1840) "to show how circumstances may unfold the inward strength of a timid woman."[25] This theme is apparent in several of Harriet Beecher Stowe's novels. Douglas prefaces her discussion of religious feminization with a section called "The Meaning of Little Eva" in which Eva St. Clare of *Uncle Tom's Cabin* is called symbolic of sickly, wilting religion in American culture. Douglas fails to mention that while the frail Eva fades away, stronger characters in Stowe's fiction survive as result of Arminian fortitude in the face of tribulation. The confident reformism which governs *Uncle Tom's Cabin* is reflected in a piety which is sentimental, but at the same time prompts courage in the face of oppression. Eliza Harris,

21 *Horse-shoe Robinson* (New York, n.d., f.p. 1835), p. 392.

22 *Selections from the Autobiography of Elizabeth Oakes Smith*, Mary Alice Wyman, Editor (Lewiston, Me., 1924), p. 42.

23 *Woman and Her Needs* (New York, 1851), p. 39.

24 Frank Forester, *pseud.* H. W. Herbert, *The Fair Puritan. An Historical Romance of the Days of Witchcraft* (Philadelphia, 1875, f.p. 1856), pp. 30, 198.

25 *Delusion; or, The Witch of New England* (Boston, 1840), p. iii.

deciding to escape the Shelby plantation upon hearing that her child has been sold, becomes "an entirely altered being from the soft and timid creature she had been hitherto."[26] Proving herself "a right brave gal" in her crossing the ice, Eliza gains "a depth of firmness and steady resolve that was never there in her earlier and happier days" (p. 189). Eliza's husband George also waxes heroic, showing that white cruelty inspires in slaves "courage, energy, and enthusiasm, where before was only the blackness of despair" (p. 173). Even Uncle Tom, despite his reputation as an obsequious character, is designed to embody religious firmness. By enduring the lash of Simon Legree for his refusal to punish a fellow slave, Tom "felt strong in God to meet death," as "the brave, true heart was firm on the Eternal Rock" (p. 474). This Christian resolution is shared by protagonists of other Stowe novels—Mary Scudder, James Marvin, Harry and Tina Percival, and Sam Lawson.

The Arminian protest against determinism and tyranny was objectified in various ways. In the historical novel about Puritan times it was evidenced by the opposition between repressive Calvinist magistrates and liberal proponents of self-determination and freedom. In contemporary fiction it surfaced as the conflict between cruel Calvinist stepparents and resolute orphans, or between idle slaveholders and sturdy slaves or abolitionists. In biblical fiction it was seen in the efforts of early Christian martyrs to resist despotic Jews or pagans. In the frontier novel it was manifested by two-fisted backwoodsmen battling with full trust in themselves and in God.

In most of its manifestations this "hard" theme of Arminian heroism was accompanied by a "soft" emphasis on aestheticism and feeling. The pious protagonist was often a paradoxical amalgam of courage and gentleness, reasonableness and warmth, firm adherence to principle and theological naïveté. As an opponent of such doctrines as total depravity and predestination, the protagonist exhibited "masculine" strength and perseverance; as a foil to polemical rigidity, he or she showed a "feminine" inclination to simplicity and warmth.

Often this paradoxical combination resulted in descriptions in which sexual stereotypes were intentionally balanced. Mrs. F. Larned tells us that "in Geraldine Sanford were united many rare

[26] *Uncle Tom's Cabin; or, Life Among the Lowly* (New York, 1967, f.p. 1851), p. 90.

and almost opposite qualities—to a dignity of mind and nobleness of sentiment much like her mother's, she united a simplicity that was almost infantine."[27] Another character possessing "almost opposite qualities," the heroine of John Neal's *Authorship* (1830), combines the features of "the child, the woman, [and] the man."[28] Similarly, Caroline Gilman describes the nature of one of her pious heroines: "These almost masculine purposes belonged to a young and seemingly fragile being; but it is wonderful how feminine enthusiasm bears up the frail and delicate, where seemingly stronger spirits fail."[29] Stowe's Alice H—— of *The Mayflower* (1843) has "the mind of a man, the heart of a woman, and the face of an angel."[30] Esther of *Oldtown Folks* (1869) also realizes the Platonic ideal of "the MAN-WOMAN."[31] Caroline Hentz's *Eoline* (1852) criticizes both a woman who is too "masculine" (Miss Manly) and one who is too "feminine" (Louisa), while lauding the independent yet gentle Eoline: "No one that looked upon the fair, sweet face, and girlish form of Eoline, would dream of the brave, undaunted spirit, the firm self-reliance, and moral courage that formed the deep under stratum of her character."[32] Gertrude Flint, the heroine of Maria Cummins' *The Lamplighter* (1854), approaches life "[w]ith the simplicity of a child, but a woman's firmness; with the stature of a child, but a woman's capacity; the earnestness of a child, but a woman's perseverance."[33]

In short, to dismiss sentimental protagonists as "innumerable pale and pious heroines," or as "a gallery of nincompoops," is to violate the complexity of the pious imagination of nineteenth-century popular writers. Scholars have noted the fundamental paradoxes of nineteenth-century American religion. In 1835 Alexis de Tocqueville commented that while American churches were divided and sectarian without state backing, they had a stronger, more unified control over society than did established European churches. Connected to this paradox is that fact that while various new sects emerged in nineteenth-century America, making religion

27 *The Sanfords, or Home Scenes* (New York, 1830), I, 122.

28 *Authorship, A Tale* (Boston, 1830), p. 110.

29 *Tales and Ballads* (New York, 1839), p. 12.

30 *The Mayflower* (New York, 1843), p. 223.

31 *Oldtown Folks* (Boston, 1869), p. 439.

32 *Eoline; or, Magnolia Vale* (Philadelphia, 1852), p. 22.

33 *The Lamplighter* (Leipzig, 1854), p. 97.

apparently more diversified, doctrinal distinctions blurred in the course of the century, making many of these sects increasingly similar. Another paradox is captured in Henry Steele Commager's statement that religion prospered in nineteenth-century America while theology went slowly bankrupt.[34] Yet another is pointed to in Paul Carter's generalization that post-1850 American culture became "more religious and more secular at the same time."[35]

To these paradoxes can be added one of special importance in light of the somewhat confused findings of recent feminist criticism: American religion became both more "feminine" and more "masculine" during the nineteenth century. The loss of theological rigor was accompanied by a valuation of "tender" sentimentality in both popular ministers and female writers. Yet the escape from the strict belief in predestination and total depravity resulted in a "tough" assertion of human capability and heroic muscularity. It is no accident that those nineteenth-century women who most closely approximated modern definitions of feminists—Margaret Fuller, the Grimké sisters, Elizabeth Oakes Smith, Elizabeth Cady Stanton, Susan B. Anthony—all stressed that Calvinist passivity and defeatism should give way to a firm trust in the human will. It is also understandable that Beecher's definition of religion was essentially paradoxical: "The end, Manhood. The means, Truth. The spirit, Love."[36] Here the spirit is "feminine," reflecting the emotionalism which would impel Orestes Brownson to mock Beecher's "religion of gush." But the end is "masculine," signaling Beecher's emphasis on manliness and self-confident activity. Beecher was voicing the paradoxical balancing of sexual stereotypes which had appeared throughout the century in the piety of Boston liberals, evangelical Calvinists, and sentimental novelists as well.

Ann Douglas has surmised that in nineteenth-century religion we find prototypes for such mawkish products of twentieth-century popular culture as Teen Angel and Miss America. If this is true, it is important to realize that we also find forerunners of Wonderwoman and Superman, characters who in daily dress seem like weak bumblers but who secretly possess godlike strength.

[34] *The American Mind* (New Haven, 1950), p. 61.

[35] *The Spiritual Crisis of the Gilded Age* (De Kalb, 1971), p. viii.

[36] *Yale Lectures on Preaching*, I, 6.

Janet Harbison Penfield

Mrs. Penfield now is a free lance journalist, after having served many years on the staffs of PRESBYTERIAN LIFE and AD magazines and Princeton Theological Seminary.

Women in the Presbyterian Church—an Historical Overview

HISTORY, OF COURSE, IS NOT SIMPLY WHAT HAPPENED. It is a selected, weighted account of what we think must have happened, derived from the bits and pieces of records preserved from the past. When it comes to recounting the history of women in their relation to any era or institution, the record tends to be sketchy, scattered, and selective. This is the case with respect to the role of women in the Presbyterian Church[1] in the U.S.A. Since some Presbyterian congregations have already celebrated their two hundred-fiftieth anniversaries, it stands to reason that women were active in Presbyterian churches long before the American Revolution. Yet their names and deeds have largely vanished. Once Presbyterian women began to form into women's groups, about the beginning of the 19th century, however, the records of women's participation in church life began to be kept in such detail and profusion that the mass of material awaiting study is overwhelming.

This paper will sketch briefly four phases of the participation of women in the life of the Presbyterian Church, any one of which might be interestingly explored at much greater length. The four aspects are:

1. The rise and development of women's "Cent Societies," or "Praying Societies"—in their early years they had a variety of names—in congregations chiefly along the eastern seaboard in the first quarter of the nineteenth century.

2. The development of regional, and ultimately national, women's boards of home and foreign missions, from roughly the time of the Civil War (1870 marked the formation of several of

these), to the reorganization of the church's boards and agencies in 1923.

3. The roles women played in the missionary field, in particular, and in some other aspects of church life, from the late 1830s, and increasingly until the close of the century and beyond—roles that would not have been permissible for women in their home churches at that time.

4. The struggle of women to achieve parity with men in the Presbyterian Church, and in particular their struggle to be admitted to offices of honor and authority in the church—the diaconate, and the ruling and teaching eldership. This struggle dates back into the 19th century,[2] and ended technically only in 1956.

It will be seen that these various phases of the life of women in the church have at times gone on simultaneously in time. For purposes of clarity, it seems better to treat these issues topically in a brief paper, but an effort will be made to relate them to one another in time, and to relate them to events of the time outside the church. Certain aspects of the role of Presbyterian women are noticeably and purposely absent from this article. Among these are: a discussion of notable women who happened to be Presbyterian, but whose fame sprang from activities not directly connected with the church; any analysis of the degree to which women have been present and influential in the organized structures of the church—as moderators of judicatories, for instance, pastors of congregations, or members of judicatory committees. Either of these areas would repay further study.

The Beginnings of Organized Women's Societies

The first national official recognition that Presbyterian women were constituting themselves into groups for the purpose of raising money to be given to various worthy causes of the church occurs in the minutes of the General Assembly in 1811.[3] The sentence has attained considerable fame, perhaps because of its uniqueness. "It has pleased God to excite pious women also to combine in associations for the purpose of aiding by their voluntary contributions, one or another of the above institutions." The institutions referred to were the missionary, tract, and Bible societies. Women had been coming together in such "associations" for at least half a dozen years when the General Assembly took note of their existence. The oldest recorded "Female Charitable Society" seems to have been founded in Newark, New Jersey, in 1803.

Others must have followed very shortly, since the 1811 Minutes speak of "associations." The long list of "Cent Societies," "Female Praying Societies," "Female Missionary

Societies," and the like, painstakingly compiled by Florence Hayes,[4] records what seems like an explosion of such groups after the recognition of the 1811 General Assembly. The first General Assembly of the Presbyterian Church on this continent occurred in 1789, coincidental with the final establishment of the United States as an independent nation. Perhaps because of a rather more settled mode of life after the end of the Revolutionary period, women began shortly to find more leisure to devote to the interests of their church. In any event, "Cent Societies" were flourishing barely twenty years later.

"Benevolence is always attractive, but when dressed in a female form, possesses peculiar charms," the 1811 Minutes go on, presumably in an effort to pay the ladies a compliment while encouraging them to raise more money. The superior effect of blandishments from a wife, mother, sister, or female friend is then alluded to, and the passage concludes, "We hope the spirit which has animated the worthy women of whom we speak, will spread and animate other bosoms."[5] Money was the name of the cent society, and the raising of money for missions and theological education, as well as the production of useful articles to clothe missionaries and seminary students, was, from the first, its primary aim.

From the point of view of the men who ran the Presbyterian Church, it would have been better if the ladies had confined their activities solely to contributing their "cents," carefully saved out of their egg money or whatever sums they could economize on the food budget. They might have done a bit of sewing as they met together, to make nightcaps for missionaries or "false fronts" for the student at the theological seminary just getting started at Princeton in 1812, but unfortunately, while they met and sewed, they listened as one of their number read aloud from an improving book, and sometimes they prayed, also aloud. A few seem even to have raised their voices in general prayer meetings, where both sexes were present.

Because of the danger that this might happen, some ministers were opposed even to the formation of female missionary groups. They preferred that the women have a collection for missions several times a year,[6] but without organizing and meeting. The General Assembly itself felt called upon to send to the churches in 1832 a pastoral letter,[7] advising that,

> Meetings of pious women by themselves for conversation and prayer, whenever they can conveniently be held, we entirely approve. But let not the inspired prohibitions of the great apostle of the Gentiles, as found in his epistles to the Corinthians and to Timothy, be violated. To teach and exhort, or to lead in prayer, in public and promiscuous assemblies, is clearly forbidden to women in the Holy Oracles.

It should be noted that the year 1832 was a time of revivals and emotionalism[8] in the church; the Assembly feared for decency and order. Indeed, the tensions between Presbyterians whose chief emphasis was on right thinking and theological orthodoxy, and others, who believed more in inner warmth, those of a more "romantic" cast of mind, were a continuous phenomenon during the eighteenth and early nineteenth century.[9] They still go on today, albeit sometimes in altered form.

One aspect of these tensions was the continual necessity under which the men seemed to find themselves to warn the ladies against arrogating to themselves any masculine prerogatives. Even in 1858, in speaking before a ladies' group, the Reverend Alexander T. McGill felt obliged to say, "The world is yours, young ladies,[10] depend upon it, only as long as you keep your sphere." And as late as 1862, an issue of *The Presbyterian* discussed the question of women's praying in public. The conclusion reached was the same as ever— "let pious females be content to walk and act in the sphere in which God has placed them. . . . If they will exercise their gifts publicly, let them have female prayer meetings."[11] It would be nearly sixty years before the Presbyterian General Assembly would go so far as to let a woman preside over an event under its immediate control.[12]

Church Women Organize on a Wide Scale

As early as 1822, Female Missionary Societies in the Synod of Albany (New York) numbered more than fifty branches.[13] As more and more such societies came into being, they began to work together. Roughly at the same time, women were included among the earliest groups of missionaries sent both to lands overseas and to work among native Americans as the great western lands were developed.[14] The church was reaching out as the country grew, and women, no longer quite so anonymous, yet not in the mainstream of the church's effort, either, extended their work.

It was apparently the experience and initiative taken by women during the Civil War that gave Presbyterian women the self-assurance to organize mission boards on a national scale. Clifford Drury, the distinguished historian of the church thinks so: "Following the war," he writes, "these women cast about for some outlet for their newly realized potentialities. Many of them found that opening in the churches. Within about sixteen years after the close of the Civil War, 6 women's boards for foreign missions and 1 for home missions had been organized within the Presbyterian Church."[15]

The fact that women were not at that point admitted to any

positions of authority on the male-dominated church boards meant that female energies could not find an outlet through regular structures. It meant also that women had a smaller vested interest in denominational structures and denominational distinctions than did men. They took, one can assume, a lesser interest in the theological splits and ecclesiological schisms endemic to the Presbyterian Church in the 19th century. For all these reasons it was natural that women should pool their mission efforts with those of other denominations (mainly Congregationalists).

The "Women's Union Missionary Society of America for Heathen Lands," for example, was founded in New York in 1861. Since its members were not solely Presbyterian, it felt that it could send out missionaries and conduct work in some places where denominational groups could not. It is also, perhaps, typical that this board was established as a result of enthusiasm engendered in participants at a "parlour" meeting where Mrs. Francis B. Mason, a missionary on furlough from Burma,[16] told of the needs in that country. The "Woman's Union Missionary Society," with branches in several places outside New York City, sent out missionaries under the American Board of Commissioners for Foreign Missions, a non-denominational group.

That there was much overlapping in the areas covered by the various women's boards of mission seems clear. Sometimes both "home" and "foreign" missions were conducted under the same board. Sometimes an object of mission would be denoted "home" for awhile and then become "foreign," or vice versa.

The Woman's Board of Missions, which was attached to the American Board, chiefly collected money from women in the New England area, though it reached down into New Jersey in a few instances. Its first annual meeting, held in Boston in 1869, attracted over 600 ladies, in "spite of inclement weather." The main speaker, Dr. N. G. Clark, called attention to the fact that there had been more missionaries serving under the American Board in 1837 than there were in 1868 (the Civil War having intervened) and called for "a revival of the missionary spirit of 50 years ago."[17] This revival was clearly on its way by 1869.

It is far more difficult to weave into a coherent story the histories of the various women's boards of foreign missions of the Presbyterian Church than is the case with home missions. This difference is largely due to the industry and determination of Dr. Sheldon Jackson, the great missionary to the Northwest and Alaska. Jackson early became convinced that there was much potential in the energy and the money of women. Disregarding the structures of the Presbyterian Church, but nevertheless cooperating with the denomination's Board of Home Missions, Jackson set out to help the women organize for the support of home missions on a national scale. Through his wise counsel and the work of a number of women, the national Woman's Executive Committee of Home Missions of the Presbyterian Church came into being in 1878. Attempts to secure the cooperation of already existing women's boards had to be made. Endless negotiations, and endless meetings for prayer, had to happen before this could come about. But Jackson saw the organizing of the women as, for one thing, a solution to the problem of financing educational work by the church on the home mission field—since the denomination's resources clearly would not stretch far enough to pay for this development. By 1894, the Woman's Board of Home Missions, successor to the Woman's Executive Committee, had 391 teachers in home missions schools, and raised $367,333 in support of the educational phase of its work.[18]

By 1917, shortly before the reorganization of all the boards of the Presbyterian Church, the women's boards of foreign missions still numbered six, regionally based. They were located in New York, Philadelphia, Chicago, St. Louis, San Francisco, and Portland. Some of these continued to raise money for home missions as well as foreign. In contrast to the Woman's Board of Home Missions, the foreign missions' boards present a kaleidoscopic picture.

The equivocal attitude of churchmen to the efforts of women on behalf of the church, already noted in the 1811 *Minutes*, continued through the events of the century. General Assembly minutes abound in sentences of gratitude, sometimes almost fulsome, to the ladies for their work.[19] When the men's boards are in financial straits, they do not hesitate to ask the women to finish paying for the statue of John Witherspoon for the Centennial, for instance,[20] or to start paying rent for offices they occupied.[21] On the other hand, one can detect a nearly audible sigh of relief when, on the reunion of the Old School and New School Presbyterians in 1870, the mission activities of Presbyterian women begin to come under strictly Presbyterian boards.

Perusal of the lists of board members of the various women's boards, and of the lists of contributions (no sum was considered too small to be listed)[22] makes it clear that these mission boards really did have a grassroots constituency. To single out any two or three of the leaders of these mid-and late-nineteenth century enterprises is invidious. But for purposes of illustrating the caliber of woman involved in this work, let us consider the contributions of Mrs. Richard Haines, and Mrs. Darwin James.

Frances Haines (Mrs. Richard), a lady from Elizabeth, New Jersey, was originally interested mainly in foreign missions. As a young woman, she had intended to go herself as a missionary to the "heathen." After she married a Christian businessman, a

Frances Haines

widower with twelve children, she devoted her considerable talents, and money, to furthering the cause of missions through mission organizations.

When, as we have seen, in 1878, Sheldon Jackson undertook to organize a national women's group for the promotion of home missions, and particularly to take on the educational mission work, Mrs. Haines was one of the original officers. She became one of the two corresponding secretaries of the group, and was, according to Mary E. Boyd, who was also one of the co-founders of the Woman's Executive Committee for Home Missions, its "guiding spirit in the formative years."[23] Mrs. Haines drew up the original "plans and regulations" for the Woman's Executive Committee, and worked tirelessly for its causes. She urged a study of teachers' salaries in the church's schools in Utah; she made a tour of the western mission fields, extending to Alaska. For some time she and Mrs. Boyd personally handled all the Board's correspondence. She was the one who urged the purchase of a "caligraph," and a typewriter—in 1883, apparently several years before the General Assembly's Missions board bought its first such newfangled machines. At her death in 1886, Mrs. Haines was said to have known by name, location, and handwriting, at least, every missionary under the care of the Woman's Committee.[24] It is undoubtedly significant that Frances Haines's name does not even appear in the index of Clifford Drury's exhaustive and thorough study of national missions history *(Presbyterian Panorama.)*

Another influential woman in the early history of the Woman's

Executive Committee of Home Missions was Mrs. Darwin James. Her husband was a representative to the United States Congress, and under her leadership (she became President of the Committee in 1885, upon the death of Mrs. Ashbel Green, the first President), the Committee took a keen interest in the question of plural marriage among the Mormons. This was one of the few public questions Presbyterian women seem to have become officially involved in. Because of her long experience in Washington, Mrs. James understood the intricacies of working through government channels. Under her leadership, more than 100,000 signatures of Presbyterian women urging Congress to deny statehood to Utah until "such time as she proves worthy," were collected. Mrs. James' personal interventions with congressmen, attempting to persuade them of the evils of polygamy, were unceasing.[25]

The heyday of the women's boards and committees of mission, the period of the exercise on the part of women of the Presbyterian Church of near autonomy in the raising, administering, spending, supervising of funds, and the developing of particular phases and fields of mission ran roughly from the close of the Civil War to the end of the second decade of the 20th Century. It spanned periods of economic prosperity, and of financial crisis. It more or less corresponds to the period of great industrial and territorial expansion of the country.

By 1920, when the General Assembly celebrated the 50th anniversary of the founding of some of the women's boards, and the Assembly for the first time permitted a woman—Miss Margaret Hodge—to preside at a popular meeting of the Assembly, it was clear that the structures of the church were becoming an uncontrollable sprawl. By then the various area women's foreign missions boards had been consolidated into one, but there were still too many boards.

In 1922, the General Assembly consolidated all the existing national church boards into four, and thus, in the salty phrase of Arthur Judson Brown, "solved the problem in its own way." Fifteen of the forty members of the Board of Foreign Missions, for example, were to be women. The staff was to be composed of women and men. "This was done without consultation with either Board," writes Brown.[26] "Some of the individual members knew of the proposal that was to be made, but the official judgment of the two boards was not asked for. So the Women's Board found itself united with the Assembly's Board and given the difficult task of choosing 15 of its 40 members to membership on the new Board." "Whether the consolidation of the Women's Board with the Assembly's Board has resulted in more and better work by women is not clear," he continues. The situation of the Woman's Board of Home Missions was, of course, similar.

That the boards were merged, and women given full membership on General Assembly boards before any women had official status in their own congregations (women became eligible to be deacon only in 1926) has indubitably had an effect on the work of women for missions. It is, however, a not unusual pattern in American church life.[27]

Varieties of Gifts

While some women were organizing themselves into "Female Praying Societies," and were later combining these societies into regional and national boards devoted to the raising of funds for missions, and were themselves administering mission work, others were involved in enterprises, chiefly on the mission field itself, that might have been thought unsuitable for females of their era.

Some of these women undoubtedly simply went to mission fields because their husbands went. Others may have been particularly independent people, or more dedicated to the spreading of the Gospel than others, or more restless and unhappy with the very limited lot of women in local congregations at the time. The story of these indomitable women runs parallel in time, though on another stage, with the story of the women's boards of mission.

Miss Narcissa Prentiss seems to have been one of those who were internally motivated toward the mission field. The query of the Reverend Samuel Parker,[28] writing to the American Board in 1834, remains famous: "Are females wanted? A Miss Narcissa Prentiss of Amity is very anxious to go to the heathen." Though the reply was in the negative, Narcissa Prentiss married Dr. Marcus Whitman, and so was enabled to be one of the first white women to cross the Rockies, and, scarcely ten years later, to be massacred by non-Christian Indians.[29]

Not only Narcissa Whitman, but many another young woman felt the pull of the unevangelized millions on this continent and across the waters. "The wives of missionaries," writes Arthur Judson Brown in *The Foreign Missionary,* "are regarded as associate missionaries, uniting with their husbands in desire and effort to give the Gospel to the unevangelized. It is expected that, so far as is consistent with their strength and household duties, they will learn the language and take part in missionary work."[30] The same expectation extended to the wives of home missionaries, although because such missionaries were often sent by synods or presbyteries, they and their wives were not officially commissioned in the same way foreign missionaries are.

The service of women on the mission field surpassed what might have been expected in numbers and devotion. W. Reginald

Wheeler writes, in *Words of God in an African Forest*, "Many a young man in America who has been drawn to service on the foreign field but who through timidity or unwillingness to endure hardship has drawn back from this call, would be ashamed of his fears if he knew the courage of the women on the foreign field."[31] The means of conveyance to overseas mission fields was, of course, the sailingship. Voyages took months, and the conditions of travel were unspeakable. In some parts of the world, the inhabitants were so suspicious of people from overseas with white faces that missionaries spent months before they could persuade anyone to give them a first clue about the native tongue. China was such a place. Babies were born to missionary families without benefit of any more skill than happened to be present at the particular mission station, and were brought up a prey to many a mysterious disease. The alternative for women on the foreign mission field was to send their children home—trusting them to missionaries returning on furlough—and give them to the care of relatives, often not seeing them for years thereafter.[32]

And yet, Brown writes, "For years women formed approximately two-thirds of the total missionary force."[33] Though there was at first a prejudice against single women on the missionary field, this quickly dissipated in the face of enthusiasm on the part of women and the great need. Some of these women, like Amanda McFarland, of Alaska fame—who served both as married woman and widow—, like Donaldina Cameron, the McBeth sisters and an impressive roster of women doctors such as Mary Niles, Mary Fulton, and Eleanor Chesnut, all of whom served in China, became well-known.[34] Others labored obscurely for the span of time the flesh could bear and earned only their names in the records of servants of the church. To single out any of these missionary women for special mention might be invidious; but there is no way to give a picture of their struggles except by mention of the following few individuals.

Mary Cloyd Latta Nassau, offspring of a long line of Presbyterian ministers, was born in 1837 and died 10 September 1870 at Benita, in West Africa. Her missionary career ran from 1860 to 1870—thus encompassing the Civil War and immediate postwar period and coinciding with the founding of most of the women's boards of mission. It is possible to know a great deal more about Mary than about many missionaries because she married Dr. Robert Nassau, who had a long missionary career in Africa, and who during and after his service wrote many books, including a detailed tribute to his wife that appeared in 1874.[35] Mary Latta applied to be sent as a missionary to Africa in 1857; she could not be sent until 1860, since unmarried women missionaries were obliged to wait until couples were departing so as to have escorts to their posts. A year after her arrival in Africa, the mission was reinforced by the arrival of Dr. Robert Nassau, whom Miss Latta married. They had three sons; Willie, the eldest, was sent home to be brought up; the second, Paull, died very young. The Nassaus were forced to go by lantern-light to re-bury his body when there was a threat that the grave might be robbed. Shortly after the birth of Charlie, the third boy, Mrs. Nassau was to be sent home, since her health had failed. On an open boat, being taken to find a sailing-ship for England, Mrs. Nassau died. She had been a great student of the Benga language, and had translated many hymns into that tongue. She had also taught the young African girls, and to meet with her students was one of the first concerns of the newly-widowed doctor.

Quite another sort of missionary was Isabella Nassau, the sister of Dr. Nassau. She served in Africa from 1868 until 1906, when she died there in service. Isabella was a determinedly single person, and determinedly devoted to evangelism in Africa. During the pregnancy of the second Mrs. Robert Nassau, another Mary whom Robert met, courted briefly, and married during a furlough, Dr. Nassau had occasion to write: " . . . the next, to whom she should turn as a repository of her happy secret would naturally be her sister-in-law. But my sister, having deliberately chosen for herself the single life, caused it to be understood that as she 'knew nothing about babies,' she could render no aid. . . ." What Isabella Nassau did know about was the training of young men for the ministry. In an account of "A Visit to the West Africa Mission," by A. W. Halsey, Secretary of the Board of Foreign Missions from 1899-1921, occur these lines:

> Evangeline Cottage [Miss Nassau's home] is the theological seminary of the mission field. Here for many years students have been taught the Word of God and fitted for their life work by the professor of didactic and polemic theology, church history, catechetics, and much else—and that professor a woman. . . . I listened to the examination of these candidates for the Gospel ministry and was well satisfied that whatever St. Paul meant when he said that women should not speak in churches, he did not mean that women should not teach in a theological seminary in Africa.[37]

About the same time (1873) Sue McBeth, joined by her sister, Kate, who arrived on the field in 1879, conducted a mission among the Nez Perce Indians. Sue, until her death in 1893, trained native teachers, preparing some Indians for ordination to the gospel ministry. She was said to be a "living theological seminary."[38] She was proficient in the Nez Perce language and put together its grammar and vocabulary. A fascinating account of mission work of that time as seen by a missionary is contained in Miss Kate McBeth's book, *The Nez Perces since Lewis and Clark.*[39]

Quite a different sort of mission was that performed for many years (1895-1937) by Donaldina Cameron (before her, by Margaret Culbertson), Miss Cameron's efforts were directed toward rescuing young Chinese girls who were brought from China especially to be the concubines of rich men, or simply to be prostitutes. At considerable risk, Miss Cameron would organize, or assist the police with, raids on opium dens and other immoral places in San Francisco, and bodily remove the girls to a place of refuge under Presbyterian auspices.[40] That this work was headed by a woman, and directed originally by women's boards of mission was perhaps due to the fact that it concerned the plight of young women. It was, particularly at the time when it began, a work rather outside the normal sphere of women's activity.

One further area in which women have long been permitted great freedom to serve the church is that of writing and editing. Perhaps because of the anonymity of the written word—no actual person faces the reader of an article, whereas the preacher in the pulpit is quite visible—, perhaps because there is no explicit "prohibition" in Scripture against women writing for and about the church, women hymn-writers and magazine scriveners abound in the nineteenth century American church. Mrs. Delos Finks, and her daughter Theodora Finks, were the sole editors-in-chief of the *Home Mission Monthly* from its beginning in 1886 to its discontinuance in 1924. Mrs. Finks was the editor for twenty-five years.[41]

From these examples, it can be seen that without being given authority in the regular structures of the church, women in the American Presbyterian church who possessed particular drive and dedication have found ways to take on tasks that men either were unable or unwilling to do, or perceived as peripheral.

Winning a Place in the Structure

It must not be thought that while women were busily erecting what some have referred to as "the church beside the church"[42] and others were finding ways to give their lives in the service of the church at home and abroad no attention was being given to securing for the women of the Presbyterian Church rights and privileges equal to those of men. As early as 1805, Miss Eliza Dunlap appealed to the General Assembly a decision of the Synod of New York and New Jersey excluding her from the "distinguishing privileges of the church."[43] But movement was slow. Frances E. Willard, in *Woman in the Pulpit,* published in 1888, refers to the "Sarah Smiley case," of 1874, which involved the fact that a woman had been permitted to preach from one of the pulpits in Brooklyn Presbytery.[44] This resulted in the Presbytery's reiterating the General Assembly's pronouncements regarding the Pauline injunctions to silence on the part of women in the churches. Miss Willard speaks of the "slow-moving Presbyterians," and alleges that only they, the Roman Catholics, and the Episcopalians continue to deny their theological seminaries to women. "Are they willing that women should baptize and administer the sacrament in the zenanas of India but not at the elegant altars of Christendom?" she inquires.[45] Inez M. Cavert, in *Women in American Church Life* suggests that only the Lutherans, Southern Presbyterians, United Presbyterians ("old U.P.s"), and Episcopalians among Protestants are more conservative on issues relating to women in the mainstream of church life than the Presbyterian Church, U.S.A.[46] It is certain that the Cumberland Presbyterian Church was somewhat quicker. As early as 1892, that church suggested that women might be ordained as ruling elders "where it shall be needful."[47] In 1893, it is recorded that there was a woman elder commissioner to the Cumberland Church's General Assembly. In 1889, Mrs. Louisa M. Woosley was ordained to the ministry in the Cumberland Presbyterian Church, but the record of her service is rather confused. Most striking in the account of the Cumberland Church's dealings with the participation of women is the simple and direct way in which the whole issue was resolved. The 1921 General Assembly of that denomination simply adopted a statement alleging that "the word 'man' with reference to a human being is a generic term," and that where it is used in church documents, it "has no reference to sex but would be construed to, and does, in fact, include the human being whether male or female."[48]

The Presbyterian Church in the U.S.A., which is a direct ancestor of the United Presbyterian Church of today found no such easy answer. Although periodically its General Assembly was asked whether women might serve as deacons or elders, or preach from pulpits, the reply consistently given was a reiteration of the sentiments of the 1832 pastoral letter.

By 1919, three presbyteries brought overtures to the General Assembly asking that something be done toward permitting women to act as ruling elders and ministers. The Assembly's majority action on these proposals congratulated the men that only three presbyteries had come forth with overtures on the topic and recommended no action. A minority felt the problem should be investigated.[49] An investigation was already under way, and in 1920, the Assembly was hearing a report of its Special Committee on the Relation of Women in the Church, through its chairman, the Reverend S. Hall Young. This committee recommended the election of women as ruling elders. The Assembly itself submitted to the churches an overture that women be accepted as ruling elders or deacons. Though more presbyteries voted for this overture than against, it did not gain a clear majority and so was defeated. By 1922, however, a new overture permitting women to be ordained as deacons had finally passed.[50]

This did not settle things, apparently, for in 1926 Mrs. Katharine Bennett and Miss Margaret Hodge (stalwarts of the old women's boards) were heading an investigation to determine "the cause of unrest among women."[51] The unrest had begun to manifest itself in a particularly clear fashion—after the consolidation of the boards, the giving of the women had begun to fall off. The report on causes of unrest, when it was presented in 1927 to the General Council of the church (which had commissioned it) was printed and "distributed to members of the General Council and to any others interested."[52]

In 1929, the General Assembly asked the presbyteries to vote on admitting to the ruling and teaching elderships women duly elected. The verdict, in 1930, was that women might be admitted to the ruling eldership.[53] At this same General Assembly, a report on marriage and divorce, and remarriage was brought in. The committee, of eleven men, no women being eligible since there were as yet no women elders, opined that, "We can preach high and unimpeachable living, can still preach Christ, glorify not the American girl but American Motherhood."[54] Marriage and motherhood might be thought to be subjects in which women take a particular interest—but American wives and mothers still had to get the official word of the church from the fathers and brethren.

By 1956 the office of teaching elder was finally opened to women. Nevertheless, an Assembly committee reporting in 1967 on the Marriage of Divorced Persons was male except for one woman. A 1966 committee on the nature of the ministry consisted of ten men; no women. If the national church has been slow to accept women into its councils, women have themselves been slow to take opportunities as have been opened to them. Several recent reports of Task Forces on Women in the Church, which have come to the General Assemblies of 1972 and later years, seem to have begun to change this situation. Although the last official survey of the UPCUSA congregations still showed a number that have never had a woman ruling elder, women are beginning to enroll in theological seminaries in considerable numbers. At the same time, the seminaries are beginning to take seriously the allegation that theological education that is conducted entirely by and for males cannot be whole. They are gradually employing more and more women faculty members and administrators.[55] Since first-class theological training was for so long very difficult for a woman to obtain, the pool of candidates qualified by traditional seminary standards for such posts is not large, but it is growing.

Lois Stair and Thelma Adair have served as Moderators of the General Assembly of the United Presbyterian Church. Several others have at least run for that office. No ordained teaching elder who is a woman has as yet taken this step. Even though seminaries are accepting women, and some schools are aiming at a student body of at least one-half women, there continues a reluctance in local Presbyterian congregations to accept women as pastors. Women seminary graduates are thus most often relegated to obscure rural parishes, to Christian education jobs, or to assistantships, from which they will experience more difficulty moving than do their male counterparts.[56] Synod and presbytery task forces on the role of women in the church, and special attention to the situation on the part of church vocation specialists are attempting to deal with this state of affairs.

Advocates of the equality of women in the church may perhaps take heart from an observation of Kathleen Bliss, in *The Service and Status of Women in the Churches*, published in 1952: "The times when the church has regarded women as a lower species, doubtfully redeemable, or as ignorant and ineducable, are always the times when the Church is dead in other matters, failing to evangelize, indifferent to human suffering. As soon as quickening life returns to the church, or to some section within it, men and women are found working at the same enterprise and new attitudes begin to prevail."[57]

NOTES

[1]"Presbyterian Church" as used in this article refers primarily to the Presbyterian Church in the U.S.A. Clifford M. Drury, in his *Presbyterian Panorama*, Board of Christian Education, Philadelphia, 1952, includes on p. 406 a schematic diagram of the many splits and mergers among American Presbyterians. Women in all the larger and smaller segments of Presbyterianism undoubtedly played roles somewhat similar to those they have played in the denomination on which, for purposes of convenience, I have chosen to concentrate.

[2]Fule, Aurelia T., "Landmarks on the journey toward human equality in the church," (New York, UPCUSA Program Agency, Dept. of Women's Program, 1975), mimeo.; and, Thiel, Mary Margaret, "Status of women in the United Presbyterian Church in the U.S.A.," (Princeton Theological Seminary, class paper, on file in Speer Library).

[3]Presbyterian Church in the U.S.A., General Assembly, *Minutes*, 1811, p. 483. Hereafter cited as *G. A.* and date.

[4]Hayes, Florence, *Daughters of Dorcas*, Board of National Missions, Presbyterian Church in the U.S.A., 1952, pp. 141-56.

[5]*G. A.*, 1811, p. 483.

[6]Hayes, *op. cit.*, p. 24.

[7]*G. A.*, 1832, p. 348.

[8]Anent revivals, ca. 1832, see Loetscher, Lefferts A., *The Broadening Church*, (Philadelphia, University of Pennsylvania Press), 1954; as well as *G. A.*, 1832, pp. 339*ff*.

[9]See Loetscher, Lefferts, *op. cit.* passim.

[10]Hayes, *op. cit.*, p. 39.

[11]*Ibid.*, p. 48.

[12]Brown, Arthur Judson, *One Hundred Years*, (New York, Fleming Revell, 1936), p. 139.

[13]Hayes, *op. cit.*, p. 149.

[14]Betsy Stockton, for example, a black woman, was sent from Princeton, New Jersey, as a missionary to the "Sandwich Islands" in 1822. *Journal of Presbyterian History*, 52 (Summer 1974), 157-66.

[15]Drury, C. M. *op. cit.*, p. 198.

[16]Brown, A. J., *op. cit.*, p. 116; Hayes, *op. cit.*, p. 53.

[17]Women's Board of Missions, *Annual Report* (1869-1870), bound with *Life and Light for Women*, p. 6.

[18]Drury, *op. cit.*, p. 204. In some years apparently the women's boards raised more money than the General Assembly's boards.

[19]See, for example, G. A., 1885, p. 612.

[20]Hayes, *op. cit.*, p. 57.

[21]*Ibid.*, p. 102.

[22]*Home Mission Monthly*, 1886-1924, any issue.

[23]*Ibid.*, Dec. 1918.

[24]Hayes, *op. cit.*, pp. 73, 91, 102. It should be noted that this admirable book, which contains a wealth of information painstakingly dug out, has no index, and no very clear scheme or organization—so it, too, must be mined.

[25]*Ibid.*, pp. 106*ff.*

[26]Brown, *op. cit.*, p. 142.

[27]See comments in Cavert, Inez, *Women in American Church Life*, Friendship Press, New York, 1949, p. 11.

[28]Drury, C. M., *Marcus Whitman, M. D.*, (Caldwell Idaho, Caxton Printers, 1937), p. 87. See also other works by Drury on the Whitman-Spalding mission.

[29]Drury, C. M., *Presbyterian Panorama*, p. 116; the train of events leading up to the massacre is treated more fully in other Drury works.

[30]Brown, Arthur Judson, *The Foreign Missionary*, (New York, Revell, 1950), p. 76.

[31]Wheeler, W. R., *Words of God in an African Forest*, (New York, Revell, Chicago, 1931), p. 272.

[32]Nassau, Robert H., *My Ogowe*, (New York, Neal Publishing Company, 1914). Other accounts of mission life tell the same story.

[33]Brown, *One Hundred Years*, p. 114.

[34]Noyes, Harriet Newell, *History of the South China Mission, of the American Presbyterian Church*, (Presbyterian Mission Press, 1927).

[35]Nassau, Robert H., *Crowned in Palm Land*, (Philadelphia, Lippincott, 1874). Details on Mary Latta Nassau are taken largely from this account.

[36]Nassau, *My Ogowe*, p. 446.

[37]Halsey, A. W., quoted in Brown, *One Hundred Years*, p. 248. See also Nassau, R. H., *Historical Sketch of Mission in West Africa*. (Philadelphia, Woman's Foreign Missionary Society of the Presbyterian Church, 1881), p. 21.

[38]Ellinwood, Frank F., "Three heroines of the Nez Percés Mission," *Missionary Review of the World*, 7 (March 1894), 193.

[39]McBeth, Kate C., *The Nez Perces since Lewis and Clark*, F. H. Revell, New York, Chicago, 1908.

[40]Wilson, Carol Green, *Chinatown Quest—Donaldina Cameron*, Stanford University (California) Press, 1931.

[41]*Home Mission Monthly*. 1886-1924.

[42]Personal conversation with a number of European women, who cannot understand the organized church life of American women.

[43] Minutes of the General Assembly of the Presbyterian Church, 1789-1820, p. 338. The General Assembly at least appears to have considered Miss Dunlap to be a person.

[44]Willard, Frances, *Woman in the Pulpit,* Lothrop, Boston, 1888, *passim.* but especially page 50.

[45]Willard, *op. cit.,* p. 55.

[46]Cavert, Inez M., *op. cit.*

[47]See Campbell, Thomas H., *Studies in Cumberland Presbyterian History,* (Nashville, Cumberland Presbyterian Publishing House, 1936), and Barrus, Ben M., *et al, A People Called Cumberland Presbyterians,* (Memphis, Frontier Press, c.1972), pp. 429*f.*

[48]Barrus, *op. cit.,* p. 430.

[49]*G. A.,* 1919, pp. 267*f.*

[50]*G. A.,* 1922, pp. 194, 196, 198.

[51]Gripe, Elizabeth, "Women, Restructuring and Unrest in the 1920's," *Journal of Presbyterian History,* 52, (Summer 1974), 196.

[52]*Ibid.,* p. 196.

[53]*G. A.,* 1930, pp. 48*ff.*

[54]*G. A.,* 1930, pp. 74-100. The turgid, pious, unremittingly masculine tone of this report is calculated to raise the blood pressure of any Presbyterian woman. It has phrases like, "The demand for self-expression in man calls for his complete passing into the life of another. He must become creator." (p. 76.) The symbolism is unmistakably male-sexual. "Man" just cannot be taken as "generic" here.

[55]A comparison of sample seminary catalogues of four or five years ago with those of 1975-76 makes this clear.

[56]Counseling with women M.Div. seniors and graduates at Princeton Theological seminary, as I have done intermittently over the past three years, is my primary source of this information.

[57]Bliss, Kathleen, *The Service and Status of Women in the Churches,* (London, S.C.M. Press, 1952), p. 17.

Religion and the New England Mill Girl: A New Perspective on an Old Theme

JAMA LAZEROW

IN April 1829, mill girls from three textile factories in Taunton, Massachusetts, abandoned their looms to protest a reduction in wages.[1] Bedecked in their colorful working attire—black silk dresses, red shawls, and green calashes—the women paraded about the town common before a shocked if somewhat amused gathering of local menfolk. Their leader was a young weaver named Salome Lincoln. Just twenty-two years old, she had spent eight years working in the Taunton mills. Marching the procession into a local public hall, Lincoln took the podium, instructed one of her lieutenants to stand guard at the door, and opened the meeting with a prayer "to the Great Arbitrator for Justice." It was an apt beginning, for her talk that spring morning was something of a sermon, as she lectured her sisters "on the subject of their wrongs" in contributing to their own predicament. On that morning, Salome Lincoln sounded more like a censorious minister than the leader of a factory "turn-out."

For this particular mill girl, however, the two endeavors were not so disparate as they might at first appear. In an age

I would like to thank William Breitenbach, Hans Ostrom, and especially Irene Scharf for their generosity in contributing their considerable literary skills to make this essay more readable. An earlier version of this article was presented at the Conference on New England: An Historical Perspective, Salem State College, Salem, Massachusetts, October 1984.

[1] Details of this strike may be found in Carolyn B. Owen, "Vignettes, No. 66," Taunton Historical Society, Taunton, Mass.; *Columbia Reporter and Old Colony Journal* (Taunton), 6 May 1829; see also, Almond H. Davis, *The Female Preacher, or Memoir of Salome Lincoln, Afterwards the Wife of Elder Junias S. Mowry* (Providence, R.I., 1843). Though we would today call these operatives "women," I often refer to them here as "mill girls" because that is how they referred to themselves.

when women rarely spoke in public, and were usually vilified when they did, the Taunton strike was not the first time Salome Lincoln had addressed a gathering of her townspeople. And it was probably not the first time her sister weavers had heard her speak. For Salome Lincoln was a lay preacher in the Freewill Baptist church, a denomination whose theology held out the possibility of salvation for all and whose clergy would play a role, disproportionate to their numbers, in subsequent labor protest in New England. Although Lincoln had no official church credentials, she had been exhorting from the pulpit of the local Freewill Baptist meetinghouse three or four times a week since 1827. In private, she was "naturally reserved and retiring in her manner," her biographer wrote, but "in the pulpit, she was bold and attracting." In 1829, she turned that boldness to the cause of workers' rights

There is little in the historical literature on women, religion, or labor that makes much sense of Salome Lincoln. We know that women constituted the majority of many church congregations in America from at least the mid-seventeenth century, and we know that by the early nineteenth century their interests and concerns increasingly dominated American religion.[2] This "feminization" of Protestantism helped define "woman's sphere" in the young republic, while it simultaneously fostered women's conspicuous involvement in a broad range of reform movements, from temperance to abolitionism to women's rights.[3] But most of what we know about this subject concerns middle- and upper-class women. We know precious little about working women in antebellum

[2] There are numerous disputes among scholars concerning the timing and precise nature of this process, but the basic trend is not in dispute.

[3] See, for example, Nancy Cott, *The Bonds of Womanhood: "Woman's Sphere" in New England, 1780–1835* (New Haven: Yale University Press, 1977); Blanche Glassman Hersh, *The Slavery of Sex: Feminist-Abolitionists in America* (Urbana: University of Illinois Press, 1978); Barbara Epstein, *The Politics of Domesticity: Women, Evangelicalism, and Temperance in Nineteenth-Century America* (Middletown: Wesleyan University Press, 1981); Nancy Hewitt, *Women's Activism and Social Change: Rochester, New York, 1822–1872* (Ithaca: Cornell University Press, 1984).

religious and reform activity, and even less about those involved in labor protest.[4]

If Protestantism played a crucial role in women's lives in the early nineteenth century, and inspired their social activism, we might fruitfully ask how religion influenced the mill girls of antebellum New England. For it was these young women who composed much of the early factory workforce in America. As textile operatives in industrial communities like Taunton, and more renowned places like Lowell, Massachusetts, and Manchester, New Hampshire, they helped make New England the hub of American industry before the Civil War. Most important, these women were often in the forefront of antebellum labor protest. Indeed, for a time during the 1840s, they were the vanguard of a region-wide labor reform movement. How did religion color *their* lives and activities?

To answer this basic, if complex, question, we begin by examining the religious beliefs and practices of mill girls generally, turning then to the impact of that piety on mill girl labor protest. For the former, we have an ample documentary record in such literary magazines as the *Lowell Offering*, written by and for female textile operatives in the early 1840s, and in such radical newspapers as the *Voice of Industry*, the mouthpiece of labor reform in New England during the same decade. For religion's role in labor protest, we can learn a great deal from radical mill women like those of the Lowell Female Labor Reform Association (LFLRA), whose activities were regularly reported in the labor press.

The *Lowell Offering* is perhaps the richest source of mill girl writings we have, and virtually every page reveals an intense spirituality. This will come as no surprise to most historians, given the historical consensus that the defenders of the factory system promoted the magazine to sell the image of the virtuous mill girl. And, to be sure, the *Offering* did enjoy the support and encouragement of local clergymen,

[4] Although Nancy Cott mentions Salome Lincoln, she is concerned primarily with "middle-class" women. *Bonds of Womanhood*, see esp. pp. 9–13, 56–57.

church leaders, politicians, and mill agents. Indeed, erstwhile contributors like LFLRA president and *Voice* editor Sarah Bagley claimed that the *Offering* refused articles critical of the factory system and that, in general, the corporations used the publication as propaganda to gain public support, attract a steady supply of labor, and quiet discontent.

But the use of the *Offering* as mill propaganda does not perforce render it a spurious source of mill girl sentiment. In fact, it is not at all clear that the magazine was as conservative as it has been portrayed by contemporaries or historians nor that these particular mill girls were at all unusual in their piety. First, the *Offering* seems to have arisen, at least in part, from the initiatives of the mill girls themselves and *then* to have been appropriated by others. Moreover, a close reading of the articles and editorials reveals a far more complex picture of the authors than that presented in most accounts. While they did not join in collective protest against what the protesters called the "factory system," their writings evinced an incisive understanding of their own oppression, both as women and as workers. But most important, their evident faith in Christianity united them with their protesting sisters who wrote in autonomous labor reform publications, such as the *Voice of Industry*, which manifested a similarly intense piety.[5]

If the *Offering* and the *Voice* provide a window onto the religious world of the mill girls, the Lowell Female Labor Reform Association offers a glimpse of that religion in action, in the service of labor protest. Part of the working-class agi-

[5] For the traditional view among historians, see Norman Ware, *The Industrial Worker, 1840–1860: The Reaction of American Industrial Society to the Advance of the Industrial Revolution* (1924; reprint ed., Chicago: Quadrangle Books, 1964), pp. 83, 85–95. For this view among contemporaries, see "Citizen of Lowell," *Corporations and Operatives* (Lowell, 1843). A more nuanced account can be found in "M" (Lucy Larcom), "Improvement Circle," *Offering*, 2d ser., no. 5 (January 1845) and Benita Eisler, ed., *The Lowell Offering: Writings by New England Mill Women (1840–1845)* (New York: Harper & Row, Publishers, Inc., 1977), pp. 33–40. For a sympathetic view by labor reformers outside Lowell, see (Cincinnati) *People's Paper*, 13 December 1843. The substantial disagreement among contemporaries and historians on both the history and meaning of the *Lowell Offering* suggests the need for a fresh and in-depth study of this important early example of female working-class expression.

tation that swept through New England's industrial communities during the mid-1840s, the association marked the first permanent labor organization among mill girls in the nation's history. Under the leadership of the charismatic Sarah Bagley and the indefatigable Huldah Stone, the LFLRA played a key role in the regional labor bodies of these years, the New England Workingmen's Association (NEWA) and its successor, the New England Labor Reform League (NELRL). The Lowell women helped establish Female Labor Reform Associations elsewhere, provided many of the correspondents for the movement's labor press, and spearheaded the major campaign of the day, the petition drive for the ten-hour workday. Numbering some five hundred members by the end of 1845, the LFLRA established a "Female Department" in the *Voice* (which they later helped edit), issued a series of widely circulated *Factory Tracts*, set up a committee to expose pro-corporation propaganda, started an industrial reform lyceum, and organized fairs, social gatherings, and improvement circles to spread their gospel and to raise money for a variety of labor causes.

What, precisely, did these labor reformers stand for? The focus of the association's protest was the factory, but they did not reject the factory per se. Rather, these women declaimed against the "unutterable woe" that capitalist industry had wrought among wage-earners. Thus, they dedicated themselves to "the improvement of the condition of the laboring masses." But the association, acutely aware of the *general* negative effects of the industrial revolution, advocated something still more fundamental than this. Like the broader movement of which it formed an integral part, the LFLRA favored not just shorter hours, higher wages, and better working conditions but various schemes for radical social change, such as utopian socialism, land reform, and producer and consumer cooperatives. Indeed, the LFLRA proposed nothing less than an entire transformation of society: the abolition of "slavery and oppression, mental, physical and religious."

Unlike the writers of the *Offering*, the women of the LFLRA openly and directly protested the conditions of life in Lowell and joined in collective action radically to transform them. But, like their sisters at the *Offering*, the labor reformers evinced a pervasive and powerful strain of piety and Christian mission. In this, the mill girls were one. When they wrote or spoke in public, activists and non-activists alike remembered the past, interpreted the present, and envisioned the future in the prevailing vocabulary of their day: the language of religion.[6]

To understand these women, and the religious world they inhabited, we must reconstruct the social context of their confrontation with the factory. They had left family and friends in their countryside homes for a strange new world of company-sponsored boardinghouses and textile machinery. What they left behind—"the green hills and fertile vales . . . where the pure air of heaven, gave life and animation to the whole being," in Huldah Stone's recollection—became at once a touchstone and a refuge for them: a standard by which they judged their present circumstances and a sanctuary to which they retreated, literally as well as figuratively, when these circumstances seemed too harsh to bear.[7] In doing so, they reconstructed their past as a kind of "Golden Age," a world that never was but one that ought to be. They thus created a model that offered legitimacy for dissent against present conditions and provided alternative visions of the future.

At the very core of this largely romanticized perception of "home" was the religious sentiment that permeated rural

[6] See Francis Early, "A Reappraisal of the New-England Labour-Reform Movement of the 1840s: The Lowell Female Labor Reform Association and the New England Workingmen's Association," *Histoire Sociale-Social History* 13 (May 1980): 33–54. Quotations are from Sarah Bagley's editorial, *Voice of Industry* (Fitchburg, Lowell, and Boston, Mass.), 15 May 1846; LFLRA Report to NEWA, *Voice*, 23 January 1846.

[7] *Voice*, 25 September 1846.

New England during the early nineteenth century. In the *Offering*, for example, one writer described her "Last Evening at Home," recalling her feelings as she prepared to leave "this sacred, this enchanted spot, and go to a land of strangers."[8] A writer in *Factory Tracts*, which claimed to publish articles too radical for the *Offering*, echoed the same theme, picturing the prospective factory girl leaving "the home of her childhood; that home around which clusters [*sic*] so many beautiful and holy associations."[9] For these young women, most of them in their late teens or early twenties, going to work in the mills was a wrenching experience; their re-creation of a peaceful, harmonious, and, most of all, pious home provided an essential frame of reference in coping with that experience.

If holiness was the lifeblood of the mill girl's home, Scripture was its heart, the source of her intellectual, moral, and spiritual energies. Lucy Larcom, a Lowell operative and contributor to the *Offering*, claimed to have learned to read by reciting from the New Testament. She also had fond memories of worshiping with her brothers and sisters as their father read to them from the family Bible. She could not touch that book, she wrote later, without feelings of "profound reverence."[10] Larcom's radical contemporary, Huldah Stone, recorded that same veneration on a trip to her childhood home in 1846. There she found the old family Bible, which her mother had turned to for "counsel, wisdom and strength," still occupying its proper place on the common room table.[11]

As it was in their childhood, so it was in their new lives as mill workers. When the *Factory Girls' Album and Oper-*

[8] Aramantha, "The Last Evening at Home," *Offering*, 2d ser., no. 4 (1844):78.

[9] Amelia, "Some of the Beauties of Our Factory System—Otherwise, Lowell Slavery," *Factory Tracts*, No. 1 (October 1845). Philip S. Foner has reprinted all that survives of this publication (the first issue and extracts of the second, which appeared in the *Voice*) in his *The Factory Girls* (Urbana: University of Illinois Press, 1977), pp. 130–41.

[10] Lucy Larcom, *A New England Girlhood* (1889; reprint ed., Gloucester, Mass.: Peter Smith, 1973), pp. 44, 150.

[11] *Voice*, 8 May 1846.

atives' Advocate appeared in February 1846, the lead article was entitled "The Bible." "It is a thing always to be had," the author wrote, "always within call, and ever at hand, and very portable."[12] The statement was more a comment on contemporary practice than advice to the unregenerate. Company regulations prohibited reading in the mills, but Lucy Larcom recalled that some of her sister operatives believed that Scripture was exempt from that ban. Indeed, Lucy herself tore pages from her Bible and carried them with her to work. She was not alone. It was common, she claimed, for a mill operative to "have a page or two of the Bible beside her there, committing verses to memory while her hands went on with their mechanical occupation." The overseer would confiscate these materials whenever he found them, and it is testimony to the ubiquity of the practice that Larcom reported that her overseer's desk was full of Bibles.[13] As we shall see, this assiduous reading of Scripture yielded effective ammunition for those operatives who protested against the system of factory labor in which they found themselves.

While the Bible was the fulcrum of the mill girls' faith, it was not the only important element of their religious heritage. The church and its subsidiary institutions figured prominently, if somewhat problematically, in their lives. "The Meeting House, as in most country villages, is conspicuous, as the greatest ornament," wrote one operative of her New Hampshire home.[14] To be sure, not all mill girls shared those memories, usually because they grew up on farms too far from the meetinghouse to make regular attendance possible. But the absence of organized worship in childhood seems to have made many that much more eager for it as adults. Sarah Bagley, the most prominent female labor leader of the 1840s,

[12] *Factory Girls' Album* (Exeter, N.H.), 4 February 1846. The *Factory Girls' Album*, unlike the *Offering*, was an open advocate for the rights of female operatives. Though edited by a man (Charles Dearborn), most of the articles were written by the mill girls themselves. It is likely that this anonymous piece was penned by one of them, as Dearborn generally signed his articles and editorials.

[13] Larcom, *New England Girlhood*, pp. 180–81; Larcom, "Among Lowell Mill-Girls," *Atlantic Monthly* (November 1881), reprinted in Foner, *Factory Girls*, p. 23.

[14] E. E. T., "Childhood's Home," *Offering* 1 (1841):69.

even insisted that one advantage of being a mill worker in Lowell was "the pleasure of being associated with the institutions of religion." "Most of us, when at home, live in the country," she pointed out, "and therefore cannot enjoy these privileges to the same extent; and many of us, not at all."[15] What all these women had in common was an acute awareness of the church's crucial role in Christian life.

To some extent, the operatives' participation in the church life of these mill towns was assured because, in many communities, workers were required "to be constant in attendance upon public worship." Although the editor of the *Offering* insisted that the regulation was not always "strictly enforced," it was generally a technical condition of both employment in the mill and residence in the company boardinghouse.[16] The mill owners no doubt conceived the rule as part of their broader design: to create (and control) a morally upright community of factory operatives as an alternative to the infamous English manufacturing system, thus countering popular fears and prejudices, and insuring a steady supply of labor. But, as Hannah Josephson observed many years ago in her classic study of the mill girls, strict rules governing morality and Sabbath observance reflected "the standards of behavior of young women all over New England at this time." Thus, textile recruiting agents traveling in the countryside would carry a copy of their company's regulations to assure parents that their daughter's virtue would be protected in the factory town. The textile corporations were not inaugurating anything new, Josephson pointed out; rather, they were bowing to the mores of the era.[17]

Still, the interests of parent and daughter seem at times to have diverged in this particular, for some operatives

[15] S. G. B. (Sarah G. Bagley), "Pleasures of Factory Life," *Offering* 1 (1840):26.

[16] See Samuel Adams Drake, *History of Middlesex County, Massachusetts*, 2 vols. (Boston: Estes and Lauriat, 1880), 2:102, for a typical "regulation paper."

[17] Hannah Josephson, *Golden Threads: New England Mill Girls and Magnates* (1924; reprint ed., New York: Russell and Russell, 1967), p. 71.

denounced the "regulation paper" they were forced to sign. "Lo! here is the beginning of the mischief," declared a writer in *Factory Tracts.*[18] At issue was the very "independence" the mill owners celebrated in their "Yankee" mill girls. "Time and labor only are bought by the employers," another *Tract* writer insisted, "and the Operative has no right to be dictated as it regards the duties he owes to himself or those of his friends."[19] Similarly, *The Factory Girl* of New Market, New Hampshire, offered this definition of "contemptible": "for an overseer to ask a girl what her religious sentiments are, when she applies to him for employment."[20] These women may have adhered to prevailing standards of piety and morality, but they protested their employers' right to compel them to do so.

It is difficult to assess the significance of the churchgoing regulation, either in promoting or in discouraging attendance.[21] In Lowell, showcase of the pious Yankee mill girl, evidence suggests that female operatives took a deep interest in organized religion. Certainly, the twenty-three churches built there between 1825 and 1850 attest to the zeal of the local inhabitants, the majority of whom were mill women. Moreover, numerous observers remarked on the workers' strong attachment to organized devotion. "Religion has thriven in this place," noted two English Congregationalists on a tour of American churches in 1835.[22] Lucy Larcom, a churchgoing mill girl herself, remembered that "the church was really the home-centre to many, perhaps to most of us."

[18] Amelia, "Beauties of Our Factory System."

[19] "Extracts from Factory Tracts No. 2," reprinted in *Voice*, 14 November 1845. Though this comment referred to the requirement that mill girls reside in a boardinghouse, it aptly summed up the resentment some of them felt over company regulations in general.

[20] *The Factory Girl* (New Market, N.H.), 15 January 1843.

[21] No detailed empirical work has been done in this area. Preliminary work by the author, linking ten-hour petitioners in Lowell with available church membership rolls, reveals the presence of female labor reformers in a range of local churches.

[22] James Matheson and Andrew Reed, *A Narrative of the Visit to the American Churches, by the Deputation From the Congregational Union of England and Wales* (London: Jackson and Walford, 1835), p. 414.

As to the question of compulsion, she declared flatly, "nearly all the girls attended public worship from choice."[23] And though Sarah Bagley pointed out that regular church attendance was a requirement for mill employment, she also boasted that "many [mill girls] were engaged as teachers in the Sunday Schools" of Lowell, not because they were compelled to but because they were of high "moral and intellectual character."[24]

Whether by choice or by compulsion, it appears that, as "Susan" concluded upon her arrival in the city, "Lowell is a church-going place." And yet, this mill girl perceived a more complex reality in her new home. "It seems as though every one went to meeting, and the streets are so full on Sundays," she reported, "*but it is not so.*" Indeed, there were some operatives, though often devout, who found it difficult "to be constant in attendance upon public worship," regulation or no.[25]

Many of these women, pious but alienated from local church life, demanded a radical change in the conditions of life, in the mill and in the mill community. At the top of their list of complaints about the churchgoing regulation was the long workday, the premier working-class complaint of the age. "Can it be reasonably supposed," Sarah Bagley asked, "that those who are called to their task every morning at half past five, and kept until seven at night, will have sufficient energy to be constant in their attendance at church on the Sabbath?"[26] Some objected as well to paying pew rent for a gospel that they believed should be dispensed "without money and without price."[27] Others warned that the pious hypocrisy of churchgoing employers, "who compel their help to labor on the Sabbath day or lose their situations," would

[23] Larcom, *New England Girlhood*, p. 209.

[24] *Voice*, 12 June 1846; Massachusetts General Court, *House Documents*, No. 50 (1845), reprinted in Foner, *Factory Girls*, p. 239.

[25] "Letters from Susan," *Offering*, 2d ser., no. 4 (1844): 148.

[26] *Voice*, 12 June 1846. See also, *Voice*, 23 January 1846.

[27] *Offering*, 2d ser., no. 2 (1842): 120. See also, letter of "An Operative," *Voice*, 22 January 1847; Bagley's letter, *Voice*, 8 September 1846.

render the Sabbath "a pastime, or a day in which the weary operatives may attend to their own private business." Moreover, these employers enjoyed the same dominant position in the meetinghouse that they held in the workplace. "Is it strange," Bagley wanted to know, "that the operatives should stay away from the churches where they see the men filling the 'chief seats,' who are taking every means to grind them into the very dust?" Ministers constituted still another obstacle: "their sanction of the system . . . disqualifies (the operatives) to attend church and cultivate the spirit of the gospel."[28]

But the most common complaint had a particularly *female* cast. Mill girls, some argued, were further discouraged by the necessity and difficulties of emulating contemporary fashions. "Our Agents and the aristocratic class to which they belong," Bagley observed, "have ordained fashions in dress and equipage, which the operative is unable to follow, and they must at any rate *ape them*, or they will be wanting in self-respect." As for those who went to meeting in their "plain country dress" because they could find neither the time nor the money to keep their "wardrobe in church-going order," Bagley said, they "are almost stared out of countenance."[29]

For most mill girls, these criticisms did not reflect an "infidel," or anti-Christian, position. Bagley, extremely influential as editor of the *Voice of Industry* and president of the Lowell Female Labor Reform Association, addressed the subject only "with painful emotions" and "regret." "We would thank God most devoutly," she announced, "if there could be found a house of worship in Lowell, where the Gospel, as preached by ancient disciples, could be heard by every operative."[30] In the absence of such a church, many simply rejected the prevailing institutions of organized reli-

[28] "An Operative," Introduction, *Factory Tracts*, No. 1; *Voice*, 6 May 1846.

[29] *Voice*, 12 June 1846. See also, letter of "Octavia," *Factory Girl*, 1 March 1843; "Abby's Year in Lowell," *Offering* 1 (1841).

[30] *Voice*, 6 May, 23 January 1846. See also, *Voice*, 12 June 1846. Bagley became a member of the First Universalist Church of Lowell in 1840. Extant church records do not indicate when she left. Records in possession of Laura Husted, Lowell.

gion while they remained pious Christians. Thus, one Lowell mill girl admitted that resting rather than attending church on the Sabbath was "trifling with holy time," but she wondered if those who worshiped alone were not "as near to the kingdom of God" as those who "worship where the useless show of vanity characterizes more the appearance of a playhouse, than of immortal beings congregating for the important purpose of enquiring what they should do to be saved." Sacrifice to God, she insisted, involved "not a change of garments but a change of hearts."[31]

As "Christians without a church," workers like this mill girl drew from a powerful tradition in European and American Protestantism that emphasized faith over forms and ceremonies. In antebellum America, one manifestation of this tradition was "come-outerism," usually associated with abolitionists who, having renounced their churches for countenancing slavery, sometimes established their own anti-slavery congregations.[32] But there were "come-outers" among labor activists as well. Some urged the mill girl "to go out upon the hills, where she might worship in the great temple of the universe, without a priest, as proxy, to stand between her and her Maker."[33] Others, combining religious devotion with the rights of labor, formed alternative churches. In the fall of 1845, for example, a Lowell newspaper reported that "*fashion*" had rendered church attendance "so expensive" that many operatives now held Sabbath meetings at the Mechanics' Reading Room where they read from Scripture, sang hymns, and discussed "topics affecting the rights and interests of the laborer."[34]

[31] *Voice*, 12 June 1846.

[32] See esp. Lewis Perry, *Radical Abolitionism: Anarchy and the Government of God in Antislavery Thought* (Ithaca: Cornell University Press, 1973).

[33] *Voice*, 2 April 1847. See also Laura S. Brigham, ed., "An Independent Voice: A Mill Girl from Vermont Speaks Her Mind," *Vermont History* 61 (Summer 1973):142–46.

[34] *Vox Populi* (Lowell), reprinted in *Young America* (New York), 18 October 1845. See also the LFLRA report to the National Industrial Congress (October 1845), describing Sabbath meetings to "discuss the great principles which pertain to human rights and human duties" (*Voice*, 7 November 1845).

But it would be wrong to infer that the discontented had abandoned the established churches altogether. Indeed, there is evidence, though fragmentary, of labor protest welling up from within mill town churches themselves. During the 1836 "turn-out" in Lowell, a local Methodist minister dispensed certificates of dismissal, in essence membership transfers, to some sixty or seventy female strikers in his church who chose to leave town rather than return to work.[35] In numerous communities, both Calvinistic and Freewill Baptists provided important support for female labor protest, suggesting that these churches maintained a following among the ranks of radical mill women. When factory girls in Amesbury, Massachusetts, "turned out" in 1836 over an increased work load, they met in the local Baptist vestry to choose officers and pass resolutions.[36] A decade later, in Lowell, a touring correspondent for the New York *Working-Men's Advocate* reported speaking before a large and receptive audience "of factory girls and working men" at the local Freewill Baptist meetinghouse.[37] And, although the Lowell clergy of the 1840s were generally recognized by contemporaries as opponents of the labor movement, the pastor of the Worthen Street Baptist Church did support the mill girls' demand for the ten-hour workday.[38] Meanwhile, Lowell's first Freewill Baptist preacher, Hiram Stevens, surfaced in 1847 as the president of the Dover, New Hampshire, Female Labor Reform Association. When Stevens opened the association's "social pic nic" with a prayer in the spring of that year, it is likely that more than a few of those in attendance were members of his congregation.[39]

Still, for many, perhaps for most, the labor movement itself was their only church. For antebellum labor reform, particularly in the 1840s, often evinced the evangelical style of its

[35] *Zion's Herald* (Boston), 5, 12 October 1836.

[36] Edith Abbott, *Women in Industry: A Study in American Economic History* (1910; reprint ed., New York: Arno and the New York Times, 1969), p. 131n.

[37] *Working-Men's Advocate* (New York), 2 November 1844.

[38] *Voice*, 9 October 1846.

[39] *Voice*, 16 April 1847.

age.[40] One poet in the Lowell FLRA exhorted her sisters to "chide the sinful, turn the erring," while another cajoled the uninitiated, "Come! join ye this worthy band / And drive oppression from the land."[41] A Lowell factory girl reminded her compatriots in the Manchester FLRA that they would probably meet many "faithless and indifferent ones," who must be shown "the error of their ways."[42] Meanwhile, the Manchester Association vowed not to suffer factory evils "without our testimony against them."[43] And, at "social gatherings" and "fairs" in Lowell, Manchester, and elsewhere, female operatives joined with male workers in "nigh fancying ourselves in a 'better land' where sin and oppression were unknown."[44]

Some thought this endeavor was a particularly *female* province, identifying labor reform with those other benevolent enterprises in which women were so prominent during these years. In a letter to the *Voice of Industry* denouncing prevailing views of the proper "sphere of woman's influence," "Olivia" insisted that there was no "good work or benevolent enterprise" outside "woman's sphere." "Shall she not be a ministering angel at the hovel of intemperance and wretchedness," she asked; "shall not her kind words and tears of sympathy recall the wanderer, and make glad the hearts made desolate by sin?"[45] Here, indeed, was one answer to the problem of church participation in the mill community: labor reform as Christian benevolence.

It should come as no surprise that mill girls in antebellum New England often spoke of labor reform in terms of Chris-

[40] On the evangelical style of the labor movement in general during these years, see my "A Good Time Coming: Religion and the Emergence of Labor Activism in Antebellum New England" (Ph.D. dissertation, Brandeis University, 1983).

[41] *Voice*, 8 May, 20 February 1846.

[42] *Voice*, 17 April 1846.

[43] *Voice*, 12 February 1847.

[44] *Voice*, reprinted in *Young America*, 28 February 1846.

[45] *Voice*, 5 December 1845.

tian benevolence. As female Americans, they had been taught that their sex had a special responsibility to protect the moral virtue of the republic; as Christian Americans, they had been taught that they had a special responsibility to save themselves and humanity.[46] Like their sisters in a host of antebellum movements, from moral reform to women's rights, radical mill women had absorbed these lessons and applied them to the cause of secular reform. They had been stirred to action, they said, by religious obligation. In its report to the New England Workingmen's Association in April 1846, the Lowell FLRA talked of a "spirit abroad in the world" that would not be stilled until justice, right, and brotherhood were established throughout the land. "Let no one disregard the holy, benevolent promptings of this heaven-derived spirit in the soul," the association cautioned, "but rather heed its kind warnings, and obey faithfully its imperative commands!"[47] The labor reform movement for which the Lowell women spoke—its style, its critique, and its social vision—provides ample evidence that this spirit had indeed taken root among certain workers. The particular cast of that movement derived at least in part from the fact that these workers were often women.

Like evangelists, radical mill women of the 1840s exhorted their constituency to do battle "in the name of God" on behalf of a "righteous" and "holy" cause.[48] True to their heritage, they made good use of the Bible. In the women's

[46] See esp. Linda K. Kerber, *Women of the Republic: Intellect and Ideology in Revolutionary America* (Chapel Hill: University of North Carolina Press, 1980) and Mary Beth Norton, *Liberty's Daughters: The Revolutionary Experience of American Women, 1750–1800* (Boston: Little, Brown and Co., 1980).

[47] *Voice*, 10 April 1846. See also, LFLRA report in *Voice*, 23 January 1846.

[48] My decision to focus on the 1840s forces me to sidestep a critical question raised by a number of recent studies: did the revivals of the 1837 depression infuse evangelical piety into the working class (and thus the working-class movement), fundamentally altering its character? All the evidence is not in on this subject, but in towns as diverse as Fitchburg and Fall River, Massachusetts, significant numbers of labor reformers during the 1840s had been members of local churches for a *decade or more*. See my "A Good Time Coming," chap. 2. On the impact of the depression revivals, see esp. Bruce Laurie, *Working People of Philadelphia* (Philadelphia: Temple University Press, 1980).

column of the *Voice of Industry*, "Juliana" roused her sisters with messianic imagery drawn from the Old Testament.

Let the thought that we are engaged in a *good* work nerve us on to duty. The battle is not to the strong, nor the race to the swift—but to the righteousness of the cause. In the strength of Elijah's God, the God of Right, let us march boldly on to the conquest. Let us take no rest until the shout shall rend the earth and heavens—"Goliath is fallen!"[49]

Similarly, Manchester FLRA leader Mehitable Eastman encouraged a group of operatives in her city to persevere if their first efforts at reform should fail. "Let us remember," she told them at a labor rally, "that the children of Israel did not arrive at the promised land, save through a journey of forty years in the wilderness."[50]

But nowhere was the mill girls' exhortatory use of Scripture more colorful and dramatic than in their poetry. Typical of this genre was "Amelia's" "The Summons," which appeared in the Lowell FLRA's *Factory Tracts*. In the last two stanzas, this poet-operative inspired her sisters with promises drawn from Isaiah and the Gospels.

Yea, be thou strong—there yet remains
A promise sure to thee,
That God will break the oppressor's chains,
And set the prisoner free.

That righteousness and truth shall reign,
Through all the peopled earth,
And heaven repeat the exulting strain,
Which hailed creation's birth.

Now here surely was a summons no faithful Christian could resist.[51]

God's presence loomed large in this rhetoric. Ending nearly all of their letters, announcements, and speeches with

[49] *Voice*, 12 June 1846.
[50] *Voice*, 4 September 1846.
[51] *Factory Tracts*, No. 1.

appeals for divine favor, the mill girls sometimes referred to the deity as the "Omnipotent power" or the "All-seeing eye."[52] In this circumvention of earthly authority, they no doubt found an antidote to their sense of powerlessness, not only as workers but as *female* workers. Certainly, some of them did not hesitate to invoke Old Testament images of a vengeful Lord. "The Warning Cry," a poem that appeared in the *Voice of Industry*, was directed at the movement's enemies.

Tremble, tremble! well ye may,
Godless tyrants of the day,
Trampling on your fellow-clay!
  Trampling human hearts to dust!

Vengeance is the Lord's! beware!
He will list the poor man's prayer,
Raise the crushed, and chase despair!
  Tyrants, woe! THE LORD IS JUST![53]

To be sure, radical mill girls also appealed to a "beneficent God," the "God of Infinite Love" and the "kind father," and to this extent they reflected the general "feminization" of Protestantism during the early nineteenth century.[54] But such images were evoked when the mill girls spoke of their blessings or when they appealed for support from the larger community. When they faced their enemies, they usually solicited the aid of a "God of Right and Justice" rather than a God of mercy and forgiveness.[55]

[52] See, for examples, notice of NELRL meeting, *Voice*, 26 February 1847; letter of "J.R.," *Voice*, 9 October 1846; letter of "Mary Ann," *Voice*, 28 May 1846; Bagley's speech at NEWA convention, *Voice*, 11 September 1845; Stone's letter to Manchester operatives, *Voice*, 26 December 1845; *Literary Wreath and Factory Girls' Album* (Exeter, N.H.), 10 July 1845, reprinted in Foner, *Factory Girls*, pp. 217–18

[53] *Voice*, 5 December 1845. See also, Bagley's editorial, *Voice*, 15 May 1846, Mehitable Eastman's report to the NELRL, in *Voice*, 12 February 1847.

[54] Stone's letter to Manchester operatives, *Voice*, 26 December 1845; Bagley's speech to NEWA, *Voice*, 9 November 1845; letter of "Juliana," *Voice*, 7 May 1849.

[55] This is, of course, a difficult point to prove, but it is worth pursuing the possibility that labor activists used a different vocabulary, perhaps rooted in different biblical traditions, depending upon the circumstances. It does appear that religious mill women could speak both the language of anger and of love, depending upon their audience. In her first column as editor of the *Voice*, for example, Sarah Bagley

Whatever the character of their appeals to God, Christianity was the mill girls' point of departure, providing them a *raison d'être*. When the LFLRA endorsed a proposal for what amounted to a general strike for the ten-hour workday in 1846, for example, it did so with the caveat that it should be considered merely "one step, towards the great end to be attained": "Christianity in its original simplicity, and pristine beauty."[56] Their religion also provided these operatives with powerful ammunition against their employers and other opponents. In her "Advice to Mill Owners," in which she advocated allowing operatives to leave work for "an hour or two, or a day even," a factory girl in Exeter, New Hampshire, chose to address her employers as churchgoing Christians. "The man who is unkind to his female help," she announced, "cannot be a christian, if he is a church member, a deacon, or even the carrier round of the contribution box."[57]

Scripture, too, proved a powerful weapon in the hands of these radicals. Huldah Stone, who saw herself as a kind of evangelist for the *Voice of Industry*, found biblical analogy particularly useful when she encountered opposition from employers. After a professedly sympathetic machine shop boss in Lawrence, Massachusetts, had refused to purchase a subscription from her because "'females are out of their *place* while soliciting names to a working man's paper,'" Stone wrote a long letter to the *Voice*, reminding both him and her sisters of the role one woman had played in biblical times. It deserves to be quoted in full.

---

echoed a note of militancy uncharacteristic of that paper's editorials, either before or after her tenure. Speaking to her constituency and announcing herself to her enemies, Bagley chastised a textile agent who had threatened to discharge a member of the LFLRA. "We will make the name of him who dares the act, stink with every wind, from all points of the compass," she warned (*Voice*, 15 May 1845). When she addressed the NEWA convention as president of the LFLRA the following fall, however, she insisted that her cause was one in which every philanthropist should take an interest, reminding her audience to "be true to the sympathies and emotions of piety which a God of Infinite Love has implanted in every human soul" (*Voice*, 9 November 1845).

[56] *Voice*, 23 January 1846.

[57] *Factory Girls' Album*, 14 February 1846. See also, Stone, "Improvement of Time," in *Voice*, 7 August 1845; Ada, "The Universal Brotherhood," *Voice*, 6 February 1846.

Only think of it, girls, how very unfeminine and "out of place" it would have been in this gentleman's eyes, had he lived in Christ's day, for Mary to have gone alone to the sepulcre where none but *Jesus* slept. No *ladies* there? Why in all probability he would not have received the news of the glorious resurrection from her lips had it been what his soul was panting to hear; for, O shameful to relate, a *female* had dared to presume to know for herself somewhat of that blessed "truth" which was to elevate and make good and happy the race, and had even stepped out of *her place* (the *back kitchen* I suppose he meant) so far, as to go out and ascertain whether Christ was indeed risen, and to proclaim the glorious news to her friends and her kindred![58]

Stone, true to her namesake, the Old Testament prophetess Huldah, was by all accounts one woman who did not remain in the "place" set aside for those of her sex.

Just as they used their religion effectively to criticize their enemies, these operatives drew upon the Bible and Christianity to assert their dignity and worth both as women and as workers. In "A Dream" (subtitled, "I had a dream which was not *all* a dream"), a Manchester factory girl described her vision of the Judgment Day. Sinners having been arrayed in groups "like criminals," the agents and owners of the Amoskeag Manufacturing Company stood before their Maker. As on earth, the agents spoke for their employers.

Judge. What were you doing on Sunday, the-day-of-1844?
Agent. Attending church.
Judge. But I am informed that you were blasting rocks.
Agent. Oh, ah, ye-yes-I, we employed some common people to do that for us, *I* attended church *myself*.
Judge. You must go below.

Then, a factory girl from one of the Amoskeag mills appeared.

Judge. What were you doing on Sunday the-day-of-1844?

[58] *Voice*, 13 July 1847. Like working men, the mill girls also used Christ as a model for emulation. See letter from Lowell, *Voice*, 11 September 1845; Bagley, *Voice*, 6 February 1846; letter of "Weaver," *Democrat* (Manchester, N.H.), 13 January 1847.

Girl. I attended church in the morning and in the afternoon I rambled off into the woods.
Judge. How came you to ramble in the woods on Sunday?
Girl. I had no time on weekdays.

After eliciting information on her working hours and the time remaining "for relaxation, religious and moral instruction, reading, social visiting and intercourse with your family," the judge decided this factory girl's fate.

Judge. You may go to Heaven.
Girl. What seat shall I take?
Judge. Any of the upper seats that you like.

Echoing Christ's prediction in Matthew that "the last will be first, and first last," this vision served to remind the mill girls that their day would come.[59]

As the foregoing attests, some mill girls had their own vision of woman's proper station in society. They based that vision on their interpretation of a fiercely debated concept in antebellum America, God's "design." In a typical recourse to this rationale, notices for LFLRA meetings invited all females "who would wish to place women in that elevated station intellectually and morally which a bountiful Creator designed her to occupy in the scale of being."[60] This "design"—the basis of labor's argument for the ten-hour workday in antebellum America—necessitated that workers have the freedom to perfect themselves (physically, intellectually, morally, and spiritually) through the cultivation of their God-given faculties, and thereby "honor the great Creator."[61] Here the mill girls advanced a class demand, on behalf of *female* workers, for the right to decide how much of their time would be their own and how much they would sell to their employer.

As women, though, these operatives also had special concerns. It is well known that the mill girl's morality was a chief

[59] *Democrat*, 5 September 1845, reprinted in Foner, *Factory Girls*, pp. 81–82; Matt. 20:16. See also, Bagley's editorial, *Voice*, 8 May 1846.

[60] *Voice*, 9 January 1846; 18 September 1845.

[61] See, for examples, *Voice*, 18 August, 18 September 1845; 26 November 1847.

interest of the *Lowell Offering*, as well as of the mill owners, the clergy, and the broader community; but it was also a major preoccupation of female labor reformers.[62] The new industrial communities, the LFLRA reported, contained thousands of "young, unsuspecting females, who are thrown upon the charities of a cold, unfriendly world, in helpless childhood, and compelled to earn their daily bread somewhere or perish in the streets!"[63] The depths to which a mill girl might sink were frightening, indeed. In her opening column as editor of the *Voice*, Sarah Bagley reminded her sisters of what awaited them should they fail to maintain their vigilance. While she and the defenders of the factory system agreed that, as she put it, "the standard of virtue in Lowell, is far above that of any other city of its size in the Union," she was hardly sanguine about the moral climate of "life among the spindles." Temptation abounded, Bagley believed, and Satan was its merchant.

Never, never, in the name of heaven, permit Lowell to boast her 'nymphs of the pave. At the dance, upon the street, at the social gathering, in church, or by your own fireside shrink as from the abyss of infamy, from the steady gaze or stealthy touch of the *fiend* in human form, who for a paltry job would rob you of bliss in your life, and destroy a lone girl's happiness, away from friends and home.

If Bagley's language here echoed pro-corporation exhortations on proper female behavior, the meaning was far different. While, as Christians, Bagley and her opponents shared an overriding concern with sin, they diverged sharply on its origins. For the mill owners and their allies, sin in Lowell was a product of individual moral failing alone. For

[62] The sinfulness that seemed to attend commercial and industrial capitalism concerned male labor reformers as well. Indeed, William F. Young, the founder of the *Voice*, referred to Lowell as a "wilderness of sin" (see *Voice*, 6 March 1846). Still, female activists seem to have been particularly troubled by this issue, because it was so often associated with the degradation of women. On Young, see my "Religion and Labor Reform in Antebellum America: The World of William Field Young," *American Quarterly* 38 (Summer 1986): 265–86.

[63] *Voice*, 19 February 1847.

Bagley, the problem was "the division of labor consequent upon the introduction of machinery."[64] On this issue, she and the defenders of the Lowell system were diametrically opposed.

Still, the labor reformers' preoccupation with sin reflected a view of woman's "place" that was not entirely at odds with the ideology of domesticity promoted by contemporary moralists.[65] Though these mill women advocated equal standing with men, in marriage as well as in society, they generally accepted the prevalent belief that men and women were fundamentally different.[66] In their view, no less than in that of their contemporaries, women had a unique moral obligation that could be fulfilled only through marriage and motherhood. Thus, at the top of "Juliana's" list of the "Evils of Factory Life" was the destruction of "all love of order and practice in domestic affairs." Female operatives would one day be wives and mothers, she reminded her sisters. But without time to cultivate the mind and form good habits, they would be "deficient in everything pertaining to those holy, *sacred* names!" They would be unprepared for their ordained responsibility to their families, "to instruct them in the great duties of life." If "'the mother educates the man,'" "Juliana" asked, what could be expected from young women "incarcerated within the walls of a factory, while as yet mere children . . . surrounded on all sides with the vain ostentation of fashion, vanity and light frivolity—beset with temptations without and the carnal propensities of nature within?"[67] The attack on the factory system here was radical, but the view of women was conventional indeed.

[64] *Voice*, 15 May 1846.

[65] On the "canon" of domesticity during this period, see Cott, *Bonds of Womanhood*.

[66] On marriage, see letters in *Lynn Pioneer*, reprinted in *Voice*, 14 August 1847; *Factory Girls' Album*, 28 February, 14 March 1846, 15 February 1847. On support for women's rights, see Foner, *Factory Girls*, p. 294.

[67] *Factory Tracts*, No. 1. See also, Clariette, "The Ten Hour System," *Factory Girls' Album*, 11 April 1846.

Clearly, much remains to be explored about the role of religion in the lives of the New England mill girls. In particular, we need to know more about their actual participation in local churches, since organized worship constituted a central part of their employers' design for a model industrial community. Were labor reformers more or less likely to be church members than their more quiescent peers? At the time of their political involvement, were they likely to be congregants of long standing or converts of a recent revival? To what denominations did they belong? Did their denominational preferences reflect theological issues or local peculiarities? What role did sympathetic (or hostile) clergymen play? Most important, how did the nature and scope of the mill girls' church involvement change over time?

Our knowledge may be limited, but we know enough to begin rethinking much of what we have assumed about religion's role in mill towns like Lowell. For the dissenters among the mill girls attacked the factory system in the name of its alleged bulwark—Christianity. There is, of course, something of a paradox here: those who protested labor conditions, indeed those who organized and led a movement radically to transform those conditions, spoke as traditionalists, calling for a return to the principles and values of a (however fancified) gentler age.[68] In seeking to stem the tide of innovations they perceived as antithetical to the life they had known in the New England countryside, they were conservatives. Moreover, their views about women's role in society, though often belied by their activities, could be traditional as well. Still, in seeking to root out the sin and vice they believed attended capitalist industrialization, they were radicals. Their vision of a Christian commonwealth where mill

[68] For interesting perspectives on this phenomenon in different historical settings during the same years, see Craig Jackson Calhoun, "The Radicalism of Tradition: Community Strength or Venerable Disguise and Borrowed Language?" *American Journal of Sociology* 88 (March 1983):886–914; William H. Sewell, Jr., "Artisans, Factory Workers, and the Formation of the French Working Class, 1789–1848," in Ira Katznelson and Aristide R. Zolberg, eds., *Working-Class Formation: Nineteenth-Century Patterns in Western Europe and the United States* (Princeton: Princeton University Press, 1986), pp. 45–70.

girls would take the front seats while the textile owners and their agents were sent "below" marked them as dissidents indeed.

Jama Lazerow, *Assistant Professor of History at the University of Puget Sound, is the author of the forthcoming* Religion and the Working Class in Pre-Civil War America.

"Female Laborers in the Church": Women Preachers in the Northeastern United States, 1790–1840

LOUIS BILLINGTON

In recent years historians have emphasized the centrality of women to religious life, especially among the older Protestant denominations in the northeastern section of the United States. In the late eighteenth and early nineteenth centuries, women and girls were usually the majority of attenders at prayer meetings and Sunday services, made up the bulk of converts at revivals and provided the greatest number of candidates for church membership.[1] They were also great fund raisers not only for their own congregations, but for a network of inter-denominational missionary agencies which sprang up during the first two decades of the nineteenth century and helped to impress a more evangelical character upon American society.[2] As Nancy Cott has argued, ministers may have seen this work as part of woman's appropriate and subordinate "sphere," but for the women themselves "evangelical religion nourished the formation of a female community that served... as both a resource and a resort outside the family."[3] Other aspects of women's involvement in the religious

Louis Billington is Lecturer in American Studies at the University of Hull, Hull HU6 7RX.
He would like to thank Rosamund Billington of Humberside College of Higher Education for her critical reading of an earlier draft of this paper which, he hopes, has enabled him to clarify and do justice to the feminist implications of women's religious activity.

[1] Barbara Welter, "The feminization of American religion: 1800–1860" in Mary Hartman and Lois Banner, eds., *Clio's Consciousness Raised*, (New York, 1974); Nancy F. Cott, *The Bonds of Womanhood: "Woman's Sphere" in New England, 1780–1835* (New Haven & London, 1977), pp. 126–29; Whitney R. Cross, *The Burned-Over District: The Social and Intellectual History of Enthusiastic Religion in Western New York, 1800–1850* (Ithaca, N.Y., 1950), p. 38.

[2] Cott, pp. 126–59; Keith Melder, *The Beginnings of Sisterhood: the American Woman's Rights Movement* (New York, 1977), pp. 30–48.

[3] Cott, p. 159.

Journal of American Studies, 19 (1985), 3, 369–394 *Printed in Great Britain*

culture of the early Republic have received much attention, most noticeably the careers of female founders of millenarian and communitarian sects, such as Ann Lee of the Shakers and Jemima Wilkinson, the Public Universal Friend, with their claims to be "Jesus Christ in the form of a woman," or " the Spirit of the Life of God." Both of these women also advocated celibacy for their followers, which has attracted the attention of historians of sexuality as well as of religion.[4] This paper offers a preliminary investigation of the lives and beliefs of a group of largely neglected women preachers who claimed a much wider "sphere" of religious activity than their sisters in the more middle-class Calvinist denominations, but who rarely advocated such startling doctrines as have made sects like the Shakers the subject of continued research. Yet these women preachers flourished in the same milieu as the Shakers.[5]

Many women preachers were "free spirits" who rejected formal religious affiliations, but in the northeastern United States the Freewill Baptists, the Christians and to a lesser degree, various small Methodist sects offered the most support for their mission.[6] These groups arose between 1780 and the 1830s and shared many common features. Most importantly, they emerged from within a tradition of popular revivalism associated in New England and the Maritimes with the "New Light Stir," a series of awakenings which continued through the years of the Revolution. Breaking away from the still-dominant Calvinism of the older denominations they offered salvation to all, often tipping over into a Universalism which also flourished at this time. Great emphasis was placed on personal religious experience, and their meetings were marked by trances, visions and miraculous healings. Signs and wonders accompanied their revivals, and accusations of witchcraft and magic were used against them. Perfectionist and millenarian movements constantly occurred, and there was a

[4] Edward Demings Andrews, *The People Called Shakers: A Search for the Perfect Society* (New York, 1953); John McKelvie Whitworth, *God's Blueprints: A Sociological Study of Three Utopian Sects* (London & Boston, 1975), pp. 13–88; Harold Wisbey, *Frontier Prophetess: The Life of Jemima Wilkinson* (Ithaca, N.Y., 1963); Lawrence Foster, *Religion and Sexuality: Three American Communal Experiments of the Nineteenth Century* (New York, 1981); Stephen A. Marini, *Radical Sects of Revolutionary New England* (Cambridge, Mass. & London, 1982).

[5] Hosea Quinby, "History of the Freewill Baptists," *Freewill Baptist Quarterly* Dover, N.H., 2 (1840), 207–09; Marini, pp. 82–101.

[6] Nancy Towle, *Vicissitudes Illustrated in the Experiences of Nancy Towle in Europe and America* (Portsmouth, N.H., 1833), pp. 1–60; Harriet Livermore, *Scriptural Evidence in Favour of Female Testimony in Meetings for Christian Worship*... (Portsmouth, N.H., 1824), pp. 85–87; Almond H. Davis, *The Female Preacher, or Memoir of Salome Lincoln* (Providence, R.I., 1843).

powerful seeking after the restoration of "primitive Christianity." Clerical titles and the need for general or theological education were questioned, and many called for the end of a separate and paid ministry. Foot-washing and the holy kiss as religious ceremonies had their advocates and were only suppressed amidst much controversy and schism.[7]

In time leaders emerged who introduced a greater degree of order and formal government, but among the Freewill Baptists and Christians this process was not accomplished until well into the nineteenth century, although a basic framework was established much earlier.[8] The smaller Methodist sects like the African Methodist Episcopal Church or the later Wesleyan Methodist Church experienced a similar slow movement towards denominationalism with accompanying schisms and disruptions.[9] Compared with the Congregationalists, Presbyterians, Regular or Calvinist Baptists, or the rapidly growing Methodist Episcopal Church, the sects under discussion were small, but their local and regional importance was often much greater than their crude membership totals might suggest. During and after the Revolution the Congregational establishments of Connecticut and Massachusetts struggled to reach the settlers of northern New England, but faced growing competition from the Freewill Baptists and the Christians.[10] The Freewillers were a large group in New Hampshire by the 1820s and had over two hundred congregations in Maine a few years

[7] Marini, pp. 1–135; J. M. Bumsted, *Henry Alline, 1748–1784* (Toronto, 1971); George A. Rawlyk, "From New Light to Baptist: Harris Harding and the Second Great Awakening in Nova Scotia" in Barry M. Moody, ed., *Repent and Believe: The Baptist Experience in Maritime Canada* (Hantsport, N.S., 1980). Nathan O. Hatch, "The Christian Movement and the Demand for a Theology of the People," *Journal of American History*, 67 (1980–1), 545–57, focuses on the wider aspects of the search for "primitive Christianity."

[8] Marini, pp. 116–35 exaggerates the speed of this process of formalization, and he ignores women preachers throughout his study.

[9] Carol V. R. George, *Segregated Sabbaths: Richard Allen and the Rise of Independent Black Churches, 1760–1840* (New York, 1973), pp. 128–29; Jarena Lee, *Religious Experience and Journal* (Philadelphia, 1849), p. 38. The first edition of this autobiography appeared in 1836. See also Ira Ford McLeister and Roy Stephen Nicholson, *History of the Wesleyan Methodist Church of America* (Marion, Ind., 1959), pp. 28–44.

[10] Calvin Montague Clark, *History of the Congregational Church in Maine*, Portland, Me, 1926, Vol. 1 gives a detailed account of Congregational missionary work in that state, and Paul Jeffrey Potash, "Welfare of the Regions Beyond," *Vermont History*, 46 (spring 1978), 109–28 provides a recent review of Congregational missions in Vermont. Two contemporary classics are Jotham Sewell, *A Memoir of Rev. Jotham Sewell of Chesterville, Maine* (Boston, 1853) and Nathan Perkins, *Narrative of a Tour through the State of Vermont from April 27 to June 12 1789* (Rutland, Vt, 1964).

later. The Christians had sixty congregations in Vermont by this time, and both sects grew among the Yankee migrants to western New York.[11]

Detailed local and regional studies of the rise of "Primitive Christianity" in the northeastern United States have not yet been made, although the numerous older town histories provide many clues, and Stephen Marini has recently indicated that in general the Freewill Baptists were recruited from all levels of a not very extended social hierarchy in northern New England.[12] Women preachers flourished in this region, the fastest growing area of the Republic between the Revolution and the War of 1812. This was a world overwhelmingly populated by small farmer-artisans and lumberers. After 1812 the settlement slowed, and many farmers began to move to the more fertile areas of New York and the Middle West. Here too, before 1830, pioneer farms predominated, and female preachers were popular.[13] Many young women flocked from rural New England to work in the new textile towns of eastern Massachusetts, but they retained close links with their families and friends back home and did not see themselves working as textile operatives for life. The mill towns were full of women saving for a marriage or for an education which would equip them to teach school. The Freewill Baptists and the Christians followed their rural members into the mill towns, where women preachers combined their calling with work as operatives.[14]

Between 1790 and 1840 probably hundreds of women had some experience of preaching, at least within their own localities, but for a few dozen women whose careers covered much longer periods of time and wider areas, it is possible from autobiographies, biographies, obituaries and other reports to build up a collective profile. These women were overwhelmingly the daughters of small farmer-artisans, possessed a common school education, and had grown up in a small-scale Yankee

[11] *Freewill Baptist Register* (Portland, Me), 1826, pp. 20–38; Clark, 2, 244; Two Hundred Vermonters, *Rural Vermont: A Program for the Future* (Burlington, Vt 1931), p. 351: *A Circular Letter Addressed to the People Denominated Christian Brethren* (Stow, Vt), pp. 8–10; Cross, pp. 14–17.

[12] Marini, pp. 96–98.

[13] Harold Fisher Wilson, *The Hill Country of Northern New England: Its Social and Economic History 1790–1930* (New York, 1936), pp. 1–15; Cross, pp. 55–78.

[14] Thomas Dublin, *Women at Work: The Transformation of Work and Community in Lowell, Massachusetts, 1826–1860* (New York, 1979) is a superior recent study with an extensive bibliography. Dublin's *Farm to Factory: Women's Letters, 1830–1860* (New York, 1981) brings out the centrality of religion in millworkers' lives, as does Claudia L. Bushman, "*A Good Poor Man's Wife,*" *Being a Chronicle of Harriet Hanson Robinson and Her Family in Nineteenth Century New England* (Hanover, N.H. 1981), pp. 41–63. For the Christians in Lowell see *Memoir of Elijah Shaw by His Daughter* (Boston, 1852), pp. 217–18.

Protestant world where settlements were often recent and class lines fluid. During the years of their active preaching careers the majority were single, or occasionally widowed. In a youthful population, most were in their late teens or early twenties when they first felt called upon to preach. Most stopped itinerating when married, though some continued preaching in their own neighbourhoods or made occasional tours. Others worked in tandem with preacher husbands, sometimes developing their own small sects.[15] Although the social origins and careers of most women preachers appear to fall into this pattern, those about whom we have substantial information suggest a somewhat more complex picture.

Harriet Livermore, perhaps the best known of these preachers, was the granddaughter of a substantial landowner who was a United States Senator from New Hampshire. Her father was a wealthy lawyer who sent her to Byfield Female Seminary at Newburyport, Massachusetts and Atkinson Academy, New Hampshire, two superior girls' schools. Nancy Towle, another popular preacher, also attended a New Hampshire academy at Hampton, where she made good progress in "literary pursuits" and became experienced in addressing large groups of girls and teachers.[16] Clarissa Danforth, who converted Nancy Towle, was described as "of good family and well educated... dignified in appearance [and] easy in manner."[17] Salome Lincoln falls into the more typical mould, the daughter of a small farmer and with a common school education. She went to work in a textile factory in Taunton, Massachusetts at the age of fifteen or sixteen, and continued there for eight years, using her wages to finance preaching tours from time to time. In 1829 the management at the mill attempted to reduce the wages in the weaving department where she worked. The women came out on strike and "bound themselves under an obligation not to go back into the mill, until the former prices were restored." The women organized protest parades wearing a common uniform – "black silk dresses, red shawls, and green calashes" – and at a

[15] The major autobiographical, biographical and periodical sources for this analysis are cited elsewhere in these notes. For a husband-and-wife team who organized their own sect see the account of Jeremiah and Almira Bullock of Limington, Maine in Helen Coffin Beedy, *Mothers of Maine* (Portland, Me, 1895), pp. 338–39 and *The Morning Star* (Limerick, Me), 31 Aug. 1836.

[16] Harriet Livermore, *A Narrative of Religious Experience in Twelve Letters* (Concord, N.H., 1826); Rebecca I. Davis, *Gleanings from the Merrimac Valley* (Portland, Me, 1881), pp. 13–34; S. T. Livermore, *Harriet Livermore* (Hartford, Ct, 1884). See also Towle, *Vicissitudes*, pp. 1–20.

[17] Gideon A. Burgess and John T. Ward, *Free Baptist Cyclopedia, Historical and Biographical* (N.P., 1889), p. 148.

strike meeting, Lincoln, who was already an experienced preacher, addressed the workers "at considerable length, on the subject of their wrongs." The strike was eventually broken, but Salome Lincoln refused to give in, and sought employment elsewhere. An interesting sidelight on class relationships at this time is provided by the fact that in her next job in a mill ten miles away, Salome Lincoln boarded with her employer, who admired her as a devoted Christian and a corrective influence on some of his other female employees "who were very rude."[18] Finally there were black women preachers such as Jarena Lee, a domestic servant, who acquired literacy in the household of her first employer whom she had joined at the age of seven.[19] Thus the socio-economic background of American women preachers reflected a society with a much greater proportion of small farmers and propertied artisans than Britain, and with class lines less clearly drawn. Often coming from rural, lower-class backgrounds, British women preachers sometimes faced physical violence, especially in communities which resented their attacks on popular local customs, and where neither squire nor parson offered much protection and occasionally encouraged the mob. In New England, violence against women preachers was very uncommon, although they frequently faced ridicule and verbal abuse. Many of the American women were familiar with long hard work on the farm or in the mills but, unless they were black, they rarely experienced the desperate poverty which was the lot of so many of those amongst whom British women preachers laboured. Having spent three months in southern England in 1829, Nancy Towle refused the request of her many friends to extend her preaching to the North, and returned to the United States. "The cruel oppression and distress of this land, I could not endure."[20]

Since the Great Awakening, women had taken a prominent part in prayer meetings, special services and revivals among New England Congregationalists, but in autobiographies and memoirs of pious women it was regularly stressed that, although passionately anxious to promote the Lord's work, such women remained subordinate to their pastors, and did not stray beyond their proper "sphere" which did not include preaching to mixed or "promiscuous" audiences.[21] At the height of a

[18] Almond H. Davis, *The Female Preacher*, pp. 20–26 and 49–53.
[19] Jarena Lee, pp. 1–5.
[20] Towle, pp. 88–89; Thomas Russell, *Record of Events in Primitive Methodism* (London, 1869); Hugh McLeod, *Religion and the Working Class in Nineteenth Century Britain* (London, 1984), pp. 26–29.
[21] *An Account of the Late Success of the Gospel in the Province of New York, North America*

revival, however, the clear lines of demarcation between the sexes became blurred, even among middle-class Calvinists. In Newport, Rhode Island, Sarah Osborn, a highly regarded local schoolteacher and organizer of women's religious work, became the central figure in a revival among slaves and young people in the mid-1760s. They crowded her house for special meetings, where she read to them from selected books and the Scriptures, or gave them individual advice. Mrs. Osborn proceeded with great caution, insisting that all who attended her meetings had the permission of masters or parents, behaved in an orderly fashion and retired at a reasonable hour, but she was still unhappy with her role. "She trembled with fear that if she encouraged their meetings at her home, it would be going beyond her sphere." She persevered in the work but remained anxious, "fearing to go beyond her line as a woman" and insisted that all formal preaching was undertaken by her minister.[22] In later Congregationalist revivals the same lines were drawn, but women with Sarah Osborn's type of experience in organizing evangelistic and charitable societies sometimes found it difficult to restrain their enthusiasm although they often apologized profusely at a later date if, at the height of a revival meeting, they spoke at length before a mixed audience.[23]

Although there were restrictions on women's religious roles in denominations with a highly educated ministry, clear structure of worship and deep suspicion of excitement, noise or physical prostrations in religious services, distinctions between the sexes often broke down completely among Methodists, "New Lights," Freewill Baptists, Christians and other enthusiastic sects in frontier settlements where settled ministers were lacking. The brief career of the Maine Methodist Fanny Newell illustrates this, and also the fluidity between denominational boundaries and practices, and the difficulty of distinguishing between praying in public, exhorting or urging sinners to repentance, and preaching, which in these circumstances

---

Contained in Letters from the Rev. Messrs. Buel, Hazard and Prime (Coventry, 1765), pp. 6–7; *Familiar Letters written by Mrs. Sarah Osborn and Miss Susanna Anthony* (Newport, R.I., 1807); Samuel Hopkins, *Memoirs of the Life of Mrs. Sarah Osborn* (Worcester, Mass, 1799).

[22] Hopkins, pp. 76–83.

[23] See Cott, *The Bonds of Womanhood*, pp 126–32, and Mary P. Ryan, "A Woman's Awakening: Revivalist Religion in Utica, New York, 1800–1835," *American Quarterly*, 30, No. 5 (1978), 602–23, for women and revivals after 1800. For the breakdown of gender divisions and later female embarrassment see Nathaniel Bouton. *Memoir of Mrs. Elizabeth McFarland* (Concord, N.H., 1838), pp. 269–71. Elizabeth McFarland was the widow of the principal Congregational minister in Concord and very prominent in female missionary and charitable societies.

often consisted not of a formal address but an impassioned harangue that could be heard for miles around. Fanny Newell was born in Maine in 1793, and after many spiritual wanderings joined the Methodists in 1808. In her spiritual quest she was much influenced by the Quaker preacher Thankful Hussey, and also by the Baptist practice, Newell's membership of the Methodists being marked by her baptism by total immersion. The following year, 1809, she married the circuit minister and became closely associated with his work: "After the preaching I felt such an impression to speak, that I did not dare to neglect it; but rose and exhorted the people, and had great liberty in so doing."[24] Although a child was born within a year of her marriage, Fanny Newell continued to exhort in various frontier circuits in Maine and Vermont. People came to meetings because they had heard "that the preacher's wife sometimes exhorted the people." She also engaged in the more familiar female roles of house-to-house visitation and the conducting of class meetings. After her death her autobiography became very popular and offered yet another model of the pious life to its readers.[25] Female exhorters like Fanny Newell although not commonly married to a minister were numerous among Methodists and other sects, and many pious individuals attributed their conversion not to a well-known minister or male evangelist, but to some obscure female exhorter.[26]

Fanny Newell was an enthusiast, but she accepted the doctrines and discipline of the Methodist Episcopal Church. Women converts among the New Lights and their Baptist and Christian successors were more dismissive of man-made order and government in the church. Among Nova Scotia New Lights in the early 1790s women played a major role in the "New Dispensationalism" which challenged ministerial authority. The preacher John Payzant reported extraordinary scenes:

> Mrs R: rose against all the orders of the Church, and that they were but outward forms and Contrary to the Spirit of God. These novelties in the Church caused many to follow the same examples, which made much trouble in the Church. Some time I conversed with Mrs R: on the subject. She told me that she had been seen by the Spirit of God, that Baptism and the Lord Supper, with all the Disciples,

[24] *Memoirs of Fanny Newell Written by Herself* (Springfield, Mass., 1833), 3rd ed. The quotation is on p. 83.

[25] Ibid., pp. 84–145.

[26] Stephen Allen and W. H. Pilsbury, *History of Methodism in Maine* (Augusta, Me, 1887), p. 237; John Stewart, *Highways and Hedges: or Fifty Years of Western Methodism* (Cincinnati, 1872), pp. 114–16; *Sketches of the Life and Times of Eld. Ariel Kendrick Written by Himself* (Windsor, Vt, 1850), p. 30.

of the Church, was contrary to the Spirit of God and his Gospel, and that Marriage was from the Divel. That she was determined to live sapate [separate] from her Husband, for it was as much a sin for her to have children by him as by any other man and she said that there were many who would follow her in it...I begged her not to advance such sentiments...She answered that I knew nothing of them therefore that I would not be proper Judge, for her mind had gone farther in these things, than mine.[27]

Support for these doctrines with their condemnation of marriage spread around the province and were echoed in New England, where New Lights joined the celibate Shakers.[28] In Nova Scotia the Regular or Calvinist Baptists gradually succeeded in imposing their own, more conventional beliefs on the majority of the scattered New Light congregations, but it was a slow struggle and some refused to follow their path.[29] A decade or more later women took a prominent part in challenging Harris Harding, originally an enthusiastic supporter of the "New Dispensationalism," but now seen as slipping into formalism. Women took particular exception to Harding's refusal to preach against frills, ruffles and adornments in dress, and kept up a prolonged campaign against him.

They attacked their minister in public, and openly contradicted him. They ascended the pulpit – even the sisters, in the heat of their inspiration, stood at his side and commanded him to hold his peace... Then these people would collect their finery, and commit it to the flames. Some would even take their crockery and china-ware from their shelves, and bury them. They would enter into minute confession of their sins before promiscuous assemblages... and parade the streets, exclaiming, "Behold the Bridegroom cometh."[30]

Although John Payzant had battled with the formidable "Mrs. R." in the 1790s, his Liverpool, Nova Scotia congregation remained in the New

[27] Brian C. Cuthbertson ed., *The Journal of the Reverend John Payzant 1749–1834* (Hantsport, N.S., 1981), p. 44.

[28] Marini, *Radical Sects*, p. 93; C. C. Goen, *Revivalism and Separatism in New England, 1740–1800: Strict Congregationalists and Separate Baptists in the Great Awakening* (1962 reprint edition, Hamden, Conn., 1969), pp. 200–02 shows the strength of the antinomian tradition in New England, but he writes in terms of "lawless elements" and ignores the roles of women.

[29] Rawlyck, "From New Light to Baptist," p. 21. Nova Scotia Baptists gained enormously in social standing with the conversion of a group of prominent Anglicans in 1827. This group played an important role in the foundation of a Baptist college. See Reginald V. Harris, *The Church of Saint Paul in Halifax, Nova Scotia: 1749–1949* (Toronto, 1949), p. 172. Yet the English Wesleyan missionary Charles Churchill could still detect "deeply rooted Antinomian prejudice" in western Nova Scotia in the late 1830s. See Charles Churchill, *Memorials of Missionary Life in Nova Scotia* (London, 1845), p. 37.

[30] John Davies, *Life and Times of the Late Rev. Harris Harding* (Charlottestown, P.E.I., 1866), p. 102.

Light tradition, and in 1821 the emotional style of worship of the women distressed the Regular Baptist leader, Edward Manning.

> No sooner was I seated than a young Woman whom I knew not screamed out, and a number below [he was in the gallery], all females, a melancholy sound to me, because I thought there was such an extravagancy of Voice, and such uncommon gesticulations, leaving their seats, running round the broad Isle, Swinging their Arms... Stretching their hands out right and left, then stretching them up as high as they could... I hope they are good, but truly wish they were more orderly.[31]

When Nancy Towle came to Nova Scotia a few years later, however, she felt quite at home with Payzant's people and among Harding's former followers, who had largely become Christians or "Arminian Baptists." With a letter of introduction from American Christian leaders she toured the province preaching and encouraging women as well as men to pray and exhort at her services.[32]

Whether exhorters or preachers, women were moved by a fierce religious conviction and sense of calling. Yet they did not undertake to challenge social convention lightly, especially as hostile ministers kept up a battery of criticism using Paul's injunction to the Corinthians as their favourite text: "Let your women keep silence in the churches: for it is not permitted unto them to speak... And if they will learn any thing, let them ask their husbands at home: for it is a shame for women to speak in the church."[33] Given the nature of the contemplatory religious culture with its strong biblical literalism, it was inevitable that women preachers were driven to defend themselves by the extended citation of Scriptural texts. Deborah Pierce, for example, wrote *A Scriptural Vindication of Female Preaching, Prophesying and Exhortation*, and Harriet Livermore wrote at even greater length exhibiting "every instance recorded in Scripture of God's

[31] *Journal of Edward Manning*, MS, 2 Sept. 1821, Acadia University Library, Wolfville, N.S.

[32] Towle, *Vicissitudes*, pp. 56–60; Davis, *The Female Preacher*, p. 103. Elias Smith, one of the founders of the Christians, was writing to the Maritimes as early as 1801. See Smith to Edward Manning, Portsmouth, N.H., 29 Oct. 1801, *Correspondence of Edward Manning*, MS, Acadia University Library, Wolfville, N.S. The Quaker evangelist Joseph Hoag found popular and able women preachers among the New Lights in the St. John river valley of New Brunswick and Maine around 1801, but their employment produced much controversy and was linked by many to the rejection of a paid ministry. See Joseph Hoag, *Journal of the Life of Joseph Hoag* (London, 1862), pp. 88–105.

[33] See, for example, Bouton, *Memoir of Elizabeth McFarland*, p. 271. By the 1830s the evangelist Charles Finney's technique of encouraging women to pray in mixed audiences had further alarmed conservatives already worried by women preachers. See Lois A. Boyd and R. Douglas Brackenridge, *Presbyterian Women in America: Two Centuries of a Quest for Status* (Westport, Ct, 1983), pp. 93–4.

special notice and regard to my sex." Salome Lincoln stressed the text "Woe to me, if I preach not the gospel," and most of the women pointed to *Joel* 11, v. 28: "I will pour out my spirit upon all flesh; and your sons and your daughters shall prophesy."[34] Other favoured texts included "There is neither Jew nor Greek, there is neither male nor female, for your are all one in Christ Jesus." Harriet Livermore in her *Scriptural Evidence in Favour of Female Testimony* went so far as to place MALE and FEMALE in heavy capitals to emphasize her point. Other women pointed to the fact that it was a woman who first preached that Christ had risen.[35]

They all emphasized both publicly and privately the overwhelming compulsion of their calling and yet the fear and dread which it produced in them. Deborah Pierce was "tormented by day and night" lest she publicly disgrace the cause of Christ, but was sustained in her sense of vocation to preach by a vision of Christ on the Cross. Other women wrote at length on the same theme.[36] Alongside Scriptural argument women preachers showed a shrewd understanding of the societal pressures which worked against them and worked hard to counter these. They emphasized that female preaching was unpopular and unacceptable because it was not the custom of the more socially prominent denominations which still took their social conventions from England.[37] Women preachers also argued that the key verses in Corinthians were deliberately misconstrued and used by men to make "still more degraded" woman's social position. Woman had been "taught for ages to understand herself but a *subordinate being*...and hence merely *passive*," without the independence which men possessed to work in their chosen sphere.[38] Given this history of

[34] Deborah Pierce, *A Scriptural Vindication of Female Preaching, Prophesying and Exhortation* (Auburn, N.Y., 1817); Almond H. Davis, *The Female Preacher*, pp. 12–17; Zilpha Elaw, *Memoirs of the Life, Religious Experience and Ministerial Travels...of Mrs. Zilpha Elaw, an American Female of Colour* (London, 1846), pp. 114ff.

[35] Harriet Livermore, *Scriptural Evidence*, p. 17; Pierce, p. 12; Jarena Lee, *Religious Experience*, p. 11.

[36] Pierce, pp. 3–4; Almond H. Davis, p. 38. So severely was Salome Lincoln's mind exercised on the subject of her call to preach that she wished herself damned rather than face the ordeal of a public ministry. Of course, many women succumbed to social pressures. In frontier New Brunswick, Mary Coy was converted in 1787 at the age of sixteen. As she readily admitted "if it were customary for females to preach the gospel, how gladly would I engage in the employment." Mary felt "much shame and confusion" over the conflict between her "calling" and the restrictions placed on women. See "Mary Bradley's Reminiscences: a domestic life in colonial New Brunswick," *Atlantis*, 7 (Fall 1981), 92–101. This consists of extracts from Mary Bradley's rare autobiography published in Boston in 1849 with a perceptive commentary. I owe this reference to Dr Susan O'Brien.

[37] Almond H. Davis, pp. 13–14.

[38] Towle, pp. 252–53.

oppression women preachers felt the need not only to find Scriptural evidence in their defence, but to rediscover their own history, and they wrote at length about female preachers and religious activists since the seventeenth century. Quaker and Methodist history provided powerful strands here, but the women were ecumenical in their quest for precedents and exemplars. Later women were attracted to the Freewill Baptists and Christians because of their defence and support of women preachers.[39]

The relationship of women preachers with the different sects varied, especially as local and regional church organization and practice was still very fluid. Some converts were baptized by itinerants and met informally for years before forming an official congregation. Ministers were loosely attached to congregations, itinerated over wide areas and shifted from one sect to another. Baptist, Methodist and Quaker practices were often mixed, while the rise of the Christians indicates the popularity of the quest for "primitive Christianity."[40] Titles of organizations, practices and ministerial status varied from group to group and over time. Many claimed the right to exhort or preach, and licensing systems were often resisted as an infringement on individual Christian liberty.[41] Most of the women preachers did not seek ordination, and some accepted that only men should celebrate the gospel ordinances of Baptism and the Lord's supper.[42] Yet women were occasionally listed or mentioned as Elders or ordained ministers, and certainly many held pastoral responsibility for preaching, organizing churches, making reports to regional meetings and acting as delegates to conferences.[43] Most of these women were licensed, and listed

[39] Harriet Livermore, *Scriptural Evidence*, pp. 85–110; Jarena Lee, p. 38.

[40] Ruth D. Bordin, "The Sect to Denomination Process in America: the Freewill Baptist experience," *Church History*, 34 (1965), 77–94; Wesley Bailey, "Reformed Methodist Church" in I. Daniel Rupp, ed., *An Original History of the Religious Denominations at Present Existing in the United States* (Philadelphia, 1844), pp. 466–68; Whitney R. Cross, *The Burned-Over District*, p. 16; Roland Sawyer, *The History of Kensington, New Hampshire, 1663–1945* (Farmington, Me, 1946), pp. 162–70. Sawyer had access to records of the local Christian church of which Harriet Livermore was a founder member. Almond H. Davis, pp. 40–41, shows Salome Lincoln moving easily between Reformed Methodists and Freewill Baptists. See also Hoag, pp. 88–89.

[41] A. Jones, *Memoir of Elder Abner Jones* (Boston, 1842), pp. 76–81; *Minutes of the General Conference of the Freewill Baptist Connection for 1832* (Dover, N.H., 1859), p. 80; Allen and Pilsbury, *Methodism in Maine*, pp. 235–72 and passim show numerous schisms by local preachers defending the right to preach, "shout" and teach extreme perfectionist doctrines.

[42] Harriet Livermore, *Scriptural Evidence*, p. 120.

[43] *Christian Herald*, 2 (Portsmouth, N.H.), 27 Nov. 1819; *Morning Star*, 7 Aug. and 11 Sept. 1829; I. Stewart, *History of the Freewill Baptists for Half a Century* (Dover, N.H., 1862), pp. 190–91; Burgess and Ward, *Free Baptist Cyclopedia*, pp. 56–57.

as unordained preachers, assistant preachers, or "female laborers in Christ." In some areas of New England and New York, they made up between 1 and 5 percent of Freewill Baptist or Christian preachers, although the impact of their work might be greater than these numbers suggest.[44] The predominant role of women preachers, however, was as itinerant evangelists, often without pastoral responsibility, and the more famous preachers like Clarissa Danforth, Nancy Towle and Harriet Livermore specialized in this work, moving between the Freewill Baptists, Christians and a wide range of Methodist sects as opportunity occurred.

Other roles of women in the government and life of the churches were equally varied and uncertain. The Freewill Baptists were still struggling with the problem in the 1840s. In 1830, their General Conference had ruled that women should be in subjection to male members, and the official weekly newspaper pontificated that:

> in *church meetings* for the transaction of the *business* of the church, women should be silent, they should learn in obedience – they should not be meddling with those affairs which are peculiarly designed for the transaction of men; at any rate, they should not usurp authority over the men.[45]

Yet fourteen years later the General Conference was asked to rule on whether females could move and carry important votes in the church against male members. Of course, Conference ruled in favour of the men, but it suggests the difference between official policy and grassroots practice.[46] Many local congregations with a preponderance of women were still informal gatherings with grave doubts about the need for a separate paid ministry, ministerial education and "literary improvements" or the exclusion from the pulpit of those whom Conference authority decided were not "qualified as scripture directs."[47]

The careers of some women preachers are well documented, but others,

[44] *Christian Herald*, 5, 22 Aug. 1822 for the term "female laborers in Christ." The same magazine listed women preachers as "unordained preachers." The Freewill Baptists also used the term "female laborers." Such women were licenced or "approbated" by their quarterly meetings. Estimates of the percentages of women preachers are taken from reports in Conference Minutes and magazines cited above.

[45] *The Morning Star*, 1 Sept. 1830.

[46] *Minutes of the General Conference of the Freewill Baptist Connection for 1844* (Dover, N.H., 1859), p. 237.

[47] *Minutes of the General Conference of the Freewill Baptist Connection for 1832* (Dover, N.H., 1859), p. 32 sets out these issues, but they kept recurring for the next decade and a half. See, for example, *Minutes of the General Conference of the Freewill Baptist Connection for 1847* (Dover, N.H., 1859), p. 260 for references to a secession movement in Maine opposed to the official *Morning Star* and the establishment of a biblical school.

though major figures, remain shadowy.[48] Many travelled with a group of women friends, or with a close female companion. Such friends plus the network of other women preachers reinforced sisterhood and presented some defence against the "severe trials" which the women constantly faced.[49] Young men and women preachers did travel and preach together, but the women were usually accompanied by a "pious friend" or "attendant" to avoid any suggestion of impropriety. Men and women could be mutually supportive. Some men, recognizing the women's "fervent love for Zion" and their skill as preachers, were also aware that "popular prejudice against female preaching" produced additional problems and tensions for their women companions.[50]

Whether working on the frontier or in older settled regions the women set themselves punishing schedules, preaching six or eight times a week for months on end. Sermons were often an hour or two long, and the meetings hot and crowded. These women also wrote regularly to friends and to the religious press, kept diaries and journals, and defended their right to preach verbally and in print.[51] They travelled long distances on foot and horseback, by coach and boat. Male preachers undertook the same routine, but without the constant questioning of the legitimacy of their role, which proved so trying for the women. Many of the women were frontier circuit riders as heroic as the better known men like Peter Cartwright.[52] For years, for example, the Christian press carried reports of the work of Sister Sarah Hodges and Elder Abigail Roberts in western New York. Sarah Hodges lost one horse to a thunderbolt, but the people quickly contributed ten dollars for a replacement to send her on her way.[53]

[48] Nancy Towle regarded Elice (Miller) Smith as the most admired female preacher in America, but I have discovered little more than passing reference to her. See Towle, *Vicissitudes*, pp. 196–200.

[49] Almond H. Davis, p. 65; Towle, pp. 53–95; Dorothy Ripley, *The Bank of Faith and Work United* (Philadelphia, 1819), p. 63. See also Carroll Smith Rosenberg, "The female world of love and ritual: relations between women in nineteenth century America" *Signs*, I (1975), 1–29.

[50] David Marks, *Life of David Marks... by Himself* (Limerick, Me, 1831), pp. 182–85; Abel Thornton, *The Life of Elder Abel Thornton*... (Providence, R.I.), pp. 110–28.

[51] Towle, p. 45 reports Susan Hume undertaking a tour of 3,000 miles around New York state, and p. 239 gives her own preaching schedule. Jarena Lee's *Journal* and press reports of Clarissa Danforth indicate constant travelling and preaching.

[52] For Cartwright and the male tradition see his *Autobiography*, which first appeared in 1856 and went through numerous editions. See also Donald E. Byrne, Jr., *No Foot of Land: Folklore of American Methodist Itinerants* (Metuchen, N.J., 1975).

[53] *Christian Herald* (Portsmouth, N.H.), the magazine of the Christian Connection, carried reports of women preachers in New York state from the first volume in 1818 through

Abigail Roberts' work was widely admired, as this report in the *Gospel Luminary* suggests: "In this country [western New York] we saw the fruit of Abigail Roberts' labours, for here she has been very useful. No candid person can travel through this region and see the fruits of this sister's labours and dispute the propriety of female testimony."[54] Martha Spalding, an unordained preacher, built up a circuit of eight churches in the Stanstead district of Quebec, just over the line from Vermont. She was typical of women preachers who moved back and forth across the Canadian border. The black preacher, Jarena Lee, who was mostly active in the Mid-Atlantic states, undertook one preaching tour as far as Ontario, and her *Journal* is very much a record of her extensive travels. Zilpha Elaw preached throughout the northeast, travelling as far as northern Maine and western New York. She also preached in the South, where she was threatened with enslavement, although a free Black, and harassed like all women ministers.[55] Blacks and whites worked closely together. Clarissa Danforth was converted by Charles Bowles, a black Freewill Baptist, and they sometimes preached in tandem, "a colored man and a woman preaching in the same town on the same day" creating great popular interest.[56] Salome Lincoln often preached in "African" chapels as did Ruth Watkins, an immigrant Englishwoman.[57] Another English immigrant, Dorothy Ripley, felt a special call to preach to the blacks, and travelled in the free and slave states in the course of her work.[58] Many women preachers were pioneer abolitionists, and among the Methodists they were later attracted to the Wesleyan Methodist Church because of its determined stand against slavery.[59]

---

the 1820s. The report on Sarah Hodge's horse is in Vol. 6 (31 July 1823). See also Mark Fernald, *Life of Elder Mark Fernald Written by Himself* (Newburyport, Mass., 1852), p. 201 for Sarah Hodges preaching at the New York Christian Conference of 1827.

54 *Gospel Luminary* quoted in *Christian Herald*, 27 Jan. 1825.

55 *The Morning Star*, 7 Aug. and 11 Sept. 1829; *Freewill Baptist Magazine* (Providence, R.I.), 3 (June 1829); Towle, *Vicissitudes*, pp. 45–60; *Minutes of the Stanstead Freewill Baptist Quarterly Meeting*, MS, 3 Feb. 1828, Wilbur Collection, University of Vermont; Jarena Lee, p. 49; Elaw, *Memoirs*, pp. 61–107.

56 John Lewis, *The Life, Labors and Travels of Elder Charles Bowles* (Watertown, Mass., 1852), pp. 30–33.

57 Almond H. Davis, p. 104; *The Primitive Methodist Magazine* (Bemersley), N.S. 1 (April 1830).

58 George, *Segregated Sabbaths*, pp. 128–29 gives a rather misleading and dismissive account of Ripley, whose own account, *The Bank of Faith and Work United*, 2nd edn (Whitby, 1822), pp. 187–303 shows how extensive were her travels in the free and slave states.

59 Almond H. Davis, p. 104; Lee, p. 72; Burgess and Ward, *Free Baptist Cyclopedia*, pp. 567–68; McLeister and Nicholson, *History of Wesleyan Methodist Church*, pp. 1–44;

Women like Abigail Roberts, Martha Spalding or Almira Bullock of Maine were well known in their sects, but they tended to restrict their evangelistic or pastoral work to one locality. This was probably the case with the majority of the women preachers, but a few like Nancy Towle, Clarissa Danforth, Harriet Livermore and Dorothy Ripley came close to being full-time evangelists and attracted widespread attention in an era when American revivalism was becoming increasingly professionalized.[60] During revivalistic periods like the 1820s, these women were particularly active and in the public eye, but for many, evangelism was a full-time activity even when popular interest declined. Danforth, for example, was a major figure among Freewill Baptists and Christians in New England. Her work was discussed at length in contemporary autobiographies and memoirs, where it was agreed that she possessed "extraordinary talents."[61] John Colby, a great revivalist himself, was among the first to publicize her work in successive editions of his popular *Life, Experiences and Travels*:

> It is generally allowed, that there never has been a preacher through these parts, that called out such multitudes, as went to hear her. Nor was this the only good effect, which was experienced from her preaching, for there was a glorious revival of the work of the Lord in almost every town, where she preached. The High Sheriff of this county was among the first of her converts.[62]

From Vermont and New Hampshire her reputation spread to southern New England, and the religious press carried lengthy reports of her campaigns. Although many turned out to hear her from curiosity, she made many converts and widespread revivals occurred. During much of 1819 she was in Rhode Island, and press reports and her own letters suggest that she was a skilled evangelist familiar with many of the classic techniques for bringing sinners to repentance.[63] Later campaigns followed,

---

True Wesleyan (Boston), 2 (1 June 1844). The latter was the magazine of the anti-slavery Wesleyan Methodist Church and a useful source on women preachers in that sect.

60 The standard histories of American revivalism ignore women preachers during this period. Timothy L. Smith, *Revivalism and Social Reform in Mid-Nineteenth-Century America* (New York, 1957) has an excellent discussion of the career of Phoebe Palmer, but she was a much more bourgeois figure comparable in many ways to the mid-Victorian British women preachers considered by Olive Anderson in "Women Preachers in mid-Victorian Britain: Some Reflections of Feminism, Popular Religion and Social Change," *Historical Journal*, 12 (1969), 467–84.

61 Lewis, pp. 30–3; Towle, pp. 19–36; Marks, p. 177; Thornton, pp. 14–18; Harriet Livermore, *Narrative of Religious Experience*, p. 209; Fernald, pp. 145–61.

62 John Colby, *The Life, Experiences and Travels of John Colby* (Portland, Me, 1815), pp. 58–59. Another edition appeared in 1819 and there were issues through 1820.

63 See the reports and letters cited in *The Religious Informer*, especially the issue for February 1820.

back in northern New England where "the anxiety of the people [was] so great to hear her" that it was difficult to find sufficiently large buildings.[64] Susan Humes, Nancy Towle and Harriet Livermore achieved similar successes and their activities were widely reported. Towle and Livermore were among a group of women who conducted a revival in Portsmouth, New Hampshire, in the Friends' Meeting House, Town Hall and schools, but there was a flood of opposition in this former capital and major seaport of the state until they received backing from the Christians.[65]

Women preachers, like their male counterparts, differed in their personal manner and style of delivery. The women, however, were a comparatively small and closely bound group, and it is evident that in time certain qualities in a woman preacher came to be admired. Unfortunately we have little evidence before the second decade of the nineteenth century, but from critics' reports it would appear that in the earlier period women as well as men cultivated an ecstatic style of repetitive, extempore preaching that resulted in converts shouting, screaming and rolling on the ground.[66] By the time more evidence appears some Freewill Baptists and Christians were moving away from these traditions, although preaching remained extempore. Reports stressed that the most admired women preachers like Clarissa Danforth adopted this more dignified style. She was frequently described as a controlled speaker using simple language and gestures. Other women were reported as having voices which were clear and full, but not boisterous, and with a pulpit manner that was deliberate and unsensational.[67] Almira Bullock was remembered as having a fine physique, clear and persuasive voice, and showing good ability in scriptural exposition.[68] Sometimes, however, an older style is indicated. In open-air

[64] *The Religious Informer*, 1 (March 1821).

[65] For Humes see Marks, pp. 182–5; Thornton, pp. 110–28, and her obituary in the *Freewill Baptist Magazine*, 1 (August 1827). For Towle, and Livermore in addition to their own writings already cited, the *Christian Herald* and *Morning Star* carry reports of their work during the 1820s. For example the *Morning Star* (26 Apr. 1827), reprinted an account of Livermore which described her as "the eloquent and gifted female preacher."

[66] Marini, *Radical Sects*, pp. 40–59; Sawyer, *History of Kensington*, p. 163. Alexander Crawford to Edward Manning, Yarmouth, N.S., 2 Oct. 1813, *Correspondence of Edward Manning*, MS, Acadia University, Wolfville, N.S. Crawford, a visiting Scot, was highly critical of Harris Harding, who preached only "to arouse passions" and was obsessed with dreams and visions. Ephraim Stinchfield, *Some Memoirs of the Life, Experience, and Labors of Elder Ephraim Stinchfield* (Portland, Me, 1819) gives a good impression of New Light preaching from 1781.

[67] Burgess and Ward, pp. 16 and 148; *Christian Herald*, 1 (Mar. 1819).

[68] Beedy, *Mothers of Maine*, p. 338; John Stevens, *Memoir of the Life and Character of the Rev. John Stevens* (Dover, N.H., 1878), p. 8.

meetings Almira Bullock could be sensationally loud, and in Susan Humes' and Nancy Towle's revival meetings their style was emotional.[69] Many of the women developed a professional persona which might contrast with their usual personality. Salome Lincoln was "reserved and retiring in manner" until she entered the pulpit, when, "warmed up in the spirit," this reserve entirely disappeared.[70] Among the Freewill Baptists and Christians the best of the women preachers were favourably compared with the men, and women were often chosen to give key addresses at services held in conjunction with local and regional conferences of church delegates.[71]

Since the women were extempore preachers few of their sermons survive. From an occasional outline taken down by a listener or recorded in the press it is evident that they followed contemporary practice in setting out the main points with clear divisions.[72] Commentators were anxious to stress that though the women preached from the heart they showed clearness of reasoning and sound argument, and male reporters seemed almost surprised that the women had a logical structure to their discourses.[73] Being primarily evangelists, sermons and texts focussed heavily on themes of repentance, conversion and holy living. Given their religious fervour and also the bitter criticism and opposition which they faced, many women were attracted to apocalyptic and often feminist themes. Nancy Towle looked for the Lord to raise up "a host of female warriors" to bring in the Lord's Kingdom, and Harriet Livermore longed for a feminist millennium: "How long, O Lord, how long, ere women shall be clothed with the Sun, walk upon the moon, and be crowned with Apostolic glory."[74] As with the members of Harris Harding's congregation, many women preachers were especially attracted to the image of Christ as the Bridegroom, and spoke with rapture on the text "Behold the Bridegroom cometh; go ye out to meet him." The image of woman as the Bride of

[69] Beedy, p. 339; Marks, pp. 180–5; Towle, pp. 42–44; Thornton, p. 114.

[70] Almond H. Davis, *The Female Preacher*, p. 44.

[71] Ibid., pp. 45–46; John Buzzell, ed., *A Religious Magazine*, 2 (Kennebunk, Me), Nov. 1820 and Aug. 1821; *Freewill Baptist Magazine*, 1, Sept. 1829.

[72] See, for example, Almond H. Davis, pp. 85–86, and the *Religious Informer*, 1 (July 1821), which gives the main headings of a sermon by Clarissa Danforth.

[73] Even Davis in his sympathetic memoir of Salome Lincoln felt obliged to stress that she was a clear and logical preacher. Towle, *Vicissitudes* gives many examples of male hostility and anger that women were often superior preachers to the local ministers.

[74] Harriet Livermore, *A Narrative of the Religious Experience*, p. 17. See also her *Scriptural Evidence*, p. 115 for female preaching as a sign of the millennium. Towle, pp. 12–13, and the *Religious Informer*, 1 (July 1821) echo the same theme.

Christ had a powerful grip upon their imaginations, as it did upon those of the Shakers and the English millenarian, Joanna Southcott.[75] Of course this was not their only theme, though a popular one, and Christ was also presented as the Great Highway or the Great Liberator.

In dress, the women favoured a plain style much influenced by Quakerism. Salome Lincoln's clothes were "plain, yet tasty", with a good judgment in colours.[76] Almira Bullock dressed Quaker-like, but changed her bonnet for a little cap without ribbons on entering the pulpit.[77] Nancy Towle and Zilpha Elaw moved much among the Quakers and the British Methodist sects, which favoured simplicity and expected their preachers to set an example.[78] By the mid-1820s some women preachers felt that this plain style, which had once been the mark of "free salvation" churches, was passing in favour of more "Babylonish garments," and Harriet Livermore was prominent in attacks on this change. Livermore preferred cleanliness, neatness and simplicity in the dress of converted women, a view shared by her colleagues.[79] However, Livermore strengthened her own reputation for eccentricity or "affection of singularity," and brought down on herself a barrage of criticism from church members as well as the worldly. Her act of deviance was to crop her hair and wear it short and brushed forward.

Despite such "singularity," the women preachers in general were very conscious of being labelled as deviants – "a female preacher was a spectacle." Harriet Livermore was constantly viewed as a lunatic, "a kind of gentle, inoffensive crazy woman," an attitude perpetuated by at least one recent historian.[80] Other women were accused of sensation seeking, hysteria, financial greed, and deliberate fraud. Suggestions of sexual irregularities dogged their footsteps.[81] More than one young woman was

[75] Almond H. Davis, pp. 47–48; John Davis, p. 102; Andrews, *The People Called Shakers*, p. 22; James K. Hopkins, *A Woman to Deliver Her People: Joanna Southcott and English Millenarianism in an Era of Revolution* (Austin, Texas, 1982), p. 19; Elaw, *Memoirs*, p. 74.

[76] Almond H. Davis, p. 21, and portrait opposite title page.

[77] Beedy, p. 338. Jarena Lee wore a white bonnet tied under the chin; see portrait in Lee, *Religious Experience*.

[78] Towle, p. 73; Elaw, pp. 143–47; Thomas Shaw, *The Bible Christians* (London, 1965), p. 15, and the photograph of Mary Thorne, 1807–83, facing page 69.

[79] Harriet Livermore, *A Narrative of the Religious Experience*, pp. 259–62.

[80] Ibid., pp. 269–72, and *Scriptural Evidence*, p. 9. For an unsympathetic view of Livermore which fails to relate her to the wider "sisterhood" of preachers see Elizabeth F. Hoxie, "Harriet Livermore" in Edward T. James, ed., *Notable American Women 1607–1950: A Biographical Dictionary* (Cambridge, Mass., 1974), 2, 409–10.

[81] Dorothy Ripley, *The Bank of Faith*, 1819 edn, pp. 55–63; Towle, p. 227; *Morning Star*, 2 Aug. 1837. Marks, *Life*, p. 184 and Almond H. Davis, pp. 40–43 both stressed the

disowned when she started to preach, and many felt family pressures to conform to a more conventional way of life.[82] Coming from a prominent family and having had a good education Harriet Livermore was particularly subject to this type of pressure. Friends became hostile when she started to attend Freewill Baptist meetings in a barn, and horrified when she commenced to preach. She felt drawn to a preaching career among the Freewillers and Christians, who gave her encouragement, but family opposition suggested an alternative career: "I had ever considered a school-teacher's lot very honorable; and I knew that a female preacher was lightly esteemed in this day, therefore thought I, on account of my relations and friends in nature's bonds, I will endeavour to be respectable."[83] Livermore quickly gave up her school, driven by her deep compulsion to be a preacher, but the public was more appalled by her defiance of convention in cutting her hair, an act which Livermore felt obliged to defend at some length. Her defence is important as an indication of some conventional constraints on women and was to be repeated by later generations of female activists in many spheres. Her hair, which was a yard and a quarter long, was dressed in a conventional manner with the assistance of servants or family. Once she was converted and began to travel, preach and write, moving frequently across the northeast from New York to Maine, she found the dressing and wearing of this mass of hair a hopeless inconvenience. Livermore claimed that from her childhood her hair had made her prone to headaches, but once a preacher, it became an intolerable nuisance:

> My comfort, ease and convenience, appeared to me far more desirable than appearance in travelling... I have never felt a sensation even of momentary regret at the loss of my hair, nor in any *place* or situation, public or social, the least ashamed of its odd appearance. My head is far more comfortable without it.

Livermore was seen in many quarters to compound her crime by refusing to cover her head with a cap in the pulpit as Almira Bullock and other women did.[84]

Athough American women preachers faced comparatively little physical

---

need for women preachers to maintain "propriety on all occasion" and to sustain "a good moral character."

[82] Towle, *Vicissitudes*, pp. 49 and 95.

[83] Harriet Livermore, *A Narrative of Religious Experience*, pp. 192–93.

[84] Ibid., pp. 269–72. The quotation is from p. 270. Elias Smith, *Articles of Faith and Church Building* (Portsmouth, N.H., 1802), pp. 14–15 while defending women's right to preach stressed that "every woman that prayeth or prophesieth with her head uncovered,

violence, ministers frequently refused them the use of their pulpits and spoke against them, but usually a venue was found in the church of a sympathetic sect, a public hall, or barn or the open air. Not infrequently, women preachers were barred from churches or local halls by church officers and local officials with much noise and confusion, and occasionally their meetings were deliberately disrupted.[85] In their writings, however, the women made clear that ridicule and verbal aggression was a much greater challenge to their activities than physical violence. Given the pressures exerted against them, they needed to build up a sense of sisterhood. Nancy Towle was converted by Clarissa Danforth, and seeking further guidance joined a group of experienced women preachers active in Maine and New Hampshire: "During my stay in these regions I had opportunity of forming some acquaintances with a number of female preachers of the Free Will Baptist persuasion viz Almira Bullock, Hannah Fogg, Judith Prescott and Mrs. Quimby. They strengthened my hand much in the Lord."[86] During the next ten years Nancy Towle built up close contacts with women preachers of many denominations from Virginia to Nova Scotia, including even that rare creature, a female preacher who was a "rigid Calvinist." Towle went to England and shared the physical hardships and legal harassment of English women preachers.[87] The lives of many other women illustrate this network of support. Although Harriet Livermore may have seemed "eccentric" in some quarters this did not lessen her friendship with other women preachers. About the time she cut her hair, Livermore visited Clarissa Danforth and was received with kindness by sister Clarissa and her whole family. Livermore also conducted revival meetings with Nancy Towle, who regarded her as "a person of distinguished genius."[88]

Nancy Towle represented only one strand in a network of connections which linked women preachers on both sides of the Atlantic. From the early 1800s the American revivalist Lorenzo Dow had encouraged female preaching as well as camp meetings in England, and worked closely with Methodists. He was angered when, in 1803, the Wesleyan Conference

---

dishonours her head." I found Rosamund Billington, "Ideology and feminism: why the suffragettes were 'wild women,'" *Women's Studies International Forum*, 5, No. 6 (1982), 663–74 very helpful on the labelling of nineteenth-century feminists as "unfeminine" and "unwomanly."

[85] Thornton, *Life*, p. 115; Towle, pp. 53, 182, 227; Almond H. Davis, p. 66.

[86] Towle, p. 33.

[87] Ibid., pp. 53–90.

[88] Harriet Livermore, *A Narrative of Religious Experience*, p. 209; Towle, pp. 42–44.

banned women preachers as not compatible with respectability. Dow made one English preaching tour with Dorothy Ripley, a famous figure on both sides of the Atlantic.[89] The daughter of a pioneer Yorkshire Methodist, Ripley became identified for a while with the Quakers, but soon became "a free spirit" responsible to no community or society for what the world saw as her "irregular" conduct. By 1819 she had already crossed the Atlantic seven times, publicizing her work through numerous editions of her journal and writings. She felt divinely called but saw her cause very much as the cause of women.[90] On her return to the United States, Nancy Towle kept up her English friendships and publicized the work of women preachers in Britain. She later went on preaching tours with William O'Bryan, the founder of the Bible Christians, during his three-year visit to the United States. O'Bryan and his daughters did much to encourage female preaching among the smaller Methodist sects, and his account of his American tour and Towle's autobiography provide a vivid picture of the radical fringes of Methodism and the importance of women preachers in that milieu.[91] A similar pattern of American contacts was built up by the Primitive Methodists, whose early American mission relied heavily on women preachers. The Black preacher Zilpha Elaw worked with English women evangelists in the United States before beginning a five-year mission to England in 1840. Elaw became popular not only among the Primitive Methodists but also with a secession group of independent-minded women preachers known as the Female Revivalists of Leeds.[92]

Although there was no sudden decline, women preachers of the type considered here had become less common by the 1840s. They faded from

[89] Arthur Mounfield, *A Short History of Independent Methodism* (Warrington, 1905), pp. 1–20; H. B. Kendal, *The Origin and History of the Primitive Methodist Church* (London, n.d.), 1, 58–61 and 312–13.

[90] Dorothy Ripley, *The Bank of Faith*, 1819 and 1822 editions, especially the latter, pp. iv and 200. See also Dorothy Ripley, *Memoir of William Ripley* (Philadelphia, 1827), and Z. Taft, *Biographical Sketches of the Lives and Public Ministry of Various Holy Women* (London, 1825), pp. 205–41.

[91] Ann Freeman, *A Memoir of the Life and Ministry of Ann Freeman... Written By Herself* (Exeter, N.H., 1831); Towle, pp. 97–180; William O'Bryan, *A Narrative of Travels in the United States of America* (Shebbear, 1836).

[92] John A. Acornley, *A History of the Primitive Methodist Church in the United States of America* (Fall River, Mass., 1909), pp. 16–49; John Walford, *Memoir of the Life and Labours of the Late Venerable Hugh Bourne* (London, 1856), 2, 313–23. *The Primitive Methodist Magazine* from 1829 to 1832 contains letters from the American mission. See also Elaw, *Memoirs*, pp. 143ff. and D. Colin Dews, "Ann Carr and the Female Revivalists of Leeds..." in Dews, ed., *From Mow Cop to Peake 1807–1932*, Wesley Historical Society, Yorkshire branch, Occasional Paper No. 4 (Leeds, 1982).

the Freewill Baptist press, and among the smaller Methodist sects they continued only at a very local level. Requests for licences to engage in wider work were generally refused. Increasing emphasis was placed on women being excluded from the official business life of the churches, where they were expected to have neither voice nor vote.[93] In a few areas where female preachers had been popular there is some evidence of continuity between the women of Salome Lincoln's generation and the women seeking regular ordination in a few liberal churches later in the century.[94] Church historians among the Freewill Baptists and the Methodist sects recalled the work of women preachers when looking back from the last decades of the nineteenth century, and a few women's groups recalled the memory of pioneer preachers like Thankful Hussey and Almira Bullock.[95] In general, however, they were forgotten, and in consequence have received little attention in the histories either of women or religion. Some possible reasons for this decline and subsequent neglect can be suggested.

Women preachers always faced the unrelenting opposition of the socially dominant churches, which had worked out a different and subordinate sphere of activity for their women members. By the 1840s the Methodist Episcopal Church in the northeast, with a recently founded university and socially ambitious congregations, was reflecting bourgeois values hostile to women acting outside "the sphere of their sex."[96] Many women found this constant and enlarging opposition daunting, questioned the validity of their own call and withdrew from preaching for long periods, or sometimes completely. Others counter-attacked, becoming in the process more "strident" or "eccentric," which seemed to confirm the dominant view that women preachers belonged to the lunatic fringe of

[93] As early as 1827 the editor of the Freewill Baptist *Morning Star* confessed that he was not "peculiarly partial to the improvement of female gifts in meetings of worship." By 1840 reports in the paper on women preachers were scarce. For Methodist sects see Acornley, p. 53; McLeister and Nicholson, *History of Wesleyan Methodist Church*, p. 69, and J. Bruce Behney and Paul H. Eller, *The History of the Evangelical United Brethren Church* (Nashville, Tenn., 1979), pp. 159–60.

[94] Phebe A. Hanaford, *Daughters of America; or Women of the Century* (Augusta, Me, 1883), pp. 417–21. Phebe Hanaford was an ordained Universalist minister from 1868.

[95] Burgess and Ward, *Free Baptist Cyclopedia*, passim; Edward Drinkhouse, *History of Methodist Reform* (Baltimore, 1899), I, 123–66; Beedy, *Mothers of Maine*, pp. 331–39. The latter was published by the Maine Federation of Women's Clubs.

[96] A classic statement of the mid-nineteenth-century conventional male view of woman can be found in the chapter entitled "Woman – Her Position in America" in Abel Stevens, *Sketches from the Study of a Superannuated Itinerant* (New York, 1853), pp. 29–44. Far from being "superannuated," Stevens was thirty-eight and a rising Methodist leader and historian. See also Whitney R. Cross, *The Burned-Over District*, p. 15 on Methodism rapidly becoming "respectable" in western New York.

religious life.[97] Women "eccentrics" were never able to command the public affection achieved by their male counterparts in an era of individualism. Idiosyncratic male preachers like Lorenzo Dow, Peter Cartwright and many others became popular "characters," part of the folk mythology of a young nation. No woman preacher was allowed such a role.[98]

Even the sects which had favoured female preaching began to change, and to seek a new respectability. The process of "embourgeoisement" was facilitated by socio-economic changes and by alarm created by a succession of antinomian and millenarian movements, including those of the Mormons and Millerites, which swept away many of their most enthusiastic members. Freewill and Christian leaders, who had long battled with such schisms, began to place emphasis on order and discipline and to copy institutional practices of the more socially prominent churches.[99] The process is most easily detected among the Freewill Baptists, who were in the process of becoming a denomination. In that process women preachers were gradually excluded and identified with an earlier, more "primitive" phase of the movement's history. Some like Clarissa Danforth were remembered with affection, though it was stressed that they were not of the "erratic type." Others were written out of history altogether as the Freewill Baptists followed new paths.[100]

[97] Similar problems faced the handful of Universalist women preachers of this period. Maria Cook, 1779–1835, who was of "genteel and commanding appearance" preached in New York state from 1811, but her friends implored her to stop. She was later arrested as a vagrant and forced into retirement. She was considered an "eccentric" both by a leading Universalist of her day, Nathaniel Stacey, and by the most recent historian of Universalism. See Russell E. Miller, *The Larger Hope: The First Century of the Universalist Church in America, 1770–1870* (Boston, 1979), pp. 546–7.

[98] Byrne, *No Foot of Land*, especially pp. 17–29 and 275–301. He includes no women in his study and ignores female autobiographies. His book is a study of male "giants and heroes."

[99] A Watcher (Ephraim Stinchfield), *Cochranism Delineated: or A Description of, and Specific for Religious Hydrophobia....* (Boston, 1819), and D. M. Graham, *The Life of Clement Phinney* (Dover, N.H. 1851), pp. 78–92 chart the alarm caused by one antinomian sect which led on to Mormonism. The impact of the Mormons and Millerites can be traced through the Freewill Baptist *Morning Star*, and in many of the biographies and autobiographies already cited.

[100] Rev. Porter S. Burbank, A.M., "Freewill Baptists" in Rupp, *An Original History*, pp. 58–69; Bordin, "The Sect to Denomination Process," pp. 81–93; Emeline Burlingame-Cheney, *The Story of the Life and Work of Oren B. Cheney: Founder and First President of Bates College* (Boston, 1907), pp. 15–16. The first edition of the autobiography of David Marks already cited has a full discussion of his work with women preachers. The second, posthumous edition published by his widow at Dover, N.H. in 1847 deletes all references to female preaching.

The broad changes can be easily identified, though they stretched over many years. Key Freewill Baptist ministers acquired degrees from the major New England colleges, and in turn pressed for academies, a seminary and ultimately a college. Conventional religious and academic titles like reverend or doctor replaced the more usual elder, and a new professionalism appeared.[101] It was reflected in a regular weekly newspaper which replaced erratic monthlies, and charted the rise of Sunday school, missionary and temperance societies. Women were organized in separate fund-raising groups, the Freewill Baptists' Female Missionary Society, for example, reflecting a process which more middle-class denominations had commenced forty years earlier. The Freewill Baptist newspaper mirrored these changes, and set up first a Female and later a Ladies' department.[102] Women's energies were channelled into these new organizations, although the associated anti-slavery movement may have led some of the younger generation into the struggle for women's rights.[103] Of course, many clung to traditional ways, and there were bitter protests and schisms, some of which led to the creation of sects in which women retained the right to preach and lead.[104]

These developments among Freewill Baptists and other revivalist sects reflected major changes in the economy of the northeast. Many native American Protestants either left the region or became more securely placed amongst the middle class of what was becoming an industrial and capitalistic nation with a predominantly immigrant working class. The hill country of northern New England, a Freewill Baptist stronghold, experienced increasing rural depopulation in many areas after 1830 as farmers left harsh marginal lands for the West or found alternative occupations in towns and cities. Those farmers who remained became, with the growth of steamboats and railroads, more market oriented, and

[101] Bordin, pp. 81–93; Burlingame-Cheney, pp. 19–29 and 83–141.

[102] I have traced this development in the *Morning Star* which has a "Female Department" from 1833. Reports of home and foreign missionary societies and the temperance movement quickly follow. The Freewill Baptist Female Missionary Society was organized in 1847. Mrs. O. B. Cheney was the first secretary, and "her husband was repeatedly called upon to read her reports," (Burlingame-Cheney, p. 171). A similar process of gender divisions and the restricting of women to subordinate roles is described for Birmingham in Catherine Hall, "Gender divisions and class formation in the Birmingham middle class, 1780–1850," in Raphael Samuel, ed., *People's History and Socialist Theory* (London, 1981), pp. 164–75.

[103] The links between Freewill Baptist women and abolition have already been indicated. Their attitude towards the women's rights movement needs investigation.

[104] See, for example, *Morning Star* (5 Oct. 1836), and Beedy, *Mothers of Maine*, pp. 338–39.

there developed local textile industries and a wide range of wood-related manufacturing enterprises.[105] Some of the capital for these came from southern New England or New York, but managers, foremen and clerks were often local and overwhelmingly Yankee. They were part of a new middle class in tune with the ideas and values emanating from the great seaboard cities. In the textile industry, at least, the workforce was increasingly Irish or French Canadian. In Lewiston, Maine, for example, immigrants replaced the Yankee population in tending the machinery at Bates Mill, while up the hill, Freewill Baptist young men and women attended Bates College. Their parents were rarely rich, and many students taught school in the winter, but only a sharply declining number had ever worked in the mills and most represented an ambitious, politically well-connected middle class very different from the immigrant workers or their own pioneering grandparents.[106] In southern New England, Yankee girls no longer flocked from the north to enter mills, but rapidly growing commercial and industrial cities offered a wide range of skilled manual and white-collar employment to their fathers, brothers and husbands. Suitable jobs for native American Protestant women were few, and they were expected to abandon them at marriage. In New York state the pre-industrial stage of production passed quickly, especially after the opening of the Erie Canal. The country where Deborah Pierce and Abigail Roberts had preached and organized churches became Mary Ryan's "cradle of the middle class" with changing family patterns and more restrictive definitions of women's roles. Among these, preaching and circuit riding were not included.[107]

[105] Wilson, *The Hill Country*, pp. 29–210; Lewis Stilwell, *Migration from Vermont* (Montpelier, Vt, 1948); Thomas Dublin, *Women at Work*, pp. 138–40; William Hutchinson Rowe, *The Maritime History of Maine: Three Centuries of Shipbuilding and Seafaring* (1948; rept. Freeport, Me, 1966), pp. 119–87.

[106] James S. Lemon, *Historic Lewiston: A Textile City in Transition* (Auburn, Me, 1976), pp. 14–19; Burlingame-Cheney, pp. 232–33.

[107] Mary P. Ryan, *Cradle of the Middle Class: The Family in Oneida County New York, 1790–1865* (Cambridge, 1981), pp. 71–104 and 191–210. Elaw, *Memoirs*, p. 128 refers to a Mrs. Jones, a female preacher from England who by the 1830s found very little popularity in Utica.

SHE HATH DONE WHAT SHE COULD: PROTESTANT WOMEN'S MISSIONARY CAREERS IN NINETEENTH-CENTURY AMERICA

BARBARA WELTER
Hunter College, CUNY

WOMAN'S ENTRY INTO A FIELD OR OCCUPATION FORMERLY CLOSED TO her was a prized goal of nineteenth-century feminists, who assumed that each new opportunity was a victory for their cause. It is possible, however, that woman's entry into certain fields represented less a victory than a strategic retreat by the opposition. Certain areas of societal concern were given over to woman not because of her efforts but because either society or the occupation had changed. As Olive Schreiner, the South African feminist, remarked with some irony, "Whenever there is a general attempt on the part of the women of any society to readjust their position in it, a close analysis will always show that the changed or changing conditions of that society have made women's acquiescence no longer necessary or desirable."[1] Through this "readjustment" of roles, certain occupations in nineteenth-century America were maintained by female succession. Three social phenomena played a part in this process: first, a need to place people in some area from which men were physically or socially barred but where women could be admitted; second, men's diminishing interest in certain work when other alternatives offered greater rewards of money or status; and third, a desire to maintain the rhetoric of certain institutions without any concomitant wish to bother with the substance. The changing role of women within the American Protestant foreign missionary movement of the nineteenth century illustrates these phenomena.

Nineteenth-century Protestantism shared the zeal for progress, the romantic optimism and heroic mythology, and the faith in manifest des-

[1] Olive Shreiner, *Women and Labour* (London: T. Fisher Unwin, 1911), 14.

tiny of other institutions. The theology and liturgy of most churches were softened and adorned, infused by ideals of love and service. The drama of the impending millennium impelled action since Biblical references required a converted world before the happy day of general resurrection could take place. Phillips Brooks called missionary activity "the apex to which all the lines of the pyramid lead up. The Christian life without it is a mangled and imperfect theory."[2] The "Spirit of the Age," a spirit of progress, heroism, and expansion, was identified as the "Missionary Spirit," and America's role was paramount and divinely ordained. The United States should export its religion, a Christianity untainted by Romanism, as it was exporting its goods, and with the same expectation of gain. America was that Christian candle which must shine far and wide. "It is selfish, it is inexcusable, it is wicked to hide that light at home. All Christendom would deplore it, and God would frown upon it."[3] The success of Protestantism abroad would, because of the principle of "reflex action," redound to the personal and economic good of the church at home. "We need the romance, the unworldliness, the heroism of foreign missions," wrote one observer, "to save us from . . . selfishness, narrowness of view, and all those pettinesses which, mosquito-like, are everlastingly buzzing and biting in the corridors of our churches."[4] The country must be up and doing and not allow other, less pure, nations to export their religion and their commodities. To that "all-important, God-ordained end," each member of the Church Militant must contribute.[5]

The Haystack Meeting at Williams College in 1806 and the founding of the American Board of Commissioners for Foreign Missions in 1810 signalled the beginning of a century of organization and action. By the time of the Columbian Exposition in Chicago in 1893, which was also the scene of a "Congress of Missions," the Americans had accomplished much, "although much more remained to be done, and the fields, white for the harvest, beckon those who wish to labor and serve in Christ's army."[6] Each Protestant denomination established machinery for popularizing the cause of missions, screening candidates, and administering work in the field, with a supportive network of publications, fund raising, and auxiliaries.

But while man created the organizations, at least in the early years, woman, as Harriet Beecher Stowe pointed out, "was left to follow with

[2] The Woman's Union Missionary Society of America, for Heathen Lands, *39th Annual Report* (New York, 1900), 19.

[3] S. C. Bartlett, "A Plea for Missions" (Boston, 1867), 10.

[4] Reuben Thomas, "Enlargement Through Service," (Boston: ABCFM, 1904).

[5] F. Wayland, "The Moral Dignity of the Missionary Enterprise" (Boston, 1824), 18.

[6] E. M. Wherry, ed., *Women in Missions: Papers and Addresses Presented at the Woman's Congress of the Missions* (New York, 1894), 3.

bleeding footsteps." The role of missionary wife, the only role within the missionary life that women were expected to fill in the first generation of service, was defined as important, self-denying, and subordinate.[7] Although from time to time Mission Boards debated the value of a celibate clergy, they invariably if unoriginally concluded that it was better to marry than to burn. Rufus Anderson, long Secretary of the A.B.C.F.M., wrote that "Wives are a protection among savages, and men cannot long there make a tolerable home without them. When well connected in respect to health, education, and piety, wives endure 'hardness' quite as well as their husbands, and sometimes with more faith and patience."[8] A Southern Presbyterian minister concurred: "A lady with a missionary spirit can be quite as useful as her husband—often more so." A woman was "even less trouble and expense than a man. Indeed I believe ladies are the cheapest missionaries the Board sends out."[9] Women were trained in submission, service, and love, all objects of the mission cause. Like women's work, the work of the conversion of nations was never done, until the last day. Christianity required submission of the will and intellect, and all for love. Love, "patient, self-denying, self-sacrificing," must, on the missions, be "the love of a mother for her children, however sickly, fretful, wayward, and self-conceited they might be." The object of this love was "the object of foreign missions . . . the conversion of the world by love, into an empire of love."[10] The ability of woman to love was the theme of many nineteenth-century novels; her search for a fitting love object was the theme of as many lives. The foreign missions provided a dramatic setting where that "perfect love, all other loves excelling" could be acted out to the final act of love, the laying down of life itself.[11]

If a woman had a call to this life of self-denying love it could, in the period before the Civil War, be fulfilled only by marriage to an appointed

[7] Harriet Beecher Stowe, *The Minister's Wooing* (Boston, 1868), 25.

[8] Rufus Anderson, *Memorial Volume of the First Fifty Years of the ABCFM* (Boston, 1863), 272. The ABCFM considered the question in its *Annual Report* (1842), 42–44, the Baptist Church in *The Helping Hand* (June 1890), 2, the Episcopal Church in *The Spirit of Missions* (Mar. 1844), 89–90.

[9] *The Missionary* (Nov. 1868), 117.

[10] Maria A. West, *The Romance of Missions: or, Inside Views of Life and Labor in the Land of Ararat* (New York, 1875), 91; Nehemiah Adams, "The Power of Chistian Gratitude" (Boston, 1855).

[11] The hymn "O Perfect Love," with lyrics by Dorothy Blomfield Gurney (1833), was a frequent wedding song, usually with the 1889 music. A popular hymn supplied the title chosen by Robert Pierce Beaver for his work, *All Loves Excelling: American Protestant Women in World Mission* (Grand Rapids: Eerdman, 1968).

missionary, with certain rare exceptions.[12] God who gave the vocation would provide the means, and the Mission Board sometimes played the role of marriage arranger or, more precisely, coordinator of marriages presumably already arranged in heaven. For the widower in the field an attempt was made to find a replacement of similar interests and, if requested, similar physical characteristics. In rare cases the Board gently but firmly suggested another prospective mate or refused one the missionary had proposed.[13] The missionary was a member of an elite corps and marriage to him provided an elevation in status, one function of marriage for nineteenth-century women. Lucy Lyons wrote of her intended husband, "I do not love him *only* because he is a missionary."[14] The ability of Adoniram Judson, aged 57 and twice a widower, to court and marry Fanny Forester, a best-selling author of 28, gives some idea of the persuasive power of the missionary adventure, and, of course, of Dr. Judson. "Dear Dr., only love me, do not see too many faults, censure gently, lead me to the enjoyment of higher religion, and to more extensive usefulness: *trust* me, and no place on earth is half so pleasant as 'grim Burmah.'" Fanny wrote a friend of her joy in resigning the "showy" pleasures of the world for something far more precious. "Did you ever feel as though all the things you were engaged in were so trivial, so aimless, that you fairly sickened of them, and longed to do something more worthy of your origin and destiny?" At last she was given the opportunity "of spending my short life in the way which would make me most happy—in doing real, permanent good." Their marriage, she finds, is discussed on every steamboat and in every hotel, but those who think she is throwing her life away are wrong; it is for sheer gain that she has accepted Dr. Judson's offer, the gain of heaven in the next world and "a dear little home in Burmah" in this one. She only hopes she will not be a "hindrance" to his work, with her "lack of the true missionary spirit," and she vows to "do all I can to make the autumn of your days brighter than their summer has been, that their winter may be glorious."[15]

Yet the young women who, like Fanny Forester, went off in an exalted state of piety to their chosen vocation as a missionary wife, found the reality fell short of their dreams. As children arrived, frequently in the

[12] Cynthia Farrar taught for the ABCFM in India from 1827 to 1837, returned home for two years, and returned to Ahmednugur to die there in 1862. R. Pierce Beaver, "Pioneer Single Women Missionaries," *Missionary Research Library: Occasional Bulletin*, Vol. 4, No. 2 (Sept. 30, 1953). Some ten other single women served in various mission fields before 1861.

[13] Correspondence Files, ABCFM, Houghton Library, Harvard University.

[14] William Dean, *Memoir of Mrs. Lucy T. Lord of the Chinese Baptist Missions* (Philadelphia, 1854), 123.

[15] "Fanny Forester" in real life was Emily Chubbuck. A. C. Kendrick, *The Life and Letters of Mrs. Emily C. Judson* (New York, 1860), 158–89.

middle of that arduous task of learning a difficult language, it became harder to function in the capacity of assistant missionary. The husband's time and energy were spent outside the home, with long hours in the study mastering the language that she was now too tired and too busy to master. Mrs. Fidelia Coan, in Hawaii, wrote to Laura Judd, "Do you not think that married ladies, mothers especially, in the multitude of their cares, are apt to lose sight of that constant improvement, that completeness of character to which we may attain? We have little time to ourselves; our spirits are often jaded; our bodies are weary; we are discouraged and believe what we have often been told, that the cares of a family leave no time or strength for intellectual efforts."[16] As one chronicler of women missionaries wrote cheerfully, "The unpretending labors of a female missionary are not of a nature to swell the historic page."[17] Emily Judson found that "This taking care of teething babies, and teaching darkies to darn stockings, and talking English back end foremost to teetotum John, in order to get an eatable dinner, is really very odd business for Fanny Forester . . . But I begin to get reconciled to my minute cares. I believe women were made for such things: though when I get settled, I hope to put in a mixture of higher and better things too."[18]

Yet these aspirations often met with little encouragement. Henrietta Shuck embarked on her adventure, the first American woman in the China field, carrying a note from her father entitled "A Few Private Thoughts for Henrietta." He might well have given her the same advice if she had married the boy next door. "*You must yield* to the *will of your husband*." He hoped she would be happy and that her handwriting would improve ("It needs it"). Should anything happen to her husband, she must immediately get in touch with her father, who would tell her what to do.[19] Lucy Lord wrote home that "It is important to a missionary wife to have her worldly cares reduced as much as possible, that she may have the more time and strength for other and higher duties." But her biographer, William Dean, in his introduction to Mrs. Lord's memoirs, criticized her for this ambition. Dean asked why so many missionary females die young, a problem with which he had some acquaintance since two Mrs. Deans were buried in mission cemeteries. Too often the young women exceeded their wifely duties and tried to do outside work. "Thus attempting to do what they cannot perform, they sacrifice health and life

[16] Laura Fish Judd, *Honolulu: Sketches of Life Social, Political, and Religious, in the Hawaiian Islands from 1828 to 1861* (New York, 1880), 155–56.

[17] Rev. S. F. Smith, "Mrs. Sarah Davis Comstock," in Hamilton W. Pierson, ed., *American Missionary Memorial* (New York, 1853).

[18] Kendrick, *Life*, 247.

[19] J. B. Jeter, *A Memoir of Mrs. Henrietta Shuck: The First American Female Missionary to China* (Boston, 1850), 37–38.

in the vain endeavor, and what is more, neglect the duties of their sacred calling and domestic relations." Succumbing to a love for heroics and encouraged by zealots, they believed that "to leave the high and romantic sphere in which they had thought to move, and come down to common duties of the wife, was leaving the dignity of their calling, and that these domestic services would not be called 'missionary work.'" The woman dies, struck down by "the secret thought that she is not accomplishing what the public expect, though that expectation may be unreasonable, which is the worm at the root of her joys, and which withers her happiness and her health." The foolish girl thus "robs the missionary of the solace of domestic life, and the sympathy he needs in his public work." Women should remember that "their principal and usually only duty is to render their home a heaven, and their husband happy by lightening his cares, training his children, soothing his sorrows, sympathizing in his stresses, and lending their counsel and support to his duties. . . ."[20] This insistence on the proper role of a wife, most particularly a clergyman's wife, increased as the century extolled the idyll of the family hearth and as the cares of missionary life proliferated. As Eunice Beecher concluded in her novel about vicarage life, such ambitions would revolt the "strong minded females of this progressive age," but regardless of their horror, "It is, I am persuaded, just what God meant woman to do."[21]

Having relinquished active evangelical work, a married woman could teach in schools "when her home duties permitted." Fears for the moral and physical safety of her children further isolated her, since it was her duty to keep her child as pure "as if in the wholesome air of our own country." Since mission policy in most cases required the parents to send the child home for education at the age of ten, the mother's life was a series of tearful partings, the poetic expression of which was called "The Missionary's Farewell" and featured in every gift annual. One historian considered these leave-takings "the greatest trauma and sorrow of missionary life." But the Board, when taxed with the policy, pointed out that the number of committed Christians and second-generation missionaries among the children was sufficient proof of the wisdom of the ordeal.[22]

When married women are mentioned in missionary reports it is most often in connection with their cheerful and holy demise. No matter how

[20] Dean, *Memoir*, 8–11.

[21] [Eunice White Beecher], *From Dawn to Daylight; or, The Simple Story of a Western Home* (New York, 1859), 293–94.

[22] The problem of the "missionary child" is discussed in poetry by Mrs. Lydia Sigourney, "The Parting of Sarah Comstock with Her Children," in J. Dowling, ed., *The Judson Offering* (New York, 1848), 195, and in painfully remembered fact in Lucy G. Thurston, *Life and Times* (Ann Arbor, 1882), and Olive Jennie Bixby, *My Child-Life in Burma* (Boston, 1880), among many others.

brief her labors, or how unrewarding her time in missionary life, the woman could be counted on to expire with the hope that her passing would not discourage newcomers to the field, and with a heartfelt statement that she was glad that she had come to Africa, or Ceylon, or India, even if only to die there. In actual fact, insofar as we have any statistics, missionary women lived about as long as their counterparts who stayed home. If they were lucky enough to be sent to Hawaii, their actuarial prospects substantially increased.[23] But death had a value to the mission cause and was exploited and publicized as a vindication of it. Of course if a married woman had no children her career was likely to be more active, and even if she had children she might choose to leave them with servants and flout her "proper sphere," claiming that she followed a higher law. After children were grown many a woman labored long beside her husband, or even remained in the field after his death, to become a "matriarch" and symbol to the new generation of missionaries and converts.

Early attempts to encourage women to become missionaries, and to support the missionary venture at home, emphasized the depraved condition of women in heathen lands. Woman was urged to respond to the plea of her sister who, "suffering as a slave or beast, knows not the meaning of womanhood." Christianity was characterized as the liberator of women; only in Christian lands were women accorded respect and dignity.[24] Bishop Thoburn believed that "the actual status of any people can be discovered readily by ascertaining the position of womanhood in the country under review . . . the Hindu, Mohammedan, and Buddhist have failed to appreciate the dignity and worth of womanhood. . . ."[25] In their attempts to show the immensity of the difference between Christian and heathen women, ministers rose to eloquence; one went so far as to refer in 1854 to the enfranchisement of the one and not the other.[26] No one ever suggested that the differences between the heathen women and the Christian ones might be in degrees of bondage, and that "the hobbled feet and minds" which so disturbed the missionaries, the "hostility to education" for females that they found, the loveless marriage, the sense of inferiority, and the female subordination to male desires and laws which so affected

[23] The literature of female missionary death is vast and uniformly edifying. Although women in the field died more often than men before 1860, these statistics were sharply reversed after 1860. William G. Lennox, *The Health and Turnover of Missionaries* (New York: The Foreign Missions Conference, 1933). For Massachusetts statistics see *Historical Statistics of the United States*, I (Washington, D. C.: G.P.O., 1976), 56. Hawaii records from Mission Children Society Archives, Honolulu, Hawaii.

[24] Richard S. Storrs, "The Prospective Advance of Christian Missions," 75th Anniversary of the Founding of the ABCFM (Boston, 1885).

[25] Bishop James M. Thoburn, *The Christian Conquest of India* (New York: Young People's Missionary Movement, 1906), 92.

[26] Charles White, "Power Belongeth Unto God" (Boston, 1854).

their sensibilities might have a counterpart even in this "favored land," where women "owed all they had to One who loved them much."[27]

Having detailed the deplorable condition of the heathen woman and the contrast with the joyful lot of her American sisters, the Missionary Boards were forced to two somewhat contradictory conclusions: however degraded she might be, the pagan woman wielded great power, and these powerful women, because of local custom and taboos, were inaccessible to male missionaries. "Woman everywhere represents the stronger element in the religious faith of the community whether that faith be true or false," concluded the report of the Presbyterian Board in 1881.[28] The women of China were more "fierce and intractable" than the men; the women of India "controlled the home and home devotions"; the African woman "at birth and marriage and death" had charge of rituals and idols; the women of Persia "were able in subtle ways to influence their children and their husbands," so that no religious change took place against their will. But the Chinese "pavilions of women," the Indian zenanas, the women's quarters in Japan, Africa, and Persia, could not be entered by a male, whether missionary or doctor. And the married women missionaries were very busy being "the light and solace" of Christian homes. The answer to the dilemma was found in recruiting single women for the mission field.

To send single ladies to the foreign missions, the Woman's Union Missionary Society of America for Heathen Lands, a nondenominational organization, was formed in New York in 1861. By 1893, 65 missionaries were in the field in India, China, and Japan. The Woman's Union served as a model for the separate women's boards which the A.B.C.F.M. and later the individual denominations set up between 1869 and 1888. It published a magazine, the *Missionary Link*, which exhorted the faithful to contribute money, to consider joining the force, or to "buy a substitute," supporting her as American males were doing during the Civil War. The women engaged in the work dutifully wrote long letters and developed a following as well as winning the support of prayers and money. Miss Marston's increasing deafness, "which made typhoons a hazard," and Miss Brittan's romantic story of a fiancé left behind in Africa because she refused to let him abandon the field just because the climate was killing her, captured the imagination and solidified support for the women's organization. The "girl," as she was called, no matter what her chronological age, was outfitted by her adoptive sisters and mothers, who continued to offer her their letters, gift boxes, prayers, and unsolicited advice.

[27] Lily Ryder Gracey, ed., *Gist: a Hand-Book of Missionary Information* (Cincinnati, 1893), 12.

[28] *Reports of the Board of Foreign Missions of the Presbyterian Church USA* (1881), 12.

The "Work of Women for Women" thus became the province of America's female churchgoers, whether at home or in the field. "From henceforth," said one history, "women's work for the welfare of women in non-Christian lands, whether physical, intellectual, or spiritual, was to be in women's hands, and was to be performed in women's way."[29] It would be more nearly the truth to say that henceforth women increased in absolute and proportionate representation in missionary life and began their struggle to translate these numbers into influence. In 1830 females made up 49 percent of the missionary force. In 1880 they constituted 57 percent of active missionaries, and the figure rose to slightly more than 60 percent in 1893.[30] Some commentators observed that the Civil War had trained women in administration, and made them aware of the superiority of organizations over individual attempts at change. The war had also dislocated the living patterns of American women, whether North or South, and drawn them into the Hallelujah Chorus of the missionary drama. One historian suggested it had demonstrated "new human fibres" which through the shared burden of grief predisposed women for the great service to their sisters.[31]

The Churches embraced the idea of separate Boards for women, once it was demonstrated that they would raise money over and above what their husbands already pledged to their church. By 1893 the "systematic giving" and thousands of "mite boxes" were contributing about one and a half million dollars to the various mission boards.[32] Publications were edited and distributed. Children were organized and they too had magazines geared to their interests. The stories of contributions "from picking potato bugs" or from the dying bequest of a saintly "little friend of Missions" increased the popularity of the missions, and parishes held sprightly fund-raising entertainments. The American paterfamilias was besieged with propaganda: his wife enlivened the dinner table by making conversation gleaned from her Monthly Meetings, his children quizzed him unmercifully as part of their "committee" assignment, and his pastor insisted on his dollar and assigned a Mission hymn to be sung during the

[29] D. L. Leonard, *Missionary Annals of the Nineteenth Century* (Cleveland and New York, 1899), 178. Helen Barrett Montgomery, *Western Women in Eastern Lands: An Outline Study of Fifty Years of Woman's Work in Foreign Missions* (New York, 1911), identifies early Sewing and Dorcas Societies as forerunners of Women's Work groups.

[30] Leonard, *Missionary Annals*, Wherry, *Women in Missions*, and Lennox, *Health of Missionaries*.

[31] M. M. Underhill, "Woman's Work for Missions: Three Home Based Studies," *International Review of Missions*, 14 (July 1925), 379–99.

[32] Figures taken from Edwin Munsell Bliss, ed., *The Encyclopaedia of Missions*, 2 vols. (New York, 1895). Bliss accepted Board reports at face value.

Offering.[33] This saturation of the country's imagination carried out by women and children, the technique of the temperance societies, had even more dramatic results with the missionary cause. Popular novels—*Rebecca of Sunnybrook Farm*, *Anne of Green Gables*, and Fannie Macauley's *The Lady of the Decoration*, for example—dwelt on the missionary theme. In the sequel to Caroline Hentz's best-selling *Linda*, the heroine goes off to an Indian mission with her new husband. The rage for the exotic in home furnishing, from the Turkish Corner to the curio cabinet, reflected the influence of missionaries as well as other travelers.

The single woman who went to the missions might have been someone who had longed for this work since childhood but had been prevented from going by home responsibilities; the death of a parent or the improvement of her economic position freed her to fulfill her vocation belatedly. Another type of young woman left school and went to the missions as a temporary "first job," with a strong sense of vocation but no clear idea of her duty. The missionary wife had been irritated when she was regarded as the missionary's cook; the single woman missionary was horrified to be considered his polygamous second wife. Many unmarried women had further complaints of their isolation as constant boarders "who have no home, no real abiding-place in the land."[34] Some felt that married women and the more formidable and virginal of the single women regarded them as husband-hunters, ready to snatch the next man made available when a wife succumbed to cholera or dysentery. It took time for men to realize that single women could be missionaries in their own right. Isabella Thoburn dutifully copied out her brother's correspondence for some months until she insisted that he leave her free to accomplish her own work. Bishop Thoburn, writing his sister's autobiography, tells how her refusal raised his consciousness. He understood for the first time that "a Christian woman sent out to the field was a Christian missionary, and that her time was as precious, her work as important, and her rights as sacred as those of the more conventional missionaries of the other sex."[35]

Those more conventional missionaries were not always pleased at the increasing number of women. A single woman was sometimes refused by several stations because the resident missionaries feared she would cause tension. An article in the May 1882 *Missionary Review* dealt with the

[33] Louis A. Cattan, *Lamps Are for Lighting: The Story of Helen Barrett Montgomery and Lucy Waterbury Peabody* (Grand Rapids, 1972); Mrs. M. A. Miller, *History of the Woman's Foreign Missionary Society of the Methodist Protestant Church* (Pittsburgh, 1896); Augustus R. Buckland, *Women in the Mission Field* (New York, 1895); Mrs. J. Howard Smith, "Mrs. Thomas Doremus," *The Missionary Link*, 14 (March 1877); *Mrs. Juliana Hayes* (Nashville, n.d.).

[34] Maria West, *Romance*, 467.

[35] Thoburn, *Life of Isabella Thoburn*, 95.

unmarried woman as a disruptive force and the puppet of the Board. Women in missions were told to exercise no direct influence but to hold "the same relation to man in the mission fields of heathendom that she holds in the most happy homes and churches of christendom, where her work is accomplished with a grace that disarms opposition, her views and plans are adopted because none better can be devised, and her influence is all the more potent because unconscious." The nominal cause for this cautionary tone was the influx of women doctors to the field, potentially, because of their education and drive, a real threat to the men.[36]

Although they complained to the Board about their problems, and letters from missionary wives frequently complained about them, single women found in the missionary field a rare combination of church- and socially-sanctioned activity and freedom. The woman doctor found a far more interesting practice, an opportunity to perform operations, to study rare diseases, and to escape a professional life as a poorly paid listener to female complaints, her probable lot had she remained at home.[37] As Susan Hale once pointed out in a slightly different context, if you could "persuade any single woman that a pleasure is a duty . . . she is secured to it."[38]

Although women had been encouraged to enter the field largely so that they could work with women, some, like Lottie Moon, protested that the logic was wrong. She felt that to get "any tangible, visible results" she would have "in some way to reach the men of the community. How to do this was the problem." She solved it by scrupulously following the Biblical injunctions against female preaching. She could not help it if "the men crowded silently behind them [her female hearers] and studied along with them." Surely, she wrote, "even Paul would not have objected." But when asked to comply with a latter-day Pauline injunction that barred even single women from voting in missionary meetings, Miss Moon flatly

[36] "Lady Medical Missionaries," *The Missionary Review*, 5 (May 1882), 183–86.

[37] The best biographical information is found in "Notebooks of Women Medical Missionaries," Medical College of Pennsylvania, Historical Collection. See also Anna M. Fullerton, "The Woman Physician in India," *Transactions Alumnae Association Women's Medical College of Pennsylvania*, 25 (1900), 55–58; Mary W. Griscom, "Medical Mission Work in China," ibid., 39 (1914), 86–89; *Clara A. Swain, M.D.: First Medical Missionary to the Women of the Orient* (Boston, 1912); Ellen C. Potter, "The Woman Medical Missionary," *Bulletin of Women's Medical College of Pennsylvania*, 65 (1914), 36; Bertha L. Selman, "Pioneer Women in Medicine: Early Service in Missions," *Medical Woman's Journal*, 54 (Apr., June, and Sept. 1947), 198–257; Mary H. Stinson, *Work of Women Physicians in Asia* (Norriston, Pa., 1884); and the work of several members of the Scudder dynasty, discussed in Dorothy Jealous Scudder, *A Thousand Years in Thy Sight: The Story of the Scudders in India*, typescript in Arthur and Elizabeth Schlesinger Library, Radcliffe College, Cambridge.

[38] E. E. Hale and Susan Hale, *A Family Flight through France, Germany, Norway and Switzerland* (Boston, 1881), 2.

refused. "To exclude the married women from the meetings might be unwise, but it could hardly be deemed unjust, as they could be represented by their husbands. To exclude the unmarried ladies would be a most glaring piece of injustice in my opinion. To such exclusion I could never submit and retain my self-respect." She asked for her return passage to Virginia since "It seems to be the purpose of the Committee to relegate me henceforth to the class of those women missionaries who must work in silence, without voice in any shaping of mission policies. I distinctly decline to be so relegated." The Board reconsidered.[39] But Miss Moon was an exception; the majority of women, even medical missionaries, had little to say in yearly meetings, even when they had the vote. According to one embittered child of Presbyterian missionaries, the "inevitable result" of this "religious subjection of women, was to breed in them an irrepressible independence and desire for self-expression, born of their innate and unconscious sense of injury and injustice."[40]

Perhaps equally inevitable was the attempt to find some compensatory form of solidarity and status. The "compound" of unmarried women sometimes filled this need, as did the isolated unit of two single women, either missionaries or a missionary and a native Bible woman who became a close friend. The "Deaconess" or "Protestant Sisterhood" associations, which gained prominence in the last years of the nineteenth century, although they had been in existence long before that, gave some women additional dignity and provided the visible bonds of habit and ritual. They were never widely popular, however, and the clergy had reservations about allowing them at all. "Sisterhoods should be under the general direction of wise *men*," was the firm advice of a British to an American bishop. "I have learned to fear female *rule*, unless it be itself under authority, able to know all and capable of controlling or overruling."[41] Lydia Fay stoutly denied her "need of a mother superior to accomplish something."[42] A better solution was to become the independent "Head of a Household," as Anna Safford did. "God has granted me the desire of my heart and given me a home of my own even in a foreign land and amongst an alien people." She added that besides her own pleasure in the arrangement, the Chinese, ever alert to status symbols,

[39] Hyatt, *Ordered Lives*, 109, and Una Roberts Lawrence, *Lottie Moon* (Nashville: Sunday School Board of the Southern Baptist Convention, 1927), 135–37 and 141–42.

[40] Pearl S. Buck, *Fighting Angel: Portrait of a Soul* (New York: Reynal and Hitchcock, 1936), the fictional biography of her father, Presbyterian missionary Andrew Sydenstricker. Her mother, Carrie Sydenstricker, was the subject of *The Exile* (New York: Reynal and Hitchcock, 1936), 187–89.

[41] Henry C. Potter, *Sisterhoods and Deaconesses At Home and Abroad* (New York, 1873), 87.

[42] Lydia Fay to Dr. Denison, Secretary, Board of Missions of the Protestant Episcopal Church, April 28, 1877, Episcopal Church Archives, Austin, Texas.

instantly treated her with more deference when they saw she was the one who gave the orders.[43]

A recent history of American religion suggests that the missionary movement diverted American Protestantism from the problems it faced at home.[44] It might be that for American women a secondary diversion sent them to "the dark, the distant and the trying fields"[45] instead of facing up to the questions raised by the women's movement. The counsels to wives not to exceed their calling, to single women not to speak out of turn, to Sisterhoods not to act without consulting the Bishop, could be construed as warnings against the ungodly doctrine of women's rights. The *Woman's Evangel* wrote of women's work in missions as a "happy solution of the difficulty" when a woman found it hard to reconcile her religion and her rights, agitating her own and "the public mind, creating warm discussion and angry debate." In expanding her role and involving her energy and enthusiasm in the drama of foreign missions women could rejoice. "In God's work, our highest sphere—Our precious, our inalienable rights are to do His will and to show forth His light and love."[46] The potential problem and the vigilance with which it was monitored are revealed in a story, perhaps apocryphal but quoted in most histories of women's boards. A pastor in Michigan insisted on being present at all women's mission meetings, because "no one knew what they would pray for, if left alone."[47] At least one parent Board expressed the fear that some "mild form" of the "women's rights controversy" might be lurking in the proposed women's group.[48]

By the end of the century women were active missionaries, distinguished by their achievement as well as their supportive Christian homes and beautiful deaths. The "muscular Christianity" of the period had not passed them by and they gloried in their militancy. "I am glad the providence of God calls us there," wrote Loanza Benton during an uprising in Syria, "It is a place where we can feel that we are really in the midst of the battle."[49] The *Encyclopedia of Missions* would have it that "The gospel

[43] Anna Cunningham Safford to her sister Janette Safford Thompson, January 1876, Soochow, Archives of the Southern Presbyterian Historical Society, Montreat, N. C.

[44] Sydney Ahlstrom, *A Religious History of the American People* (New Haven: Yale Univ. Press, 1972), 423–24.

[45] Beth Bradford Gilchrist, *The Life of Mary Lyon* (Boston: Houghton Mifflin Co., 1910) and Louise Porter Thomas, *Seminary Militant: An Account of the Missionary Movement at Mount Holyoke Seminary and College* (South Hadley, Mass., 1937), discuss in context this phrase often used by Mary Lyon in her "nursery of missionaries."

[46] *The Woman's Evangel*, 4 (May 1878), 2.

[47] For example in Ellen C. Parsons, "History of Women's Organized Missionary Work As Promoted by American Women," in Wherry, *Women in Missions*, 85.

[48] Mrs. M. A. Miller, *History of the Woman's Foreign Missionary Society*, 37.

[49] "A Diary and Some Reminiscences of Loanza Goulding Benton," Oct. 28, 1847. Typescript in Sophia Smith Collection, Smith College, Northampton, Mass.

had developed them and set them in honor; given them security and moral power; made them intellectually free, and queens of happy homes. . . . They undertook to carry the gospel where without them it could not go."[50] David Abeel's report of the piteous cry of the Chinese women, "O bring us some female men," had been more successful and more potentially upsetting than he realized.[51] When men abandoned the zenana, the harem and purdah to women they also abandoned much of their Biblical superiority. In everything but name women became full-fledged preachers. Mrs. Bishop Boone begged the Episcopal Board Secretary to "appreciate the fact that Miss Fay . . . has been doing a man's work, and that it will be next to impossible to find any woman to succeed to her work." In fact, "a young man should be her successor."[52] But male vocations were declining, just as women were becoming more numerous and prominent in the field.[53]

The logic of women influencing women did not bring about converts; nothing the missionaries did, with few exceptions, paid off numerically. But the recruiting of women for nineteenth-century Protestant missions created a new role and status for them within one of the most important movements of organized religion. Although women entered the missionary ranks largely in response to social change at home and the faulty strategy which made it seem desirable to replace men with women, they made valuable strides not only in professional but in personal growth. The cultural confrontation which was a necessary part of missionary life worked on both sides, and many missionaries were never quite the same afterwards. The ethnocentric attitude and national and religious absolutism of these men and women cannot be denied. In almost every case, however, if they remained in the field any length of time, there was identification with and sympathy for some aspects of the host culture. Missionaries were far more sensitive to the societies in which they worked than is generally believed. The ladies of the Chinese mission who stayed up all Christmas Eve replacing the blond hair on the dolls in the mission box with straight black wigs were making a small but affirmative statement. Sarah Smith wrote perceptively about the way in which mission life forced "a taking to pieces, if I may so speak, of all former habits

[50] "Woman's Work for Women," *The Encyclopaedia of Missions*, 2:479.

[51] David Abeel, *Journal of a Residence in China, and the Neighboring Countries* (New York, 1834). The philosophy and method was also open to criticism from another point of view. Flora Annie Steele, a bestselling author who lived in India 22 years and wrote about its customs and history, believed the "zenana mission" a great mistake, because without it India would have come out of purdah." *The Garden of Fidelity* (London, 1929).

[52] Henrietta Harris Boone to Denison, Nov. 22, 1875. Episcopal Archives.

[53] This was a matter of concern to the Boards. See, for example, "Where Are the Young Missionary Men of the Church?" *The Missionary Advocate* (June 1869), 220–24.

and associations, and modes of action and the constructing of new. . . . " The process was valuable both for work in the field and for personal growth. "This demolition and reconstruction, gives one the opportunity to study his own character and attainments . . . not a little calculated to produce humility and self-distrust."[54] Like other expatriates the missionaries could see some aspects of their own country all the more clearly once they left it. For women the experience provided a jolting examination of their vocation which carried with it a reassessment of their nature and role.

The twentieth century offers similar examples of ways in which new fields have been opened to women. Franz Boas encouraged his Barnard students to enter anthropology largely because he needed access to certain rites available only to women. Women became dominant in elementary school education when it paid badly; when the pay increased, the percentages of women in teaching began to decline. Women at universities may wonder at the workings of this social law which has given them professional status just in time for a shrinking job market and numerous academic and economic crises.

Even when men opened the doors for their own purposes, they could not and cannot now control the consequences. The missionary woman of the nineteenth century was indeed filling a role in a field abandoned to her somewhat late and with many restrictions. She was achieving prominence in an institution which was itself declining in prestige. She was keeping alive a rhetoric, just as President McKinley and Senator Beveridge were, at a time when the substance of American expansion was devoted to commerce and not to conversion. But for the individual woman the substance was very much a part of her life. The doctor who treated 200 patients a day, (including five who were already dead) and the itinerant preacher who spoke until midnight and was off in her jinrikisha at dawn, felt herself necessary and important. Unlike many American women she defined herself in terms other than those of her husband and children. The historian of the religious experience must always consider that, however much religion involved the working out of social, political, and economic necessities, it was also a matter of individual will and conscience. For the nineteenth-century American woman, on the foreign mission field her life had meaning and joy and was infused by a sense of privilege at being the special recipient of God's grace. As they said on their gravestones, "She hath done what she could."

[54] Edward W. Hooker, *Memoir of Mrs. Sarah L. Huntingdon Smith: Late of the American Mission in Syria* (New York, 1840), 308.

Outside the Mainstream: Women's Religion and Women Religious Leaders in Nineteenth-Century America

Mary Farrell Bednarowski

ABSTRACT

In order to understand fully the status of women in a particular religious tradition, it is helpful to consider the views held within that tradition on four topics: the character of the divine, human nature, the function of the clergy, and the nature of marriage. While the assumptions which have been held by mainstream religious groups on these topics appear to be linked to the absence of female leadership, certain marginal religious movements have taken positions which seem to have a positive relation to leadership roles for women. These marginal groups are characterized by (1) a perception of the divine that deemphasizes the masculine, (2) a tempering or denial of the doctrine of the Fall, (3) a denial of the need for a traditional ordained clergy, and (4) a view of marriage which does not hold that marriage and motherhood are the only acceptable roles for women. In this analysis of Shakerism, Spiritualism, Christian Science, and Theosophy, the author examines the particular manner in which each manifested these doctrinal positions and explores the roles which women occupied within the four groups.

The article concludes with some observations on the causal relationship between doctrine and leadership roles for women and on how the concerns expressed in the four movements discussed parallel those of contemporary feminist theology.

Mary Farrell Bednarowski (Ph.D., Minnesota) is Assistant Professor of Religious Studies and Director of the Master of Arts in Religious Studies Program at United Theological Seminary of the Twin Cities. She is the author of "Nineteenth-Century Spiritualism in Wisconsin" (*The Wisconsin Magazine of History*).

It is nearly impossible to summon the names of individual women who have achieved fame within the context of American religious history. The experiences and contributions of women have gone largely unrecorded in the standard American religious histories. Cotton Mather spoke of women as the "hidden ones" as far as religion was concerned, and contemporary scholars note that the situation remains much the same in the twentieth century as it did in the seventeenth, eighteenth, and nineteenth centuries; the women go to church and the men exercise the authority as members of the clergy and as professional theologians./1/

There is growing agreement among scholars that certain aspects of institutionalized religion, especially Christianity, have been responsible for excluding women from positions of leadership in American religion. These are the pervasive use of masculine language for the divine, which has tended to link the male with the numinous and exclude the female; the belief that the Fall resulted in human depravity and serves to prove the moral weakness of women, particularly; the insistence that the divine "plan" for women was revealed in St. Paul's admonition that women keep silent in church; and the assumption that woman's subordination to man was divinely ordained and revealed in Scripture and that this subordination has implications for marriage and for woman's place./2/

There are numerous examples of women's exclusion from acknowledged positions of religious authority from the seventeenth century to the present. In 1636 Ann Hutchinson was accused not only of teaching heresy, but of stepping beyond her place: she was told, "*You have rather bine a Husband than a Wife and a Preacher than a Hearer; and a Magistrate than a Subject*" (Hall: 382–83). Little had changed for women by the early nineteenth century. R. Pierce Beaver gives numerous examples of the controversy over whether Protestant women even had the right to gather to pray for the missions, much less form their own missionary societies. The struggles of mid-nineteenth-century women like Congregationalist Antoinette Brown (Solomon) and Methodist Anna Howard Shaw (Flexner) illustrate the firmly rooted assumption that women were by nature unsuited to be members of the clergy. Our own time is witness to a profusion of activity regarding the ordination of women in many denominations. The expressed need of these denominations to demonstrate Scriptural approval—or at least lack of disapproval—of women's ordination; the theological controversies over the ordination question; and the subsequent difficulties of placing women who have been ordained in some of the denominations all give evidence that the aforementioned assumptions about the rightful place of women in organized religion are still in operation.

In the so-called marginal or nonmainstream religions, however, it has often been a different story in regard to female leadership./3/ Individual women who have achieved prominence in American religious history have usually been those associated with marginal religious movements whose sources of doctrine and inspiration have been outside the Bible or in addition to it: Ann Lee, founder of the Shakers; the Fox sisters, who are closely associated with Spiritualism; Ellen G. White of the Adventist movement;

Mary Baker Eddy, founder of Christian Science; and Helena P. Blavatsky of the Theosophical movement.

Why is it that women were able to achieve positions of leadership in some religious movements, contrary both to established tradition and to cultural assumptions about the proper role of women as well? It is my contention that women achieved leadership positions and equal status with men in religious movements which embodied assumptions about the divine, about human nature, about the function of the clergy, and about marriage which ran counter to those in the mainstream traditions:

1. a perception of the divine that deemphasized the masculine either by means of a bisexual divinity or an impersonal, nonanthropomorphic divine principle;
2. a tempering or denial of the doctrine of the Fall;
3. a denial of the need for a traditional ordained clergy;
4. a view of marriage that did not stress the married state and motherhood as the proper sphere for woman and her only means of fulfillment.

My isolating of these characteristics grew out of an attempt, first, to identify American women religious leaders and, second, upon finding most of them in the marginal movements, to understand what these movements might have in common that made them sympathetic to female leadership. As a result of my survey of religious movements in which women were prominent, I chose to analyze four in detail—the Shakers, the Spiritualists, the Christian Scientists, and the Theosophists—because they were founded by women (that statement must be qualified in regard to Spiritualism); because of the high degree to which women participated in them; because of their insistence that woman's spiritual equality must be embodied in practice; and because they exhibit in various ways the four characteristics described above. I had originally intended to include the Oneida Perfectionists in my analysis, but discovered that in spite of such characteristics as group marriage, the practice of birth control, and an understanding of the divine as bisexual, founder John Humphrey Noyes was highly patriarchal in his expressed understanding of woman's nature (Thomas:119–28).

The four nineteenth-century American religious movements mentioned above produced a number of women leaders whose concern with the spiritual and social status of women has not been so strongly articulated again until the present feminist movement. The movements address in somewhat less cohesive form the very same concerns that feminists are voicing today in their critique of organized religion: the detrimental effect on women of the pervasiveness of the masculine in God language; the stereotype of women as morally weak as a result of the doctrine of the Fall; the virtual exclusion of women from the ordained clergy on the basis of essential unsuitability; and the narrow circumscribing of woman's proper sphere within marriage and motherhood.

By contrast, in spite of sometimes bitter rivalries among them as well as different sources of doctrine, Shakerism, Spiritualism, Christian Science, and

Theosophy all put forth doctrines about the divine, the human, the clergy, and marriage which provided a situation conducive to female leadership.

The Shakers

The American Shakers provide the first example of a religious movement whose beliefs and their practical working out gave women leadership status equal to that of men. Ann Lee brought her small group of followers to New York in 1774. She died in 1784, but the flowering of the Shaker communities, formed on the basis of her revelations, occurred during the first half of the nineteenth century. During their history, which is not yet ended, the Shakers attracted approximately 16,500 followers (Andrews:292).

Shaker doctrine embodied two beliefs which insured that women would assume roles of spiritual leadership: first, that God was both male and female in nature; and second, that "concupiscence" was the sin in the Garden of Eden and thus celibacy was the proper relationship between the sexes. Out of these two beliefs grew the necessity for female leadership as well as male among the Shakers: not only to reflect in practice the dual nature of the divine, but to provide religious leadership for the female members of the communities. In addition, these two beliefs prevented the denigration of women that often occurs in religions which stress the sinful nature of sexual relationships. The Father/Mother God kept the feminine aspect of the divine constantly before the Shakers, and the fact that celibacy was practiced by both sexes prevented the association of the feminine alone with the temptations of the flesh.

The Shakers based their belief in a Father/Mother God both on Ann Lee's revelation and on a kind of common sense theology which developed over the nineteenth century. Ann Lee emerged from prison in England convinced that she was to be the leader of the Shaking Quaker sect of which she was a member—that she was to represent the "female line" of divinity. It was revealed to her also that the cause of human suffering and depravity was the indulgence of the flesh through sexual intercourse (Andrews:11–12).

Both the doctrines of the Father/Mother God and of celibacy developed gradually during Shaker history. At the time of her vision Ann Lee did not articulate a sophisticated theology of a Father/Mother God or of its implications for the status of women in her religious movement. She did, however, claim divine approval of her own religious leadership as a woman. Defending herself in 1779 against Calvin Harlow's accusation that she could not reconcile her leadership "with the Apostle's doctrine," Ann Lee used an analogy with nature to answer him:

> The order of man, in the natural relation, is a figure of the order of God in the spiritual creation. As the order of nature requires a man and a woman to produce offspring; so where they both stand in their proper order, the man is first, and the woman the second in the government of the family. He is the father and she the Mother; and all the children, both male and female, must be subject to their parents; and the woman, being second, must be subject to her husband, who is the first;

> but when the man is gone, the right of government belongs to the woman: So is the family of Christ. (Andrews: 19)

The above is not a ringing affirmation of the equal standing of women in the family of Christ—Ann Lee's defense of her leadership implies authority by default. In addition, the reference to procreation seems an inappropriate defense of female leadership in view of the Shaker doctrine of celibacy. Nevertheless, at this time Ann Lee articulated a theological defense of the right of women to religious leadership.

It was for later generations to be more specific in using the analogy with human parents to defend the Shaker belief in the Father/Mother God. In 1849 Paulina Bates of the Canterbury, New Hampshire, community spoke of the dual role of male and female in the nurturing of children. "Will the infant receive nourishment at the breast of a tender father?" she asked, and goes on to say that "equally inconsistent would it be, to argue the uselessness of the mother in the natural birth, and rearing of the natural family, as it would be to argue the uselessness of the spiritual mother in the family of Christ: for the necessity of both are equally evident." Bates becomes more insistent as she continues: "And ye who think to be born and reared by the exertions of my beloved Son, exclusive of the aid of my beloved Daughter, the Bride, the Lamb's wife, know ye, your hope is vain; for this can never be" (153).

Closer to the end of the nineteenth century, Elder Frederick Evans spoke of the complementary functions of the male and female natures of divinity reflected also in the natural arrangement: "Man is to Woman *her* God, in physical and intellectual power, as revealing the Father in Deity—Wisdom. And Woman is to Man *his* God and Saviour in affectional power, and in Divine spiritual intuition, as representing the Mother in Deity—Love" (101). That description of the alternating and mutually complementary functions of the father/mother deity does not depart from the cultural stereotypes of the male as cognitive and the female as affectional. Nor does Bates's earlier description modify the notion of Father as begetter and Mother as nurturer. What is striking, however, is to see both male and female qualities incorporated into the Shaker concept of the divine: the Shaker insistence that the feminine qualities of the divine are as necessary as the masculine.

The Shaker defense of a Father/Mother God on the basis of an analogy with natural marriage did not strike the Shakers as incongruous with the practice of celibacy. Perhaps that is because the belief in celibacy underwent some modifications in the course of Shaker history. In the eighteenth century Ann Lee said to a young man that "the marriage of the flesh is a covenant with death and an agreement with hell" (Andrews:22). One hundred years later Frederick Evans explained the Shaker life as merely one way of proceeding in order to achieve salvation, not as the only way. He claimed that Shakers were not absolutely opposed to marriage, but that there were two orders, that of generation (marriage) and that of regeneration (Shaker) and that each contributed to the unfolding of the divine plan (101).

The Shaker practice of celibacy has inspired numerous speculations and explanations, among the most detailed that of Henri Desroche, who sees a direct connection between the Shaker practice of celibacy and the granting of leadership roles to women. Desroche elaborates on this connection in a chapter of *The American Shakers* on what he calls "ascetic feminism" and claims that a rejection of society of those roles assigned to women in mainstream society—to marry, to have sexual intercourse, to bear children—is always accompanied by the demand that there be a religious role for women (140). Thus, the fact that men and women led sexually separate lives within the Shaker communities fostered not only the physical, but also the psychic need for a female spiritual leadership which would function equally with that of the males.

Dual leadership took official shape after the death of Ann Lee when Joseph Meacham, her successor, appointed Lucy Wright to take leadership responsibilities at Niskeyuna, New York, in 1787. Edward Deming Andrews cites her appointment as a recognition of the need for the "Mother Gift"(56). Wright and Meacham formed the first central ministry of the Shaker communities. The ministers formed the highest echelon of Shaker leadership and their power and influence was substantial. They appointed the elders, of both sexes equally, who presided over the separate families within communities, and the trustees, also of both sexes, whose sphere was temporal.

This dual system of leadership gave rise to a new class of woman, according to Desroche: the eldress. Anna White describes her in *The Motherhood of God* as bishop, pastor, and family mother: "To her come the members of her flock, soul by soul, with the burden of sin, the frailty of nature, the weakness of character. To God, before her as witness, is confession made. . . . She must focalize the rays of divine love, connect the soul to God, impart the germ of heavenly life" (Desroche:176). The eldress had all the rights and privileges of the elder. She functioned as a representative of the divine on earth for her Shaker sisters, and she was visible evidence that to the Shakers God was mother as well as father.

The Shakers had a strong sense that their system of dual-gender leadership was superior to that of the outside world in which women functioned in religion in ways that were hidden from public view. Aurelia Mace, a Maine Shaker, claimed that "in the Shaker Community woman has taken her place as an equal with man, by intellectual, if not by physical strength. Where there is a Deacon, there is also a Deaconess, and they are considered equal in their powers of government" (95).

In spite of the visibility of their female leadership, the Shakers were not able to step out of nineteenth-century American culture completely. The work in Shaker communities reflected a sex role bias, and property settlements to departing Shakers favored husbands over wives and sons over daughters (Andrews:67). Nor is it possible to say that all women found happiness in Shaker communities, as is attested by Mary Dyer with her bitter accusations against Shakerism. But the combination of Shaker beliefs and the way that those beliefs were put into practice gave women the opportunity to participate in the communal ownership of property, to have roles in their society other than that of wife and mother, and to participate equally with men in the spiritual leadership of their communities. The high visibility of the feminine demanded by Shaker beliefs functioned to offset the Shaker conviction that the body was sinful and that its concupiscent tendencies must be curbed—a belief that is often detrimental to women aspiring to religious leadership.

The Shakers set themselves up as a society separate from the rest of the world, a society in which they believed they could reform the corruptions they saw in the world they had left. One of the specific corruptions was the inequality of women, and they intended to remedy it. As Mary Antoinette Doolittle of the community of Mt. Lebanon explained, she was taught to look back to the apostolic church for the source of truth, but with one exception: "It still lacked one pillar to give it permanency and cause it to stand erect; i.e. the recognition of woman's rights, and her capability as a counselor and co-worker with man in all that pertains to physical and spiritual life" (35).

The Spiritualists

Nineteenth-century American Spiritualism is a second religious movement where women found opportunities for leadership. Although spiritualism had appeared previously in many forms and in many cultures, including manifestations among the Shakers, the movement which came to be known by its followers as Modern American Spiritualism originated with two young girls, Kate and Margaret Fox, in Hydesville, New York, in 1848. The basic Spiritualist belief that the spirits of the dead could return to earth to communicate with the living necessitated the services of mediums, persons thought to be particularly suited by nature to receive and convey the messages of the spirits. From the beginning the role of medium was open to women, and, in fact, women were thought to be particularly suited to it. In addition, Spiritualism attracted a large number of women followers. Historian Robert Riegel remarks not only on the number of women drawn to the movement, but particularly the number of feminists. Although striking, the connection is puzzling to Riegel: "Possibly the type of mind receptive to feminism also was prone to be impressed by Spiritualism, but such a connection is difficult to support by any normal process of reasoning" (191).

Actually, the connection is not difficult to understand, given the fact that Spiritualism provided a professional role, that of medium, for women to assume, and in addition had all of those characteristics which are conducive to the support of equal status for women: a nonmale deity; a denial of human depravity; a deemphasis on an ordained clergy which approached the anticlerical in many cases; and a nontraditional interpretation of marriage. The highly optimistic and essentially nonjudgmental doctrines of Spiritualism concerning both the deity and human nature provided no theological barriers to keep women from functioning as mediums. The anticlerical attitude of Spiritualism coupled with the accessibility of mediumship to women resulted in the large number of women who achieved prominence in the movement; and the liberal Spiritualist notions about marriage and the relationship between the sexes provided an atmosphere of further support for women in

Spiritualism who sought to step beyond the ordinarily prescribed roles of wife and mother. To be sure, the role of medium was not a breaking away in every sense from the cultural stereotype of what a woman ought to be, as will become evident. Nonetheless, as R. Laurence Moore points out, mediumship provided women with one of the few professional options in nineteenth-century America (1975:200-221).

Any discussion of Spiritualist theology needs to be preceded by the caution that its tenets were highly derivative and eclectic. In addition, Spiritualism was never very highly institutionalized, so any generalization about beliefs is always subject to qualification. For example, although the trend in Spiritualism was to deemphasize the personal God of Christianity, there were Spiritualists like Charles Beecher who considered themselves Christian and spoke unhesitatingly of the mercies of the Father. Further, in spite of an intensely anti-institutional fervor, especially during the early years, by the end of the nineteenth century there were Spiritualist churches served by pastors, many of them women such as Cora L. V. Richmond (Moore, 1977; Bednarowski, 1973). In spite of these cautions, however, it is still possible to proceed responsibly in speaking of certain patterns of belief that run through Spiritualism as a whole.

To begin with, the Spiritualist concept of the divine seems to have benefited women by its insignificance. The Spiritualist God was neither mother nor father, but Spirit, an impersonal entity which did not figure prominently in Spiritualist theology. This was a God who did not judge or function as an image whose perfection was an incentive to human striving. Nor was this a God who necessarily performed any functions of consolation; that role was filled chiefly by the spirits. No doubt the most appealing feature of Spirit, at least to those Spiritualists weary of the angry God of much traditional Christianity, was that it didn't interfere much in human affairs. The advantage for woman in this kind of by-the-way, impersonal God lay in the fact that she was not likely to be found wanting in qualification for roles of leadership because she did not sufficiently reflect the divine image.

Further, the Spiritualist denial of the Fall, of human depravity, did away with any concentration on the sin of Eve and obviated the need for a redemption by a male incarnation of the deity. "Spiritualism," Robert Dale Owen explained, "disavows (or, more usually, ignores) . . . that all men and women are originally depraved, therefore objects of God's anger, and that they can be justified before him only by the blood of one of the Persons of the Godhead, to wit, Jesus Christ; who was made to suffer for the sins of the human race" (729). While the theological doctrines of Spiritualism regarding deity did not actively promote the need for female leadership, neither did they set up obstacles to such leadership.

The Spiritualists' anticlerical attitude grew in part out of a rejection of human depravity, the reality of the devil, and the possibility of human damnation. The Spiritualists maintained that the ordained clergy had badly misled their flocks about such falsehoods and had terrorized them into religious belief. Spiritualist accusations extended further to hypocrisy and elitism. One medium, Lizzie Doten, kept track of public mention of "ministerial delinquencies, ecclesiastical abominations, and human frailty," and claimed to find that "where one spiritual sheep . . . had gone astray, I have found ninety and nine of the Shepherds of Israel in great need of repentance" (1870:7). Another Spiritualist exclaimed, "What wonder that ministers who are flattered, petted, and caressed, as though they were not like other men, should, when weighed in the balance, be found wanting!" (Carra:3). A third writer asked that ministers open their pulpits to Spiritualists, men and women alike: "Gentlemen and Brothers! . . . Will you open your churches to some of our earnest and eloquent workers in the spiritual ranks? Such as Harrison D. Barrett . . . Mrs. Petter, an eloquent speaker and test medium; Miss Margaret Gaule, also a fine speaker and test medium?" (Allen:2).

This anticlerical sentiment resulted in a disdain and a distrust of the professional clergy and a willingness on the part of Spiritualists to look upon mediums as the conveyors and interpreters of truth. The Spiritualists had no intention of fostering an elite corps of clergy within their own ranks, and the role of medium was open to whoever could fill it and attract a following. Since gender was not a prohibitive factor for mediumship, many of the mediums were women. The *Banner of Light* for April 15, 1876, printed a list of Spiritualist lecturers around the country. Out of a few less than three hundred, 127 were obviously women's names, among them Lizzie Doten, Emma Hardinge Britten, Nettie Colburn Maynard, Victoria Woodhull, Cora L. V. Scott Tappan, Mrs. Livermore, and Mrs. Severance. None of their names appears in standard American religious histories, but all of them are familiar to persons who have done research in nineteenth-century Spiritualism.

Like their anticlerical attitude, the Spiritualists' antagonism toward marriage stemmed from several sources: a concern, if not a very effective one, with women's rights that was evident from the beginning of the movement (Moore, 1977:83–84); their doctrine of "spiritual affinities" which dealt with the nature of sexual attraction; and the constant need to defend themselves, particularly mediums, from the accusation of loose sexual behavior.

The Spiritualist criticism of marriage as it operated in nineteenth-century America was based on the knowledge that the husband rather than the wife had most of the legal advantages. Spiritualists recognized that the dissolution of a marriage was a social, even if not a legal, impossibility particularly for women. A woman trapped in an unhappy marriage had two choices: to remain and continue to be unhappy, or to divorce and suffer public scorn, as did Mrs. P., "one of nature's noblewomen," whom Spiritualist Warren Chase cites in his autobiography. Mrs. P. divorced the husband who deserted her and married another man, who unfortunately died a few weeks later. "Of course," said Chase, "it was not the duty of any Christian to aid or comfort her, for she had broken their sacred tie of legal marriage; and they not only let her suffer, but heaped slander on her with their scorn" (192–94).

The Spiritualists spoke of the "marriage law" or the "love principle" as something different from the legal institution of marriage. For Spiritualists love and sexual attraction had both a physical and a spiritual basis. According to Lizzie Doten, trance speaker and lecturer, the virtuous Spiritualist did not deny the reality of physical attraction, but rather cultivated a relationship based foremost on spiritual attraction: "And when you begin to know the Divine Unity, when you begin to be attracted toward each other, not from the law of the flesh, not from the first law of nature, but by the law of the spirit, the spirit acting first; then you shall know what it is to have this combination of two natures, so harmonious, so perfect, so undivided, that you are, indeed, one—most emphatically one" (1867:11). The trouble, the Spiritualists maintained, lay in the fact that too often people married at a very young age or based marriage contracts on financial concerns and thus were trapped for life with persons other than their spiritual affinities. For them, divorce should be a possibility.

Given these unconventional views, it is not difficult to see why Spiritualists were accused repeatedly of advocating free love and divorce. The Spiritualists claimed that they did not want to abolish marriage, but to institute a higher form. Lizzie Doten clarified that she was not in favor of "free lust," and her advice to those who found themselves unhappily married was temperate indeed: "Bear your misfortune" (1867:11). On the other hand, the views of Victoria Woodhull were not so moderate. She said of marriage that "the very safeguards that you have thrown around the family to make it pure and holy have made instead a community of little hot hells" (9). Woodhull's is admittedly an extreme view. More typical is that expressed by William Hepworth Dixon, who devoted an entire book to a discussion of "spiritual wives" and who echoed Lizzie Doten in his insistence that any relationship between the two sexes must have both a physical and a spiritual basis: "Can there be a true marriage of the body without a binding covenant for the soul? Are not all unions which are of the body only, false unions?" (1868:71). Again, Dixon's criticism was not so much one against marriage itself, but against the impossibility of escape, particularly for women, from a contract that was in no way a marriage of souls.

Whatever the variety of opinions within the Spiritualist ranks regarding the dangers of marriage, the prevailing view was one which afforded women more freedom and approval to seek careers other than marriage, or else to function as a medium in addition to being married, putting into effect the hope of one Spiritualist advice columnist who said, "We will not rest content until we have set her [the young girl's] soul agrowing and seen her coming into her full strength for any career" (Soule:4).

For all their unorthodox views on theology, the clergy, and women's roles, female Spiritualist mediums nonetheless conformed in a surprising way to nineteenth-century America's view of what a woman should be, as is indicated by the following excerpt from the *Banner of Light* for April 8, 1876: "Mediumship is closely identified with spiritual refinement, and all the delicate and poetical and lovely attributes of humanity, excepting those which give strength and resisting power. It is like the delicate bloom of the flower, something which is unfit to bear the contact of coldness or harshness, and generally disqualifies its possessor for exercising the necessary force and stern resistance which should be exercised in an ungenial society" (1). From this description one could assume that the Spiritualist medium was the epitome of nineteenth-century womanhood with her attendant virtues of docility, passivity, and demureness. But because she functioned as a religious professional in a society which rejected that as a suitable role for a woman, she was subject to accusations of immorality and stepping beyond her station. R. Laurence Moore suggests that to offset these criticisms, the medium emphasized her femininity by insisting that she was not responsible for her actions, that she was controlled by higher powers (1975:200–221). Mediums frequently maintained that they were as surprised as anyone else that the spirits had chosen such a frail vessel through whom to communicate. Lizzie Doten said of herself, "My brain was fashioned, and my nervous system finely strung, so that I should inevitably catch the thrill of the innumerable voices resounding through the universe, and translate their message into human language as coherently and clearly as my imperfections would allow" (1864:viii).

Moore catalogues and interprets the ambiguous position of the female medium. On one hand, she enjoyed a certain measure of independence, freedom from traditional female responsibilities, an income, even if small, and the adulation of audiences and followers. On the other hand, she often endured social ostracism, frail health, which may have been deliberately cultivated, and exploitation by audiences and managers. In a very real way, mediumship involved exploitation by both the medium herself and her audience of passivity and helplessness, but as Moore says, "The frail sensitiveness that characterized nineteenth-century womanhood was put to worse uses" (221). In sum, for the woman Spiritualist the option to function as a medium was there if she wanted it and if she thought it was worth the price. There were no theological injunctions to prevent her from doing so, and there was a great deal of encouragement for her to proceed.

The Christian Scientists

In 1867, nineteen years after the beginnings of Modern American Spiritualism, Mary Baker Eddy discovered, as she said, Christian Science, a religious movement whose root belief is that reality is in essence spiritual and that matter, sickness, and evil do not exist. Recognition of what Eddy called this spiritual fact makes possible the healing of both spiritual and physical ills. Like Spiritualism, Christian Science rapidly attracted many women followers, a fact remarked upon by historians and interpreters of the movement. Frank Podmore mentions that women constituted the majority of Christian Science patients, at least in the early years (1910:279); and Donald Meyer speaks of the "ubiquity" of women in Christian Science and other mind cure movements: "Not only was its most famous exponent a woman; scores of its lesser exponents were women, as founders, writers, preachers, teachers, healers. Mind cure gave jobs to women by hundreds and thousands." Meyer concludes his comments with the question, "Was there something wrong with women?" (46). The question might more accurately be phrased, "Was there something wrong with the position of women?"

Mary Baker Eddy discovered Christian Science at a time when women were virtually excluded from positions of political, economic, or religious power. Their influence in these areas was to be exerted obliquely through motherhood and family life. Motherhood had taken on almost cultlike proportions of what Ann Douglas calls "an extravaganza of self-immolation" (85), and a woman was expected to find fulfillment by a system of vicarious living through husband and children. A woman's life was one of physical and emotional dependence on others. In many ways Mary Baker Eddy herself epitomized the difficulties and helplessness of nineteenth-century women: she suffered early widowhood, poverty, an unhappy second marriage and subsequent divorce, and a brief third marriage. She experienced constant physical illness as well as emotional instability and seemed unable to care for the son of her first marriage. Her discovery of Christian Science marked the end of her years of illness, at least until old age, and of dependency; and although her life from then on was marked by controversy, she did not suffer the poverty and helplessness of the first half of her life.

Mary Baker Eddy's radical ontology—the total denial of the reality of matter and evil—promised an independence from specific debilitating circumstances such as sickness, poverty, and gender. The sphere of Christian Science activity was the mind, a reflection of Divine Mind, an arena open to all regardless of physical situation. The appeal of Christian Science for women lay primarily in its stress on self-help rather than helplessness, and on the possibility of healing without dependence on the dictates of doctor or clergy. Reinforcing its appeal for women was the fact that Christian Science gave access to its offices—reader, practitioner, and teacher—regardless of gender. Further, Christian Science incorporated into its doctrine of healing those same characteristics which portend well for women in a religious movement: a divinity other than father/creator; a shunning of the doctrine of human depravity; an absence of ordained clergy; and a nontraditional view of marriage.

Two aspects, particularly, of the Christian Science concept of deity have significance for women. First, Eddy stressed that God is nonanthropomorphic, but nonetheless incorporates the feminine as well as the masculine. Human philosophy had erroneously "made God manlike" (1909:269); nonetheless, she said, the divine is constituted of certain characteristics of personality. One of these is love. It was from love that the feminine aspect of God proceeded: "In divine Science, we have not as much authority for considering God masculine, as we have for considering Him feminine, for Love imparts the clearest idea of Deity" (1909:517)./4/ Second, Eddy divorced God from responsibility for the world's ills: God is not the creator of the material world—that is the work of mortal mind. The Christian Science God is not the author of human suffering; does not send sickness as a trial to the faithful; has not meted out death as a punishment for the sin of Eve. This God is not the stern judge of those who fall into sin, helpless in their own depravity to keep from doing so.

The deity of Christian Science affirms the feminine aspect of the divine. God becomes both mother and father, an infinite fount of love, not seeking retribution for sin, but desirous only that human spirits come to understand the perfection they already possess. Women could see themselves, then, not as weak and helpless, but as reflecting the image of the divine feminine. They did not need to interpret their relatively weak position in the world as a sign of God's particular disfavor. Nor was there any reason that women should be kept from full participation in Christian Science because they did not sufficiently mirror the divine nature.

The Christian Science view of human nature further reinforced a highly optimistic estimate of human capabilities, regardless of gender. Eddy taught that the human person is not a duality, made up of matter and spirit, but a totally spiritual being, a reflection of the divine: "Man is not matter! He is not made up of brain, blood, bones, and other material elements. . . . Man is spiritual and perfect; and because he is spiritual and perfect, he must be so understood in Christian Science. Man is idea, the image of Love; he is not physique" (1909:475).

It is not difficult to understand the appeal, particularly for women, of a religion which told them, first, that the body with all its limitations was merely an illusion, and second, that spiritual perfection was already theirs. For the Christian Science woman spiritual exercise involved not self-abnegation or lament over perfection not achieved, but cultivation of the understanding of the human person as already perfect. Sin, or error, in Christian Science, was to put too low an estimate on the powers of human spirit. Gender became unimportant if the body was not real. There was no moral or spiritual or physical weakness peculiar to women if the female body, like the male body, was illusory.

That gender was not prohibitive in the qualifications for leadership in Christian Science is evidenced by the fact that in the early years women practitioners outnumbered men five to one (Gottschalk:244). In addition, the offices of reader and teacher were open to women. These positions were not clerical in nature, since Christian Science considered itself a religion of laypersons, and it reflected that same bias against the ordained clergy that was evident in Spiritualism—a bias that is common in religious movements in which women have equal status. Eddy saw the clergy as perpetrators of error rather than truth, and she blamed the priestly caste for the misunderstanding in Christianity of the nature of reality: "The pride of priesthood is the prince of this world. It has nothing in Christ" (1909:270). Eddy claimed that Jesus administered to his disciples without benefit of ordination, and she did not want to "organize materially Christ's Church" (1896:90–91). Eddy's wish was that the offices of Christian Science should reflect the dual nature of deity, and the *Manual of the Mother Church* specifies that the two readers at the weekly services must be a man and a woman (29).

Nineteenth-century Christian Science gave evidence of a final likeness to other religious movements granting equal status to women in that the attitude of Mary Baker Eddy toward marriage might be called lukewarm. Her antagonism to marriage was not as strongly expressed as that of the Shakers or some of the Spiritualists, but Eddy's writings indicate that she saw marriage as a necessary encumbrance for the present state of human development: "Marriage is the legal and moral provision for generation among human kind" (1909:56). The chapter on marriage in *Science and Health* reveals an ambivalence about marriage. There are numerous typical admonitions about the need for fidelity, patience, and endurance. There is certainly no hint that Eddy had revolutionary ideas about the roles of men and women in marriage. "Men," she says, "should not be required to participate in all the annoyances and cares of domestic economy, nor should women be expected to understand political economy" (1909:59). Eddy even expressed the belief that the need for sexual union to perpetuate the race would eventually disappear: "As human generation ceases, the unbroken levels of eternal harmonious living will be spiritually discerned, and men, not of the earth, earthly, but co-existent with God will appear" (1909:68–69). Stephen Gottschalk points out that for Christian Science marriage was a human, not a spiritual, institution, and there is no provision for marriage in the *Manual of the Mother Church* (241–42).

If the evidence concerning Eddy's antipathy toward marriage seems ambiguous, her critics nonetheless were convinced of her views. In an often quoted article in *McClure's Magazine* Georgine Milmine takes Eddy to task for "her qualified disapproval of marriage," as well as her failure to say anything about children in her chapter on marriage in *Science and Health*./5/ Milmine quotes Eddy further on the subject: "Human nature has bestowed on a wife the right to become a mother; but if the wife esteems not this privilege by mutual consent, exalted and increased affections, she may win a higher" (n.p.). In *The Religio-Medical Masquerade* Frederick W. Peabody criticizes Eddy's views on marriage and children, and accuses Christian Science of causing estrangement between husband and wife. Peabody claims that "it is a part of Mrs. Eddy's teaching and the teaching of her students, that a woman cannot be an effective healer, if she really loves a man and be a true wife" and that the same was true of men (161–62).

Mary Baker Eddy's own life as a wife and mother, as both Milmine and Peabody point out, was an irregular one. It is difficult to know what kind of valid cause-and-effect relationship to set between Eddy's personal life and her tepid views on marriage and children. Suffice it to say that she herself did not function as a role model for wife and mother for her followers. Nor did Christian Science in the nineteenth century extol the high calling of the married state and motherhood as the only fulfilling options for women.

In conclusion, Mary Baker Eddy's religious doctrines had implications for the evaluation of women both spiritually and physically. She was firm in her stand for women's rights, saying that Christian Science "equalizes the sexes" (1909:340). She recognized and spoke out against the fact that "civil law establishes very unfair differences between the rights of the two sexes" (1909:63). Stephen Gottschalk claims that it would be inaccurate to call Eddy a feminist, but he speculates that her followers saw Christian Science as giving expression to a "higher concept of divine womanhood," as well as providing an example of a female religious leader (269).

Mary Baker Eddy's religious discovery evolved into a highly authoritarian structure, one which nonetheless gave women a place not usually afforded them by traditional Christianity./6/ Christian Science demanded of women that they give up the claim of reality for their material bodies, but in return it gave them a connection to the numinous in the Father/Mother God, and it promised them power over their own lives as well as equal participation in the religion they had chosen.

The Theosophists

Helena P. Blavatsky and Colonel Henry Olcott founded the Theosophical Society in New York in 1875, the same year that *Science and Health* was published for the first time. The first objective of the Society was "to form the nucleus of a Universal Brotherhood of Humanity, without distinction of race, creed, sex, caste, or color" (Blavatsky:24); and so from the beginning there was a specific identification with women and a concern for equality—this in spite of the fact that at the formation of the Society Henry Olcott served as president and Madame Blavatsky as secretary.

Blavatsky supplied the doctrinal basis for the Society, which had its origins in Eastern religious traditions, the occult, and "ancient religions." In spite of generally different content and origins, Theosophy shared with Shakerism, Spiritualism, and Christian Science the same propensities to see the divine as other than masculine; to interpret human nature in a highly optimistic manner; to dismiss the need for an ordained clergy; and to view marriage as a less than desirable state, particularly for women. The Society attracted many women of high intellectual capabilities, many of whom had had a strong allegiance to Christianity at one time in their lives; who had worked actively for women's rights; and who had experienced unhappy marriages—women like Annie Besant, Katherine Tingley, and Alice Bailey. Bailey later left Theosophy to form the Arcane School.

Blavatsky's doctrine of deity stressed its impersonal nature. She considered the Christian God "a bundle of contradictions and a logical impossibility." She saw the God of Moses as "but the gigantic shadow of *man*, and not man at his best, either" (35). Blavatsky described the God of Theosophy as a "universal Divine Principle, the root of All, from which all proceeds, and within which all shall be absorbed at the end of the great cycle of being" (36). She rejected the need for abjectness and humility on the part of human beings in their dealings with the divine, and claimed that prayer offended the dignity of human nature and "kills self-reliance." Blavatsky insisted that "this idea of passing one's whole life in moral idleness and having one's hardest work and duty done by another—whether God or man—is most revolting to us, as it is most degrading to human dignity" (42). Blavatsky did not see either men or women as suppliants: "We *act*," she said of Theosophists, "instead of *talking*. . . . We call it WILL-POWER, and it is rather an internal command than a petition" (38).

The Theosophical view of human nature proceeded from this impersonal view of the divine as a principle: "Grant us our postulate," said Blavatsky, "that God is a universally diffused, infinite principle, and how can man alone escape from being soaked through, *by* and *in*, the Deity" (Judah:120–21). Theosophists coupled their belief in the human person as permeated by deity with a belief in karma and reincarnation. The combination resulted in a denial of human depravity and a stress on individual power and responsibility regardless of gender or particular situation.

To illustrate, women found the Theosophical interpretation of karma and reincarnation particularly appealing because it deemphasized the importance of gender: reincarnation could occur in either a male or a female body, depending upon what karmic ties from past lives needed to be worked out. As Theosophist Margaret Cousins explained: "According to the doctrine of Reincarnation, which is generally accepted by Theosophists, the same ego which has incarnated as a woman several times, takes later a man's body, and vice versa; and the experiences gained in one kind of form are carried over in consciousness to the other" (215).

Like Christian Science, then, Theosophy promised women an escape from gender, but by different means. Well aware that woman's body had kept her from positions of spiritual leadership in Western Christianity, women could turn to Theosophy for aid: "A temporary function of the body [child-bearing] is made an excuse for closing off many avenues of world-service to women," said Cousins. "It is an expression of that 'Curse of Eve' which it is part of the great mission of Theosophy to reverse" (217). Because of their work in India, Theosophists knew that the doctrines of karma and reincarnation had not had a salutary effect on the roles of women in countries where the beliefs were indigenous. Transplanted to the West, however, these same doctrines seemed to promise that women could define their roles in a way that was broader than those imposed upon them by traditional Christianity. Taken together, the Theosophical interpretations of karma, reincarnation, and the essential divinity of the human person gave women an opportunity to dispense with the Christian emphasis on sin and repentance and to look forward to the redressing of the wrongs they had suffered, even if it be in another life. This was an understandable attraction for many women in a position to feel that one lifetime was too short for the strides they needed to make.

In addition to providing women with satisfactory beliefs of a personal nature, Theosophy afforded them the opportunity of exercising spiritual leadership equal to that of men. Like the Spiritualists and the Christian Scientists, the Theosophists claimed that dogma, clergy, and hierarchy distorted religious truths, and Theosophy thus had no ordained clergy. Their truths, they said, came from the masters or mahatmas, "great souls" who had passed beyond the need to be reincarnated (Blavatsky:159). The mahatmas favored women as well as men with their messages, although I am not aware that any mahatmas have ever been women; and according to Annie Besant, "Those on whose heads but for a moment the touch of the Master has rested in blessing can never again look upon the world save through eyes made luminous with the radiance of the Eternal Peace" (1893:364).

Women attracted away from Christianity to Theosophy were often those resentful of the traditional churches' attitudes toward women as well as of their refusal to ordain women. According to Margaret Cousins, "The Churches and their priesthoods have ever been the enemies of the freedom of women" (218). Theosophists countered the policies of the churches with examples from among their own members: "The writings of Madame Blavatsky, Anna Kingsford, Annie Besant, and several other women have given ample evidence that the science of theology has not been made a masculine preserve by Mother Nature, but was arbitrarily appropriated by those persistent suppressors of womankind, the world's materializing priesthoods, for their own sex" (Cousins:218). Women Theosophists encountered resistance even among their own kind, however, in the refusal to ordain women to the priesthood of the Liberal Catholic Church, to which many Theosophists belonged: "Some occultists . . . maintain that the line of magic for a man is quite different from that of a woman, and infer that the magic of the Mass could not take place through the female organism" (Cousins:220). Nonetheless, women joined the Theosophical movement expecting to participate "on terms of entire equality with men in its ideal of the family of Humanity, in its terms of membership, in all its offices, and in every facet of its teachings" (Cousins:214). The fact that there was no clergy in Theosophy itself made this an easier fact to accomplish.

Like other religious movements sympathetic to full participation by women, Theosophy had in its teachings a resistance to the traditional marriage relationship that was somewhat subtle, but detectable nonetheless. Theosophists did not deny the validity of marriage. Madame Blavatsky said, "Surely you cannot believe us so absurd and fanatical as to preach against marriage altogether" (154). But Theosophists saw the potential of marriage in the nineteenth century for the degradation and legal helplessness of women, and Madame Blavatsky also spoke of taking "the risks of that lottery where there are so many more blanks than prizes" (154). Blavatsky further spoke of marriage as detracting from spiritual development, but it is interesting to note that her remarks appear to have been addressed to men: "Can a man serve two masters? No! . . . practical Occultism is far too serious and dangerous a study for a man to take up, unless he is in the most deadly earnest, and ready to sacrifice *all, himself first of all, to gain his end*" (154–55).

Annie Besant gave another aspect of the Theosophical view of marriage. Besant was very much concerned with women's rights, particularly in the area of marriage and divorce reform and birth control, saying that in marriage a woman "loses her legal existence" and "loses control over her own body; it belongs to her owner, not herself" (1970:9). Besant was not shy about blaming the churches for the sufferings women endured in unhappy marriages and as a result of having numerous children, saying that "both the New Testament and the Church have insisted on the inferiority of the female sex" (1970:13).

Besant was convinced of the views expressed above even before she joined the Theosophical Society. Her opinions after that remained the same, but they had a different basis. After her study with Madame Blavatsky, Besant claimed that humans had let sexual passion brutalize them to the extent that their spiritual essence had been obscured. Now it was time to "hold this instinct in complete control, to transmute it from passion into tender and self-denying affection, to develop the intellectual at the expense of the animal, and thus to raise the whole man to the human stage, in which every intellectual and physical capacity shall subserve the purposes of the soul" (1893:242–43).

Because Theosophists believed that matter had its place in the scheme of human spiritual development—they did not see the body as an illusion, but as a vehicle of learning for the spiritual essence—women like Madame Blavatsky did not express the expectation that marriage would fade away entirely. Rather, they tended to reduce marriage to a passionless, utilitarian setup necessary only for carrying on the species and providing bodies for waiting "egos." But included in the insistence of Theosophists on the need for the spiritual elevation of marriage was the goal of alleviating the physical suffering of marriage for women.

The profeminist implications of Theosophical doctrines did not make the movement immune to cultural biases. For example, Arthur Sinnett's *Mahatma Letters* include an antifeminist strain, and Alice Bailey apparently felt no compunction about saying in her *Unfinished Autobiography*, "I have women friends and am devoted to them but, as a general rule, I prefer the masculine mind . . . a woman will give you lots of silly little troubles all the time and I can't be bothered" (77). But the number of female leaders and writers among Theosophists provides good evidence that in the various facets of the movement women did indeed achieve prominence as spiritual leaders and interpreters.

Conclusion

A study such as this one involves a chicken-and-egg problem. It is difficult to know exactly what cause-and-effect relationships existed between the women who were drawn to Shakerism, Spiritualism, Christian Science, and Theosophy, and the doctrines of the movements. Were women attracted to them because of their teachings about God and human nature and their distaste for an ordained clergy and for marriage? Were the doctrines, instead, shaped by the large number of women participants? Or might not both be the case? There seems little doubt that at the very least women were drawn to these four movements because of the possibility of assuming positions of leadership which were denied them in the mainstream religions.

What is striking about these four movements in which women played such important roles is that the similarities of doctrine and attitude are apparent in spite of often bitter rivalries among the groups themselves, particularly the Spiritualists, the Theosophists, and the Christian Scientists. For example, many Spiritualists were of the opinion that Madame Blavatsky's mahatmas were "undoubtedly myths"; Blavatsky spoke of the "gross materialism" of Spiritualism and downgraded the spirit manifestations as subhuman in nature; and Mary Baker Eddy devoted a chapter in *Science and Health* to discussing the evils of Spiritualism. But in spite of all the disagreements, these movements showed obvious similarities in their attempts to demasculinize the deity, to elevate human nature, and to do away with the power of the ordained Christian clergy. They differed in their views of how to reform marriage, but were unanimous in their agreement that the institution as it was lived out in nineteenth-century America was harmful to women on a variety of levels.

Another impressive fact about these four movements is the extent to which their concerns parallel those of contemporary feminist theologians. These similarities make even more salient Robert Ellwood's recent remarks to the effect that "a possible American feminine religion has already been limned by certain common features of these movements, and that when its day comes it could break out of marginality with surprising speed" (72). Missing from the nineteenth-century religious movements is the emphasis on total separation of women from the churches that is characteristic of a theologian like Mary Daly. But even that note was present to a minor extent. In *New America* William H. Dixon speaks of Eliza Farnham of Staten Island, founder of the Truth of Woman movement, based on the inherent superiority of the female in all spheres, particularly the religious: "Man is but the paragon of animals, while woman, by her gifts of soul, belongs to the celestial ranks." Farnham rewrote the story of the Fall, and in the new version Eve gave Adam the benefit of her strength: "She finds Adam in bonds and she sets him free" (1867:379–86).

Nineteenth- and twentieth-century women concerned with equal participation in religious movements appear to share a common understanding, although it is less self-consciously articulated in the nineteenth century, that a God pictured in wholly masculine images is not conducive to an understanding of the feminine as participating in the divine; that a doctrine of human nature as depraved through the Fall seems to be even more detrimental to women than to men; that an ordained male clergy is not likely to open its ranks willingly to women; and that marriage interpreted in the traditional Christian sense will confine women to a particular sphere of influence which does not include positions of religious leadership. In the nineteenth century attempts to act upon these realizations were confined almost exclusively to religious movements considered marginal. In the second half of the twentieth century these understandings are beginning to affect the practice of mainstream Christianity.

NOTES

/1/ Laurel Thatcher Ulrich quotes Mather's reference in "Vertuous Women Found: New England Ministerial Literature, 1668–1735," and says further that "well-behaved women seldom make history" (20). A survey of American religious histories shows that Ulrich is correct. One can hardly find references to women or the religions in which they achieved prominence prior to Sydney Ahlstrom's *A Religious History of the American People*, and even there the references to women are relatively few and restricted mostly to the marginal traditions. As another current example, Henry Warner Bowden's *Dictionary of American Religious Biography* mentions few women who are not connected with marginal traditions. He omits, for example, Antoinette Brown, first woman ordained in the Congregational Church in the United States.

/2/ Gayle Graham Yates summarizes the attitudes of institutionalized religion toward women and the reaction of feminist theologians in *What Women Want: Ideas of the Movement* (65–73). Analyses of antifeminism and profeminism in specific religious traditions can be found in *Signs: Journal of Women in Culture and Society* (1976); Ruether, ed. (1974); Plaskow and Romero, eds. (1973); Gross, ed. (1977); and Christ and Plaskow, eds. (1979). The Winter 1978 issue of *American Quarterly* deals with women in American religious history (see James, 1978), and *Quest: A Feminist Quarterly* (1975) contains essays on women in less traditional religious forms such as astrology and witchcraft.

/3/ The terms "mainstream" and "marginal" are fraught with controversy as to what they mean exactly. R. Laurence Moore suggests that "mainstream" is a "societal invention that has no necessary relation to an actual consensus of values and therefore its use is inappropriate, as is the use of 'marginal'" (1977:xii–xiii). I am using the term "marginal" to designate groups whose teachings are perceived by Protestants and Catholics alike to be outside the bounds of orthodox Christianity.

/4/ Not all critics see Mary Baker Eddy's concept of the Father/Mother God as particularly helpful to women or even conducive to well-being. Meyer speaks of the God of Christian Science as an extreme manifestation of the accepting parent: "Father/Mother was the child's wish about his parents, perfect in their gratification of every need" (82). Gail Parker interprets Christian Science as the "Sentimental Heresy institutionalized," and "the holiness of motherhood evolved into a species of mariolatry" (18). Susan Setta, although she affirms the incorporation of the feminine into the deity, points out that Eddy had to deny the reality of her own female body in order to do so (289–301).

/5/ This quotation is from chapter 14 of a series that began in *McClure's* in January 1907 and was entitled "Mary Baker Eddy, The Story of Her Life and the History of Christian Science." The page numbers of the copy I used at the American Antiquarian Society were cut off for chapter 14.

/6/ There seems to be an understanding that the authority in the structure of Christian Science has passed to male leadership, something which is bound to happen as a religion becomes more assimilated into a patriarchal culture. The most recent mention of this I've seen is in Heilbrun (1979:203). But the very fact that all my doctrinal quotations are taken from Mary Baker Eddy's writings rather than from a variety of interpreters illustrates the skill with which she insured that her views alone would persist.

ACKNOWLEDGEMENTS

I am grateful to the National Endowment for the Humanities for the assistance of a summer stipend in the researching and writing of this article; and I wish to express my appreciation to Professors Jean Ward and Roland Delattre of the University of Minnesota and Patricia Wilson-Kastner of the United Theological Seminary of the Twin Cities for advice while the manuscript was in process.

WORKS CONSULTED

Ahlstrom, Sydney
1971 "Mary Baker Eddy." In *Notable American Women*. Vol. 1, pp. 551-60. Cambridge, MA: Belknap Press.
1972 *A Religious History of the American People*. New Haven, CT: Yale University Press.

Allen, Milton
1904 "To Ministers Everywhere." *Banner of Light*, 16 January, p. 2.

Andrews, Edward Deming
1963 *The People Called Shakers*. New York: Dover.

Anonymous
1876 "Rights of Mediums and Rights of Philosophy." *Banner of Light*, 8 April, p. 1.

Bailey, Alice
1951 *The Unfinished Autobiography*. New York: Lucis Publishing Co.

Bates, Paulina
1849 *The Divinity Book of Holy and Eternal Wisdom, Revealing the Word of God out of Whose Mouth Goes a Sharp Sword*. Canterbury, NH.

Beaver, R. Pierce
1968 *All Loves Excelling: American Protestant Women in World Mission*. Grand Rapids, MI: Wm. B. Eerdmans.

Bednarowski, Mary Farrell
1973 "Nineteenth Century American Spiritualism: An Attempt at a Scientific Religion." Ph.D. dissertation, University of Minnesota.
1975 "Nineteenth Century Spiritualism in Wisconsin." *The Wisconsin Magazine of History* 59:3-19.

Besant, Annie
1893 *An Autobiography*. London.
1928 "The Position of Women, A Sermon Delivered in the Liberal Catholic Church at Adyar." *The Theosophist* 49:451-55.
1970 "Marriage: As It Was, As It Is, and As It Should Be: A Plea for Reform." In *Selections of Social and Political Pamphlets of Annie Besant*, edited by John Saville. New York: Augustus M. Kelly.

Blavatsky, H. P.
1972 *The Key to Theosophy: An Abridgement*. Ed. Joy Mills. Wheaton, IL: Quest Publishing Co. Original edition 1889.

Bowden, Henry Warner
1977 *Dictionary of American Religious Biography*. Westport, CT: Greenwood Press.

Carra, Emma
1857 "The Old Church and the New." *Banner of Light*, 18 April, p. 3.

Chase, Warren
1857 *The Life-Line of the Lone One or Autobiography of the World's Child.* Boston: Colby and Rich.

Christ, Carol P., and Plaskow, Judith, eds.
1979 *Womanspirit Rising: A Feminist Reader in Religion*. San Francisco: Harper and Row.

Cousins, Margaret
1918 "Without Distinction of Sex." *The Theosophist* 40:213-23.

Despard, C.
1913 *Theosophy and the Woman's Movement*. London: Theosophical Publishing Society.

Desroche, Henri
1971 *The American Shakers: From Neo-Christianity to Presocialism*. Amherst: University of Massachusetts Press.

Dixon, William Hepworth
1867 *New America*. Philadelphia: J. B. Lippincott.
1868 *Spiritual Wives*. Philadelphia: J. B. Lippincott.

Doolittle, Mary Antoinette
1880 *Autobiography of Mary Antoinette Doolittle*. Mt. Lebanon, NY.

Doten, Lizzie
1864 *Poems from the Inner Life*. Boston: Colby and Rich.
1867 "Free Love and Affinity: A Discourse Delivered Under Spirit Influence at the Melodean, Boston." Boston.
1870 *Poems of Progress*. Boston: Colby and Rich.

Douglas, Ann
1978 *The Feminization of American Culture*. New York: Avon.

Dyer, Joseph
1826 *A Compendius Narrative Elucidating the Character, Disposition, and Conduct of Mary Dyer, From the Time of Her Marriage in 1799 Till She Left the Society Called Shakers in 1815*. 2d ed. Pittsfield, MA: M. Beckwith.

Dyer, Mary
1822 *A Portrait of Shakerism*. Concord, NH.

Eddy, Mary Baker
1896 *Miscellaneous Writings, 1883-1896*. Boston: Published by the Trustees under the Will of Mary Baker Eddy.
1909 *Science and Health with Key to the Scriptures*. Boston: Allison V. Stewart.

Ellwood, Robert S., Jr.
1979 "The Study of New Religious Movements in America." *Bulletin, The Council on the Study of Religion* 10:69-72.

Evans, Frederick
1849 *Autobiography of a Shaker*. Albany, NY.

Flexner, Eleanor
1971 "Anna Howard Shaw." In *Notable American Women*. Vol. 3, pp. 274-77. Cambridge, MA: Belknap Press.

Gottschalk, Stephen
1974 *The Emergence of Christian Science in American Religious Life*. Berkeley: University of California Press.

Greenwalt, Emmett A.
1955 *The Point Loma Community in California, 1897–1942: A Theosophical Experiment*. Berkeley: University of California Press.

Gross, Rita, ed.
1977 *Beyond Androcentrism: New Essays on Women and Religion*. Missoula, MT: Scholars Press.

Hall, David, ed.
1968 *The Antinomian Controversy, 1636–1638: A Documentary History*. Middletown, CT: Greenwood Press.

Heilbrun, Carolyn
1979 *Reinventing Womanhood*. New York: Norton.

James, Janet Wilson, ed.
1978 *American Quarterly*. Winter.

Judah, J. Stillson
1967 *The History and Philosophy of the Metaphysical Movements in America*. Philadelphia: Westminster.

Mace, Aurelia
1907 *The Aletheia: Spirit of Truth*. Farmington, ME: Knowlton and McLeary Co.

Manual of the Mother Church
1895 Boston: Christian Science Board of Directors.

Meyer, Donald
1965 *The Positive Thinkers*. Garden City, NY: Doubleday.

Milmine, Georgine
1907–8 "Mary Baker Eddy, The Story of Her Life and the History of Christian Science." *McClure's Magazine*.

Moore, R. Laurence
1975 "The Spiritualist Medium." *American Quarterly* 27:200–221.
1977 *In Search of White Crows: Spiritualism, Parapsychology, and American Culture*. New York: Oxford University Press.

Nethercott, Arthur
1960 *The First Five Lives of Annie Besant*. Chicago: University of Chicago Press.
1963 *The Last Four Lives of Annie Besant*. Chicago: University of Chicago Press.

Owen, Robert Dale
1874 "Some Results of My Spiritual Studies." *Atlantic Monthly* 34:719–31.

Parker, Gail
1970 "Mary Baker Eddy and Sentimental Womanhood." *New England Quarterly* 43:3–18.

Peabody, Frederick W.
1910 *The Religio-Medical Masquerade*. New York: Hancock Press.

Peel, Robert
1966 *The Years of Discovery*. New York: Holt, Rinehart and Winston.
1971 *The Years of Trial*. New York: Holt, Rinehart and Winston.
1977 *The Years of Authority*. New York: Holt, Rinehart and Winston.

Plaskow, Judith, and Romero, Joan Arnold, eds.
1973 *Women and Religion*. Rev. ed. Missoula, MT: Scholars Press.

Podmore, Frank
1902 *Modern Spiritualism, A History and a Criticism*. 2 vols. New York: Charles Scribner's Sons.
1910 *From Mesmer to Christian Science: A Short History of Mental Healing*. London: Methuen.

Quest
1975 *Quest: A Feminist Quarterly*. Spring.

Riegel, Robert
1963 *American Feminists*. Lawrence: University of Kansas Press.

Ruether, Rosemary Radford, ed.
1974 *Religion and Sexism*. New York: Simon and Schuster.

Setta, Susan
1977 "Denial of the Female—Affirmation of the Feminine: The Father/Mother God of Mary Baker Eddy." In *Beyond Androcentrism: New Essays on Women and Religion*, edited by Rita M. Gross. Missoula, MT: Scholars Press.

Signs
1976 *Signs: Journal of Women in Culture and Society*. Winter.

Sinnett, Arthur
1923 *The Mahatma Letters to A. P. Sinnett from Mahatmas M. and K. H.* Transcribed and compiled with an introduction by A. T. Barker. London: T. Fisher Unwin, Ltd.

Solomon, Barbara
1971 "Antoinette Louisa Brown Blackwell." In *Notable American Women*. Vol. 1, pp. 158–61. Cambridge, MA: Belknap Press.

Soule, Minnie Meserve
1904 "Our Home Circle." *Banner of Light*, 16 January, p. 4.

Thomas, Robert David
1977 *The Man Who Would Be Perfect: John Humphrey Noyes and the Utopian Impulse*. Philadelphia: University of Pennsylvania Press.

Ulrich, Laurel Thatcher
1976 "Vertuous Women Found: New England Ministerial Literature, 1668-1735." *American Quarterly* 28:20-40.

"Women and Holy Orders"
1925 "Women and Holy Orders By a Member of the Church Militant." *The Theosophist* 46:201-9.

Woodhull, Victoria
1873 "The Scare-Crows of Sexual Slavery, An Oration." New York: Woodhull and Claflin.

Yates, Gayle Graham
1975 *What Women Want: Ideas of the Movement*. Cambridge, MA: Harvard University Press.

"Together and in Harness": Women's Traditions in the Sanctified Church

Cheryl Townsend Gilkes

All human communities contain enterprising and historically aware members who struggle to maintain the cherished values, statuses, roles, activities, and organizations of earlier generations that serve to structure the group's presentation of self and, therefore, constitute tradition. Within the black community in the United States, women have been some of the most enterprising agents of tradition. Since sociologists have seriously neglected study of tradition, women, and black people, black women's traditions in community institutions represent the most underdeveloped topic of social inquiry.

Black women and men have perceived racial oppression to be the most pervasive source of their individual and group suffering, but it has not been the sole catalyst for their collective action. In addition to mounting organized responses to problems of political subordination, economic exploitation, and social exclusion, black people have constructed a historical community that has provided a context for traditions, distinctive ethnic identity, and group consciousness. When pressure to abandon tradition has come from outside the black community, maintaining tradi-

Earlier versions of this article were presented to the Women's Studies in Religion Program of the Harvard Divinity School and to the *Signs* Communities of Women Conference, held February 18–20, 1983, at the Center for Research on Women, Stanford University. I wish to acknowledge the support of Boston University's Faculty Research Program, the Women's Studies in Religion Program of the Harvard Divinity School, the Inter-University Research Group on the Intersection of Gender and Race, and the Bunting Institute of Radcliffe College for their contributions at various stages of the research and writing. I also wish to thank Paule Verdet, Thomas Koenig, and two anonymous *Signs* reviewers for criticisms and editorial suggestions.

[*Signs: Journal of Women in Culture and Society* 1985, vol. 10, no. 4]

tion has become a matter of political resistance, even though this struggle may take place in parts of the community that typically avoid confrontation with the dominant culture. For example, religion and religious activity have been the most important spheres for the creation and maintenance of tradition. Black women have invested considerable amounts of time, energy, and economic resources in the growth and development of religious organizations.

Recognition of the variety of strong traditions that black women have established in the religious and secular affairs of their community has been obscured by sociologists' exclusive focus on family roles and on black women's deviation from patriarchal expectations in a sexist and racist society. The tendency to view black churches only as agencies of sociopolitical change led by black male pastors also obscures the central and critical roles of black women. Throughout all varieties of black religious activity, women represent from 75 to 90 percent of the participants; yet there is little documentation or analysis of their role in the development of this oldest and most autonomous aspect of black community life.[1] This article examines the place and importance of black women and their traditions within one segment of the black religious experience, the Sanctified Church.

The Sanctified Church, a significant but misunderstood segment of a very pluralistic black church, comprises those independent denominations and congregations formed by black people in the post-Reconstruction South and their direct organizational descendents. In contrast to those Baptist and Methodist denominations organized before the Civil War, the Sanctified Church represents the black religious institutions that arose in response to and largely in conflict with postbellum changes in worship traditions within the black community. Although these congregations and denominations were part of the Holiness and Pentecostal movements of the late nineteenth and early twentieth centuries, the label "Sanctified Church" emerged within the black community to distinguish congregations of "the Saints" from those of other black Christians. This label not only acknowledges the sense of ethnic kinship and consciousness underlying the black religious experience but also designates the part of the black religious experience to which a Saint belongs without having to go through the sometimes dizzying maze of organizational histories involving at least twenty-five denominations.

The importance of the Sanctified Church lies in its relationship to

1. Teressa Hoover, "Black Women and the Churches: Triple Jeopardy," in *Black Theology: A Documentary History*, ed. Gayraud Wilmore and James Cone (Maryknoll, N.Y.: Orbis Books, 1979), pp. 377–88; James Tinney, "The Religious Experience of Black Men," in *The Black Male*, ed. Lawrence E. Gary (Beverly Hills, Calif.: Sage Publications, 1981), pp. 269–76. See also Pearl Williams-Jones, "A Minority Report: Black Pentecostal Women," *Spirit: A Journal of Issues Incident to Black Pentecostalism* 1, no. 2 (1977): 31–44.

black history, its normative impact on the larger black religious experience, and its respect for and positive redefinition of black women's historical experience. When black people were first making choices about their cultural strategies as free women and men, the Sanctified Church rejected a cultural and organizational model that uncritically imitated Euro-American patriarchy. In the face of cultural assaults that used the economic and sexual exploitation of black women as a rationale for their denigration, the Sanctified Church elevated black women to the status of visible heroines—spiritual and professional role models for their churches. At a time when Baptist and Methodist denominations relegated Christian education to the structural margins of their organizations, the Sanctified Church professionalized this activity, and women were able to use their roles as educators and the "educated" as a source of power and career opportunity. At a time when employment opportunities for black women were the worst possible, the Sanctified Church presented "professional" role models for black working women to emulate. Higher education and work were identified as legitimate means of upward mobility for black women, and they were encouraged to achieve economic power through white-collar employment. As a consequence, the women's growing economic power helped to maintain their collective autonomy and reinforced their heroic role in the church. Finally, taking their cue from the feminist infrastructure of the black women's racial uplift movement, churchwomen created an institutional basis for women's self-consciousness. The result was an alternative model of power and leadership within the most authoritarian and least democratic of formal organizations—the episcopally governed church. These religious organizations transformed the negative and contradictory experiences of black women into an aspect of community life that maintained tradition and fostered social and individual change.

Within the Sanctified Church, black women have created for themselves a variety of roles, careers, and organizations with great influence but with variable access to structural authority. Their activities and their consciousness represent a part of the black religious experience that underscores both the dynamic and unsettled nature of gender relations in the wider black community and the historical centrality of gender as a public issue within it. Although the women in the Sanctified Church have worked within structures that range from egalitarian to purely patriarchal, they have neither ceased nor relaxed their efforts to improve their status and opportunities within these organizations. In a variety of ways, their efforts are related to those of women in other black religious and secular organizations.

Women's experience in the Sanctified Church has been part of the larger historical role of black women, a role that emphasizes independence, self-reliance, strength, and autonomy and that contradicts the dominant culture's expectations and demands of women.[2] Like many of the black community's activities of the late nineteenth and early twentieth centuries, the rise of the Sanctified Church contained a gender-conscious response to the problems of racial oppression. Concern about the status and role of women was reflected in one among a number of cultural debates within the post-Reconstruction black community. In a response to black women's suffering and role demands in the context of violent racial oppression, the Sanctified Church took account of at least four specific aspects of their history when developing churchwomen's roles: the devaluation of black women by dominant culture, the education of black women and their recruitment as educators of "the Race" during the late nineteenth and early twentieth centuries, the "relative" economic independence of black women through sustained participation in the labor force, and the autonomous political organization of black women between 1892 and 1940.[3]

The rise of the Sanctified Church also occurred when "liberation of the race was the immediate goal of blacks, [and] the men attached great importance to the females' roles in the effort."[4] In 1896, black women formed the National Association of Colored Women after several years of autonomous organizing. Their efforts earned them W. E. B. DuBois's admiration and praise as the "intellectual leadership of the Race."[5] The ethic sustaining their efforts supported women's leadership as a necessary part of the overall effort to benefit the community and the world. Clubwoman Josephine St. Pierre Ruffin stated this clearly in 1892: "Our women's movement is a woman's movement in that it is led and directed by women for the good of women and men, for the benefit of all humanity. . . . We want, we ask the active interest of our men; . . . we are not alienating or withdrawing, we are only coming to the front, willing to

2. Bonnie Thornton Dill, "The Dialectics of Black Womanhood," *Signs: Journal of Women in Culture and Society* 4, no. 3 (Spring 1979): 543–55.

3. On the dominant culture's devaluation of black women, see Bell Hooks, *Ain't I a Woman: Black Women and Feminism* (Boston: South End Press, 1981). On the role of black women in education, see Linda Perkins, "Black Women and Racial 'Uplift' Prior to Emancipation," in *The Black Woman Cross-culturally*, ed. Filomena Chioma Steady (Cambridge, Mass.: Schenkman Publishing Co., 1981), pp. 317–34; Angela Y. Davis, *Women, Race and Class* (New York: Random House, 1981); and Gerda Lerner, ed., *Black Women in White America: A Documentary History* (New York: Random House, 1971). On the "relative" economic independence of black women, see Dill; and Davis. On the political organization of black women, see Perkins; Davis; and Cheryl Townsend Gilkes, "Living and Working in a World of Trouble: The Emergent Career of the Black Woman Community Worker" (Ph.D. diss., Northeastern University, 1978).

4. Perkins, p. 321.

5. W. E. B. DuBois, "Votes for Women," in *The Crisis Writings*, ed. Daniel Walden (1912; reprint, Greenwich, Conn.: Fawcett Publications, 1972), pp. 339–40, esp. p. 340.

join any others in the same work."[6] "The Saints" carried this ethic and a positive perception of the role of the "Race woman" into their new denominational structures as they separated or were ejected from the more established Baptist and Methodist churches. Specific women's tradition reflected the high value placed on women's political and educational leadership.

Leaders of the early Sanctified Church were also responsive to the fact that the majority of job opportunities for black women were in domestic service and agricultural work. As black people migrated and the church became more urban, this consciousness generated a concern for the problems of black women as household domestics. As household workers, black women were subject to sexual exploitation by white men who assumed that all black women were morally loose and appreciated male advances. Many black parents saw the education of their daughters as a strategy to avoid such risks. As a result, white observers often criticized black parents' failure to discriminate against their daughters. These educated women were expected to play a role in elevating their sisters, and black women's gatherings were the settings of just such "uplifting" socialization. Church and community activities were organized around household domestics' "time off" as alternatives to the entertainments available in the world of "sinners." Churches encouraged both the educated and the uneducated to be "ladies." While not entirely feminist, these strategies fostered a high degree of woman consciousness within the black religious community.

The black women who responded to Holiness and Pentecostal preachers and evangelists represented the broad spectrum of Afro-American women. These women were as militantly pro-black, pro-woman, and pro-uplift as their Baptist and Methodist sisters were, and their political consciousness was fueled by spiritual zeal. They were somewhat more successful than Baptist and Methodist women in gaining access to the pulpit or lectern; in those churches where they failed, the "double pulpit" emerged as a compromise between the women's spiritual militance and biblical patriarchy. In some cases, Baptist and Methodist women defected to the Sanctified Church in order to exercise their gifts.

The militancy of organized women in the Sanctified Church led to the almost total divergence of women's leadership roles from that of the "pastor's wife." Such separation of marital role from leadership status came more slowly in black Baptist and Methodist churches than in the Sanctified Church, where women's opportunities for leadership became more and more diverse, offering a wide choice of religious careers. In

6. Elizabeth Lindsey Davis, *Lifting as They Climb: A History of the National Association of Colored Women* (Washington, D.C.: Howard University, Moorland Spingarn Research Center, 1933), p. 19.

those denominations in which women were unable to become elders, pastors, and bishops, they assumed the roles of church mothers, evangelists, missionaries, prayer band leaders, deaconesses, and, most important, "teachers"; these alternatives were also available in those denominations in which women were eligible for all leadership roles. Where churchwomen were officially "the second sex," they achieved quite powerful positions of influence and structural authority.

The various women's traditions existing within these churches are as much a response to the sociohistorical realities of black womanhood as to perceived biblical mandates and doctrines. One could almost argue that these traditions are more woman-centered than religious. Although all Protestants read the same King James Bible, the black interpretation of scripture had radically different organizational consequences than did the white male reading of the same texts. Whatever the degree of patriarchal control, black churches have been influenced in some way by the militancy of the women of the Sanctified Church.

"Women God Raised Up": The Elevation of Black Women

At the time when white Americans were calling black people a nation of "thieves, liars, and prostitutes,"[7] Sanctified Church members were calling each other "Saints." They perceived themselves to be set apart for sacred purposes; these men and women were confident that God "had raised them up" for a special calling. Regardless of the intensity of racial oppression, it was the responsibility of the "Saints" to do everything in their power to prevent whites from casting them down. Black women represented the overwhelming majority of "Saints" in need of elevation and protection from the physical and cultural assaults of white racism.

The church's resistance strategies have included the adoption of distinctive dress codes and the refusal to use first names in any public settings that could be interracial. Even cornerstones and signs listing church officers give only first initials and surnames. It is important to recognize that this tactic to achieve personhood applies to women as well as men: if male elders are listed with initials, church mothers are similarly listed. In church publications, elders, church mothers, and all others are also identified in this way. All this was (and still is) intended to prevent white racists from calling black Saints by their first names, a white practice used as a strategy to depersonalize and to devalue black people. Although largely overlooked as a tactic in cultural resistance, the Saints' use of initials rather than first names remains a very forceful answer to the daily irritations and abrasions of southern race relations. Accommodation to

7. Ibid.

racism is, in the context of the preaching of the Sanctified Church, an accommodation to sin.

Although white people withheld ordinary titles of respect for blacks, such as Mr., Mrs., and Miss, they relaxed such overt racism when using the religious titles of fellow southern Protestants. In the Baptist and Methodist churches, such courtesies were often extended only to the black preacher. The Sanctified Church, however, saw as ministry those roles reserved exclusively for women and therefore included women when contemplating the problem of interracial protocol. This failure to exclude women from protocol is clear testimony to the woman consciousness of the Sanctified Church, a consciousness evident in the glowing terms used to describe both women's and men's activities in denominational newspapers and reports. If images of the Sanctified Church were derived solely from such reading, one could almost believe that the roles of mothers, evangelists, and missionaries were structurally equivalent to those of the male elders, bishops, and pastors. Unlike men in other churches, men in the Sanctified Church have not ignored or trivialized women's roles. Thus these women with their expanded roles, important careers, and influence have been perceived as "the women God raised up."

The Church of God in Christ (COGIC), largest denomination of the Sanctified Church, ostensibly does not permit the ordination of women, and churchwomen have never let the matter rest. While there is a widespread agreement to disagree within the church, Bishop O. T. Jones represented the quintessence of the truce when he wrote, "The proper place of women in the church is an age old debate and from all appearances it seems that it perhaps will be an eternal one—for most mortals at least."[8] Despite its sexism, the church became the structural paradigm for other denominations. Despite or because of women's exclusion from pulpits, the most powerful Women's Department of any black denomination arose within the COGIC.

The Women's Department is a characteristic feature of the Sanctified Church denominations. James Shopshire argues that a defining characteristic of the power structures of these churches is their control by "a board of bishops" and the prevalence of an independently organized "women's work . . . where female leaders assume much authority, but with deference and loyalty to the bishops." Although these churches adopt the terminology associated with episcopally governed churches, they reflect the Baptist roots of their leadership in a tendency toward a Presbyterian style of more or less sharing power between the laity and the clergy. As a result, "a person may be upwardly mobile . . . to regional and

8. Charles H. Pleas, *Fifty Years of Achievement (History): Church of God in Christ* (Memphis, Tenn.: Church of God in Christ Publishing House, n.d.), p. 35.

national positions of relative independence from local congregations."[9] This is especially true for Women's Departments, which offer career mobility for a wide range of women.

Women leaders include those called to the ministry and denied access to pastoral positions, women who prefer the role of evangelist to that of pastor, women who actually have charge of churches in the absence of a pastor, and women who are Spirit-filled religious activists and congregational leaders. The political skill of the early Women's Department of the COGIC was such that nearly all women's roles, including that of "laywoman," were eventually included in that denomination's official definition of the ministry. The term "layman" was not so included. Thus the avenues of social mobility for women in the church branched out and were officially recognized. The diversity of roles allowed women to exercise influence beyond their congregations, which laymen were not organized to do. Women's Departments today retain unparalleled power in matters of policy and practice for all laywomen and continue to provide ladders of career mobility. They communicate both to the women of the church and to the male leadership and, regardless of restrictions, determine the role models available to churchwomen. This means that the choice of heroines of the Women's Department, and thus of the church as a whole, reflects churchwomen's values and view of reality.

In order to contribute to the construction of those role models in the early days of the Sanctified Church, women needed to attend the regional and national conventions and convocations. For the black women of the late nineteenth and early twentieth centuries, such travel was full of risks, and Jim Crow laws made these undertakings all the more difficult. Since women played a large part in developing individual congregations, the church recognized as issues of common concern the problems of their travel and need for respect in public places. In order to counter the stereotypes used as rationales for the abuse of black women, Sanctified Church women were encouraged to "dress as becometh holiness." One early bishop was convinced that the sight of women of the COGIC dressed according to the dictates of the Women's Department would restrain the most ardent racists.

There was a decided contrast between the ecstatic style of worship of these churches and the formal style of dress. Women wore black or white uniformlike dresses, and evangelists and church mothers devised a uniform or "habit" called "the Saint" to wear in services and on trains. At regional or national meetings, the highest ranking woman—the district missionary, the district supervisor, or the national supervisor—determined the dress of all other women present and decided whether they

9. James Shopshire, "A Socio-historical Characterization of the Black Pentecostal Movement in America" (Ph.D. diss., Northwestern University, 1975), pp. 144–4F.

wore white on a particular day. While this may seem a rather trivial matter, the problem of discipline was not, and clergymen were required to adhere to equally stringent dress codes.

Thus the women of the early COGIC and other Sanctified Church denominations achieved such a position of respect and autonomy that they defined the content of their own roles. Furthermore, church members could not advance ideologies of patriarchy that contradicted standards of holiness since "holiness" was the most important achieved status in these churches—and a status not humanly conferred. Biblical debate concerning women was confined to structural norms, not the nature, quality, or character of women per se. Denominations that ordained women to be elders and pastors argued about women becoming bishops; in others in which all roles were open, there was no controversy. However, the egalitarian denominations would not recognize a woman's call at as early an age as they would a man's.[10] Within the COGIC, the church was forced to argue that women were completely capable but that the COGIC did not recognize the feminist biblical argument.[11]

Since women evangelists or revivalists founded or "dug out" many churches, they could not be excluded from church histories; they were too important to the tradition of holiness and to church growth. When male church leaders identified in their spiritual biographies those preachers who effected their conversions, the revivalists were often women. Thus the personal and congregational accounts passed down in written records and oral tradition placed a high value on the contribution of women and men to the most important goal of the church—salvation and holiness.[12]

The extension of women's spiritual contributions into autonomous leadership networks and careers fostered the development of heroines and myth, the most important pillars of tradition. In a social setting that placed a primary value on spirituality, "the women God raised up" as "Mothers in Zion" could not be excluded simply for the sake of male domination. The many tensions created by the intrusion of patriarchal norms were eased by the fact that both men and women placed a high value on holiness, and women played a heroic role in upholding that value. Women's allusion to Deborah who "arose a mother in Israel" in their self-descriptions provided a legitimate counterideology to the pa-

10. Church of the Living God, Christian Workers for Fellowship, *Glorious Heritage: The Golden Book—Documentary and History* (n.p.: Church of the Living God, Christian Workers for Fellowship, 1976).

11. Church of God in Christ (COGIC), *Official Manual with the Doctrines and Discipline of the Church of God in Christ* (Memphis, Tenn.: COGIC Publishing House, 1973).

12. Lucille Cornelius, *The Pioneer History of the Church of God in Christ* (Memphis, Tenn.: COGIC Publishing House, 1975); Church of the Living God; Pleas.

triarchal desires of churchmen.[13] Finally, elevation to clearly articulated roles of spiritual leadership guaranteed that female heroines were part of the culture of the church shared by both men and women.

"Women May Teach": Education as a Source of Power

Education has represented a supreme cultural value in the black church and community. The Sanctified Church arose during the height of the struggle for black education, which led to the expanded role of women as educators. The parents of church founders were slaves who had made their children's education a life's goal that was often not realized. Church officials' personal accounts of conversion echo laments over their own lack of education. Because the Sanctified Church became stereotyped as the sects and cults of illiterate black masses and disaffected urban migrants, both black and white observers failed to apprehend the high value these denominations placed on literacy and higher education. Thus it is important not to view their teaching ministries as a devalued area of female segregation. Male denominational leaders recruited educated women precisely because of their importance to the future.

The Sanctified Church's emphasis on biblical authority made learning "the Word" an important means for living a sanctified life. Educational goals therefore comprised general literacy, biblical literacy, advanced academic and professional achievement, and biblical expository skills, and these goals apparently ranked second in priority after salvation and holiness. The Saints were encouraged to acquire "the learning" without losing "the burning." Those able to teach biblical and general literacy skills and to provide appropriate spiritual role models were chosen as teachers.

The growth in women's roles as teachers resulted from a combination of male decisions and female enterprise. The male church organizers shared the larger cultural value of education, and their decisions to recruit female educators converged with the women's desires for important roles in their churches and with trends toward black women's education in the wider community. Recruitment occurred during that period in black history when the education of women was a conscious response to aspects of their oppression and when they were also being encouraged to act as educators of "the Race." Thus the deployment of women teachers in black education was carried out with almost total disregard for the dominant culture's norms; these women were not limited to teaching children or relegated to roles subordinate to men's. Black women capitalized on their leadership in church education. The early Women's Departments

13. Judg. 5:7.

revolved around the Prayer and Bible Study Bands, which expanded the literacy skills of women collectively; these groups paralleled the clubs and seminar groups that were part of the early National Association of Colored Women. This collective self-education was reflected in the expansion of women's leadership roles in denominations and in the growth of the Women's Departments.

Although engaged in conflict with the larger black community over the importance of ecstatic worship, the Sanctified Church admired the same heroines in racial uplift and black education. The examples of prominent churchwomen such as Mary McLeod Bethune, Nannie Helen Burroughs, Ida B. Wells, and Mary Church Terrell prompted the founder of the COGIC, Bishop C. H. Mason, to recruit Mother Lizzie Woods Roberson, a Baptist teacher and academy matron, to be the first "overseer" of the women's work. Encouraged to travel in order to enlist and appoint women leaders, she also conducted revivals as an organizer. Another woman, Arenia C. Mallory, was hired as a teacher at Saints' Academy in Lexington, Mississippi. Church histories describe her as a protégée of Mary McLeod Bethune. After the death of the first principal of Saints' Academy, Mallory became head of the school, which then grew from a primary academy to an accredited junior college. For a while, she was the only black woman college president. As conflicts over theology, doctrine, biblical interpretation, and church polity fostered differentiation within the Sanctified Church, women's importance as educators and the high value placed on educated women were not diminished. When denominations argued about the ordination of women, those that chose to ordain preserved the teaching roles of evangelist and missionary.[14]

In addition to their role in developing attitudes about and organizations for formal education, Sanctified Church women were permitted to teach the Gospel. Teaching the Gospel involved setting forth biblical doctrine, church polity, and duties; conducting revivals; presenting teachings in the morning service in lieu of and in the style of a sermon; and "having charge of a church in the absence of the pastor."[15] The tasks of the teaching role differed very little from the task of the preaching role reserved for men. In some denominations, evangelists not only could have charge of churches but also, as in the case of Pentecostal Assemblies of the World, could serve communion and perform marriages. In some instances, the difference between women's and men's credentials was merely internal; for all practical and legal purposes, women evangelists were clergy. Often members of particular congregations have been hard-pressed to distinguish between men's preaching and women's teaching. One young woman I interviewed observed, "I went to the service and the

14. COGIC; Church of the Living God.
15. COGIC.

elder preached. Then he invited the women to speak. They preached, and they were much better than the man."

In the COGIC, women developed their own standards for examining and promoting evangelists. While it is conceivable that a COGIC churchman may be ordained as an elder with very little preaching and administrative experience, the Women's Department sets radically different requirements for women aspiring to become national evangelists. In order to receive such a license, a woman must preach revival successfully in seven states.[16] COGIC churchwomen are strongly motivated to develop their gifts and to develop a national reputation as revivalists in order to receive approval from the Women's Department.

The most widely shared value in the total black religious experience is the high premium placed on good preaching, which is as important in the black church as good music—another area in which women are not restricted. In the COGIC, the women's system guarantees that their "teaching" skills are superior. The dynamic and effective teaching of these women stands in stark contrast to the official stance of the COGIC that women are not called to preach. The availability of women evangelists who are in theory skilled "teachers" but in reality excellent preachers allows the elder with minimal skills in the pulpit to provide good preaching for his congregation. Since black Baptist and Methodist denominations tend to call all evangelists "Reverend" and to call male pastors conducting revival away from their own churches "Evangelist," the uninitiated may believe that these women are preachers. In the formative days of the Sanctified Church, the role of evangelist was an alternative for those women in Baptist and Methodist denominations who were unable to exercise their gifts either from the pulpit or from the floor. Such women went "over" into the Sanctified Church. Contemporary changes among Baptists and Methodists have reversed this earlier trend.

Women's concentration in educational roles in the early Sanctified Church was not simply a form of female segregation; instead it was the basis for alternative structures of authority, career pathways, and spheres of influence. More important, those leaders and historical accounts that provide the church with normative legitimacy and modify the stereotype of its members as poor and illiterate credit the influence of women's educational work. Given the overall, sometimes exaggerated, respect and deference that the black community confers on educators, these women have legitimized the image of the "professional" woman throughout the church. As a result, women in the Sanctified Church have established a more differentiated model of social mobility and occupational aspiration than have the men.

16. Women's Department, COGIC, *Women's Handbook* (Memphis, Tenn.: COGIC Publishing House, 1980).

"$10,000 in a Paper Bag": The Economic Limits of Subordination

In the black community, educated women work outside the home. Contrary to trends in the dominant culture, the higher the social class of black women, the greater their rate of labor force participation.[17] Organizers of the black Holiness and Pentecostal churches were children of freedwomen who worked for wages and thus were more sympathetic to the problems and stereotypes black women faced. These church leaders learned that it was working churchwomen who decided what proportion of their earnings would go to the church. However, black churchwomen did not wait for their pastors to discover their economic importance; they demonstrated their economic power collectively. After 1906, black congregations, conventions, and denominational convocations became acquainted with Women's Day, when women take charge of the program and turn over to the congregation, the convention, or the denomination the money they have raised. In one church I visited, this contribution was one-third of the church's budget for the year. While black congregations also hold Men's Days, men have rarely matched the contributions of the women. The fund-raising ability of women remains a traditional source of male-female rivalry in black churches.

The overwhelming female majorities in the early Sanctified Church meant that women's economic enterprise and labor force participation were essential for church growth and survival. Thus women's financial power was a major contradiction to the ethic of male domination and control. This contradiction was intensified by the dynamics of economic decision making in black families and black women's relatively greater economic independence.

Strong Women's Departments retained control over the disbursement and allocation of their funds. Women paid the expenses of their leaders and staff members, collected offerings for the evangelists and church mothers "teaching" in the churches and representing districts and congregations at national meetings, and provided benevolence for unemployed men, women, and their families. Sanctified Church women raised money for their pastors' and bishops' wives to travel to conventions and simply to have some funds of their own. These women believed in economic cooperation with men, not in economic dependence on them.

Black women have a history of handling financial matters efficiently. Early Women's Departments often assessed each member an equal amount of money to meet goals, one of several monetary practices that paralleled those of the clubs of the National Association of Colored

17. Priscilla Douglas, "Black Working Women: Factors Affecting Labor Market Experience," Working Paper (Wellesley College, Center for Research on Women, 1980).

Women. As their activities grew, Sanctified Church women adopted the practice of contributing money throughout the year and then presenting this collection at the end of Women's Day or of a convention. Such practices had their roots in benevolent and mutual aid associations, with the sacred and secular practices becoming mutually influential. In a sense, churchwomen extended their domestic economic practices to their households of racial uplift and their households of faith.

By 1951, the COGIC Women's Department had grown to such an extent that the women began meeting in a separate convention under the leadership of Lillian Brooks Coffey. Using the structure of state and district supervisors, Mother Coffey collected money prior to and during the convention and then presented it to the church at the end of the convention. She inaugurated this practice at a convention where she surprised the church by presenting Bishop Crouch with "thousands of dollars" in a paper bag.[18] The women's importance to the survival of congregations led some to the false belief that black women were better off economically than black men. Since women tithed faithfully and prominently, it was easy to perceive them as the most powerful economic segment of the black community. Such perceptions made the image of the matriarch so believable to black men.

Whatever their beliefs and ideologies concerning female subordination, men in the Sanctified Church ultimately have been confronted with the economic necessity of maintaining good relationships with their female members. At some point during the church year, it has been in the interest of the most sexist and domineering pastor to advocate financial support for the local, district, and national women's work. Like almost all black pastors, these men also have acknowledged the collective economic power of churchwomen on Women's Day—and they often have vacated their pulpits to do so. Finally, the collective economic power of women has been reinforced at the district, jurisdictional, and national levels when the superintendents and bishops receive the quarterly or annual "reports" from the Women's Department.

"The Women Stuck Together": Collective Autonomy

Women's economic power has limited attempts by bishops and pastors to impose themselves directly on the activities of women. Churchwomen have thus been free to discuss issues and problems that churchmen may not have wanted to hear. While the dynamics and degree of male domination of local congregations varies, black women, because of

18. Cornelius (n. 12 above), p. 24. Oral tradition and interviews set the amount at a minimum of $10,000.

their autonomous organizations, occasionally remind their brethren, "If it wasn't for the women, you wouldn't have a church."

Although many denominations were formed between 1895 and 1950, those that survived and flourished were those with strong Women's Departments. Structures of female influence enabled denominations with charismatic male founders to grow after those founders died; other denominational movements with high visibility but no structures of female influence almost disappeared. The Women's Department of the COGIC was formed at approximately the same time that the denomination was reconstituted as Pentecostal in 1907 and after women's auxiliaries, missions, societies, and clubs had grown and developed in black Baptist and Methodist churches. The founder of the COGIC, divorced from a woman who was still living, could not remarry. His position as an unmarried head of a church was almost unique in black church history, a marked departure from the traditional pattern of a preacher married to a professional woman leader (usually a teacher). This historical "accident" generated the model of a nearly autonomous women's organization. Mason not only recruited Mother Roberson to head the women's work but also on her advice appointed women's overseers along the same jurisdictional and district lines as the male overseers who later became bishops. The title "overseer," a literal translation of the Greek word usually translated as "bishop," was used in the early days of the church for both men and women leaders in the church. Such usage implied that the founders of the COGIC and other denominations initially envisioned a church organized in parallel structures of both male and female overseers. This vision was closer to the dual sex political systems characteristic of some West African societies than to the patriarchal episcopal polities of European origin.

The founding of the Sanctified Church coincided with the most extensive and energetic period of organizing by black women. In the 1890s, the Fire Baptized Holiness Church of God of the Americas was founded as an egalitarian denomination. The COGIC began as a Holiness church in 1895 toward the end of, but distinct from, the Church of God movement that established an interracial and egalitarian denomination. In the same year, black women began holding national conventions focused on the problems of "the Race" and of black women. Women were eligible for ordination in the A. M. E. Zion Church, the church of Harriet Tubman. During this period, they organized major women's auxiliaries among black Baptists and Methodists, and they formed the National Association of Colored Women, which assembled women across the boundaries of religion, class, and intensity of skin color. By 1907 and the beginning of the Pentecostal Movement, the black woman had a prominent image as Race woman, clubwoman, churchwoman, and educator in the black community. Black clubwomen and schoolteachers in the Sanctified Church were prepared to assume roles of leadership and possessed the skills to do so.

The period between 1895 and World War II was the era of "racial uplift." In addition to race relations, female employment, and the multiple problems of group advancement, black women made the "status of the ministry" a central concern of their national programs, first in the Colored Women's League and the Federation of Afro-American Women and, after the merger of these organizations, in the National Association of Colored Women.[19] Women in the Sanctified Church were committed to the cause of racial uplift. They retained their commitment to ecstatic worship, which black Baptists and Methodists were rejecting. They also retained an emphasis on women's interests, education, professionalism, and the cultivation of a black female image that contradicted the dominant culture's stereotypes.

Some of the organizational features of the Sanctified Church Women's Departments have since disappeared in the black women's clubs where they may have originated. One such example is the Women's Purity Class, where women still learn their "proper place" in their churches and homes. A Baptist clergywoman I interviewed who visited such a class remarked, "Those classes are interesting. One woman told me, 'The Bible says that I should be in subjection to my husband, but that's the *only* man!'" In these classes—as well as the meetings of the evangelists, missionaries, and church mothers; the Prayer and Bible Bands; the Sewing Circles; and the organizations of the Deacons' Wives, the Bishops' Wives, and the Pastors' Wives—women are able to develop a perspective on their position in their churches that includes important critiques of church politics and structure. In such settings, women learn the language of biblical feminism and maintain their collective autonomy, arguing that it is not "proper" for pastors "to teach . . . things that women should know."[20]

In structuring their activities, women in the Sanctified Church retained the features of organizations founded during the most intensive era of Afro-American feminism; the network of small groups they organized around churchwomen's specialized roles formed a feminist infrastructure within a patriarchal organization. Many women belonged to several of these groups, which provided multiple perspectives on women's roles in the form of direct statement and biblical allusions. When churchwomen showed their strength, it arose from these many networks and was described in biblical terms.

The role of the Women's Department in the COGIC during the crisis precipitated by the founder's death illustrates the importance of the

19. Elizabeth Lindsey Davis (n. 6 above).

20. Women's Department, COGIC (n. 16 above), p. 21.

women's infrastructure to the survival of the denomination. During that crisis, while the men were fighting constitutional battles in the courtrooms, the Women's Department continued to function under the leadership of Mother Anna Bailey. While sources are cryptic, the Women's Department seemed to exercise veto power over the direction of policy, structure, and choice of leaders. The women also participated in the election of the bishops, who in turn elected the presiding bishop. Finally, the church's newspaper took special note of Mother Bailey's approval of the final choice of the board.[21]

Writing later in an official church history, Lucille Cornelius emphasized the contribution of the Women's Department to the survival and integrity of the COGIC. She emphasized that "the women stuck together and held the church in harness until the brethren could find their identity in the form of leadership that we must have in this time."[22] The phrase "in harness," a biblical term meaning "prepared or organized for war," referred to the children of Israel leaving Egypt. The statement reflects some of the disdain that the well organized feel for the relatively disorganized; the women knew that they could do better. Cornelius's tone also suggests the frustration of many black women who, regardless of conflicts and inequities, were reluctant to abandon institutions they played a major role in building.

Churchwomen have advanced a public strategy of cooperation with men. While their oral tradition is militant, their written tradition is indulgent, eschewing overt conflict. Recently, church mothers were admonished to "remember . . . [that the pastors] are the Lord's people."[23] It seems that the biblical ethic of love and of church unity has reduced the temptation toward open rebellion. Yet these women are aware that other denominations have been founded by women more militant in opposing subordination. Examples of female leaders within the denomination heighten women's sense that entire congregations and perhaps the entire church could continue in the absence of male leadership. However, racial oppression serves to remind black women of the importance of unity. The tension generated by a hostile dominant culture encourages women to adopt a cooperative model of gender relations and to support male leadership that, as Cornelius wrote, is necessary "in this time."

Men in the early Sanctified Church were aware of the tension between women's leadership skills and the structural realities within their institutions. Although bishops and elders married evangelists and missionaries, historically a woman's marital status did not determine her access to leadership; only one of the four national supervisors of women was married to a man nationally prominent in the church. In a very few but significant cases where pastors died and were therefore "absent" from

21. Cornelius (n. 12 above), p. 27.
22. Ibid.
23. Women's Department, COGIC (n. 16 above), p. 21.

their churches, bishops did not appoint any other male leaders to replace them but left the widows, licensed evangelists, in charge. The COGIC discovered that such congregations were more efficiently managed.[24] Finally, while churchwomen today admonish their sisters to cooperate with pastors, many pastors head congregations that were "dug out" and managed by women until those women sent for a pastor.

In other denominations that do not restrict women, female evangelists have become elders or pastors through the prompting and encouragement of women's organizations. In the Church of the Living God, Christian Workers for Fellowship, for example, women recognized that the sacred traditions of the wider black community did not encourage women in ministry in the way they encouraged men.[25] Both churchwomen and clubwomen depended on their autonomous organizations to achieve positions of leadership.

The women's methods of leadership have evolved in direct contrast to the authoritarian style demanded by the nature of episcopal polity: hierarchical, individualistic, and dominating.[26] In comparison, women's leadership tends to be consensus oriented, collective, and more inclusive, involving larger numbers of people in decision making. Visible women leaders have been able to represent large organizations of women in both sacred and secular settings. Black churchwomen have thus transformed their autonomy into the form of power best described as influence and created a pluralist political structure in an episcopally governed church where pluralism was never intended.

The collectivism and autonomy of organized women has been the most significant historical factor in the survival of denominations within the Sanctified Church. In churches with structures derived from male positions, women's organizations with parallel structures maintain the visibility of female leaders. Finally, this collectivist orientation has also kept alive a cooperative model of gender relations and pluralist political practice in an elitist organization.

Beyond "This Time": Tradition, Cooperation, and Prospects for Change

Women's standing in the Sanctified Church presently ranges from subordination in the COGIC to equality with men in the Fire Baptized Holiness Church of God of the Americas and the Mount Calvary Holy

24. James Tinney, "Black Pentecostals: The Difference Is More Than Color," *Logos Journal* 10, no. 3 (1980): 16–19.

25. Church of the Living God (n. 10 above).

26. Jualynne Dodson, "Black Women as an Unknown Source of Organizational Change" (Providence, R.I., Society for the Scientific Study of Religion, 1982, mimeographed).

Church of America. While access to authority is a problem for these churchwomen, they do not experience structural marginality, a major difficulty for women in white churches. According to Rosemary Ruether, churchwomen were marginalized because they "seldom controlled the processes of the cultural interpretation of their actions," which led to their exclusion from the myths and heroic accounts central to church tradition. Women's exclusion from leadership followed, except "in those areas where roles based on gifts of the Spirit were recognized."[27] Both men and women in the Sanctified Church attain leadership through their expression of gifts of the Spirit, which perhaps explains in part why marginality and exclusion do not characterize the type of subordination women experience in black Pentecostal and Holiness denominations. Where the processes of cultural interpretation have been external to the church, the entire Sanctified Church has suffered. Where the interpretive process was internal to the church, black women influenced and, in some cases, controlled that process.

The politics of sexism in the Sanctified Church are the politics of incomplete male domination, and the politics of feminism are the politics of cooperative protest, collective enterprise, and assertive autonomy. Therefore, strong and visible women's traditions are part of the total church culture that is passed on in the socialization of new members. Recruits and young people learn beliefs, values, and ways of thinking that depart from the dominant culture's notion of women's place in churches and other formal organizations. Church members also learn to admire the distinctive aspects of black women's experience and their historical role without accepting the negative images and stereotypes imposed by the dominant culture.

By writing symbolic accounts of women's participation in the extraordinary events that made the growth and development of these denominations possible, churchwomen continue to reinforce these heroic images. In American society, women have been permitted more expression of gifts of the Spirit, the most important aspect of these denominations' identities. Clearly, women must be included in the symbolic accounts or myths strengthening the norms of holiness that define the unique position of the Sanctified Church on the continuum of black religious experience.

The presence of prominent female heroines in holiness has prevented churchwomen from becoming alienated by their structural subordination in the Sanctified Church. The collective and self-conscious politics of female influence modify the politics and pain of male domina-

27. Rosemary Radford Ruether and Eleanor McLaughlin, eds., *Women of Spirit: Female Leadership in the Jewish and Christian Traditions* (New York: Simon & Schuster, 1979), pp. 16–17.

tion. Over time, black women in the Sanctified Church have drawn on the strength of their skills and historical experiences to create structural conditions tending toward equality. Yet even in denominations where women have full access to authority, some of which were formed in protest against discrimination, black women and men have not pursued a course of antagonism or separatism. Instead, a model of dual-career religious leadership has emerged. Where women church members have a higher status than their husbands ("Mr. and Rev.," or "Deacon and Elder," or "Mr. and Elder"), men express pride in their wives' achievements. Through a combination of heroic accounts, symbolic leaders, and an alternative organizational setting, black women have maintained a tradition of protest and cooperation—a dialectical tradition—within the Sanctified Church.

The Sanctified Church and its women's traditions are an important resource for the entire range of the black religious experience. Churchmen cannot ignore the written tradition of women's achievement, and they ignore the oral tradition of cooperative protest with great difficulty. In denominations that do not ordain women, female members point to their tremendous records of service and continue the conflict over their role in the church. If and when these denominations change their stance—and there are a variety of reasons to be pessimistic about this prospect—ordained women will have a greater impact than they now do as unordained evangelists. As has been the case in the area of music, the Sanctified Church continues to have normative impact on the larger black experience greater than would be expected from its actual number of members, and that number is growing.

A major problem exists concerning the values of churchmen, which range from a commitment to patriarchy, domination, and hierarchy to a belief in male-female cooperation and mutual influence. The history of the Sanctified Church demonstrates that both sets of values exist in the world of black men. In the Sanctified Church and beyond, many black men want to achieve the pure patriarchy they have never truly experienced. The functional necessity of women to the very survival of congregations, convocations, and denominations opposes such a tendency. James Tinney suggests that some black men absent themselves from churches precisely because of authoritarian male domination.[28] However, such male resistance to religious patriarchy is undermined by the dominant culture's persistent denigration of black women as matriarchs who are too assertive, powerful, and aggressive. Such labeling feeds a sexist backlash within the black community that encourages a rejection of the

28. Tinney, "The Religious Experience of Black Men" (n. 1 above).

model of womanhood black women represent and deepens intragroup hostilities.[29]

Thus it has become fashionable since the civil rights movement to dismiss the achievements of black women in church, community, and society at large as a mere consequence of economic necessity. Unfortunately, many black men perceived the message of the 1960s to be, If you will be sexist, we white men won't be racist. Such ideological assaults led to attempts to enforce European or dominant culture patriarchy where it had been effectively resisted.

The disestablishment of sexism in the dominant culture remains a threat to many black males who perceive the traditional model of gender relations as a component of the goal of assimilation. In order to persist in this thinking, such men must reject as unseemly and inappropriate any institutional record that suggests a tradition of heroism by black women. They must refuse to transform their observations of women's church and community roles and of the historical records of the churches into an internalized norm of egalitarian gender relationships. The saving grace for black women in the Sanctified Church is that, even in a context of structural subordination, they do control the record books and therefore the written record of their role. As long as women are involved in this process of cultural interpretation, there exists a strong egalitarian potential within the Sanctified Church. Additionally, black women do have their allies among pastors who have never adopted or who have abolished the separate lectern or "double pulpit" and among sympathetic bishops who will ordain them to take a charge outside the church (e.g., military chaplaincies) or to begin new churches.

Racial oppression and its gender-specific racist ideologies still invade the black experience. Black women who do not conform to patriarchal traditions have been particularly victimized. Unless black women's image in the dominant culture changes radically, their struggles against racial oppression must proceed both inside and outside the black community; they will continue to be tied to internal struggles to maintain what power they now have in the face of embarrassed black male opposition, as well as to the external struggles with white racism. As long as racism limits opportunities for black men, black women will continue to express some ambivalence about competing with black men inside the black community and will also strive to avoid direct confrontation and overt conflict. As long as racism and patriarchy operate as combined forces in the oppression of black women and men, black women will not abandon those institutions that are responsive to the shared aspects of the problems. The

29. Dill (n. 2 above); Pauli Murray, "The Liberation of Black Women," in *Voices of the New Feminism*, ed. Mary L. Thompson (Boston: Beacon Press, 1970), and "Jim Crow and Jane Crow," in Lerner, ed. (n. 3 above), pp. 592–99; Hooks (n. 3 above).

history of formal and informal organization within the black community suggests that the cooperative and egalitarian model of male-female leadership would be the preferred outcome. Black women's traditions in the Sanctified Church yield great hope for the transformation of structures that alienate and trivialize women's experiences. In the meantime, black women will maintain their solidarity and organizational strength—"stuck together [holding] the church in harness"—until deliverance comes.

Department of Sociology
Boston University

"CHRISTIAN WOMAN, PIOUS WIFE, FAITHFUL MOTHER, DEVOTED MISSIONARY": CONFLICTS IN ROLES OF AMERICAN MISSIONARY WOMEN IN NINETEENTH-CENTURY HAWAII

PATRICIA GRIMSHAW

At seven o'clock on the Friday evening of 29 May 1840, the members of the Maternal Association of the Sandwich Islands Mission met at the home of Mrs. Laura Fish Judd, wife of the mission physician, in Honolulu, Oahu. All the women present had volunteered at some time during the previous two decades for missionary service under the auspices of the American Board of Commissioners for Foreign Missions, which had maintained a mission to the Hawaiians since 1820. The topic posed for this evening's discussion, and continued over subsequent days, was "The influence of natives upon the characters of our children."[1] The discussion was energetic, and its vigor indicated the centrality of this question in their days and lives.

The questions raised in the evening's debate indicate the tension the issue generated in the lives of missionary women. The first and crucial question received a prompt answer. "It was asked in what *particular* was native influence most prejudicial? One of the ladies replied—to the *moral purity* of the children." Was any mother present willing that her children should communicate *at all* in the Hawaiian dialect? The reply was unanimously negative, although the practical problems of preventing such language acquisition were acknowledged to be formidable. Did their children at an early age manifest a fondness for native society? Then "mothers should redouble their efforts to render themselves agreeable companions for their children," and attempt to keep Hawaiians and mission children apart by prescribing the areas of the house to which Hawaiians had access. When one woman announced that her husband devoted all his time to the Hawaiians,

Feminist Studies 9, no. 3 (Fall 1983). © by Feminist Studies, Inc.

she to her children, another queried the effect of this separation of duties on the mission women's work for the "heathen." One woman thought that "since the ladies of the misssion had withdrawn to such an extent from the service, the native women do not appear so well as the men." Should the missionary women divert time and attention from their children to labor more directly for the natives? One solitary voice was raised in favor of the sisters' returning to their respective stations "with new resolutions to increase their efforts for the poor and needy natives, and not feel that their children demanded their whole time and thought."[2]

The occasion for the convening of the Maternal Association was the annual General Meeting of the Sandwich Islands Mission, which drew families from the outlying stations of Maui, Kauai, Molokai and the island Hawaii to the busy port town of Honolulu. Each day the general sessions were held in the schoolhouse near the mission premises. The women attended, seated amidst the men, with their work at hand, their infants and young children close by, while the older children fought and played in the yard outside the windows. They listened with intense interest; they were not permitted to speak or vote.

Since 1834, the women had also convened separate meetings in their own Maternal Association, where they could discuss together those issues affecting their lives that were ignored in the men's deliberations. Women presented papers; debate followed. The subjects they raised ranged from details of childbearing to broader social issues: the proper use of the rod, the right age to inform children of "the connection of the sexes," the influence of fiction on children; the propriety of older children exercising authority over younger, the temperance movement, the implication of Paul's injunction that wives should submit themselves to their husbands.[3] Through all their gatherings, one subject, posed for the major debate in 1840, was constantly raised and never satisfactorily resolved: the tension between the women's commitments as missionaries and their wish to protect their children from the influence of the very "heathens" they were committed to reforming. This tension indicated a more general conflict for women between public undertakings and maternal obligations, a conflict deepened in this instance by the inevitable ethnocentrism with which both public commitment and private duty were defined. The experience of these missionary women, then, has broader implications for understanding the efforts of white, middle-class women in the nineteenth century to widen their engagement in the public sphere. These efforts were limited both by an ideology that valorized women's moral qualities but insisted that these qualities, once a woman had children, be exercised primarily in the home; and by the cultural rigidity that isolated white, middle-class women and prevented them from finding value and alliance in any social world but their own.

The involvement of women in social reform in nineteenth-century America; in the antislavery movement and abolition; in temperance; and in a variety of urban, religious, educational, and moral reform societies has come increasingly to the attention of serious historical inquiry.[4] Such social initiatives by women are interesting in themselves, but historians seek too to find in them an avenue for understanding the emergence of one style of feminism from within the ranks of reform movements, a style which gave Victorian feminism its special character. Those women who engaged in American Protestant missionary activity deserve attention within this same context. They shared with their sisters in other movements a similar passion to reform the habits, inform the minds, and modify the world views of those whose life-styles differed markedly from the model established by New England Protestantism. Some reformers looked to undermine the power of oppressive and dissolute southern whites; others fastened their attention on unregenerate drinkers, the neglected children of the urban poor, or male seducers of hapless females. In social background, religious belief, and education, missionary women were markedly similar to these other reformers, and indeed in speech and writing upheld the same goals. Their own choice, however, was the reform and conversion of distant "heathen savages." A burning conviction that their personal destiny lay in the mission field, experienced during a few years of their early maturity, had led them into an exile's lot.

Years of exile did not distance these women from their American origins. Ten, twenty, forty years of life in the Polynesian environment left them little altered, undaunted by notions of moral or cultural relativism. A small tract issued for Sabbath schools in 1829, *Conversations on the Sandwich Islands Mission,* gives insight into their attitude toward the indigenous population. A pious matron, Mrs. Barton, is pictured telling her children of the Hawaiian Mission, and producing a map showing the islands of Polynesia. "Jane's curiosity was roused, and she drew up to her mother, and inquired 'what sort of people they were who seemed to dwell in the midst of the ocean.' 'Heathen,' observed Mrs. Barton."[5] To the missionary women, "heathen" the Hawaiians were, and to a large extent "heathen" the Hawaiians remained when acceptance of the gospel alone did not effect the moral reform the women sought. Their task would be considered accomplished only when Hawaiians behaved in ways that made them recognizably social beings in terms of American cultural expectations.

The experiences of the missionary women provide insight into the attempts by women to become involved in public activities in the nineteenth century and into the barriers that continued to frustrate those initiatives. Newly industrializing societies slowly began to offer women enlarged areas of involvement in public life both in the paid work force, and in the greater engagement of middle-class women in charitable and religious societies and pressure groups. Women had to test for themselves the limits on their public activities and discover what would be the boundaries of legitimate behavior. The women who departed for the Sandwich Islands mission in the decades from 1820 onwards believed that they had made a lifelong commitment to teach the "heathen."

Yet the same newly industrializing societies that afforded women entry into the public sphere witnessed simultaneously the articulation of ideologies stressing the supreme moral and spiritual worth of home and family and sanctified the role of the mother in nurturing the finest qualities of human behavior. Nowhere was such sentiment more pronounced than in New England with its Puritan heritage. While a sense of an exalted female influence underwrote women's acceptance into public roles, such an underpinning of women's activism contained within it the seeds of potential conflict.

The group of young, married social reformers who set sail for Hawaii had not long to wait before a second obligation was added to their duties to teach the "heathen:" to train their own growing children to be fit subjects of Christian grace and worthy laborers in a Christian society. The outcome was a painful conflict in which their roles as wives and mothers all but usurped their vocation as teachers. The story of the female missionaries to the Sandwich Islands offers a simple yet revealing tale of the foundering of female ambition for an independent public role on the rocks of sacred maternal obligation.

* * *

During the long voyage to the islands around Cape Horn in 1837, Angeline Tenney Castle recounted to her shipmate Charlotte Knapp the means by which she had responded to the missionary call. After she had become a member of the Oberlin Institute in Ohio, she said, the subject of missions was often brought up and sometimes pressed upon her "till she came to the conclusion it was her duty to become a missionary if Providence should open the way. She was in this state of mind when Mr. Castle proposed to her to accompany him about the last of August and was accordingly prepared to decide immediately."[6] The steps by which Angeline Castle had joined missionary service were typical of missionary women as a whole. Concern about the unevangelized peoples of the world was fostered in many seminaries in the North East and West now open to women, and at Oberlin she had developed a conviction that she had a personal responsibility for the "heathen." Finally, when a male missionary about to depart on the mission proposed marriage to her, the means were presented by which this personal conviction could be translated into reality. She accepted, and they departed soon after.

For most of the women, further education had been part of their effort to improve their qualifications as schoolteachers in the growing common school system in the North East, or in the West. That some teachers should have been drawn toward serving the "heathen" was not surprising. Evangelical Protestantism, which attempted to imbue the work of teaching with moral and spiritual values, served to legitimate prolonged education for girls and young women.[7] Women who volunteered for the Sandwich Islands mission were for the most part schoolteachers, who came primarily from the New England states and from western New York State, with a sprinkling from New Jersey and Pennsylvania.[8] Their education had often been acquired through considerable personal struggle. A few specific examples indicate the backgrounds of these women.

Clarissa Chapman Armstrong, for example, was raised in a struggling farmer's family in Russell, western Massachusetts, where she had learned domestic work and helped with the lighter farm work and with the cows and sheep. Her father was partly crippled with rheumatism. To attain further education, she boarded at a farm near the Westfield Academy, and worked in the dairy to pay part of her board while she attended college. Thereafter, she was able to teach in the local school in Russell, and after training in the new infant school system, worked in a neighboring town.[9] Laura Fish Judd came from a similar farming background from Plainfield, Oswego County, in the west of New York State. She began teaching at sixteen, suffered the ordeal of "boarding around," and at nineteen entered the Clinton Female Seminary under Miss N. Boyce. "I was very anxious and ambitious to secure a thorough education — I was poor — entirely dependent on my own exertions for support — not a friend to furnish me with a dollar; I was obliged to dress very plain and practice the most rigid economy in order to purchase books, pay my board, ½ tuition. My friends were kind, and waited till I raised money by teaching. I struggled hard — I suffered many mortifications — shed many tears, but my aim was high — I was proud and independent as I was poor."[10]

That this personal effort to attain an education and an independent livelihood had feminist implications is suggested by Lucy Goodale Thurston's account of her struggle to obtain an education. She pitted herself quite explicitly against the notions of woman's place embedded in the society in which she was reared. The daughter of a substantial farmer in Marlborough, Massachusetts, she developed a sense of grievance at the treatment of females in the family economy of surrounding districts. Although sons and daughters both provided significant labor, sons were paid for that labor in maturity, but adult daughters worked unremunerated like children. While sons were trained for future employment, no calculation was made for the daughter except that "some one of the sterner sex would take her by the hand, and lead her forth into the mazes of human life." She had been mortified to hear the minister say, at the local public school examination of the girls of the senior arithmetic class, that "there is no use in girls going as far in arithmetic, other than setting themselves up as candidates for the wives of merchants."[11] She, Lucy Goodale, vowed she had higher ambitions than to make education a matrimonial ticket. She was determined to enter the Bradford Academy, forty miles away. With trepidation she approached her father, a figure of patriarchal authority, for permission. In the matter of female education would he, the deacon, go ahead of the minister? Summoning up all her resolution, she asked him: "Father, I have a strong desire to attend the Bradford Academy. May I?" To her amazement and delight he agreed to the scheme, and her years at Bradford secured, as she saw it, the avenue to an independent and honorable livelihood.[12]

It was no coincidence that educated women with a sensitivity to the status of women in their own society might be especially interested in the work of foreign missions. Whatever women's place in America, they believed that the *true* gospel of Christ upheld a high status for women. The place of women in "heathen" societies, by comparison, was painted as desperately degraded; hence such women urgently needed the benefits of Christianity to raise them from misery. In an address to the Princeton Female Society for the Support of a Female School in India, one of numerous female mission support groups, Dr. Ashbel Green presented the case in typical fashion. *All* "heathens" and Mohammedans were in a state of wretchedness, but their womenfolk were debased far below even their lords and masters, as drudges, slaves, and the instruments of male sensuality. Surely there was a call to lift such women "from bestial ignorance, degradation and servility, to a state of rationality, intelligence, happiness, dignity and the hope of heaven. Christian women must feel this on behalf of their sex, whose feelings they must best know, and in whose wretchedness and sorrows they can best sympathize." He wondered that the known condition of these women had not operated with an "electrical force" on the whole enlightened part, and particularly the Christian part, of the sex, to arouse them to the most vigorous action.[13]

Some of the sex were so roused, through their participation in missionary societies, conversion at revival meetings, or contacts at such female seminaries as those run by Mary Grant and Mary Lyons. The strong sense of sisterly bonds with female friends, often formed in such seminaries, also motivated a few women to enlist in the missionary cause. Lucy Goodale's Bradford experience indicated how the decision of one stalwart scholar could inspire others to emulate her. Lucy Goodale Thurston departed for the Sandwich Islands in 1819, "an affecting and solemn scene," reported her close friend Elizabeth Edwards, who despaired of ever again beholding her dear friend's face, as she wrote in her diary.[14] Three years later, her diary records an urgent desire to follow in her friend's path. "An opportunity presents for me to go to the heathen; the question is to be decided immediately. My soul is struggling within me." Three days later she writes, "I have made the all important decision, have at last concluded to go to the heathen. O my God thou knowest my motives all my motives. Search me, O God, and know my heart. . . and if there be an unholy motive within my heart O show it unto me and lead me in the right way."[15] The way took her to marriage with Artemas

Bishop and to Kailua, on the island of Hawaii, to her friend Lucy Thruston's mission station. To another Bradford friend, Miss Parker, Lucy wrote in jubilation at her choice of mission work, and of her love. "Would that I could again feel the embrace of those loved arms, again enjoy the long solitary walk. My heart thrills at the thought it might be so. . . . I embrace her with an overflowing tide of affection. She reciprocates. . . ." Alas, Miss Parker was not so lucky and was not sent to the Sandwich Islands mission.[16]

Similarly when Charlotte Fowler Baldwin left for the Sandwich Islands, her friend Mary Barker, wrote in her diary that there was only one beam of hope, "I think I shall see that beloved sister, yet again on earth—Then it must be—*We meet on that distant Heathen shore!* Roll on Ocean, bear thy freight far hence; and soon I will follow! If *God* will."[17] Two years later she wrote, "Today—my heart is stirred within me,—It quivers strangely. I seem to hear a voice saying who will go to the Marquesas!—who?—*Lord I will* Send me—is the heart's reply—Poor poor pagan!"[18] She was in fact, about to marry one Henry Parker, who was departing for the Sandwich Islands and thence possibly to the Marquesas. She reached her dear friend and in the 1860s was still writing with deep affection to "dear, dear Charlotte," and of her longing to visit with her at her station as soon as possible.[19]

In all these stories of enlistment in the cause very little is made of the relationship with the male missionary. The American Board seldom sent single female missionaries abroad in the early decades of its activities. Most of the women believed it was impossible to go to the field unmarried. They were, however, prepared to marry men who were total strangers to them, when the men were on the point of departing for the mission. Usually fresh graduates of Yale, Princeton, Amherst, or Williams, these men, once accepted as missionaries for the Sandwich Islands were immediately faced with the requirement that they go to this field as married men for as it was fraught with dangers for the celibate. Seldom did they already know a woman willing to make such a sacrifice. They would make discreet inquiries about women with a known interest in missions; introductions would be arranged; proposals made and accepted. It then remained for the board to investigate the credentials of the proposed female missionary, and sometimes the newly married pair would be on a ship sailing for the Pacific within a month or two of first meeting. Before her departure one such bride, Clarissa Chapman, wrote a lengthy farewell letter to her friend Ludentia, informing her of her enlistment as a missionary, and added virtually as an afterthought, "Tomorrow evening in Church, I expect to become the wife of Rev. Richard Armstrong."[20] These women appear to have made their momentous decisions with remarkable coolness and determination.

These women were not passive entrants to the missionary field. They believed they had a strong call in their own right to teach the nations. Marriage to a male missionary was the means of fulfilling their ambition to engage in the reform work that seemed to them of the highest importance. A ship owner who watched the first white women embark for the Sandwich Islands ordered his captains to give them free passages back home again. "Those women are fools. They cannot live there, and will, every one of them, be back within a year."[21] But the women set off with high hopes. "Who would not be willing to endure the scorching heat of a sultry region, a few fleeting days if thereby they may be instrumental of plucking immortal souls from the scorching of eternal burnings?" asked Nancy Ruggles as the brig *Thaddeus* approached the shores of Hawaii.[22] Who indeed? These American women were eager to plunge into their task. Mindful of the board's admonition to departing missionaries to beware the indolence common in sultry climates, the first contingent of women set to work in the islands with alacrity, watched at first by curious crowds of Hawaiians who seemed much excited even to observe their cooking operations on an open fire in the mission yard. Urged by the mission board to enlist the favor of the female chiefs, the women found that their sewing skills also attracted admiration. They cut out and made up satin gowns for high-born women, pantaloons and ruffled shirts for the chiefs. Mercy Whitney managed thirty garments in the space of a few weeks. "In cutting and making clothes for them, etc. I have so gained the confidence of many, that they think that whatever I do is right, and are willing to confess themselves ignorant."[23]

Many of the women, shortly after arrival, enjoyed finding themselves central actors in a scene encapsulating the essence of their mission. They sat on stools in the midst of a circle of Hawaiian women or of Hawaiian children seated on mats on the floor, teaching an attentive audience, gratified to be bringing enlightenment to the natives. Louisa Ely experienced this at Kaawaloa. "I had the happiness of commencing a sabbath school for the little heathen children. Altho [*sic*] it was not known until the close of morning exercises, I had the pleasure of seeing 15 little children seated around me listening to instruction. . . . What can be pleasanter than to labor to enlighten the dark minds of these ignorant heathen?"[24] Similarly placed, Lucy Thurston at Kailua wrote of her enjoyment at "the delightful experience of presenting truths to the dark minds of these untutored natives. . . to see the look of intelligence, of wonder, of gratitude and love."[25] To Sybil Bingham, teaching the women in a chief's hut near Honolulu, "It seemed like being where my thoughts had often in past years placed me — *on heathen ground*."[26]

Their pleasure was usually short-lived, defeated by their horror of the easygoing ways of the Hawaiians whose deviations from the norms of their own society they saw as sin. Lucy Ruggles Holman found Hawaiians "sunk to the lowest depth of sin and depravity—they appear to glory in what should be their greatest shame. There is no sin, the commission of which disgraces them but work. . . ."[27] A usual response was a spontaneous expression of disgust at the Hawaiian life-style, swiftly suppressed by some hastily summoned up reiteration of their pious intentions, of reform activity in store. Julia Brooks Spaulding, who had been a pupil of Mary Lyons and then a scholar and teacher of the Ipswich Seminary, wrote, "In their lack of clothing and in their wild vociferation they were repulsive, but we remembered that we went for their good, and not for our own gratification, and therefore felt that we could be content in their midst."[28] Another had a similar reaction. "It is true that I knew but little before my arrival of the character if they may be said to have any, of a heathen people. Language cannot convey to you a just idea of their ignorance and stupidity; nor can I say that our intercourse with them is in any way particularly pleasant but as [*sic*]we enjoy the happiness of seeing them improve by our efforts."[29] Maria Loomis witnessed a hula. "We hope the time is not far distant when we shall see them engaged in more noble employment," was her immediate reflection.[30] One must hate the sin, but try desperately hard to love the sinner.

They came with the goal of raising the supposed abject status of Hawaiian women. The situation was not, however, quite what they had visualized. Forty years of contact with American and European sailors, beachcombers, and traders had initiated changes in Hawaiian culture, culminating shortly before the first missionaries arrived in the overthrow of traditional laws, laws which had indeed incorporated notions of women as profane and polluting.[31] The Americans discovered not only a diminution in the restrictions of laws governing women's lives, but also the enormous, astonishing prestige and power of women of the chiefly class; in this highly stratified society highborn women, as well as men, were accorded high status. New England republicanism was offended by the hierarchic nature of Hawaiian society. So too were notions of proper feminine behavior, particularly as both sexes were polygamous in the highest ranks, and it was difficult to discover to which husband a female chief ought to show due deference. Though they complained in private, publicly the mission women submitted to treatment from the female chiefs that seemed to them humilating. The stature of the chiefs even enabled them to dandle these slight American brides on their knees in an affectionate mood, like pets.

To the American eye, signs of degradation remained, even if they were not the anticipated marks of female subordination. The Hawaiian sexual division of labor, and particularly Hawaiian sexual practices elicited American reforming zeal. The missionary women had expected to discover Hawaiian women as drudges for the men: they were shocked to discover that in a society where material wants were in any case easily satisfied, the women performed *insufficient* labor. "Indolence may be considered as a native characteristic." observed Maria Loomis. "Little to excite them to action [,] they spend many precious hours in sleep. Their women do no work of any consequence [;] they think it rather a disgrace."[32] Hawaiian men undertook the bulk of the manual labor, including preparation of food in ovens in the ground. The women principally prepared cloth from bark. They seemed disinclined to rouse themselves energetically to change the family's living style in ways prescribed by missionaries. Nor, in fact, was childcare an onerous burden for Hawaiian women. They reared the infants, though not necessarily their own; babies were often adopted by kin. Abortion and infanticide reduced the numbers of children the women reared. Older children, with their sleeping mats in a roll under their arms, changed homes frequently among the carefully preserved extended kinship network.

The sexual arrangements of ordinary Hawaiians were even more severely censured. Marriage was a flexible arrangement. Girls and boys past puberty engaged in sexual activity with a number of partners. Around the age of eighteen they settled into marriages which were sometimes enduring but could be dissolved easily if alternative relationships were desired. Girls and women discussed and presented their sexuality in an open, public fashion, revealing a frank enjoyment of things of the body foreign to the American women. The mission women deprecated such sexual indulgence, even more vehemently when the sexual relationship involved American and European sailors, who rewarded sexual favors with Western material goods (and with Western venereal disease, the nasty part of the bargain).

The first brake on the single-minded efforts of missionary women was applied by the pull of their own domestic obligations as married women. Many of the marriages of these hastily matched couples turned out to be remarkably close. Clarissa Chapman Armstrong spoke for many when she said after eight months of marriage that she feared the painful separation of her husband and herself by death, which she often thought might soon be their punishment as "we are so much inclined to idolatry—this is a sin, that I hope grace, will enable us to overcome."[33] Their husbands' absences were dreaded. Romantic Elizabeth Edwards Bishop had clearly transferred her strong emotions to her husband when she wrote in her journal of seeing in her mind's eye, day and night, the form of her beloved bosom friend—her husband. "Indulgent God, protect, preserve, bless, return to my waiting heart my dear husband, my soul's delight, support, and joy."[34] Juliette Cooke, who had demanded testimonials from her suitor when he proposed, wrote in Amos Cooke's absence, "May God return that dear one safe to my arms and make me a better wife than I have ever been before [.] How desolate the widow."[35] "I am one *alone* in the midst of company. Oh! I am alone!" wrote Maria Patton Chamberlain, eighteen years married and mother of eight. "When will my beloved companion return?"[36] In fact, the men could not face this alien wilderness without wives, and even miserably bereaved widowers would have to seek another wife, or abandon the mission.[37]

Neither deep emotional bonds nor transplantation to an exotic setting, however, had been sufficient to alter the traditional demarcation of labor within their own marriages. Except in crises such as childbirth and illness, husbands dissociated themselves from routine domestic chores and minor social obligations, despite their apparent sympathy for their wives' desire to teach. However well-educated and willing their wives might be, it was the men who would learn the language, write the translations, and study, abstracted from the tedious a repetitious work of the physical and material maintenance of the family. Once their families had roofs over their heads and some rudimentary furniture, the men labored for the "heathen" in uninterrupted blocks of time.

Women's study and teaching, on the other hand, would be squeezed into a day and a week constantly broken by the multifarious demands of the good housewife, painfully and laboriously performed in an environment bereft of their accustomed aids. The time-consuming character of these chores, and the physical toll they exacted, clearly surprised these hopeful brides, as they sewed all the family clothing, cooked meals, cared for the sick, or entertained visiting captains or local Americans at meals. They attempted to initiate curious Hawaiians into the mysteries of American housekeeping, but servants seldom stayed long, and never did this assistance match the requirements of maintaining the semblance at least of American standards of living in a frontier and alien situation. Within three years Sybil Bingham was bewailing the constant interruptions to her time that prevented her improvement in the language and continued study. "Perhaps my life may be spared to labor yet more directly for the heathen. You may wonder, sometimes, what, in this corner of the earth, I can find to be doing, if it is not laboring for the heathen." What indeed, except that the demands of American housewifery had not been left behind with their kindred. She had already fallen back on the role of the good helpmeet as compensation. "I have this consolation,—I am allowed to aid one whose constant employment is in the way of direct efforts for their good."[38]

While the missionary women remained childless they were able to undertake a fair amount of teaching, despite the domestic burdens that fell to their lot. Indeed, they usually commenced teaching on a grand scale. Adult women, even more than the young children, were keen to learn to read and acquire books in the Hawaiian language printed by the mission. Frequently, the women confronted classes of one hundred or more in two shifts, morning and afternoon. With enormous resourcefulness, the teachers sought ways to overcome the problems posed by lack of writing paper, desks, pencils, and equipment to teach counting, and they discovered local materials and new methods as substitutes. Conscious always of the need to interest their pupils and develop their curiosity about the world of Western learning, the women labored hard to involve their students, training some as monitors to cope with the huge classes. As more ordinary Hawaiians followed their chiefs in indicating an attachment to the Christian faith, women conducted prayer meetings and Sabbath schools, as well as the inevitable sewing classes which would insure that their pupils would be baptized fully clothed and behatted. (Hats they worried about, but not shoes.) The women swapped notes on the teaching methods they found successful, and sent home for urgently needed equipment to broaden the basis of their curriculum. They were clearly equal to the demands of a highly unusual situation and managed capably. On odd occasions when their husbands substituted for them in their young children's classes, male admiration knew no bounds. How did they have the patience and resourcefulness to keep such restless little beings interested and working?

Their teaching initiatives sometimes survived the birth of one baby, seldom the birth of a second. With fertile couples, first infants arrived as early as nine or ten months after marriage, and usually no later than by eighteen months, unless a miscarriage had intervened. Second and subsequent births occurred at around two-yearly intervals. A number of women at this stage experienced continuous ill-health as homesickness, the unaccustomed warm and humid climate, and untreated gynecological problems like profuse menstruation or frequent miscarriages left them debilitated and depressed. Some died. Some were forced to return home for medical treatment, seeking the care of mothers and sisters. Those who survived and persevered in the mission bore on average between six and seven children. They had not been young brides, for the median age of marriage had been nearly twenty-five years, so those who had the largest families of eight, nine, or ten were bearing children over their fertile period into their early forties.[39] Sometimes they sounded slightly embarrassed at reporting yet another birth to their parents back home. Abner Wilcox said, when informing his parents of Lucy's bearing a second child only sixteen months after the first, "This, for your cold climate would be thought premature, but in a tropical climate like ours, it is nothing unusual to have one or two crops in one year."[40] Maria Chamberlain probably spoke for most of the women when she responded to a married daughter's request for advice on birth control. "You ask what I did? I frankly tell you, I never did anything to prevent having a family. I thought it was all of the Lord to give life, and I never did anything to destroy it."[41]

Although one infant in ten died before the age of five, and a smaller number between five and twelve, the burden of child-rearing was considerable. The missionary women would often take first babies along to school with them, a distraction, but not a total obstacle to teaching duties. When a second infant appeared eighteen months or two years later, the serious difficulty arose. Who was to care for the older child, now beginning to talk and show awareness of the surrounding world? This question led the missionary women to a soul-searching reappraisal of their various obligations as Christian women. Increasingly, they comprehended the gulf that separated their own notions of childrearing from the Hawaiians and realized that even religious conversion generated change in this area very slowly. Further, there was the unnerving discovery that their own young children were strongly attracted to Hawaiian society. As a result, they were forced to the reluctant conclusion that if their children were to grow up as American Christian children should, they would need to be insulated as completely as possible from Hawaiian society. This recognition precluded the use of Hawaiian women as nurses and child minders.

Accounts of the undisciplined life of the Hawaiian child were legion. "You might see them," wrote Sheldon Dibble, "from morning to night, ungoverned by their parents, almost naked, ranging the fields in companies of both sexes, sporting on the sanddunes, bathing promiscuously in the surf, or following in the wake of some drunken sailors, and learning all their profaneness, obscenity and swaggering behaviour."[42] Betsy Curtis Lyons at Waimea had established classes for Hawaiian mothers to teach them their duty with regard to their children, and her husband gave the reason."Many evils existed among mothers. They were accustomed to give away their children in their earliest infancy. They neglected parental government. Their children were disobedient, their passions unrestrained, the mother trampled underfoot, and the domestic circle a scene of confusion, to which happiness was a stranger. Children were growing up in sin, and plunging into sin."[43] The common practice by which infants were adopted away from biological parents was seen as a root cause of this apparent disorderliness: children had too many parents, adopted or natural, and could move readily if their parents curbed their behavior.

Nothing, however, alarmed the missionary women more than the fact that the openness about sexuality of Hawaiian adults extended to their children. Their language and topics of conversation indicated a knowledge of sex and a fascination with it that the missionaries found appalling. Even very young children could be seen indulging in intimate and "immodest acts," quite happily and openly. Even more disconcerting was the reluctance even of Hawaiian church members to accept the importance of keeping children ignorant on "certain subjects." "It is common," one missionary told the board, "for children here at all ages to hear and see and talk of everything that is transacted from the sick chamber of parturition to the hour of marriage and from the obscene practises of the brothel and debasing intercourse of the street to the hall of judgement; of course none of the scenes mentioned, even the 'hall of judgement' or 'sick chamber' are in this land managed with any modesty at all. Modesty is an anomaly in heathen character."[44]

That conversion to Christianity was not going to bring reform naturally in its train, even when Hawaiian and half-Hawaiian children were taken into the bosom of the Christian family, had been a discovery of the first missionary groups. They had clearly expected that by taking such children under their wing, by teaching them and training them in the arts of the household, they would produce an important pool of converts to American ways. Young William Beals, a ten- or eleven-year-old lad when Sybil Bingham "picked him up" near her fence in 1820, showed like others exceptional advances in American manners, in language and learning. He was exhibited to visiting sea captains and he was chosen to teach high chiefs. In his writing book, he diligently practiced "I not go in the way of a bad boy. . . . For a bad boy cannot go to God. . . . See not my sin O God and let me not go to the pit. . . . I may die today, all men are to die."[45] A bad boy, alas, he proved to be, three years later with fourteen-year-old Hannah Holmes, doyenne of the girls' class, despite the fact that both had been presented with Bibles at the school examination for reciting the Ten Commandments. Poor William died from an infection ("of licentiousness," according to Clarissa Richards), telling Hannah how he and she had "done wrong," and that he would soon go to hell.[46] Most of the girls went to another "hell;" once the girls were neat, smart, and literate, the local foreign element benefited from Sybil Bingham's labors by snapping them up as mistresses.[47]

The missionary women chafed at the apparent impossibility of keeping the mission children from observing the open sexual practices of the Hawaiians. From the time babies were capable of noticing objects around them, wrote Clarissa Richards, they were "constrained to witness scenes which would shock the feelings of parents of ordinary sensibility. . . . What care and watchfulness, untiring vigilance is necessary for parents to render them faithful to their trust, and to preserve their infant off-spring from defilement in a land where modesty—chastity, virtue and terms synonymous, are words unknown."[48] How were they to keep their children from being corrupted by the words, gestures, and customs so threatening to American notions of propriety?

They were disconcerted to discover the aptitude of their own young children in imitating Hawaiian ways, including the language itself. Their first words were Hawaiian; they learned the language very quickly, finding it much easier than English. They liked Hawaiians; they were fascinated by their gestures, facial expressions, and movements, and as soon as they could walk alone, would sneak out to be with them and laugh with them. Caroline Armstrong's mother anxiously reported that by the age of three the child imitated *all* that the natives did. "She knows considerable of the language—does not speak it much but will tell in english[*sic*] what they say, or what we say to them. . . . In imatating [*sic*] she scratches her head, squats on the mats, spits, and clear her nose, and many other things just like the natives—and it is exceedingly difficult to prevent it."[49] The infant Henry Parker used facial gestures like Hawaiians' before he could walk; his insistence on crawling only backwards symbolized to his mother a moving backwards in civilization, surrounded as they were day by day with "a low grovelling people, and they our only society."[50] By age two he could speak Hawaiian very fast. "You can little conceive," Mary Parker said, "what a native's influence is over such a child—their language and conduct—I speak of the children of his age, is corrupting and ruinous."[51]

The apparently perverse attraction of Hawaiian ways for their children seemed all the more alarming because it coincided with the missionaries' belief in the birth of their infants into sin from which they must be redeemed. By the time Mercy Whitney had four young children, the connection between their sinful natures and their interest in Hawaiians was clear. Divine grace was able to keep them in some measure from the pollutions of the heathen, she asserted somewhat doubtfully, but "I have reason to believe both from observation and experience that nothing short will keep them effectually from giving loose to the sinful profanities of a depraved and wicked heart."[52] And where would it stop? The missionaries reminded themselves that even back home, the children of the same neighborhood tended to share the same general habits and tastes and language, even though there might be considerable difference in the characters of their parents.[53]

The "pollution" evidenced by their young children dimmed in comparison with the dangers in store when their children reached puberty. An English mission to the Society Islands (Tahiti) had been established since 1797 and veterans of that field had many a woeful tale to relate when they visited their Sandwich Islands brethren. According to them, British children in Tahiti were almost as much strangers to chastity as the natives: daughters were prostitutes and sons were vagabonds.[54] Sons ran away from school to join Tahitian boys in initiation ceremonies in the mountains. Boys had been expelled from the South Sea Academy for seducing native girls. A mission daughter gave birth to a baby of Tahitian extraction. One mission mother, hearing a noise one night in the room where her three daughters slept, had fainted on finding *three* Tahitian men in the chamber.[55]

The American women pitied their sisters in the South Seas, but they were certainly not going to repeat their mistakes. The significance of childrearing was a highly important component of their own religious and cultural heritage. The books they read, the sermons they heard, and Maternal Association publications reinforced their belief in the period of early education as critical for the child's future well-being. If the souls of the unevangelized were precious (and their very presence in the Sandwich Islands testified to this belief), were not the souls of those who lived within the fold equally precious? They could scarcely be happy in the work of converting the heathen while their own children grew up unredeemed. They were surrounded by heathen families. "Placed in such circumstances," wrote Laura Judd to the New York *Mother's Magazine,* "how bright should be the light of our example. Like a city set on a hill, truly."[56] A very dim light it would be, indeed, if instead of their converting Hawaiians to Christianity, the Hawaiians made heathens of the missionary children.

Some of these missionary women believed that fathers should take a more than nominal part in childrearing. Lucia Smith, as yet unmarried, had watched with dismay how seasick missionary mothers were dispatched to the hold on interisland voyaging with their miserably vomiting children, while selfish fathers sat in peace on the deck. "I found myself revolving the question in my own mind many times, why all this thrown on the mother? Is it right? I fear if I had been in the place of some of them I should have said Aloe no. Enough of this!!"[57] When an *Address to*

Mothers was read at the Honolulu Maternal Association stressing the incessant duties of mothers from morning to night till they reached the grave, while they might expect no return for their labors except consciousness of duty done, "some objections were made to the recent practice of authors throwing *all* the care and responsibility of training on the Mother."[58] Over and over women hoped that their husbands would soon be able to play a more active part in the training of the children, but at present they seemed particularly busy. The time seldom seemed to arrive.

In practice, women devoted themselves fully to the care of their children through their early years. When the children were infants, they often relied on the services of a Hawaiian woman to care for the baby under the mother's close supervision. By the time the children became "prattlers," they were removed entirely from the Hawaiians' care, to be looked after physically and educated in a more formal sense by the mother. Every attempt was made to prevent their learning the language, that gateway to an alien culture. They were with the mother all day, at their books or playing in a walled yard adjacent to the bedrooms known as the *tabu* yard, and forbidden to Hawaiians.[59] If the mother went out to visit or take some exercise, the children accompanied her. Some of the earliest women on the field panicked to such an extent that they sent children as young as six, seven, or eight back to America, despite heart-breaking separations and uncertain guardianship. Other children were sent at eleven or twelve. Because successive infants kept appearing, these departures relieved the mother's burden only marginally. Lucy Goodale Thruston stood out against such unnatural separations, and cloistered herself with her children until the oldest was eighteen—not because she enjoyed it, but because she believed it to be her duty. She was servant, playmate, mother, and preceptress, she said, to her children.[60] "Crucifixion is the torture of days. This maternal anxiety, which hourly preys upon the heart, and produces so many sleepless nights, is the *anguish of years*."[61] Caroline Bailey described the pressure as debilitating. "This is one thing that breaks down ladies here so fast. It is the constant care which presses, by day and by night. If one goes to Meeting, their children must go with them, if one goes visiting, their children must be of the party, and so of everything else, thus keeping up the pressure. I often think if I could leave them for a day or two with a trusty person, it would help me wonderfully."[62]

To Mary Parker arriving in the Sandwich Islands in 1833, the missionary children appeared interesting, and as well advanced in their studies as the children at home. "Most of them would suffer nothing compared with the children in America, they are easy, intelligent, and free from such vulgarity common with children at home. This last fact is owing probably to the never having been entrusted to servants."[63] The educational prowess of these children certainly was impressive. Introduced at as early an age as possible to reading, even at two years and under, to wean them away from Hawaiian speech, the children found in books the best occupation for so many confined hours. By four years of age, most could read a chapter of the Bible and commit a long passage to memory, and were ready to commence the courses in history, geography, and botany their parents devised. By ten or eleven they were proficient in mathematics, chemistry, sometimes Latin or Greek. After 1841, Punahou School in Honolulu catered for the education of children over ten.

The mothers now turned their ingenuity to discovering ways of keeping restless children occupied. Boys as well as girls learned to ply their needles at patchwork and simple clothing. Mothers of farming backgrounds bemoaned the absence of chores like harvesting and animal husbandry to occupy the children's time as they grew older—small vegetable plots and a cow were poor substitutes.[64] They could and often did dispense with Hawaiian domestic assistance altogether so that the children could learn the discipline of washing floors, setting tables, baking bread. Job efficiency was not remarkable, and the women's cares again were only marginally relieved.

In fact the women worried, too, about the effects of this separation from the Hawaiians on the children's characters. Would children not be in danger of becoming selfish and circumscribed in their affections if they were not able to sympathize with Hawaiians in their afflictions?[65] Were they in danger of inducing in children a contempt and disgust for the Hawaiians rather than love and pity?[66] Mercy Whitney was proud that her three-year-old daughter would sit at the window watching Hawaiian children play, without attempting to join them, and would even reprove them for playing on the Sabbath.[67] Most mothers began a complicated indoctrination process by which children were taught to understand their own privileges, so as to pity the natives for their deprivation. A dictated letter to grandma from young Gerrit Judd shows this procedure in motion as early as seventeen months. "I have many play things, but native children haven't any. I have a basket of clothes but native children haven't any and I have parents to teach me and take care of me and a nice trundle bed to sleep in, but native children have not any. I feel sorry for poor native children."[68]

By no means all the husbands, nor the board, were prepared to accept the women's choice as necessary. When the board was critical of Martha Goodrich, who was accused with her husband of failing to exert herself sufficiently in the field, William Richards wrote in her defense that, although it might injure the reputation of the other ladies at the mission to say so, no married woman after three years on the mission ground had ever spent as much as two hours a day working directly for the Hawaiians. "Nearly all, when they first come on mission ground, commence schools, and some have continued them till they have two or three children, but after that, it is out of the question."[69] Jeremiah Evarts pleaded for the board with the missionaries, in vain, not to be so anxious about their children. As all their experience as parents had been at the islands, undoubtedly missionary parents believed that all difficulties in controlling and educating their children stemmed from their peculiar circumstances. The truth was that parents found it difficult to bring up their children anywhere.[70]

Laura Judd herself began to discern dangers for the missionary children in being taught to think that their mothers' entire attention should be devoted to watching, quieting, and directing "its own little self," instead of appreciating that others had claims on their mothers' time.[71] But anxious the mothers were, and tension between their duties as missionaries and as mothers continued to press. Ursula Emerson described the situation to the *Mother's Magazine*. "We have many trials, as mothers, in this heathen land. We sustain an important relation to the native mothers and children around us, as well as to our own dear offspring; and it is not unfrequently a question of deep interest how we shall rightly divide the claims of each upon us."[72] Most women attempted some public activity. They continued classes in sewing, or spinning, or braiding hats. They gave out medicine and nursing advice, occasionally visiting the sick, or called on church members to inspect the cleanliness of their homes. They met with Hawaiian women for prayer meetings, and in mothers' meetings to dispense good advice. Where their husbands were attached to a boarding school they usually conducted classes intermittently.

Outside observers commented on the women's efficiency. One young American visiting his aunt in the 1830s found her a formidable character.

> My aunt could work, scold, preach, wash, bake, pray, catechize, make dresses, plant, pluck, drive stray pigs out of the garden. There was nothing useful in this wilderness which she could not do.
> She exercised an influence from her energy and practical virtue which bordered on absolute authority. As I walked with her through the village, her presence operated as a civilizing tonic. True, the effect in many cases was transient. But the natives knew what she expected. As she appeared, tobacco pipes disappeared, idle games or gambling were slyly put by, Bible and hymn books brought conspicuously forward and the young girls hastily donned their chastest dresses and looks. . . ."[73]

For the women themselves, however, what they accomplished seemed spasmodic, ineffectual, and inadequate. It was not really the satisfying labor they had left mothers, sisters, and beloved New England to perform.

They consoled themselves as best they could. Clarissa Armstrong wrote her brother of her sadness at not doing more directly for the natives, "but husband tries to comfort me by saying, I may perhaps be raising missionaries, who will do much more than I could. However it may be, I know it is all ordered by providence. . . . If it is my duty to raise a family, it is my duty to do so cheerfully. Oh, to be a better *missionary wife* and *mother.*"[74] Fanny Gulick, convert of Charles Finney, graduate of the Westfield Academy, and pioneer teacher of slum infants in New York, was similarly consoled with the thought that if she raised a large family of good moral character, she would not have lived in vain.[76] A disappointed Mary Ives told her aunt how little she accomplished compared with the expectations when she left America. She only looked after her own family, but then, that was as much as most women did in civilized lands, and here at least she could feel more, pray more, and have a greater influence in turning the heathen to the Lord than she could if she did not live among them, even if she wasn't able to teach school.[76] What could a mother with five children six years of age and under do for the natives in a land where she must be housekeeper, teacher, and seamstress for her family, asked Maria Chamberlain? She and others at least did something, doubtless, by way of example. "By being sober, loving our husbands, loving our children, being discreet, chaste, keepers at home, obedient to our husbands, virtues which converts from heathenism would be slow to learn without living examples set before them."[77]

Their submission to the dictates of maternal duty was by no means without severe personal struggle, for no more than their husbands, were they noticeably meek, gentle, or passive by nature. When a fellow missionary was reprimanded by the board for returning home without permission, Juliette Cooke was enraged. "Though Missionaries we are *New Englanders* still, and the love of *liberty* is woven into every fibre of our hearts. It will take something more than an unjust law to quench this love of freedom."[78] But as they burned with anger from afar about slavery, or confronted drunken seamen or angry chiefs with resolution, concern for the spiritual and temporal future of their small offspring won the day.

As mothers at least they were highly successful in reproducing their young in their own image. The children proved clever, excelling eventually even in the prestigious eastern colleges back home, at Yale and Princeton and Mt. Holyoke. They turned out pious too, and many daughters and sons became the teachers and ministers of their mothers' dreams. Little Henry Parker, who had once crawled backwards, strode forward in maturity to the pulpit. On the Californian goldfields, a group of mission sons donned Sunday best and read their Bibles. Samuel Chapman Armstrong fought with other mission lads for the North in the Civil War, and founded the Hampton Institute after it, while his sister and her mission friends taught freed slaves' children in Virginia. Six Gulick sons became missionaries, and in 1852 children of missionaries formed the Hawaiian Mission Children's Society to support a new mission in Micronesia (women had equal rights in the organization).[79] Many mission sons, full of Yankee initiative, astuteness, and zeal for hard work, were poised to take advantage of land and business opportunities in the new state of Hawaii. Undoubtedly, in later years, the women derived satisfaction from all this, yet a pervasive sense of failure marked their evaluation of their life experience.

In fact, however, the vision of a glorious enterprise in an independent capacity was unrealistic from the very beginning. The American board quite clearly saw the men's activity as primary and the women's as ancillary. This attitude was clearly spelled out by the secretary to the board, Rufus Anderson, when in 1836 he wrote an introduction to a memoir of the English missionary Mary Ellis. He laid out the grounds for sending women as wives to the mission field. First, it was not good for man to be alone, no less among the "heathen" as at home. His nature demanded a wife, and he needed a friend, counselor, and companion to lighten his toils, nurse him in sickness, secure comfort in his home, and provide adequate food and clothing. Otherwise he would waste precious time, and the loneliness and vexations of his situation would waste his spirits, curtail his efforts, perhaps shorten his days.[80] In other words, the wife's primary role was to assist the man to be "a more contented, zealous, faithful, useful missionary." The second reason for sending women to the mission field was so that the "heathen" should have an opportunity of seeing Christian families. The missionaries perceived the Hawaiians' own domestic constitution as dreadfully disordered, and the degraded womenfolk as needing the models of the virtuous, useful, praiseworthy wives and mothers. Only last did Anderson state that women would be useful as teachers of women and children, that they should go out trained for the work, and that indeed such successful activity would shorten the work of missions by one or two generations.[81] He hastened to add that of course these duties must remain subservient to their primary obligation, the care of their households.

The men in the mission field themselves remained attached to traditional notions of demarcation of work in the family, and for the most part they were vociferous in criticizing women who stepped outside their appropriate sphere. Lucy Goodale Thurston had to defend herself sharply on a number of occasions where she was seen as having disregarded appropriate womanly behavior, once when she presented the station's annual report at the General Meeting during the illness of her husband.[82] Mary Tenney Castle, stepmother to her sister's child and mother of ten, a seeker of Garrisonian perfectionism, aroused animosity by praying aloud at a prayer meeting attended by both women and men, and for a time was virtually ostracized.[83] In later life she supported women's suffrage. In 1847, during her husband's absence, Clarissa Armstrong conducted religious worship in meetings where men were present. She was dubbed "Abby Kelley" after the prominent abolitionist as a term of reproach for preaching in a pulpit and praying in public. She was called insane by some, a heretic by others, and was told she might as well "wear the pants," that she was in favor of women's rights, that she neglected her family. She remembered the experience with bitterness into her old age. "I knew the Theology was 'let your women keep silence.' My husband, like others, learned the same Theology, but encouraged me. . . . I have often wondered why men who have studied for years, through a course of Theology etc. and never discussed the freedom Christ gave women." God, she believed, blessed her efforts: Christ had never taught such sentiments.[84]

The drama of the lives of the American missionary women in Hawaii was played out in an exotic setting remote from the eastern seaboard of the United States from which they came. Their experience, however, has implications for understanding the efforts of women in antebellum America to enlarge the sphere of influence beyond the domestic circle. The distant location and the confrontation of American women with participants in an utterly different social system serve to isolate, reinforce, and magnify features inherent in early American feminism that were not always so clearly delineated in the American social context.

In the first place, the outcome of the missionary women's pursuit of an independent career, purchased at no small personal cost, reflects the ambiguities and tensions in the movement of nineteenth-century American women into public life. The justification of a public role for women was grounded in the elevation of women's role within the family, and in the desire to see such supposedly ennobling influence extended in the work of uplifting community standards as a whole. Such a justification for female public activity inevitably contained within it a potentially contradictory message that would thwart women who sought independent endeavors. Nowhere was this illustrated more plainly then in the Hawaiian mission experience. These missionary women were prepared to leave America (for which they grieved all their days), and to marry virtual strangers, in order to pursue a lifetime career. But their aspiration to such a future had been possible only because it fell within a socially acceptable ideological framework, one essential aspect of which was that married women should serve as the moral focus of their families, and should devote themselves selflessly to the nuture and guidance of their children. These women fully embraced their maternal duty, but in fulfilling it found their teaching efforts inexorably frustrated. The parameters of married women's participation in the public sphere were starkly revealed. And the frustration was not less cruel because the women themselves had for the most part thoroughly internalized such values.

Second, the experience of these female missionaries reveals something significant about the attitude of many American female social reformers to those whom they sought to assist. Such women could display undeniable courage, a determined spirit, and a capacity of altruistic endeavor. That a group of such women, however, should have designated Hawaiians as appropriate subjects for their attention, defining every feature of the Hawaiian social system as defective, indicated an unyielding attachment to their own world view. A self-assurance bordering on arrogance armed many of these American women at home or abroad to impose their own perceptions of reality on their protégés. The missionaries shared the tough set of armor that enabled Americans, along with other representatives of capitalist, industrializing countries, to initiate and survive innumerable cross-cultural encounters. Racism was part of that cultural armor.

The mission women could be warm, loving, and sympathetic among their own kind, qualities they were prepared to share with Hawaiians, but at a price. The Americans believed that Hawaiians were significant human beings, with souls of equal worth with their own in the eyes of God, beings whose education was a socially important labor. But they also viewed Hawaiians as sadly misguided children,[85] and offered them (as they offered their own offspring) affection and support in exchange for the Hawaiians' adoption of American values and behavior. The Hawaiians, however were fully-fledged members of a different cultural system; they might make concessions, but they could not make the fundamental change that the missionaries demanded. When Hawaiians did not display swift conversion to all things American, the mission women preferred unhappy isolation for themselves and their children, rather than to adjust, still less to see their children adjust, to a different cultural system. Female reformers in America did not face the test of exposing their children to the value systems of those they sought to help, to the values of slum children or freed slaves, for example, yet certainly a similar blinkered attitude to their protégés' cultural systems underwrote many such women's reform activities. Their utter conviction of the unassailable integrity of New England values was starkly revealed on this American frontier, where the mission women were incapable of appreciating that the Hawaiians' cultural system was as valid in its own terms as was American culture.

For these mission women, the effect of such racial attitudes was critical for their life experience: such an uncompromising view of Hawaiian society effectively undermined the women's hopes for a public role, or any chance that they might have withstood the force of their maternal obligations. The mission women's experience thereby adds another dimension to our understanding of the character of early American feminism. A genuine chance for the emancipation of women awaited not only an assault on powerful domestic ideologies, but also an assault on a narrow vision of issues of race and class which was endemic to nineteenth-century middle-class women's struggle for sexual equality.

NOTES

This paper was presented at the Australian and New Zealand American Studies Association Conference held at the University of Queensland, Queensland, Australia, 9-13 May 1982.

I would like to thank Mary-Jane Knight, Lela Goodell and Barbara Dunn of the Hawaiian Missions Children's Society Library in Honolulu and Dr. Charles Sowerwine and Professor Greg Dening of the History department, University of Melbourne, Australia, for their kind assistance in the preparation of this paper. The quotation in the title is drawn from Rufus Anderson, in his introduction to William Ellis, *Memoir of Mary Ellis* (Boston: Crocker & Brewster, 1836), xxii.

1. Records of the Maternal Association of the Sandwich Island Mission, 1834-41, 29 May 1840, Church Records, Hawaiian Mission Children's Society Library (hereafter cited as HMCSL), Honolulu, Hawaii.
2. Ibid., 29 May, [3 June], [5 June] 1840.
3. See, for example, the list of forty-four subjects for essays assigned to members at the annual meeting of 1835. Ibid., Annual Meeting 1835.
4. Among the influential works on women in the period are: Carroll Smith-Rosenberg, "Beauty, the Beast, and the Militant Woman: A Case Study of Sex Roles and Social Stress in Jacksonian America," *American Quarterly* 23 (October 1971): 562-84; Gerda Lerner, "The Lady and the Mill Girl: Changes in the Status of Women in the Age of Jackson, 1800-1840" in *A Heritage of Her Own: Toward a New Social History of American Women*, ed. Nancy F. Cott and Elizabeth H. Pleck (New York: Simon & Schuster, 1979); Barbara Welter, ed., *Dimity Convictions: The American Woman in the Nineteenth Century*, (Athens, Ohio: Ohio University Press, 1976); Gerda Lerner, *The Grimké Sisters from South Carolina: Pioneers for Woman's Rights and Abolition* (Boston: Houghton Mifflin, 1967); Nancy F. Cott, *The Bonds of Womanhood: "Woman's Sphere" in New England, 1780-1835* (New Haven, Yale University Press, 1977); Ellen Du Bois, *Feminism and Suffrage: The Emergence of an Independent Women's Movement in America, 1848-1869*, (Ithaca: Cornell University Press, 1978); Ann Douglas, *The Feminization of American Culture* (New York, Knopf, 1977); Kathryn Kish Sklar, *Catherine Beecher: A Study in American Domesticity* (New Haven, Yale University Press, 1973); Mary P. Ryan, *Cradle of the Middle Class: The Family in Oneida County, New York, 1790-1865* (New York: Cambridge University Press, 1981). A recent study of missionary women is Barbara Welter, "'She Hath Done What She Could': Protestant Women's Missionary Careers in Nineteenth-Century America," in *Women in American Religion*, ed. Janet W. James (Philadelphia, University of Pennsylvania Press, 1980), 111-26.

5. A Lady, *Conversations on the Sandwich Islands Mission* (Boston: Massachusetts Sabbath School Union, 1829), 6.
6. Charlotte Knapp, 10 March 1837, Journal, December 1836-June 1838, Journal Collection, HMCSL.
7. See *Panoplist and Missionary Magazine* 15, no. 2 (Ferbuary 1819): 67. An article in this evangelical journal gave support to the higher eduation of women teachers with an argument which illustrated such a justification for women's public role. Women might go "where men would not be supported. Their influence might be felt in the most secluded parts of our country. And, in some remote spot, which a traveller's eye may never survey, the angels of God may behold a pious female, in her little circle of affectionate pupils, laboriously and anxiously instructing the objects of her care to fear, and love, and serve their God." In no way was such advanced education to be considered wasted if these women married and withdrew from public teaching to rear their own children. The article continued: "It is paganism to keep the female sex in ignorance. Christianity has restored to women many of their rights, and has raised them from a wretched state of degradation, and abject servitude. The light of the Gospel irradiates their hearts as well as the hearts of men. Then let the light of science illuminate their minds, nor let women be compelled to think that their sphere is that of the butterfly, to flutter in useless gaiety, and wandering thoughtless."
8. Of the eighty-five women who joined the Sandwich Islands Mission in the years 1819 to 1845, twenty-one were from Massachusetts, fifteen from Connecticut, six from New Hampshire, three were from Maine, and five were from Pennsylvania; five from New Jersey; one each from Ohio, Delaware, Kentucky, Scotland, and England. See Hawaiian Mission Children's Society, *Missionary Album* 1937; reprint, (Honolulu: Hawaiian Mission Children's Society, 1969). [1934]
9. Helen W. Ludlow, "Clarissa Chapman Armstrong," in *American Heroes on Mission Fields*, ed. Hiram C. Haydn (New York: American Tract Society, 1894), 256-58.
10. Judd Family, *Fragments: Family Record of the House of Judd* (Honolulu: Privately printed, 1903), 27.
11. Lucy G. Thurston, *Life and Times of Mrs. Lucy G. Thurston* (1882; reprint, Honolulu: The Friend, 1934), 245-47.
12. Ibid., 248.
13. *Missionary Herald*, November 1825, pp. 360-61. For further background material, see Page Smith, *Daughters of the Promised Land* (Boston: Little, Brown & Co., 1970), chap. 13, and Welter. For a study of the American Board of Commissioners for Foreign Missions in its early years, see John A. Andrew III, *Rebuilding the Christian Commonwealth: New England Congregationalists and Foreign Missions, 1800-1830* (Lexington: Kentucky University Press, 1976).
14. Elizabeth Edwards Bishop, 28 October 1819, Journal, Journal Collection, HMCSL. Lucy Goodale had previously written to Elizabeth Edwards from the Bradford Academy, "O, Elizabeth, it is impossible to describe the sensations which pervade my mind. I know not how to compose myself to study. . . . My feelings are, however, some tried while contemplating what our feelings must be while passing thru [*sic*] the deep waters through which we must, me thinks, shortly be called to wade."
15. Ibid., 28 August and 3 September 1822. When Elizabeth Bishop died in 1828 in Hawaii, a collection of letters was discovered in a secret drawer of her writing desk, all affectionate notes from female friends of the Bradford Academy. For example, there was a poem written on 10 October 1816 by Nancy Batchelder:
May guardian angels all your steps attend
And every blessing crown my dearest Friend

In every state may you most happy be
And when far distant, sometimes think of me.
Bishop, Missionary Letters, HMCSL. See treatment of female friendship in Carroll Smith-Rosenberg, "The Female World of Love and Ritual: Relations between Women in Nineteenth-Century America" *Signs* 1 (Autumn 1975): 1-29.

16. Lucy Goodale Thurston to Miss A. Parker, 31 January 1822, ABCFM-Hawaii Papers, HMCSL. The Houghton Library, Harvard University, Cambridge, Mass., holds the originals of the American Board of Commissioners for Foreign Missions' Hawaii papers.

17. Mary Parker, [1830], Intimate Notebooks B, 1824-86, Journal Collection, HMCSL.

18. Ibid., [1832]. She did not refer to her husband by name in her diary. She noted her marriage thus: "I take myelf new and solemn vows—teach me Lord to fulfil [*sic*] them as unto thee."

19. Mary Parker to Charlotte Baldwin, 27 January [1864], Journal Collection, HMCSL.

20. Clarissa Chapman [Armstrong] to Ludentia [?], 25 September 1831, Missionary Letters, HMCSL.

21. Samuel Castle, "A General Review of the Mission Work in Hawaii," in Hawaiian Mission Children's Society, *Jubilee Celebration of the Arrival of the Missionary Reinforcement of 1837* (Honolulu: Daily Bulletin Steam Print, 1887), 111-12.

22. Nancy Ruggles, 24 February 1820, Samuel Ruggles and Nancy Wells Ruggles, Journal on Board the Brig *Thaddeus*, 1819-20, Journal Collection, HMCSL.

23. Mercy Whitney, 28 March 1823 (typescript), Journal, 1821-60, Journal Collection, HMCSL.

24. Louisa Ely to Elizabeth Bishop, 14 May 1824, Missionary Letters, HMCSL.

25. Lucy Thurston to Miss A. Parker, 31 January 1822 ABCFM-Hawaii Papers, HMCSL.

26. Sybil Bingham, 13 July 1820 (typescript), Journal on Board the *Thaddeus* and First Years in the Islands 1819-23, Journal Collection, HMCSL.

27. Lucia R. Holman, *Journal of Lucia Ruggles Holman* (Honolulu: Bernice P. Bishop Museum, Special Publication no. 17, 1931), 32-33.

28. Julia Spaulding, "Autobiographical Sketch," ABCFM-Hawaii Papers, HMCSL. They were at the same time often conscious that the Hawaiians showed considerable kindness towards them. Commenting on the warmth of the Hawaiians' greeting of her when she returned to Kaneohe after a visit to Honolulu, Mary Parker wrote: "I think after all we wrong the natives' character some, by giving them credit for so little heart. If they are not ladies and gentlemen they are friendly, and as my thoughts ran over the jars and discords of more polite, but less sincere friendship, I could not but feel that these poor people were worth caring for, and I came home to them quite contented." Mary Parker to Maria Chamberlain, [late 1830s], Missionary Letters, HMCSL.

29. Maria Dibble to Mary [?], 9 September 1833, Missionary Letters, HMCSL.

30. Maria Sartwell Loomis, 30 January 1821, Journal, 1819-28, Journal Collection, HMCSL.

31. See Sybil Bingham's response to the news on her arrival in the Sandwich Islands in 1820. "The taboo system is no more—men and women eat together — *the idol gods are burned!!*" Sybil Bingham, Journal, 30 March 1820. Descriptions of Hawaiian society, either traditional or in the early culture contact period, may be found in: E.S.C. Handy and others et. al., *Ancient Hawaiian Civilization* (Honolulu: Kamehameha Schools, 1933); David Malo, *Hawaiian Antiquities* (Honolulu: Bernice P. Bishop Museum, Special Publication no. 2, (Indeed) 1951; John Papa Ii, *Fragments of Hawaiian History* (Honolulu: Bernice P. Bishop Museum, 1964); Samuel Manaia-Kalani Kamakau, *The*

People of Old (Honolulu: Bernice P. Bishop Museum, Special Publication no. 51, 1964).
32. Loomis, Journal, 21 June 1820.
33. Clarissa Chapman Armstrong, 7 May 1832 (typescript), Journal, 1831-38, Journal Collection, HMCSL. Compare Mary Barker Parker who wrote to her sister on the voyage to the Sandwich Islands that her husband was "Just what you saw him, better than I am but not perfect. I am not proud enough to think he is, nor vain enough to wish others to think so, but he is a good husband and that is enough for me." Mary Parker, 19 February 1833, Journal of Voyages to Hawaii and Marquesas, 1832-33; A, Journal Collection, HMCSL. She wrote on another occasion that she had been ill, and he looked after her. "However, I expect soon to be well enough to be his prime minister and legate with him; then our administrations will be admirably conducive to health. . . ." Ibid., 14 February 1833.
34. Bishop, 12 August [1823], Missionary Letters.
35. Juliette Cooke, 24 September 1837, Journal, 1837-[1839], Journal Collection, HMCSL.
36. Maria Patton Chamberlain, 22 May 1846, Journal, 1846-47, Missionary Letters, HMCSL.
37. The dead woman's missionary sisters disapproved if the remarriage was too hasty. See Clarissa Amstrong's comment on the search of Edmund Rogers for a second wife in 1836, his first wife having died in 1834. "Mr. Rogers, one of our printers, is going to America, *for a wife I suppose*, and will then return. You will percieve [*sic*] that wives are important articles of household furniture here. They cannot easily be sent in boxes, so it costs some time and trouble, to obtain them." Clarissa Armstrong to Reuben Chapman, April 1836, Missionary Letters, HMCSL.
38. Bingham, Journal, 16 February 1823.
39. I considered thirty-eight women who had joined the mission between 1819 and 1845, selecting those women who lived at least nine years on the mission, who were fertile, and whose childbearing was not terminated before they reached the age of thirty-five because they, or their husbands, had died. The average number of children was between 6 and 7. Seven couples had 4 children; six couples had 5 children; one couple had 6 children; nine couples had 7 children. Of those who had larger families than the average, nine couples had 8 children, three couples had 9 children, two had 10 children and one had 11 children. Of these 257 children, 26 infants died before the age of seven years, and 4 more children died between the ages of five and twelve years. Twenty-six women bore children at forty years and over. Three ceased bearing children by the age of thirty-two. Ages of marriage ranged from twenty-one to thirty-five years, with the median age falling between twenty-four and twenty-five years. Of seventy-six marriages of missionaries of those who enlisted between 1819 and 1845, thirteen ended with the wife's death. Eight couples bore no children. See *Missionary Album*, supplemented by additional information from the Journal Collection, HMCSL.
40. Ethel Damon, ed., *Letters from the Life of Abner and Lucy Wilcox, 1836-1869* (Honolulu: Privately printed, 1934), 113.
41. Maria Chamberlain to Bella Chamberlain Lyman, 7 June 1867, in Maria Chamberlain, "Letters to Her Daughter, Bella Chamberlain Lyman, 1850-1875," 2 vols. (typescript), Missionary Letters, HMCSL. She continued with an interesting comment on birth control methods. "If by mutual consent you both agree to wait 14 days or so, I do not think there is wrong in that, and if after that you should find yourself in such circumstances, I should say it is of the Lord, and if he gives you a large family, *he will provide*, and it is no matter what people say—it is none of their business." She later cautioned her daughter to be very careful in her activities so as not to risk a miscarriage, for "then you are a broken-down woman. It is alarming, even in the early stages, to have a flowing come down, and I would rather go through two regular confinements than have one abortion." Ibid., 18 August 1867. A small group of couples had four or five children in swift succession, and then no more although the wife was

only in her early thirties. This probably indicated use of coitus interruptus, although in one or two cases where the wife's health was very poor, one could not rule out the possibility of cessation of sexual intercourse.

42. Sheldon Dibble, *A History of the Sandwich Islands* (1843; reprint, Honolulu: Thos. G. Thrum, 1909), 267.

43. Lorenzo Lyons to ABCFM, 18 September, 1837. ABCFM-Hawaii Papers, HMCSL.

44. Cochran Forbes to ABCFM, 10 October 1836, Missionary Letters, vol. 8, (typescript) ABCFM-Hawaiian Papers (Houghton Library, Harvard), HMCSL. Compare William Richard's opinion: "In New England there are three great barriers against female licentiousness, which are almost unknown here, and without which chastity would even with you, be comparitively [*sic*] rare. 1st Public opinion. 2nd *Modesty* and reserve, 3rd *Real ignorance*. The latter is not the least. Here there is no such thing as ignorance, not even among children, and the sexes play together in every immodest manner without the least reserve. The construction of their houses and manner of sleeping, are also very unfavorable to chastity." William Richard to ABCFM, 7 December 1832, Missionary Letters, vol. 6, ABCFM-Hawaii Papers (Houghton Library, Harvard), HMCSL.

45. William Beals, Notebook, 1823, Children of the Mission, HMCSL.

46. Clarissa Richards, 19 February 1824, Journal from Lahaina, 1824, Journal Collection, HMCSL.

47. Charles S. Stewart, *Journal of a Residence in the Sandwich Islands* (New York: John P. Haven, 1828), 119.

48. Richards, Journal, 10 February 1824.

49. Clarissa Armstrong to Reuben Chapman, April 1836, Missionary Letters, HMCSL.

50. Mary Parker to Fanny Gulick, 31 December 1834, Missionary Letters, HMCSL.

51. Mary Parker to Mrs. Lyman Frisbie, April 1836, Missionary Letters, HMCSL.

52. Whitney, Journal, 18 September 1828.

53. Minutes of the General Meeting of the Sandwich Islands Mission, 1819-1828 p. 51 (typescript), Sandwich Islands Mission Collection, HMCSL.

54. See William Richards to ABCFM, 7 December 1832, ABCFM-Hawaii Papers, (Houghton Library, Harvard), HMCSL. The Sandwich Islands Mission deputation had just returned from the Society Islands. "Chastity is almost as rare among the children of the missionaries as it is among the natives!! How much good will those children do the cause of missions!!!" See Niel Gunson, "The Deviations of a Missionary Family: The Henrys of Tahiti," in *Pacific Islands Portraits*, ed. J.W. Davidson and Deryck Scarr (Canberra, Australian National University Press, 1970), 31-54.

55. Lucy Thurston to William Goodell, 23 October 1834, ABCFM-Hawaii Papers, (Houghton Library, Harvard), HMCSL.

56. *Mother's Magazine*, February 1839, p. 41. For a study of the emergence of the nineteenth-century domestic ideology in Oneida County, New York, see Mary P. Ryan, *Cradle of the Middle Class*.

57. Lucia Smith [Lyons] to Juliette Cooke, 1 September [1837], Missionary Letters, HMCSL.

58. Records of the Maternal Association of the Sandwich Island Mission, 1834-41, 6 October 1841, Church Records, HMCSL.

59. Compare Mary Parker's account. "Tabu yards—every house has a Tabu yard where no native is allowed to enter. They are indispensible [*sic*] where there are children, who must never be allowed to be with a native after they can talk. Do you ask why? *Pen cannot tell you* understandingly. I will point you to broken hearted parents at the Society Isles *who can*. They know how to weep over fallen, ruined children who have been allowed to learn the native language, and as a consequence have learnt their practices. My sister, you can never feel for a moment as do the missionaries at the Islands

without exclaiming. My children, o my children. . . .The sin—the various sins of the land is dreadful." Mary Parker, Journal, A, 31 March 1833.

60. Lucy Thurston to William Goodell, 16 October 1829, ABCFM-Hawaii Papers. (Houghton Library, Harvard), HMCSL.

61. Persis G. Taylor, "Shifting Views of the Life of Your Mother, from 1821 to 1894," pp. 2-3 Children of the Mission, HMCSL.

62. Caroline Bailey to Mrs. James Bailey, 23 October 1849, Missionary Letters, HMCSL.

63. Mary Parker, Journal, A, 31 March 1833.

64. For example, Whitney, Journal, 17 March 1829.

65. Records of the Maternal Association of the Sandwich Island Mission, 1834-1841, 9 June 1840, Church Records, HMCSL.

66. Ibid., Annual Meeting, June 1835.

67. Whitney, Journal, 17 September 1823.

68. Judd Family, *Fragments IV: Family Records of the House of Judd* (Honolulu: Honolulu Star-Bulletin, 1928), 78.

69. William Richards to ABCFM, 4 September 1834, Missionary Letters, vol. 6 (typescript), ABCFM-Hawaii Papers (Houghton Library, Harvard), HMCSL.

70. Jeremiah Evarts to Missionaries at the Sandwich Islands, 27 October 1827, ABCFM-Hawaii Papers (Houghton Library, Harvard), HMCSL.

71. Records of the Maternal Association of the Sandwich Islands Mission, 1834-1841, Annual Meeting 1839, Church Records, HMCSL.

72. Ursula Emerson to the Editor, *Mother's Magazine*, April 1839, p. 88.

73. James Jarves in *Confessions*, cited in Henry Restarick, *Hawaii 1778-1920: From the Viewpoint of a Bishop* (Honolulu: Paradise of the Pacific, 1924), 50-51.

74. Clarissa Armstrong to Reuben Chapman, April 1836, Missionary Letters, HMCSL.

75. Fidelia Coan to Fanny Gulick, November 1841, Missionary Letters, HMCSL.

76. Mary Ives to Aunt Rossiter, 12 May 1841, Missionary Letters, HMCSL.

77. Maria Chamberlain to sister Jane, 27 December 1835, Missionary Letters, HMCSL.

78. Juliette Cooke to her mother, Mrs. Montague, 8 June 1839, Missionary Letters, HMCSL.

79. See Hawaiian Mission Children's Society, *First Annual Report, presented May 21st 1853* (Honolulu: Government Press, 1853); Charlotte P. Dodge and Arthur L. Silverman, *Hawaiian Mission Children's Society, 1852 to 1970* (Honolulu: HMCSL, 1969).

80. Rufus Anderson, introduction to William Ellis, *Memoir of Mary Ellis* (Boston: Crocker & Brewster, 1836), ix. Of two men who remained single in the Sandwich Island Mission, one went mad and the other developed a dangerous habit of dandling Hawaiian girls on his knees.

81. Ibid., xii-xv.

82. Information from Ms. Lela Goodell, librarian of HMCSL.

83. William R. Castle, *Life of Samuel Northrup Castle* (Honolulu: Samuel N. and Mary Castle Foundation, 1960), 109.

84. Clarissa Armstrong to Lucia Lyons, 8 July 1880, Missionary Letters, HMCSL. She reported the original incident to Mr. and Mrs. Reuben Chapman on 8 March 1848, Missionary Letters, HMCSL.

85. Compare Mercy Whitney reporting on 13 May 1837 on the Maternal Association she organized for Hawaiian women at Waimea, Kanai: "It will be long however before we can hope for much *permanent* good from our labors except in occasional instances, as the natives are so accustomed to do evil, that it is no easy task for them at once to change their inveterate and long indulged habits of life. . . . Often when reminding them of their duty, they will reply, 'you have repeatedly told us so before—we know that is right, but we are so accustomed to our *old* ways, we soon forget what you say to us.' They are indeed like children—need line upon line and precept upon precept. . . ." See Missionary Letters, HMCSL.

The Local Parish as a Female Institution: The Experience of All Saints Episcopal Church in Frontier Minnesota

JOAN R. GUNDERSEN

In recent years historians have begun exploring the feminization of religion in nineteenth-century America. While much of the published debate has centered on the particular definition presented by Ann Douglas in her study, *The Feminization of American Culture*, other scholars have adopted the term but applied it in different ways.[1] Douglas based her argument on a small sample of liberal Protestant female writers and clergymen in New England whom she saw as giving cultural expression to a new popular theology. She did not explore its impact upon any particular congregation, and much of the controversy surrounding her thesis has focused on the narrow base upon which she made expansive claims.[2] The concept of a feminized church, however, has attracted a number of scholars. Some, like Gerald Moran, have found evidence of the process much earlier in New England, while Mary Ryan and others have explored church membership during the Second Great Awakening of the early nineteenth century.[3] The research continues the Northeastern focus, however, in terms of both geography and denomination. Thus historians still have no sense as to the universality of these trends. In addition, the focus has remained on church membership and cultural perceptions of women's religious role. We have precious little information on how women translated ideas about their role into the life of an ongoing religious institution.

1. For an outline of the basic debate, see Ann Douglas, *The Feminization of American Culture* (New York, 1979); David Schuyler, "Inventing a Feminine Past," *New England Quarterly* 51 (1978): 291-308; David S. Reynolds, "The Feminization Controversy: Sexual Stereotypes and the Paradoxes of Piety in Nineteenth-Century America," *New England Quarterly* 53 (1980): 96-106; Richard Shiels, "The Feminization of American Congregationalism, 1736-1835," *American Quarterly* 3 (1981): 46-62.
2. David Reynolds, for example, critiques Ann Douglas's thesis of feminization by stressing the continuation of a "masculine" religion. One of his examples for such "masculine" religion was the frontier; Reynolds, "Feminization Controversy," p. 99. David Schuyler is among the scholars who have criticized Douglas for the smallness of her sample and its New England nature; Schuyler, "Inventing a Feminine Past," p. 293.
3. See for example Gerald Moran, "Conditions of Religious Conversion in the First Society of Norwich, Connecticut, 1718-1744," *Journal of Social History* 5 (1972): 331-343; Shiels, "Feminization of Congregationalism," pp. 46-62; Mary Ryan, *The Cradle of the Middle Class: The Family in Oneida County, New York, 1780-1865* (Cambridge, 1981), pp. 75-104.

Ms. Gundersen is associate professor of history and director of women's studies in Saint Olaf College, Northfield, Minnesota.

This essay blends two areas of theoretical concern. The first area is the debate over the extent and nature of feminization of nineteenth-century religion. The second arises from recent emphasis on the role of the laity in the church and a rediscovery of the meaning of such phrases as "the priesthood of all believers" and "lay ministry," which spring from an emphasis on the church as the body of Christ. This emphasis mandates an exploration of the role of the laity in the past and a church history that transcends chronicles of the hierarchy. By looking at the actual experience of a parish, it is possible to regain a sense of the role of the laity and to see in what ways women, as a part of the laity, shaped the religious parameters of a community. Church history that has defined its subject matter as the institutional hierarchy and has emphasized the role of ordained clergy has been part of the process, described by Rosemary Ruether and Eleanor McLaughlin, by which women's experiences have been "edited out" of the past. This editorial process has extended to histories of the local congregation or parish which have defined the parish as an extension of male governing bodies and periodized according to clerical adminstrations.[4]

All Saints Parish in Northfield, Minnesota provides the scholar with an opportunity to consider the feminization of religion in a tangible form by studying a single congregation from a neglected denomination in a neglected region. The Episcopal church has been ignored in scholarly discussions except as a comfortable liberal home for some Northeastern elites. Yet the Episcopal church had an evangelical bent both in the South and after 1840 on the frontier which was fostered by the missionary impulses of New York church leaders, especially in western New York. (The great missionary bishops of Minnesota and Wisconsin, Henry Whipple and Jackson Kemper, both were sent to the frontier from western New York.) Furthermore, the Episcopal church is the most hierarchical of American Protestant churches and thus provides the extreme test for whether the laity, especially women, could have leadership roles in the church.[5] Also, the location of All Saints Parish on the midwestern frontier allows for regional comparisons and for questions of the impact of the frontier on culture. Finally, Ruether and McLaughlin have argued that women's religious leadership either has been marginal and subversive or has relied on spiritual authority to transcend hierarchy. While they have stressed that historians of women in religion need to rethink old categories, they have not explicitly redefined the parish based

4. Rosemary Ruether and Eleanor McLaughlin, *Women of Spirit: Female Leadership in the Jewish and Christian Traditions* (New York, 1979), p. 16.
5. Mary Farrell Bednarowski, for example, has argued that the hierarchical nature of mainstream Protestant churches excluded women from leadership roles; Bednarowski, "Outside the Mainstream: Women's Religion and Women Religious Leaders in Nineteenth-Century America," *Journal of the American Academy of Religion* 48 (1980): 207-231.

on the way it functions.[6] By studying a single parish, it is possible to see how a functional definition exposes the threads of female participation in the fabric of church life.

The usual accounts of the growth of Episcopal churches on the Minnesota frontier focus on the arrival of heroic missionary clergy, their efforts to work with American Indians and to found schools and seminaries, and the many weary journeys they made to provide services in scattered frontier towns.[7] In these accounts the local community remains the passive but fertile soil waiting for the seed of religion to be planted by the missionary. Even local parish histories have been the chronicles of the clergy who served them. While in no way intending to deny the labors of these missionaries, I would submit that this is only part of the story. The missionary clergy were, after all, transitory. Even resident Episcopal priests spent much time on the road serving neighboring congregations, and because of the heavy workload, most clergy stayed at a parish less than three years.[8] In Northfield, Minnesota, when the focus is shifted to All Saints Parish as a community institution, a different picture emerges: the laity, especially the women of the parish, are active, central participants in religion, and the feminization of religion is given tangible rather than intellectual form.

The founding of All Saints Parish is inextricably tied to the founding of Northfield as a community. The first settlers arrived in the Northfield area of Rice County in 1854, four years before Minnesota became a state. By 1856 John W. North had planted a town along the Cannon River, bought out the early claims, and begun selling lots. North had close connections to New York reformers and envisioned his town as a reformed New England village, free from alcohol and built around a town square. By 1860, however, that dream had collapsed for North and others. The Panic of 1857 did not immediately affect frontier Northfield, but in 1859 reality arrived when a railroad line to the settlement went bankrupt and was left unfinished. North and other investors were ruined. Some pioneers moved on; others retreated to nearby towns such as Hastings for a few years; some returned East, but others stayed. The community's population thus was highly unstable in the founding years, with settlers coming, leaving, and returning continually.[9]

6. Ruether and McLaughlin, *Women of Spirit*, pp. 17–28.
7. The standard history of the diocese is George Tanner, *Fifty Years of Church Work in the Diocese of Minnesota, 1857–1907* (Saint Paul, Minn., 1909). The other basic works covering the founding period are all studies of the missionary clergy. See, for example, Henry Benjamin Whipple, *Lights and Shadows of a Long Episcopate* (London, 1900); Anson R. Graves, *The Farmer Boy Who Became a Bishop* (Akron, Ohio, 1911); Hugh Burleson, *An Officer of the Line in the Conquest of the Continent* (Hartford, Conn., n.d.).
8. For example, All Saints Church was served by seventeen different priests in its first thirty years. The longest stay of any one was six years. Several stayed less than a year.
9. John North and his family moved on to California. The mobility of others was equally high. Olive Josephine Hull came with her grandmother to Northfield in 1857. She taught school for two years and then returned to New York. A year later she married, in New York,

The Northfield experience was not unique. Frontier communities in general had a rapid turnover of settlers. What is important to note, however, is that the creation of community institutions such as churches did not wait for stability. One of the challenges to any denomination was to establish itself despite a constantly mobile membership.[10]

Frontier Northfield was an extension of the Northeastern states. The early settlers were mostly from New England and New York, with a seasoning of Canadians. John North himself was from Utica, New York. All of the counties along the Erie Canal contributed to the migration. While for some settlers Northfield was a secondary move, many came directly from the East to the raw frontier. In religion, the settlers reflected their home areas in the heart of New York's burned-over district and in New England Protestantism. Congregational, Baptist, and Methodist ties were common. The earliest settlers included Episcopalians, however, and the itinerant Episcopalian missionary Timothy Wilcoxson baptized Emma Minerva Jenkins, the infant daughter of one of Northfield's first settlers, on 9 March 1856.

When on 21 April 1858 a group of women met at the home of J. S. Allen to elect officers and draw up a constitution for the Ladies Social Circle, Northfield already had a lyceum (which served as library, school, and debating society) and Methodist and Congregational societies. Emma Hodges Jenkins, the mother of Emma Minerva, became the first president. The women, "feeling the need of some effort on our [their] part to commence the work of building a church," were assuming the leadership in founding an Episcopal parish. Reversing usual roles, the Ladies Social Circle allowed men to be honorary members (at double the women's dues), but allowed only women to vote, conduct meetings, and hold office. Unlike a typical male institution, the women shared leadership by requiring the election of new officers every three months; the frequent rotation of officers also allowed the circle to function in the transient conditions of the town.[11] Twelve women and two men promptly became members by paying their dues.

The lyceum and the churches thus became the first institutions of the Northfield community. In the 1860s a group of men founded a masonic lodge and a volunteer fire company. The churches and education, however, came first for the settlers who formed these primary institutions before they had decent roofs over their heads. At the time the churches began to organize, the

---

Charles N. Stewart, another New Yorker who had settled in Northfield. They then returned to Minnesota together to live in the Northfield area. Hiland H. White claimed a farm outside of Northfield in 1855, then moved to Hastings to run a hotel with his brother and returned to Northfield in 1861; Mrs. C. N. Stewart obituary, *Northfield News*, 29 June 1923, p. 4; Hiland H. White obituary, *Northfield News*, 26 May 1900, p. 1.

10. For more on the pressures of mobility on frontier institutions see Julie Roy Jeffrey, *Frontier Women: The Trans-Mississippi West, 1840–1880* (New York, 1979), pp. 79–84.

11. All Saints Parish Register, (5 vols.) vol. 1, mss., All Saints Episcopal Church, Northfield, Minn. (hereafter cited as ASC); Secretary's Book of the Episcopal Social Circle, ASC, 21 April 1858, 5 May 1858, pp. 1, 6.

only dwellings in the community were log huts. The "town" consisted of a large flour mill, a saw mill, and some hastily built shacks. The hotel run by Herman Jenkins had a canvas roof. Not until 1878, when a chapter of the Women's Christian Temperance Union formed in Northfield, did any organization compete for the time of Northfield women. They could attend the lyceum and edited its literary magazine, but only men could debate.[12]

Over the summer months of 1858 there was a flurry of activity as the women led efforts to create a parish. In June the Episcopalians rented the only public meeting hall in town, the lyceum, for two Sundays a month, at a rent of $100 a year. They had hopes of more regular services because Faribault, only fifteen miles to the southwest and the Rice County seat, had been selected in the fall of 1857 by a group of Episcopal clergy as the site of a mission, seminary, and school.[13] On 22 September 1858 the Rev. David Sanford and his wife attended the social circle meeting. Sanford had arrived recently in Faribault to organize a parish there. He apparently discussed plans for formal organization with the women of Northfield, too, for on 1 November he returned to town to preside at the organizational meeting of All Saints Parish.[14] Formal parish organization, of course, required male leadership to fill the offices of churchwardens and vestry. The women apparently spent the month and a half between Sanford's visits recruiting men to fill these positions. Before 22 September only Harvey Allen and George Loomis had attended the ladies' meetings. At the October meetings, however, five more men joined. One month after the parish officially had been formed, fifteen men and thirteen women attended the social circle meeting. The men continued to attend the women's meetings until they were pulled away by the Civil War. Women, however, presided and elected officers.[15]

The men were not attending these meetings out of simple courtesy, but rather because these were the only parish meetings other than Sunday services. All Saints has no vestry records before 1903, but not because records are missing. Such records never existed. In the first thirty years of parish life, the vestry had no business except to handle contributions for clergy salaries and fuel. The Ladies Social Circle contributed about one third of these costs, and, in addition, it oversaw all the other items normally covered by a modern parish budget: outreach, fellowship, christian education, music, and building repair. The vestry budget had routine expenses with no discretionary power;

12. Northfield Bicentennial Committee, *Continuum: Threads in the Community Fabric of Northfield, Minnesota* (Northfield, Minn., 1976), pp. 41–42; Bessie Lathe Scovell, *A Brief History of the Minnesota Women's Christian Temperance Union from Its Organization September 6, 1877 to 1939* (1939), pp. 44–54.

13. Northfield Lyceum Minute Book, Typescript, Northfield Public Library, 16 June 1858; Tanner, *Fifty Years*, pp. 135, 297.

14. Secretary's Book, Ladies Social Circle, 22 Sept. 1858, ASC, p. 8; Parish Register, vol. 1, ASC.

15. Secretary's Book, Ladies Social Circle, ASC, 6 Oct. 1858–26 Nov. 1863, pp. 8–9.

the social circle paid for all the items in which there was parish discretion, and their total contribution was far more than a majority of parish expenses.[16] While control over a minister's salary usually meant control over the choice of minister, in this case Seabury Mission in Faribault decided who would give services in Northfield. For many years the vestry also had no building to maintain or rent to pay. In 1860 George Loomis forgave the lyceum a large debt in exchange for use of their building, rent free, by All Saints Parish.[17] When the parish did build a church in 1866, the women raised the money and paid for most repairs or improvements, so the vestry continued to have little to do.

In fact, the men elected to the first vestry included several who were not active members of the parish. Hiram Scriver, for example, was never a member of the parish, although he was courting Clare Olin, who was a member. Scriver helped to found the Congregational Church in Northfield. Likewise, Abraham Mynders was never confirmed or a communicant at the parish. These men seemed to consider the office more a public trusteeship than a religious commitment.[18]

The women of the Ladies Social Circle, however, were active members of the parish. Moreover, the Ladies Social Circle offered both parish fellowship and one of the few forms of entertainment available in temperance-supporting early Northfield. Aside from the lyceum meetings, there were no other organized social activities for the first few years except those sponsored by churches. Eventually there would be lodges and other organizations, but throughout the nineteenth century the churches sponsored most of the social events. While many of the members were married couples, a number of single men and women were members. For a lonely young man on the Minnesota frontier, female companionship was at a premium. Felix Collet, Jr., for

16. Jeffrey has mixed feelings about women's financial role in frontier churches. She states both that women's financial aid was substantial and that ministers still expected the majority of funds to come from men. However, Jeffrey continues to view the women's contribution as aid rather than to recognize the full range of discretionary activities covered by that term. I would argue that the use of the word "aid" is a social fiction that allowed women to exercise informal power behind the scenes; Jeffrey, *Frontier Women*, pp. 98–99.

    The records of All Saints have not been at risk. The parish has occupied the same building since 1867, and few things have been thrown away. Records before 1866 are sparse, since nonresident clergy served the parish. It was the custom for clergy to keep personal records of births, marriages, and so on, and these records disappeared with the clergy. The women, however, kept control of their own records and thus they survive for the founding years.

17. The proposal also covered forgiving the parish the money already owed for rent. The parish probably had not paid the rent owed from the time it organized; Northfield Lyceum Minutes, Northfield Public Library, 20 Jan. 1860.

18 All Saints was not the only parish forced to recruit nonmembers for its first vestry. The first vestry of the Episcopal Church in Keokuk, Iowa in 1850 included no church members. There, too, women had gathered the first church society; Jeffrey, *Frontier Women*, pp. 98–99. In Northfield, the vestry included several of Northfield's leading entrepreneurs but also others who were more obscure; Parish Register, vol. 1, Families, ASC; Julie Walstad, "Northfield's Wealthy Residents of 1870," Saint Olaf Student Essays on Northfield History (1977), Northfield Public Library, p. 15.

example, was not a member of the parish, but he attended the meetings of the social circle regularly until he married Susan DeLancey. She was treasurer of the circle. Charles Stewart was Congregationalist, but he too courted his bride at the Episcopal Ladies Social Circle.[19]

The attendance and leadership patterns evident in the parish's early history suggest different explanations for feminization of religion than those recently offered by Richard Shiels. Shiels posited that men might be less active in older, more settled areas and more active in frontier areas because in the older areas other organizations already existed for men to join. In Northfield the leadership patterns were established before there were many competing organizations, but frontier enterprise certainly occupied men's time. Men would eventually found other social organizations, but the leadership patterns in the church were well established before this competition began. In fact, the ties between the first masonic lodge and the Episcopal church were strong. The founders of the lodge either were members of All Saints or had wives who were. Episcopal clergy graced many early lodge events with their presence and conducted masonic funerals.[20] In other words, the lodge functioned as an alternative social focus for men of the parish, but men did not develop this alternative until after female leadership had established itself in the parish. Men, who outnumbered women in frontier Northfield, made up a majority at many of the Social Circle meetings, but leadership remained with women. The first vestry included men such as Hiram Scriver who had many other competing public responsibilities. Thus the feminization of parish leadership in Northfield did not have an inverse relationship to the number of other opportunities for community leadership by men. Rather, men eventually created other leadership and social organizations; women still controlled the parishes.

Women's leadership opportunities in frontier Northfield centered around the church. Unlike their eastern counterparts, Northfield women did not found a variety of humanitarian organizations with overlapping memberships.[21] Education also provided no incentive for women to organize. From 1857 on women taught at local schools, but the very existence of schools at

19. John North had restricted the deeds in Northfield so that no liquor could be served in town. See Rice County, Abstracts of Titles—Deeds, Northfield and Village, 1856–1885, Rice County Court House; Secretary's Book, Ladies Social Circle, ASC, 1 Nov. 1860–11 Dec. 1862, pp. 34–57; Charles Stewart obituary, *Northfield News*, 19 Jan. 1917, p. 1; Mrs. C. N. Stewart obituary, *Northfield News*, 29 June 1923, p. 4.

20. Shiels, "Feminization of Congregationalism," pp. 58–60. A recent study of masonic membership in western New York documents the close ties between the Episcopal church and the masonic orders there. It also suggests that the lodges provided important leadership opportunities to its male members of all social classes; Kathleen Smith Kutolowski, "Freemasonry and Community in the Early Republic: the Case for Antimasonic Anxieties," *American Quarterly* 34 (1982): 543–561.

21. For a study of such groups in an area from which many Northfield women came, see Nancy Hewitt, *Women's Activism and Social Change: Rochester, New York, 1822–1872* (Ithaca, N.Y., 1984); Barbara Leslie Epstein, *The Politics of Domesticity: Women, Evangelism, and Temperance in Nineteenth-Century America* (Middletown, Conn., 1981).

such an early stage in Northfield's history relieved women of any obligation to form organizations to foster education. When Northfield College (soon renamed Carleton) opened in 1867 and Saint Olaf's School opened in 1873, each was a denominational project, and women channeled their support for these ventures through existing denominational groups. In 1878 the WCTU became the first organization for Northfield women other than a denominational circle or guild, but even it operated as an extension of the Congregational and Baptist churches. There is no evidence of any Episcopal membership in the Northfield WCTU. Also, many of the pioneer women of All Saints did not live in town, but rather on surrounding farms. Elizabeth Friar Jenkins and Catherine Archibald had a five-mile trip one way; Sophia DeLancey and her daughter Hannah and daughter-in-law Mary Archibald had a seven mile wagon ride from their farm. Clearly it required great effort to attend meetings in Northfield. Since the women put the church first in their priorities, the precious little time they could spare went to the church.[22]

The fact that the Ladies Social Circle functioned as the parish meeting suggests something else about power in the parish. Women had taken the lead in forming the parish and even in laying plans for the formal election of a vestry on which they could not serve. By setting up a traditional vestry that acted merely as a front for the active women's organization, the women of All Saints Parish avoided the problems faced by Grace Church, Clearwater, in 1860. Grace Church applied for recognition by the diocese in that year with a set of by-laws which made women voting members of the parish. This issue created a division at the diocesean convention that led to the challenge of the credentials of Deacon J. Johnson Emmegahbowh (the only American Indian cleric in the diocese) when he voted to admit Grace Church. The Northfield delegate also sided with Grace, as did a majority of other lay delegates, but the clergy vetoed admission of the parish. After the rejection, Grace Church collapsed. It was years before Episcopalians organized again in Clearwater. Northfield's solution allowed the women to have a major voice without violating church canons, or challenging the clergy. The forms remained traditional, although the substance was not.[23]

The greatest power of the ladies' circle was financial. The women provided most of the money available to the parish, and they controlled its disburse-

22. Jeffrey argues that community institutions developed after the initial stage of settlement and finds women involved in a variety of activities. In Northfield the development of congregations coincides with the first settlement; Jeffrey, *Frontier Women*, pp. 79–84; Scovell, *Women's Christian Temperance Union*, pp. 44–54, 249; U.S. Census 1860, Rice County, Bridgewater and Northfield Townships; Minnesota State Census 1865, Rice County, Bridgewater and Northfield Townships.

23. *Journal of the Proceedings of the Third Annual Convention of the Protestant Episcopal Church in the Diocese of Minnesota* (1860), pp. 27–29. Ann Douglas argues that the clergy and their female parishioners were allies, although the clergy had ambivalent feelings due to their loss of power to the women. The clergy of Minnesota were hardly ambivalent when it came to Grace Church; Douglas, *Feminization*, pp. 116–119.

ment. Members paid not only yearly dues, but a small sum each time they attended. By 1860 the women were raising about three dollars each time they met and felt confident enough to vote to "hire an amount sufficient to" purchase a "Melodium for the Episcopal Church, the cost not to exceed $125."[24] The women's financial control was strong enough to impose their will upon Seabury Mission and Bishop Whipple. In 1865 the women paid $250 for a lot owned by Sarah Wing, one of the members of the circle. The Seabury Mission had purchased a lot in 1857 as a Northfield church site, but apparently the women had their own opinion about where the parish should build its church. They ignored the lot already purchased and selected another for the site. While the deed officially listed the Seabury Mission as the purchaser of the new lot, the Rev. Solomon S. Burleson reported to the diocese that the women of the church had raised $300 to purchase the lot and to provide supplies to start construction of a building. The church building rose on the site the women preferred, and Seabury Mission quietly sold its rejected lot several years later.[25]

Throughout 1866 and early 1867 the parish built its frame rural gothic church. Men of the parish, including the minister, donned overalls to help in the construction, while the women raised the money and solicited contributions, including some from easterners interested in missionary work. On 11 April 1867 Bishop Henry Whipple consecrated the new church and confirmed a class of twenty-one members. He reported that Rector Burleson's "success is due greatly to a band of loving daughters of the Church."[26] The women were not finished, however, as gifts from women in Tennessee and New York added a fence to the churchyard and linen to the altar.

Not until 1871 did the national Episcopal church authorize the formation of the Women's Auxiliary to their Board of Missions, although agitation for a national women's wing had begun as early as 1850.[27] Thus women had to rely on informal networks to mobilize support for the church. Informal networks of family and friends, however, were a well-established feature of

24. Secretary's Book, Ladies Social Circle, ASC, 16 June 1860, p. 30.
25. The Rev. James Lloyd Breck had purchased lots in both Northfield and nearby Dundas in 1857. He and his wife gave these to the Seabury Mission in 1860. Holy Cross Church eventually was built on the Dundas lots. The plan to purchase lots early in frontier towns is outlined in a letter by N.I.T. Dana to Bishop Whipple. Sarah Wing, an active member of the Social Circle, purchased a lot one block closer to the town center in 1861; she and her husband, Samuel, sold it to the Seabury Mission in 1865. The parish built its church on this lot in 1867. The Seabury Mission then sold the Breck lot in 1869; Rice County, Abstracts of Deeds, Northfield, pp. 98–99, 62–63; *Journal of the Proceedings of the Eighth Annual Convention of the Protestant Episcopal Church in the Diocese of Minnesota* (1865), pp. 19–20; N.I.T. Dana to Bishop Whipple, 11 May 1860, Benjamin Henry Whipple Papers, Box 2, Minnesota Historical Society.
26. *Journal of the Proceedings of the Tenth Annual Convention of the Protestant Episcopal Church in the Diocese of Minnesota* (1867), p. 15.
27. Mary Donovan, "Zealous Evangelists: the Women's Auxillary to the Board of Missions," *Historical Magazine* 51 (1982): 371.

nineteenth-century women's lives.[28] By the Civil War, Protestant women throughout the east belonged to local church groups. As some of these women moved west, they naturally founded similar groups, though they also continued to write to their friends in the east. The major difference between east and west was the local orientation of the western groups in their early stages. Rather than forming to foster outreach to distant areas or others within their community, the women in the frontier towns were the subjects of their own activism. They were missionaries on the scene, building for their own families. They solicited help from eastern women for themselves, not others. Within twenty years, this focus would change, and All Saints women would raise money for missionary work in newer areas even while their own clergy were receiving missionary boxes from the east.

The Ladies Social Circle, renamed the Parish Aid Society in 1863, moved on to other projects. By 1868 they had purchased a temporary parsonage. Within another three years they had started a fund to build a new rectory and enlarge the church. After sponsoring innumerable socials, Mother Goose parties, and oyster suppers, the women had enough to build a rectory in 1875 on the lot behind the church. Although records are sparse for these years, there is no doubt that the rectory was the project of the women. They paid the county taxes on the building (the receipts are pinned in their secretary's book) and paid for all later repairs.[29]

Nowhere was the role of women more evident than in the church enlargement project of 1879. On 6 October the new rector, A.J. Yeater, went to the ladies to plead for a larger church building. The women "unanimously resolved to make an effort to enlarge the church building. Mrs Handy and Mrs Mosher were appointed a committee to raise funds,—who after a few hours of successful work, turned the paper over to Mr. Yeater who carried it to completion." Maria Handy and Rosella Mosher were skilled fund raisers. The subscription list shows that they went after the big contributors first. The first six names contributed one-sixth ($75) of the sum needed. The women not only turned to members of the parish, but to leading business and churchmen of Northfield. Excluding one memorial bequest, the first twenty-

28. There is an extensive literature on women's networks, including Nancy Cott, *The Bonds of Womenhood: "Women's Sphere" in New England, 1780–1835* (New Haven, 1978); Carroll Smith-Rosenberg, "The Female World of Love and Ritual: Relations Between Women in Nineteenth-Century America," *Signs* 1 (1975): 1–29; Ann Firor Scott, "What, Then, is the American: This New Women?" *Journal of American History* 65 (1978): 679–703; Hewitt, *Women's Activism*. Polly Welts Kaufman's recent study of the letters of evangelical teachers sent to the frontier has illustrated the power of these networks to bind the east and the frontier together; Kaufman, *Women Teachers on the Frontier* (New Haven, 1984).

29. The names of vestrymen, naturally, appear on the deeds, but the women's records show that the women had been contributing regularly to a building fund; Rice County, Abstract of Titles, Deeds, Northfield and Village, 1856–1885, vol. 1, pp. 114–115; Rice County, Deed Book 36, p. 337; Rice County Deed Book 32, p. 435; Secretary's Book, Ladies Social Circle, ASC, Oct. 1875, 1 Nov. 1875; *Rice County Journal*, 14 April 1875, p. 4.

three names read as a business directory of Northfield, including John and Jesse Ames, owners of the local flour mill (Jesse was a Baptist, John an Episcopalian). Even the Congregational minister contributed $5. The women's groups themselves contributed another one-third ($157) of the cost. This was undoubtedly the women's project, although they designated the Reverend A. J. Yeater as their business agent. The subscription list and a detailed accounting of all expenses was carefully recorded in the Ladies Aid's minutes.[30]

The fine distinction between what was women's private role in the church and the public image of the parish in best illlustrated by the way the local newspaper reported on this same church enlargement. The *Rice County Journal* reported on the enlargement almost every week from 16 October to 4 December. All reports are taken from Yeater, and the articles repeatedly praise Yeater for his skill at raising the needed money.[31] The women had, after all, appointed Yeater their business manager and given him the subscription list to finish. Thus the community-at-large conveniently could ignore the actual leadership of the women and instead could focus on the traditional leadership of the male clergy.

Yeater needed a boost to his public image. He had arrived in September 1879, a former Presbyterian who had left that denomination when he rejected its Calvinism. Yeater, however, was a temperance advocate. While Northfield was a temperance town—and All Saints Parish included some prominent temperance advocates—the parish was also the home of the "wet" faction in town. In late December Yeater preached on temperance; less than a week later he had resigned and left town. Charles Wheaton, the editor of the *Rice County Journal*, was a temperance advocate, and he may have been trying to help the minister out by making him seem too valuable to lose. Ironically, Wheaton's plan backfired. The women had been supporting Yeater even while the "wet" men withdrew from church services. But the newspaper's constant efforts to credit the minister with the fundraising done by the women undercut the women's support of Yeater. Without that support, he had to leave. Yeater was one of only two rectors forced out by parish disputes before 1900.[32]

The women's control of finances was not limited to building and maintaining the church structures. The "Melodium" the Ladies Social Circle voted to

30. Secretary's Book, Ladies Social Circle, ASC, 5 Oct. 1879, pp. 88–90.
31. *Rice County Journal*, 16 Oct. 1879, p. 3; 30 Oct. 1879, p. 3; 6 Nov. 1879, p. 3; 20 Nov. 1879, p. 3; 27 Nov. 1879, p. 3; 4 Dec. 1879, p. 3.
32. This is a reconstruction pieced together from bits in the newspaper. The editor made a point of noting which men had returned to the church after Yeater left. Several of the vestry were members of the anti-prohibition slate in town elections for 1880; *Rice County Journal*, 1 Jan. 1880, pp. 2, 3; 4 March 1880, p. 3. The turnover of ministers in Northfield was due to financial problems, diocesan politics, and exhaustion. With the exception of Yeater and J.D. Ferguson, all other changeovers were for reasons not under the control of the parish.

purchase in 1860 was in place by 1864, when Solomon Burleson reported that the parish owned a "Prince's double bank melodeon" worth $140. From 1883 to 1889 the women of the parish put on a series of dramatic entertainments and musicales at the opera house to raise money for a cathedral reed organ to replace the original instrument. In 1913 women purchased a pipe organ for the parish.[33]

The women not only provided the means by which the parish could enjoy music, they provided the music. Susan DeLancey Collett, who had joined the circle by 1860, became the parish's first organist, serving for nearly thirty years. The women hired and paid the organist's salary on their own for over a hundred years. Even the parish priest had little say in the matter until nearly 1900.[34] Women also did most of the singing in the choir. Charles Wheaton described the start of services at All Saints on a bitterly cold November morning: "Mrs. Collett was not on her throne at the organ, and no singers in their places; but soon Mrs. Collett appeared and going to the organ she was followed by Misses Mary Lawrence and Frankie Bushnell, and this effective combination gave us all sufficient music. They sang well."[35]

The Sunday School was another area the women controlled through their organizations. Anna Sophia DeLancey founded the Sunday School long before the parish had a rector or a building. Frances Sophia Metcalf Allen served as Superintendent for ten years before her death in 1881. Although a male might occasionally serve as director, the women taught most of the classes and their organizations provided the funds for supplies, picnics, Christmas parties, and other activities. In 1864, for example, Burleson reported to the diocese that there was one male and four or five female teachers. He went on to note that the Sunday school met every week, "conducted by several earnest female communicants, to whom much of the present vitality of this parish is due."[36]

The reason that Burleson ignored the male teacher in his later comments is simple. He was the male. He had begun teaching while still an unordained seminary student at Seabury. He commuted to Northfield in 1864 to conduct Morning Prayer until he was ordained. Thus the women were the only resident teachers. His report is confirmed by memories of others. A former

33. *Rice County Journal*, 8 March 1883, p. 3; *Northfield News*, 16 Feb. 1889, p. 3; 20 April 1889, p. 3; 29 June 1889, p. 3; *Minnesota Missionary and Church Record* 27 (Sept. 1903), p. 13; Saint Agnes Guild Minute Book, ASC, 10 Sept. 1912, p. 23; 11 Nov. 1912, p. 31; *Northfield News*, 4 July 1913, p. 8.

34. For payment of the organist's salary, see the Secretary's Book, Ladies Social Circle, ASC 24 Dec. 1879, p. 94; Ladies Guild Minute Book, ASC, 5 Oct. 1889, 16 Dec. 1889, 21 Jan. 1890, 20 Feb. 1890.

35. *Rice County Journal*, 25 Nov. 1880, p. 3.

36. *Journal of the Eighth Annual Convention*, p. 19. For the Sunday School expenses, see *Rice County Journal*, 13 Nov. 1879, p. 3; 20 Nov. 1879, p. 3; Mrs. Anna Sophia DeLancey obituary, *Northfield News*, 28 April 1900, p. 1; Mrs. J. S. Allen death notice, *Rice County Journal*, 3 March 1881, p. 3.

parishioner, Jane Harris, reminisced in 1917 that when she first "knew Northfield in 1861 the small society of Episcopalians held service and Sabboth School in the Lyceum building, with a student from Seabury as Lay Reader and conductor of the Sunday School ably assisted by the Mothers as Teachers. Once a month Prof. Manney or Dr. Buck came to preach us a sermon, administer communion, baptize the babies & the progress of the war taking most of our citizens, only two male members were left in the church, William Stuart and Grandpa De Lancey, but the Mother's kept the Sunday School together."[37] Similarly, Silas Judd wrote in 1897 that their three children had received their "first Teachings" at the Episcopal Sunday school "which was held in the old Lyceum building by the Pioneer Lady Members of All Saints Church—Old Lady Delancey, Mrs. Seymour Allen, Mrs Minders, Mrs. H. H. White, Mrs. Susan Collett & a few others All Ladies: there were no male members at that time save Old Mr. Delancey."[38]

While Silas Judd and Jane Harris remember the Civil War years slightly differently (Harris recalls two male members and Judd only one), the general outlines of their story are the same. The women were the parish. The Civil War did create special circumstances that drew Northfield's men away, but the war does not provide a complete explanation of the absence of males. While All Saints Parish included a number of men who served in the army at sometime during the Civil War, many men did not. Silas Judd, after all, had to be in Northfield during the war to remember the church then (though he did not count himself among the church members). Women simply invested more time in parish activities, and their preponderance in church membership is documented in several ways.[39]

The Ladies Social Circle records provide the only lists of parish members before 1864, when Solomon Burleson became resident rector and started a parish register.[40] The Social Circle records, however, include many men; the records list every person who attended a meeting, since each had to pay dues. Until September 1862, men outnumber women at the social circle meetings. Then they almost disappear from the records. Men never again attended the regular meetings in any great number because the nature of those meetings had changed. The Social Circle had mixed parish planning with "a good time." Its records, then, are not strictly lists of members, for some of those attending, especially among the men, might be interested purely in the polite company. In 1862 the women voted to hold their first fair to raise money, and the ordinary meetings became work and planning sessions for separate social

37. Jane E. Harris to F. M. Garland, 28 April 1917, ASC.
38. Silas Judd to Mrs. Estell Henderson, 20 May 1897, ASC.
39. The membership patterns resemble those found by Mary Ryan in her study of western New York; Mary Ryan, *The Cradle of the Middle Class*, pp. 257, 75–104.
40. Burleson apparently tried to reconstruct the earlier records of the parish by filling in the baptisms and confirmations from 1856 to 1864. There are gaps, however, and the membership list for the parish is from 1864; Parish Register, vol. 1, ASC.

events. Shortly afterward they changed their name to the Parish Aid Society.[41]

The diocesan and parish records give a more accurate listing of affiliated members. In these records the women's role is clearer, and they confirm the impressions of Judd and Harris. All Saints Parish had 23 confirmed members, 45 families, and a total of 142 people when Solomon Burleson became rector in 1864.[42] Of the twenty-three communicants Burleson lists, only five were males, one of whom was a minor. Only nineteen of the twenty-three were active communicants in 1864. Two were men. Burleson made his parish register retrospective and included several pioneer communicants who had left, had died, or were in the army; thus the register has different figures than his parish report.[43] Burleson recorded a total of sixty-seven families who were part of All Saints Parish from 1864 through 1871. Of these, thirty women were listed as more active in the church than their husbands, and only in four families were the husbands more active. In another three families other adult females were the most active members. Thus the feminization of church membership helped to support the women's organizations as the power of the parish. While Ann Douglas claims that ministerial perceptions of feminized congregations were more a result of women's assertion of power through their societies than any shift in actual numbers, All Saints clearly had both a numerical superiority of women and strong women's guilds.[44]

By late 1879, when All Saints Parish finished enlarging the church, the town of Northfield was moving out of its frontier stage. Businessmen were replacing their original rude frame structures with buildings of brick and stone. And while the infamous James-Younger raid in Northfield was but three years in the past, the town was more interested in the fame it had won as a premier flour milling center and in its institutions of higher learning, Carleton College and Saint Olaf.[45] The legacy of the "Pioneer Lady

41. Secretary's Book, Ladies Social Circle, ASC 23 Sept. 1861, p. 42.
42. The printed version of the diocesan report gives the number of confirmed members as 28, but the parish records list 23. There is probably a transcription error in the printed version; Parish Register, vol. 1, Communicants, ASC, p. 162; *Journal of the Eighth Annual Convention*, pp. 19–20.
43. John DeLancey, the "Grandpa Delancey" of Jane Harris's letter, died in 1863. His daughter Hannah DeLancey had gone to Saint Barnabas House, New York. Both appear on the list. Herman Jenkins Jr., and Sr., also were listed but were absent from Northfield. Women from these families were still in Northfield and probably ensured that Burleson listed the absent members. DeLancey's death is not listed in the parish register, but the date appears on his tombstone and on a church window. The Parish Register communicants' list notes what happened to the others.
44. My measurement for activism was church status. The records list a person as baptized, confirmed, or communicant, representing an ascending order of commitment. My findings parallel those of Richard Shiels for New England Congregational churches; Douglas, *Feminization*, pp. 116–117; Shiels, "Feminization of Congregationalism," pp. 51, 59–60.
45. In the twentieth century the college presence had a strong effect on All Saints Parish, but the parish had no members from either college until after 1880, since Carleton was Congregational and Saint Olaf was Norwegian Lutheran.

Members" was strong, however. Women would continue to serve as the parish leadership at least until 1900. After 1900 the vestry would begin to share power with the women, eventually becoming the major decision-making and financial body of the parish.

The success of the All Saints women in the nineteenth-century came from several sources. First, the women were expected to be pious and religious. Their very attempt to live up to this role made them the majority of the parish. Second, the women worked cooperatively in shared leadership by rotating officers frequently. Thus the rapid changeover common to any frontier town did not leave the women's organization without leaders. Third, the women did not challenge directly the image of male leadership. Rather, they used the men as a screen behind which they could work effectively. Fourth, not only did the women have the power of numbers, they had the power of finances. In the nineteenth century the means available for women to raise money filled a major social gap in the life of the town. Hence they actually controlled most of the parish money. But as the forms of entertainment changed after 1900 in a well-established college town, the women could not maintain this social position. Last, and most important, the very exclusion of women from the church governmental structure left them free to develop independently their own leadership, an experience repeated in many church groups, both in Northfield and in other communities.[46] After 1896 women were pulled in two directions because the diocese granted them the vote in parish meetings. Being enfranchised split the women's focus; they looked both toward their guilds where women traditionally led, and towards the parish meeting where they could vote but only men could hold office. The decline in power was very slow, however, for the "Mothers" of All Saints had left a tradition of power to their daughters.

How, then, does the experience of All Saints Parish illuminate the extent and forms of feminization of religion in nineteenth-century America? The answer may depend on whether or not the experience of the Northfield parish was unique. The evidence suggests that while Northfield women were notable, other parishes in Minnesota shared parts of this experience. Just as in Northfield, women's organizations led the way to parish formation for Gethsemane Parish (1858) in Minneapolis and Ascension Parish (1846) in Stillwater. Women were so prominent in the early years of the Episcopal church at Chatfield that a correspondent in 1888 summed up the parish's first twenty-five years by saying, "It might be called a womens church." When the Reverend G. W. Dunbar arrived in Cannon Falls (nineteen miles east of Northfield) in 1867 to become first resident rector of Holy Redeemer Parish, he found that "the little church was finished, and paid for. I soon gathered the particulars as to how it had been done. Mrs. Wheat, Mrs. Tanner, and Miss

46. Donovan, "Zealous Evangelists," p. 372. Rosemary Keller, "Lay Women in the Protestant Tradition," in *Women and Religion in America: The Nineteenth Century*, ed. Rosemary Radford Ruether and Rosemary Skinner Keller (San Francisco, 1980), pp. 242–243.

Love, were faithful communicants, and they had first enlisted the interest of Mr. Tanner and Mr. Wheat, and through them gained Mr. and Mrs. Ellsworth, J. E. Chapman, J. H. Abbot and others." Not only in Northfield and Cannon Falls did women lead their husbands into church roles. At Chatfield, Fanny Ripley convinced her Unitarian husband to serve as Episcopal sexton for many years. Most parishes in Minnesota have similar experiences. The fund-raising abilities of the women at All Saints also were part of a larger pattern. In 1884 two women served as parish collectors in Perham. In fact, short histories compiled as part of the Minnesota Episcopal Church Women's convention in 1981 show a consistent pattern of women's leadership and financial control in the founding years of the diocese.[47]

The letters of evangelical women who were sent to the Illinois and Iowa frontiers as teachers in the 1850s indicate that women played much the same role in forming churches and Sunday Schools in those communities. Julie Roy Jeffrey has found evidence from scattered communities throughout the trans-Mississippi west which demonstrates women's leadership in the formation of congregations and predominance in attendance and membership there as well.[48]

The feminization of the local parish was concrete, not merely abstract. Not only were women the majority of members, but they exercised a wide range of powers through separate women's organizations that both complied with the restrictions of a proper woman's sphere and built upon the networks of that separate sphere. Even hierarchical denominations such as the Episcopal church were shaped at the parish level by powerful women's organizations. Yet institutional structures gave little indication of this power. The women formed a shadow church with its own leadership. Theoretically, male vestries controlled church property and male clergy determined liturgy. Yet both depended upon the support—financial and pyschological—of the women. Women used that dependence to fashion local parishes centered on their interests and in their sphere.

47. Mrs. H.C. O'Ferrall to George Tanner, 20 Nov. 1888, Papers of the Diocese of Minnesota, Minnesota State Historical Society Archives, Box 2; Typescript Memoir of Fanny Ripley, n. d., Papers of the Diocese of Minnesota, Minnesota State Historical Society Archives, Box 1; E. Steele Peake to Henry B. Whipple, 19 July 1884, Henry Benjamin Whipple Papers, Minnesota State Historical Society Archives, Box 17; George Tanner to Henry B. Whipple, 18 Dec. 1880, Henry Benjamin Whipple Papers, Minnesota State Historical Society Archives, Box 15; Episcopal Church Women Convention, *Faribault Republican*, 14 Oct. 1981, suppl.

48. Kaufman, *Women Teachers*, pp. 32–33, 192–193, 209; Jeffrey, *Frontier Women*, pp. 95–104.

Women's Response to Plural Marriage

Kahlile Mehr

Plural marriage was a complex phenomenon in both theology and practice. It was no less complex psychologically. Some LDS women ardently accepted it as a divine principle. Others viewed it as an unwelcome but necessary sacrifice to achieve salvation. A few loathed it. There were women who coaxed reluctant husbands to take an additional wife. Others quietly acquiesced — either in initial discussions or when presented with a *fait accompli*, and still others left the household rather than accept a sister wife. Sometimes the inner and outer persons were in conflict. Inwardly repelled and outwardly obedient, many women faced a struggle that for some led to triumphant self-control and for others to shattering disillusionment.

The principle of plural marriage was promulgated unofficially both before and after its public life. Introduced in the 1830s, it emerged officially in 1852 after the Latter-day Saints had relocated in Utah, putting a geographical buffer between themselves and larger society. Officially terminated in 1890, the practice continued sub rosa until 1904 when it was completely disavowed by Church authorities and membership.

Those living the principle did so counter to the commonly held mores of Western society. This required them to justify their actions to themselves as well as others. For some, the justification was obedience to religious principle. For others, it was the pursuit of celestial glory. Some sought a larger posterity. Many accepted the counsel of ecclesiastical leaders or the urging of associates to live plural marriage. The satisfaction of romantic desires motivated at least some. (I have no evidence of sexual gratification motivating women.) For others, practical needs made the system feasible. At least a few women were tricked or even coerced.

KAHLILE MEHR is a professional librarian. He has degrees in Russian and library science and is a candidate for an M.A. in family and local history from Brigham Young University. This article was written to gain a personal understanding of his own polygamous forebears. He lives in Bountiful, Utah, with his wife, Marolyn Price Mehr, and their five children.

A quantitative study has yet to be made, but this essay reviews the motivations that led to acceptance of plural marriage among Mormon women based on anecdotes, family histories, and surviving first-person accounts. Not only does this study illuminate the complexity of plural marriage as a feature of the LDS heritage, but it raises larger issues of the dilemma confronting all who profess religion and reason while coping with their own humanity.

"If any man espouse a virgin, and desire to espouse another, and the first give her consent, and if he espouse the second . . . then is he justified" (D&C 132:61). This revelation established the divine mandate to marry plurally. After forty years of practicing it, when the Church was confronting national opposition, 2,000 LDS women gathered at the Capitol Theater in Salt Lake City on 6 March 1886 to address the reports that they were violating Christian marriage principles. Among other speakers, Ellis Shipp of Salt Lake City, a physician and the first of Milford Shipp's four wives, explained: "True we practice plural marriage, not, however, because we are compelled to, but because we are convinced that it is a divine revelation, and we find in this principle satisfaction, contentment, and more happiness than we could obtain in any other relationship" (Shipp 1886, 37). Numerous other public statements by LDS women affirm their feeling that they lived the principle in adherence to divine mandate.

One might be tempted to dismiss such statements as propaganda designed to appease anti-polygamy critics. However, similar feelings are expressed in the personal papers of many participants. Leonard Arrington and Davis Bitton summarize: "That its primary justification — and the primary motivation of its practitioners — was religious obligation, no one who has examined the diaries and letters of the time can deny" (1979, 199).

Yet, not everyone accepted the principle full-heartedly and without qualm. This was particularly true during the early years in which it was practiced clandestinely. Eliza Partridge Lyman, a plural wife of Joseph Smith, reminisced in 1877 in Salt Lake City:

> A woman living in polygamy dare not let it be known and nothing but a firm desire to keep the commandments of the Lord could have induced a girl to marry in that way. I thought my trial was very severe in that line and I am often led to wonder how it was that a person of my temperament could get along with it and not rebel, but I know it was the Lord who kept me from opposing his plans although in my heart I felt that I could not submit to them, but I did and I am thankful to my Heavenly Father for the care he had over me in those troublous times. (1846–85, 13–14)

The primary motivation in both this and the statement of Ellis Shipp is obedience to divine revelation.

While visiting Utah in 1872, Elizabeth Kane accompanied her husband Thomas and Brigham Young on a tour of LDS settlements from Salt Lake to St. George. A non-LDS observer, she tells of a plural wife she named Delia J. of Parowan married to a husband twice her age. Though childless, Delia was an earnest advocate of plural marriage as a divine institution. Elizabeth asked if she could support a Congressional act forbidding any further plural marriages but legalizing those already in existence to secure the social position of all wives. Delia exclaimed: " 'Secure my social position! How can that satisfy me! I want to be assured of my position in God's estimation. If polygamy is the Lord's order, we must carry it out in spite of human laws and persecutions' " (1974, 105). Yet, Elizabeth reports that the first wife had told her Delia "could not bring her mind for a long time to see it to be her duty. But she is reconciled now" (1974, 104).

Helen Mar Whitney, a plural wife of Horace K. Whitney, wrote *Why We Practice Plural Marriage*, an important defense, in 1884. Her personal justification was included: "Had it not been for the powerful testimony from the Lord, which gave me a knowledge for myself that this principle is of celestial birth, I do not believe that I could have submitted to it for a moment." Her own resistance had been physically debilitating: "During that season I lost my speech, forgot the names of everybody and everything, and was living in another sphere" (1884, 9; Crocheron 1884, 112).

Romania Bunnell Pratt Penrose, a plural wife of Parley P. Pratt and later of Charles Penrose, experienced an intense struggle as well but termed living plural marriage as cathartic: "Were it lived according to the great and grand aim of its author, though it be a fiery furnace at some period in our life, it will prove the one thing needful to cleanse and purify our inmost soul of selfishness, jealousy, and other mundane attributes" (1881, 6). Though Romania dissolved her sealing to Pratt in 1881, she continued to accept the principle, marrying plurally as the third wife of Penrose in 1886.

As a woman contemplated plural marriage, she had to come to terms with its centrality to salvation in the Mormon view: "For behold, I reveal unto you a new and everlasting covenant; and if ye abide not that covenant, then are ye damned; for no one can reject this covenant and be permitted to enter into my glory" (D&C 132:4).

Although the twentieth-century Church interprets the new and everlasting covenant as celestial marriage, the nineteenth-century Church most often understood it as plural marriage. Not only did one have to be married in the temple (celestial marriage) but it had to be done plurally for each male and his wives to reach the highest degree of celestial glory. Annie Clark Tanner, a plural wife of Joseph M. Tanner remembers, "It was taught at that time [1880s] that the second wife opened the door of salvation in the Celestial Kingdom not only for herself but for her husband and his first wife" (1976, 62).

Bathsheba B. Smith, the first wife of Apostle George A. Smith, alluded to this doctrine when she said, "Being thoroughly convinced, as well as my husband that the doctrine of plurality of wives was from God and having a fixed determination to attain to celestial glory, I felt to embrace the whole gospel. . . . Accordingly I gave to my husband five wives, good, virtuous, honorable young women" (Tullidge 1877, 320–21).

Elizabeth Fuhriman was twenty-four, single, and being courted by a young single man who would call on her at work in Logan's ZCMI. This perturbed the manager, Isaac Smith, who also had an eye for Elizabeth. He eventually forbade the youth to continue his store visits. Smith was fourteen years her senior and married, but he proposed and she accepted even though the year was 1894 and plural marriage was officially discouraged. When later asked by her daughter, Elva, why she had chosen the one over the other, Elizabeth said he was a good talker, good looking, a good dancer, and that he convinced her "how many more blessings she would receive in the life hereafter if she married into polygamy" (Shumway 1980). Kimball Young reported that one wife felt so strongly that her own glory would be lessened by her husband's refusal to be married plurally that she divorced him after two years and became the plural wife of a man many years her senior (1954, 108).

However powerful the motive of salvation, it was not equally compelling to all. When the principle was announced in 1852, Fanny Stenhouse, then on a mission with her husband in Switzerland, retired to her room to read the revelation more closely. "Before I had got through one half I threw it aside, feeling altogether rebellious against God. I now began to feel perfectly reckless, and even willing to throw aside my religion, and take 'my chance of salvation,' rather than submit to Polygamy, for I felt that that new doctrine was a degradation to womankind" (1872, 34). Fanny permitted her husband to marry again, but later, both left the Church and lectured stridently against plural marriage.

While few went so far as Fanny, perhaps a little of her rebelliousness is to be found in many of those that confronted the principle. Many women like Delia J. and Helen Mar Whitney became more convinced of their faith through the practice of polygamy even though, as we have seen, they sometimes harbored feelings of doubt or rebellion. The reality for most women was probably a mixture of faith and frustration.

Some LDS women saw plural marriage as a means to increase the number of children reared in a knowledge of gospel principles, a view supported by Section 132: "[Plural wives] are given unto him to multiply and replenish the earth, according to my commandment, and to fulfil the promise which was given by my Father before the foundation of the world, and for their exaltation in the eternal worlds, that they may bear the souls of men" (D&C 132:63). Helen Mar Whitney felt children were "stars" in their mother's "crown" and each added to the glory of the woman and her husband in the afterlife (1884, 9). Eliza Martin Allen of West Jordan, the first wife of Daniel R. Allen, echoed these feelings, preaching to her reluctant husband during the 1850s that it was essential to their glory for him to have more wives and to rear and properly train a large number of children (Jensen 1948, 52). Daniel eventually married five other women between 1857 and 1872.

When the first wife was barren, she felt particularly obligated to permit the husband to have another wife. Jennie Harrington Tanner, first wife of Brigham Young Academy professor Joseph Marion Tanner, consented to his marriage with Annie Clark in 1883 because she had no children (Tanner 1976, 63–64). Wealthy Richards Clark of Farmington, the wife of Edward Barrett Clark, was childless during the first six years of their marriage. She received a priesthood blessing in 1885 which promised her children only when she permitted her husband to marry again. She acquiesced and permitted him to marry Alice Randall that year. The blessing was fulfilled, though it exasperated her that Alice bore a child before she had hers (Clark 1979, 5). Childless Muzetta Porter Burton of Ogden was miserable during the first four years of her marriage to John F. Burton. In 1903, even after the banning of plural marriage, she felt strongly enough about the need to have children that she persuaded her husband to take her sister Florence as a wife. She pursued a career but continued to assist in the education and upbringing of the five children that came from the second marriage (Burton, 1929). Thus, some first wives salved the wound of barrenness by sacrificing their monogamous marriage.

Subsequent wives likewise found motivation in the desire to have posterity. Sarah Rogers of Snowflake, Arizona, older and with no prospects for marriage during the late 1880s, heard Charles Edmund Richardson speak in church and was impressed. One of Charles's daughters relates that Sarah greatly desired to have a family. Sarah's own daughter reports that Sarah's mother pressured her to marry Charles polygamously. A third of Charles's children report that Sarah finally approached the stake president and expressed her feelings. When the stake president delivered the message, Charles was beset with doubt and confusion. He paced the floor at nights protesting to Sadie, the first wife, that he could not do it. Sadie responded, "You know that you should be entering into this principle and you have no right to deprive that good woman of having a family" (Shumway 1980, 5; Blau 1980, 10; Richardson 1980, 13). Charles told Sarah that he did not love her but would agree to the marriage. Sarah became the second wife in 1887. Third and fourth wives joined the family in 1889 and 1904.

Many of those who entered plural marriage reported experiences that conveyed divine confirmation. For Louisa Greene Richards, founding editor of *Woman's Exponent* and wife of Levi W. Richards, after earnest prayer came an inner witness — "not suddenly, as it comes to some but gradually and unmistakably" (1882, 94).

For others the witness was more startling. Sarah Kendall Durfee of Springville, the first wife of Jabez Erastus Durfee, had rebelled against her husband's desire to remarry, became ill, and received a visitation from the other world. Her son reports that the person said: " 'Sarah, you're awful sick, aren't you . . . Listen, your husband wants to take a second wife and you're opposing him, bitterly opposing him and that is a true principle. . . . He should stand at the head of the home and you should go with him and your children should go with him. If you don't, when you pass out of this life you'll be just canceled out' " (Durfee 1979, 3). Sarah promised to relent, and in 1880 Jabez married the second wife of five additional wives to be added to the family through 1902.

Emma Mortenson, working in Colonia Diaz as a teacher after the Manifesto, was unmarried, twenty-four, and concerned. She fasted and prayed about a husband and was comforted in a dream where she was shown the picture of the man she was to marry. Although she had previously vowed not to marry a redheaded man, she noted in her dream that her husband-to-be had red hair and a small moustache. She later went to Colonia Juarez and boarded with the Skousen family. She was shocked to recognize James Skousen as the man of her dream. She had not only vowed never to marry a redhead but also never to marry into plural marriage. She became his second wife in 1901 (Skousen 1979, 11).

The impressive spiritual manifestation to Vilate Kimball, first wife of Heber C. Kimball, should not be overlooked. Joseph Smith had revealed the principle to Heber but Vilate knew nothing of it. She was perplexed at the turmoil in her husband's mind. Depression settled over them both and she prayed fervently to know the cause: "Her mind was opened, and she saw the principle of Celestial marriage illustrated in all its beauty and glory, together with the great exaltation and honor it would confer upon her in that immortal and celestial sphere if she would but accept it and stand in her place by her husband's side" (Whitney 1881, 74). Their mutual gloom lifted when she went to Heber, aware now of his unexpressed concerns.

Their mutual revelation represents the ideal. In general, this thorny problem was not easily resolved. Kimball Young recounts that a man in Paragonah, Utah, told his wife "he had had a revelation to marry a certain girl and that in the face of such divine instructions, she must give her consent. The next morning she announced that in the night she, too, had received a revelation 'to shoot any woman who became his plural wife' " (1954, 123).

Women's responses to dreams, visions, divine mandates and the promise of celestial glory were influenced greatly by their perceptions of the connections between this life and the afterlife. There were, however, other more down-to-earth motives that influenced Mormon women.

The counsel of ecclesiastical superiors was often decisive for women entering plural marriage. Young notes that in thirty-three instances where a motive is mentioned, thirty attributed their decision to the counsel of Church authorities (1954, 106). This motive is also mentioned commonly in the interviews of the LDS Polygamy Oral History Project. Sarah Williams of Cedar City responded to the advice of Church leaders and incurred the hostility of her family. When she left home to marry Benjamin Perkins in the fall of 1881, her father disgustedly said he had no desire to even wish her goodbye if she left to come back a plural wife. When she returned married, her mother scolded her. Sarah picked up her sister's baby, but the sister snatched it away and slapped her. Finally, Sarah's mother gave her a quilt and a blanket and asked her to leave permanently. Sarah felt that since she had been advised by her Church leaders to get married plurally, she was doing right and must take "the consequences" (A. Lyman 1930, 7–8).

Ecclesiastical leaders preached plural marriage consistently from the pulpit. Catherine Pond, married to Brigham Pond in 1885 as his second wife, explained to her son that her principle motive was to follow the counsel of Church authorities. She said that she had been taught by these authorities to accept the proposal of a worthy man if he asked her to marry into polygamy (Pond 1980, 16). Hyrum Clark proposed to Ann Eliza Porter on condition that she accept another wife later. Ann went to her father, Alma Porter, a bishop, and confided to him that she thought it was terrible. He said, "No, that is very noble and unselfish. If he wants another wife, you must be equal to it" (Ericksen 1980, 16–17). Kimball Young quotes a nineteenth-century Mormon: "We'd heard it preached all our lives and we believed it was the true Principle. It was preached and preached and preached at us. When they weren't preaching that, they preached marriage" (1954, 203).

Frequently, when men were given positions of leadership, a Church leader would request that a man, and by implication his wife, enter the principle. Prior to being called as seventy's quorum leader, Andrew Lars Hyer of Lewiston, Utah, was told by Apostle Marriner Merrill to take a second wife. He conferred with his wife, Ellen Gilbert, and proposed a possible second wife. Ellen suggested instead their maid, Elizabeth Telford, whom he married in 1885 (Hyer 1978, 1).

The archetype for this private persuasion can be found in the experience of Isaac Robeson Farley of Ogden. When he and his fiancée Madeleine Malan came to Brigham Young in 1858 for the ceremony, President Young told him to bring her twin sister, Emily, as well. Isaac obeyed, and Emily agreed (Farley, n.d.). On another occasion, Brigham Young advised a man to marry a specific immigrant girl of sixteen before he departed to the Dixie Mission. The girl refused since her parents had not yet arrived. Brigham had the girl brought to his office where he explained that it was a commandment, that they would be blessed if they kept it and condemned if they did not. His counsel had the desired effect, and the two were wed (Young 1954, 109).

Blessings of ecclesiastical leaders sometimes encouraged plural marriage. We have already noted the blessing of Wealthy Richards Clark that promised her children if she accepted the principle. Emily Crane of Fillmore, Utah, was already engaged to George Penny, a single man, when Lorenzo Dow Watson proposed to her. She was undecided. Her parents sought a blessing from the stake patriarch for her. The blessing advised her to reconsider her choice and stated that she would marry plurally. Emily asked George if he would ever approve of plural marriage and, when he said no, she broke the engagement and married Watson (Driggs 1975, 4).

Sometimes friends, relatives, and other Church members provided the necessary emotional support, even when it came ambiguously. Ellen Elvira Nash Parkinson of Preston, Idaho, was eight months pregnant with her third child in 1887 when her husband, William C. Parkinson, married Louisa Benson. Ellen found the situation difficult to accept and sought her mother's counsel. The mother had been married plurally and responded to Ellen's plea, "You are no better than I to stand it." Ellen finally accepted the marriage because the Church urged it and the family all "approved" it. "There was nothing to do but make the best of it" (Parkinson 1965, 208). Ellen Gilbert Hyer of Lewiston, Utah, first wife of Andrew Lars Hyer, counselled her children, "Think nothing of it. It is just our religion" (Hyer and Ririe 1978, 19). Rudger H. Daines of Logan commented similarly that the plural marriage of his parents, William Moroni Daines and Chloe Hatch "was just a natural thing in their lives" (1976, 19).

The pressure to conform was at times intense. Elijah Nicholas Wilson courted a young woman whom he does not name in Cache Valley. Elijah had spent an unusual youth, growing up with the Shoshone, and was regarded by some as a renegade. They attempted to thwart his suit and encouraged the girl to marry a man of good standing in the community who was already married. She told Elijah "her folks and the bishop and all of the neighbors had turned loose on her and she saw no peace until she promised to marry him [Elijah's rival]" (1971, 194–203).

Economic security or status was an acknowledged motivation for some LDS women. Conditioned by modern society to accept romance as a primary motive to marry, we tend to forget that "pioneer people were motivated by elementary survival interests," as Nels Anderson suggests, "and none were more practical than some of these pioneer women, many of whom favored men who were more secure economically and able to provide the substance for living" (1942, 403). An unmarried woman may have been attracted to a polygamous man because, as Vickey Burgess-Olsen notes, polygamous husbands were usually better off occupationally than their monogamous peers and held higher positions in the Church (1975, 125).

Elizabeth Kane relates an instance where Sarah Comstock, a maid, obtained a jesting promise from the first wife that she could marry the husband after seven years of service. At the end of the seven years, she broke an engagement to another man, reminded the wife of her promise and claimed it, sharing the home and goods of the well-to-do husband (1974, 104).

A first wife might find some short-term economic advantage if her husband married a domestic who would continue her service to the family. Thus, Melvina Greer Skousen encouraged her husband, Daniel, to marry a hired girl saying, according to her daughter, "You might as well marry her and keep the money in the house" (Walser 1976, 22). Financial advantage was not the only benefit. Phylinda Loverage Terry of Union, Utah, sorrowed so deeply at the death of one of her children in 1848 that her health failed. Her husband Charles brought in Sarah Hammond, a neighbor's daughter, to assist the family during the wife's illness. She cared lovingly and competently for the children. Phylinda continued to fail and consented for Charles and Sarah to be married in 1851, thereby providing for the stability of her family once she was gone. She soon died (Blair 1937, 11).

A first wife usually had the most status among the wives. According to her daughter, Caroline Romney Eyring of Colonia Juarez, Mexico, was willing to permit a second marriage because she believed "that the way they would get their celestial glory was by living this principle." However, she expected to be "queen bee" as her own mother, a first wife, had been. She was disappointed when Edward, the husband, decided that Caroline and Emma, the second wife and Caroline's sister, would be treated equally (Calder 1980, 5; Eyring 1976, 11).

Sometimes a plural marriage offered escape from a difficult situation. Pearl Dean Taylor of Colonia Juarez worked "real hard" to tend her invalid parents until she married Samuel Walter Jarvis as a plural wife in 1902 (Augustus 1976, 8). Emmeline B. Whitney, a widow, wrote in 1852 to Daniel H. Wells, who had five wives, requesting that he "consider the lonely state" she faced and "return to her a description of his feelings for her." They were married that year (Eaton-Gadsby and Dushku 1978, 459). Nancy Gibbons was forty-eight and John D. Lee was thirty-five when, according to his report: "She told me she was without friend that she could in reality claim as a counselor or lodge the secrets of her breasts with, and that she had thought rather hard of me for I was one of the first elders that brought the gospel to her and a man in whom she always reposed the most exquisite trust and confidence" (Lee 1938, 99). She became his twelfth wife.

First wives, likewise, found themselves looking at the situation from a practical point of view. Viewing plural marriage as inevitable, one anonymous wife encouraged her husband to marry: "If you're going to get married, I want you to do it while I'm young. I don't want you to wait until I'm old and good for nothing and then bring in a young wife" (Young 1954, 113).

From a scriptural perspective, love was not a prerequisite to plural marriage. As Section 132 observes: "If any man have a wife, who holds the keys of this power, and he teaches unto her the law of my priesthood, as pertaining to these things, then shall she believe and administer unto him, or she shall be destroyed" (D&C 132:64). When asked by her son if she loved her husband, second wife Catherine Pond responded that she did not but that she learned to love him (Pond 1980, 11). One peppery prospective second wife in St. George (identified only as Carolyn Y.) refused to have romance mixed up with her religion: "Yes, religion that was what it meant to me. I wouldn't have no courtin'. Before we was married he used to want me to go out walkin', but I wouldn't have it. 'No courtin', I says to him. 'If you've got anything to say to me, you know how to say it and where. Come to the house and say it out straight, no strollin' around like young lovers. I don't go walkin' with any woman's husband' " (Sarah Comstock in Mulder and Mortensen 1954, 433).

These two traditional views coexisted with the generally accepted role of love as prelude to marriage increasingly adopted by American society in general throughout the nineteenth century.

A third wife had love as her first priority in marriage: "I don't think I thought anything about the Principle . . . when I married. . . . I fell in love with my husband and married him, just as a girl would today, only it was in polygamy. He was twenty years older than I was, but he never seemed old. I think I loved him even when I was a little girl" (Young 1954, 117). Sarah Crossley, baptized as a child in England, knew many of the missionaries including Peregrine Sessions. Sarah immigrated with the Willie handcart company at the age of thirteen and suffered severely. Peregrine took her into his Bountiful home, cared for her, and when she was eighteen, married her. She relates, "I think I had loved him from my very childhood, and although I was his fourth wife and many years younger I was the happiest woman in the world" (Burningham 1979, 1-3).

Such happiness could create its own disruptions. According to the son of Betsy Lowe Allen of Cove, Utah, when she found her husband, James Carson Allen, "spooning" with her younger sister Ellen a year after her own marriage, she cried so long and so heartbrokenly that she could no longer produce milk for her baby (Allen 1980, 22). Ann Doney Lowe of Franklin, Idaho, confided in her son that she deeply loved his father, James Galloway Lowe, but when he married Elizabeth Kingsford in 1885 after five years of monogamy, it was nearly unbearable for her (Lowe 1976, 8).

Kimball Young suggests that wives not romantically attached to their husbands were better able to adjust to plural marriage (1954, 209). One of the strongest advocates of plural marriage, Zina D. H. Young, advised that a successful polygamous wife "must regard her husband with indifference, and with no other feeling than that of reverence, for love we regard as a false sentiment; a feeling which should have no existence in polygamy" (Van Wagoner and Walker 1982, 417).

There is no evidence to suggest that sex motivated women to accept plural marriage over monogamy. Commenting on this, Romania Pratt Penrose said in 1886:

> It cannot be true, as asserted, that plural marriage is entered into as a rule for sensual motives. It is self-evident that it is not the case with women, and it is unreasonable to suppose that men would bring upon themselves the responsibilities, cares and expenses of a plural family, when they could avoid all this, yet revel in sin. (Penrose 1886, 31)

Even anti-Mormon literature portrayed Mormon women as victims of lust rather than proponents of sensual designs.

Not all women were given a choice, either to accept a plural wife or to become one. Young reports two cases. One man, after sixteen years of marriage, requested his wife to ready his temple clothes. When she inquired the reason, he said it was to remarry (1954, 122). One son reports hearing his father tell his mother that the authorities threatened to release him from the bishopric if he did not take another wife. The mother reluctantly consented (1954, 74).

Fourteen-year-old Anna Eliza Berry in 1879 accompanied her mother and stepfather to St. George, ostensibly to tend the younger children and to enjoy the ride. Once while feeding the team she asked her stepfather why he was taking her to the temple. He said to marry her. She writes, "Well I just felt horried [sic] and thought but never dare say is that the way a woman gets Married cant a woman say who she wants." She went through the temple for her endowments. While she was in the sealing room, she writes, "I was lookin at the pretty rooms and I remember of knelling on the alter and a man talking. Mr. H. C. said yes and after they said to me to say yes I wispered yes not noing what I was saying." On the return journey the stepfather put his arm around her shoulder and called her his "little wife." She was aghast and said, "Why, be I your wife? He said yes, but I said well I never new [sic] that. He said dont tell a sole or we will half to be put in prison for living in poligmey and I did feel so bad I wondered if all girls got married that way and would like to run away" (Day 1899–1907, 4).

Uneasy decisions and unsettling adjustments confronted many women in plural marriage. Dropped into the balance of a woman's decision were the weights of faith, emotion, and reason. When the factors had been weighed, the women decided on various courses, ranging from outright acceptance and encouragement of the system to adamant rejection.

Theresa Thompson, an example of the first extreme, questioned her husband-to-be, Anson Bowen Call, at the time of his proposal in 1885: " 'Do you believe in polygamy and would you practice polygamy?' He didn't hardly know what to say because he wanted to gain her favor. He said, 'I believe in the principle and if the opportunity comes I would practice it.' She said, 'I am thankful of that' " (Alder 1976, 27). Theresa later consented to three more wives entering the family after the Manifesto. She outlived them all.

Many women responded cooperatively, though hesitantly. For some plural marriage was a violation of beliefs and feelings they could not accept. Belief in the principle helped other plural wives deal with their negative emotions. Sadie Richardson, of Colonia Diaz, the first wife of Edmund Richardson, struggled with jealousy as two more wives joined the family, but claimed "that woman who believes in continued revelation, could not be far off in accepting the principles of polygamy. They might have different attitudes in their living of it, but not in the divinity of it" (Richardson 1980). The third wife in Edmund Richardson's family, Rebecca Jacobson reported, "I have been happy and blessed as a polygamist wife. . . . Any sacrifice we made for each other was rewarded ten-fold." In the words of Annie Richardson Johnson, Edmund and Rebecca's daughter, "Like Joseph Smith, polygamists had sealed their testimony, not with their blood, but with the power of acceptance when the principle of Plural Marriage was revealed" (Johnson 1972, 292, 294). With such an attitude, many women felt deeply affirmed in their decision.

Mary Jensen, a fifteen-year-old living in Cottonwood, Utah, recorded that "one morning she found her mother sorely depressed with her older sister, Annie, looking very serious." She was shocked to learn that her stepfather felt "it his duty" to take seventeen-year-old Annie as his second wife. Affronted, Mary convinced her mother and her sister to refuse. She persuaded them that "the Lord doesn't want a man to marry a lot of women." Simply stated, this was the argument that Church members faced from the outside and, because of their Western heritage, from the inside. Mary's case was an argument that gave way with the passage of time. Both she and Annie were married two years later as sister wives to Joseph Moulton (Moulton n.d., 11–12).

Wilford Woodruff, while an apostle, complained in October conference in 1875 that "we have many bishops and elders who have but one wife. They are abundantly qualified to enter the higher law and take more, but their wives will not let them" (Cowley 1909, 490). Juanita Brooks's grandfather went wooing in vain when his first wife appeared at the home of the prospective wife and left after a door-slamming scene. The second woman refused the proposal (1922, 300). Ann Riter Young, first wife of Seymour B. Young, went to George Q. Cannon, counselor to Church president Wilford Woodruff and said, "I don't give my consent." She pleaded that they had a child with cerebral palsy to take care of and that her husband was already too occupied to find time for another family. This did not preclude Seymour's marriage to Abbie Wells (Hammond 1980, 8). When Charles Ora Card, stake president in

Logan and later founder of Cardston, Canada, remarried, his first wife, Sarah Ann Birdneau Card, left him and did all she could to help the federal marshals find and imprison him (Card 1980, 27).

Given the potential problems in a monogamous marriage, it is reasonable to suspect that plural marriage would generate more. Statistics indicate that plural marriage ended in divorce more commonly than single marriages. Studies of family group sheets in the Genealogical Society Library, show a 9 percent divorce rate among polygamists as compared to a 1 percent (0–9) rate among monogamists (Kunz 1980, 68–69). These statistics are probably symptomatic of the unseen, unresolved struggles that beset those so married.

An intimate glimpse of those complex feelings comes from the Leavitt family of Bunkerville, Nevada. The first wife, Mary Abbott Leavitt, had given her consent for Thomas Dudley Leavitt to remarry; but as she awaited his return with his new bride, Ada Waite, she went outside in the moonlight and "asked the Lord to give me strength that when they came I would be able to bear it. I told him how I felt in my heart and asked him if he would bless me so that this feeling would leave me, so I wouldn't have that jealous feeling and that terrible feeling. I couldn't endure it. I shed bitter tears, and I prayed with all my heart and soul." She heard the wagon, hurried back to her house, and waited in the dark. Thomas entered and struck a match. Seeing her in the shadows, he approached and, noting that she had been crying, he embraced her and said, "I want you to know that you are my first love. . . . No one can take your place, nobody" (Waite 1980, 5).

In summary, then, women accepted plural marriage for reasons both spiritual and temporal. It brought great self-mastery to some. In others it unleashed emotions that were hardly containable. Ultimately, it required the resolution of conflicting demands placed on the individual woman in response to her faith, emotion, and reason. The struggle to resolve the tension felt within each soul and acted out in each life is a matter that requests only our understanding and not our judgment. As Marinda Bateman explained to her daughter who objected to the practice of plural marriage, "Do not say you do not believe it, say you do not understand it" (Jensen 1948, 51).

BIBLIOGRAPHY

Church Archives refers to the Historical Department Archives, Church of Jesus Christ of Latter-day Saints, Salt Lake City, Utah. LDS Polygamy refers to the LDS Polygamy Oral History Project, Charles Redd Center for Western Studies Oral History Program, Manuscript Division, Harold B. Lee Library, Brigham Young University, Provo, Utah.

Alder, Lorna Call. Interviewed by Jessie Embry. 28 June 1976. LDS Polygamy.

Allen, Clarence. Interviewed by James Comish. 1980. LDS Polygamy.

Anderson, Nels. *Deseret Saints*. Chicago: University of Chicago Press, 1942.

Arrington, Leonard J. and Davis Bitton. *The Mormon Experience: A History of the Latter-day Saints*. New York: Knopf, 1979.

Augustus, Pearl J. Interviewed by Jessie Embry. 1 June 1976. LDS Polygamy.

Blair, Elizabeth T. "Women of My Early Pioneer Home." In Kate B. Carter, comp. "The Other Mother." *Daughters of Utah Pioneers Lesson for December 1937*. Salt Lake City: Daughters of Utah Pioneers, 1937. Pp. 11–12.

Blau, Teresa Richardson. Interviewed by Leonard Grover. 25 April 1980. LDS Polygamy.

Brooks, Juanita. "A Close-up of Polygamy." *Harper's Magazine* 168 (Dec.–May 1933): 299–307.

Burgess-Olsen, Vicky. "Family Structure and Dynamics in Early Utah Mormon Families, 1847–1885." Ph.D. diss., Northwestern University, 1975.

Burningham, Hannah Sessions. "Story and Life of Sarah Crossley Sessions." 1979. Church Archives.

Burton, Muzetta Porter. Genealogical Survey, 24 Oct. 1929, bound with other surveys in "Genealogical Surveys of L.D.S. Members," Genealogical Library, LDS Church Genealogical Department, Salt Lake City, Utah.

Calder, Rose Eyring. Interviewed by Leonard Grover. 12 July 1980. LDS Polygamy.

Campbell, Eugene E. and Bruce L. Campbell. "Divorce Among Mormon Polygamists: Extent and Explanations." *Utah Historical Quarterly* 46 (Winter 1978): 4–23.

Card, Orson Rega. Interviewed by Maureen Ursenbach Beecher. Salt Lake City, Utah. 1980. Church Archives.

Carter, Kate B., comp., "The Other Mother." *Daughters of Utah Pioneers Lesson for December 1937*. Salt Lake City: Daughters of Utah Pioneers, 1937.

Clark, Walter. Interviewed by Leonard Grover, 12 Oct. 1979. LDS Polygamy.

Cowley, Matthias F. *Wilford Woodruff: Fourth President of the Church of Jesus Christ of Latter-day Saints; History of His Life and Labors as Recorded in His Daily Journals.* Salt Lake City: Deseret News, 1909.

Crocheron, Augusta Joyce. *Representative Women of Deseret*. Salt Lake City: J. C. Graham, 1884.

Daines, Rudger H. Interviewed by Jessie Embry. 16 July 1976. LDS Polygamy.

Day, Anna Eliza Berry. Reminiscences, 1899–1907. Church Archives.

Driggs, Alice Nevada Watson. Interviewed by A. Hamer Reiser. Salt Lake City, Utah. 1975. Church Archives.

Durfee, Charles. Interviewed by Dean May. 24 Nov. 1979. LDS Polygamy.

Eaton-Gadsby, Patricia Rasmussen and Judith Rasmussen Dushku. "Emmeline B. Wells." In Vicky Burgess-Olsen, ed. *Sister Saints*. Provo, Utah: Brigham Young University Press, 1978.

Ericksen, Edna. Interviewed by Leonard Grover. 18 Oct. and 15 Nov. 1980. LDS Polygamy.

Eyring, Joseph. Interviewed by Jessie L. Embry. 1976. LDS Polygamy.

[Farley.] "A Life Sketch of Isaac Robeson Farley." Typescript. Copy in possession of author.

Hammond, Hortense Young. Interviewed by Leonard Grover. 15 March 1980. LDS Polygamy.

Hyer, Dorris Dale. Interviewed by Tillman S. Boxell. 30 June 1978. LDS Polygamy.

Hyer, Merle Gilbert and Estell Hyer Ririe. Interviewed by Tillman S. Boxell. 30 June 1978. LDS Polygamy.

Jensen, Juliaetta Bateman. *Little Gold Pieces: The Story of My Mormon Mother's Life.* Salt Lake City: Stanway Printing, 1948.

Johnson, Annie R. *Heartbeats of Colonia Diaz*. Mesa, Arizona: Annie Johnson, 1972.

Kane, Elizabeth Wood. *Twelve Mormon Homes Visited in Succession on a Journey through Utah to Arizona.* Salt Lake City: University of Utah Library, Tanner Trust Fund, 1974.

Kunz, Phillip R. "One Wife or Several? A Comparative Study of Late Nineteenth-Century Marriage in Utah." In Thomas G. Alexander, ed., *The Mormon People: Their Character and Traditions*, Charles Redd Monographs in Western History, No. 10. Provo, Utah: Brigham Young University Press, 1980. Pp. 53–73.

Lee, John D. *Journals 1846–1847 and 1859*. Charles Kelley, ed. Salt Lake City: Western Printing, 1938.

Lowe, Glen Doney. Interviewed by Jessie Embry. 18 June 1976. LDS Polygamy.

Lyman, Albert Robeson. "Notes on the Life of Sarah William Perkins." 1930. Church Archives.

Lyman, Eliza Marie Partridge. Reminiscences and Diary, 1846–85. Church Archives.

Moulton, Jensine Marie Jensen. "History of a Polygamist Wife in Heber Valley." N.d. Church Archives.

Mulder, William, and A. Russell Mortensen, eds. *Among the Mormons*. New York: Alfred Knopf, 1958.

Parkinson, Ellen Elvira Nash. "Ellen Elvira Nash Parkinson." *Our Pioneer Heritage* 8 (1965): 201–18.

Penrose, Romania B. Pratt. "Memoir of Romania B. Pratt, M.D." 1881. Church Archives.

———. *Mormon Women's Protest: An Appeal for Freedom, Justice, and Equal Rights....* Salt Lake City: Deseret News, 1886.

Pond, George S. Interviewed by Leonard Grover. 16 Feb. 1980. LDS Polygamy.

Richards, Louisa Greene. "Personal Experience, Etc." *Woman's Exponent* 11 (15 Nov. 1882): 94.

Richardson, Ivan R. Interviewed by Leonard Grover. 20 Aug. 1980. LDS Polygamy.

Shipp, Ellis. *Mormon Women's Protest: An Appeal for Freedom, Justice, and Equal Rights* ... Salt Lake City: Deseret News, 1886.

Shumway, Elva R. Interviewed by Leonard Grover. 24 April 1980. LDS Polygamy.

Skousen, Karl. Interviewed by Leonard Grover. 31 Oct. 1979. LDS Polygamy.

Smith, Elva Fuhriman. Oral interview by Kahlile Mehr. Bountiful, Utah. 1980. Audio tape in possession of author.

Stenhouse, Fanny. *Exposé of Polygamy in Utah: A Lady's Life Among the Mormons*. New York: American News, 1872.

Tanner, Annie Clark. *A Mormon Mother*. Salt Lake City: University of Utah Library, Tanner Trust Fund, 1976.

Tullidge, Edward W. *The Women of Mormondom*. 1877. Reprint ed., Salt Lake City: 1975.

Van Wagoner, Richard S. and Steven C. Walker. *A Book of Mormons*. Salt Lake City: Signature Books, 1982.

Waite, Glenna. Interviewed by Jessie Embry. 3 Jan. 1980. LDS Polygamy.

Walser, Asenath Skousen. Interviewed by Jessie Embry, 26 May 1976. LDS Polygamy.

Whitney, Helen Mar. "Scenes and Incidents in Nauvoo." *Woman's Exponent* 10 (15 Oct. 1881): 74.

———. *Why We Practice Plural Marriage*. Salt Lake City: Juvenile Instructor Office, 1884.

Wilson, Elijah Nicholas. *Among the Shoshones*. 1910. Reprint ed. Medford, Ore.: Pine Cone, 1971.

Young, Kimball. *Isn't One Wife Enough?* 1954. Reprint ed., Westport, Conn.: Greenwood, 1970. He gives individuals in his study pseudonyms. I have avoided quoting these names here so that there will be no confusion between historical and pseudonymous persons.

Zenanas and Girlless Villages: The Ethnology of American Evangelical Women, 1870–1910

Joan Jacobs Brumberg

On February 4, 1896, a petition representing 600,000 American women was presented to his "Excellency" Grover Cleveland beseeching the president "to interpose . . . for the protection of Christian women" in the Turkish Empire. This appeal, which represented the joint efforts of women in all the major foreign-missionary societies of the Protestant churches, followed by two weeks a similar petition authored by Frances E. Willard and the national leadership of the Woman's Christian Temperance Union (WCTU), an organization that claimed in 1896 a "following of not fewer than a million persons."[1]

The subject of concern in both national petitions was the fate of Armenian Christian women and their children who, as a result of the uprisings of Armenian men against the Muslim sultan of Turkey, had become the victims of a vicious nationalistic and religious war. "We believe, upon unimpeachable authority," stated the February document, "that our Armenian sisters have been so dealt with that they have, in at least one large company, drowned themselves in the Euphrates River to escape a fate worse than death." Armenian women were reported as "hav[ing] been turned out by scores into winter snow," without adequate clothing, food, shelter, or male protectors. The WCTU petition noted "the agony and outrage inflicted by Moslem savages" on women and families "whose only fault [was] their devotion to Christ and their loyalty to a pure home." Early in 1896 an Armenian relief organization

Joan Jacobs Brumberg is assistant professor in the Department of Human Development and Family Studies and Women's Studies Program at Cornell University and 1982–1983 Fellow at the Charles Warren Center for Studies in American History, Harvard University. A portion of the research for this study was supported by a faculty research grant, College of Arts and Sciences, Cornell University.

[1] "Petition of the Woman's Foreign Missionary Societies of the United States of America," *Woman's Work for Woman*, 11 (March 1896), 59–60; *New York Times*, Jan. 21, 1896, p. 5. The relationship between foreign-missionary organizations and the development of the Woman's Christian Temperance Union is presented in Ruth Bordin, *Woman and Temperance: The Quest for Power and Liberty, 1873–1900* (Philadelphia, 1981).

asked: "Is it not natural that the woman-heart of the West should be touched by the unparalleled affliction and peril of the women of Armenia?"[2]

Whatever the exact nature of the "atrocities" against the Christian population of Turkey, the 1896 peititions constituted an explicit call for action on the part of national leadership, revealing women's assumptions about their own vulnerability. Declaring that one million WCTU members believed "the protection of the home is the supreme duty of statesmen," their petition went on to implore Congress "to take such action as shall put our home-loving republic on record as having used its moral and material influence for the relief of Armenia." The petition emanating from the church groups echoed the same program, urging the "protection" of Armenian women by those who, it was stated, enjoyed life in a nation "where woman's home and honor are secure."[3] Whether we choose to regard these petitions as an expression of confidence or read them as a strategic prod to the national conscience, motivated by anxiety rather than assurance, the fact is that large numbers of women in late Victorian America made a litany of the claim that their own position was both protected and unique.

The values and assumptions incorporated in the 1896 petitions suggest that we give closer attention to those post-Civil War social experiences which generated such a pervasive interest in women abroad, activating this type of double vision. We also need to know what cultural information underlay the perception that American women occupied a safe place in a unique "home-loving" republic. In other words, we must consider both how and what American women came to think about themselves in relation to other women of the world. This process of describing, classifying, and interpreting the distinguishing characteristics of other races, was, after all, the central activity of ethnology, a branch of anthropological study that began to have scientific and scholarly credence in the last decades of the nineteenth century. Yet masses of American women, with only the slightest notions of scientific rigor, embraced the study of ethnology as early as the 1870s, precisely because they were interested in the similarities and dissimilarities in women's position in other cultures of the world.

The kind of cultural yardstick implied by the 1896 petitioners was actually generated by rudimentary ethnological descriptions emanating from American missionaries in foreign fields. In fact, the public plea for the specific protection of Armenian women came near the close of what has been commonly called the "Century of Missions." Foreign missionary activity by Americans began in 1812 when New England Congregationalists endorsed and sent out their first youthful evangelization workers, some of whom, like Adoniram Judson, shared both public attention and national affection with their wives.[4] In the

[2] "Petition of Woman's Foreign Missionary Societies," 59; *New York Times*, Jan. 21, 1896, p. 5; *ibid.*, Feb. 17, 1896, p. 5.

[3] *New York Times*, Jan. 21, 1896, p. 5; "Petition of Woman's Foreign Missionary Societies," 59.

[4] Joan Jacobs Brumberg, *Mission for Life: The Story of the Family of Adoniram Judson, the Dramatic Events of the First American Foreign Mission, and the Course of Evangelical Religion in the Nineteenth Century* (New York, 1980); Oliver Wendell Elsbree, *The Rise of the Missionary Spirit in America, 1790–1815* (Williamsport, Pa., 1928).

1820s the missionaries of the evangelical Protestant churches began to ply their supporters at home with firsthand descriptions of social life among the heathen they were attempting to convert. By the late nineteenth century, missionary ethnologists found an attentive public in the swelling middle-class, and predominantly female, reading audience.

Distinguished from professional or scientific ethnography by the fact that it employed the paradigm of an antithetical "other," the missionary ethnology was essentially didactic in purpose.[5] Ethnological descriptions of manners, family life, politics, and culture were used, first and foremost, to articulate distinctions between Christians and heathens. Not surprisingly, the complexities of intercultural contact were ignored, as reports from the field increasingly developed a formulaic vocabulary for describing women's place in non-Christian societies. By 1900, American women were familiar, if not conversant, with an entire vocabulary that implied the degradation of women: zenanas and harems; the seraglio and the bagnio; female infanticide and suttee; concubinage and polygamy; bride sale; foot-binding and ear and nose boring; consecrated prostitution and sacrifice; bastinado; child marriage and slavery.[6]

In essence, the evangelical ethnology encouraged a notion of "characteristic atrocities" and, in the process, revitalized cultural stereotypes that were either dormant or had never really disappeared. In antebellum America, women had already developed some notion of lives beyond their own as they heard travel lectures, popular on the lyceum circuit. But the religious ethnology, embraced by women after 1870, gave new credence to long-standing cultural observations, such as the polygamy of Indian rajahs or the foot-binding of Chinese girls, first made prominent in the era of colonialist exploration. Thus, the evangelical ethnology was significant not for any substantive contribution to scientific or professional anthropology but for its distinctive focus on women's status and roles.[7] And, in the hands of nineteenth-century religious women, old observations were given both a new gloss and a new currency, reflecting anxieties and assumptions about women's place among the American middle class.[8]

[5] In anthropology the idea of antithetical other is associated with symbolic and structuralist approaches to cross-cultural comparisons, particularly those of Claude Levi-Strauss. For discussions of the continuities in cultural stereotyping in a single area see: Bernard S. Cohn, "Notes on the History of the Study of Indian Society and Culture," in *Structure and Change in Indian Society*, ed. Milton Singer and Bernard S. Cohn (Chicago, 1968), 3–28; and A. Leslie Willson, *A Mythical Image: The Ideal of India in German Romanticism* (Durham, N.C., 1964).

[6] A seraglio is the portion of a Muslim house where women are secluded not unlike a Hindu zenana or a Muslim harem. Bagnio refers to a brothel, a bathing house, or both. Suttee is the self-immolation of the Hindu widow on her husband's funeral pyre. Consecrated prostitution is defined below. Bastinado refers to an oriental mode of punishment, especially blows with a stick to the soles of the feet or buttocks.

[7] It should be noted that elements of the missionary ethnology were incorporated in the work of anthropologists such as Alexander Francis Chamberlain, *The Child and Childhood in Folk-Thought (The Child in Primitive Culture)* (New York, 1896); Otis Tufton Mason, *Woman's Share in Primitive Culture* (New York, 1894); Samuel M. Zwemer, *Childhood in the Moslem World* (New York, 1915).

[8] Evangelical women were not alone in using cross-cultural analysis. Feminists in the nineteenth century also employed cross-cultural information to argue that the subjection of women

The vehicle for the popular dissemination of this catalog of heathen atrocities was the women's foreign-mission crusade, a powerful and multifaceted sisterhood of agencies that took shape at the close of the Civil War. Between 1868 and 1873, in each of the major American Protestant evangelical denominations, women separated from what were called "parent boards" of male directors and generated their own foreign-mission organizations headed by a national directorate of exclusively female leadership. In 1868, Congregational churchwomen coalesced to form the Woman's Board of Missions. A year later, Methodist Episcopal women followed suit, creating the Woman's Foreign Mission Society. In 1870, women in the Presbyterian fold organized the Ladies Board of Foreign Missionary Societies of their church; in 1873, the Woman's Baptist Foreign Missionary Society was formed.[9]

In the hands of women, the foreign-mission crusade took on new life and was transformed in a number of significant ways. At a very basic level, the post-Civil War women's mission crusade stopped making male missionaries the focus of their fund-raising efforts and began to generate funds for the specific support of women in the field. The Congregationalist women stated explicitly: "The object of this Society is to engage the earnest, systematic cooperation of . . . women . . . in sending out and supporting unmarried female missionaries and teachers to heathen women."[10] The women they chose to sponsor were largely unmarried or widowed, giving women without benefit of family support an opportunity to combine religious zeal with the means of making a living, if but for a few years. In the first decade of operation Congregationalists sent out 103 female missionaries of whom over 60 percent had never been married at the time of departure. In the Woman's Baptist Foreign Missionary Society the pattern was almost the same; 60 percent of their missionaries were unmarried at embarkation. Among Methodists, the percentage was even higher: 98 percent of the women sponsored by the Woman's Foreign Mission Society had not been married. By 1909, each of the major groups supported a sizable force of women missionaries: the Methodists, for example, who had only 2 women missionaries at their founding in 1869, had 312 four decades later. N.G. Clark, an officer of the Congregationalists' American Board of Commissioners for Foreign Missions, sang the praises of the women's

had no historical or universal validity precisely because it took different forms. This kind of thinking, which William Leach calls "cultural cosmopolitanism," led feminist reformers out of the evangelical churches and down a very different path than their religious sisters. William Leach, *True Love and Perfect Union: The Feminist Reform of Sex and Society* (New York, 1980), 13. An important antebellum example of feminist attention to cross-cultural information is in Sarah M. Grimke, *Letters on the Equality of the Sexes, and the Condition of Woman* (Boston, 1838), 27–45.

[9] The best nineteenth-century summary of these organizational histories is *Historical Sketches of Womans' Missionary Societies in America and England* (Boston, 1879), which was published by Mrs. L. H. Daggett, subscription agent for *Heathen Woman's Friend* until 1882. This information on their founding is confirmed by separate organizational histories and by the missionary magazines. Helen Barrett Montgomery links the formation of these organizations to experiences in the Civil War. See Helen Barrett Montgomery, *Western Women in Eastern Lands: An Outline of Fifty Years of Women's Work in Foreign Missions* (New York, 1910), 10.

[10] *Historical Sketches*, 44.

organizations, calling them "a great uprising of Christian women in behalf of their sex."[11]

In fact, Clark's perception of a "great uprising" was accurate. Between 1870 and 1910, the women's foreign-mission crusade experienced extraordinary organizational growth which has been hidden until now by the particularistic perspectives of denominational church history. When we look across the denominations, however, and follow the course of organizational development into the twentieth century, it becomes clear that foreign missions were, among women at least, a veritable growth industry. For example, between 1873 (when the organization was founded) and 1909, the Woman's Baptist Foreign Missionary Society grew from 255 to 5,000 auxiliaries. Organizational growth was even more dramatic among Congregationalists, Methodists, and Presbyterians, the latter group expanding from 100 auxiliary sections in 1870 to 10,869 in 1909. And where auxiliaries were planted, revenues grew. Although foreign-mission giving increased among all women's groups, the Methodists outdid all others: by 1909, contributions from the Woman's Foreign Missionary Society of the Methodist Episcopal Church were close to $1 million a year.[12]

The success of foreign-missionary fund raising was inextricably linked to the rise of the middle class. "If every Methodist woman who goes to her summer cottage would take a mite-box and drop in a thank offering for each 'good time,'" wrote one missionary publicist, "there would be plenty of money to send out all the dear girls God is calling."[13] This assumption that families had

[11] For a discussion of the marital status of missionaries, see Barbara Welter, "She Hath Done What She Could: Protestant Women's Missionary Careers in Nineteenth-Century America," *American Quarterly*, 30 (Winter 1978), 624–38. Percentages of unmarried women are extracted from the list of missionaries sponsored by woman's organizations between the time of organizational origin and 1879 in *Historical Sketches*, 31, 52–54, 107. Barbara Welter charts the general move to women missionaries in this way: in 1830, females made up 49 percent of the missionary force; by 1893 women represented 60 percent. Welter, "She Hath Done What She Could," 632; Montgomery, *Western Women*, table following 286; *Life and Light for Heathen Women*, 1 (March 1869), 6.

[12] The data presented here represents only the six major women's foreign-mission groups. In 1910, at the time of Montgomery's compilation of statistics on which this study is based, there were at least thirty-five national or regional women's missionary organizations in the United States. See Montgomery, *Western Women*, table following 286. I have excluded from consideration any organizations outside the Baptist, Congregationalist, Methodist, and Presbyterian churches as well as those within these churches that were not autonomous women's groups, for example, Women's Missionary Auxiliary to the Southern Baptist Convention (1888). Typical of the denominational accounts of organizational growth are Frances J. Baker, *The Story of the Woman's Foreign Missionary Society of the Methodist Episcopal Church, 1869–1895* (Cincinnati, 1898); and Mary Sparkes Wheeler, *First Decade of the Woman's Foreign Missionary Society of the Methodist Episcopal Church, with Sketches of Its Missionaries* (New York, 1883). Each of the denominations has an equivalent set of individual organizational histories. A somewhat broader approach was taken in 1893 at the World's Columbian Exposition. The papers from the missionary congress were collected in E. M. Wherry, comp., *Woman in Missions: Papers and Addresses Presented at the Woman's Congress of Missions, October 2–4, 1893, in the Hall of Columbus, Chicago* (New York, 1894).

[13] "Home Department," *Heathen Woman's Friend*, 27 (July 1895), 20. *Life and Light for Heathen Women*, 1 (March 1869), 5 has the same theme; the Congregationalists, however, wrote about laying aside jewelry and other "superfluities" in life in order to keep the treasury of the

the means to support both women's charity work and their own leisure pervades accounts of the formation of the women's crusade. A Methodist audience in the 1870s was told that because "woman regulates the family expenses . . . it is for her to say whether the entire income shall be expended in luxury and needless self-indulgence, or whether there shall be sufficient left for benevolent purposes." In 1910 Helen Barrett Montgomery, later the first woman president of the Northern Baptist Convention, attributed the inauguration of an autonomous women's foreign-mission organization to an essential economic transition: the change from the collection of "beautiful self-denials," in the form of ad hoc gifts culled from the wife's "egg . . . butter . . . and rag money," to systematic gifts levied from the household budget.[14] Thus, the cluster of women's foreign-mission organizations about 1870 should be regarded as more than a simple organizational development within the realm of religious history. In fact, the origin of these groups after the Civil War reflects the larger socioeconomic transformations that were recasting the work roles of men and women and, consequently, the nature of the family itself.

The essentially middle-class spirit of the women's foreign-mission crusade is further revealed in the theory and content of auxiliary programming. Beyond all else, the foreign-mission crusade in the hands of women became a means of self-education; consequently, women's groups increasingly moved into the business of publishing materials designed for an audience of middle-class women readers. Magazines such as *Life and Light for Women* (Congregational), *Woman's Work for Woman* (Presbyterian), *The Helping Hand* (Baptist), *Heathen Woman's Friend* (Methodist), and *Woman's Missionary Advocate* (Southern Methodist) were created and disseminated by each of the denominational women's groups with monies drawn from their own revenues.[15] Before 1870 missionary literature had generally taken two forms: the pietistic memoir and biography of dead or returned missionaries and their wives or the ponderous anniversary sermon and annual report of the denominational board. The magazines that came after 1870, however, were part of a new "light infantry of missionary literature" which had a distinctly different tone. Underlying the new materials was the assumption that there

society full. Typical of the 1890s appeal was the suggestion that Christian "economizing" did not mean canceling the missionary magazine but rather balancing the demands of fashion, amusements, carfares, and charity. *Life and Light for Women*, 25 (June 1895), 271–72.

[14] Mrs. M. C. Hickman, "Woman's Foreign Missionary Society," *Heathen Woman's Friend*, 2 (May 1871), 130; Montgomery, *Western Women*, 11–12. See Winthrop S. Hudson's biography of Montgomery in Edward T. James, Janet Wilson James, and Paul S. Boyer, eds., *Notable American Women* (3 vols., Cambridge, 1971), II, 566–68.

[15] The titles of these magazines often varied. *Life and Light for Women* (1869–1922) was known as *Life and Light for Heathen Women* until 1872. *Woman's Work for Woman* (1871–1924) became *Woman's Work* in 1905. *The Helping Hand* (1842–1914) began as *Macedonian*. *Heathen Woman's Friend* (1869–1940) became *Woman's Missionary Friend* in 1896. *Woman's Missionary Advocate* (1880–1910) retained its name throughout its publication. In addition, there were children's magazines sponsored by the women's groups (the Presbyterians' *Children's Work for Children*, 1876–1893; The Congregationalists' *Mission Dayspring*, 1882–1913; the Baptists' *Little Helpers*, 1883–1885; the Methodists' *Heathen Children's Friend*, also known as *Children's Missionary Friend* and *Junior Missionary Friend*, 1890–1939), as well as at least one foreign-language magazine that the Methodists published out of St. Louis, *Der Heiden-Frauen-Freund*, later *Der Frauen-Missions-Freund*, which first appeared in 1885.

was a body of knowledge, a "uniform study," to be learned and mastered by every foreign-missionary supporter. In addition to nonfiction reports and letters from the field, the missionary magazines for women featured stories, poems, and graphic visual materials, reflecting the evangelicals' flexibility and wide-ranging interests in adapting print media to their message.[16]

"Taking the magazine" consequently became a major part of the membership process. Some of the magazines could boast circulations of nearly 25,000, and while the number of subscriptions never approached the number of members, local auxiliaries never relented in their push to make every member a subscriber.[17] Increasingly, the national leadership regarded the magazine as the centerpiece of the auxiliary system, encouraging a program of active self-study and group study of every issue. Weekly or monthly meetings were encouraged to offer "systematically-arranged programmes of essays, readings, recitations, and music." "We must have something to talk about better than cake-making or flounces," wrote an 1873 Methodist contributor to *Heathen Woman's Friend*, revealing a certain impatience with the traditional notion of women's singular commitment to domesticity. "We must have missionaries' letters, when we can get them,—anything, everything that will bring this most noble and Christly work close to our slow, selfish hearts." As for the nature of the missionary letters, the organizational leadership clearly expected them to be "frank and confiding, such as can only be written to mothers and sisters." A Mrs. Anderson of Boston, a Congregationalist, had urged as early as 1869 the creation of a missionary curriculum based on these field reports. "What we need," she wrote, "is to make the missionary work a study . . . [we need] to take up missions, one after another, becoming acquainted with geography, history, etc. Few know how much the minds and hearts of our women may become enlarged, enlightened and quickened in duty, by such a course." In this way, women's foreign-missionary societies took on the function of both "lyceum and prayer-meeting" at least two decades before the formation of the General Federation of Women's Clubs, usually regarded as the great agency of female self-culture.[18]

As early as 1878, Methodist women, under the leadership of Harriet Merrick Warren, editor of *Heathen Woman's Friend*, inaugurated an outline "Uniform Study" which was designed to assist local societies in "pursuing a systematic course of study of missionary subjects." Typically, readings focused on the geography and social customs of the heathens about to be Christianized. The Methodist reading course, for example, was devoted in April 1896 to "Social

[16] Montgomery, *Western Women*, 38. For a discussion of evangelical communications theory, see Brumberg, *Mission for Life*, 64–68, 70–78, 219–21.

[17] Circulation figures are extremely difficult to ascertain. *Heathen Woman's Friend* had a circulation of 25,000 in 1872 and 22,000 in 1895. See Baker, *Story of the Woman's Foreign Missionary Society*, 74–76.

[18] E. J. K., "One of Many," *Heathen Woman's Friend*, 5 (Aug. 1873), 510; J. F. W., "Missionary Sociables," *ibid.* 509; I. H., "Uniform Readings," *ibid.*, 13 (Aug. 1881), 39; *Life and Light for Heathen Women*, 1 (March 1869), 6; *ibid.* (Dec. 1869), 132. For the history and structure of the General Federation of Women's Clubs, see Ellen M. Henrotin, "The Attitude of Women's Clubs and Associations toward Social Economics" *Bulletin of the Department of Labor*, 4 (July 1899), 501–45.

Life among African Women," in May it was given over to "Girl Life in the Orient," and in June it featured reading and discussion of "High-Caste Woman in India." Didactic reading, however, was not the only pedagogical technique. The "moral map" of the world, a colorful graphic device for illustrating the alarming presence of heathenism around the globe, was a popular teaching aid, as was the chalkboard. "We believe," wrote an 1881 contributor to the Methodist magazine, "the time has come when a blackboard exercise will have a place on the programme of every missionary meeting. The work need not be very elaborate till the ladies become accustomed to handling the crayon. A mere outline of the country under attention, with the principal natural features, . . . would form a basis for a few minutes' paper or remarks."[19]

The concept of "uniform study" was designed to substitute information for sheer sociability at meetings; it also implied authority, legitimatizing time spent on missionary activity. Uniform study ultimately fostered the gratifying conclusion that a study group really did approximate a formal classroom. Members were encouraged to discuss the information and master a variety of facts about the world evangelization movement. A typical "Question Meeting," sponsored by the Newark, New Jersey, branch of the Woman's Foreign Mission Society in 1881, revolved around a number of questions published in the magazine, such as: "How does our Society compare as to organization and efficiency with similar societies in other churches?" "Has the gospel been preached in every nation?" "What is the greatest barrier in the mind of a Chinese in receiving Christ as his present Saviour?"[20] Other formats were based on questions with stock answers which were then used as responsive readings, a technique that heightened the individual's sense of participation in the group and strengthened the conviction of common ideals. For example, the auxiliary leader might pose the question: "What event of this century is most important and far reaching in its power for good to the human race?" In this case, a self-congratulatory answer was supplied by the group: "The higher education of woman, and her service in giving the gospel to the secluded women of the world; in a word, the organization of Woman's Boards of Missions." Much of the self-study, however, focused on the mastery of fac-

[19] Baker, *Story of the Woman's Foreign Missionary Society*, 75–76; "Study for the Month," *Women's Missionary Friend*, 27 (April 1896), 289; *ibid.* (May 1896), 318; *ibid.* (June 1896), 349; I. H., "Uniform Readings," 38–39; *Life and Light for Heathen Women*, 1 (Dec. 1869), 132; *ibid.* (March 1870), 165–66; "Home Department," *Heathen Woman's Friend*, 12 (April 1881), 235. For a detailed pedagogical guide to foreign-mission study for women's groups, see Helen Barrett Montgomery, *How to Use: A Handbook of Suggestions to Accompany the Text-book Western Women in Eastern Lands* (Boston, [1910]). Montgomery was particularly fond of visual devices; for example, she described a chart in pyramid form, which represented, in the form of colored blocks of varying lengths, the expenditures of American women. At the base, representing the largest amount, was candy (178 millions) followed by ice cream sodas (107 millions), tea and coffee (98 millions), patent medicine (75 millions), jewelry (60 millions), chewing gum (15 millions), and, in the smallest category, foreign missions (4 millions). *Ibid.*, 58. Montgomery reported on a number of techniques for demonstrating the possible resources of the churches for missionary work.

[20] "Home Department," *Heathen Woman's Friend*, 12 (April 1881), 233; Lilly Ryder Gracey, ed., *Gist: A Handbook of Missionary Information Pre-eminently for Use in Young Women's Circles* (Cincinnati, 1893), 12.

tual material, generally of a quantitative nature, which was designed to produce a sense of urgency about evangelization work. For example, missionary study groups were fond of memorizing the ratio of Christians to heathen worldwide and then calculating the rate at which the evangelization of the world might occur.[21]

Materials geared to developing women's overall conception of the emancipatory nature of Christianity versus the oppressions of the "ethnic religions" were pervasive. "We live in a country where the discussion of 'Woman's Rights' is ever to the front," wrote Montgomery. "We are to study lands where they are just beginning to recognize woman's wrongs—lands where the slogan 'Ladies First' is consistently and persistently 'Ladies Last.'" Unlike the United States, where "wrongs against women" were set in contradistinction to Protestant Christianity, the "wrongs of Hindu, Chinese, and Moslem women [were] buttressed behind the sanctions of religion, and . . . indorsed by the founders of their faith."[22] Having established an angle of double vision, the mass of American women came to use cross-cultural information to support rather than to challenge gender and family arrangements in their own country. Churchgoing American women, largely preoccupied with ameliorating what they considered to be the degraded condition of their non-Christian sisters, were generally skeptical of, if not downright hostile to, the emergence of an indigenous feminist political movement and its critique of sexual subordination at home.[23] Rather than examine their own social relations, the bulk of American Protestant women sought to define themselves by what they were not. Indeed, the "otherness" of the non-Christian became the central message of their ethnology.

The catalog of heathen activities against women constituted the central proof of the evangelical charge that heathens were, by definition, misogynous. Although the word *misogyny* never appeared in these texts, hatred of women was identified as a central tenet in a number of faiths. For example, after having studied the work of Manu, a Hindu lawgiver, an Indian Christian convert proclaimed "I have never read any sacred book in Sanskrit literature without meeting this hateful sentiment about women." According to reports, Hindu abasement of women was so extreme that the government of British India was forced to exclude from the mails, "as obscene matter," the sacred scriptures of Hinduism. Muslims and Buddhists were also considered misogynous; as proof, missionary ethnologists were fond of reporting how demeaned Buddhist women prayed for the reward of being born a man in a future transmigration. Given their faith in the misogynistic core of all who were not Christian, the female readership pursued discussions of the relative merits and demerits of being born in China as compared to Africa, in Turkey as compared to India. Missionary enthusiasts structured their discussions around questions such as: "In what non-Christian lands do girls receive as good an education as boys?"

[21] Gracey, ed., *Gist*, 9–12.

[22] Montgomery, *Western Women*, 45–46.

[23] The relationship between evangelicalism and feminism is discussed in Brumberg, *Mission for Life*, 79–106.

"In what lands do women eat with their husbands at a family table?" "If you were to be born a woman in a non-Christian land, where would you choose to be born?"[24]

In the vast missionary literature of heathen female debasement, three general categories of reportage consistently emerge: intellectual deprivation, domestic oppression, and sexual degradation. In each category there were specific social practices upon which American Protestant women chose repeatedly to focus their attentions. Therefore, the assumption here is that these formulaic descriptions are less than random and that they reveal as much about the experiences and values of the ethnologists as about the society being studied.

Not surprisingly, the absence of the Bible among non-Christians underlay all observations about the general intellectual deprivation of heathens, be they female or male. The missionary's essential task was, after all, to supply the Gospel to the unenlightened; "How can they know, if they have not heard?" was the popular evangelical refrain. Consequently, Bible reading was part and parcel of the evangelical program to extend literacy to both men and women. Observers typically reported a sexual differential, however. "In India," reported one missionary, "only one man in 42 and one woman in 858 can read or write."[25] Women's inferior access to educational opportunities was uniformly noted, while the work of women missionaries in establishing schools for heathen girls was touted as an important cultural advance. In fact, religious women reveled in the way in which their organizations were ringing the world with educational institutions where heathen girls might function "as if they were at Mt. Holyoke."[26] Evangelical reports moved beyond simple illiteracy, however, to the description of a pervasive intellectual vapidity among women, a vapidity fostered by the heathen social practice of the zenana.

The zenana was, in fact, one of the primary instruments of woman's seclusion in the larger purdah system. In both Muslim and Hindu societies, purdah, meaning curtain, set limitations on interactions between women and men outside certain well-defined categories. Among Muslims, for example, women were accessible to male kin; among Hindus they were not. The zenana, a segregated living space for the exclusive use of women and the men they could see without violating rules of modesty, varied with social class. Among the very wealthy, the zenana meant separate entrances and, often, sumptuous private apartments; among the urban poor, where economic resources could not support separate residences, purdah might be observed by seclusion within a single room, by limiting male entrance to the house, or by simply hanging a curtain. In addition to variations in physical form, zenanas incorporated different female age groups. Among Muslim women the restrictions of purdah

[24] Montgomery, *Western Women*, 47, 58–59, 65, 75–76; *Life and Light for Women*, 25 (April 1895), 12.

[25] Gracey, ed., *Gist*, 33.

[26] Mount Holyoke Seminary was the model for Congregationalist activity. See *Life and Light for Heathen Women*, 2 (Sept. 1869), 85; *ibid.* (March 1870), 156.

commenced at puberty; among Hindus seclusion generally began with marriage. Within the zenana women engaged in traditional women's work: cleaning and maintenance of house and possessions, child care, food preparation, spinning, sewing, weaving, and other handicrafts. Women in strict purdah did not, of course, leave their homes to purchase daily food supplies or to negotiate with artisans or merchants.[27]

Among missionary ethnologists, distinctions between zenanas, based on class, locale, and religious tradition were flattened, resulting in a formulaic portrait. In the hands of the evangelicals, the zenana was never rendered as a collective workplace but as a symbol of enforced female isolation from the world. This kind of involuntary seclusion, it was argued, had serious intellectual consequences for women. The zenana was uniformly pictured as a place of indolence and monotony. "Try seriously to contemplate ourselves within the doomed circle [of the zenana]," urged a missionary pedagogue. "All day long, and every day, for years in and years out, in one room; four bare walls, and nothing more to look at but a square patch of sky occasionally. What should we think about?" Selections from Evelyn Baring, Earl of Cromer and the British ambassador to Egypt, lent authority to Montgomery's perspective on the zenana: "[it] cramps the intellect and withers the mental development of one-half the population of Moslem countries." According to Baring's firsthand report, when an Englishwoman asked an Egyptian lady how she passed her time, the Egyptian responded in a languid manner: "I sit on this sofa . . . and when I am tired I cross over and sit on that."[28]

As symbol of purdah, mental torpor, and physical lethargy, the zenana loomed large in the missionary ethnology, explaining why it became a focal point of so many evangelization activities emanating from the United States and Great Britain. In fact, the zenana was used to rationalize the very creation of an autonomous women's foreign-mission crusade. Women missionaries might enter these private female domains while male missionaries could not. Thus the penetration of the zenana by Christian womanhood became an important strategic implement in the evangelical arsenal. Methodist American women, for example, made "zenana visiting" central to their proselytization efforts as did the members of the Church of England's Zenana Missionary Society. The missionary magazines carried stories of attempts, both successful and failed, of American women who sought to introduce "spiritual" or gospel themes among ignorant and cloistered women. "This is . . . the work," reported Isabel Hart, "through which the social foundations of heathen nations are being undermined."[29] Clearly, the way to affect the stagnation im-

[27] For ethnographic descriptions of the contemporary zenana and its place in the purdah system, see Hanna Papanek, "Purdah: Separate Worlds and Symbolic Shelter," *Comparative Studies in Society and History*, 15 (June 1973), 289–325; Patricia Jeffery, *Frogs in a Well: Indian Women in Purdah* (London, 1979); Elizabeth Warnock Fernea, *Guests of the Sheik* (Garden City, N.Y., 1965). Keith Hjortshoj touches on the zenana and the architecture of seclusion in Old Lucknow (pre-1856) in Keith Hjortshoj, *Urban Structures and Transformations in Lucknow, India* (Ithaca, 1979), 46–47, 50–51, 61–62, 64.

[28] Gracey, ed., *Gist*, 38; Montgomery, *Western Women*, 81.

[29] *Historical Sketches*, 86–87.

plied by the zenana was acceptance of the Christian message with all the self-study components of which middle-class American women were so fond.

The American woman's horror of female social isolation in the zenana can also be read as a subconscious criticism of the nineteenth-century cult of domesticity. By 1900, American middle-class women were in obvious tension with the notion of separate spheres. Although home life was mostly a world of women, children, and servant girls, with men absent a good portion of the day to professional and business offices, an expanding interest in athletics and physical fitness, nature, popular entertainments, and civic affairs moved many women beyond sheer domesticity. For some, these new activities forced recognition of woman's very real isolation from the centers of power in industrial America. Yet, for the most part, the middle-class American woman regarded the nuclear family environment in America, however much it was privatized, as something quite distinct from the seclusion implied by the zenana. Her private world demanded that she cultivate and refine her skills as both domestic manager and mother in order to extend the sphere of her influence.[30]

With this distinction in view, evangelical observers were struck by the fact that among heathen women there were, allegedly, no codified, formal rules of wifely or domestic behavior. "The duties of a perfect housewife for a Hindoo family are, indeed, not defined," wrote a woman missionary; "consequently . . . women enter on their earthly career quite ignorant of the responsibility attached to it."[31] Clearly, illiterate women in less developed areas of the world operated in their homes without benefit of the authoritative domestic guidebooks, such as Catharine Beecher's well-known *Treatise on Domestic Economy*, which were linked in the American context to the formation of the middle class. Given the evangelicals' religious predisposition to the authority of text, the lack of both domestic guidebook and Bible compounded the heathen woman's cultural handicap. The assumption that a lacuna was created by the absence of these texts informs the development of the evangelical ethnology and its subsequent description of female behavior both within the zenana and without.

In the literature of heathen domestic oppression, Protestant women's essential faith in monogamy and companionate marriage served as bedrock for further elaborations.[32] Most reports attested to the authoritarianism of heathen husbands and the acquiescence of their wives:

[30] The notion of separate spheres underlies these works: Nancy F. Cott, *The Bonds of Womanhood: "Woman's Sphere" in New England, 1780-1835* (New Haven, 1977); Ann Douglas, *The Feminization of American Culture* (New York, 1977); Mary P. Ryan, *Cradle of the Middle Class: The Family in Oneida County, New York, 1790-1865* (Cambridge, Eng., 1981); Kathryn Kish Sklar, *Catharine Beecher: A Study in American Domesticity* (New Haven, 1973); Barbara Welter, "The Cult of True Womanhood: 1820-1860," *American Quarterly*, 18 (Summer 1966), 151-74; and Barbara Welter, "The Feminization of American Religion: 1800-1860," in *Clio's Consciousness Raised: New Perspectives on the History of Women*, ed. Mary S. Hartman and Lois Banner (New York, 1974), 137-57.

[31] "The Education of the Hindoo Women," *Heathen Woman's Friend*, 3 (Nov. 1871), 200.

[32] I rely here on the conception of companionate marriage in Lawrence Stone, *The Family, Sex and Marriage in England, 1500-1800* (New York, 1979), 234-45, 262-63.

"A woman [in India] has no other god than her husband. Though he be aged, infirm, a drunkard, or debauchee, she must still regard him as her god. If he laughs, she must also laugh; if he weeps, she must weep; if he sings, she must be in ecstasy; she must never eat till he is satisfied. If he abstains from food, she must fast; and she must abstain from whatever food he dislikes." Under such bondage, is it any wonder that there are millions of women to whom the words "love" and "home" have no meaning?

George Washburn, a Congregationalist missionary in Constantinople, told the readership of *Life and Light for Heathen Women* that in Turkey women had no authority within marriage because they "are not recognized in society save as the servants and slaves of men." A report from China concluded that marital relations in that country were also shaped by "the idea that woman exists only for the convenience of man, and scarcely shares the same nature." Notably, these reports specified the authoritarianism of husbands rather than fathers, and the denominational magazines included stories and pictures of women consigned to routinely fanning their husbands or walking behind them in the street.[33]

Formulaic reports from a variety of areas also noted how women patiently served meals but were forbidden to eat with their husbands.[34] This interest in the social relations of eating was tied to the reality of middle-class family life in the late nineteenth century. By the 1870s middle-class families were apt to be brought meals cooked and served by domestic servants who ate apart from the family. As Faye Dudden has demonstrated, these immigrant girls and women, hired in an impersonal labor market, had a strikingly different relationship to the family than had the perennial hired girl or "help" who characterized an earlier era. Because of their need to manage these servants, middle-class women were absolutely familiar with the statuses implied by the social relations of eating. In addition, the meal itself had taken on a new social significance. As relationships within the family were reshaped by the husband's daily absence to a separate place of work, the children's attendance in public schools, and the wife's commitment to religious and secular charitable activities beyond the home, family meals among the middle class became veritable "seasons of privacy."[35]

The use of women as beasts of burden in agricultural areas of Africa and Persia was also an element in the missionary ethnology. One report, typical of many others, observed that women in Africa looked "like pack-mules rather than women." From the Orient came another metaphoric description lamenting the lot of "helpless woman, priced as cattle in the market, crippled, led in

[33] Gracey, ed., *Gist*, 39–40, 20–21; *Life and Light for Heathen Women*, 1 (March 1869), 7–8; *Heathen Woman's Friend*, 4 (May 1873), 453.

[34] *Heathen Woman's Friend*, 4 (May 1873), 453; Ione Barbee, "Women without Opportunity," *Woman's Missionary Friend*, 29 (April 1898), 313; *Life and Light for Women*, 1 (June 1870), 191; *ibid.*, 25 (March 1895), 6.

[35] Catharine Beecher recommended explicitly that servants should eat in the kitchen and not with the family. Catherine Beecher, *Letters to Persons Who Are Engaged in Domestic Service* (New York, 1842), 87–89; Faye Evelyn Dudden, "From Help to Domestics: American Servants, 1800–1880" (Ph.D. diss., University of Rochester, 1981), 1–97; Harriet Beecher Stowe [Christopher Crowfield], *The Chimney-Corner* (Boston, 1868), 18.

flesh-encrusted chains." This conception of the non-Christians' exploitative use of female labor and the female body was perpetuated in the responsive readings that young women supporters of missions were encouraged to commit to memory. To the question "What is the condition of women among the Muslims?" the readers replied that Muslim women, in addition to being generally "degraded and ignorant," were "made to labor in the fields like animals; and treated as slaves."[36]

The domestic oppression of heathen women in their marriages was documented further by material that stressed the inequality of power and status within the conjugal relationship. The most dramatic examples of this, of course, were citations of wife abuse and wife beating, the latter being tied most directly to Muslim countries where, purportedly, the Koran sanctioned "scouring and beating" of wives. In Syria, Lilly Ryder Gracey reported that the murder of women and girls within the Muslim family went virtually unnoticed. When male tyranny was combined with opium use, as in the Chinese case, women fared very badly, often losing both their material possessions and their children to satisfy the husband's noxious habit. A particularly lurid 1910 report by Montgomery told of a wife who, after losing her home and her infant son, was hired out by her depraved spouse as a wet nurse; when, in time, her breasts became dry, the husband sold her to a leper.[37]

Still further but less dramatic evidence of women's oppression within marriage was the fact that heathen men in social situations throughout Africa, the Middle East, and the Orient never introduced their wives to either friends or strangers. That women were regarded as socially invisible flew in the face of the middle-class American woman's perception of her own important social and cultural role, personified in the hyperbolic "Cult of True Womanhood."[38] Consequently, the social affront symbolized by nonrecognition was a persistent theme in the evangelical ethnology, and women missionaries were proud of reporting how a general Christian influence affected manners. When at a public reception in 1895 a Korean official for the first time introduced his wife by name, Mrs. M. F. Scranton wrote enthusiastically of the meaning of this small gesture: "Perhaps this may seem an insignificant affair to you, but to us who are here and who know about the secluded and narrow lives of Korean women, it seems a most important and significant event."[39]

Reports of polygamy enlarged the conception of domestic oppression in non-Christian society. Actual numerical descriptions of the number of wives held by heathen men varied widely; Montgomery wrote in 1910 that in Palestine

[36] Gracey, ed., *Gist*, 53-54, 106, 113; *Life and Light for Women*, 25 (April 1895), 10; *Life and Light for Heathen Women*, 1 (June 1869), 53.

[37] Gracey, ed., *Gist*, 101-02; *Life and Light for Heathen Women*, 1 (March 1869), 7-8; Montgomery, *Western Women*, 78. Montgomery's report was excerpted from Official Minutes of 1908 Foochow Woman's Conference, 1908.

[38] See Welter, "Cult of True Womanhood," 151-74; Mary P. Ryan, *Womanhood in America: From Colonial Times to the Present* (New York, 1975), 139-91; Barbara J. Berg, *The Remembered Gate: Origins of American Feminism: The Woman and the City, 1800-1860* (New York, 1978), 75-94.

[39] Mrs. M. F. Scranton, "A Social Advance," *Heathen Woman's Friend*, 27 (Sept. 1895), 65.

"ten or eleven wives [was] not at all uncommon," but a very early missionary report recalled how the forty-seven wives of the Prince of Marava were all burned together on their husband's funeral pyre.[40] In a very basic sense, polygamy was treated as unacceptable because it was seen as the social construction of sexually insatiable men. This was the common leitmotiv in the virulent domestic campaign against Mormon polygamy which paralleled the flowering of the women's foreign-mission crusade.[41] The critique of polygamy abroad, however, had a somewhat different emphasis in that it highlighted the ways in which the practice poisoned relations among women. For example, missionary ethnologists were fond of pointing out that for women in the Middle East there was an inverse relationship between money and happiness precisely because Muslim males inevitably translated their financial success into sexual excess, meaning additional wives. In this situation, competition among the wives for resources and affection was unavoidable. Thus, polygamy deprived women in their role as wives of the "domestic felicity" that was part and parcel of the Christian companionate marriage. "Who can describe the wretchedness and wrong, the untold degradation and corruptions, hidden in the harems of Turkey?" asked Gracey. "Shut in completely to themselves, [women are] the prey of jealousy, envy, and every evil passion."[42] Implicit in this ethnological account was the belief that monogamy's value lay in its elimination of competition among women.

Pervasive accounts of patrilocal living arrangements throughout the Middle East and the Orient contained further elaborations of the notion that there was a competitive rather than a cooperative spirit among heathen women. In particular, mothers-in-law and daughters-in-law were described as intrinsically hostile to one another. The daughter-in-law's structurally weak position in the patrilineal, patrilocal family was symbolized in reports that told of her deferential relations with the mother-in-law. In 1869, for example, *Life and Light for Heathen Woman* informed its readers that Turkish brides forced to leave their natal families were forbidden for over one year to even speak out loud in the presence of the mother-in-law.[43] From the perspective of middle-class American women, among whom marriage generally meant a separate household of one's own, patrilocalism, in particular, raised enormous problems of home management. In addition, new research on the kinship systems of nineteenth-century American families reveals how much American women invested in matrilocal rather than patrilocal networks; a study of Michigan families between 1820 and 1920 indicates that women—despite enormous geographic distances—relied heavily on their own mothers and sisters for eco-

[40] Montgomery, *Western Women*, 53; "Horrid Pagan Customs," *Massachusetts Baptist Missionary Magazine*, 3 (Dec. 1813), 355-56.

[41] See Klaus J. Hansen, *Mormonism and the American Experience* (Chicago, 1981), 140-46. According to Sen. Frederick T. DuBois (Idaho), "There was a universal detestation of polygamy, and inasmuch as the Mormons openly defended it we were given a very effective weapon with which to attack." *Ibid.*, 145.

[42] Gracey, ed., *Gist*, 92-93.

[43] *Life and Light for Heathen Women*, 1 (March 1869), 7-8; "Education of the Hindoo Women," 201; Montgomery, *Western Women*, 78-80. The report on education of Hindu women observed that so long as their in-laws are alive, women "exercise no influence."

nomic and emotional support across the individual and the family life cycle.[44] Immersed in what Carroll Smith-Rosenberg has called a "female world of love and ritual," middle-class Protestant women belabored the vulnerability of the heathen female who appeared to be without a similiar system of social or economic support.[45]

The ethnological descriptions of generational relations among non-Christians also underscored a lack of common interest and even a duplicity among women. For example, the short magazine biographies of heathen girls adopted by Methodist missionary groups regularly included accounts of how these young women came to be orphaned. More often than not, the attribution of blame fell not to natural causes but to an older woman—a mother, grandmother, aunt, or village hag—who subjected young girls to some kind of indignity. One converted adoptee was allegedly rescued at age eight from "an old woman who had trained [her] for [a] dancing [girl], and intended to make her fortune" from her.[46] So, too, physical mutilation of girls, primarily in the form of Chinese foot-binding and Burmese ear and nose boring, was also linked to the initiative of older women, particularly mothers. In both cases, mothers were described as implicated in the act of mutilation because of concern for their daughter's attractiveness as a potential marriage partner. Among the heathen, so the thinking went, the mother's self-hatred and low expectations resulted in the passing-on of her afflictions. For example, foot-binding, reported an 1897 magazine, was "inflicted by the mothers, buoyed up by the hope that this coveted charm will secure [for the girls] a good position in life."[47] Rather than treat ear boring as a classic rite of passage, accounts were used as testimony that relations among heathen women were nonsupportive: "amid the shrieks of the young lady victims and the shouting of the older women, who hold them down, the holes are made, and pieces of string are inserted."[48] Thus, it was implied that heathen women contributed to the victimization of their daughters, insuring that the cycle of female abuse continued.[49]

[44] George Peter Murdock, *Social Structure* (New York, 1949), 16, 18. The matrilocal nature of American family life was asserted by Ellen M. Henrotin, "The Social Status of American Women," in Kate Byam Martin and Ellen M. Henrotin, *The Social Status of European and American Women* (Chicago, 1887), 38. See also Marilyn Ferris Motz, "True Sisterhood: The Female Family in Nineteenth-Century Michigan" (Ph.D. diss., University of Michigan, 1981), 157-77, 230-35.

[45] Carroll Smith-Rosenberg, "The Female World of Love and Ritual: Relations between Women in Nineteenth-Century America," *Signs*, 1 (Autumn 1975), 1-29.

[46] Mrs. M. A. Thomas, "Sketches of the Orphan Girls Supported by the New York Branch," *Heathen Woman's Friend*, 2 (May 1871), 123; Fannie J. Sparks, "Sketches of the Orphan Girls Supported by the New York Branch," *ibid.*, 4 (Jan. 1873), 394; Wilma H. Rouse, "A Modern Hannah," *ibid.*, 27 (July 1895), 3.

[47] Mrs. C. M. Jewell, "Footbinding," *Woman's Missionary Friend*, 29 (Oct. 1897), 112-14; S. H. Woolston, "Dress of Chinese Women," *Heathen Woman's Friend*, 4 (Jan. 1873), 402; "Family News," *ibid.*, 27 (July 1895), 13; *Life and Light for Heathen Women*, 1 (Sept. 1870), 223-24. A Natural Feet Society, founded in the 1890s by women missionaries and enlightened indigenous Chinese, received attention in the magazines.

[48] Gracey, ed. *Gist*, 122.

[49] For a related analysis see Nancy Chodorow, "Family Structure and Feminine Personality" in *Woman, Culture, and Society*, ed. Michelle Zimbalist Rosaldo and Louise Lamphere (Stanford, 1974), 43-66.

In this sense, both heathen patrilocalism and the mutilation of girls were used to set the American middle-class experience in relief. Only in Christian society, so the thinking went, did women's shared concerns and networks form the basis of community social life. Nineteenth-century American women were, in fact, prone to exalted testaments to the associative power of their sex, congratulating themselves for the plethora of women's organizations that represented the formalization of their cooperative tendencies. The heathen woman's failure to create any comparable sisterhood of agencies was seen, from the perspective of the didactic ethnology, as proof of the debilitating effects of heathen culture on the development of female personality.[50]

Accounts of woman's sexual degradation, the third and final category of evangelical reportage, were more oblique. Neither heterosexual intercourse nor rape, for example, was ever detailed or called by name. In fact, with the exception of a few accounts of "consecrated prostitution" (that is, girls who inhabited religious shrines in India, offering themselves to male pilgrims as part of the worship), literal or graphic descriptions of women's sexual lives or of heathen sexual practices were nonexistent.[51] Victorian standards of propriety among the missionary ethnologists and their readership precluded overt discussion of sexual acts. The question then is how did the evangelicals create an impression of generalized sexual degradation among heathen women without resort to explicit information about it?

The answer lies in the evangelical conception of the relationship between culture and the female life course. Not only woman's personality but the timing and sequencing of her life events were related to cultural considerations. This focus on the life course of heathen women provided a less explicit but nonetheless effective way of talking about sexual degradation. The exploitation of heathen women was implied in a single transitional event that violated middle-class American values and contrasted sharply with middle-class American experience. In essence, the evangelical case for female sexual degradation centered on the early loss of virginity through child marriage, which in turn implied the absence of "girlhood" or adolescence as well as premature aging.

Women's missionary periodicals were uniformly preoccupied with the heathen practice of child and infant marriage—what one commentator called "legalized lust."[52] The awful fate that awaited girls in non-Christian lands was a popular justification for the missionary school program overseas. An article by Abbie B. Child, in an 1871 missionary edition for children, stated the case quite clearly:

[50] See May Wright Sewall, ed., *The World's Congress of Representative Women* (Chicago, 1894), xxiv, 15, 19, 37–38, 147–48, 258, 297.

[51] Montgomery, *Western Women*, 65. The sale of "girls and women for all sorts of purposes" was mentioned in the magazines. See, for example, "Mosaic," *Heathen Woman's Friend*, 5 (March 1874), 622.

[52] Montgomery, *Western Women*, 60; Louise Ellwanger, "Another Zenana Convert," *Heathen Woman's Friend*, 2 (May 1871), 121; Mrs. E. E. Baldwin, "Celebration of a Chinese Betrothal," *ibid.*, 4 (May 1873), 456; "Mosaic," 624; Rouse, "Modern Hannah," 3–4; *Life and Light for Women*, 30 (Oct. 1900), 437; *ibid.* (March 1900), 109.

I wonder if the girls in America, as they trudge along to school with their mother's good-by kiss still warm on their lips, with their heads full of ambition to be at the head of the class, or busy with merry sports . . . could ever guess the reason that the little Hawaiian girls want to go to school. I don't think you could, if you should try a long, long time. I will let you peep into one of Mrs. Bingham's letters, and see if she can tell us. Oh yes! this is it. She says that one day one of the natives came to her, holding a small brighteyed girl by the hand and said, "Won't you take my little Ruth, away from her sister's husband? He is determined to have her—not for his adopted daughter, not for a playmate for his children, but—for his wife!" That doesn't seem to be such a very strange thing in that country for Mrs. Bingham says that there is another child by her side who wants to go [to school] for the same reason.[53]

Magazine stories and reports also detailed the family circumstances and the exotic weddings of child brides. In 1896, Clara A. Swain, a well-known Methodist medical missionary, wrote of a spectacular wedding ceremony that included 2,500 persons, 300 camels, 500 horses, and 9 elephants. Swain said of the child bride: "Poor little Bai, only twelve years old, with such a host of things to take charge of."[54] Commentary on the child bride's new responsibilities rarely included explicit mention of the consummation of the marriage, although the implication was clear, particularly in those cases where the age of the husband testified to his capability to perform adult heterosexual activity.

Child marriage was portrayed as a consistent evil across cultures, giving the reports a formulaic aspect: child brides forced from their natal homes were subjected to the tyranny of mothers-in-law and abused by husbands; sexual relations were generally initiated at about age thirteen or fourteen, at the instigation of the mother-in-law; first children were born by age sixteen; when future births resulted in a succession of girls, the heathen mother was led to the unthinkable—the strangulation of her own infant daughter. Female infanticide in this rendering was as much the result of woman's desperation as it was a pure expression of misogyny.[55]

Child marriage also resulted in a large number of "child widows," of whom there were an estimated half million in 1901.[56] The "child widow," as presented in the magazines, was a young Hindu woman whose early marriage had never been consummated; yet she was forced unfairly to live a marked and dreary life as a widow because of her spouse's death. A "child widow" could

[53] Abbie B. Child, "Hawaiian Girls," *Life and Light for Heathen Women*, 2 (March 1871), 44-45.

[54] Clara A. Swain, "A Marriage in High Life," *Woman's Missionary Friend*, 28 (Aug. 1896), 35-36.

[55] One woman destroyed seven female children by "her own hand," according to Gracey, ed., *Gist*, 20-21. For general references to infanticide, see *ibid.*, 34; J. M. Thoburn, "Contradictory Missionary Reports," *Heathen Woman's Friend*, 3 (Nov. 1871), 198-99; Elsie Marshall, "Child-Life in China," *Woman's Missionary Friend*, 27 (June 1896), 332; *Life and Light for Women*, 10 (April 1880), 122-23. Montgomery, *Western Women*, 47-48, also reports that in addition to female infanticide, girls committed suicide in groups rather than consent to early marriages. Among feminist reformers, Elizabeth Cady Stanton was known for her defense of Hester Vaughn, accused of infanticide in 1868. See Alma Lutz, *Created Equal: A Biography of Elizabeth Cady Stanton, 1815-1902* (New York, 1940), 162-63.

[56] For an estimate of close to 400,000 under 15 years of age, see Montgomery, *Western Women*, 62. An estimate of 667,000 widows below the age of nineteen appears in Gracey, ed., *Gist*, 41.

not remarry. Gracey told her readers: "Practically, every Hindu girl of good caste is either a wife or a widow before she reaches the age of fourteen. In hundreds of thousands of cases the child [widow] has never known what it is to be a wife." Thus, the "child widow," according to the Christian view, was a wife only on a technicality. Consequently, evangelical women were strenuous in their efforts to improve her lot, giving both emotional and monetary support to the campaign for a "child widow" school led by Pundita Ramabai, an educated, high-caste Indian convert to Christianity and herself a widow. Ramabai, who presented an authoritative voice on the general debasement of Hindu women, visited the United States on at least two occasions, telling the "child widow" story to missionary groups. Her school at Poona, India, pictured and described in the missionary magazines, was a bucolic and overtly Christian antidote to the social ostracism that followed the "child widow."[57]

According to evangelical ethnologists, the demographic consequences of child marriage were to be found in the "girlless villages" of the Middle East and Far East. A typical report, from a Congregationalist missionary named Olive Parmelee, noted that in Turkey "one sees among the heathen only little girls and older women." A Methodist bishop acknowledged the same reports in 1871. The "girlless village," which at first hearing might seem to refer to the effects of female infanticide, was actually a trope, signifying the perceived absence of female adolescence in non-Christian society. "The women marry so very young," explained Parmelee, "that they are deprived of all those pretty girlish years from twelve to twenty." In a similar vein, Ella J. Glover, a Methodist missionary in Tientsin, reported that "there is hardly such a thing [as girlhood] known in China, outside of Christian schools."[58] The "girlless village," then, was the ethnologists' way of reporting that among the heathen there was no observable period of dependency in which young women capable of reproduction were sheltered and protected by family or community.

The absence of girlhood among the heathen was used to set the American middle-class experience in relief. "Think of our careless happy girls in their early teens in contrast with this little Hindu wife and mother," wrote a missionary in her life history of one Anandabai Joshee, "who was a mother at twelve." In 1906, a missionary council's description of Muslim women contrasted their "failing brain power" at fourteen or fifteen to the Christian girl's receptivity and quickness. The heathen girl "is like a flower closing," they wrote, "so far as mental effort goes." Provoked by the tragedy of a teenage Turkish mother, Parmelee told her readers: "As I look at her delicate face, with its almost childish look, I am reminded of dear little girls of thirteen or fourteen in America, whom we should shelter very carefully in the home circle for many years."[59] In fact, American middle-class families were doing just

[57] Gracey, ed., *Gist*, 41–43; *Life and Light for Women*, 30 (March 1900), 97–100.

[58] *Life and Light for Heathen Women*, 1 (Sept. 1869), 87; Thoburn, "Contradictory Missionary Reports," 198–99; *Life and Light for Heathen Women*, 1 (Sept. 1869), 87; "Our Post-Office Box," *Woman's Missionary Friend*, 27 (June 1896), 347.

[59] *Life and Light for Women*, 30 (March 1900), 101; Montgomery, *Western Women*, 56; *Life and Light for Heathen Women*, 1 (March 1869), 88.

what Parmelee prescribed. By the 1890s, adolescent girls among the middle class were delaying marriage until their mid-twenties, attending public high schools in disproportionately high numbers, and leaving traditional forms of female work, such as domestic service, to newly arrived immigrant girls. Moreover, their time outside of school was increasingly organized around institutionally sponsored programs for girls, often cast in the model of their mothers' religious, charity, and reform work. All of the national women's foreign-missionary groups, for example, encouraged the formation and development of young ladies associations.[60]

Unable to identify any comparable experience among non-Christians, women cast heathendom both as girlless and as conducive to premature aging. Gracey told her young readers that women age rapidly under heathendom: "As a rule, youth is past at twenty-five; and at thirty or forty a woman looks sixty or seventy."[61] Repeatedly, the magazines linked premature aging to early marriage. Asked why Indian women had "no constitution" and died young, an evangelical writer responded:

> How can she [survive] with a child mother, child grandmother, and all her female ancestry in their teens? In the training of a little girl there are some things unspeakable which undermine her physically and morally; she herself may know the throes of childbirth while a little girl of thirteen or fourteen. . . . I think I am safe in saying that the number of physical wrecks is not much lower than that of healthy well-developed women . . . the[se] women are old while their sisters in this country are in their prime.[62]

When premature wifehood and motherhood were combined with the burdens of wearing awkward personal ornaments in a hot climate, the ethnologists believed they had found a reasonable explanation for the differences between the life expectancies of heathen and American Christian women.[63] "The Hindu women, married at eleven or twelve, a grandmother before thirty, becomes a worn out drudge or a scolding terror by forty, if she lives so long," reported a 1900 magazine, "while our girls gain the whole happy period of girlhood and schooldays before their much later marriage."[64]

Simply put, female vulnerability was seen as the consequence and the burden of life in a non-Christian society. Woman "is still regarded as of old, in a non-Christian environment, as a scandal and a slave, a drudge and a disgrace, a temptation and a terror, a blemish and a burden," read the 1910 missionary

[60] The median age of marriage for all classes in 1900 was 21.9. In the same year, girls accounted for 60 percent of the high school graduates in the United States. Department of Commerce, Bureau of the Census, *Historical Statistics of the United States: Colonial Times to 1970* (2 vols., Washington, 1975), I, 19, 379. On the decline in domestic service among middle-class, native-born daughters see Dudden, "From Help to Domestics," 79-84; David M. Katzman, *Seven Days a Week: Women and Domestic Service in Industrializing America* (New York, 1978), 46, 73; Carol Groneman, "Working-Class Immigrant Women in Mid-Nineteenth-Century New York: The Irish Woman's Experience," *Journal of Urban History*, 4 (May 1978), 255-73.

[61] Gracey, ed., *Gist*, 54.

[62] *Life and Light for Women*, 30 (Oct. 1900), 437.

[63] "Why Indian Women are Early Old," *Woman's Missionary Friend*, 28 (Aug. 1896), 43.

[64] *Life and Light for Women*, 30 (March 1900), 109.

audience. Montgomery's double vision led her to confirm the correctness of James Shepard Dennis's observation in *Christian Missions and Social Progress* (1906) that woman is "at once the touchstone and stumbling block of human systems, the sign and shame of the non-Christian world."[65] "A nation can never rise to any greatness when her women are not respected," reported a Christian convert from China; training manuals told youthful religious workers that "no race . . . has ever risen above the condition of its women."[66] On the basis of the comparative ethnologies generated in the foreign-mission crusade, the status of women came to be regarded by evangelical Protestants as an index of national accomplishment. Totally self-congratulatory in this respect, the ethnologists' comparisons supported the status quo, fueling the social Darwinist claim that the treatment of women in Protestant Christian lands marked the Anglo-Saxon race as further up the ladder of social evolution. In this sense, the ethnology created by American evangelical women simultaneously reinforced deference for patriarchy at home while encouraging a critical perspective in looking abroad.

Popular interest in the antithetical "other," provoked and sustained by religious self-study, had additional policy implications. Given that middle-class women in the foreign-mission crusade focused their attentions on alien cultures and distant locales, they constituted the kind of attentive public that came by the 1890s, according to Ernest R. May, to see American expansion as in their interest.[67] Undoubtedly, the popularization of the notion of female exploitation at the hands of non-Christians is an inseparable part of the story of how public opinion in the United States shifted from anticolonialism to genuine imperialism.

Although it is nearly impossible to pinpoint the extent to which women, as a disenfranchised group, influenced foreign policy, a number of prominent late-nineteenth-century policy makers were tied to the foreign-mission crusade. For example, in 1896 President Cleveland appeared before an enormous Presbyterian gathering in New York's Carnegie Hall where he urged his fellow religionists to give generously to both domestic and foreign missions. "Our missionary impulse should be large enough and strong enough for both," he told an enthusiastic audience of men, women, and children waving handkerchiefs, hats, and programs. Three years later, William McKinley, a supporter of Methodist causes, attended the baccalaureate ceremonies at Mount Holyoke, the oldest and most prestigious of the nation's missionary training schools for women. There, in a chapel filled with ferns and palms, McKinley sang the hymn "Angels of Light," and M. W. Jacobus of the Hartford Theological Seminary implored the graduates to help others by following "this country of ours" as it goes out "with its unselfish civilization to bless the nations of the world." In September 1898, at the conclusion of the war with Spain, the cor-

[65] Quoted in Montgomery, *Western Women*, 77.

[66] Jewell, "Footbinding"; Gracey, ed., *Gist*, 11.

[67] Ernest R. May, *American Imperialism: A Speculative Essay* (New York, 1968), 187–89. Although Ernest R. May found religious support for imperialistic ventures, as demonstrated in sermons, he all but ignored women's religious organizations.

responding secretary of the Missionary Society of the Methodist Episcopal Church wrote the president expressing concern for "religious liberty" in the Philippines; "there is a strong feeling among the people against returning those islands to the political control of Spain," he said.[68] While religious women were neither voters nor policy makers, they were an important constituency with great interest in the resolution of the Spanish-American War and in foreign policies generally. Consequently, we should not obscure their significance as the wives and daughters of manufacturers, merchants, and investors who promoted colonial expansion in the service of wider markets.[69] Women's concerns, after all, provided merchant imperialism with a humanistic or religious rationale, explaining, in part, the American propensity for moral rhetoric.

Ultimately, what is most surprising about the missionary ethnology is the extent to which it fueled the Progressive outlook. When, in the 1896 appeals to President Cleveland, women praised the Christian state for its protection of women and children, they were not so much stating a fact as staking out a claim and providing a secular agenda for the future. From a generational perspective, the reform leaders of the Progressive period came to maturity within a women's culture that had long regarded child marriage as a litmus test for barbarism. A literature directed at girls and written by both Christian converts and Anglo-American women was widespread. Books such as *The Third Daughter*, *Pomegranate*, and *The Love Story of a Maiden of Cathay* circulated in schools and libraries, promoting the notion that crippled feet and absolute filial obedience were the twin burdens of Chinese girls.[70] Descriptions of women in foreign cultures were also widely disseminated in the secular periodical literature for women. The popular *Ladies Home Journal* regularly included stories such as "The Life of a Japanese Girl," "What Girl-Life in Italy Means," or "The Engaged Girl in China." Although the contributors were not missionaries, but rather foreign-born observers in the United States, the message was essentially the same: American women enjoyed a unique and enviable position. For example, in extolling the happiness, freedom, and security of women in the United States, Wu Ting-fang, envoy extraordinary and minister plenipotentiary from China, reported in 1902 that the American woman "walks as does no other woman on earth."[71] Even Flora Annie Steel, who was

[68] *New York Times*, March 4, 1896, pp. 1–2; *ibid.*, June 19, 1899, p. 7; L. B. Leonard to William McKinley, Sept. 6, 1898, Records of Board of Managers of the Missionary Society of the Methodist Episcopal Church (Commission on Archives and History Library, United Methodist Church, Lake Junaluska, N.C.).

[69] The importance of women has often been ignored. See, for example, Walter LaFeber, *The New Empire: An Interpretation of American Expansion, 1860–1898* (Ithaca, N.Y., 1963).

[70] See Lu Wheat, *The Third Daughter: A Story of Chinese Home Life* (Los Angeles, 1906); Jennie Beckingsale, *Pomegranate: The Story of a Chinese School Girl* (London, 1910); [Florence Rush Nance], *The Love Story of a Maiden of Cathay, Told in Letters from Yang Ping Yu* (New York, 1911).

[71] See Onoto Watanna, "My Impressions of American Women," *Ladies Home Journal*, 16 (April 1899), 7; Marchesa Theodoli, "What Girl-Life in India Means," *ibid.*, 18 (Aug. 1901), 14; Sui Sin Far, "Engaged Girl in China," *ibid.*, 19 (Jan. 1902), 14; Wu Ting-Fang, "My Impressions of American Women," *ibid.* (Feb. 1902), 10. It should be noted that both Jane Addams and Florence Kelley wrote, on occasion, for *Ladies Home Journal*. See Jane Addams, "When Youth Seeks a Mate,"

known as the "Female Rudyard Kipling" and who personally deplored the zealotry of missionaries in India, produced a number of popular short stories, such as "Mussumut Kirpo's Doll," that dealt with the lot of the Hindu child-wife and the problems of premature motherhood.[72]

This is not to say that Progressives and missionary supporters were one and the same. Rather, it is to point out that in the 1920s, when women activists and social workers made legislation for the protection of women and children the sine qua non of their social program, they were confirming a set of assumptions that were already at the heart of the American religious community.[73] The best known of these Progressive efforts is, of course, the child-welfare movement, which enlisted Jane Addams, Julia Lathrop, Mary Anderson, Lucy L. Flower, Lillian Wald, Grace Abbott, and Florence Kelley in the push for wide-ranging legislation to protect children from the exploitation and abuse of both employer and family. Moreover, social-welfare workers and sociologists in the 1920s, allying themselves against eugenicists, began a reform campaign against child marriage in the United States, a campaign that raised the spectre of female sexual degradation, domestic oppression, and intellectual deprivation just as the missionary ethnologies had done over the preceding half century.[74]

Railing against the fact that in 1925 twenty-three states allowed girls to be married at fourteen or even twelve years of age, the Progressive reformers also chastised the courts of the United States for allowing men who committed sex offenses against young girls to marry their "youthful victims" in order to avoid fines, incarceration, and even death.[75] Progressive reformers argued that

ibid., 26 (Nov. 1909), 22; Florence Kelley, "Why Working-Girls Fall into Temptation," *ibid.*, 15-16.

[72] See Flora Annie Steel, *The Flower of Forgiveness* (London, 1900). On Flora Annie Steel herself, see Daya Patwardhan, *A Star of India (Flora Annie Steel, Her Works and Times)* (Poona, India, 1963); and J.R.H. Weaver, ed., *Dictionary of National Biography: 1922-1930* (London, 1937), 809-10. Steel was the author of *On the Face of the Waters* (1896), which was a best seller in the late 1890s.

[73] For some, the popular conventions of the missionary ethnology provided a departure for critical scholarly and artistic works. See, for example, Elsie Clews Parsons, *The Old-Fashioned Woman: Primitive Fancies about the Sex* (New York, 1913). This is an anthropologist's attempt to negate the power of the religious ethnology by stressing continuities, rather than differences, in the treatment of women cross-culturally. In Edwin R. A. Seligman and Alvin Johnson, eds., *Encyclopedia of the Social Sciences* (15 vols., New York, 1930-1935), III, 395-97, Ruth Benedict offered a professional anthropological view of child marriage, observing that the popular emphasis on prepubertal sexual relations among non-Christians distorted the complexity and variety of child marriage arrangements. Benedict was clear to point out that the existence of child marriage did not necessarily imply low status for women, as evangelicals believed. Also interesting is D. W. Griffith's film *Broken Blossoms* (1919), which depends upon the viewer's prior familiarity with the missionary ethnology in order to understand the "missionary-in-reverse" scenario.

[74] The campaign against child marriage is related to but not the same as the effort to raise the age of consent. See David J. Pivar, *Purity Crusade: Sexual Morality and Social Control, 1868-1900* (Westport, Conn., 1973), 139-46.

[75] Arthur W. Towne, "Young Girl Marriages in Criminal and Juvenile Courts," *Journal of Social Hygiene*, 8 (July 1922), 287-90. Arthur W. Towne was superintendent of the Brooklyn (New York) Society for the Prevention of Cruelty to Children. See also Mary E. Richmond and Fred S. Hall, *Child Marriages* (New York, 1925), 20, 45-54; and Women's Protective Association of Cleveland, *School-Girl Brides: A Study of the Ohio Marriage Laws Relating to Minors* (Cleveland, 1926), 34-37. For a eugenicist taking a different point of view, see Paul Popenoe, "Early Marriage and Happiness," *Journal of Social Hygiene*, 12 (Dec. 1926), 544-49.

concern for the future moral and educational development of the girl (and not the notion of "saving" her individual or family reputation) should determine judicial actions. Mary E. Richmond, the founder of social case work and co-author of *Child Marriages*, claimed that between 1890 and 1924 more than a third of a million American women began their married life as child brides, under the age of fifteen.[76] Published case studies of both native and foreign-born parents pushing their daughters into deleterious premature marriages gave the drive to raise the marriageable age and maximize enforcement of existing laws an enormous sense of urgency. Parental consent to child marriages was uniformly regarded as a sign of ignorance, greed, or depravity; Richmond argued persuasively that where parental insight and guidance were lacking "the state must be able to throw some safeguard around the young."[77] While sociological studies of marriage and the family debated the most appropriate age for marriage (within a range of respectable options), there was never any doubt about the state's role in the process. "Marriage is a matter which should be regulated by the state, not by parents," wrote Ruth Reed, a professor of economics and sociology at Mount Holyoke in 1929.[78]

Between 1919 and 1930, the "tragic mischief" of child marriage came under increasing scrutiny and control: the marriageable age was raised in at least half the states; advance notice of marriage was increasingly required; and proof of age was standardized and strengthened. Significantly, courts began to intercede in preventing child marriages; in Monroe County, New York, for example, parental consent to the marriage of a girl under sixteen was regarded as proof of improper guardianship, resulting in the girl's removal from the home.[79]

Although child marriage in the United Stated never involved the kind of numbers claimed by the Progressive reformers, it was a popular rallying cry with a direct appeal to large numbers of middle-class Protestant women already conversant with the missionary ethnology and its didactic use of the antithetical "other." From lessons learned in foreign-mission study, women extracted the principle that an intrusive role for the state was in their best interests; in effect, protection by the state, rather than equality in it, became a central concern.[80] American girlhood, so the thinking went, could be insured

[76] Richmond and Hall, *Child Marriages*, 57. This figure is, apparently, inflated. See Thomas P. Monahan, *The Pattern of Age at Marriage in the United States* (2 vols., Philadelphia, 1951), I, 47.

[77] Richmond and Hall, *Child Marriages*, 92.

[78] Ruth Reed, *The Modern Family* (New York, 1929), 120. Child marriage was a subject of interest and concern in the sociological writing of the period. See Elsie Clews Parsons, *Social Freedom: A Study of the Conflicts between Social Classifications and Personality* (New York, 1915), 33; Willystine Goodsell, *Problems of the Family* (New York, 1928), 109; Ernest R. Groves, *Marriage* (New York, 1933), 124–31; Ray E. Baber, *Marriage and the Family* (New York, 1939), 114–15, 175–78. Unlike the earlier missionary ethnologists, sociologists linked child marriage to the rising divorce rate. The cry for more uniform marriage laws was generally based on an analysis of legislation in Fred S. Hall and Elisabeth W. Brooke, *American Marriage Laws in Their Social Aspects: A Digest* (New York, 1919); and George Elliott Howard, *A History of Matrimonial Institutions* (3 vols., Chicago, 1904).

[79] Richmond and Hall, *Child Marriages*, 110, 147.

[80] In the 1980s the evangelical community continues to adhere to the notion that a truly Christian state protects women, children, and the family. This kind of thinking is evidenced in the

by force of laws regulating marriageable age, school attendance, age of consent, and employment. Thus, middle-class women, who, a generation earlier, wishfully touted protection of their sex and their children as the distinctive characteristic of the Christian state, embraced Progressive reform, as they embraced imperialism, precisely because it actualized their understanding of the world. In sum, the popular ethnology developed by evangelical women in the post-Civil War foreign-mission crusade had a life beyond the local auxiliary where it was first infused into the larger culture, and ultimately, it helped to shape an American self-definition.

Laxalt Bill, alternatively known as the Family Protection Act. Moreover, the opposition of "the evangelical right" to the Equal Rights Amendment is based on the notion that the amendment would remove "protections" from vulnerable women.

Sisters of St. Joseph: The Americanization of a French Tradition

Patricia Byrne, C.S.J.

On 25 March 1836 the first Sisters of St. Joseph ever to leave France arrived in the nine-year-old diocese of St. Louis. Those six women brought with them the rich heritage of a nearly 200-year tradition that had roots in the renewal of the Catholic Church in France during the seventeenth century. Like other immigrant groups, the sisters found that success in the new world depended upon adjustment to changed conditions. Challenged by the necessity of cultural assimilation, they were able to draw upon the legacy of their particular history in France in order to form a style of religious life that worked remarkably well for them as a way of being Catholic and American. The history of the Congregations of St. Joseph in the United States can be viewed as the Americanization of that French tradition.[1] This study explores several elements in the nineteenth-century experience of Sisters of St. Joseph which highlight the interaction of French background and American milieu. The data is taken primarily from six of the United States congregations established before 1870: Carondelet (1836), Philadelphia (1847), Wheeling (1853), Brooklyn (1856), St. Augustine (1866), and Ebensburg, Pennsylvania (1869).

1. Twenty-five congregations of St. Joseph now in the United States can be traced to six foundations made from motherhouses in France: Carondelet, 1836 (Lyons); New Orleans, 1855 (Bourg); St. Augustine, 1866 (Le Puy); Lee, Massachusetts, 1885 (Chambéry); Fall River, Massachusetts, 1902 (Le Puy); and Jackman, Maine, 1906 (Lyons). Only the latter and the Chambéry foundation remain provinces of the original congregations. Margaret Quinn, C.S.J., and Patricia Manning, C.S.J., "Federation of the Sisters of St. Joseph in the United States of America and Canada: Historical Development of the Congregations" (Brentwood, New York: By the authors, 1985).

Patricia Byrne, C.S.J.

French Origins

The Congregation of St. Joseph came to America on one of several waves of expatriated French Catholicism which affected the Catholic Church in the United States during its formative years. The nineteenth-century French influence on the American Church was the result of the contemporary religious revival in France, activist in color and missionary in scope, exemplified in the organization of the Society of the Propagation of the Faith at Lyons in 1822.[2] The Society was to play an important part in the foundation of the Sisters of St. Joseph in the United States.

The origins of the Sisters of St. Joseph considerably antedate their coming to America, going back to the middle of the seventeenth century. A fruit of the immense spiritual and organizational energies of the Counter-Reformation in France, the Congregation of St. Joseph was in the vanguard of the modern movement of women's congregations which, in spite of ecclesiastical law, were directed specifically toward the service of the

2. *Dictionnaire de spiritualité ascétique et mystique, doctrine et histoire*, s.v. "France: 8, De la Révolution au début du 20ᵉ siècle," by André Rayex, and S. Delacroix et al., *Les missions contemporains (1800–1957)*, vol. 3 of *Histoire universelle des missions catholiques*, ed. S. Delacroix (Paris, 1958), 20–71.

neighbor and therefore did not observe canonical cloister.[3] The precise date of the foundation of the Sisters of St. Joseph is unknown. It was an evolutionary event, connected with the labors of the Jesuit priest Jean-Pierre Médaille in the mountainous and poverty-stricken areas of south central France.[4] Between 1646 and 1651, six women took over the administration of the hospital-orphanage in the rue de Montferrand in Le Puy and became Sisters of St. Joseph. They obtained ecclesiastical approbation from Henry de Maupas, bishop of Le Puy, 10 March 1651. There were at the same time other foundations in the diocese of Le Puy—the earliest recorded being that of Dunières, where Anne Deschaux, a woman of the parish, began a community of St. Joseph on 29 September 1649.[5]

Father Médaille envisioned "this new way of life" as at once deeply spiritual and eminently practical. He defined its purpose in terms of the perfect love of God and neighbor: "Our selfless congregation . . . tends to achieve [the] total double union of ourselves and the dear neighbor with God, and of ourselves and all others, whoever they may be, of all others among themselves and with us, but totally in Jesus and in God his Father." In order to make this ideal tangible within the social order of the day, the Sisters of St. Joseph were to practice "all the spiritual and corporal works of mercy of which woman is capable."[6] Not restricted to any specific work, they were free to respond to the needs of a situation—a fact that was to have great importance for their history in America.

During the century and a half of their existence before the French Revolution, foundations of Sisters of St. Joseph spread rapidly in the Massif Central and some surrounding areas to the south and east. At no

---

3. The Council of Trent and subsequent papal legislation had required cloister and solemn vows for all women religious. Sess. 25, 3–4 December 1563, decree *De Regularibus et Monialibus*, in *Concilium Tridentinum: Diariorium, Actorum, Epistularum, Tractatuum*, ed. Societas Goerresiana, 13 vols. (Freiburg, St. Louis, 1901–1938), 9(1924): 1077–1085; and Pius V, constitution *Circa Pastoralis*, 29 May 1566, in *Codicis Iuris Canonici Fontes*, 1:112, cited in James R. Cain, "Cloister and the Apostolate of Religious Women," *Review for Religious* 27(1968):272.

4. *Dictionnaire de spiritualité*, s.v. "Médaille, Jean-Pierre," by Marius Nepper, S.J.

5. Compte rendu par Estienne Treveys des recettes et dépenses acceptées par lui pour la maison des filhes orfelines de St. Joseph de la rue Montferrand du Puy, April 1646–March 1648, 8 A 1, Archives of the Sisters of St. Joseph of Le Puy (hereafter cited as ACSJLP); Lettres de provision données par Monseigneur Henry de Maupas du Tour evesque du Puy en faveur des Filhes de la congregation de St. Joseph du Puy touchant leur establissement 10 mars 1651, 12 H 1, Filles de St. Joseph-Hôpital de Montferrand, Departmental Archives of the Haute-Loire, Le Puy; and Constitution de dot soy faite par soeur Anne Deschaux superieure de la congregation des filles de St. Joseph, 10 February 1662, Dunières papers, ACSJLP.

6. *Règlements*, no. 5; *Lettre eucharistique*, no. 29; and *Constitutions primitives*, no. 49, in Soeurs de Saint Joseph, eds., *Textes primitifs* (Clermont-Ferrand, 1981), 105, 8, 23. Translations by the Intercongregational Research Team, Federation of the Sisters of St. Joseph, U.S.A.

time before the Revolution did they have a centralized organization. Each house was independent, and one may speak in a true sense of parish communities. Although the bishop was the ultimate authority in regard to each community, the curé often acted as the local ecclesiastical superior. Community records show that he gave the habit, received vows, confirmed elections, and sometimes kept the books.[7]

Membership was drawn largely from the parish, and communities tended to be small, numbering perhaps six or seven.[8] Surviving acts of association show that Sisters of St. Joseph were most often daughters of laborers or farmers with small holdings, but there were considerable differences from house to house. Only in the larger towns, and late in the eighteenth century, did their dowries exceed those typical for women of the lower classes.[9] The sisters supplemented their meager income through cottage industry, usually lace- or ribbon-making.[10]

Sisters of St. Joseph did what was needed in the parish: they operated primitive grade schools, catechized the women, took care of the sick and orphans in small local "hospitals," visited homes of the needy, and were sacristans for the parish church. Listing the useful activities of the Sisters of St. Joseph there in 1761, the citizens of Job concluded: "Since there is no one other than the *filles associées* . . . to instruct and train the young girls, it is very important that this community exist as being very advantageous for the said parish."[11] Their sentiments are echoed in the judgment of the social historian, Gabriel Le Bras, who asserted that without the

7. Acte d'association, 1660, Boisset Papers, ACSJLP; Profession de Marie Limousin, 8 March 1734, Registre, Aurec papers, ACSJLP; Registre, Bas papers, ACSJLP; Acte d'association de Claudine Antoinette Montaland, 25 May 1744, C-2, Aubépin papers, Archives of the Sisters of St. Joseph of Lyons (hereafter cited as ACSJL); and Registre, C-12, Izieu papers, ACSJL.

8. Due to the extensive destruction during the Revolution, French congregational sources do not permit a statistical analysis; these figures represent an impression formed by examining papers of the pre-Revolutionary communities contained in the motherhouses at Le Puy, Lyons, and Clermont-Ferrand.

9. Dowries from 300 to 500 *livres* are typical of acts of association found in many of the houses represented in ACSJL and ACSJLP; some larger city houses show dowries of 1,000 *livres* or more. Registre des délibérations des actes des administrateurs de la maison du Refuge, 18 August 1758, H 7, le Bon Pasteur, Departmental Archives of the Puy-de-Dôme, Clermont-Ferrand; and acte d'ingrès de Catherine Jouve, 2 August 1769, Craponne Papers, ACSJLP. See F. Gouit, *Une congrègation salèsienne: Les Soeurs de Saint-Joseph du Puy-en-Velay* (Le Puy, 1930), 138; and Olwen H. Hufton, *The Poor of 18th Century France (1750–1789)*, (Oxford, 1974), 28.

10. Most pre-Revolutionary documents identify the Sisters of St. Joseph as "filles dentellières" or "filles rubanières," as in Petition addresse a M Verardier, con[seill]er du Roy, president en l'Ellection de St. Etienne, 13 April, 1719, C-30, Saint-Genest-Malifaux papers, ACSJL.

11. Deliberation of the inhabitants of Job in favor of *lettres patentes* for the Sisters of St. Joseph, 1761, "12-Débuts des soeurs de Saint-Joseph à Job, près d'Ambert (1742–1761)," in Roger Sève, Jean Perrel, and Jean Chapelle, eds, *L'enseignement sous l'Ancien Règime en Auvergne, Bourbonnais et Velay* (Clermont-Ferrand, 1977), 28–29, my translation.

The city of Le Puy-en-Velay, France, where the Sisters of St. Joseph were founded

sisters there was often no one in a village to provide this kind of social assistance, the parish being the sole source of such service.[12] In addition to parish work, sisters also staffed institutions—including general hospitals, *hôtels-Dieu*, a few detention homes for *filles repenties* such as the Refuge du Bon Pasteur in Clermont, and some schools which, in the scheme of Louis XIV, served for the indoctrination of recently "converted" young Protestants.[13]

In its pre-Revolutionary development, the Congregation of St. Joseph was characterized by membership drawn from people of the most ordinary means and education. No personal letters of Sisters of St. Joseph before the Revolution survive; the only evidence of literacy is from convent registers and legal documents, which demonstrate merely the ability to execute a signature. These reveal that, like four-fifths of the French population at the end of the seventeenth century, many Sisters of St. Joseph were illiterate.[14]

---

12. *L'église et le village* (Paris, 1976), 149–52.

13. Notes of A. Achard, Tence and Saint-Paulien papers, ACSJLP: Lettres patentes, 1754, Privas papers, Archives of the Sisters of St. Joseph of Viviers, Aubenas, and *Dictionnaire d'histoire de l'Eglise de France*, s.v. "France: 4, Les 17e et 18e siecles," by Andre Latreille, col. 88

14. Pierre Goubert, *The Ancien Régime: French Society 1600–1750*, trans. Irene Cox (New York, 1973; 1974), 262, citing Maggiolo, *Etat récapitulatif et comparatif*. . ., published by the Ministère de l'Instruction publique, n.p., n.d., Bibliothèque Nationale, 4° Lf 242–196.

Without benefit of privilege or education, through their activities in parishes, rudimentary hospitals and schools, congregations like the Sisters of St. Joseph achieved the direct participation of women in the pastoral care of the Church. Significant for this study is their integral role among the common people in the society of the *ancien régime*, and the history of intense localization, the strong identification of communities with the local Church, which seemed to become a habit, and was to re-emerge in the American scene.

The aftermath of the French Revolution found the Sisters of St. Joseph with a handful of martyrs, many quiet heroines, a few apostates, and the majority who tried to survive the storm without compromising themselves.[15] In many parishes where they had been before the Revolution, a few of the old guard struggled to reorganize their community life, and were joined by new recruits. Under the Napoleonic system these communities found themselves at first independent of each other, and later, for the sake of utility, pressed into a centralized organization under diocesan motherhouses.[16]

Cardinal Joseph Fesch, uncle of Napoleon and archbishop of Lyons, is credited with authorizing the re-establishment of the Sisters of St. Joseph in his archdiocese in 1807 at Saint-Etienne. To be more exact: there were many separate communities of St. Joseph being founded or refounded in the diocese of Lyons after the Revolution. Under the administration of Fesch and his vicar-general, Claude Cholleton, former pastor at Saint-Etienne and spiritual director for a group known as the *Filles Noires*, the latter were transformed into Sisters of St. Joseph. They were an unofficial community of pious women, some of them ex-nuns, who had been practicing an ascetic life at Saint-Etienne for about six years, waiting for the day when they could become cloistered. Contemplatives, however, were despised by Napoleon, and the needs of the vast archdiocese demanded, above all, workers. In order to change the direction of the *Filles Noires* into an active vein, in 1807 Mother St. Jean Fontbonne, former superior of the Sisters of St. Joseph at Monistrol, came to Saint-Etienne. Im-

15. Four, possibly five, Sisters of St. Joseph were executed during the Terror: Marie-Anne Garnier and Jeanne-Marie Aubert at Le Puy, 17 June 1794; Antoinette Vincent, Marie-Anne Sénovert, and Madeleine Dumoulin at Privas (Ardèche), 5 August 1794. (Although tradition has identified Jeanne-Marie Aubert as a Sister of St. Joseph, there is no documentation to prove it.)

Like their eccentric bishop, Charles Lafont de Savines, fourteen of the sixteen sisters at the hospital of Aubenas in the diocese of Viviers took the constitutional oath. Extraits des Archives de l'Hôpital d'Aubenas, CS V 10, 135, Archives of the Sisters of St. Joseph of Viviers, Aubenas.

16. Roger Aubert, *The Church between Revolution and Restoration*, trans. Peter Becker, vol. 7 of *The History of the Church*, ed. Hubert Jedin and John Dolan (New York, 1981), 66–67; and Paul Nourisson, *Histoire légale des congrégations religieuses en France depuis 1789*, 2 vols. (Paris, 1928), 1:82–83, 100–103.

Sister Febronie Fontbonne

Sister Delphine Fontbonne

prisoned during the Terror, and reputedly slated for execution, she had been spared by the fall of Robespierre.[17] After a year's novitiate under Mother St. Jean, seventeen of the *Filles Noires* received the habit as Sisters of St. Joseph on 14 July 1808, and the nucleus of the Lyons Congregation took shape. By 1816, Mother St. Jean had moved from Saint-Etienne to the episcopal city of Lyons, and in 1829 a centralized novitiate was established there for all the houses of the Sisters of St. Joseph in the diocese.[18]

17. The history of Mother St. Jean Fontbonne is problematic, making it difficult to sort legend from fact. Her correspondence was reportedly destroyed in a fire while in the possession of her first biographer, whose account of her life is undocumented and strictly hagiographic: J. Rivaux, *Vie de la Reverende Mere Saint Jean nee Fontbonne* (Grenoble, 1885), trans. and ed. by [M. Assissium Mc Evoy, S.S.J.], under the title of *Life of Mother St. John Fontbonne: Foundress and First Superior-General of the Congregation of the Sisters of St. Joseph in Lyons* (New York, 1887). A second biography, which makes corrections and significant additions to Rivaux's material while borrowing much of it is [Marie-Stephanie Hervier, C.S.J.], *Simple et grande: Mere Saint-Jean Fontbonne, fondatrice de la congregation de Saint-Joseph de Lyon, restauratrice de l'Institut* (Paris-Bruges, 1929), trans. and ed. by A Sister of St. Joseph of Brentwood, New York [M. Leonilla Cleary], under the title of *Mother Saint John Fontbonne: Foundress of the Congregation of the Sisters of St. Joseph of Lyons* (New York, 1936). See [Hervier], *La congregation de Saint-Joseph de Lyon*, Les ordres religieux (Paris, 1927), 44–45.

18. Prise d'habit 14 juillet 1808, Registre "Profession," unclassified papers, ACSJL; and Ordonnance sur le Noviciat des Soeurs de St. Joseph, Jean-Paul Gaston de Pins, Archèveque d'Amasie, Administrateur Apostolique du Diocèse de Lyon et Vienne, 23 December 1828, 1 0 III, Mère Saint-Jean papers, ACSJL.

In the post-Napoleonic era, the Sisters of St. Joseph retained the parish orientation and the variety of occupations which they had had before the Revolution.[19] The motherhouse structure added the dimension of mobility and a larger pool of personnel, which made possible greater specialization in works and expansion through deployment of sisters who had received uniform religious training in the central novitiate. The stage was set for a missionary venture.

Foundations of an American Identity

The American foundation of the Sisters of St. Joseph in 1836 resulted from a conjunction of circumstances, and there were quite a few fingers in the pie. There was the city of Lyons, during the thirties a center for American connections in Europe, due to the location there of the headquarters for the Society of the Propagation of the Faith. There was a countess, Félicité de Duras, the pious and philanthropic wife of the Count de la Rochejaquelein. She, like many Catholics of her day, was a reader of the *Annales* of the Society of the Propagation of the Faith.[20] The Mission of Missouri was a regular feature in the *Annales*, with letters from priests in the field, including a number from Joseph Rosati, the Bishop of St. Louis, with vivid descriptions of life in America, as well as appeals for missionaries and funds.[21] Mme de la Rochejaquelein, determined to do something for the foreign missions, decided to finance a group of Sisters of St. Joseph for America. She enlisted Fr. Claude Cholleton, ecclesiastical superior of the Sisters of St. Joseph in Lyons and European agent for Rosati, to convince the latter that what he needed on the Missouri frontier were Sisters of St. Joseph.

The countess had a definite project in mind. "I would send six Sisters of St. Joseph to North America," she wrote to Rosati, "with a view to their converting the savages, instructing the little ones, and educating and converting the children of Protestants."[22] The dual emphasis on savages and

19. Etat des maisons des soeurs de St-Joseph existant dans le Diocèse de Lyon, 10 April 1812, V 262, Cultes, Departmental Archives of the Rhône, Lyons.

20. *Annales de la Propagation de la Foi* (Paris, 1822–). For their impact on French Catholics in the nineteenth century, see Edward J. Hickey, *The Society for the Propagation of the Faith: Its Foundation, Organization, Success (1822–1922)*, The Catholic University of America Studies in American Church History, no. 3 (Washington, 1922; reprint, New York, 1974), 140–142, 169–172.

21. Mgr. Rosati, evêque de Saint-Louis et administrateur de Nouvelle Orléans à M l'abbé P., 3 août 1828, *Annales de la Propagation de la Foi* 28 (May 1929): 545–571; idem à M Cholleton, vicaire général, St. Louis, 8 mai 1832, *Annales* 36 (April 1834): 101–102.

22. Félicité de Duras to Bishop Rosati, Chambéry, 10 June 1835, copy and trans., Archives of the Sisters of St. Joseph of Carondelet, St. Louis (hereafter cited as ACSJC); original, Archives of the Archdiocese of St. Louis (hereafter cited as AASL).

sectarians reflected the reports which filled the *Annales* at the time. The countess' visions of an evangelizing enterprise were rooted in her confidence in the ability of the Sisters of St. Joseph to adjust in America, which she rightly associated with the flexibility of their rule,[23] and the diversity of their occupations:

> They give themselves to all the works of mercy, they take charge of free schools or boarding schools, hospitals, asylums for foundlings or for the aged: they may look after prisoners; attend on the poor and the sick in their houses; take care of the infected—they are ready for anything.[24]

Mme de la Rochejaquelein described what she had seen in France, but her perception of the sisters as a pious and versatile labor force was to prove a constant in their history in America.

The American experience of the Sisters of St. Joseph begins in 1836, when the first six came to St. Louis, accompanied by a priest. Two more were to follow in 1837. With the exception of one sister sent in 1860, these eight were the extent of the French personnel to be supplied from the motherhouse at Lyons.[25] The original band were all between the ages of twenty-one and thirty-one; five had been professed in France and three came to America as novices. One was a lay sister.[26] There were connections of family and bonds of friendship among the group. Two were blood sisters—Febronie and Delphine Fontbonne—nieces of Mother St. Jean in Lyons; the priest who came with them was their brother, Jacques Fontbonne. Although they did not realize it at the time, these pioneering sisters were no longer able to look to Europe for support; they would have to make their own way in a new world.

When the sisters arrived in 1836, their Frenchness determined their role in the St. Louis diocese. They began work in two settlements with French-Canadian and Creole populations: at Cahokia, on the Illinois

---

23. "It will fructify there all the more because in this Order a foundation according to rule is not so restricted as in some other Orders; it accommodates itself to times and circumstances." *Ibid.*

24. *Ibid.* The same theme appears in a letter of Jean-Paul Gaston de Pins, Administrator of the Archdiocese of Lyons to Bishop Rosati, 1 January 1836: "They will be excellent catechists, good nurses for the sick, perfect sacristans, zealous teachers." Copy and trans., K–A–23, ACSJC; original, AASL.

25. Sisters Fébronie Fontbonne, Delphine Fontbonne, Marquerite-Félicité Bouté, Marie-Fébronie Chappelon, St. Protais Déboille, Philomène Vilaine, and Father Jacques Fontbonne arrived in 1836; Sisters Célestine Pommerel and St. Jean Fournier, 4 September 1837, and Sister Marie de la Sainte-Croix Bennelin in 1860. Dolorita Marie Dougherty, C.S.J. et al., *Sisters of St. Joseph of Carondelet* (St. Louis, 1966), 421–422. (In the text, the pioneers' names appear in their anglicized forms.)

26. In a report of Bishop Rosati, Philomene Vilaine is listed at the end of the community, after the single novice as "Soror Conversa-Philomena (Marie Vilain) emisit vota die 3 Januari 1838." Excerpt from Status diocesis 1838, copy, ACSJC; original, AASL.

bank of the Mississippi, and a place with the unpromising epithet of *Vide poche* a few miles south of St. Louis—better known today as Carondelet. In her old age, Sister St. Protais Déboille recalled in still-broken English that the people of Cahokia had venerated the sisters as women "come from the same mother as them, the Catholic France, to have care of their sick, their poor, their children . . . they think of them as their mother."[27]

The French language was to be an advantage in promoting the sisters' schools. One of the first boarders at the enlarged log cabin in Carondelet, popularly known as "Madame Celestine's School," explained that her mother sent her there because "she was anxious of my acquiring a French education in all the purity of the language."[28] In 1839, the institution at Carondelet was a French convent school with a large dose of Missouri frontier—in winter the sisters' duties included shaking snow from the boarders' beds in the middle of the night. By 1841, however, there was a three-story brick building, and the French character of St. Joseph's Academy attracted daughters of Southern planters until the Civil War.[29] French was also a drawing card for the select schools, established in conjunction with a free school as a means of support until the parochial system was established later in the century. In 1858, recently arrived in Oswego, New York, the Sisters of St. Joseph placed an ad in the September 6 edition of the *Palladium Times:*

> *New Advertisements: Select School and Private Lessons.* The Sisters of St. Joseph, having taken the direction of St. Mary's School, will also open, on the 13th inst., a Select School for Young Ladies, in their house, No. 68 West Sixth Street, where they will teach all the branches generally taught in the best Academies. They will also give private lessons in French, Music, Embroidery, Painting, etc., to young ladies who may desire. For terms apply to SISTER STANISLAUS Sup'r.[30]

It was the presence, in the Oswego community, of Sister Hyacinth Blanc, a missionary from Moûtiers, which enabled them to offer French in addition to their basic curriculum. Although their French background provided

27. Memoirs of Sister St. Protais Déboille, n.d., D–M–7a, ACSJC.

28. Memoirs of Eliza Mc Kenny Brouillet, D–M–5b,c, ACSJC. Apart from a number of letters to Bishop Rosati, there is little documentation for the initial period at Carondelet. Many details are known only from later recollections, many recorded at the request of Sister Monica Corrigan around 1890 and preserved in ACSJC; also a long letter containing notes on the American foundations which had been requested by the Lyons superior: Soeur St. Jean née Fournier à la Supr Gle des Soeurs St Joseph de Lyon [1873], ACSJL (reproduced with English trans. in Marie Kostka Logue, S.S.J., *Sisters of St. Joseph of Philadelphia: A Century of Growth and Development 1847–1947* [Westminster, MD, 1950], 326–353).

29. Brouillet and Déboille memoirs; and Mary Lucida Savage, C.S.J., *The Congregation of Saint Joseph of Carondelet: A Brief Account of Its Origin and Its Work in the United States, 1650–1922* (St. Louis, 1923), 59.

30. Cited in Dougherty et al., 218.

Sister Febronie Chapellon

Sister Marguerite-Felicite Boute

them an entree in the diocese of St. Louis, the Americanization of the Sisters of St. Joseph began almost immediately, through the introduction of American membership in the congregation and interaction with the wider civic and ecclesiastical communities.

The first American woman joined the community at Carondelet in October 1837, just one year and a half after the United States foundation She was Anne Eliza Dillon, who had met the Sisters of St. Joseph as a boarder at the convent school of the Sacred Heart in St. Louis, where two of the St. Joseph Sisters had come for English lessons in the summer of 1836. She was to provide an American element within the community from the dawn of its history in this country; life under the rigorous French regime entailed compatible conflict. In March 1838, the new Sister Mary Joseph wrote to Bishop Rosati protesting the severity of Sister Delphine's governance and the hardships which threatened her health:

> The superior requires me to do work, for which I have not strength sufficient My health is not very good and at times I have severe pains in my breast and side Mother is forever scolding me, she says as a novice I ought to be employed in the kitchen and that it is an honor for me to teach.[31]

31. Sister Mary Francis Joseph Dillon to Bishop Rosati, Carondelet, 22 March 1838, copy, ACSJC; original, AASL.

Sister St. Protais Deboille

Mother Celestine Pommerel

In truth, the sisters could hardly do without her teaching at that time, since she was the only one in the community who spoke fluent English.[32] When Sister Mary Joseph Dillon died of her pains at twenty two years of age, 30 October 1842, she was replaced as English teacher in the Academy by Sister Mary Rose Marsteller, an American novice who was a native of Alexandria, Virginia.[33]

The incipient process of Americanization was promoted when the sisters became involved with civic structures through the services they offered. Two of them, Sisters Celestine Pommerel and St. John Fournier, had been trained for a year in France in methods for teaching the deaf-mute. This skill earned a government subsidy from the State of Missouri for the "asylum" at Carondelet—in reality a conglomeration of deaf-mutes, boarders, orphans and sisters who managed to pursue their goals elbow-to-elbow.[34] The sisters also functioned for a time as public school teachers,

32. "Nous n'avons mis aucune conversion ni aucun bapteme parce que nous sommes encore dans l'impossibilite d'instruire des americaines." Sister Febronie Fontbonne to Bishop Rosati: Cahokia, February 1838, copy, ACSJC, original AASL. Eliza McKenny Brouillet recorded that during her years as a boarder at Carondelet (1839–45) none of the French sisters could speak English well. Sister St. John Fournier being the most conversant. Brouillet Memoirs.

33. Savage, 61.

34. *Missouri Session Laws*, 8 February 1839, 334 cited in Dougherty et al., 67, and "Cahier de fondation-1838," C-M-1a, ACSJC.

The Deboille and Brouillet memoirs relate that before the brick structure of 1841, everyone shared the same dining and recreation rooms—pupils, mutes and orphans at two tables and sisters at a third. These rooms served by turn as dormitory, classroom, parlor and chapel, with beds stored in a loft during the day.

First students at Mt. Gallitzin Academy, Ebensburg, Pa., 1869

being paid by the Corporation of Carondelet for the education of girls of the town.[35] Although these arrangements with the government were not permanent, they provided incentive to learn English and provoked interaction with the American milieu.

The sisters in St. Louis were also reaching beyond their French context by teaching only nationality groups in the diocese. In 1845 they opened

35 Minutes of the Board of Trustees, 23 April 1839, cited in Savage, 53. Mother St. John Fournier related, "We had all the children of the village in our school. The city paid us every year in land." Logue, 328-329.

their first mission in the city of St. Louis, a school for Black children on Third and Poplar Streets. There they taught free Blacks a general curriculum, but were restricted to catechetical instruction for the slaves of Catholic families. Under pressure of racial prejudice, city officials urged Bishop Kenrick to abandon the project, and the school was closed the following year.[36] Also in 1845, the sisters opened a school in St. Vincent de Paul parish, which at that time was composed of German- or English-speaking members, the latter chiefly Irish immigrants.[37]

In 1846, in a significant and ironic twist of events, the French Sisters of St. Joseph took over the boys' orphan asylum in St. Louis which had been abandoned by the American Sisters of Charity. The latter had been obliged to withdraw from this institution when they affiliated with the French Daughters of Charity whose rule forbade the care of male orphans. The same procedure was to be repeated the following year in Philadelphia, extending the works of the Sisters of St. Joseph beyond the limits of the St. Louis diocese.[38] Although there was no clear precedent for the care of boys by the Sisters of St. Joseph in France, there was nothing explicitly against it in their rules, and they did in fact take charge of boys in this country whenever it was necessary. This was to be an important factor in the history of their expansion in the United States, for bishops were anxious to have sisters for male orphanages, and pastors often preferred a community who could teach boys in the parochial school, since a parish could ill afford separate institutions for boys and girls.[39] The decision to take on unprecedented works and to move into new areas gave the Sisters of St. Joseph greater visibility in the Catholic Church in America and enlarged their ranks with additional members.

Despite the hardships aggravated by their poverty and the somewhat Jansenist leanings of a rigorous French piety, the Sisters of St. Joseph

---

36. Extract from the Records of St. Louis Diocese, entry signed by Edmund Saulnier, Book 1, A.D. 1845, K–A–8, ACSJC; Letter of Mother St. John Fournier in Logue, 330–332; and Dougherty et al., 123–124.

37. Peter Richard Kenrick to Archbishop Milde of Vienna, St. Louis, 10 December 1844, *Berichte der Leopoldinen Stiftung*, 18:6–14, original in English; retranslated from the German in John Rothensteiner, *History of the Archdiocese of St. Louis: In Its Various Stages of Development from A.D. 1673 to A.D. 1928*, 2 vols. (St. Louis, 1928), 1:822.

38. Logue, 28; and Savage, 66.

39. A letter of Mother Clement Lannen to Rev. John W. Shanahan, 29 May 1889, reveals that objections to the sisters' teaching boys above twelve or thirteen years came not from them, but from Archbishop Ryan. M–29–1–4, 3.441, Archives of the Sisters of St. Joseph of Philadelphia (hereafter cited as ACSJP). Further correspondence shows that pastors managed to get around the episcopal objections: John W. Shanahan to Mother Clement Lannen, Philadelphia, 26 December 1889; idem, 25 September 1849; and William A. Duffy to Mother Clement Lannen, Pottstown, Pa., 8 August 1889, M–29–1–3, 3.390; M–29–1–4, 3.451–52, ACSJP.

continued to attract American candidates.[40] By 1845 the number of sisters in the community who could not speak French necessitated the translation of the constitutions into English. The profession of novices was delayed until the completion of this translation, an indication of the importance of an English document for the life of the community at this time.[41] The English *Constitutions of the Congregation of the Sisters of St. Joseph* printed in 1847 signifies not only a shifting pattern of membership in the community, but an implicit decision to become American, since in fact the French language and culture had not been imposed on novices as a condition for being a Sister of St. Joseph. By the end of their first decade in this country, the Sisters of St. Joseph had an English rule, a growing American membership, and a ministry which included a variety of ethnic groups. The foundations were in place for the emergence of a community with a properly American identity.

Separation from France

The single most important element in the rapid Americanization of the Sisters of St. Joseph was the independence of American communities from the motherhouse in France. Although congregational histories explain the separation of the French and American congregations as a result of mutual agreement, archival sources are curiously silent on this matter.[42]

The decade between 1847 and 1857 was a time of tremendous expansion for the Sisters of St. Joseph, with foundations in the dioceses of Philadelphia, St. Paul, Toronto, Hamilton, Wheeling, Buffalo, Brooklyn, and Albany. This growth necessitated the definition of lines of authority, and brought into focus the question: Who is the superior? Since the constitutions of Sisters of St. Joseph at the time provided for both a sister

---

40. By the beginning of 1845, five American-born women, plus one each from Ireland and Germany had entered the community. Register of Professions, ACSJC.

41. Sister Aloysius Fitzsimmons (received 1839, professed 1845) reported that during the five years while "Bishop Barron of Savannah" [Edward Barron] was translating the rule, she had to wait to make vows. Memoirs, 1879; and Register of Professions, ACSJC. The English version was published under the title of *Constitutions of the Sisters of St. Joseph* (St. Louis, 1847). Page iv reads: "translated from the French edition of Lyons, 1827," referring to *Constitutions pour la petite congrégation des Soeurs de saint Joseph*, Nouvelle édition (Lyons, 1827), which is essentially the same as the first edition printed at Vienne, 1693.

42. Dougherty et al., 363; Logue, 173; Savage, 108; and M. Evangeline Thomas, C.S.J., *Footprints on the Frontier: A History of the Sisters of Saint Joseph, Concordia, Kansas* (Westminster, MD, 1948), 59–60, all suggest some kind of formal separation from France, but neither the archives at Lyons nor at Carondelet yield any correspondence between the congregations regarding separation. Savage, 108, cites correspondence from Father S. Auguste Paris, C.M., to Mother Celestine as early as 1856 which indicates that a form of government centralized at Carondelet was already under consideration.

Sister Petronilla Stibolitski and her nephew, Johnstown, Pa., 1881

superior and a male ecclesiastical superior, the question had to be answered in terms of each.

The ecclesiastical superior—the bishop or some priest designated by him—exercised extensive powers over the life of a community: the constitutions gave him the right to impose corrections, confirm elections, and even to appoint or remove the sister superior.[43] The legal unity of a congregation of more than one house depended on the bishop rather than on the sister superior. Canonically, this meant that when the sisters left Lyons and came under the jurisdiction of the bishop of St. Louis, they were in fact a separate community.[44] The juridical situation notwithstanding, the Sisters of St. Joseph remained connected with France in mind and heart for some time. In 1848, Sister St. John Fournier, became superior in Philadelphia, puzzled as to why there had been no new recruits from Lyons for the American missions; in Lyons, congregational communiqués continued to report the deaths of sisters "in our community at Carrondelet (America)."[45] The conscious realization that the sisters in America had

43. Part I, chap. 6, *Constitutions* (1847), 9–11.

44. Such a separation is implied in a letter of Father Claude Cholleton to Sister Delphine Fontbonne, Lyons, 4 April 1837: "Sister St. John is yet a novice. When she appears to you sufficiently proven and well disposed, you shall ask Monseigneur Rosati . . . to be kind enough to receive the vows himself. . . . You will follow the same procedure in the future for the admission of subjects who by the divine goodness will be confided to your maternal care." Copy and trans., K–A–7, ACSJC; original, AASL.

The Lyons constitutions were not revised to provide for a sister as superior general until 1858. *Constitutions pour la petite congrégation des Soeurs de Saint-Joseph établies dans le Diocèse de Lyon,* Deuxième édition (Lyons, 1858).

45. Francis Patrick Kenrick to Peter Richard Kenrick, Philadelphia, 15 December 1848, in *The Kenrick-Frenaye Correspondence: Letters Chiefly of Francis Patrick Kenrick and Antony Frenaye 1830–1862,* trans. and ed. Francis E. Tourscher (Lancaster, Pa. 1920), 289.

in fact become an independent foundation with distinct authority structures, membership, and cultural identity developed only gradually, and in relation to the role played by the sister superior vis-à-vis the bishops.

The original French constitutions did not define the role of a sister as Superior General; no sister exercised authority beyond her particular house. This was the practice adopted in America at the beginning. Each of the two houses, Cahokia and Carondelet, had a sister superior; each received novices.[46] Neither house had precedence over the other, the bishop being superior over both. At the beginning of 1845, however, when they started to open other missions in the St. Louis diocese, the Sisters of St. Joseph had only one house in this country: Cahokia had been flooded out the previous June and Sister Febronie Fontbonne, the superior there, returned to France.[47]

Thus, precisely at the moment when expansion began, there was only one sister superior—Celestine Pommerel at Carondelet; of necessity it was she who made assignments to the new houses. Sister Celestine was a charismatic leader, much respected and loved by the sisters, and she continued in this role, appointing superiors and assigning personnel, when foundations were made in dioceses outside St. Louis. She was acting as a virtual superior general, without constitutionally possessing such authority.[48] Following the untimely death of Sister Celestine at forty-four years of age, 7 June 1857, a movement to regularize the situation resulted in a provisional constitution drafted in 1860, which called for a provincial structure of government with the motherhouse at Carondelet, and granted extensive powers to the archbishop of St. Louis over houses in other dioceses.[49]

Most of the bishops who already had congregations in their dioceses vigorously opposed the centralization. John Timon of Buffalo went to Philadelphia and spoke against it at the sisters' annual retreat in 1863, as

46. Archival sources indicate that Sister Febronie Fontbonne opened a novitiate at Cahokia, where Sister Antoinette Kincaid received the habit 6 March 1842. MS notes, K–A–15, ACSJC. The date of the establishment of the novitiate at Carondelet is given as 1844 in *Constitutions* (1847), iv.

47. She and Sister Marie-Febronie Chapellon, her close friend, returned to France in October of 1844. They both lived at Chagny, where Febronie Fontbonne was superior until her death, 10 April 1881; Marie-Febronie Chapellon died there 3 January 1890. Dougherty et al., 60–61.

48. *Rules and Constitutions of the Sisters of St. Joseph*, Approved of and adopted by, the Most Reverend the Archbishop of St. Louis, for the Diocess [*sic*] of St. Louis (Carondelet, MO, 1860), 291, explains that the sisters have "regarded the Mother Superioress of that house [Carondelet] as being virtually our Superioress-General."

49. The section of the *Constitutions* of 1860 (part 1, chap. 7, 24–25), which made the Archbishop of St. Louis in effect superior general over all houses, in whatever diocese, was changed by Rome as prejudicial to the jurisdiction of other bishops. Observations of Cardinal Quaglia on the constitutions, 1863, K–K–11, ACSJC.

did Bishop Loughlin at the community elections in Flushing, New York.[50] A paper drafted by Bishop James F. Wood of Philadelphia, replete with citations from Roman documents, identifies the neuralgic point:

> The general principle is that the rights of an Ordinary cannot be encroached by his equal. . . . And this is the danger perpetually recurring. Where a Bishop pretends to jurisdiction over religious Communities in another diocese, even where they subject themselves freely and willingly to the exercise of such authority.[51] [*sic*]

It was in part a power struggle among bishops, and Thomas L. Grace, O.P., of St. Paul, at odds with the plan for centralization endorsed by his metropolitan, Peter Richard Kenrick of St. Louis, earned himself a reprimand from the Propaganda Fide for interfering with the constitutions of sisters.[52]

The end result was the formation of independent diocesan congregations in Philadelphia, Toronto, Hamilton, Wheeling, Buffalo, and Brooklyn, while Albany and St. Paul became provinces of Carondelet. Some of the women who had entered at Carondelet returned there when the various communities chose independent status; others deplored the change and repudiated the "new" rule:

> Six of our religious were weak enough to let themselves be seduced by the attraction of a false liberty and have left our congregation in the course of the last two years. Thanks to Divine Mercy two have already recognized their error and have re-entered the straight road of dependence.[53]

Such was the view from Carondelet. In Wheeling, where the small community was jeopardized by the exodus of sisters to Carondelet, the writer of the annals lamented, "All that had been done before was undone by the action of the Carondelet House."[54]

The events occasioned by centralization demonstrate the proprietary attitude of bishops toward the communities, and the considerable effects of their insistence on indigenous diocesan congregations in the process of

50. "At Retreat Bishop Timon spoke of St. Louis' seeking approval. He is against it." First Council Book 16 January 1863, C–B–1, ACSJP; and Annals, 24 August 1863, 1:17, Archives of the Sisters of St. Joseph of Brentwood, New York (hereafter cited as ACSJB).

51. "Jurisdiction of Bishops over Religious Communities Outside of Their Diocese," [post 1864], ACSJP.

52. Propaganda Fide to Thomas L. Grace, bishop of St. Paul, 26 April 1866, Lettere, vol. 357, fol. 379 v; and Peter R. Kenrick, Archbishop of St. Louis, to PF, 13 January 1864, Scritture riferite nei Congressi, America Centrale, 1866–1867, vol. 21, fols. 73 r, 74 v, Archives of the Congregation for the Propagation of the Faith, Rome.

53. Mother St. John Facemaz to Cardinal Quaglia [1869], K–B–25, ACSJC.

54. Record of profession, 6 August 1861 [probably written in 1864 by Sister de Chantal Keating], Annals. Archives of the Sisters of St. Joseph of Wheeling (hereafter cited as ACSJW).

Americanization. This dynamic would be epitomized at the turn of the century in St. Augustine, when the ailing bishop, John Moore, enforced separation of the Sisters of St. Joseph, who had been in Florida since 1866, from the Le Puy motherhouse. His letter to the superior in France explains his frame of mind:

I believe I see a necessity to have only Sisters who are entirely diocesan, Sisters who obey the Bishop of the Diocese. . . . I repeat, I want Sisters who obey me like their Bishop; and who are not in any manner subject to orders of a Superior in another distant country.[55]

As in Florida at a later date, the bishops' maneuvers in the 1860s punctuate how important the contributions made by sisters were in the face of exploding needs in the young dioceses, which were desperately short of personnel, and had already begun to feel the impact of immigration. The episode indeed points out the sisters' own identification in many cases with the local setting, since they too played a part, and their motives were influenced by psychological and sociological realities. Most telling of all, by 1860, twenty-four years after their arrival in the United States, there was no longer any question of formal dependence on France for these Sisters of St. Joseph. The matter at hand was strictly the clarification of lines between several flourishing American congregations.

Cultural Tensions

By 1860 the Congregations of St. Joseph had become American-based communities, with a numerical dominance of American members. In at least two of the largest congregations, however, sisters still looked to their French component for leadership. Mother St. John Fournier, one of the pioneers, was the superior in Philadelphia until her death, 15 October 1875. At Carondelet, a new influx of missionaries from the congregation of Moûtiers, in Savoy, continued to supply novice mistresses, provincial superiors, and a superior general, Sister St. John Facemaz, who served in that capacity from 1857 until her resignation in 1872.[56]

At the death of Sister Celestine Pommerel in 1857, the community elected an American, Sister Seraphine Coughlin, a native of New York

55. John Moore to Reverend Mother [Pélagie Boyer], St. Augustine, Florida, 31 January 1900, copy, Archives of the Sisters of St. Joseph of St. Augustine; original, ACSJLP; trans. Mary Albert Lussier, S.S.J., St. Augustine.

56. Between 1854 and 1887 the Sisters of St. Joseph of Moûtiers sent thirty-nine missionaries to the United States who were incorporated into the Carondelet congregation. Dougherty et al., 113, 223, 424–425.

who had entered the novitiate at Carondelet in 1846.[57] When she declined the office, begging inability and poor health, Archbishop Kenrick of St. Louis acted on his authority as ecclesiastical superior to appoint Sister St. John Facemaz, who had come from Moûtiers just three years previously. His announcement hardly met unanimous approval. According to the report of a contemporary, "The sisters screamed, threw themselves on the floor, etc., etc.—. The Archbishop left immediately, even ran from the chapel and would not hear or see anyone."[58] Perhaps this scene in the Carondelet chapel demonstrated the reaction of an increasingly American (if undisciplined) community to what they feared would be a severely Gallic rule.

The French sisters were a minority in the growing congregations. As early as the 1850s and throughout the century, the greatest number of candidates were Americans, followed by a large element of Irish-born women, with a smaller but significant group of Germans, and a sprinkling of other nationalities.[59] Ethnic patterns in congregations reflected the Catholic populations of areas where the sisters worked. By the fourth quarter of the nineteenth century, for many communities derived from Carondelet, the French character of the congregations would have been hearsay.

Yet the French women had proved indomitable forerunners, and they carried Sisters of St. Joseph to nearly every frontier of American Catholicism. At the end of the Civil War, when Augustin Verot sought educators for the freed Blacks in his episcopal jurisdiction, he obtained Sisters of St. Joseph from his native Le Puy:

> I want you to understand clearly and thoroughly, that it is for the Negroes, and for them almost exclusively that I am having the sisters of your Order come to my Diocese. I have five to six hundred thousand Negroes without education and without religion and without baptism for whom I wish to do something.[60]

The labors of the French sisters contributed toward making Georgia and Florida the scene of the only organized effort on the part of the Catholic Church for the education of Blacks during the Reconstruction period.[61] The seven Sisters of St. Joseph, whose adventurous trek across the desert

57. Savage, 89.
58. Memoirs of Sister Febronia Boyer, n.d., D-M-5a, ACSJC.
59. Registers of Profession, ACSJC and ACSJP.
60. Augustin Verot to Madame la Supérieure et très-chère en N. S. [Léocadie Broc], Savannah, 21 February 1866, my translation; also *idem*, Brest, 25 August 1865; and *idem*, Atlanta, Georgia, 18 September 1865, copies, Archives of the Sisters of St. Joseph of St. Augustine; originals, ACSJLP.
61. Michael V. Gannon, *Rebel Bishop: The Life and Era of Augustin Verot* (Milwaukee, 1964), 138; see 131–144.

A lay sister, St. Augustine, Florida, 1887

from San Diego to Tucson in 1870 was dramatized in a *Playhouse 90* production starring Helen Hayes, included five missionaries from Moûtiers.[62] One of the original volunteers from Lyons, Sister St. Protais Deboille, spent the last twenty years of her long life among the Chippewa at St. Francis Xavier Mission in Baraga, Michigan, where she was buried in 1892.[63]

Significant as the works with native American or Black populations were, they formed a scant part of the whole. Most Sisters of St. Joseph found themselves among the urban Catholics of the United States. There they shared the poverty of an immigrant church. Like other women of their day, sisters stretched their income by plying the needle. At Carondelet, the pioneers sewed powder sacks which sold for one cent; the Flushing account books show receipts for sewing scapulars and "habits" (shrouds). The St. Augustine sisters survived by making the beautiful bobbin-lace for which Le Puy is still famous: "We would have starved," they reported starkly, "but for the sale of our lace."[64] Sisters also took on menial tasks

62. [Corrigan] Taggert, Sister Monica, "Diary of the Journey of the Sisters of St. Joseph to Tucson, Ariz. 1870," *St. Louis Catholic Historical Review* 2 (April-July 1920) 101–113. Sister Monica, born Annie Taggert, was the widow of John Corrigan. St. Claire Coyne, C.S.J., "The Los Angeles Province," in Dougherty *et al.*, 289–294.

63. Dougherty *et al.*, 134. During the nineteenth century the Sisters of St. Joseph of Carondelet staffed missions among native Americans in Michigan, Wisconsin, Minnesota, Arizona, and California.

64. Déboille memoirs; sample entries from 1858 to March 1860, Expenses and Receipts, ACSJB; *Living Waters*, a commemoration of the centennial of the Sisters of St. Joseph (St. Augustine, 1966); and Sister Louise Antonia to Worthy and good Reverend Mother, Ybor City, Florida, 12 February 1900, copy and trans. Archives of the Sisters of St. Joseph of St. Augustine, original, ACSJLP.

in church institutions. While they humbly contributed to providing basic necessities of civilized life for clerics and scholars, at least one sister understood the social ramifications of these roles. In a notarized statement dated 14 March 1900, Sister de Chantal Keating testified regarding property rights of the Wheeling congregation which were being disputed by a diocesan priest:

> None of us would have felt we were receiving more than our due had the deed been presented to use for a dollar in the time of Bishop Whelan: he knew the amount of slavish work that was performed by the Sisters in the College where such a number of Boarders and Seminarians were cared for in health and sickness: the washing and mending for them and the Cathedral, etc., and all this where there were so few conveniences.[65]

"Slavish work" was the price paid by many sisters to secure a niche in the society, both ecclesiastical and civil, of the United States of America.

Integral as they were to the great system-building of nineteenth-century Catholicism, sisters were an oddity to the larger population. Until the Civil War, Sisters of St. Joseph wore lay clothing for travel; the Brooklyn community disguised their veils with a sunbonnet even in their own yard. In 1875, the first sisters in New Castle, Pennsylvania were met with a vulgar display of bigotry.[66] Their participation in the Civil War won a qualified acceptance for Catholics as a bona fide part of American society, and heightened their own sense of identity as citizens. In February of 1864, the United States government rented space in Wheeling Hospital and hired the Sisters of St. Joseph who staffed it to care for the wounded soldiers. When Washington failed to pay, the superior took action. "Despairing of justice without a personal application," she wrote in the community annals, "Sr. de Chantal left Wheeling today [6 February 1865] for Washington City accompanied by an Orphan child, an insane soldier & guard, also received Govt. transportation." [*sic*] There she made the rounds of the War Department, and within two weeks had word that all arrears would be paid.[67]

Many women, lay and religious alike, who served in camps and on the battlefield were not trained nurses. They worked primarily as cooks and ward managers. Dr. Henry H. Smith, Surgeon-General of Pennsylvania,

---

65. St. John's home [Brooklyn], 14 March 1900, [signed] Mother M. de Chantal Keating, ACSJW.

66. The Philadelphia archives contain a record of Mother St. John Fournier's going to the Chapter in St. Louis in 1860 "dressed in secular attire." Council Book 1, C–B–1, ACSJP; Mary Ignatius Meany, C.S.J. *By Railway or Rainbow: A History of the Sisters of St. Joseph of Brentwood* (Brentwood, NY, 1964), 46–47; and Adele Whaley, S.S.J., *Salute to the Pioneers: Pages in the Early History of the Sisters of St. Joseph of Baden, Pennsylvania* (Pittsburgh, 1952), 29.

67. Annals, 26 February 1864–18 February 1865, ACSJW; and Rose Anita Kelly, S.S.J., *Song of the Hills: The Story of the Sisters of St. Joseph of Wheeling* (Wheeling, 1962), 213–222.

was insistent in his letter to the Philadelphia superior regarding sisters for Camp Curtin, new Harrisburg: "Good cooks & house keepers rather than nurses are required. Sister Philomene and two lay sisters would make an excellent party."[68] Letters of one of the ten Sisters of St. Joseph of Carondelet who served in the Spanish American War reveal (in addition to unadorned generosity, good humor, and common sense) the simplicity of her education: "Yesterday nine of us was swoming [*sic*] in to serve Uncle Sam which we will loyally I hope." Their tour of duty took them to Camp Hamilton, Kentucky, Americus, Georgia, and Matanza Bay, Cuba.[69]

Despite the sisters' intimate involvement in the most convulsive events of the century in American history, they showed an extraordinary reserve in discussing them afterward. "[They] resumed their former duties as if they had never left them," wrote an admiring sister in Philadelphia. "Seldom did they allude to their war experiences . . . nor did they ever record their story."[70] Their reticence was likely inspired by a desire to avoid "singularity"—a considerable transgression of convent manners. It also reflected the "world within a world" ethos which permeated Roman Catholicism, and particularly convent life. Although immersed in the concerns of education, social work and health care for nineteenth-century Americans, within their own houses sisters had a separate culture, which operated according to its own dictates. A curiously Catholic variety of civil religion appears in an 1894 decree permitting the sisters to observe national holidays as feasts "of the II. class."[71] (A second class observance meant, unlike other days, that talking was allowed at dinner and supper, and for most of the evening). The comic element in this juxtaposition does not hide the fact that Sisters of St. Joseph in the United States never enjoyed the same kind of complete integration with the prevailing culture which had been second nature for them in their "mother . . . the Catholic France."

The American identity of the Sisters of St. Joseph did not emerge in perfect harmony with the spirit of the older tradition. There were tensions

68. To Madame St. John, Surgeon-General's Office, State of Pennsylvania, 22 January 1862. In a letter of 14 April 1862, Dr. Smith reiterates the need for "*hardy* . . . or *strong* Sisters." *Idem*, Fortress Monroe, 21 April 1862 alludes to "friendly competition with a party of females directed by Miss Dix." M-27-1-4, 1.71, 74, 79, ACSJP; see Logue, 119-134.

69. Sr. Ligouri [McNamara] to Mother Agatha Guthrie, Camp Hamilton [Kentucky], 5 October 1898, D-M-4a, ACSJC; and Dougherty et al., 128-129.

70. "Brief account," MS, n.a., n.d., M-27-1-1, ACSJP.

71. Decrees of the General Chapter 1894, 2-1, S17, ACSJP; the same is found in "Regulations of the Sisters of St. Joseph, c. 1915, Archives of the Sisters of St. Joseph of Baden, Pennsylvania.

caused, on the one hand, by the general conflict in the Roman Catholic Church in this country between the republican, democratic spirit of its American context and the inherited European forms;[72] on the other by the specific differences of French and American cultures.

Sisters of St. Joseph had to balance French custom and American sensibilities in their religious life. Their spirituality had been formed in Europe, and they preserved the Gallican idiom in practices such as kissing the floor, praying *les bras en croix*, and using penitential instruments like the discipline. Aware of their abrasiveness to Americans, sisters confined such things strictly to the privacy of the convent. Even there, however, old world etiquette sometimes proved uncomfortably at odds with the American way. On 30 December 1884, the day of her re-election as superior general of the Philadelphia congregation, Mother Mary John Kieran noted in her diary, "I asked to be dispensed with the Srs. kissing the hand as they had before. He [Archbishop Ryan] allowed it to be dispensed with. That was a relief."[73]

Conflict between an authoritarian regime and a strong spirit of independence was not the preserve of Americans. Some of the more notable nonconformists among the nineteenth-century Sisters of St. Joseph were Irish, or daughters of Irish immigrants. Outstanding among them was Anna Fogerty, a native of County Louth. Professed in 1854 at St. Louis as Sister Mary Blanche, she transferred to the Wheeling community in 1869, "desirous of returning to the old Rule"—in other words, objecting to a central government. She had further objections to ecclesiastical centralization, for on 19 May 1871, she "left the Com'ty dispensed from her vows, and at the same time left the Church, obstinately refusing to accept the dogma of Papal Infallibility."[74]

The period after 1875 in the history of the congregations is marked by a certain stabilization among the older ones, and at the same time by a restlessness that went in search of new frontiers. The eight permanent foundations which were made after 1880 are related to the enterprising activity of two women, both first generation Irish born in New York, whose separate and arduous peregrinations covered this country from East to West. They were Sisters Stanislaus Leary and Mary Herman (alias Margaret Mary) Lacey. Mostly, they were on the run in conflicts

72. James Hennesey, S.J., "American History and the Theological Enterprise," *Proceedings of the Catholic Theological Society of America* 26 (1977): 94–95.

73. Diary of Mother Mary John Kieran, vol. 1 (1873–1885), M-28-1-6+, ACSJP.

74. Register of Professions, ACSJC; and Annals, 4 February 1869, 19 May 1871, ACSJW [where she is identified as Anne Gogerty].

A choir sister, St. Augustine, Florida, 1887

with bishops or major superiors.[75] The history of these and other mavericks in the congregations deserves to be written for it shows how the diocesan structure of communities indirectly promoted extension, since one could seek escape from an oppressive regime by removing to another jurisdiction. It also represents the French tradition in perhaps its most American pose.

If qualities of individualism, activism, aggressiveness and adventure can be considered typically American, then the American spirit had more than a few exponents within a scheme of convent life which called for hiddenness, obedience, and docility. Few were as outspoken as Sister Assissium Shockley, superior of the Albany province from 1866 to 1869. She took great pride in the fact that her forebears on both sides dated to the Revolution. Worthy of her ancestry, Sister Assissium put a quite American appreciation of progress to work in building the provincial

75. Sister Stanislaus Leary, first postulant at Canandaigua, New York, and subsequently superior of the Rochester congregation, founded the congregations of Concordia, Kansas (1883) [whence Wichita (1888)], and La Grange, Illinois (1899) [whence Orange, California (1912)]. Thomas, 81-98, 198.

Sister Lacey was originally Sister Mary Herman of the Albany province of Carondelet. As Sister Margaret Mary, she established the congregations of Watertown, New York (1880), and Kalamazoo, Michigan (1889), aiding that of Tipton, Indiana (1888). She returned to Carondelet in 1890, and died a member of that congregation in California. Emily Joseph Daly, C.S.J., "Part Four: The Albany Province," in Dougherty *et al.*, 226-229.

house and novitiate at Troy, New York. Her enthusiasm for the up-to-date set her at odds with the higher authorities at Carondelet: "The bone of contention," reported Sister Assissium, "seems to have been the introduction of modern improvements. . . . Even the wise Jesuits could not quiet their scruples on this point." Her troubles may have been at bottom a cultural conflict—of the five members of the general council at that time, two were French and one German.[76]

Along with her sense of national pride and her broad-minded approach to modernity, Sister Assissium simply enjoyed being the boss. Having returned to Carondelet in 1869 on the very day her term as provincial expired, she was informed of the fact and told to resume her ordinary rank in the community. Forty years later she still remembered that she had accepted her demotion with dignity: "I thanked them," she wrote, "and did as I was told without showing the least mark of emotion, which I had every reason to feel."[77] It is possible that only the immense conservative strength of the Roman Catholic Church was able to temper the enterprising pragmatism native to these American women, in some cases by giving them work to do worthy of their energies. At least in the role of superior, one had plenty of opportunity for the baptized exercise of the "American" virtues.

The Lay Sister Issue

The conflict of a democratic spirit with European notions of a stratified society came to a painful focus among the Sisters of St. Joseph over the issue of lay sisters, and the history of law sisters in the American congregations serves as a prime example of how pressures from the new sociocultural context served to change the received French tradition. In France by the nineteenth century, there were two classes of membership, the choir sisters, who wore a veil and guimpe and carried on the white collar occupations of the community such as teaching and administration, while lay sisters, usually women with minimal education and dowery, wore a bonnet and paid their way by doing housework.[78] Lay sisters had no voice in community elections and occupied the lowest rank, after the choir novices.[79]

---

76. Memoirs of Sister Assissium Shockley, 1912, D–M–9c, ACSJC; and Dougherty et al., 366.

77. Shockley memoirs.

78. *Kenrick-Frenaye Correspondence*, 289.

79. *Constitutions* (1860), 28. The Carondelet customs book of 1868, 33–34, reads: "Postulants and novices are required to pay $100.00 for their board during the probationary & Novitiate term, plus another $100.00 dowry. Lay sisters need bring only the $100.00 dowry." ACSJC. See p. 26 for the difficulties caused by dowry in the American setting.

The system of class distinction meant trouble for the sisters from their beginnings in the United States. Although one of the original group, Sister Philomene Vilaine, was a lay sister, they adopted a uniform habit at the suggestion of Bishop Rosati who advised them to avoid any outward marks of inequality.[80] Lay sisters nevertheless continued to do the menial work in communities, in which they enjoyed responsibility without privilege. According to Father Edmond Saulnier, voluble pastor at Carondelet and self-appointed monitor of the community there, they were treated "like Negro women."[81]

Distinctive garb for lay sisters was reintroduced around 1853, partly as a result of Mother St. John Fournier's concern to bring the American practice in line with the French.[82] She believed the American innovation to be a cause of the unwillingness of the superiors in France to send more subjects. The role of the bonnetted sisters is concisely summarized in a letter of Mother St. John to Bishop Bayley of Newark in 1872. "When we open a mission," she explained, "we generally send a lay sister so as not to be troubled with servant girls."[83]

What seemed quite compatible to a French mentality never sat well in the American milieu. Miss Eliza Gilligan, accepted as a choir postulant in Wheeling (apparently because her brothers had agreed to pay $500 for her education), "Left of her own accord August 9th 1868 unfit for the Choir, & unwilling to embrace the Lay rank." Another member of the Wheeling community, Sister Mary Magdalen (Julia) Quill, an Irish immigrant, was professed as a lay sister, 28 December 1868. In 1870, her superiors had her rank changed to choir, citing "evidence of capacity sufficient to bear us out in believing that the change is for the glory of God and the advantage of the Com'ty." Eight years later she was elected superior general of the Wheeling congregation.[84]

There is ample testimony to a rising tide of dissatisfaction with class distinction in the communities as the century progressed. Mother Mary John Kieran's diary reveals that it ran high on the day of her election as superior of the Philadelphia congregation in 1875. "All the professed sisters and novices voted," she observed; "All the lay sisters were in very bad humor all day."[85] As a Redemptorist, William H. Gross, bishop of

80. *Kenrick-Frenaye Correspondence*, 189. See n. 36, above.

81. Edmund Saulnier to Joseph Rosati, Carondelet, 29 November 1837, copy and trans., ACSJC; original, AASL.

82. Boyer memoirs; and *Kenrick-Frenaye Correspondence*, 289.

83. Mother St. John Fournier to James Roosevelt Bayley, Chestnut Hill, 15 June 1872, M-27-2-5, 1.42, ACSJP.

84. Annals, ACSJW.

85. Diary, vol. 1, 21 October 1875, M-28-1-6^{+}, ACSJP.

Savannah (1873–1885), had first-hand experience of community life, and forbade the reception of lay sisters. When his successor reinstated the practice, the American superior of the Sisters of St. Joseph there thought she would have to appeal to France for a lay sister, and in 1888 expressed her anxiety to Le Puy: "You know our first Lay Sister . . . became insane on the subject of her habit and they all hate the cap." Conflict over the incompatibility of the *converses* with American mores plagued the Le Puy foundations in Florida and Georgia from their beginnings. As a missionary in Savannah had reported triumphantly to France in January of 1868, "We finally succeeded in giving the lay habit to one of our postulants; this was a real *coup d'ètat;* no one wants to be a 'lay sister.'" Mother Helene Gidon, commenting to the European superiors on the same event, put her finger on the heart of the dilemma: "It was feared we should be criticized; we are in a country which esteems equality so much."[86]

Mother St. George Bradley (an Irish-born woman of independent mind who had left Carondelet following centralization), solved the problem in her own way. The Sisters of St. Joseph of Cleveland, established by her in 1872, never had lay sisters.[87] In fact, indigenous American sisterhoods such as the Sisters of Loretto did not, as a rule, form a separate servant class within their communities.[88] (Some antebellum congregations in the South did, however, follow the American tradition and had slaves.) For the Sisters of St. Joseph, cut off from their European roots, a separate class within the community grew more and more problematic. Part of the difficulty involved public image, in cases where lay sisters were needed for teaching and catechetical works, but the variations in their dress advertized them as servants.[89] By 1898 the sisters at Ebensburg, where a Jacksonian air breathed from the beginning, decided in one stroke to suppress the lay habit and limit the term of the mother superior.[90]

86. Sister St. John [Kennedy] to Rev. Mother de Sales [Pays], St. Joseph's Convent, Washington, Ga., 19 September 1888; *idem,* 13 December 1888; Sister Josephine Déléage to Mère Agathe, Savannah, [January], 1868; and Sister Helene Gidon to Ma bonne et excellente Mère [Léocadie Broc], Savannah, 9 January 1868. Copies, Archives of the Sisters of St. Joseph of St. Augustine; originals, ACSJLP, translation by Sister Mary Albert Lussier.

87. Sister Dorothy Glosser, Archivist, Sisters of St. Joseph of Cleveland, to author, June 1985. References to Mother St. George [Mary Bradley, received at Carondelet as Sister Georgiana; Provincial at St. Paul (1865–68) as Mother George] and the sisters who joined her in Cleveland are found in the Register of Professions; and MS notes, D–M–6c, ACSJC.

88. Correspondence of the author with archivists of Sisters of Loretto; Sisters of Charity of Nazareth; Sisters of Mercy of Charleston; Dominican Sisters of St. Catherine, Kentucky; and Sisters, Servants of the Immaculate Heart of Mary.

89. John Ireland, MS, 1908, K–K–43, ACSJC.

90. "Questions regarding the change of habit," 26 July 1898, [signed] Rev. John Boyle, Ecclesiastical Superior; Rev. John Boyle to Mother Joseph Burke, Johnstown, Pa., 12 August 1898, and *idem,* 29 August 1898, Archives of the Sisters of St. Joseph of Baden.

Nurses at Camp Hamilton, Kentucky, 1898

The Ebensburg decision created ripples in other congregations. From Philadelphia the superior went to Washington in December of 1899 to consult the Apostolic Delegate on community matters, including "the threatened change in lay Sisters' dress."[91] The same ferment was at work in other congregations, and the clergy were involved. From St. Paul, Archbishop John Ireland sent a letter in his own hand to the General Chapter assembled at Carondelet, proclaiming the unequal status of lay sisters simply un-American:

the spirit and customs, prevailing in the United States are much contrary to such distinctions in dress and appearance, and the enjoyment of rights and privileges, as indicate social classification. Whatever the arguments for distinctions of this kind may have existed in other times or may exist in other countries, such argument is scarcely to be found in the United States.[92]

The sisters themselves concurred with Archbishop Ireland's judgment on lay status as "antiquated and practically meaningless," for it was suppressed by the Carondelet Congregation in 1908. Although a distinctive dress was abandoned by the other congregations at nearly the same time,

91. "Answers on Constitutions," notes by Sister M. Assissium McEvoy, 25, S-9-1, ACSJP.
92. Ireland MS.

it was not until later in the century that lay sisters were completely integrated in all congregations through the assumption of rank and vote.[93] The issue of lay sisters remained sensitive long after the practice was dead, a kind of skeleton in the closet—in reality a sin against the American way of life.

I have suggested the Americanization of a French tradition as an interpretive framework for the history of the Sisters of St. Joseph in the United States during the nineteenth century. How to assess that process of adaptation? How well did the sisters really adjust to the American way of life? To what extent did they remain true to their French origins?

Adaptation in America was a function, at least in part, of what the sisters did *not* bring with them from France. The lack of persistence of French culture or language among the American Sisters of St. Joseph must be accounted for by their early separation from France, but also by the social composition of the congregations. Neither the French sisters nor the Americans who joined them in this country were drawn from the upper classes. In 1869, requesting release from the obligation of demanding a dowery, Mother St. John Facemaz explained the American situation to an official in Rome: "Generally, there are many vocations for the religious life, but they are especially from the class which is less wealthy, since wealth is principally in the hands of Protestants in this country."[94] The poor are generally not so invested in preserving a cultural tradition as those who have reaped the benefits of a given social system. Like the Irish immigrants who flooded their ranks during the last century, the French Sisters of St. Joseph were more ready for social adaptation in America than other groups who with their European cultural connections had something to lose.[95]

What the Sisters of St. Joseph had brought from France was a congregational heritage of remarkable openness and flexibility that enabled them in many ways to be at home in the American context. The long history in France had provided a model for adaptation to the exigencies of the local situation. Their spirituality, at least in its authentic interpretation, provided a coherent identity for women involved intimately with people through all kinds of service. The French tradition supported the readiness of sisters in this country to become involved in every dimension of parish life and to take on an enormous variety of institutional endeavors. They even fulfilled the dreams of the Countess de la Rochejaquelein by working with Indians. Protestants, however, were another story.

93. Dougherty et al., 369.

94. To Cardinal Quaglia, K–B–2, ACSJC.

95. Dennis Clark, *The Irish in Philadelphia: Ten Generations of Urban Experience* (Philadelphia, 1973), 26.

The essentially Protestant cast of American society in the nineteenth century spelled the limitation of genuine accommodation of the Sisters of St. Joseph to life in the United States. Like many other sisters, they suffered nativist hostility. At the end of the century, in 1895, they were barred by a special act of the Pennsylvania legislature from teaching in the public schools because of their distinctly religious garb.[96] The lack of fit in the American society was due, not to the fact that the Sisters of St. Joseph were French, but that they were Roman Catholic. In some ways the sisters epitomized the separateness of the Catholic Church in the United States.

The real assimilation of Sisters of St. Joseph in this country was not so much to the American way of life as to the American Catholic Church. The Sisters of St. Joseph became American in the sense that the Catholic Church became American—that is, ambivalently.[97] Within the ecclesiastical enclave, however, the fit was hand in glove. Like the larger church, the sisters' membership and professional orientations were shaped by the press of immigration; they, like their Catholic matrix, formed a masterpiece of institutionalization which was, for the most part, urban and separatist.

The role of the bishop in the American church, often that of benevolent tyrant, was the most influential factor in shaping the place of sisters within the American Catholic culture. The bishop considered the Sisters of St. Joseph as "agencies that he might summon to his aid." Their flexibility of organization and diversity of works allowed them to respond readily, and they became identified in the United States as a group on whom the bishops could rely for effective and loyal assistance.[98] There is no denying the price which was paid by sisters for a place in this paternalistic system in terms of subservience and real limitation in forming their own policies. They learned, however, to use this controlling relationship with the bishop to advantage. In congregations which were for the most part diocesan, Sisters of St. Joseph became deeply involved with the life of the locality. Although they formed, to be sure, an exotic part of the congregation, Sisters of St. Joseph attended the parish church. And the church which they knew conferred upon them a certain dignity and prestige. The numbers who joined their communities attest to the attractiveness of the Sisters of St. Joseph as a way of life for young Catholic women.

96. Act 282, 27 June 1895, *Pennsylvania State Reports*, 164:657, cited in Whaley, 33–34.

97. James Hennesey, S.J., *American Catholics: A History of the Roman Catholic Community in the United States* (New York, 1981), 4.

98. John Ireland, *Sermon on the Occasion of the Fiftieth Anniversary of the Sisters of St. Joseph in St. Paul, Minn. (August 20, 1902)* (New York, n.d.); and John J. Wright, *The Sisters of St. Joseph: A Sermon Preached at a Solemn Pontifical Mass in Saint Paul's Cathedral, Worcester, Commemorating the Three Hundredth Anniversary of the Sisters of St. Joseph, Saturday, October 21, 1950* (Worcester, MA, n.d.).

By 1900 there were twenty-one independent American Congregations of St. Joseph, as well as four in Canada. The history of these groups forms a pattern consistent with the French origins in their being closely woven into the fabric of the local church, identified with the common people they served, and "ready for anything."[99] It is a paradox that distance and detachment from the French structures enabled the Sisters of St. Joseph, in the conditions of nineteenth-century America, to remain faithful to the original French inspiration of service to the neighbor through whatever they could do as women in a given time and place.

99. Félicité de Duras to Bishop Rosati.

CATHOLIC WOMEN RELIGIOUS AND WOMEN'S HISTORY: A SURVEY OF THE LITERATURE

SR. ELIZABETH KOLMER, A.S.C.
St. Louis University

ALTHOUGH CATHOLIC SISTERS HAVE BEEN ACTIVE ON THE AMERICAN scene since the eighteenth century, the story of their life and work remains largely untold. In particular, we know little of their history in relation to that of women in general or to the cycles of feminist thinking and action. On first thought, one might suspect that few such connections existed. Catholic sisters of the nineteenth and much of the twentieth centuries lived in relative seclusion from society at large, their lives centering in the institutions they staffed and managed. In addition, the women's movement until recent times was almost exclusively Protestant and middle-class. Nevertheless significant opportunities exist for serious researchers in this untouched area of social history.

This essay will evaluate the existing literature on the history of Catholic nuns, identify bibliographical aids, and indicate the archival and other sources available for investigation of the history of women religious. First I will survey scholarly works on American religious history in general, histories of individual congregations and biographies of their foundresses, and unpublished dissertations on the role of sisters. Second, I will comment on materials available for study of the relationship of Catholic sisters and their congregations to the women's movement of the 1960s and 1970s. In conclusion I will offer some recommendations for future study.

* * *

General histories of religion in America say little if anything about Catholic sisters or sisterhoods. Sydney Ahlstrom's wide-ranging *Religious*

History of the American People mentions the work of women's orders and their contributions to Catholic education in America, citing very briefly the Ursulines, the Carmelites, and Elizabeth Seton and her Sisters of Charity. In the second edition of his *Religion in America*, Winthrop Hudson also mentions Seton and gives passing recognition to the "sacrificial devotion of the members of numerous sisterhoods" who became the backbone of parochial education in America. Otherwise Hudson gives space only to radical stances taken by some religious organizations of women in the 1960s vis-à-vis the authority of the Church.[1]

Lack of space might account for the brevity of coverage in the general religious histories, but publications centering on the Catholic Church in the United States similarly neglect women religious. John Gilmary Shea, the classic early historian of the American Church, touched upon the sisters in each of his four volumes, but mostly in passing reference to their work in the schools and other Catholic institutions. More recently, Thomas T. McAvoy wrote a *History of the Catholic Church in the United States* almost without mentioning the sisters, let alone their work in such an important Church institution as the parochial school. John Tracy Ellis in his short *American Catholicism* also gives them very little attention. While Theodore Roemer discusses the sisters' place in the history of the Church, his interpretation is limited and the book has other weaknesses.[2] Where these and others do discuss women, they treat the sisters by individual orders and in descriptive terms emphasizing their works. Only when recounting their service as nurses in the Civil War do these authors consider women in orders as a single sociohistorical group.

The researcher will find two bibliographies more helpful: Ellis' *Guide to American Catholic History* and Edward R. Vollmar's *The Catholic Church in America*.[3] Ellis' noteworthy second chapter describes manuscript repositories and his sixth chapter discusses some of the histories of the foundation of women's communities. Critics generally consider the Vollmar work (1956) the most complete bibliography on the Catholic Church in the United States; the second edition includes unpublished

[1] Sidney E. Ahlstrom, *A Religious History of the American People* (New Haven: Yale Univ. Press, 1972), chap. 32. Winthrop S. Hudson, *Religion in America*, 2d ed. (New York: Scribner's 1973), 249–50, 420–21.

[2] John Gilmary Shea, *History of the Catholic Church in the United States* (New York: John G. Shea, 1886–1892). Thomas T. McAvoy, C.S.C., *A History of the Catholic Church in the United States* (Notre Dame: Univ. of Notre Dame Press, 1969). John Tracy Ellis, *American Catholicism* (Chicago: Univ. of Chicago Press, 1956). Theodore Roemer, O.F.M. Cap., *The Catholic Church in the United States* (St. Louis: B. Herder, 1950), 156, 192ff, 216ff, 235ff, 253, 258, 284, 339, 354.

[3] John Tracy Ellis, *Guide to American Catholic History* (Milwaukee: Bruce, 1959). Edward R. Vollmar, S.J., *The Catholic Church in America: An Historical Bibliography*, 2d ed. (New York: Scarecrow, 1963).

masters' theses and doctoral dissertations written at Catholic colleges and universities. Vollmar's entries are alphabetical, but the book contains an excellent topical index, as well as a 40-page historiographical essay. "A Selected Bibliography of the Religious Orders and Congregations of Women," by Joseph B. Code, published in the *Catholic Historical Review* (1937), lists the source material then available on orders of religious women founded in the United States before 1850. Though limited in its usefulness today, the article represents an early effort to assist in the study of religious women and their work.[4]

Most of the periodical literature published on the history of women religious has appeared in the Catholic press. One can readily locate these articles through the *Catholic Periodical Index*. Their concern has been either with the sisters' devotional lives or with the history of women's orders or provinces within the larger congregations. Essays in the scholarly journals, the *Catholic Historical Review*, published by the American Catholic Historical Association, and the *Records of the American Catholic Historical Society of Philadelphia* have the same limitations as the longer historical studies: they have not considered nuns from the viewpoint of their common identity or their relationship with other groups of women.

A large number of the some 450 orders of American sisters listed in the *Official Catholic Directory* for 1976 have provided a biography of their foundress or a history of their congregation. Many of these works have been privately printed, and are available primarily to members of the particular congregation or can be found in libraries of Catholic institutions. In quality they run the gamut from scholarly studies to popular episodic sketches. Most have drawn upon letters and papers relating to the congregation, but these are often used to poor advantage, either because of the writer's deficiencies or because of gaps in the congregation's archives. Often the book will not even list these sources.[5]

A few selected titles will suffice as a sample. Excellent both in scholarship and style is *The Society of the Sacred Heart in North America* by Louise Callen (1957). *With Lamps Burning* by Mary Grace McDonald

[4] Joseph B. Code, "A Selected Bibliography of the Religious Orders and Congregations of Women Founded Within the Present Boundaries of the United States (1727–1850)," *The Catholic Historical Review*, 23 (Oct. 1937), 331–51. An extended form of this bibliography is found in *CHR*, 26 (July 1940), 222–45.

[5] Titles of many of these works can be found in Vollmar's bibliography and Ewens' dissertation noted below. Ewens estimates that 45 percent of the books she examined (59 titles) were of scholarly value, with generous use of primary sources and good documentation; another 8 percent (11 titles) were diaries, letters, or journals; 20 percent (26 titles) used primary sources, but without documentation; and 27 percent made no use of scholarly technique.

(1957), a history of the Benedictines in Minnesota, and *Not With Silver or Gold* (1945), an account by the Dayton Precious Blood Sisters of their foundation in Ohio, are also works of distinction. In *We Came North* (1961), Julia Gilmore draws upon congregation archives, local newspapers, and personal interviews to recount the history of the Sisters of Charity of Leavenworth, Kansas.[6] Veronica McEntee's *The Sisters of Mercy of Harrisburg, 1869–1939*, gives evidence that there are ample resources in the houses of the Mercy Sisters, though the book is undocumented, as is *Mother Caroline and the School Sisters of Notre Dame in North America*. Other histories are written in a more popular style, among them Covelle Newcomb's *Running Waters* and *Builders by the Sea* by S. M. Johnston. One final example is Angela Hurley's *On Good Ground*, semipopular in style and written primarily from secondary works and newspaper sources.[7]

Biographies of such outstanding women as Elizabeth Seton and Philippine Duchesne are readily available. In addition, the pages of the histories mentioned above are full of other strong, fearless women who faced great odds and dangers in founding their convents and institutions. Poverty, the threat of starvation, overdemanding bishops, and hostile neighbors were some of their trials. Among the many "nameless" women in our pioneer history we should not forget the sisters who built not only schools but hospitals, foundling homes, and shelters for the sick and poor which served as the chief charitable resources of many nineteenth-century American communities.

Did the nineteenth- or early twentieth-century nun identify with the problems of women outside the cloister, or with secular women's movements of the time? Perhaps not. Her sequestered existence would make this unlikely, and in any case many congregations of that time were still in the building phase, struggling to establish themselves. In this effort they seem to have worked alone. We do not know if they recognized a need for bettering the position of women in society whether inside or outside convent walls; certainly there is little evidence that they looked to an or-

[6] Louise Callan, R.S.C.J., *The Society of the Sacred Heart in North America* (New York: Longmans, Green, 1937). Mary Grace McDonald, O.S.B., *With Lamps Burning* (Minn.: St. Benedict's Priory Press, 1957); Dayton Precious Blood Sisters, *Not with Silver or Gold* (Dayton: Sisters of the Precious Blood, 1945); Julia Gilmore, S.C.L., *We Came North* (St. Meinrad: Abbey Press, 1961).

[7] Mary Veronica McEntee, R.S.M., *The Sisters of Mercy of Harrisburg, 1869–1939* (Philadelphia: Dolphin Press, 1939); School Sisters of Notre Dame, *Mother Caroline and the School Sisters of Notre Dame in North America* (St. Louis: Woodward and Tiernan, 1928), 2 vols; Covelle Newcomb, *Running Waters* (New York: Dodd, Mead, 1947); S. M. Johnston, *Builders By the Sea: History of the Ursuline Sisters of Galveston, Texas* (New York: Exposition, 1971); Angela Hurley, *On Good Ground: History of the Sisters of St. Joseph* (Minneapolis: Univ. of Minnesota Press, 1951.)

ganized women's movement for inspiration or aid in dealing with their own problems. If they refused to accept a bishop's categorization of them as weak, inexperienced, and ineffective, they worked, so far as we know, on a practical level as individuals or individual congregations to prove him wrong, rather than looking for intellectual or moral support in the broader society. It would be an interesting undertaking to determine whether a feeling of solidarity existed among the sisters earlier than the mid-twentieth century with contemporary secular women and, if so, with which classes of women they identified.

The availability of source material on this topic is an important consideration. The headquarters of most congregations have some archival material, but little of it has been catalogued. Furthermore, there has been no guide indicating how much and what kind of material is to be found in any given religious house such as that to the Canadian religious archives published by the Canadian Religious Conference, or Abbé Charles Molette's guide to religious women's archives in France.[8] Some of these needs, however, are soon to be met.

The Leadership Conference of Women Religious has initiated a program to promote the preservation and organization of the records of sisterhoods in the United States. As a first step, the Conference in 1977 and 1978 held six workshops in basic archival training for designated members of religious orders. Directed by Evangeline Thomas, C.S.J., the workshops were funded by the National Historical Publications and Records Commission. The Conference has now embarked upon a survey of some 650 convent archives in the United States, under a grant from the National Endowment for the Humanities. They expect to complete the survey by late 1980, and publish a *Guide to Source Materials in Repositories of Women Religious in the United States.* The *Guide* is designed as a research tool for scholars not only in women's history but also in related fields in the humanities and social sciences.

Meanwhile, a researcher would have to contact individual congregations for information. One can find the most readily available list of these houses in the annual *Official Catholic Directory*. A few other volumes might be helpful. Although certainly dated, *Religious Orders of Women in the United States* (1930) provides a brief historical and institutional account of many congregations. More up to date but less complete in information are Thomas P. McCarthy's *Guide to Catholic Sisterhoods in the*

[8] Canadian Religious Conference, *Abridged Guide to the Archives of Religious Communities of Canada* (Ottawa, Canada); Molette, *Guide des sources de l'histoire des congregations feminines francaises de vie active* (Paris: Editions de Paris, 1974).

United States (1952) and Joan Lexau's *Convent Life: Roman Catholic Religious Orders for Women in North America* (1964).[9]

Of great value and directly related to the topic of this essay is Mary Ewens' "The Role of the Nun in Nineteenth Century America," an American Studies dissertation, from the University of Minnesota.[10] Ewens concludes that sisters were generally regarded with hostility in the early part of the nineteenth century, largely because the Protestant public's concept of them had come from European literature which portrayed a distorted image. Following the public's first hand experience with sister nurses in the Civil War, however, the nuns became highly regarded for their commitment to Christian living and humane concerns.[11] By the end of the century, they had moved to a stronger position in the sense that realistic questions were being asked about their cloistral practices and their adaptation to American society. Throughout her study Ewens examines the image of the nun in the serious literature of the times and compares it with the actual lives and work of the sisters. The bibliography contains a wealth of material about sisters in the profession of nursing and in popular and serious literature, as well as works of a broader scope on the Catholic Church in America. One section lists biographies and histories of individual religious congregations.

Limited material can be found in other dissertations in history, education, and sociology. Those in history are largely studies of the foundations of specific orders, although there is one on the Sisters of Mercy as nurses in the Crimean War.[12] Those in the second group deal with the education of sisters, the education of children by sisters, or the educational contributions of individual orders. The sociology dissertations have a special interest since they approach a religious situation from a different perspective, as part of a larger social structure. Some of the themes treated in these studies are the religious community as a social system; power, status, and institutionalization in the occupational milieu of the Catholic

[9] Elinor T. Dehey, *Religious Orders of Women in the United States* (Hammond, Ind.: W. B. Conkey, 1930); Thomas P. McCarthy, *Guide to the Catholic Sisterhoods in the United States* (Washington, D. C.: Catholic Univ. of America Press, 1952); Joan Lexau, *Convent Life: Roman Catholic Religious Orders for Women in North America* (New York: Dial, 1964).

[10] Mary Ewens, O.P., "The Role of the Nun in Nineteenth Century America: Variations on the International Theme" (1971), to be published by Arno Press.

[11] For example, when a statue of Abraham Lincoln was erected at Oak Ridge Cemetery in Springfield, Ill., President Grant, who himself was being honored by the citizens of Illinois on the same occasion, insisted that two nuns unveil the statue, in acknowledgement of the country's debt to sisters for their wartime services to the wounded. The story can be found in Sister Thomas Aquinas Winterbauer, O.P., *Lest We Forget* . . . (Chicago: Adams Press, 1973).

[12] Mary Gilgannon, R.S.M., "The Sisters of Mercy As Crimean War Nurses," (Diss. Univ. of Notre Dame, 1962).

sister; the process of socialization in a religious community; and the integration of dual professional roles in sisters.[13]

* * *

The historian who seeks to record and interpret the effects of the women's movement in recent Catholic religious history will face several difficulties. So far there has been little written on the subject, and the literature that does exist tends to have a wider perspective. Sisters of today do not see themselves as set apart from other religious women, or even from other women generally. In the sixties and the seventies, in contrast to the past, there has been a pronounced expression by many Catholic sisters of feelings of solidarity with women in all walks of life, professional or otherwise, as well as with religious women of all faiths. Yet the impact of the feminist movement, in varying degrees, has been a common experience for the Catholic sisters in this country, 130,000 in number according to the 1978 *Official Catholic Directory* and constituting a more or less homogeneous group.

The inquiring student might begin with Sarah Bentley Doely's book entitled *Women's Liberation and the Church* (1970).[14] This deals with the question of women and religion on an interdenominational level, and from several different aspects. One essay discusses Catholic sisters, choosing as an example the Immaculate Heart Sisters of California, who wished to determine their own destiny in terms of lifestyle and apostolic work. When their male superiors in the Church disapproved of their plans, the group renounced their canonical status in the church and formed a lay association. Many sisters today are struggling for and gaining greater self-determination, but most strive to remain within the traditional structures of the religious congregation and Church authority. Study of these developments in the lives of women religious has hardly begun.

The subject of sisters and the women's movement is treated, but only briefly, in several books published in the late 1960s, such as Elsie Culver's *Women in the World of Religion*, *Women in Modern Life* by William Bier,

[13] Mary George O'Toole, *Sisters of Mercy of Maine—A Religious Community as a Social System* (Washington, D. C.: Catholic Univ. of America Press, 1964); Rosalma G. Wedhe, "The Occupational Milieu of the Catholic Sister" (Diss. St. John's Univ., 1966); Blake Hill, "Women and Religion: A Study of Socialization in a Community of Catholic Sisters" (Diss. Univ. of Kentucky, 1967); Mary Brigid Fitzpatrick, "The Sister Social Worker: An Integration of Two Professional Roles" (Diss. Univ. of Notre Dame, 1962).

[14] Sarah Bentley Doely, *Women's Liberation and the Church* (New York: Association Press, 1970).

and *Women of the Church* by Mary Lawrence McKenna.[15] Culver makes a case for the importance of the sister's role when she says that "within these orders women have an unusually good opportunity to develop special talents for religion, administration, the arts and professions, though they may not have the temporal power some did in earlier ages" (221). *Women in Modern Life*, dealing with women in general, discusses sisters only in connection with a survey of priests' attitudes toward them and another survey of attitudes of young girls toward sisters (55–96). McKenna, too, concentrates on the general topic of women in the Church, only briefly discussing the role of sisters. She concludes that active religious today perform real functions but no longer belong to the Church's hierarchic structure, only to her "life and holiness." She sees the present position of women in the Church as less than it was in the primitive Church, although the status of women in society at large has supposedly been bettered. "What is lacking today is the status of ecclesiastical order, and the attendent sense of having a definite place and function in the Church's official structure" (147).

Two other books represent the 1960s in still another way. *The New Nuns* and *New Works for New Nuns*[16] were written at the height of the renewal in the Catholic Church, when sisters were asking what they should be doing to meet the needs of present-day society. The informal essays in *New Works* discuss the ways of reaching those who need help—in education, social justice, or any other form. *The New Nuns* (1967) consists of essays gleaned from the "Sisters' Forum" of the *National Catholic Reporter*, which surveyed the sisters' life as it was a decade ago and their growing involvement in new areas of work. Both are now dated, but they do reflect the development of thought that women religious went through to come to renewal in the Church and greater participation in society. A final publication to mention is *The Role of Women in Society and in the Church* (1975), the work of the Canadian Religious Conference. Basically this is an extended annotated bibliography on several themes dealing with women; some twelve pages are devoted to the life of sisters.

Probably the most valuable source of material regarding nuns and the women's movement is the periodical literature of the recent past. Increasingly, magazines devoted to sisters are featuring articles that deal specifi-

[15] Elsie T. Culver, *Women in the World of Religion* (Garden City: Doubleday, 1967); William Bier, S.J., *Women in Modern Life* (New York: Fordham Univ. Press, 1968); Mary Lawrence McKenna, S.C.M.M., *Women of the Church: Role and Renewal* (New York, 1967).

[16] Mary Charles Muckenhirn, O.S.C., *The New Nuns* (New York: New American Library, 1967); Mary Peter Traxler, S.S.N.D., *New Works for New Nuns* (Saint Louis: B. Herder, 1968).

cally with the movement in one form or another. *Sisters Today*, a popular journal devoted chiefly to their religious lives, occasionally publishes personal reflections, such as Evelyn Mattern's "Woman—Holy and Free," or informative pieces like Angelita Fenker's "Sisters Uniting," which explains the function of the organization of that name, formed in 1974 as a forum for exchange of information.[17]

Review for Religious deals with feminist issues more frequently, and while its articles do not always relate specifically to religious women the implications are clear enough. Judith Vollbrecht's "The Role of Women in Social Change"[18] is of special interest for its anthropological approach to American social structure. She suggests a more radical living of the vows professed, through which the sister might be a voice that bespeaks values not totally accepted by her society. An article with a contrasting point of view is Rose Marie Larkin's article on "Religious Women and the Meaning of the Feminine" in *Communio*.[19] Larkin believes that radical feminism has obscured the true feminine and that faith is the most important element in its restoration. Surrender and the veil symbolize the essence of womanhood, the secret wisdom which the woman is to use through compassion, love, and sharing and in this way fulfill her vocation. Larkin's very nineteenth-century definition could have little appeal for today's feminists, religious or nonreligious. The literature on sisters and the women's movement does not usually take such a conservative position, except for some of the articles on the issue of the ordination of women in the Catholic Church.

Another periodical that deserves mention is *Benedictines*, which presents articles on Benedictine history and spirituality, as well as reporting on recent efforts of these sisters to redirect their lives and work. A look through the index discovers no articles on nuns and the women's movement, yet the periodical itself attests to women's independence. That these women have published a magazine of high quality for 30 years with almost no support from the male sections of the Church indicates some degree of liberation. The *Church Woman* is another kind of magazine, published by Church Women United, an international ecumenical group

[17] Evelyn Mattern, I.H.M., "Women—Holy and Free," *Sisters Today*, 47 (May 1976), 553–57; Angelita Fenker, "Sisters Uniting," *ST*, 45 (Apr. 1974), 465–73.

[18] Judith Vollbrecht, R.S.C.J. "The Role of Women in Social Change," *Review for Religious*, 35 (Mar. 1976), 265–71. One also finds in the periodical press bibliographies more or less complete; the same issue of *Review for Religious* prints a list of 30 books and 100 periodicals dealing with "every phase of womanhood." Though less than exhaustive in any of these areas, it gives some idea of what is available, particularly in the popular Catholic press, and could be a starting point for some types of research.

[19] Rose Marie Larkin, "Religious Women and the Meaning of the Feminine," *Communio, An International Catholic Review*, 3 (Spring 1976), 67–89.

of women united in faith who work to effect better participation of women in society through social action. Their 1971 pamphlet by Joan O'Brien entitled *Goal in Common* deals with the relation between Church Women United and Roman Catholic sisters. The magazine publishes many articles on social justice, and discusses aspects of the women's movement in all churches.

Newer periodicals are *Probe* and *Origins*, both started in the early 1970s. *Origins* is published by the National Catholic News Service (Washington, D. C.), and though it deals with a larger spectrum of religious considerations, articles by sisters on the women's movement are included from time to time, for instance "The Role of Women in the Church" (July 3, 1975) by Margaret Farley, and Margaret Brennan's "Women's Liberation/Men's Liberation" (July 17, 1975). Lora Quinonez addresses herself to "The Women's Movement and Women Religious," (November 21, 1974). In her view the feminist movement and the renewal of life for Catholic sisters reflect some of the same concerns: for personal maturity, new ministries in the Church, and a new vision of celibacy. She says in conclusion: "I see affinities between our search and that of other women—a desire to experience ourselves and to be experienced as persons, not as symbols or mythic figures. . . ." *Probe* is the official magazine of the National Assembly of Women Religious (NAWR). This too deals largely with the social concerns of sisters in their work, but also from time to time publishes articles on feminism as it affects their lives.

Almost any of the general Catholic magazines carries articles on women's issues, women in the Church, and sisters in particular. These vary in depth and scholarship, the differences more often than not determined by the type of readership. One of the best has been the December 1975 issue of *Theological Studies*, devoted to women and religion. Though this is not confined to women religious, it presents some excellent scholarly essays by some of today's most prominent Catholic sisters. Particularly valuable is the bibliographical article on "Women and Religion: A Survey of Significant Literature, 1965–1974" by Anne E. Patrick, which includes books on historical analysis and works on selected issues such as canon law, ministry, and ordination, as well as some publications on constructive efforts and radical challenges. This is an insightful essay which makes a real contribution toward further research.[20]

Any discussion of sisters and the women's movement must include the issue of women's ordination, the debate over proposals that they be admitted into the traditionally male role of priest. Literature on this issue

[20] Anne E. Patrick, S.N.J.M., "Women and Religion: A Survey of Significant Literature, 1965–1974," *Theological Studies*, 36 (Dec. 1975), 737–65.

has been so abundant in the past few years that it is impossible to do justice even to part of it in this essay. At the conference on the ordination of women held in Detroit in November 1975, some of the speakers were among the most distinguished sisters in the country, who have written much on the issue of women in the Church. The meeting made available an eight-page bibliography, compiled by Donna Westly, of works since 1965 on the ordination of women. Related to this is the bibliography on women and ministry published in *Origins* in May 1972. The work of this initial conference was continued through an organized group, the Women's Ordination Conference, which held a second meeting in November 1978. Some 2,000 women and men attended from forty-three states and thirteen foreign countries. Following the conference a delegation of women proceeded to Washington, D. C. to attempt the beginnings of dialogue with the Bishops at their annual meeting. Since December 1976, WOC has sponsored a *Newsletter* which keeps interested parties abreast of developments, alerts them to needs for action, and informs them of happenings elsewhere. The objective of WOC is not simply the ordination of women in the traditional priest role. Rather it seeks to "explore how priesthood should and could be transformed in the twentieth century and how the ministry-style of women will help bring that about" (*Newsletter*, June, 1978). Anyone interested in this aspect of sisters and the women's movement should contact this group, whose headquarters are in Rochester, New York.[21]

Finally we call attention to a production of a very different type, "Women of Promise," by Kay Schwerzler and Joyce Fey. This is a slide presentation available through the Leadership Conference of Women Religious which deals with sisters and the women's movement. It celebrates the great figures such as Frances Xavier Cabrini, Philippine Duchesne, and Elizabeth Seton, as well as the many nameless sisters who risked their lives caring for the sick and homeless and who "invented, administered, planned . . . who did 'men's' work without waiting to be permitted." The style of this presentation is visual and poetic; its scholarly base is inconspicuous. Most of the research was done in the Church History collection at the University of Notre Dame, a source which no researcher should overlook.[22]

[21] Women's Ordination Conference, 34 Monica Street, Rochester, N. Y. 14619.

[22] Because of the number and quality of manuscript collections housed in its University Archives, Notre Dame ranks second in importance to Baltimore as a research center for American Catholic history. The collection includes the early papers of the Archdioceses of Cincinnati, Detroit, Indianapolis, and New Orleans, as well as the personal papers of a number of leading Catholic laymen, and is well indexed and calendared. See Ellis, *Guide*, for descriptions of other depositories in the United States, 7–12.

Anyone seriously considering research in the areas discussed in this essay should contact some of the key organizations of sisters. Two are especially prominent. The Leadership Conference of Women Religious (LCWR) with headquarters in Washington, D. C. represents mostly those sisters who hold administrative positions in their congregations. More of a grass roots organization of the rank and file is the National Assembly of Women Religious, publishers of *Probe*. From its headquarters in Chicago, NAWR attempts to mobilize sisters for service to their Church and nation. Many of the religious active in these organizations are among the most competent and knowledgeable women leaders in the country and would be helpful to the researcher. Other organizations that could be contacted are the Black Sisters Conference, whose publication is *Signs of Soul*, and the National Coalition of American Nuns.[23]

* * *

Anyone interested in studying women and religion should find a rich mine in the American Catholic sisters, a group large and homogeneous enough to permit research to be carried on with some facility and valid conclusions to be drawn. It is well to remember in dealing with religious women of any faith that, if indeed they are interested in the women's movement, they also have another motivating force, namely their religious commitment. Also, in the natural order, their lives are probably less immediately dominated by men, although they too ultimately are subjected to some of the same discrimination suffered by other women. The following are some suggested areas for research.

1) One of the first that could be explored is the pioneer or founding experience. Just as colonial women performed many tasks and carried on businesses from sheer force of necessity, so did Catholic religious women in setting up their congregations and institutions. Most of these foundations were made in the nineteenth century, yet these women were apparently oblivious to concepts of "the Victorian lady" and "the cult of domesticity." With or without the support of men of the Church, they did what needed to be done. As mentioned above, many of these stories are separately recorded but the Catholic woman religious as a type has not been studied. The question might well be asked how free were these women to determine their own existence and policy. Staffing hospitals, schools, colleges, asylums for children, and other kinds of institutions gave them a certain degree of autonomy; still we know that they often encountered difficulties in their relationships with Church authorities.

[23] Further information (addresses, officers, etc.) is available in the current issue of *The Catholic Almanac*.

2) Certainly an extension of Mary Ewens' work would be of value—to ascertain attitudes towards sisters in the twentieth century through experience and interviews with sisters and through the serious and popular literature of the times.

3) If the Roman Catholic girl always had the choice of a career in religion, does this explain why Catholic women were not attracted to the women's movement, especially in the nineteenth century? In a day when women were expected to marry, the life of the sister possibly constituted an appealing, respectable alternative. We know that, in the mid-twentieth century, many of the college presidents who were women were Catholic sisters. This seems to indicate that sisters enjoyed a freedom of movement, self-determination if you will, that other women did not have at that time.

4) Looking back a bit, and outside the confines of the United States, one might test McKenna's thesis that because the sister lacks an ecclesiastical order in the Church the status of women now is probably lower than it was in the early Church. Did religious life for women evolve in order to give those interested in working in the Church some kind of "status," but a status which at the same time removed them from such an official position as deaconess? In developing societies women frequently have roles that are later denied them when the society becomes more complex. Did this happen in the early Church, that once the primitive period passed and Church structure became more complex, the official position of deaconess was abandoned and women were relegated, so to speak, to the "life and holiness of the Church" (McKenna, 147)? Or in other words, were they given some "status" as sisters but, lacking an ecclesiastical order, no power of determining policy or making decisions?

5) It would also be interesting to ascertain what forces in the 1960s really brought about the change in the lives of sisters. Vatican II and the women's movement converged at some point, yet one wonders just how the motivating forces worked for individual sisters.[24] Accompanying this inquiry should be an assessment of attitudes towards feminism, not only the leaders' attitudes, but also those of the rank and file.

These topics and others could make a significant contribution not only to the religious history of the United States but to our knowledge of women and their roles in American society. The source material is available and abundant, a ready field for the interested researcher.

[24] This question is partially pursued in the Fitzpatrick dissertation noted above, in which she concludes that the role of the religious takes first place in the hierarchy of role obligations. Conflict is solved by making decisions in favor of the religious role. If an integration of the two is achieved, she says (as in this case, social work), a redefinition of the role of religion to include the occupational role is necessary.

TRANSITIONS IN JUDAISM: THE JEWISH AMERICAN WOMAN THROUGH THE 1930s

NORMA FAIN PRATT
Mt. San Antonio College

"TO BE A JEW IN THE TWENTIETH CENTURY IS TO BE OFFERED A GIFT," wrote Muriel Rukeyser, the New York–born Jewish poet. "If you refuse, wishing to be invisible, you choose death of the spirit. . . ."[1] Most American Jewish women accepted this gift, even though the tenets of Judaism circumscribed the role of women in worship and community activity. Women had never been encouraged to examine the nature of their own religious beliefs, nor had the traditional assumptions about their inferiority and subservience to men been challenged. In the late nineteenth and early twentieth centuries, however, a minority of women began to redefine their place within Jewish life, and in the 1920s and 1930s patterns perceptibly changed for the majority. Women became participants in the synagogue, the schools, and the social institutions which expressed the new culture of American Jewry. Nevertheless they continued to face limitations and intolerance; by the 1940s, a new pattern had been established with its own forms of inclusion and exclusion.

* * *

In order to distinguish the ways in which women altered their role, it is important to consider the nature of American Judaism and its course of development. American Jews never centralized their religious institutions. What could be termed "organized" Judaism was congregational. Essentially, public rituals were practiced in local synagogues whose con-

[1] Muriel Rukeyser, "To be a Jew in the Twentieth Century," in Abraham Chapman, ed., *Jewish-American Literature* (New York: New American Library, 1974), 342–43.

gregations selected a mode of worship and expressed their preference for certain Jewish theological interpretations. In popular parlance, the types of worship came to be categorized as Orthodox, Conservative, and Reform. National synagogue unions were formed at the turn of the present century.[2]

In the seventeenth century, Sephardic Jews brought to British America from Spain and the Middle East a variation of the ritual and theology of medieval Judaism practiced by their co-religionists in Western and Eastern Europe. A few Sephardic women took an active part in business and in the high cultural life of American urban centers. German Jews arrived in considerable number just before the middle of the nineteenth century. Between 1840 and 1880 some 250,000 settled in the eastern and midwestern United States, mainly in the cities. Many had already been influenced by secular European culture and in America they created their own version of Reform Judaism. The Reform synagogues, now called temples, eliminated some of the ancient ritual, substituted English for Hebrew, altered the theological emphasis of the liturgical literature, and departed substantially from the traditional orthodox service.

Reform Jews initiated radical innovation in the position of women. The temples permitted the desegregation of the sexes; women and men now sat together in the family pews. Women were allowed to sing in the choir. Girls were confirmed. The Reform prayerbook eliminated the male benediction thanking God "that I am not a woman." Women were counted as part of the *minyan* (the ten-person quorum necessary to hold services). Through the temple "sisterhood" organizations women participated in the administration of charitable and other social services; they were granted the privileges of tending to temple upkeep and to the religious education of children.[3] These changes did not come without opposition. One dissenter posed the argument familiar in the Judaeo-Christian tradition in his article "God's Curse on Womanhood," published in 1864 in the popular Philadelphia German-Jewish English-language periodical, *The Occident*:

> Now when Eve was created she was made equal to Adam in every respect, and by no means had he any power or authority over her whatever. . . . But after she had induced him to break the commandment of God, and he was cursed to labor and to toil for his living, and to support her, to supply all their wants through hard work, she was also cursed by losing her right to be equal

[2] Maurice J. Karpf, *Jewish Community Organization in the United States* (New York: Block Publishing, 1938), 51–56.

[3] Charlotte Baum, Paula Hyman, and Sonya Michel, *The Jewish Woman in America* (New York: Dial Press, 1976), 17–53, deals with German Jewish Reform Judaism.

> to him. . . . Now this was the curse pronounced against her, that she should always remember and repent of what she had done. She shall always desire to be equal with him, as before she sinned, but he shall rule over her. . . .[4]

By 1900, many middle-class Jewish American women of German descent had assumed responsibilities in the work of their Reform temples. A National Federation of Temple Sisterhoods was founded in 1913 with a membership of 5,000, representing 52 local groups.[5] Sisterhoods met both for recreation and for temple and community work. Contemporary feminist thought has variously interpreted such voluntarism as a cult of the leisured woman; as an aspect of middle-class conspicuous consumption; as an outlet for female energies which did not conflict with home duties and which in fact translated women's work in the home into social terms; as an expression of a feminist consciousness; or as a factor of labor division in a developing capitalist economy.[6] While all these theories might be applied to the women of the Reform movement, as well as to the voluntary work of American women of other faiths, the leadership of the Federation understood their own purpose in specifically Jewish terms. "The increased power which has come to the modern American Jewess ought to be exercised in congregational life," stated the NFTS constitution.[7] Another motif, the future of Judaism, pervaded their ideology. "Woman is the bearer, the guardian and the preserver of the nation," the feminist Bertha Pappenheim proclaimed. This is her "primary function—on which depends the welfare and continued existence of the people, Israel. . . ."[8] But guardianship was not enough. By the 1890s German Jewish American women also defended the faith. The founding convention of the National Council of Jewish Women in 1893 stood aggressively against anti-Semitism. Along with religious understanding, philanthropy, and education, the purpose of the NCJW was "to secure the interest and aid of influential persons in arousing the general sentiment

[4] January 21, 1864.

[5] XXIV Biennial Assembly of the National Federation of Temple Sisterhoods, *The Days of Our Years* (Chicago, Ill., Nov. 1963), 24.

[6] See, for example, Doris B. Gold, "Women and Voluntarism," in Vivian Gornick and Barbara K. Moran, eds., *Woman in Sexist Society* (New York: New American Library, 1971), 533–54.

[7] *The Days of Our Years*, 24. Joseph Leiser, *American Judaism* (New York: Block Publishing, 1925), 174–203, discusses the "modern American Jewess."

[8] Bertha Pappenheim, "The Jewish Woman in Religious Life," pamphlet reprinted from *The Jewish Review* (Jan. 1913) by the Jewish League for Woman Suffrage. For biographic studies of Pappenheim see Marion Kaplan, "Bertha Pappenheim: Founder of German-Jewish Feminism," in Elizabeth Koltun, ed., *The Jewish Woman* (New York: Shocken Books, 1976), 149–63.

against religious persecutions whenever and by whomever shown, and in finding means to prevent such persecutions."[9]

German Jewish women also defended the faith by taking measures to prevent assimilation. Although, like the men, they responded to the temptations of Americanization by adopting aspects of the dominant culture, they also wanted to retain their individuality as Jews. Zionism served this purpose. Hadassah, the women's division of the Zionist Organization of America, founded in 1912, planned to foster Judaism at home through the propagation of Zionist ideals. Books for young women explained that the chief problem for Jews in America was "finding a way back to the original Jewish National life and thereby defeating assimilation."[10] The solution was "a return to the sources of Jewish culture, to the Bible and to the study of Hebrew and by contact with the living Jewry of the East."[11] Ida Adlerblum, the head of Hadassah's Cultural Committee, boasted in 1930 (when the organization had the largest membership of any Zionist group in the United States) that "The future historian of the twentieth century will reckon Hadassah among the forces which operate in creating Judaism anew. . . . From a mere organization, Hadassah has become a spiritual historical movement knitted with the life of Palestine as well as with Jewish life in America."[12]

The migration of Eastern European Jews began in 1880; by the early 1920s more than 2½ million had immigrated.[13] The place of Eastern European immigrant women in Judaism was far different from that of their American German-Jewish co-religionists. Some inequalities, explicit and implicit, still existed in the Reform community (for example, women could not join the rabbinate or hold administrative posts in their temples), but in the orthodox system segregation and subordination of women was the rule.

Orthodox men and women were responsible for different spheres of religious behavior. Men were obligated to say prayers at three specific times during the day, to participate in synagogue worship and maintenance, and to study not only the Bible in Hebrew but also the Talmud.

[9] Rebekah Kohut, "Jewish Women's Organizations in the United States," *American Jewish Year Book*, 1931–1932 (Philadelphia: Jewish Publication Society, 1931), 33:175, hereafter referred to as *AJYB*.

[10] *Junior Hadassah Yearbook*, 1924–1925 (New York: Junior Hadassah, 1925), 24.

[11] Ibid.

[12] Ida S. Adlerblum, "Cultural Committee," in *Reports* of the National Board, Standing Committee and Regional Units to the Sixteenth Annual Convention of Hadassah, Buffalo, N. Y., Oct. 26–28, 1930, p. 19.

[13] Karpf, *Jewish Community Organization*, 1–8. The most recent study, Irving Howe, *World of Our Fathers* (New York: Harcourt, Brace, Jovanovich, 1976) gives limited attention to the woman immigrant.

Unlike men, orthodox women were not required to pray at appointed times or to attend the synagogue regularly. When women did attend, they were segregated from men by a specially constructed partition. Of course, an orthodox woman could not become a rabbi nor could she sing in the synagogue, since the ancient rabbis considered the female voice to be profane in a holy place. Women did not count as part of a *minyan*. Male children were given a religious education by male teachers after the age of five or six, but girls were not obligated to study. One could find in the Talmud adages which warned: "Whoever teaches his daughter Torah is as though he taught her folly," or "Let the words of the Torah rather be destroyed by fire than imparted to women."[14] Orthodox women were restricted to observing only particular rituals. They were permitted to light Sabbath and holiday candles, to separate the *hallah* portion from the bread dough in preparation for the Sabbath, and to bathe in the *mikva* (ritual bath). Interestingly, orthodox women were encouraged to become involved in the business enterprises of the marketplace, and they often supported their Talmudic scholar husbands who tended the sacred sphere.[15]

Orthodox Judaism encompassed civil as well as religious life. Thus marriage, divorce, inheritance, and the administration and execution of justice were all regulated within the jurisdiction of *halakah* (Jewish law) as expressed in the *Talmud* and interpreted by the rabbis. The *halakah* regarding women were the dictates of a patriarchal society. Woman's role in life was defined as caring for her husband, children, and home. For satisfaction of her needs she depended upon father, husband, or son. "It says in the Torah," wrote the immigrant novelist Anzia Yezierska in her novel *Bread Givers* (1925), "only through a man has a woman an existence. Only through a man can a woman enter Heaven."[16]

Women's spiritual sphere was the moral purity of the household, and this was assured by observing dietary laws of *kashruth* and by keeping to a strict system of bodily cleansing. A woman's word regarding *kashruth* of her home or her attendance at the *mikva* was sufficient but the testimony of a woman in court was not acceptable. Legal dicta regulated sexual behavior by defining a close relationship between sexual performance and the so-called cleanliness of the female body. For example, the *Shulchan*

[14] For a discussion of women in the Talmud see Judith Hauptman, "Images of Women in the Talmud," in Rosemary Radford Ruether, ed., *Religion and Sexism* (New York: Simon and Schuster, 1974), 184–212.

[15] See Charlotte Baum, "What Made Yetta Work? The Economic Role of Eastern European Jewish Women in the Family," *Response*, No. 18 (Summer 1973).

[16] Quoted by Alice Kessler-Harris in her introduction to Anzia Yezierska, *Bread Givers* (New York: George Braziller, 1975), vi.

Aruch, a code book of laws culled from the Talmud for daily use as a guide to behavior, contains numerous chapters dealing specifically with sexual cleanliness, "Laws concerning Chastity," "Laws forbidding the being alone with Women and other familiarities with them," "Laws concerning a woman menstrually unclean," "Laws concerning the regulation of the Menses and the examination before and after cohabitation."[17] Often, however, crucial aspects of women's lives were not celebrated. As a feminist recently remarked, "There are blessings in Judaism for almost everything including going to the bathroom, but there isn't one for menstruation or for a healthy pregnancy."[18]

Not all Eastern European immigrant women remained orthodox Jews. A minority had rejected some or all of the ancient practices even before coming to America. Many young women became "enlightened" when their parents enrolled them in Eastern European non-Jewish state schools.[19] In the United States the degree of strict religious observance varied. With the desire to Americanize, some of the more foreign-appearing practices were eliminated. For example, orthodox married women shed the traditional headcover *(shaytl)*; *kashruth* and the Sabbath might not be strictly observed. The prestige of the rabbis as interpreters and executors of the rabbinic law was undermined; for women, American civil law often appeared more efficient and more fair. Katya Govsky recalled her discovery that her husband was a bigamist. "I went to the criminal court and the man said, 'In twenty-four hours, you can get a divorce.' And that's what happened; but Pa says, 'You have to get a Jewish divorce.'" It took her more than a year to obtain a rabbinic decree. Furthermore, Govsky remembered, "I wanted to adopt my son (you know, a child belongs to the father). Pa had to take the rabbi to New York and talk to my husband, fill out all kinds of papers. And I had to go to four rabbis. . . ."[20]

Despite the greater freedom for women within the Reform movement, very few Eastern European women joined the Reform temples. To them as well as to the men, Reform seemed too Christian in style, and the wealth of German Jews appeared to place them in a higher social class. It was not until the 1930s that any significant number of Eastern European

[17] Rabbi Solomon Ganzfried, *Shulchan Aruch* (Code of Jewish Law), Hyman E. Goldin, trans. (New York: Hebrew Publishing, 1927), 13–42.

[18] K. S., "Judaism is not for men only," *Brown Alumni Monthly*, 19, cited in Anne Lapidus Lerner, "'Who Has Not Made Me a Woman': The Movement for Equal Rights for Women in American Jewry," *AJYB*, 1977, 8.

[19] Patterns of education for Jewish girls in Eastern Europe are discussed in Celia Heller, *On the Edge of Destruction* (New York: Columbia Univ. Press, 1977), 157–58.

[20] Sydelle Kramer and Jenny Masur, eds., *Jewish Grandmothers* (Boston: Beacon, 1976), 70–71.

Jews joined in worship with those of German ancestry,[21] and then they often were accused of social climbing. Esther Bengis, a young orthodox *rebetsn* (rabbi's wife) in a small town in Connecticut in the early 1930s, complained that some members of her husband's congregation held "dual membership"—in the Orthodox *shul* and in the Reform temple.[22] German and Eastern European Jewish women, however, began in the 1920s to work together in areas not directly religious, such Zionist or social service organizations, contributing to a growing homogeneity in American Jewish life.

For nearly 40 years after 1880, Jews who were no longer orthodox and yet could not accept Reform Judaism had no form of Judaism through which to express their changing mode of behavior. Conservative Judaism, a movement attracting mainly second and third generation American Jews of Eastern European background, was still in its formative stages. The majority of Conservative congregations were established during or soon after World War I, their synagogues located in the newer non-ghetto neighborhoods where the Jewish population was in the minority and where living conditions expressed middle-class tastes. Marshall Sklare has described Conservatism as a mediation "between the demands of the Jewish tradition. . .and the norms of middle class worship."[23] The new patterns altered the liturgy, showed tolerance toward personal deviation from traditional practices like *kashruth* or rest on the Sabbath, and created social clubs as part of the function of the synagogue. Following somewhat the practice of Reform Judaism, Conservatives adjusted the status of women. Men and women were seated together. Women's synagogue organizations participated in the upkeep of the synagogue and in the religious education of the children. Women, however, still were excluded from significant parts of the worship, for instance the rituals surrounding the handling and reading of the Torah. In the 1920s and 1930s Conservative women wrestled with a felt dichotomy between the new position in synagogue life and the traditional home. Some thought that things had gone too far. "At the risk of being declared a reactionary, a menace to women's freedom," wrote Rose Goldstein in the Conservative Women's League paper *Outlook*, "I maintain that the greatest part the

[21] Author's interview with Jane Evans, Executive Director of the National Federation of Temple Sisterhoods, New York, June 30, 1977.

[22] Esther Bengis, *I am a Rabbi's Wife* (Moodus, Conn.: Esther Bengis, 1934), 14.

[23] Marshall Sklare, *Conservative Judaism: An American Religious Movement* (New York: Shocken, 1972), 75.

Jewish woman can play in the future of a healthy American Judaism is through the conduct of her own household."[24]

Beside the Orthodox, Conservative, and Reform modes, a secular form of Judaism developed in the late nineteenth century which offered women a different place in Jewish society. While secular Jews rejected most theological values, they retained *Yidishkayt*, a sense of Jewishness embracing a respect for the Yiddish language and traditions and for the contemporary common Jewish fate. One could observe secular Judaism without prayer and without joining a special group. The *veltlekhe* (secular) Jews did organize, since they not only accepted a Jewish identity in theory but put this into practice by creating a cultural life for themselves and their children. The study of Jewish history, appreciation of Yiddish and Hebrew literature, celebration of Jewish holidays, and support of a Yiddish theatre were characteristic expressions.

A vital part of the secular movement, which divided along sectarian lines, was radical political ideology in such forms as socialism, Zionist-socialism, and anarchism. Actually, the roots of secular Judaism were found in Eastern European Jewish radical and labor movements that provided doors through which working-class men and women entered the secular world. Some radical groups like the Marxist Jewish Labor Bund discouraged workers from following religious customs since religion was held to reflect the Jewish bourgeois power structure. Bund ideology transformed the special Jewish religious identity into a national one, urging Bundists to work for a socialist revolution in which Jews would obtain cultural autonomy.[25]

Radical Jewish movements accepted equality between the sexes and this made political radicalism attractive to women. Because Jewish women had been excluded from those male sanctuaries, the orthodox synagogues, women intellectuals and workers joined radical organizations expecting to find equality within the movement. For these women, a nonreligious mode of life within a Jewish community became bound with socialism and equality. When an increasing number of Eastern European radicals emigrated to America after the unsuccessful Russian revolution of 1905, many of the politically conscious women began participating,

[24] Rose B. Goldstein, "Women's Share in the Responsibility for the Future of Judaism," *Outlook*, (May 1938), 3. For a more recent statement of a woman's ambivalence regarding inclusion of women in the synagogue see the historian Lucy Davidowicz, "On Being a Woman in Shul," *Commentary* (July 1968), 71–74.

[25] Ezra Mendelsohn, *Class Struggle in the Pale: The Formative Years of the Jewish Workers' Movement in Tsarist Russia* (London: Cambridge Univ. Press, 1970), 107. For the Bund see also Henry Tobias, *The Jewish Bund in Russia From Its Origins to 1905* (Stanford, Cal.: Stanford Univ. Press, 1972).

soon after their arrival, in the feminist and suffrage movements. Esther Luria, a Bundist who in Europe had engaged in revolutionary activities, played a role in the suffrage and labor movements among Jewish immigrant women in New York. Far less known than Emma Goldman, Luria tried to provide Jewish women with role models through her writings and the example of her own life. Her biography had the romantic ring of that first generation of immigrant radical intellectuals. Born in Warsaw in 1877, Luria completed the Russian gymnasium and studied at the University of Bern in Switzerland where she received the degree of doctor of humanistic studies. In Bern she joined the socialist movement, and she returned to Russia as an active member of the Bund. Arrested there several times, she was sent to Siberia in 1906. She escaped in 1912 and came to New York City. Luria made her debut in the Yiddish-language socialist literary and political monthly *Zukunft* (Future). She wrote more than sixty articles about Jewish and non-Jewish women who broke out of traditional molds, including "Famous Jewish Women in America and England," "Marx's Wife and Daughter," "The Russian Women and the Revolution," and the "Life and Works of Liebknecht and Luxemburg." Her contributions to the International Ladies Garment Workers' Union Yiddish weekly *Glaykhhayt* (Equality) advocated political activism for women in America. Without a family, impoverished, and in poor health, Luria disappeared in the early 1920s and her fate is unknown.[26]

Women in these Jewish circles had more equality with men than their sisters in the Orthodox, Conservative, and even Reform movements. In theory, at least, they were unencumbered by religious traditions, restrictions, and ancient prejudices. As a consequence, working-class women joined trade unions and occasionally were trade organizers[27]; literary women wrote fiction or poetry and were employed on the staff of the Yiddish press and in the Yiddish theatre; women were active within political groups. Nevertheless there were inequalities. Ambivalent or negative attitudes toward the "emancipated" Jewish woman existed in subtle, perhaps unconscious form, and the contradiction between the ideal and the real would become more apparent by the 1920s. Such attitudes could be found in the literature of the time. The novel *Worshippers* (1906) by Henry Berman (who was sympathetic to socialism and thus to the rights of women) centers upon Katherine Bronski, the creatively frus-

[26] Biographic information in *Leksikon fun der nayer yidisher literatur*, 7 vols (New York: Congress for Jewish Culture, 1956), V, 30. Khaim L. Fuks, "Vegn eynegste shriber fun der *Zukunft*," *Zukunft*, 11–12 (Nov.-Dec. 1962), 494–95.

[27] Alice Kessler-Harris, "Organizing the Unorganizable: Three Jewish Women and their Union," *Labor History*, 17 (Winter 1976).

trated and sexually unsatisfied wife of a Philadelphia pharmacist. Katherine leaves her husband to follow a stage career and to engage in an extramarital affair with a New York Yiddish socialist poet. According to Berman, Katherine's emancipation illustrates the fallacy of the socialist aspiration for sexual equality. Katherine's freedom is merely a mask for her egotism, her desire to dominate males, and her inability to understand political commitment. Berman assigns all the affirmative values to her lover, whose virtues include intelligence, idealism, compassion, and a sense of responsibility. In the end Katherine, a failure on the stage, deserts her lover to return to Philadelphia and the pharmacist.[28] Berman's novel focused some of the traditionally negative attitudes upon the so-called emancipated woman: her intellectual inferiority, the superficiality of her political and artistic purpose, and her destructive sexual powers.

* * *

By the early 1920s Jews had ceased to be an immigrant nation in America. Increasing numbers left immigrant work to enter business and the professions. Jewish women and men moved out of the old ghetto-like neighborhoods into newer, more middle-class parts of town. Although occasional anti-Semitism created feelings of insecurity, social mores in the United States permitted Jews to retain their religion, sacred or secular, and still become American. In fact the American partiality for religious affiliation encouraged Jews to identify themselves in religious terms. Concurrently, most became convinced that an American style of life was appropriate for all citizens.[29]

Far from merging into their surroundings, however, the Jews developed a particular culture during the years between the two world wars. A myriad network of institutions demonstrated this adherence to what Horace Kallen called "cultural pluralism"[30]: Jewish congregations (3,118 in 1927),[31] theological seminaries, religious schools and secular Yiddish culture schools, local and national philanthropic agencies, and social and recreational groups. At least four organizations dealt with the problem of

[28] Berman's book is discussed in Carole S. Kessner, "Ghetto Intellectuals and the 'New Woman,'" *Yiddish*, 2:2–3 (Winter-Spring, 1976), 23–31. Kessner accepts Berman's view of the emancipated woman uncritically.

[29] For a recent study of problems of assimilation see Deborah Dash Moore, "Jewish Ethnicity and Acculturation in the 1920s: Public Education in New York City," *Jewish Journal of Sociology*, 18 (Dec. 1976), 96–104.

[30] Horace Meyer Kallen, *Cultural Pluralism and the American Idea: An Essay in Social Philosophy* (Philadelphia: Univ. of Pennsylvania Press, 1956).

[31] Karpf, *Jewish Community Organization*, 54. For statistics on religious and community organizations see the annual *AJYB*.

Jewish rights in America and abroad. The Jewish socialists and communists ran their own political sections, children's schools, camps, and cultural and social groups, and published books and periodical literature.

Within this structure the functions women performed expanded. The status of all American women had been enhanced by their enfranchisement in 1920. Jewish women had benefited both economically and educationally during the movement into the middle class and were now capable of shouldering the burdens and privileges of community life[32]; many accepted civic duties. One slogan of a girl's youth organization in 1930 declared: "Every member of Junior Hadassah is an American, a Jew and a Zionist. She is not one time one, another time another; she is all three in one."[33]

Changes in the practice of Judaism itself contributed to the new involvement of women. Orthodox Judaism, regulating all daily life (secular and sacred) by religious law, made heavy demands upon the male. The Reform movement of the nineteenth century and the new Conservative movement, by separating the sacred and secular, left only the actual religious service in the realm of the sacred. The male was no longer required to uphold the faith of his fathers by daily worship, religious study, and synagogue attendance. Jewish education, philanthropy, social services, and sociocultural expression had moved out from under Talmudic-rabbinic regulation. Under these circumstances, women became more participant in all areas of Jewish life while men became less so.[34]

Women in some numbers also began writing about their feelings toward Judaism in general and about being an American Jew in particular. The articles, memoirs, novels, and poems were the first candid disclosure of distinctly female religious sentiment since the *tkhines* (devotional prayers) written by women for women in the late Middle Ages.

One women's vehicle for the ideas of Jewish women was a mixed Yiddish-English emulation of the *Ladies' Home Journal: Der yidisher froyen zhurnal*, published in New York, which lasted from May 1922 to October 1923. It was intended for a first-generation immigrant audience of middle-class status. The *froyen zhurnal* printed sentimental poetry but

[32] The columns of *Who's Who in American Jewry*, 3 vols. (New York: National News Association, 1927, 1928, 1938) show the increasing number of Jewish women who received college educations and went on to participate in community and professional affairs. Also see "Professional Tendencies Among Jewish Students in Colleges, Universities and Professional Schools," *AJYB* 1920–1921, 22:383–86, which describes the educational pattern of women students.

[33] *The Story of Junior Hadassah on its Twentieth Anniversary* (n.p., 1940), 22. This pamphlet is in the collection of the Jewish Division of the New York Public Library.

[34] Sklare, *Conservative Judaism*, 87.

also ran articles about marriage, infant care, women's organizations, mother-daughter generational conflicts, college girls and their careers, achievements of outstanding American Jewish women, and women in politics. Each number included at least one article about women and religion, almost all of which lauded the woman's role in Jewish holiday celebrations. In the first issue, Ella Blum's "Pesakh un di yidishe froy," (Passover and the Jewish woman) reminded the reader that Moses' mother and sister and the Pharaoh's daughter all played active roles in the Jewish struggle for freedom from Egyptian slavery.[35] Ethel Judensen, writing about Chanukah, explained that "The highest pinnacle of success in life is achieved by consecration of one's self to an ideal and the readiness to make sacrifices for it. In the possession of this particular virtue, we feel sure, the Jewish woman excelled."[36]

In poetry and memoirs women expressed their intimate feelings about their Jewishness. One of the finest Yiddish poets, Anna Margolin, wrote about her ambivalence toward the past in "Mein shtam redt" (My Ancestry Speaks). She described her female forebears, "a few of whom I am ashamed," tramping through her "like through a dark house" so that she could not recognize her own voice.[37] In "A mentsh" (A Human Being) published in the experimental magazine *In zich* (Introspection) in 1923, Margolin sardonically chided God as she forgave Him for creating an imperfect human being and for creating a Jew. Describing the *mentsh* she wrote:

> Er iz a nit farendikter eksperiment
> In groyse laydnshaftn, emes, poze,
> A nit derbakene metamorfoze
> Fun hoykhn glutikn gedank
> In orem fleysh un blut,
> Mit milyonen andere halb-rizn un halb gnomen
> A shpotisher umnitslekher bavayz
> Az der almekhtiker ken shvakh
> Zayn fakh.
>
> He is an unfinished experiment
> In great passion, truth, pose,
> A half-baked metamorphosis
> Of glowing thoughts

[35] *Der yidishe froyen zhurnal*, I (May 1922), 3.
[36] "A Miracle of Chanukah," ibid., I (Dec. 1922), 3.
[37] Anna Margolin, "My Ancestry Speaks," in Joseph Leftwich, ed. and trans., *The Golden Treasury: A Worldwide Treasury of Yiddish Poetry* (New York and London: Thomas Yoseloff, 1961), 668–69.

In paltry flesh and blood,
Along with millions of other half-giants and half-gnomes
A scornful unnecessary proof
That the Almightly did not know
His trade.[38]

Margolin's chastisement of God gave voice to an ancient strain in the Jewish tradition as well as to her own private revolt.

Leah Morton, a social worker and author, published her memoir, *I am a Woman—and a Jew,* in 1926. In the tradition of prodigals, she described her odyssey from the total rejection of her immigrant parents' orthodox Judaism, through her marriage to a non-observant Christian and years of indifference to religion, to her renewed interest in organized Jewish practices when, in her late thirties, she returned to a personal identification with Jewishness. She wrote: "As a Jewess, I had found a creed not mine to believe, and I had put it aside, but I had not been able to put my Jewishness aside. . . . I am a Jewess, though I do not belong to any church, nor has my world enclosed my people. The divisions are in my memories, in my heart."[39]

What did ordinary women think and feel about religion—apart from professional writers? One glimpse into their thoughts is given in a master's essay written at the New York School of Social Work in 1937 by Sadie Josephson. The author examined how six New York women understood the influence of Jewishness in their lives. The "subjects" were between the ages of 26 and 46; two were Eastern European immigrants and four the children of immigrants. Josephson's information suggests interesting patterns. All the subjects believed that their Jewish identity was of central importance in determining their lives. Josephson noted in her summary, "The tendency . . . was to feel that they had made their own adjustment through their own thinking, yet none of them had thought through very clearly ideas and feelings about religion or Jewishness." Each woman had decided points of view. Subject "E" felt that she had been unsuccessful in her career and personal relationships because she was born a Jew. Yet she would not change her religion. Subject "D", an ardent Yiddishist, said she was not religious and was interested in Judaism only as a cultural expression. As a child she had spoken Yiddish but had been unaware of Jewish religion until five years before the interview, when her grandparents had come to America. Subject "S" remained orthodox and, as Josephson commented, "carried out in her ways

[38] Margolin, "A mentsh," *In zich*, 3 (Mar. 1923), 5.

[39] Leah Morton (pseud. Elizabeth Stern), *I am a Woman—and a Jew* (New York: J. H. Sears, 1926), 361–62.

of living as many customs as she finds convenient." Subject "J" claimed indifference to religion but expressed guilt about not keeping the traditional customs and so observed the Sabbath and High Holy Days. Subject "R" had married a Catholic but stated that "since her marriage she feels more Jewish than before." Subject "G", the only woman in this group to emigrate to the United States in her late teens and to work at a menial job, was critical of Jews. She felt persecuted by her Jewish employers and she made anti-Semitic comments about them. Except for the Yiddishist, who taught at a Sholom Aleichem Folkschule, none of the subjects appeared to be active in organized Judaism.[40]

Such lack of formal ties—the problem of the unaffiliated Jew—was a source of anxiety among leaders of this era, apprehensive that Judaism might not survive in America because of the changes that already had taken place. Women often were blamed by rabbis and other male writers for their share in this so-called decline of Judaism. David Goldberg took the mother to task in 1921 in an article in the *Jewish Forum*: "There is no time for the Sabbath . . . as her boys 'must' attend one or the other of the mediocre social 'events,' a musicale or a dance which, counting on the lack of backbone of the modern Jewish mother, her gentile friends invariably arrange for Friday evening."[41]

Adopting a more analytic but equally patronizing tone, Rabbi Mordecai M. Kaplan of the Jewish Theological Seminary echoed Goldberg's admonition. "[T]he Jewish Emancipation, or the change in the civic status of the Jews, has alienated the Jewish woman from Judaism far more than the Jewish man," he lectured the annual convention of the Hadassah in 1932. Kaplan contended that men had managed to deal with Emancipation without loss of their Jewish identity. "There are very few women who can claim the credit," he said. The rabbi attributed this female failure to resist assimilation to "the fact that she had been ill-prepared to play an active part in the process of Jewish adjustment." Passive and conforming to man's guidance, "she did not know how to make even a single stroke to save her Jewish selfhood." Culturally neglected, "she had turned to other cultures. . . ." Hungry for acknowledgement, she had given "undue significance to social advancement. . . . To the Jewish woman, therefore, the Jewish Emancipation has meant not freedom for her people from bondage of fear and oppression, but rather the chance to win a place for herself and

[40] Sadie Josephson, "Adjustment Histories of Six Jewish Women: A Study of Life History Material with Special Emphasis on the Problems of Jewish Adjustment," manuscript in the Jewish Division of the New York Public Library, 370, 36a, 94–97, 129, 182, 223, 360.

[41] David Goldberg, "Woman's Part in Religious Decline," *Jewish Forum* (May 1921), 871–75, cited in Rudolph Glanz, *The Jewish Woman in America* (New York: Ktav, 1976), 187.

her family in the so-called higher circles of Gentile society." Rabbi Kaplan urged the Hadassah to amend for their failures through Zionism. "Hadassah," he preached, "will save the soul of the American Jewish woman. . . ." She "needs Zionism if her personality is to achieve that normal and complete growth which living up to one's historic heritage makes possible."[42]

To the contrary, Jewish women had not lost their souls, had not abandoned Judaism. If, for example, intermarriage was an indication of assimilation, then statistics for the period suggested that far fewer women than men married outside their faith.[43] The predominance of male over female intermarriage was even more striking when one realized that in accordance with *halakah* a child's religion in a mixed marriage was determined by the religion of the mother. The child of a Jewish mother and a non-Jewish father was still considered a Jew. The popular literature of the 1920s and 1930s was replete with novels dealing with intermarriage between Jewish men and non-Jewish women. Sholem Asch, Ludwig Lewisohn, Ben Hecht, and others worried the question. Elmer Rice's Broadway play *Counsellor at Law*, about a Jewish lawyer and his gentile wife, came to the silver screen with John Barrymore as the romantic lead.[44] The literary critic Leslie Fiedler has suggested that these Jewish writers were investigating the ramifications of assimilation through the male-female relationship. In fiction and perhaps in life, the *shiksa* (non-Jewish woman) represented the aspirations and conflicts inherent in the blending of two different cultures.[45]

The literature dealing with marriage between a Jewish woman and a non-Jewish man was meager. An anonymous autobiographical statement published in the *Menorah Journal* in 1929 offered the testimony of a "Nordic" biology professor who married an Eastern European immigrant

[42] Mordecai M. Kaplan, "What the American Jewish Woman Can Do For Adult Education," *Jewish Education*, 4 (Oct.-Dec. 1932), 139, 140, 146.

[43] *AJYB* 1972–73, 295. The following sources are helpful: Julius Drachsler, *Intermarriage in New York City* (New York: Columbia Univ. Press, 1921); Reuben B. Resnick, "Some Sociological Aspects of Intermarriage of Jews and Non-Jews," *Social Forces* (Oct. 1933), 94–102; Milton L. Barron, "The Incidence of Jewish Intermarriage in Europe and America," *American Sociological Review*, 11 (Feb. 1946), 6–13; Erich Rosenthal, "Some Recent Studies About the Extent of Out-Marriages in the U.S.A.," in *Intermarriage and Jewish Life: A Symposium* (New York: Herzl Press and Jewish Reconstructionist Press, 1963), 84–89.

[44] For novels that deal with intermarriage see Sholem Asch, *East River* (1938); Ludwig Lewisohn, *The Island Within* (1940); and Ben Hecht, *A Jew in Love* (1931). There is an interesting discussion of intermarriage and the Jewish male in Bernard Cohen, *Sociocultural Changes in American Jewish Life as Reflected in Selected Jewish Literature* (New Jersey: Fairleigh Dickinson Univ. Press, 1972), 129–34. See comments about Barrymore in *Counsellor at Law* in Axel Madsen, *William Wyler* (New York: Thomas Y. Crowell, 1973), 90–93.

[45] Leslie Fiedler, "Genesis: The American Jewish Novel through the Twenties," in *Jewish-American Literature*, 570–86.

Jew. In the academic community where the couple lived, anti-Semitic sentiments were expressed on social occasions. He described their plight in this way:

> My wife has no desire to pass as Nordic. Whenever she is due to meet people, it is my duty to let such people know that she is Jewish. She regards it a duty to tell all new acquaintances thus to disarm them or to warn them. . . . Telling people in advance often avoids embarrassment. Once we sat at a table where the guest of honor regaled the party with Jewish jokes. I have learned that Jews prefer to have Jewish jokes told by Jews; at least my wife feels that way. The guest of honor was greatly mortified when someone warned him. . . .[46]

It seems that a mixed marriage could painfully increase the woman's sense of Jewishness.

The number of national women's organizations founded in the 1920s and 1930s testified to the vitality of Jewish women and to their interest in religion and community affairs, as well as to the strength of the separatist tradition. The list includes Junior Hadassah (1921); Conference Committee of National Jewish Women's Organizations (1923); Women's Branch of the Union of Orthodox Jewish Congregations of America (1924); Women's Division of the Communist Workers' Order (1924); Women's Organization of the Pioneer Women of Palestine (1925); Women's American ORT (1927); Women's League for Palestine (1927); American Beth Jacob Committee (1928); Mizrachi Women's Organization of America (1930); and the Menorah League (1935).[47]

Along with the older groups like the National Council of Jewish Women, the National Federation of Temple Sisterhoods, or the Women's League of the United Synagogues of America (1918), all these associations provided a complex Jewish "woman's world." She could choose to work at several levels—congregational or civic, national or international. The range of her activities might encompass personal study of history, politics, and religion; mundane social events; teaching children; social work in the community with the poor, with recent Eastern European immigrants or, in the 1930s, with refugees from Germany; programs to aid impoverished Eastern European girls or to settle Jews in Palestine; assistance to universities and Jewish libraries; or the publication of periodical

[46] Anonymous, "My Jewish Wife," *Menorah Journal*, 16 (May 1929), 460–61. For a Jewish father's response to his daughter's marrying an Italian Catholic see New York *Jewish Daily Forward*, Jan. 22, 1921.

[47] The women's organizations and their purposes are listed in the *AJYB*. For the Women's Division of the Communist Workers' Order see Yiddish-language *Almanac* (New York: International Workers Order Cooperative, 1934), 461; for the Women's Organization for the Pioneer Women of Palestine see "Constitution," *The Pioneer Women*, I (Mar. 1927), 7.

literature. Not all commitments were alike: some women contributed money to their favorite cause, while others joined the rank and file or took active leadership roles. These positions were exacting and prestigious, and women like Henrietta Szold emerged as heroic role-model figures.[48] Nor were all workers volunteers. Jewish social services were becoming professionalized; the Graduate School of Jewish Social Work was organized in 1925 and attracted young women in search of socially approved careers.

Trends in Jewish education generally reinforced women's interest in perpetuating their religious, social, and cultural life. By the 1920s, the example of American coeducational public schooling, the increased number of organized Jewish women, and changes in rituals like the introduction of a *bas mitzvah* or female confirmation ceremony in the Conservative synagogues all encouraged the inclusion of girls in Jewish educational programs. These were held after regular school hours or on Sunday. Hebrew or Yiddish and Jewish rituals, holidays, and history were the major subjects. The Conservative schools, however, emphasized the male *bar mitzvah* and offered girls a less intensive and hence less socially important program. By the 1930s one third of the pupils enrolled in Jewish schools were girls. The Reform Sunday schools and the secular Yiddish schools had still higher female enrollments, mainly because their programs were not *bar mitzvah* oriented.[49]

Orthodox Jews, whose sons attended daily religious schools and received a more rigorous theological training than the children of their coreligionists, included girls in their Talmud Torah or yeshivas only with reluctance. They did, however, voice concern about the preservation of their faith; as a pamphlet of the Agudath Israel read: "While the Jewish boy was relatively safe from the onslaughts of assimilation in the yeshivas . . . the girls were easier prey for the Enlightenment."[50] By the late 1930s, a few schools for girls were in operation in New York City and girls were occasionally accepted as students in the traditionally all-male orthodox schools. Nevertheless the study of the Talmud remained a male privilege, girls being restricted to studying Hebrew, Jewish history, and the literature of the Bible. A new concept of educating orthodox women, the Beth Jacob schools, originating in Poland during the 1920s,[51] combined the

[48] See, for example, Susan Dworkin, "Henrietta Szold—Liberated Woman," in *The Jewish Woman*, 164–70.

[49] *AJYB* 1936–37, 40–41. Also see Azriel L. Eisenberg, "A Study of 4473 Pupils Who Left Hebrew School in 1932–33," *Jewish Education*, 7 (April–June 1935), 91–96.

[50] Joseph Friedenson, *A History of Agudath Israel* (New York: Agudath Israel, 1970), 22.

[51] For a discussion of the education of girls among the Orthodox see Zvi H. Harris, "A Study of Trends in Jewish Education for Girls in New York City," (Diss. Yeshiva University, 1956).

study of religion with the training for a vocation. These schools attracted the interest of American Jewish women's organizations, which raised funds to assist the experiment. Dora Edinger, visiting Cracow in 1937 as a representative of the Conservative Women's League, was favorably impressed by the religiosity of the Beth Jacob students. "I heard two of these girls give marvelous sermons on the Sedra," she observed.[52]

In America, female students and teachers were involved in experimental programs to improve education in the part-time Reform, Conservative, and secular Jewish schools which supplemented regular public school. Since the boys' teachers were wary of tampering with the traditional curriculum and methods, innovative approaches to learning languages or new subjects were tried out on the girls. In this way, as one historian noted about the Orthodox and Conservative schools, though "Jewish education for girls generally lagged behind that of boys, girls . . . strangely enough made a unique contribution to Jewish education."[53]

Women teachers, who by 1935 made up about one-third of the teaching force, were in the forefront of developing not only new methods but a new philosophy for Jewish education. For example, Fannie R. Neumann, an articulate educational theoretician at the Brooklyn Jewish Center, hoped to create a method of rearing Jewish children which would offer them a "cultural synthesis." She envisioned a way to educate "a new type of Jew—steeped in Jewish culture, yet thoroughly at home in . . . [the] American milieu, disciplined yet free, adjusted to the machine age but saved from its serfdom by a critical eye and a sentient heart."[54]

In the 1930s, girls seemed to respond more enthusiastically than boys to Jewish education. This was especially true in the secular Jewish schools, where preparation for the *bar* or *bas mitzvah* was not the final goal and where girls were taught the same curriculum as boys. In fact, Leibush Lehrer, a leading educator in the Yiddishist Sholom Aleichem Folkschule, was struck by the differences in male and female reactions to Jewish interests. Interviewing former students, Lehrer found young women to have a more tenacious identification with Yiddish. Many more women than men continued to read Yiddish fiction and poetry and to attend Yiddish theatre after they had ceased their formal education. Discussing the possible reasons for the differences, Lehrer suggested that the female students were more intellectually mature than the males during the ages from 8 to 14 when they were studying Yiddish culture. He attributed

[52] Dora Edinger, "A Visit to Beth Jacob," *Outlook*, 7 (May 1937), 1.
[53] Zvi Harris, "Trends in Jewish Education," 66.
[54] Fannie R. Neumann, "A Modern Jewish Experimental School—in Quest of a Synthesis," *Jewish Education*, 4 (Jan.–Mar., 1932), 27.

the male students' lack of interest to an overemphasis on sports in American culture. Not being involved in sports, the girls had time for languages and literature.[55] It was likely, too, although Lehrer did not state this, that Jewish girls were encouraged to study humanistic subjects as part of the feminine ideal of a "cultured lady," while the boys rejected these subjects for that very reason.

Although by the end of the 1930s women were thus taking a prominent part in public aspects of American Jewish life, the extent of their exclusion and segregation continued to be profound. In fact the changes tended to mask the remaining inequalities. The unresolved problems in the most "progressive" Jewish sectors illustrate the biases that operated throughout the community. Reform Judaism, for instance, had integrated women into the temple and into the religious service for almost a hundred years. Reform women were lawyers, judges, and doctors. Nevertheless, in 1922 when Martha Neumark, a student at the Reform seminary, Hebrew Union College, expressed her intention to seek ordination as a rabbi, her request was denied. The lay members of the Board of Governors who opposed her ordination argued that such a departure from tradition was too radical and might alienate the Conservative and Orthodox co-religionists. The calling of rabbi required strenuous full-time activities and complete devotion; the essential role of the Jewish woman was to cultivate a Jewish home life and family. The board could not encompass the thought of combining the two. Dr. Jacob Z. Lauterbach, one of the more articulate members, assured the rejected candidate that there was "no injustice done to woman by excluding her for this office. There are many avenues open to her if she chooses to do religious and educational work."[56]

But women who were active in the "work" of the Jewish community discovered that a male bureaucratic hierarchy firmly controlled finances, policies, and plans. In Jewish schools male principals directed female teachers who were often paid less than their male counterparts. Female membership in the B'nai Brith, the mutual aid society, rose in the 1930s as did their financial contribution to the organization; at the end of the decade about a third of the B'nai Brith members were women. But, as in most other Jewish organizations, the B'nai Brith women were relegated to auxiliary sections and had no representation on the national executive board, which controlled finances and policy. At the 1938 B'nai Brith convention, as a historian of this organization has noted, "the rapid

[55] Leibush Lehrer, "Di tsey yidishe doyres in amerike." (The Two Jewish Generations in America), *Zukunft*, 36 (Sept. 1931), 593–99.

[56] Jacob Z. Lauterbach, "Responsum on Question 'Shall Women Be Ordained Rabbis?.'" *Central Conference of American Rabbis Yearbook* (Cape May, N. J., 1922), 32:162.

growth of women's activities emboldened them to seek representation at Supreme Lodge conventions. But the best the delegates . . . could do for them was—conveniently without changing the Constitution—to permit each women's District at the next triennial convention to designate one representative to attend, with voice but no vote, and at her own District's expense.''[57]

Radical secular groups upheld sexual equality in theory throughout this period, but the socialist and communist organizations in particular followed in the footsteps of their bourgeois brethren by encouraging women's auxiliaries[58] and by allowing males to dominate party bureaucracies. The woman's voice was heard mainly on the woman's page of the Sunday edition of the paper. In the socialistic *Jewish Daily Forward* or in the more feminist-conscious communist *Freiheit*, women were not on the editorial boards and only rarely wrote on political or economic issues. Occasionally an individual, especially a poet, would question aspects of Jewish tradition. Lily Bes made an open call in *Freiheit* in 1929 for rebellion against *tsnies* (modesty), a supposed female virtue incorporating the traditional notion of discreet behavior.[59] Writing in Yiddish the poet said:

> Es hot geplatst in mir di tsnies fun mayn bobe
> Es brent in mir revolt vi zummerdiger vayn
> Zol gute layt mikh shultn oder hasn
> Ikh ken shoyn ander nit zayn.
>
> Within me has burst my grandmother's sense of modesty
> Revolt burns in me like effervescent wine
> Let good folk curse and hate me
> I can no longer be otherwise.[59]

Rebellion, however, did not extend to criticism of the position of women in the radical movement. For the most part, social relationships within the Jewish movement were similar to those outside radical circles.

* * *

Jewish women in the 1920–1940 period lived within a pattern of seeming acceptance combined with implicit exclusion that remained characteristic of American Judaism until the 1970s, when Jewish feminists pressed for

[57] Edward E. Grusd, *B'nai Brith: The Story of a Covenant* (New York: Appleton-Century, 1966), 217–18.

[58] The development of female auxiliaries in the *Arbeiter Ring* (Workmen Circle) is discussed in Maximilian Hurwitz, *The Workmen Circle: Its History, Ideals, Organization and Institutions* (New York: The Workmen's Circle, 1936), 212–14.

[59] Lily Bes, "Fun eygene vegn" (On My Own Path), New York *Freiheit*, Jan. 20, 1929.

new changes. Obviously they were not unique. Women were socially and organizationally segregated for the most part in American Protestant and Catholic society as well. But American Judaism did not merely imitate American culture, although imitation was an aspect of Jewish historical development. The perspective which Jewish women faced in the 1920s was complex. For most Jewish women secularization was of recent origin. The traditions of orthodox Judaism explicitly, even legally, maintained separate worlds for women and men. The meeting of these worlds within a secular frame of reference had brought about a radical change. Comparing their own position with that of their grandmothers, most women believed themselves to be already living a revolution; few developed much insight into the contradictions of their situation.

It was difficult, too, for women to form a common ground upon which to base criticism of their role within Judaism. The myriad women's organizations reflected the structural decentralization of the faith. Identification as a Reform, Orthodox, Conservative, Yiddishist, or Socialist Jew obfuscated the sense of being a Jewish woman at odds with a set of common limitations. Furthermore, since the Jewish education of women was not grounded in theological literature, they did not feel qualified to muster arguments in their own defense.

Despite their many successful adjustments, Jews additionally did not feel secure in their newfound homeland in the 1920s and 1930s. The sense of existing as foreigners, as immigrants, was still a part of Jewish thinking. The threat of anti-Semitism combined with the apprehensions regarding assimilation had marked ramifications for women. Anti-Jewish sentiments were commonly expressed during the First World War, and immediately following the war restrictions were placed upon Jewish immigration to the United States. In the 1930s the rise of Nazism and echoes of fascism in the Coughlinites, Pelley's Silver Shirts, and others intensified Jewish anxiety. Anti-Semitism acted as a centripetal force exacting solidarity. In the face of external hostility, Jewish women were not able to begin their own crusade as women.

Concurrently, the perceived threat of assimilation kept Jewish women in their place. Since Biblical times Judaism had been inherited genetically through the mother. In America women had increasingly shouldered the responsibility of preserving a faith which men often found burdensome. The school and the social institutions became part of the domain of women—even if men controlled the upper reaches of power. Thus as newly installed defenders of the faith, it seemed contradictory for women also to be critics of that faith.

In the early 1970s Jewish feminists began to battle these contradictions. They questioned power relationships in Jewish institutions, religious inequality in Judaic practices, and anti-female bias expressed in some traditional Jewish literature. Concurrently, feminists sought Jewish precedent to legitimize the concept of equality of the sexes in Judaism. Like many religious reformers in the past, feminists have turned to a reinterpretation of the Bible. Rabbi Laura Geller, one of several women ordained in Reform Judaism, noted during a recent interview that Jewish feminists can look to another creation story than that of a masculine God creating in male terms. The first chapter of Genesis reads, "in the image of God created He them, male and female . . . , and he called their name 'adam' (human beings)." thus all human beings are created in the image of God. "Just as God is the father, God is also the mother," said the Rabbi.[60]*

[60] There are two good bibliographies on Jewish women related to the contemporary woman's movement: Aviva Zuckoff, *Bibliography on the Jewish Woman*, 2nd rev. ed. (New York: Jewish Liberation Project, 1972) and *The Jewish Woman in the Community: A Selected Annotated Bibliography* (pamphlet prepared by the Blaustein Library for the American Jewish Committee, 1976). The interview with Rabbi Laura Geller is by Tova Feder in the Los Angeles *Jewish Federation Council Bulletin*, Aug. 15, 1977.

*The author wishes to thank Marsie Scharlatt, Hillel Kempinski, Janet Hadda, Ariela Erhlich, Kenneth Pratt, and the library staff of YIVO Institute For Jewish Research for their kind assistance.

In Search Of Unconventional Women:

Histories of Puerto Rican Women in Religious Vocations Before Mid-Century

VIRGINIA SÁNCHEZ KORROL

Oral history is frequently used to document the lives of people deemed typical or representative of their group or community. The three women whose stories form the core of this essay, however, can help us understand a broader history precisely because they are unconventional: at a historical juncture in the development of Puerto Rican *barrios*, when women's roles were circumscribed by social custom and occupation, they chose to break new ground. Each followed a personal calling for spiritual and humanitarian reasons, and came to play an important pastoral and religious role. Though unknown outside of their respective religious communities, their important role in the history of the Puerto Rican community is just beginning to be understood.

The life histories of these unconventional women, as recorded through oral history, illuminate the professional and to a lesser extent, the personal life experiences of each individual, while also

VIRGINIA SÁNCHEZ KORROL is an Associate Professor in the Department of Puerto Rican Studies and co-Director of the Center for Latino Studies, at Brooklyn College, CUNY. She is the author of *From Colonia to Community: A History of Puerto Ricans in New York City, 1917-1948.*

documenting their contributions at specific historical points in Puerto Rican community development. In this sense, the oral histories do more than add to our growing knowledge of individual Puerto Rican lives: they are especially valuable in enabling historians to begin to construct an inter-generational view of the Puerto Rican experience.[1]

Two of the women, Sister Carmelita and Reverend Leoncia Rosado, began their careers in the 1920s and 1930s, respectively. A vulnerable period in the development of the young community, it was also a time when women were expected to follow traditional roles and remain in the home as wives and mothers. The third woman, the Reverend Aimee García Cortese, is representative of the transitional second generation of Puerto Ricans, born in the U.S.A., which internalized many of the old customs while accommodating to a mainland reality.

The period between 1917 and 1950 was highly significant for Puerto Ricans in New York City. Under the leadership and influence of the earliest substantial migration from the island's rural and urban sectors, the community in New York City began to take shape as identifiably Puerto Rican. As early as 1910, over a thousand Puerto Ricans were said to reside in the United States. American citizenship, conferred in 1917, stimulated and facilitated migration, and within a decade all of the forty-eight states reported the presence of Puerto Rican-born individuals. Estimates indicate substantial population gains throughout the 1930s and 1940s, culminating in a total population of some 425,000 by mid-century, 80% of whom lived in New York City.[2]

Women formed an integral part of the migration experience, comprising over half the migrant flow in some decades. A partial tabulation of representative Hispanic districts in the New York State Manuscript Census of 1925, provides some insights into the earlier migrant population. Of 3,496 women listed in the census,

[1] Oral histories with the Reverends Leoncia Rosado and Aimee García Cortese were taped during the winter of 1985 by the author and Dr. Benjamín Alicéa, New Brunswick Theological Seminary, with the purpose of elucidating a little-known period in the history of the Puerto Rican community in New York City. The interview with Reverend Rosado was conducted in Spanish and translated by the author for this essay. The interview with Sister Carmelita was conducted and taped, by Professor John Vazquez, New York City Technical College, when he directed one of the earliest oral history projects on the Brooklyn Puerto Rican community in conjunction with the Brooklyn Historical Society.

[2] Joseph P. Fitzpatrick, *Puerto Rican Americans: The Meaning of Migration to the Mainland*. Second Edition. (Englewood Cliffs, New Jersey: Prentice-Hall, Inc., 1987), p. 135.

the majority were young housewives, under thirty-five years of age, who had resided in the city for less than six years. For the most part, Puerto Rican family traditions defined women's place in the early New York community. Expected to fulfill traditional roles as wives and mothers, women were conditioned to accept these roles as their primary life functions, regardless of their degree of involvement in community, career, or work-related activities.[3]

However, when confronted with the economic realities of an overwhelmingly poor community, close to 25% of the migrant women went to work outside the home in factories, laundries, and restaurants. This figure would rise in the coming decades, and parallel the demand for workers in the garment and other industries. Many women worked as seamstresses and domestics; others found ways to combine homemaking with gainful employment by taking in lodgers, caring for the children of working mothers and doing piecework at home.

While the majority of the migrant women fit into the above categories, a handful—less than 4%—established a foothold in other areas. These were the women who were either formally educated, skilled or bilingual, or who, by virtue of their community involvement, exercised leadership roles. Some sought and secured white-collar, office employment upon their arrival in the city; the status inherent in that work was sufficient to raise them above the ordinary. Others proceeded to launch supportive community enterprises, or to form volunteer organizations in response to the special needs of the community, as they had previously done in Puerto Rico. Still others, writers, poets, essayists and journalists, expressed themselves through their creative and artistic talents.[4] Finally,

[3] Virginia Sánchez Korrol. *From Colonia to Community: The History of Puerto Ricans in New York City, 1917-1948*. (Westport, Connecticut: Greenwood Press, 1983.) Chapter 4. See also: "On the Other Side of the Ocean: Work Experiences of Early Puerto Rican Migrant Women in New York," in *Caribbean Review*, January, 1979, pp.23-30. Altagracia Ortiz explores the role of women in the garment industry from the 1940s to the fifties in "Puerto Rican Women in the ILGWU, 1940-1950." Paper presented at the Women's Studies Conference, Brooklyn College, April, 1984. For a broader and comparative analysis see Palmira Ríos, "Puerto Rican Women in the United States Labor Market," in *Line of March*, No. 18, Fall, 1985.

[4] Numerous articles have appeared on notable women in Puerto Rican society. Among the most substantive are Isabel Picó de Hernández, "The History of Women's Struggle for Equality in Puerto Rico," and Norma Valle, "Feminism and its Influence on Women's Organizations in Puerto Rico," in Edna Acosta-Belén, *The Puerto Rican Woman: Perspectives on Culture, History and Society* (New York: Praeger Press, 1986.) For an overview of exceptional women in New York, see: Virginia Sánchez Korrol, "The Forgotten Migrant: Educated Puerto Rican Women in New York City, 1920-1940," in Acosta-Belén, 1986.

there were the women who chose the church, and in their own way contributed towards— and help us understand—Puerto Rican community development.

Carmela Zapata Bonilla Marrerro was born in Cabo Rojo, Puerto Rico in 1907. Raised in a rural atmosphere on the western coast of the Island, she belonged to a family composed predominantly of middle-class farmers and property owners. After the premature death of her mother in 1918, a move to Mayaguez, the island's third largest city, enabled her to receive a Catholic school education. During this tender period in her life Carmelita first articulated the desire to enter a convent. At sixteen, she made the decision to become a missionary nun in the Roman Catholic Church. Leaving her home and family for Georgia, the conventual center of the Trinitarian Order, in 1923, she hardly imagined that this would be the first of many trips between Puerto Rico and the U.S.

What impressions and images must have crossed the girl's mind as she made the five-day journey alone from San Juan to Brooklyn, where the ship was due to make port! She believes she left on a Thursday because the steam ship lines always sailed from Thursdays to Mondays; she remembers traveling second-class which offered the same menu as first, but without the dancing; and she recalls that the nuns met her ship at the Columbia Heights Promenade at Fulton Street. Carmelita spent her first night at the Brooklyn convent painfully aware that she was in strange surroundings, and anxiously anticipating her trip to Georgia, where she would enter the Convent of the Holy Trinity to begin her novitiate. Two years later, she was given her first assignment and sent to her Order's Court Street Center, in Brooklyn, the first Puerto Rican nun in their community. As a young nun, she had little choice in the matter, but the assignment proved to be propitious for the Brooklyn Puerto Rican community. As she recalled, her first impressions were:

> that center was two old houses and they were put together for the purpose of having clubs—we had boy scouts, girl scouts, brownies, sewing clubs, manual work for the children, mother's clubs, library, arts, crafts, all that. We had hundreds of children. We had no Puerto Ricans in this neighborhood then. We had lots of Polish, Irish. It was called Irishtown. . . [There were] Polish, Lithuanian, Chinese, Filipino.[5]

---

[5] Interview with Sister Carmelita Bonilla, Puerto Rican Oral History Project, Brooklyn Historical Society, Brooklyn, New York, 1977. See also: Anthony Stevens-Arroyo, "Puerto Rican Struggles in the Catholic Church," in Clara E. Rodríguez et al, *The Puerto Rican Struggle: Essays on Survival in the U.S.* (Maplewood, New Jersey: Waterfront Press, 1984).

Although her earliest missionary work was carried out among the poor multi-ethnic children of Brooklyn, it was the plight of the Puerto Rican migrants that sparked Sister Carmelita's imagination and dedication:

> During those years it was when they use to put them, you know, out — dispossess them—and it was very hard. And I thought that it was my duty to save every Puerto Rican that I found—from anything. I felt that terrible, you know, so I remember seeing them on the sidewalk, with all their children, and their beds, and all their things—dispossessed. Then we had no welfare. So then I remember a friend of mine—in 176 Sand Street—she owned that building and one day I met her. And I use to visit Puerto Ricans there. "Sister," she said, "I have this building and nobody pays rent so I'm gonna give you the key to this building. When you see a family dispossessed, you bring them to this building." That's what I did. I had that building filled with people—no heat, but anyway, they had a house for a while.*

Sister Carmelita remained in Brooklyn until 1949, active in numerous social welfare programs. A familiar sight in the local precincts and hospitals, she was frequently called upon to intercede on behalf of the Puerto Rican community, to translate for them and guide their general welfare. But her return to her native Puerto Rico allowed Sister Carmelita the opportunity to teach and pursue her own academic interests within the structure of her convent. She earned a Bachelor's degree as well as a Master's from the University of Puerto Rico, concentrating on the study of social work, an area in which she was experienced. In time, a personal desire to return to the Brooklyn community and the families she had left behind, motivated Carmelita to request a transfer to the mission center where she had initiated her career.

During the fourteen years that Carmelita spent in New York, a diverse Puerto Rican community—the *Barrio Hispano*—developed. It straddled the East River with *colonias*, or neighborhoods, on both sides. Puerto Ricans predominated among the city's Spanish-speaking population. As American citizens, they were unaffected by the immigration barriers that restricted aliens from coming to the U.S. In terms of actual numbers, however, census figures varied depending on who was taking the count. Puerto Ricans could easily fit into several groupings. They could be counted as blacks or whites or racially-mixed, as citizens or immigrants. To further com-

*Interview with Sister Carmelita Bonilla.

plicate matters, as residents of a U.S. possession, Puerto Ricans did not figure into immigration counts.

A report issued by the New York Mission Society in 1927 estimated a total of between 100,000 and 150,000 Spanish-speaking inhabitants of whom approximately 85,000 were Puerto Ricans engaged in the cigar-making industry.[7] Overwhelmingly working-class, theirs was a tightly-knit, introspective community whose neighborhood organizations boasted substantial audiences of one or two hundred persons at any given function, and where Spanish language newspapers and magazines found an appreciative reading public.[8] Culturally, the Puerto Rican community identified strongly with Spanish America. The Spanish language and the Roman Catholic faith served to weld close bonds. The institutionalization of common customs and tradition insured both the insulation and isolation of the nascent *colonias*. Advocacy in their interest frequently rested with the organizations that structured the community.

The work of Sister Carmelita and her Trinitarian Sisters notwithstanding, the Catholic Church was slow to respond to the needs of the growing Puerto Rican settlements, most of which were nominally Catholic. The first church to offer masses in Spanish was Nuestra Señora de la Medalla Milagrosa, founded in East Harlem in the 1920s. La Milagrosa was followed by Santa Agonia and St. Cecilia, both of which were established during the 1930s.[9]

By 1939, the Catholic Diocese initiated reforms based on the premise that all parish churches should become integrated or multinational. Previously, the Diocese had favored ethnic or nationality-oriented churches, and these had adequately provided

[7] One of the best sources for the Puerto Rican experience in the U.S. during this early period is Cesar Andreu Iglesias (ed.) *Memorias de Bernardo Vega*, (Rio Piedras, Puerto Rico: Ediciones Huracán, 1977). English translation, *Memoirs of Bernardo Vega*, by Juan Flores, Monthly Review Press, 1984. See also History Task Force, Centro de Estudios Puertorriqueños, *Labor Migration Under Capitalism: The Puerto Rican Experience*, (New York: Monthly Review Press, 1979), and Sánchez Korrol, *From Colonia to Community*, chapter 2.

[8] Sánchez Korrol, *From Colonia to Community*, Chapter 3. Another account of the community from the twenties to the forties is Jesús Colón's *A Puerto Rican in New York and Other Sketches* (New York: International Publishers, 1982). The Federal Writers Project, *The WPA Guide to New York*, (New York: Pantheon Books, 1982), offers interesting observations regarding the Manhattan Puerto Rican community.

[9] Fitzpatrick, *Puerto Rican Americans* , Chapter 8.

guidance, pastoral services and a sense of cultural identity for earlier Polish, Irish, and Italian immigrant groups. Influential and respected institutions, the nationality churches cushioned the immigration experience of their congregation by fostering ties with the native land, language, and customs. Moreover, the churches functioned as brokers or mediators between the immigrant and the dominant society. However, in the case of the Puerto Ricans, the new policies that argued against differential treatment were rationalized on several counts. First, unlike other immigrant groups before them, Puerto Ricans did not bring clergy with them to the New York settlements. Indeed, the Church failed to understand the point that in the island there had never been sufficient numbers of native-born Puerto Rican priests. Non-native, Spanish-speaking clergy had been imported to Puerto Rico for decades. Second, and more significant, the Catholic Diocese in New York had weathered a decline in third-generation national church membership. It argued that the already existing clergy, as well as schools and churches, could simply be re-trained and re-structured to accommodate the Puerto Ricans.[10] Partly because of the failure of this policy, many of the spiritual and social welfare needs of the Puerto Ricans defaulted to numerous community organizations. These included charitable groups such as the Catholic Settlement Association, the New York City Mission Society, Casita Maria, and the protestant churches.

Throughout the years, Sister Carmelita utilized the organizations, as well as the church, in her work. She was one of the founders of the settlement house Casita María, and she is directly credited with influencing and motivating the academic growth and aspirations of numerous youngsters of that period.[11] Her recollections evoke images of a dismally poor and needy community. She was frequently called upon to advocate for the non-English speaker; to mediate between migrant parents, intent on maintaining island customs, and their rebellious U.S.-born children; and to confront

[10] Ana María Díaz Ramírez, "The Roman Catholic Archdiocese of New York and the Puerto Rican Migration, 1950-1973: A Sociological and Historical Analysis." Ph.D. Dissertation, Fordham University, 1983. See also Anthony Stevens-Arroyo, "Puerto Rican Struggles in the Catholic Church," in Rodríguez et al, *The Puerto Rican Struggle*, and Fitzpatrick, *Puerto Rican Americans*, Chapter 8.

[11] Interview with Sister Carmelita Bonilla. A number of individuals interviewed in my research, including Elizabeth Guanill, former Commissioner of Human Rights, Suffolk County, New York, credit Sister Carmelita for guiding and encouraging them.

the authorities on behalf of the community. Her vocation dictated expertise in teaching, counselling, and religion, and her dedication to the people she served sharpened her knowledge of the law, public health, the penal system and housing. Her office in St. Joseph's on Pacific Street was open to everyone and she developed a resource network rooted as much in the leadership of the Puerto Rican *barrios* as in the church. She states:

> I was a friend of the politicians. I must admit I used to ask the politicians for help, you know, especially those that sold *bolita* (numbers racket)—the bankers—and they used to help me a lot for the poor people. And then the politicians that didn't belong to the *bolita* were right there, in Borough Hall so they were good to the Puerto Ricans. I use to visit everybody who was Spanish-speaking, no matter what it was or when it was and that's how I met all those people. I use to ask them to please help me out, like when Thanksgiving came —*el dia del pavo*— [the day of the Turkey] they used to give me two or three hundred dollars. I used to spend that in food and for Christmas. It was the same for *Reyes* [Three Kings' Day.][13]

Until poor health forced her retirement in the early 1970s, Sister Carmelita continued to do what she could to influence the social, cultural, and educational development of the Brooklyn Puerto Rican community. The number of Catholic institutions providing spiritual and material resources specifically for Puerto Ricans throughout the 1930s and 1940s was clearly limited.

By contrast, there were some twenty-five Puerto Rican protestant churches, most of them pentecostal. These were fundamentalist sects which adhered strictly to a literal interpretation of the Bible and encouraged rejection of worldly concerns among the members. The American invasion had facilitated the protestantization of the island, accelerating a process already evident in the late nineteenth century. By the mid-1930s one observer noted that some of the protestant churches in New York were located on the second floor of various types of buildings, and that as one approached Upper Harlem, these become more numerous. Some religious congregations met in private homes, while others rented store fronts for prayer and worship. Although the origin of the pentecostal movement in New York remains unclear, an estimated five percent of the Puerto Ricans living in the city during this period were pro-

[13] The Puerto Rican Oral History Project yielded other life experiences which supported Sister Carmelita's perspective. Among these was the interview with doña Honorina Weber Irizarry.

testant.[13] And within a decade, the pentecostals had become the fastest-growing protestant group among Puerto Ricans.

Dependent on a grass-roots tradition for their leadership, ministers often came from the ranks of the congregants. Sects were frequently self-starting and self-sustaining, supervised by ministers who were working class themselves. Small and intimate, many pentecostal or evangelical churches provided a sense of community not found in the more traditional denominations.[14] Women played a pivotal role in this phase of church and community development, as they did within the structure of the Catholic Church. However, if conventual roles were limited under the strict, formal policies of that complex institutional structure, they were also restricted by gender. As a nun, subordinate to a male hierarchy, Sister Carmelita's professional and private life was circumscribed. By contrast, the pentecostal faith permitted the ascendancy of a few women to the pulpit. Among these was the Reverend Leoncia Rosado Rosseau.

Born on April 11, 1912 in Toa Alta, Puerto Rico, Leoncia Rosado Rosseau believes that she was destined for the ministry from birth. The second of five children born to Señora Gumersinda Santiago Ferrer and don Manuel Rivera Marrerro, Leoncia received her religious calling in 1932 at the age of twenty. Then followed a period of evangelism in the poorest *barrios* of Puerto Rico. A small and slender young woman, she was not afraid to enter the most alien and hostile environments because she was convinced that it was all part of God's mission. Foretold in a vision that she was destined to carry God's word across the ocean, in 1935 she left the island for New York to continue her work as a missionary and evangelist. By 1937 she had received her first certificate in Divinity.[15]

In New York City, life was firmly anchored in church and community. Reverend Leoncia preached on street corners and delighted in debating scripture with non-believers. She offered testimony to the glory of God, visited the sick, and assisted in the general

---

[13] Lawrence R. Chenault. *The Puerto Rican Migrant in New York City* (New York: Russell and Russell, 1970), p. 129. Refer also to the dissertation in progress of Reverend Benjamin Alicéa, "The Puerto Rican Protestant Churches in East Harlem: 1912-1980," Union Theological Seminary, Columbia University, New York City.

[14] Fitzpatrick, *Puerto Rican Americans*, pp. 135-136.

[15] Interview with Reverend Leoncia Rosado Rousseau. First Reformed Church, Queens, New York, November, 1985.

organization of her church. She traveled to the Dominican Republic and other Latin countries in the service of her church. There too she continued in her dual roles as missionary and evangelist. But while her spiritual gifts and fervent dedication were acknowledged by her fellow congregants, she was limited by tradition to addressing the congregation from the floor, and not the pulpit. On the eve of the Second World War she married a church elder, Roberto Rosado, and added to her life the dimensions of wife and homemaker.

About this time, the Puerto Rican community in New York City witnessed a decline in the numbers of individuals coming from the island and a rapid dispersement of those already residing in the city into all five boroughs. Puerto Ricans continued to fill the ranks of the working class and competed for the meager unskilled employment of the depression period. But this situation changed radically in the 1940s, when women, minorities, and foreign nationals from bordering countries were vigorously recruited for factory and farm work. The labor shortages of the Second World War precipitated the large-scale Puerto Rican migration of the period just before and after the war. But this was only part of a broader expansion: close to 400,000 foreign contract workers entered the country in response to the demands of the labor market between 1942 and the end of the war, very few of whom were Puerto Rican. Some scholars argue that despite the general postwar contraction, the departure of many of those workers after the war created a vacuum in particular sectors of the labor market to which Puerto Rican workers responded. Between 1947 and 1949, a yearly net average of 32,000 individuals migrated from Puerto Rico, many destined to work in the garment and needle-trade industries.[16] They continued to be concentrated in blue-collar, low-paying sectors, especially in light industry. By 1948, the Migration Division of the island's Department of Labor established programs to aid potential migrants and to inform them about New York City. And by the start of mid-century, the great migration from Puerto Rico was well underway.[17]

---

[16] Sánchez Korrol, *From Colonia to Community*, chapter 2. See also: History Task Force, Centro de Estudios Puertorriqueños, 1979, chapter 2.

[17] Numerous studies have appeared on the migration experience of Puerto Ricans during the fifties and sixties. Among these are C. Wright Mills, Clarence Senior and Rose Goldsen, *The Puerto Rican Journey: New York's Newest Migrants* (New York: Harper & Bros., 1950). Also, Elena Padilla, *Up From Puerto Rico* (New York:

For the charismatic Reverend Leoncia, this period represented a turning point in her life. It signalled the beginning of her ministry as Pastor of the Damascus Christian Church and it brought the church directly into the social service of the community through the creation of the Christian Youth Crusade.

According to the Reverend Leoncia, both events were foretold in a vision in which The Lord took her to the edge of a river where He indicated that she was to retrieve enormous quantities of carrots from the waters. She agonized over her task and exclaimed that she could not do it but He replied, "Yes, you can. Continue. Take them out."[18]

> Finally, I got them all out of the river and when I turned around I saw that all the carrots had become people and most were young. Then we walked in front of the multitudes which were uncountable and we were going to find Damascus. I don't know what had happened to them, but they had a small congregation. We had loudspeakers to take the message to the entire world. That's how far I went with the Lord and I wondered what this all meant.
>
> Within a short time my husband was drafted. He was already an ordained minister. My husband at that time weighed 105 pounds because he was sick with a heart condition. And he did everything possible, even writing to the President of the United States, not to go into the army. I prayed that he wouldn't have to go but the Lord responded, "Do not pray for this—it is my will that he go, but he will return." He [Rosado] was sure that the army would not take him. When he went for his induction, weighing 105 pounds more infirmed than ever, he was accepted. It never crossed my mind to take over for him because I had forgotten my dream, and I could not seriously think or suggest this to him, and so we spoke of Brothers Fernando Noriega and Belén Camacho as possible substitutes. And I would assist them as I had helped (my husband). And so we went to meet with them to discuss this but they said, "No, not us. The one who should remain here is Sister Léo." and that's how I came to be pastor of the Damascus Christian Church.[19]

Even though precedents for women to act as missionaries and evangelists existed in Puerto Rico and in the New York Puerto

---

Columbia University Press, 1958), and Dan Wakefield, *Island in the City: The World of Spanish Harlem* (Boston: Houghton Mifflin, 1959). Personal narratives include Piri Thomas's *Down These Mean Streets* (New York: Alfred Knopf, 1967), Nicholasa Mohr, *Nilda* (New York: Bantam, 1973), and Edward Rivera, *Family Installments* (New York: William Morrow & Co., 1982).

[18] Interview with Reverend Leoncia Rosado Rousseau.

[19] Ibid.

Rican *barrios*, it was extremely rare for women to become ministers. In Puerto Rico, Juanita García Peraza, or "Mita" as she was known to her followers, epitomized the role of women as evangelists and ministers.[20] There are few objective accounts of Mita's life and work, but her achievements were known on both sides of the ocean. In the early 1940s she inaugurated her own sect and pentecostal church, which engaged in the operation of cooperatives and provided social services for its congregants. Her disciples believed she was God's incarnation on earth and referred to her as the "Goddess."

In the daily operations of pentecostal churches in New York, women were also indispensable. They supervised Bible study classes, succored the sick, comforted families in distress and performed countless acts of charity. Missionaries participated in street ministries and proselytized aggressively from door to door. Yet, despite the high degree of visibility and responsibility that women undertook in church matters, their involvement, by tradition, seldom extended to the pulpit.[21]

Although the Reverend Leoncia encountered resistance and discrimination towards her calling because of her gender, it was nothing compared to the obstacles she faced in orienting her church to the social/economic problems of the community. Until that point, pentecostalism among the Puerto Ricans in New York had served as a sanctuary from the cultural and social malaise inherent in the migration experience; it basically shielded the congregants from spiritual contamination by the outside world. Leoncia Rosado's ministry opened the way for new definitions.

When the Christian Youth Crusade was initiated in 1957, Damascus Christian Church had expanded to include branches in other boroughs. One of the earliest grass-roots programs to fight drug abuse, it was sustained by funding from within the church. It provided a refuge for gangs, addicts, alcoholics, and ex-convicts, and its philosophical base was strictly religious. The addict was viewed as a sinner and only repentance and acceptance of the Lord would bring about a cure. The major center for treatment was in

[20] Anthony Stevens-Arroyo, "Religion and the Puerto Ricans in New York," in Edward Mapp (ed.) *Puerto Rican Perspectives* (Metuchen, New Jersey: The Scarecrow Press, Inc., 1974), pp.119-131.

[21] Interviews with missionaries, doña Virginia Martínez, New York City, doña Celina Díaz, Brooklyn, New York, and the Reverend Aimee García Cortese, Cross Roads Tabernacle Church, Bronx, New York, December, 1985.

the Damascus Christian Church in the Bronx but there was also an upstate site, Mountaindale, to which recovering addicts would go. In spite of its success, however, the church was most reluctant to engage in such community-oriented tasks. Reverend Leoncia recalled the confrontation with the church leaders on this matter:

> Our church was a church like any other. It did not work with alcoholics, etc. Sophisticated, illuminated with the Holy Spirit, yes, but it did not work with alcoholics. I came and told them of my vision. I understand these are alcoholics and lost souls, and the lowest people in society. But God wants us to do this work and they said, "Not here, no, no, not here," and I said to them, "Yes here! Because God mandates it of us." The church which closes its being and heart to the clamor of lost souls does not have a right to a place in the community. What do you think you're here for? Here is where the work is to be done and if you don't do it, I'll present my resignation. I was the pastor there then. My husband had returned from the army, and he was a bishop with the church council. Then they (the congregation) gave me a place that we called the Tower of Prayer, which was a long room and there I placed beds and cots which I found.
>
> Imagine a person like me, who had never even smoked a cigarette, unworldly, working with addicts, breaking their habits cold turkey, without aspirin or anything. My husband Roberto and I and the brothers and sisters of the church who helped us there. . . legs full of sores, and then when an addict is breaking the habit, their stinking sweat, that fever, the cold, the trembling, the heat, their screams... it was a tremendous thing!
>
> And that bunch of kids—about fifteen, sometimes twenty or twenty-five, and their crying Mama—that's where I got the name, Mama Léo—Mama, it hurts here, rub there, or there, and when I would treat their legs and feet, oozing, full of sores, I would think, I held the feet of Our Lord.
>
> I would make them a banquet for Thanksgiving and they would come dirty, strung-out, sick, anyway at all but before feeding them I would provide a religious service with the other youths already saved. The kids would say, "Mama, we came for the bird and you gave us the Word!"[11]

An estimated two hundred and fifty to three hundred young people, mostly Hispanic, who were rehabilitated through that program went into the ministry. Many of them are active today in youth-oriented programs. Close to eighteen programs or schools

[11] Interview with Reverend Leoncia Rosado Rousseau. Reverend Rosado Rousseau's achievements, particularly with the Christian Youth Crusade, were highlighted in an article by Howard Broady, "The Power of Faith," Associated Press, 1959.

have been established by them worldwide. Reverend Leoncia considers this her greatest and most rewarding mission.

If the community service programs begun by Mama Léo served to initiate the church's role in the streets, her example as a pastor and as a woman illustrated new directions for some of the young Puerto Rican women growing up in New York during this period. One of these was the Reverend Aimee García Cortese. Aimee García Cortese was born, in 1929, raised, and educated in the New York Puerto Rican *barrio* of the South Bronx. Her close-knit and religious family offered Aimee and her two brothers and sister a stable and loving environment in which to grow. At thirteen, Aimee encountered pentecostal outreach efforts for the first time, when local church members offered prayers and services for her ailing mother. Soon afterwards, the family became active in church affairs. As New York teenagers, steeped in the world of movies and other social activities, the Garcías at first resisted the rigor, discipline, and sacrifice expected of pentecostal youth. However, by the time Aimee was fifteen, she confided her intention to become a minister to her pastor, the Reverend Manuel López. He replied, "las mujeres no predican"—women do not preach! His pronouncement notwithstanding, and fortified by her personal belief that she was named after the American preacher, Aimee Semple McPherson, she returned to him and proceeded to systematically badger him into letting her preach. She received permission to do so before her sixteenth birthday.[23]

> He told me that the next Sunday I would be preaching. Well I was so proud that I was going to preach, I never thought that I had nothing to say, I never thought that I wasn't prepared to face a crowd but I was so proud of the fact that I was going to preach that I got down on my knees and said Lord, you know you've got to bless me. Well next Sunday came and he told me to be at church at 5:30 a.m. I said that's a little early. When I got there, there were four other young people. One had a flag, one had a tambourine, one had a license in his hand and he (the pastor) said to me "Now you go out to Brook Avenue and 134th Street and you preach." Oh, I thought it was going to be in church. "Oh no, mi hija, ahi es donde se aprende" [no, my daughter, that is where you'll learn] and it was there on that corner that I realized the strangest thing in the world: what do I say? I only knew two verses. All my friends were coming out of the holes, like cockroaches out of a wall. All of a sudden I'm surrounded by eighty, ninety kids of the neighborhood that had never seen me in this posture, and there was

[23] Interview with Reverend Aimee García Cortese, December, 1985.

> the crowd! I recited John 3:16, and then I went on to this other verse about God gives peace. I said this is very important that you know it. So then I went back to John 3:16, and then I went back to God is going to give you peace. I did that about five times and then I realized I had nothing to say. And I looked at the people and said, "Something great's happened in my life but I don't know how to say it. One of these days I'm gonna come back and tell you," and I started to cry. One young man tapped me on the shoulder and said, "vámonos" [Let's go]. And they took me back to the church. When I arrived, I was still crying, and the pastor said, "te di'te gusto nena?" [Did you enjoy yourself?] I had nothing to tell them. "Well," he replied, "get ready to tell them something." And that was it. And he taught me my first year, 365 Bible verses.[34]

Aimee García Cortese went on to tell the people something. She was ordained by the Wesleyan Methodist Church in Puerto Rico in 1964, became a missionary evangelist for the Spanish Assemblies of God, Associated Minister of Thessalonica Christian Church in the South Bronx, and the first female chaplain for the New York State Department of Corrections. Reflecting on her past experience, Reverend García Cortese credits Reverend Leoncia Rosado Rosseau, as well as other ministers and missionaries, with opening the way for women in religious life and providing experiences from which to learn.

> There were women in ministry, but different types of ministry. Like, take la hermana Cartegena. She was the missionary of our church. She will be eighty years old, come 1986. Now there was a woman, deep in the Word, a woman dedicated to visitation, and dedicated to doing God's work. To watch her, to be with her. . .and as I grew in the Lord, I grew out of proportion, in terms that I did not go with the young people. They didn't satisfy me. What they were doing didn't satisfy me. What satisfied me was what la hermana Cartagena was doing. She would visit the sick, knock on doors, give out tracts, and I thought to myself, this is God's work! I was kind of ahead of my day. I was a young girl with a "little old lady" mentality. Now I realize it wasn't a "little old lady" mentality, it was "kingdom" mentality, but I didn't know what it was then. I didn't know I wanted to reach the world for Christ. I didn't know the extent of my drive. But now as I look back, I realize.
>
> Elisa (Alicéa) was also a tremendous role model in the sense of daring to be innovative, in music, in leadership. [She] would pick up a trumpet and wake up a whole Puerto Rican town, in Ciales, and she did with music, you know, what, later on, I did with the Word. Just stirred people, woke them up, brought them into a "Hey, here's young people and we're doing something for God."

---

[34] Ibid.

> And there was Mama Léo. I don't ever think there was a moment I wanted to be [exactly] like her. I just loved her for what she was, but, it looked like her walk was a much more difficult walk than what I could do. In other words, to me, Léo was somebody to learn from, but never to want to be. Maybe because Léo was one hundred years ahead of her time. On a one-woman scale, she did what, later on, organizations like Teen Challenge did, or an organization like Odyssey House did in the secular [world]. You're talking about a little lady, all by herself taking on the world.[25]

The congregations directed by Reverend García Cortese, from the 1960s to the present, have incorporated many of the outreach programs that were considered radical in Reverend Leoncia Rosado's period. Today, youth and community programs are naturally included in church planning. Contemporary urban music plays a major role in attracting, and encouraging, religious expression among the youth. In Spanish or English, music has become an integral part of street ministries. If Reverend García Cortese's role as minister is no longer questioned because she is a woman, neither is the direction that she foresees for her congregation challenged. She envisions her church of the future to be a religious complex, including a community center with a swimming pool, gymnasium, physical fitness space, and Bible and Sunday schools. The building of the sanctuary would come last because a congregation's priority should be its youth and community. All of this she believes to be a legitimate part of worship.

From Sister Carmelita's period to Reverend García Cortese's, attitudinal changes towards church and community are apparent. They resulted from a combination of the external transformations of the 1960s, the maturation of the Puerto Rican community, and differing perspectives regarding women's roles. At the same time, similarities abound in the experiences of all three women. The utilization of these oral histories, in conjunction with an analysis of specific historical periods, offers a unique inter-generational perspective. They provide a significant variant on the history of Puerto Ricans in New York City, and more importantly they allow us to understand the continuity of our experience.

The task of recovering and defining women's histories in the New York Puerto Rican community before mid-century is clearly underway. From the 1920s to just after the Second World War, Puerto Ricans struggled to lay the foundations of a distinctive communi-

[25] Ibid.

ty with formal and informal coping structures, internal leadership, businesses, professions, common cultural interests and modes of behavior. The population movements alone, punctuated by the unique circular nature of the Puerto Rican migration, brought repeated ruptures and renewals of ties, dismantling and reconstructions of familial, individual, and communal networks. We have identified a small segment of the population that contributed to the process of community development, assumed the reins of leadership, and embraced demanding social commitments. Through their ministries and work with young people, women like Aimee García Cortese, Leoncia Rosado Rousseau, and Sister Carmelita aided in the stabilization of the Puerto Rican community at significant points in its historical development.

Catholic Laywomen in the Culture of American Catholicism in the 1950s*

Jeffrey M. Burns

In 1960, Paul Goodman, in his now classic *Growing Up Absurd*, enunciated a commonly held intellectual assessment of the 1950s—American society was absurd. Goodman argued that American children were destined to grow up "absurd" because American society and American parents could not provide their children with enough meaningful and significant work. American society offered no outlet for creativity, grace or intellect, making "honor" and "dignity" unobtainable. America was a "closed room," whose members were caught in a "rat race."[1] With no creative outlet, the American male was readily molded into the Organization Man, as another analyst dubbed him.

If American society offered few creative outlets for men, it offered even fewer outlets for women who ventured outside the confines of the home. After having entered the work force in vast numbers in support of the war effort, American women were once again told to return to the home to allow the returning veterans to resume their civilian jobs. Women who did work were relegated to the "traditionally female" occupations—nursing, teaching, secretarial work, or social work—jobs with little power and prestige and less pay.[2]

Besides receiving less remuneration and credit for their work, American working women were accused of subverting American family life, and in so doing subverting America. The 1950s witnessed a revival of "tradi-

*Presented at the Cushwa Center Conference on American Catholicism, October 4, 1985.

1. Paul Goodman, *Growing Up Absurd* (New York, 1960), 17, 160.
2. Richard Pells, *The Liberal Mind in a Conservative Age: American Intellectuals in the 1940s and 1950s* (New York, 1985), 210.

tional family values," and as such, woman was instructed to resume her role as "Nurturer" and "guardian of culture."[3] If woman was unhappy, (and the oft cited *Fortune* poll of 1946 suggested she was), it was not because she was tied to the home, as the feminists argued; it was because she refused to accept her "biological destiny" to be mother and homemaker. The widely popular text by Ferdinand Lundberg and Marynia Farnham referred to modern woman as "the lost sex,"[4] and berated feminist activists who sought (in the words of historian William Chafe paraphrasing Farnham and Lundberg), "to reject their natural sex based instincts in a futile attempt to be imitation men. . . . Passivity, dependence and the desire to raise children comprise the formula for female contentment."[5]

Indeed, American society in the 1950s did demonstrate an increased commitment to family life—between 1940 and 1960 the birth rate for the third child in a family doubled, and tripled for the fourth child. Magazines offering helpful homemaking hints flourished in the blossoming cult of domesticity. Despite feminist criticism to the contrary, many women did enjoy their role as wife and mother—the family provided women with satisfactions often unobtainable in the work place, namely responsible and rewarding work, and intimate companionship.[6] Even as avant garde a social critic as Paul Goodman could write, "A girl does not have to make something of herself. Her career does not have to be self-justifying, for she will have children which is absolutely self-justifying."[7]

Despite the rewards of family life, many women continued to look beyond the family for meaning. As historian Richard Pells asserts, women sought jobs outside the home because "employment offered women their only chance to fashion an identity and sense of independence outside the home."[8] Traditionally women were taught to submerge their identity in the family. Eugenia Kaledin suggests in her study of American women in the 1950s, that women were relegated to living vicariously—through their husbands and children. A woman who wanted to be a doctor, would marry a doctor; women were not allowed to have separate selves.[9] Throughout the 1950s, the proper place of woman in American society was debated, and on this matter the Catholic Church in American was quite vociferous.

---

3. Eugenia Kaledin, *Mothers and More: American Women in the 1950s* (Boston, 1984). From the Preface.
4. Ferdinand Lundberg and Marynia Farnham, *Modern Women: The Lost Sex* (New York, 1947).
5. William Chafe, *The American Woman: Her Changing Social, Economic and Political Roles, 1920–1970* (New York, 1972), 203, 205.
6. Kaledin, *Mothers*, 17.
7. Goodman, *Absurd*, 13.
8. Pells, *Liberal Mind*, 214.
9. Kaledin, *Mothers*, 43.

Patty and Pat Crowley, founders of the Catholic Family Movement

Since the 1920s, American Catholics, the last defenders of "American innocence" as William Halsey phrased it,[10] had been alerting Americans to the existence of a "family crisis." Increasing divorce rates, declining birth rates, and the ultimate evil, birth control, were all conspiring to subvert family life. As the family was the basic unit of society, a culture hostile to the family was an unhealthy culture. In this, American Catholics reflected and reinforced those values articulated by other conservative elements of the society or by what William Chafe calls the "anti-feminists."[11] Catholics believed that feminism was a major culprit in the subversion of the family. Feminism was a "false philosophy" that confused the proper spheres of male and female as dictated by the natural order. While it was fine for women to have the vote, the Dominican journal *The Torch* conceded, it warned that feminists had now gone overboard. "Women they said must have the same rights as men in all areas—which of course is nonsense."[12] The theory of family disseminated by Catholics asserted that while men and women were equal in the eyes of God, they were different: each possessed certain distinct sexually based characteristics and qualities which, while different, complemented one another. In the family, masculine and feminine complemented one another perfectly, creating a new unity, with the father serving as head of the household

10. William Halsey, *The Survival of American Innocence: American Catholicism in an Era of Disillusionment* (Notre Dame, 1980).

11. Chafe, *American Woman*, 199–200.

12. E. J. Keegan, "Woman and the Church," *The Torch* (March 1950): 2.

Integrity *focused its September 1953 issue on the emerging Catholic woman*

while the mother served as the heart of the family. This theory of the family was taught in all Catholic marriage preparation and family education programs, and received its clearest articulation in the Cana and Pre-Cana Conference Movements.

Cana participants were counselled that man was the protector, the provider, who must earn his living in the world. He was aggressive, courageous; interested in "objects and projects, facts and figures," more interested in things than persons. Man analyzed, calculated, and put things in logical order. Woman was the homemaker, "spontaneously and easily" given to the service of her husband and children. Woman was more sympathetic and sensitive than the male and had an intuitive faculty whereby she was able to take a wider view of things. Woman was more interested in persons than things, having "an insight into human souls . . . because her task is to form the plastic personality of the child." Together, man and woman, complemented one another, each supplying strengths and covering for the other's weaknesses. The family unit created this supportive unity.[13]

13. Walter Imbiorski, *The New Cana Manual* (Chicago, 1957), 74.

By 1960, a whole range of Catholic organizations were concerned with the preservation of a healthy family life.[14] Concern for the family at the abstract level reflected the arrival of a significant number of American Catholics to middle-class America. Long characterized as an urban, immigrant, working class group, Catholic Americans now entered the middle class and joined the flight to the suburbs. The long quiescent laity began to "emerge" from its slumber at the 1950s enjoyed the burgeoning of the Catholic lay apostolate, or what had been called Catholic Action in the 1930s; the Grail Movement, YGS, YCW, CFM, Cana, and the continued apostolate of the Catholic Worker Movement and Friendship House Movement, as well as the blossoming of several significant lay magazines—*Integrity, Jubilee, Cross Currents,* and *Commonweal.* In all these lay activities women played an important and integral role.

Despite what feminists would consider a restrictive ideology, Catholic women of the 1950s demonstrated a new independence and assertiveness. For the rest of the paper, I would like to briefly develop three points. First, beyond being the "heart of the family," Catholic lay women of the 1950s made a significant impact on American Catholic culture, particularly liberal, Catholic culture. Second, a new class of Catholic women emerged, whom I shall call the "emerging Catholic laywoman." The emerging Catholic laywoman continued to articulate the Catholic theory of the differences of the sexes, while her activities suggested a growing disjuncture between ideology and practice. Modest attempts were made to reassess the role of woman in the 1950s, but a sustained re-evaluation would not occur until the 1970s. Finally, to escape the absurdity of 1950s American and the restrictions of Catholic ideology, Catholic women had to adopt radical lifestyles—this is exemplified in the lives of Dorothy Day and Catherine de Hueck Doherty, the two most influential Catholic women of the decade.

Point one: Catholic lay women in the 1950s made a significant impact on American Catholic culture. As James J. Kenneally's work has pointed out, women in prevous eras, could, "despite the restrictions of Catholicism . . . achieve intellectual independence, a sense of self-worth, dignity and happiness;"[15] however, these women had less impact on their culture than the Catholic lay women of the 1950s. Though the emerging Catholic laywoman was working for the same goals as her predecessors, she had far greater success in achieving them. Garry Wills goes so far as to say

14. See Jeffrey M. Burns, "American Catholics and the Family Crisis: the Organizational and Ideological Response, 1930–1962" (Ph.D. diss., University of Notre Dame, 1982).

15. James Kenneally, "Catholic and Feminist: A Biographical Approach" *U.S. Catholic Historian* 3 (Spring 1984): 237.

(albeit somewhat cryptically) that the world of the Catholic liberal in the 1950s, "was largely shaped and cared for by female heroines and attendants."[16] Wills lists twenty-one women who made a significant impact in the 1950s indeed many of their names became (if you will excuse the expression), household words—Dorothy Day, Catherine de Hueck Doherty, Edith Stein Sigrid Undset, Raissa Maritain, Dorothy Dohen, Carol Jackson, Maisie Ward, Barbara Ward, and Patty Crowley among them. Many of these women were not merely Catholic activists, but were important for the symbolic role they played for Catholics during the 1950s. Devotion was paid to Edith Stein, a Jewish convert who had become a Carmelite nun, and later, a victim of Nazi persecution. The cult of the Little Flower, St. Therese of Lisieux, flourished, with stress placed on her "little way" to sanctity. Dorothy Day and the Baroness, Catherine de Hueck, whom Willis dubs "earth mothers" for the era, became symbols of heroic sacrifice and devotion to the poor, demanding greater efforts on the part of all Catholics, liberal and conservative alike. And the greatest female symbol of them all was, of course, Mary. In a decade noted for its Marian devotion, Mary became "all things to all people." Mary was cited by nearly everyone to justify their own view of the role of woman—feminists stressed her strength and position, while conservatives stressed her humility and willingness to serve. In any case, Mary and an assortment of other women operated as important symbols for Catholics in the 1950s.

Woman's role was more than symbolic, however. Although Catholic women were denied positions of power within the clerical, hierarchical structure of the Church, Catholic lay women did attain positions of power and influence, particularly in the lay Catholic movements. The popular Christian Family Movement (CFM) was directed largely by Patty Crowley, who founded and directed the Movement with her husband, Pat. Both CFM and Cana were important in that women were given a significant role in the movement as husbands and wives operated together as the unit of membership.[17] Mary Jerdo and Ann Harrigan ran Friendship Houses. Janet Kalven and Lydwine van Kersbergen directed the Grail Movement in America. Scores of women became actively involved in Friendship Houses, the Catholic Worker, CFM, Cana, Young Christian Students and Young Christian Workers, and the Grail. In all these movements women made a significant impact.

---

16. Garry Wills, *Bare Ruined Choirs: Doubt, Prophecy and Radical Religion* (New York, 1972), 59.

17. Patty Crowley tells the story that CFM became a "couples movement" because she and other wives became tired of their husbands running off for study groups with Msgr. Reynold Hillenbrand. The women wanted a form of Catholic Action in which they could participate with their husbands.

Dorothy Day, founder of the Catholic Worker Movement, addresses a group at one of the hospitality houses.

Perhaps the greatest outlet for Catholic lay women was journalism—writing and editing. One is struck by the ubiquitous presence of women writers in Catholic journals during the 1950s. Some, like Flannery O'Connor, received recognition from non-Catholic sources. Equally impressive is the number of women who advanced to editorial status. At the top of the list is Dorothy Day, editor of the *Catholic Worker*. Besides Day, several women operated as editors or co-editors, or assistant editors. The popular liberal magazine *Integrity* was co-founded and co-edited by Carol Jackson. Later, Dorothy Dohen would become sole editor of *Integrity*. *Integrity* also featured several regular women contributors—Elaine Malley, Marion Mitchell Stancioff, Mary Reed Newland and Dorothy Willock. The liberal magazine *Jubilee*, while retaining its top three editorial positions for men, did list two female editorial associates—Rita Joseph and Kathleen Goess, and six of the seven members of *Jubilee*'s

Patty and Pat Crowley discuss the Catholic Family Movement with Cathy and Bob Burggraf

staff were women. Sally Cuneen was a co-editor of *Cross Currents*, Betty Miller served a brief stint as co-editor of *The Critic*, and Anne Freemantle was an associate and contributing editor for *Commonweal*. Naturally, women were involved in the Grail, Cana and CFM publications. In symbol, writing, editing and action lay women made a significant impact on the culture of American Catholicism in the 1950s.

Point two: The increased activity of women, and the expansion of their traditional roles and spheres created a disjuncture between ideology and practice. A new breed of Catholic woman developed in the 1950s—middle class, college educated, devoutly Catholic, activist in spirit and articulate. The "emerging Catholic laywoman" was not content in simply being a housewife and mother, but was reluctant to challenge traditional Church teaching regarding the role of women. No significant Catholic feminist criticism emerged in the 1950s: liberal Catholic women seemed content to reiterate the company line about the role of women. On a practical level, Catholic women continued to expand their activities, and in those rare moments when the traditional teaching as regards women was questioned, it was done so within the bounds of the traditional Catholic rhetoric.

The ambivalence and subterranean contradiction which resulted went unnoticed, for the most part. In the April 1954 issue of the liberal Catholic journal *Jubilee* the disjuncture is evident. In a pictorial essay entitled, "The Role of Woman" a series of photographs are presented depicting woman in her many roles. The photos include a housewife praying, a mother teaching her children to pray, a mother taking down her family's clothes, a mother and child, a group of women religious, a woman teaching children, a nurse helping an invalid, a wife preparing to embrace her husband, and another mother and child. In no picture do we see a woman working in anything other than a traditional woman's role. The implication is clear: woman is mother, helper, teacher, wife; she lives for others. In case we miss the point of the pictures, short quotes and aphorisms are printed next to the pictures to leave us no doubt. One writer is aglow, wondering at the immense beauty of woman's "patience," which no man can hope to equal. "Watch her as she washes socks. . . . There is a willingness to be quietly bored, a tacit acceptance that a dull task must be done. . . ."[18] In contrast to these images and sayings, on the second page of the same issue is a picture of one of *Jubilee*'s editorial assistants, Kathlene Goess. She is pictured seated at her desk in the office, in a neat business suit, pencil in hand ready to work. As if to reassure traditionalists the accompanying description tells us that Kathleen is "editorial assistant" and "secretary-receptionist."

The Grail Movement also reflected the growing disjuncture between ideal and practice. The Grail, begun in Europe in the 1920s, imported to American in the 1940s, and firmly established in Loveland, Ohio by the 1950s, established a training center for young women who wished to become involved in the lay apostolate. Grail sought to train women in accord with their true nature. Thus trained, women would inspire a renewal of the womanly virtues in the world, thereby balancing the excessively masculine character of modern culture. While Grail reiterated the common Catholic understanding of the differences and complementarity of the sexes, it exposed young Catholic women to a wide variety of ideas and endeavors—the domestic arts, drama, music, liturgy, theology, missionary work, publishing and writing. As Alden Brown points out in his study of Grail, the Grail provided Catholic lay women with a distinct and autonomous role within the Church, providing a significant outlet for Catholic women, no where else possible. As members of Grail came to do more and more, the restrictive ideology of sexual spheres would have increasingly little relation to the reality of the experience of Grail women. The experience of autonomy enjoyed by Grail women in the 1950s would lead ultimately to a radical questioning and rejection of the traditional ideology by the 1970s.

During the 1950s, however, there was no systematic re-examination of the role of woman. As creative as the Grail got was to suggest that mas-

18. "The Role of Woman," *Jubilee* (April 1954): 40–47.

culine and feminine virtues were not in exclusive opposition to one another. Lydwine van Kersbergen could suggest that "everyone possessed both (masculine and feminine virtues) to some degree," and that the great person, the saint or genius, developed both, still "in the man the masculine pole should be dominant and in the woman the feminine."[19]

The most innovative thinking as regards the role of woman was done by the *Integrity* magazine group, a magazine which, as pointed out earlier, had allowed women significant roles. Under the editorship of Ed Willock and Carol Jackson, *Integrity* proposed a severe, radical personalism designed to renew corrupt modern society. As part of their renewal program, men and women were required to return to their natural spheres. Willock and Jackson both saw a generation of castrated men, and since men refused to be manly, women had been forced to take on more and more masculine tasks. Willock complained that "the family had lost its head."[20] In order for men to become men again, women had to return to their natural feminine sphere. To guide women was the image of Mary: one *Integrity* writer counseled, "through the practice of Mary's most neglected virtues, modesty, humility, poverty and silence, we can stage our small revolt (against) the modern perversion of the woman's status."[21] A return to Mary would restore the proper notion of womanliness, which in turn, would restore manliness. (It is interesting to note that editor Carol Jackson wrote most of her articles under the pseudonymn "Peter Michaels," which she did according to one historian "to lend an air of authority to her opinions."[22] But whether writing under her own name or that of Peter Michaels, Jackson remained staunchly "anti-feminist.")

The tone and style of *Integrity* underwent a shift under the editorship of Dorothy Dohen (1951–1955.) *Integrity*'s radical personalism shifted from an insistence that the individual conform him or herself to the ideal, to a policy of stressing the primacy of the human person against the requirements of the institution. *Integrity*'s attitude toward woman also changed. In contrast to the old *Integrity* line that women belonged in the home, *Integrity* contributor Abigail McCarthy exhorted women to "be present" in and to modern society.[23] McCarthy, citing papal directives, argued that women had a right to be in public life, and to participate in government.

19. My discussion of Grail is based on Alden Brown's study, "Women in the Lay Apostolate: The Grail Movement in the United States," *Cushwa Center Working Paper* Series 15, Number One (Spring 1984). Kersbergen quote cited on p. 34.

20. Ed Willock, "The Family has Lost its Head," *Integrity* 1 (1947): 40.

21. Elaine Malley, "Springboards for Sanctity," *Integrity* 3 (1949): 15.

22. James Fisher, "The Evolution of Personalist Catholicism in America, 1933–1960." Unpublished manuscript in possession of the author.

23. Abigail McCarthy, "Be Present!" *Integrity* 7 (1954): 41.

The role of Catholic women is captured in this illustration from Integrity

Women were called to be leaders of popular causes—civil rights, migrant labor, low income housing—realms previously considered as beyond woman's normal sphere. Another *Integrity* regular, Marion Mitchell Stancioff argued that nineteenth century Victorian pieties had drastically restricted the sphere of middle class women—working class and aristocratic women were never so isolated. The twentieth century had come to accept as normative the rigid Victorian restrictions on the activities of women.[24]

The same held true for single women. In a 1954 issue devoted to "Single Women," *Integrity*, while acknowledging that all women were called at least to spiritual, if not physical motherhood, denied that this could be achieved only through the married or religious life. Nor were single women restricted to the service of families. Single women were encouraged to participate in social and political life, and urged to recognize that remaining single was "part of the Divine Plan," and not an aberration. Ironically, the final article of the "Single Women" issue was written by former editor Ed Willock and entitled, "Single Men—Afraid to Marry?" which undercut the articles which preceded it. Willock contended that unmarried men, by remaining single, "perpetuated the evils of individualism" and "in choosing individualism he is condemning some girl to the same predicament." Implicit in Willock's argument is the belief that women are dependent upon men to give their lives meaning. Moreover, women remain single because of the selfishness of men, and not because of the Divine Plan.[25]

24. Marion Mitchell Stancioff, "People Are People Are People," *Integrity* 7 (1954): 14ff.
25. Ed Willock, "Single Men—Afraid to Marry?" *Integrity* 8 (1954): 36.

The most innovative statement in regard to women was made by Marion Mitchell Stancioff in an article, "People Are People Are People." While acknowledging the complementariness of the sexes, Stancioff argued that "complementarity" had been abused, used to shackle both men and women rather than contributing to their growth. Grounding her argument in personalistic terms, Stancioff asserted that women had come to be considered "things." Rather than teaching that certain traits were masculine or feminine, she argued that human traits should be taught. Both sexes were equally capable of vice and virtue and both could attain full freedom only in God. Stancioff wrote, "There is so much of her father in every woman, so much of her mother in every man that it would be rash in the labyrinthine darkness of the human soul to seize on this or that as specifically and immutably masculine or feminine." Man and woman both were looking for something beyond themselves. The peculiar merit of Christianity was its "transcendence of sex." Woman had a dignity independent of man; "the soul of woman is not a spiritual rib, a by-product of man's spirit, but a direct work of God." Stancioff arrives at what must have been considered an unorthodox conclusion:

> For although man and woman have always been thought of as complementary they are not only that. If we start thinking of ourselves as complements rather than people, we will never take heaven by storm. We should never think of ourselves as "writer," "woman," "leader," or "mother" etc. Such thinking tends to make us act rather than be. We are each of us men and women, but we are all of us people, people with souls that are curiously and gloriously unique. Men and women are saved by the same virtues, the same sins are deadly to both.

Stancioff's article reflects the caution with which an innovative argument had to be set forth in the pre-Conciliar Church. In any case, Stancioff's article began a questioning of the role of woman that would not reach a crescendo until the 1970s.[26]

In a similar article, sociologist Father Joseph Fichter S.J. addressed the problem, "Why Aren't Males So Holy?" Fichter echoed the feminist stance of the 1950s[27] by arguing that women appeared more concerned about religious matters because of the way the culture perceived religion and trained women. Fichter asserted "religion in itself is neither masculine nor feminine." Religious values were "theoretically meant to have the same significance for both sexes . . . The liturgical and sacramental ideals and the social virtues are bi-sexual in content and intent," but the way these values were interpreted was different for each sex. The "expected

26. Stancioff, "People Are . . .": 17–20.
27. See William Chafe, *American Woman*, 210ff.

Catholic workers at the hospitality house in San Francisco, 1971

patterns of behavior," the way men and women are "supposed to act" as dictated by the culture, were extremely influential in the way men and women *do* act. Much of what was thought to be masculine and feminine was culturally determined, and would change as the culture changed.[28]

Integrity writers who made forays into the theology of the sexes were constrained to argue within the boundaries of traditional Catholic rhetoric as regards the sexes, and were constantly subjected to the serious criticism that there work was "not Catholic." And though the articles cited above went virtually unnoticed by all but a few American Catholics, they do represent a significant development in the attempt to reduce the disjuncture of ideology and practice as regards the "emerging Catholic laywoman."

Point three: to escape the absurdity of modern America, and to overcome the restrictive Catholic family ideology, Catholic laywomen were required to adopt a radical stance and lifestyle—this is exemplified in the lives of Dorothy Day of the Catholic Worker Movement and Catherine de Hueck Doherty of Friendship House. Day and de Hueck were the two most influential Catholic laywomen of the 1950s, but they betrayed little interest in feminism as a movement. Day and de Hueck regarded their work as neither masculine nor feminine—they were simply responding as best they could to the commands of Jesus. While they may have assented in theory to the notion of "proper spheres," their actions largely ignored masculine or feminine characterizations. Their influence lay not in their

28. Joseph Fichter, S.J., "Why Aren't Males So Holy?" *Integrity* 9 (1955), 5–6.

being women and thus, mother figures. Their influence lay in their personal bearing, in their unwavering conviction, in their spiritual authority (much as Jesus was regarded as one who spoke with authority despite having no official title).

John Cogley marvels of Day (and also of de Hueck), "No one seemed to think it odd that a woman should be leading a vigorous social movement in the very male-centered Catholic Church."[29] No one thought it odd because Day and de Hueck simply acted and their strength and self-assurance burst any limiting notion of "proper spheres." Michael Harrington, foremost American socialist and former Catholic Worker, wrote of Day, "Dorothy is a presence. When she comes into a room even a stranger who had never heard of her would realize that someone significant had entered the room."[30] And Thomas Merton could write of Catherine de Hueck, "The way she said some things was as moving as a propaganda movie . . . and left you ready to do some kind of action . . . renounce the world, live in total poverty."[31] The presence of Day and de Hueck was neither masculine or feminine, but human.

In the preceding paragraph I have cited John Cogley, long-time editor of *Commonweal*, Michael Harrington, and Thomas Merton to demonstrate the enormous influence of Day and de Hueck and their ability to inspire. All three men—the journalist, the socialist, and the monk—have made significant impacts on American culture, and each of them was inspired onward by Day or de Hueck. The influence of Day and de Hueck transcends their own actions, and includes the good deeds of the vast number of people they have inspired—men as well as women.

Both Day and de Hueck chose to stand on the margins of society, with the outcast, the alienated, and the poor. In so doing they were in line with what Kaledin calls the tradition of "women as apostles of moral indignation."[32] Women had long been involved in social and charitable work, which was considerd an extension of their sphere. The radical commitment and severity of lifestyle followed by Day and de Hueck, if considered in terms of proper spheres, stretched those spheres to the breaking point. Both women chastised modern culture for abandoning the poor. They rejected the prevailing ethos of middle-class, suburban, consumer culture. Such a culture could only produce death and absurdity. If men and women could find no significant and meaningful work within the system,

29. John Cogley, *A Canterbury Tale: Experiences and Reflections, 1916–1976* (New York, 1976), 12.

30. Michael Harrington, *Fragments of a Century* (New York, 1973), 19.

31. Thomas Merton, cited in Michael Mott, *The Seven Mountains of Thomas Merton* (Boston, 1984), 187.

32. Kaledin, *Mothers*, 103.

then they needed to go outside the system, or at least to its margins. America needed more than just patchwork reform—it needed to be transformed at its roots. The severity of Day's rejection of the prevailing ethos is witnessed in her unyielding pacifism during World War II and the Korean "police action," stands which were unpopular with Catholic and non-Catholic alike. The radical quality of the life Day lived and demanded all to follow clearly exceeded what would have been thought of as a proper woman's role.

If Day shattered the traditional bounds of a woman's sphere, she did so because of the crises of modern life, not because she was asserting some abstract right or pursuing some illusory self-fulfillment. Day clearly saw her role as that of "mother." The birth of her own daughter, Tamar, was one of the most crucial and exalted moments in her life. Her own experience of childbirth spurred her to enter the Catholic Church and to reject her bohemian life and common law husband. In her autobiography *The Long Loneliness*, she rejoices of her Catholic Worker experience, "I found myself a barren woman, the joyful mother of children."[33] Day was both physical and spiritual mother. Only the demands of the time made Dorothy pursue her radical work. John Cogley reports that when asked what she would like to do for eternity, "Dorothy Day said she would like to be a simple wife and mother, charged with the care of an ever growing family."[34] Dorothy Day was not a radical feminist, just a Christian radical and radical Christian.

Nonetheless, Day and de Hueck offered both men and women a way out of the absurdity of the 1950s—the injunction to "sell all and give to the poor" and to love as Jesus did were neither masculine nor feminine injunctions; they were commands required of all who wished to be called followers of Christ, and offered the only real alternative to the corrupt modern world.

In conclusion, what can be learned from a brief overview of the role Catholic lay women in the culture of American Catholicism circa 1950? For one thing, women did play a significant role in that culture beyond being housewives and mothers. Moreover they did this despite an excessively male-centered, clerical, ecclesiastical structure, and a restrictive ideology of the family and the sexes. Historians of the 1950s culture would do well to pay closer attention to the efforts of Catholic lay women during this decade. Indeed, the present feminist ferment in the Church has its roots in the 1950s with the arrival of what I have called the "emerging Catholic laywoman." As American women in general became less satisifed

33. Dorothy Day, *The Long Loneliness* (New York, 1952). Postscript.
34. Cogley, *Canterbury Tale*, 20.

with their subservient role, so too would Catholic women, having grown more assertive and independent during the 1950s, bristle at the traditional ideology and structure of the Church. Nonetheless, one lesson we might glean from the lives of Dorothy Day and Catherine de Hueck Doherty is that a middle class rebellion, which fails to change the structures and attitudes of society, is destined to frustration. A society which is essentially absurd, will continue to be absurd, whether or not women are allowed a full and equal role. A society which cannot provide its male members with meaningful and significant work can hardly hope to offer its female members meaningful and significant work. Only a radical Christianity can provide men and women with a sense of meaning and direction to survive the absurdity of American culture.

Copyright Information

Shiels, Richard D. "The Feminization of American Congregationalism, 1730–1835." *American Quarterly* 33:1 (Spring 1981): 46-62. "©1981, 1978, 1986, 1984, 1971, 1970, 1976, 1985, American Studies Association, Washington, D.C., USA." Reprinted with permission of the Association and the author.

Cott, Nancy F. "Young Women in the Second Great Awakening in New England." *Feminist Studies* 3 (Fall 1975): 15-29. ©by Feminist Studies Inc., Women's Studies Program, University of Maryland, College Park, Maryland, USA.

Loveland, Anne C. "Domesticity and Religion in the Antebellum Period: The Career of Phoebe Palmer." *The Historian* 39:3 (May 1977): 455-471. ©Phi Alpha Theta International Honor Society in History, Allentown, Pennsylvania, USA.

Ryan, Mary P. "A Women's Awakening: Evangelical Religion and the Families of Utica, New York, 1800–1840." *American Quarterly* 30:5 (Winter 1978): 602-623. "©1981, 1978, 1986, 1984, 1971, 1970, 1976, 1985, American Studies Association, Washington, D. C., USA." Reprinted with permission of the Association and the author.

Mannard, Joseph G. "Maternity . . . of the Spirit: Nuns and Domesticity in Antebellum America." *U. S. Catholic Historian* 5 (Summer/Fall 1986): 305-324. ©U. S. Catholic Historical Society, Baltimore, Maryland, USA.

Boylan, Anne M. "Evangelical Womanhood in the Nineteenth Century: The Role of Women in Sunday Schools." *Feminist Studies* 4:3 (October 1978): 62-80. ©by Feminist Studies Inc., Women's Studies Program, University of Maryland, College Park, Maryland, USA.

Reynolds, David S. "Memoranda and Documents: The Feminization Controversy: Sexual Stereotypes and the Paradoxes of Piety in Nineteenth-Century America." *The New England Quarterly* 53 (March 1980): 96-106. ©The New England Quarterly Inc., The Colonial Society of Massachuetts, Northeastern University, Boston, Massachusetts, USA.

Penfield, Janet Harbison. "Women in the Presbyterian Church—An Historical Overview." *The Journal of the Presbyterian Historical Society* 55:2 (1977): 107-123. ©Presbyterian Church (USA), Department of History, Philadelphia, Pennslyvania USA.

Lazerow, Jama. "Religion and the New England Mill Girl: A New Perspective on an Old Theme." *The New England Quarterly* 60 (September 1987): 429-453. ©The New England Quarterly Inc., The Colonial Society of Massachusetts, Northeastern University, Boston, Massachusetts, USA.

Billington, Louis. "'Female Laborers in the Church': Women Preachers in the Northeastern United States, 1790–1840." *Journal of American Studies* 19:3 (December 1985): 369-494. ©*Journal of American Studies.* "Reprinted with permission of the Cambridge University Press, New York, NY, USA."

Welter, Barbara. "She Hath Done What She Could: Protestant Women's Missionary Careers in Nineteenth-Century America." *American Quarterly* 30:5 (Winter 1978): 624-638. "©1981, 1978, 1986, 1984, 1971, 1970, 1976, 1985, American Studies Association, Washington, D. C., USA." Reprinted with permission of the Association and the author.

Bednarowski, Mary Farrell. "Outside the Mainstream: Women's Religion and Women Religious Leaders in Nineteenth-Century America." *Journal of the American Academy of Religion* 48 (June 1980): 67-91. ©*Journal of the American Academy of Religion*, University of Rochester, Rochester, New York, USA.

Gilkes, Cheryl Townsend. "'Together and in Harness': Women's Traditions in the Sanctified Church." *Signs: Journal of Women in Culture and Society* 10:4 (Summer 1985): 678-699. "©1985 by The University of Chicago. All rights reserved." Chicago, Illinois, USA.

Grimshaw, Patricia. "'Christian Woman, Pious Wife, Faithful Mother, Devoted Missionary': Conflicts in Roles of American Missionary Women in Nineteenth-Century Hawaii." *Feminist Studies* 9:3 (Fall 1983): 489-521. ©by Feminist Studies Inc., Women's Studies Program, University of Maryland, College Park, Maryland, USA.

Gundersen, Joan R. "The Local Parish as a Female Institution: The Experience of All Saints Episcopal Church in Frontier Minnesota." *Church History* 55:3 (1986): 307-322. ©1986, The American Society of Church History, Chicago, Illinois. USA.

Mehr, Kahlile. "Women's Response to Plural Marriage." *Dialogue* 18:3 (1985): 84-97. ©1985 by the Dialogue Foundation, Salt Lake City, Utah, USA.

Brumberg, Joan Jacobs. "Zenanas and Girlless Villages: The Ethnology of American Evangelical Women, 1870-1910." *The Journal of American History* 69:2 (September 1982): 347-371. ©Organization of American Historians, 1962, Indiana University, Bloomington, Indiana, USA.

Byrne, C.S.J., Patricia, "Sisters of St. Joseph: The Americanization of a French Tradition." *U.S. Catholic Historian* 5 (Summer/Fall 1986): 241-272. ©U.S. Catholic Historical Society, Baltimore, Maryland, USA.

Kolmer, A.S.C., Sr. Elizabeth. "Catholic Women Religious and Women's History: A Survey of the Literature." *American Quarterly* 30:5 (Winter 1978): 639-651. "©1981, 1978, 1986, 1984, 1971, 1970, 1976, 1985, American Studies Association,Washington, D.C., USA." Reprinted with permission of the Association and the author.

Pratt, Norma Fain. "Transitions in Judaism: The Jewish American Woman through the 1930s." *American Quarterly* 30:5 (Winter 1978): 681-702. "©1981, 1978, 1986, 1984, 1971, 1970, 1976, 1985, American Studies Association,Washington, D.C., USA." Reprinted with permission of the Association and the author.

Korrol, Virginia Sánchez. "In Search of Unconventional Women: Histories of Puerto Rican Women in Religious Vocations before Mid-Century." *Oral History Review* 16:2 (Fall 1988): 47-63 . ©Oral History Association, State University of New York at Buffalo, Buffalo, New York, USA.

Burns, Jeffrey M. "Catholic Laywomen in the Culture of American Catholicism in the 1950s." *U.S. Catholic Historian* 5 (Summer/Fall 1986): 385-400. ©U.S. Catholic Historical Society, Baltimore, Maryland, USA.

Index

Bei Fragen zur Produktsicherheit wenden Sie sich bitte an:
If you have any questions regarding product safety,
please contact:

Walter de Gruyter GmbH
Genthiner Straße 13
10785 Berlin
productsafety@degruyterbrill.com